On Jewish Folklore

On Jewish

Raphael Patai

Folklore

Wayne State University Press
Detroit, 1983

Library of Congress Cataloging in Publication Data

Patai, Raphael, 1910–
  On Jewish folklore.

  Includes bibliographical references and index.
  1. Jews—Folklore—Addresses, essays, lectures. I. Title.
GR98.P375 1982   398'.089924   82–11034
ISBN 0–8143–1707–3

The author and publisher are grateful to the American Folklore
Society, the Folklore Society, the Hebrew Union College Annual,
Indiana University Press, the Jewish Quarterly Review, Midstream
and the Herzl Press, Mouton Publishers, and the New York Academy
of Sciences for permission to reprint the articles in this volume that
originally appeared in their publications.

Contents

III. The Marranos of Meshhed

IV. Sephardim and Oriental Jews

V. From the Four Corners

VI. On the Peripheries

Preface

The studies included in this volume have been selected from writings I originally published in Hebrew, Hungarian, German, and English over the course of half a century. They fall into six parts.

Part I contains four papers outlining the general issues confronted by Jewish folklore, ethnology, and mythology. In 1945, when the first of the papers was written, the scholarly study of these subjects was in its infancy, despite the valuable work done among European Jews by such early pioneers as Max Grunwald (1871–1953), Judah Bergman (1874–1956), and Judah L. Zlotnick (later Avida, 1887–1962), the friendship of all three of whom I was privileged to enjoy in Jerusalem. In that year I founded the Palestine Institute of Folklore and Ethnology in Jerusalem, whose primary purpose was to study the folk life and folklore of the Jewish communities in Jerusalem and other parts of Palestine. "Problems and Tasks of Jewish Folklore and Ethnology" was intended to outline the little that had been done up to that time and the much that still remained to be done in those fields of study, and at the same time to present an outline of what Jewish folklore and ethnology are all about. Today, thirty-five years later, this programmatic article can serve as the base line from which to measure the not inconsiderable progress which has since been made in these no longer neglected fields. The article was first published in Hebrew in the first issue of *Edoth: A Journal for Folklore and Ethnology*, which I launched to serve as the organ of the institute and edited, during the three short years of its existence, with the participation of my friend and former teacher, Professor Yosef Rivlin (1889–1971).

In the fall of 1947, I received a fellowship from the Viking Fund (now the Wenner-Gren Foundation for Anthropological Research) which brought me to New York, where I have made my home ever since. For more than a decade thereafter, I was occupied with studying cultural processes in the contemporary Middle East and Palestine, and not until 1959 was I able to return to Jewish folklore. "Jewish Folklore and Jewish Tradition" served as the introductory essay to *Studies in Biblical and Jewish Folklore* (1960), which I edited together with my friends and colleagues Francis L. Utley and Dov Noy; it is a direct sequel to "Problems and Tasks of Jewish Folklore and Ethnology." In it I focused on the relationship between folklore and tradition, and, among other things, repeated the warning that with the extermination of Jewish communities in eastern and central Europe and the dismantling of Jewish communities in the lands of the Middle East, the traditional forms of Jewish folk life were becoming rapidly and irrevocably lost.

About 1960, I became deeply involved in the investigation of one aspect of ancient Jewish folk culture, that of mythology. Biblical mythology had been a highly controversial subject ever since the pioneering nineteenth-century mythologists began to pay attention to it. Not only religiously conservative Jews, but the Jewish establishment as a whole, frowned upon any attempt to treat biblical narrative as myth. Ignaz Goldziher (1850–1921), the great Islamologist, had to pay dearly throughout many decades of his life for his youthful and precipitate attempt to follow in Max Müller's footsteps and trace solar mythology in the Bible. I, writing three generations later, still encountered sporadic denunciation of my temerity in considering certain biblical stories as myths, which I did in *Hebrew Myths* (1964), written jointly with Robert Graves. I was also criticized for joining forces with an author who, although generally recognized as a great poet and novelist, was regarded as eminently unscientific by the scholarly world. I don't know what my scholarly reputation suffered in consequence, but for me biblical, talmudic, and later Jewish mythology was and remains a fascinating subject.

"What Is Hebrew Mythology?" originally was read to the 26 October 1964 meeting of the Division of Anthropology of the New York Academy of Sciences; it presents the understanding I had reached at that time of the meaning and character of Hebrew mythology—to which, incidentally, I fully subscribe to this day. "The Goddess Cult in Hebrew-Jewish Religion" is a summary statement of the conclusions I reached in *The Hebrew Goddess*

(1967; 2d enlarged ed. 1978), which deals with the role, worship, and myth of a female deity in Judaism. When speaking of this subject, I still cannot help feeling amazed at the tenacity with which popular Jewish religion, despite all orthodox strictures, retained an essentially identical image of the goddess from early biblical to late hasidic times.

Part II of this volume contains some of my earliest scholarly papers. "The Rainbow" (1937) and "*T'khelet*—Blue" (1939), both originally written in Hebrew, discuss the beliefs and customs connected with the rainbow and the blue dye and color in ancient Jewish life. In translating them into English I had to tone down the stylistic exuberance which was due partly to my youth and partly to the nature of Hebrew phraseology as I then understood it. The collection of Hebrew legends of the sea was written in 1936 and represents my first attempt at a scholarly paper in English. When I wrote it my knowledge of English was rather limited, so that before reprinting it here I had to subject it to some stylistic revision, but I have refrained from making any other changes.

The common feature of all six papers in Part II is that they deal with specific manifestations of ancient Jewish folk culture. Taken together, these papers, I believe, afford an insight into those elements of Hebrew and Jewish folk life which were either ignored or unrecognized by the official religious authorities, were scorned and opposed by them, or else were reinterpreted and incorporated into the body of orthodox religious belief and practice.

Part III contains five papers dealing with the Jadid al-Islam (New Muslims), as the Marrano community of Meshhed, Iran, was called. I myself have never been to Iran, and I collected the material on which these studies are based in Jerusalem, in interviews with the leaders and members of the community of Meshhedi Jews there. In addition, I frequently attended the Sabbath and holiday services in the Meshhedi synagogue in the Bokharan quarter of Jerusalem, in which I resided from 1940 to 1947. The only comment I have today on these papers is that I regret not having been able to supplement those on marriage, death, and historical traditions with others on birth customs, religious observances, and similar topics, and to collect more than a very few of the folktales still current while I lived there. The generation to which my informants belonged having passed away, I am afraid there is little chance for present-day folklore students to retrieve this material.

Part IV consists of a general introductory article on the scope of Sephardi folklore, collectanea of folk customs among Sephardi, Moroccan, and other Jews, and three papers on Sephardi and oriental Jewish magical procedures.

Part V contains only one rather lengthy study. It is a detailed collection of charms, folk remedies, and other customs associated with childbirth all over the Jewish world, in the past and in what I define below as the "ethnographic present." The material shows that, in order to satisfy the overwhelming desire of Jewish couples for children, folk custom resorted to an almost infinite variety of charms and remedies (the so-called *s'gullot*). While the utilization of every imaginable *s'gulla* to obtain "the blessing of the womb" is in line with the high valuation put on children ever since biblical times, it comes as a surprise that Jewish women living in such an emphatically pro-natalistic atmosphere nevertheless also used a rich assortment of charms for the opposite purpose. While we have reason to doubt the efficacy of the magical means for conception or for contraception, the very use of the latter indicates that there were women who wished to remain childless or to stop bearing children. It is equally remarkable that there were rabbis and *hakhamim* who sympathized sufficiently to include contraceptive charms in their books of charms and remedies. This shows a relatively liberal approach to family planning, of which little has survived among Orthodox rabbis today. It would seem that if a woman desired to resort to contraception, the spiritual leaders of the community assumed that she must have weighty enough reasons for doing so, and, far from condemning her, lent a hand by including recipes in their very popular books of *s'gullot*.

Part VI deals with two communities which I had the opportunity to study on the spot: one which is on its way in from the periphery toward the mainstream of Judaism, and another which became detached from the body of Jewry several centuries ago. The two papers on the Jewish Indians of Mexico are the result of field trips I took to Mexico in 1948 and 1964; the paper on the Chuetas of Majorca is based on interviews I conducted while I stayed on that island as a guest of Robert Graves.

Most of the written sources used in the studies contained in this volume date from the second half of the nineteenth century or earlier. The oral and written personal communications which are the sources of part of the data date from the 1930s and early 1940s. This being the case, it must be assumed that the customs and beliefs described have since fallen into desuetude. In most cases the Jewish communities within which these customs and beliefs once lived have themselves fallen victim to the Nazi Holocaust and no longer exist. It might, therefore, seem proper to use the past tense in referring to these customs and beliefs, so as to indicate that I am dealing with manifestations of Jewish folk life from a bygone era. If I nevertheless employ the present tense, I have done so for three reasons. One is the generally accepted anthropological usage of offering data in what is referred to as the "ethnographic present." The second is my determination to reproduce as faithfully as possible the language of my sources, whether written or oral, and in these sources, as a rule, the present tense is used. The third is my desire to present Jewish folk custom and belief as what it was in the period described in the books and manuscripts and in the oral or written information supplied by a dozen or so informants—a vibrant, living, organic whole and an integral part of everyday life.

The essays reprinted below have been edited, as far as was practical, to bring them into conformity with the publisher's house style, but otherwise they appear substantially as they were first published. All translations, unless otherwise noted, are my own.

In the preparation of this edition I received bibliographical help and advice from Dina Abramowicz, head librarian of YIVO, New York City; Sylvia Landress, director of the Zionist Archives and Library, New York City, and its staff; Dr. Leonard Gold, chief of the Jewish Division of the New York Public Library, and its staff; E. Christian Filstrup, chief of the Oriental Division of the New York Public Library, and its staff, and especially its Arabic expert, Dr. Houssam Khalil. I wish to express my thanks to all of them, as well as to Dr. Bernard Goldman, director, and Dr. Sherwyn Carr, editor, of Wayne State University Press, for their meticulous attention to the preparation of this difficult manuscript for the press.

Raphael Patai
Forest Hills, New York

Abbreviations

I.
Introductory and Programmatic

1. Problems and Tasks of Jewish Folklore and Ethnology

1.

If we wish to approach our subject methodically, we shall have first of all to define what folklore is, then what ethnology is, and only after having delimited the provinces of these sciences shall we be in a position to delineate the problems and tasks specific to Jewish folklore and ethnology.

The term "folklore" was coined in 1846, by the English antiquarian William John Thoms, to replace the earlier expression "popular antiquities." The new term soon established itself in countries outside England, and was definitively adopted by Nordic scholars, among them the Finns, who are to the present day first and foremost in this study. As to the precise scope of the science of folklore, there was some divergence in the views of its students (which it is unnecessary to describe here), until finally there emerged a consensus of opinion of the majority, to the effect that folklore is the study of the mental equipment of the simple folk in civilized countries. This definition requires some explanation. By mental equipment, as distinguished from technical skill, are understood mainly the traditional beliefs, customs, songs, stories, and sayings, while the technical skill of the people is expressed in popular artifacts such as buildings, furnishings, and clothing, as well as utensils, implements, ornaments, and the like. These latter lie, accordingly, outside the scope of folklore proper, and are studied by its sister science, ethnology. But of this later. The simple folk, whose mental equipment folklore studies, is marked by its stationary and tradition-bound character, in contradistinction to the cultured classes, whose mental equipment is determined by the ever-changing and developing achievements of modern arts and sciences. The limitation of the scope of folklore to the simple folk in civilized countries excludes the customs and beliefs of the population of backward countries and savages, these being the province of certain branches of anthropology.

Notwithstanding this threefold ideal limitation in topical, social, and cultural respects, the scope of folklore remains a very wide one. Moreover, it is not always desirable or even feasible to remain within these ideal limits when tackling an actual problem. In dealing with beliefs and practices in connection with agriculture, for instance, it is often necessary to study also the forms of the agricultural implements, though these already belong to the material culture, in which the technical skill of the people expresses itself. Or, in following up the development of games and sports, to take another instance, it is mostly impracticable to confine oneself to the simple folk, as such pastimes know neither social nor cultural barriers. Again, myths or magical practices appear among the simple folk in civilized countries and primitive peoples, in form so closely related as to preclude exclusive study of the one without the other. But even without taking into consideration this often necessary transgression of its ideal limits, the science of folklore within its most legitimate bounds has quite a formidable kingdom to explore. It would be too technical to name all the departments of this kingdom, so let us confine ourselves to giving only the barest outline of three of its chief provinces. The study of folklore devotes its attention to the great domain of customs connected with certain fixed dates in the calendar, such as feasts and fasts, with the decisive turning points in the life of the individual, such as birth, marriage, and death, and with occupations, games, and social institutions. Another great domain, that of beliefs, comprises beliefs about the origin and structure of the world, about inanimate things, about the vegetable and animal kingdoms, about human, half-human, and superhuman beings, about the corporeal remains and the spiritual manifestations of the dead, as well as beliefs which are expressed in the diverse practices of the magic arts, white and black, in divination, witchcraft, and leechcraft. The third and last of the great domains of folklore consists of numerous types of folk literature, such as folk stories and tales, legends and myths, songs, ballads and epics, riddles and proverbs.

In depreciation of this neat threefold division, however, it must be said that as soon as it comes to the actual classification of an item of folklore, one is only too often reminded of the fact that living phenomena are essentially refractory to classification. A simple item like the worldwide practice of rainmaking, which in its usual form consists of pouring out water, unites in itself traits which belong to each of the three main divisions of folklore. It is based on a belief in the sympathetic effect of the water on the rain; it is a customary ceremony regularly performed each time rain is needed; and it is accompanied by songs and sayings special to it. In addition to these traits, rainmaking ceremonies often display features which are outside the scope of folklore proper as defined above, but which must not be detached or neglected if one be intent on giving a picture, as complete and true as possible, of this item in popular life. These features, such as the erection of special buildings for the rainmaking ceremony, or the use of special costumes and implements, fall under the heading of ethnology, and it is to the definition and characterization of this science that we next devote our attention.

II.

The term "ethnology," meaning "the science of peoples," is the continental designation for that science which in English-speaking countries is more commonly called social or cultural anthropology, and which is regarded as a part of anthropology, the general comprehensive science of man. Anthropology, to quote a definition which found its way into the *Encyclopaedia Britannica* and has thus some claim to general acceptance,

> is the science of man and of his culture at various levels of development. It includes the study of the human frame, of racial distinctions, of civilization, of social structure and of man's mental reaction to his environment.[1]

It may be worthwhile to add a second definition, or rather characterization, of anthropology, which carries the authority of Franz Boas, who was the leading figure among American anthropologists.

> Anthropology deals with man as a social being. The races, languages and cultures found in different localities and following one another in the course of time are the material and contain the problems of anthropological study. The historical events that have led to modern conditions and the sources of the differentiated forms of social life, whether sprung from a common source or of multiple origin; the processes by which modifications of race, language and culture come about by the action of inner forces and by mutual influences; the

interrelations between man and his environment and those between race, language and culture; the types of mental activity found in distinct cultures; the relations between individual and society—these present some of the problems that anthropology is trying to solve.

Its subject matter includes all the phenomena of the social life of man without limitation of time and space. From an anthropological viewpoint human life of the earliest times and of the remotest parts of the world is no less important than that of historic times and of our own race. The geographical distribution of forms of human life and their historic sequence from earliest time to the present must be included in the scope of anthropological researches. The first task of the science is therefore the reconstruction of the history and distribution of mankind and the forms of human life.

This material must be supplemented by the investigation of the physiological reactions of the body determined by heredity and environment; of the mental processes of the individual under the stresses of natural and social environment; and of the behavior of society. The analysis of static types, languages and cultures alone is insufficient for an understanding of their development. The dynamic conditions of change require a knowledge of the sequence of events and of the functioning of society and of its component individuals.

The life forms of any given people exhibit three distinct phenomena: bodily form, language and culture. Culture itself is not a unit, for the manifestations of social life are diverse in character. Bodily form is determined by biological conditions, by the influences of heredity, environment and selection. Language is largely dependent upon linguistic processes. Although these are intimately related to other cultural phenomena they are so unique in their character that the linguistic processes may be considered separately. Culture in the narrow sense of the term is highly complex, for the conditions under which economic life, inventions, social forms, art and religion develop are not analogous, although in many respects interrelated.[2]

After these penetrating observations it will be easier to understand how it came about that the same science should be called by two names so different as cultural anthropology and ethnology. Cultural anthropology deals with speech and implements, with the modes and methods of obtaining food, with marriage and the family, with social organization and religion, with beliefs and arts—and it is precisely these traits which characterize people, by which social entities can be distinguished from one another, and which can thus be appropriately regarded as the subject matter of a science of peoples, ethnology.

It will also be clear that the two sciences, folklore on the one hand and ethnology or cultural anthropology on the other, are, in some respects, overlapping. Some attempts, it is true, were made to assign mutually exclusive territories to the two sciences. Sir James George Frazer, for instance, maintained that folklore is the anthropology of civilized peoples, while anthropology is the folklore of savages. Such demarcations, however, seem inadequate when one is confronted with the obvious fact that mankind is not composed of either civilized or savage peoples, diametrically opposed to each other, but of communities which belong to a great number of different cultural levels lying between these two poles, and ranging from the lowest hunters up to the highest representatives of modern civilization. Moreover, while the majority of folklorists claim as their territory only the simple folk within civilized countries, the anthropologists, in general, show by no means a corresponding modesty, and though in practice they deal only with primitive and backward peoples, they never cease to assert that the ideal scope of anthropology is the study of man on every cultural level. Anthropology would thus include folklore as one of the geographical as well as topical subdivisions of its cultural department.

III.

Having stated the respective provinces and tasks of folklore and ethnology, one may perhaps be inclined to think that thereby the special problems and tasks of folklore and ethnology as applied to the Jewish people have also been stated. The general principles of a science should, after all, be applicable to a special case; otherwise the science does not deserve to be called a science, nor the principles to be called principles. Now, folklore and ethnology are sciences and their principles possess validity and applicability in a no lesser degree than those of other sciences in the social field. So, if in spite of all we find that the problems and tasks of Jewish folklore and ethnology require special statement and treatment, the hitch would seem to be neither in the sciences in question nor in the formulation of their principles, problems, and tasks, but—in the Jewish people. And right we shall be in making this assumption, for there is a fundamental difference between the Jewish people and any other people or social unit which, as a rule, form the subject of ethnological research. Any other people on whom ethnology may focus its attention will prove a unit, if not in every, at least in some respects. In some cases they will prove a unit in racial and linguistic and cultural and geographical aspects, such as for instance a great number of the so-called primitive tribes in Africa or America, in Australia or Oceania. In other cases one or more aspects of this fourfold unity will be found missing; a case in point are the Arabs, who constitute a more or less definite unit regarding race, language, and culture, but not regarding geography. Again, cases may be found in which the human subject matter of ethnology could be pronounced a unit on the strength of one single aspect, for instance the geographical one, which would give sufficient justification to a study of, say, the ethnology of India, even though this would embrace peoples of different races, languages, and cultures. However, without basing the study on one at least of the four fundamental aspects of ethnological unity, it would seem to be, to say the least, extremely difficult to find a definite group to be subjected to investigation, short of mankind as a whole. Yet it is precisely this theoretically so impracticable a case which is presented to the ethnologist in the unique phenomenon of the Jewish people.

It may be a commonplace, but for the sake of clearness I should like to repeat that the Jews constitute a unit neither geographically, culturally, linguistically, nor racially. They are scattered over the five continents, are permeated with the cultures of their respective habitats, speak the languages spoken in their surroundings, and possess no uniform physical type, but show in many cases racial affinities to the peoples of the countries in which they live. Against these four negatives—no common country, no common culture, no common language, and no common race—they possess one positive asset which is common to them all. This positive asset is their tradition, mainly religious, which, generally speaking, was until quite recently vigorous enough also to mark the culture and the personality of the Jew with a peculiar and distinctive flavor. The fundamentals of Jewish tradition are common to all Jewish communities the world over. They constitute first of all a religious bond which was strong enough to prevent the breaking up of Judaism into confessions. Jews are not organized in a church; they possess no common religious authority; but nevertheless there exists only one Jewish religion. Closely bound up with religious tradition is national tradition: previous to the dispersion Jewish tradition looks back to a common history running through approximately two millennia and beginning with one single person, Abraham the Hebrew. Jewish tradition never ceased to look to Palestine as the Land of Israel, and never gave up the hope of returning to it some day. Firmly rooted in religious tradition on the one hand and in national tradition on the other is racial tradition: traditionally every Jew is the descendant of Jews and of Jews only, and he is bound to pass on this heredity to his children untainted.

All this, naturally, has its negative side too. Jewish tradition favored only external, formal, but not internal, sentimental acclimatization to the often changing homelands of the Jews. Wherever they went, the Jews remained a distinct entity, a foreign body, and as such they evoked antagonism. They were forced by circumstances to develop a faculty most disagreeable to their gentile neighbors: the competitive faculty. Many causes interplayed to determine their special occupational groupings. Bitter experiences taught them to be cautious, mobile, alert. Even those of them who were ready to give up their religion for the benefit of total assimilation were mostly rejected by gentile society. Thus, partly by choice and partly by force of circumstances, Jewish tradition was kept alive wherever Jewish communities were formed. The original common traits continued to develop locally, often absorbing non-Jewish influences from the surroundings, until finally the Jewish tradition of any Jewish community acquired a very distinct local coloring.

Thus it would seem that from an anthropological viewpoint the common link between the many Jewish communities scattered the world over is their tradition alone, a tradition fundamentally the same but everywhere locally colored. Therefore, when speaking of the study of the folklore and ethnology of the Jews, one substitutes for the usual criteria of geographical boundary, race, language, and culture, a new criterion, tradition. Jewish tradition, though it evidently belongs to the sphere of culture, cannot be regarded as the culture of the Jews, for in fact it constitutes everywhere only a small part of their culture, the great bulk of which is borrowed from their gentile neighbors.

These cursory remarks concerning the Jewish people may indicate that the subject matter of Jewish folklore and ethnology is in itself more intricate and complex than that which folklorists and ethnologists have to deal with as a rule. When one comes to cope with problems or to study processes, the difficulties increase. Be this as it may, the work has to be done. The folklore and the ethnology of other peoples are studied by great bodies of students and scholars, occupying chairs in seats of learning and organized in societies and institutes. In the Jewish counterpart of this important work only the slightest beginnings have been made. It would, of course, be best to assign the study of the folklore and the ethnology of each Jewish community to a special group of field workers. But no such groups of field workers exist at present, and even under the most favorable circumstances it will take considerable time until the facilities can be made available for their training. So it is up to the few of us who have specialized in this field to tackle Jewish folklore and ethnology as a whole, even if our work can only have the character of a preliminary survey, and even if we know that each one of us in his lifetime can contribute but a small portion to the solution of the innumerable problems connected with these studies.

IV.

Let us delineate these problems and tasks in the sequence usual in handbooks of anthropology and in ethnological monographs. Accordingly, we shall begin with physical anthropology. Instead of mentioning technical and statistical details, I should like to state in brief some of the main problems and tasks which confront us when we wish to apply to the Jews the methods and viewpoints of physical anthropology.

Investigations have shown that in accordance with the preponderant racial type found in a community, the community can be assigned a more or less definite place in the racial variations of mankind. The Jews, in general, belong to the Caucasian or "white" stock. This stock comprises races as different as the very white-skinned, blue-eyed and blond-haired Nordic race on the one hand, and the dark brown-skinned, black-eyed and black-haired Hindu race on the other; and even the Abyssinians, after due allowance has been made for the infusion of black blood, are, by some students, assigned to this stock. Any of the peoples belonging to this stock consist of one, two, or at the utmost three racial elements, near enough to each other to permit of imperceptible transitions and mergings into each other. The Jews, however, though they comprise mainly communities belonging to the Alpine race (white skin, brown eyes, brown hair), include in European countries a fair percentage of individuals exhibiting the Nordic type,[3] and at the other end of the scale, pure—that is, for many generations endogamous—types such as the dark-brown Yemenites, and various quite black communities. The complementary side of this great variety in physical type is the affinity existing between the average Jewish types in any country and the preponderant types of the non-Jewish population. The evidence of such measurements as exist shows that the Jews evince little hereditary racial type, but approximate in each country the physical type of the general population.

Faced by such a great variety, the mere technical work which is incumbent on Jewish anthropometry is enormous. Yet it is not until this work has been done that problems relating to the racial composition of the Jews can be scientifically approached. These problems are both historical and actual, and they range from the question of the original racial elements of the ancient Hebrews, through the problems of the descent and the racial affiliation of the extreme light and dark types, to issues of policy in inter-marriage and eugenics.

Before leaving the intricate problems of the Jewish race, which give rise to so much heated discussion, I should like to say a few words about a piece of research which, though the Jews were only incidentally involved in it, indicates a most valuable research lead for Jewish anthropometry. In 1907 Professor Franz Boas of Columbia University was entrusted by Congress to conduct investigations concerning the changes in bodily form of the descendants of European immigrants in the United States. In order to conduct his inquiry within the limits of the time and money available, Boas restricted his investigation to immigrants in New York City. He further restricted the range of the groups investigated to five racial subtypes, the Scots, Bohemians, East European Jews, and two types of Italians. The measurements taken comprised height, standing and sitting; weight; cephalic index; facial index; color of the eyes; and color of the hair. The individuals investigated were the immigrants themselves born in Europe and their children born in Europe and in the United States. The results were surprising and very significant. To take only one instance, it was found that in the descendants of the immigrants born in the United States, the difference in the shape of the head tended to diminish. The Sicilians born in Sicily are long-headed, their cephalic index being about 78. Their descendants born in America showed a rise in the index to 80; that is, they became more broad-headed. The cephalic index of the Jews born in eastern Europe is about 84, which is a round or broad head. Among the children of these Jews who were born in America, the index sank to 81; that is, they became more long-headed.[4] As to the interpretation of this most interesting phenomenon of definite bodily changes from one generation to the next, science is as yet groping in the dark. As no corresponding change was exhibited by the European-born brothers and sisters of the American-born children, the change must have been due to the immigration to a different environment, however obscure the precise channels may be along which environment affects bodily form.

The results of this inquiry open up new vistas of the origin of the human races in general. Much of what is problematical about the diversity of the physical types of Jewish communities could be elucidated by investigations conducted along these lines. For inquiries of this kind Palestine readily offers itself as a great natural laboratory. In Jerusalem alone are to be found immigrants from some thirty oriental Jewish communities, ranging from Morocco in the west to Afghanistan in the east, from the Caucasus in the north to Yemen and Aden in the south. These, and in addition to them the less varied but quantitatively more important European Jewish communities, should be subjected to thorough anthropometrical investigations as long as the foreign-born parents are to be found among the living together with their Palestinian-born children.

V.

The next point to consider is that of the languages of the Jews. The languages spoken by the Jews will be the special concern of Jewish ethnology only insomuch as they either are spoken exclusively by Jews or have undergone certain changes in the mouths of the Jews, in which latter case only the divergences between the Jewish and non-Jewish idioms will be of special interest. A further restriction follows from the preoccupation of anthropology in general with primitive, that is backward, cultures. Accordingly, the study of those of the specially Jewish languages which have reached a high literary standard, such as Hebrew, and the various Judeo-German and Judeo-Spaniolic dialects, will have to be exempted from the surveillance of anthropology and conceded to the respective philological studies. What remains after these self-imposed limitations is still far from meager.

There are mainly three languages of which special Jewish dialects are spoken to this day in various oriental Jewish communities. These three languages are Arabic, Aramaic, and Persian. Special Jewish-Arabic dialects are spoken by several Jewish communities in North Africa and in Yemen and Aden. Some of these dialects also possess a certain amount of literature of their own, parts of which are committed to writing in an entirely phonetic manner. Jewish-Aramaic dialects are spoken among the Jews of Sacho, north of Mossul in Iraq, and of Urmia, west of the great Urmia Lake in Asserbeidjan, and other places in Kurdistan around the Iraqi-Persian frontier. The existence of a Hebrew-Aramaic dialect mixed with Arabic also was reported from Libya in North Africa. The most important of these dialects are those of Sacho and Urmia. They both possess full translations of the Bible which were traditioned orally in fixed wordings and were but recently noted down by Dr. Yosef Rivlin, who also put into writing a great number of Aramaic poems, epics about great biblical figures as well as lyrics collected by him from the mouths of a few aged Kurdish Jews, and thus saved from oblivion in the twelfth hour. The third group, the Jewish-Persian one, consists of dialects spoken by Jews in various parts of Persia proper, in Bokhara and in the Caucasus. These dialects are almost entirely unknown to science, and their investigation is one of the urgent tasks of Jewish ethnology.

In addition to these three groups, there are quite a number of other languages spoken by peripheral or exotic Jewish communities, such as the Indian Jews, the Falashas—that is, the Abyssinian Jews—and the like, concerning whom the first task would be to establish if their language differs from that spoken in the vicinity, and if it does, in what respects.

VI.

The third department of anthropology, that which deals with man as a cultural and social being, is in many respects more ramified and more complex than the two dealing with the human frame and the languages of man. Physique and language are, when all is said, homogeneous and uniform groups of phenomena when compared to the great variety of social and cultural phenomena. The enumeration of the different topics which constitute the subject matter of the social and cultural branch of anthropology would be a catalogue of practically everything that man is, does, and experiences. When wishing to speak of the special problems and tasks which confront this department of anthropology as applied to the Jews, our survey will of necessity have to be even more cursory than previously.

It can be generally stated that the main difference between a non-Jewish people and the Jewish people will also here be that of multiplicity. That is, while normally one can speak of the culture of any given community, one cannot do so when one comes to deal with the Jews. Just as they speak various languages, they also possess a plurality of cultures. Moreover, the cultures of the various Jewish communities are so different from each other that they are best studied piecemeal. What is required is a series of ethnological monographs on the Jewish communities, written by trained ethnologists. Such ethnologists should specialize on a certain community, learn its language, and spend some months or even years living as one of the community in its original home, insofar as this original home still exists. I may mention here in passing that the Palestine Institute of Folklore and Ethnology has set as one of its chief tasks the technical training of students who will later be given financial support to accomplish this work.

The ethnologist working on a Jewish community has to take into account the special circumstances in which such a community usually lives. A cultural unit among the oriental Jews mostly constitutes a small community numbering a few hundred members. In a greater community, or in one relatively isolated because living in a compact block—such as ethnologists generally deal with—external influences remain peripheral, and are as such relatively negligible in research. A small Jewish community, however, living in close daily contact with a non-Jewish community many times its size, is as a rule thoroughly permeated with external, non-Jewish influence. It is therefore incumbent upon the investigator to make himself acquainted, not only with the culture of the Jewish community, but also with that of the surrounding non-Jews. In other words, the study of one who investigates a Jewish community will in the great majority of cases be not only a study in local culture, but a study in culture contact, cultural change, and other cultural processes as well.

On the other hand, in order to gain a thorough understanding of the culture of a Jewish community it is necessary to be familiar with its history. The ethnological survey of a Jewish community will thus in most cases be inseparable from its historical study. The ethnologist, however, will be interested not so much in a chronological enumeration of the rabbis and heads of the community and their works and deeds as in the general aspects of life, thought, and culture of the community in the course of the ages. It is astonishing how much of such historical material sometimes remains preserved in memory up to the present, or rather the passing, generation. From some of the Persian Jadidim in Jerusalem, for instance, those Jews of Meshhed who under threat of death outwardly adopted Islam, I have collected data as to the different sets of burial customs which were in vogue among them in various ages, reaching as far back as the fifteenth century. Though Jewish historical ethnology is still awaiting methodical treatment, valuable work has already been done by, among others, two of the copresidents of the Palestine Institute of Folklore and Ethnology, Yitzhak Ben-Zevi, the president of the General Council of the Jews in Palestine, and Dr. Max Grunwald, who was for over thirty years the editor of the chief periodical publication devoted to Jewish folklore.

When coming next to sketch briefly the scope of a Jewish ethnological monograph, I have in mind an oriental Jewish community, and for this there are weighty reasons. First of all, only oriental Jewish communities are typical; that is, only they exhibit special features in all or most of the data with which ethnology is concerned. Modern western civilization is a great leveling force; it absorbs cultural traits, or rather stamps them down into a uniform and continuous surface. Jewish communities in the great cities of the West were the first to succumb to its pressure. What remained of their specifically Jewish culture consists of little more than the synagogue, with ever diminishing frequentation, and the cemetery; while their ever-present philanthropic institutions and their schools have retained only a minimum of peculiarly Jewish traits. In eastern Europe and in smaller places remote from the cultural centers, original Jewish culture was somewhat better preserved. I say was, because Nazism and the war, even where they did not exterminate Jewry altogether, blotted out such remnants of specifically Jewish culture as still existed. Culture is to a great extent attached to the spot. When a few individuals or even small groups out of great communities have had to flee for their lives, only small fragments of the culture of these communities could be transplanted to their places of refuge. It was mostly young people who succeeded in escaping from concentration camps or stealing through frontiers, but it was the old who were imbued with the traditional culture of their community, and the majority of the old people perished before they could transmit their cultural heritage.

But even if the Jewish culture of eastern Europe does not exist any more as a living thing, this does not mean that traces of it are lost. The ethnology and folklore of East European Jews has been studied for the past thirty years, valuable work having been done by societies as well as by individuals. This work should be continued most energetically. Jews from eastern Europe have emigrated in times of peace under relatively favorable conditions, which enabled them to take with them a fair share of their home culture in the form of customs and legends, stories and songs, proverbs and reminiscences, and the like; and wherever they settled, be it Palestine or America, Australia or South Africa, there is still ample opportunity to collect and note down, to study and reconstruct. On the other hand, we shall not find in these communities more than the scantiest remains of a specifically Jewish material culture. Thus the ethnological study of East European Jewry will have to be confined by the very nature of the available material to those fields of research which, as pointed out earlier, are the proper domain of folklore. Therefore, if one wishes to be scrupulous in the use of terminology, one would better speak of the folklore of East European (Ashkenazi) Jews, while the term "ethnology," or its equivalent, "cultural anthropology," should be applied only to oriental Jewish communities.

VII.

To turn now to the subjects to be dealt with by an ethnological monograph on an oriental Jewish community, let us first of all recapitulate in brief that the first chapters should be devoted to the history of the community, the physical type or types exhibited by it, and the language or languages spoken by it. In most cases it will also seem advisable to give right at the outset an epitomizing account of the environment, touching upon its various aspects, such as physical geography, botany, zoology, and anthropology. These peripheral subjects being duly accounted for, the first part of the monograph should be devoted to "material" culture. In doing so the procedure usual in ethnological monographs is best followed. Accordingly, the following main topics should be discussed:

1. Food, kinds, modes of obtaining, preparation, and so forth
2. Houses and furnishings
3. Clothing and adornment
4. Tools and materials, implements, and weapons

Though many of the items to be collected under these headings will be found identical with the corresponding items of the surrounding non-Jewish population, they should nevertheless be submitted to thorough scrutiny and should, moreover, be illustrated by photographs and sketches as amply as possible. The same applies to products of plastic and graphic arts, which will be found mostly connected with religious life, such as ornaments of the Tora, of the synagogue in general, and things used in connection with feasts, as well as tombstones and the like. Productions of vocal and musical arts as well as examples of idiom and pronunciation should be recorded by phonograph. Since one cannot expect the ethnologist to be a musicologist as well, the records taken by him should in due course be submitted for transcription and interpretation to the expert in this field, but the phonograph as well as the camera should be indispensable equipment for the ethnologist, without which no field work should ever be undertaken.

When turning next to the social aspects of culture, one will have to deal with marriage and the family, and with the structure, functionaries, and working of the Kehilla, the community organization and its bodies. One will have to conduct statistical inquiries as to the occupations pursued by the members of the community in order to obtain a living. The description of the occupations and industries, the manufactures and processes, though belonging in part to the subjects of material culture, will best be treated here together with such phenomena as trade, transportation, and travel. The social standing of the various occupational groups will have to be touched upon, as well as property, ownership, and inheritance. Social life, social control, education, and entertainments will largely be bound up with religion, but they have, at the same time, a communal-functional aspect of which account should also be taken.

The third great division of cultural anthropology, that of spiritual culture, will be permeated to an even greater extent with religion. Though Jewish religion, at the height of its vitality, is a sort of general code of conduct, having its say in every phase of life, in things material as well as social, its proper domain is spiritual culture, and its influence is felt most of all in mental equipment and outlook. Customs which accompany man during his whole life, from birth through childhood and puberty to marriage, from procreation through illness and recovery to death, all have a religious flavor and are inseparably interwoven with codified religious precepts. Even that most obscure side of folk life which tends to express itself in the belief in, and the use of, charms, talismans, amulets, witchcraft, and leechcraft, omens and divinations and other manifestations of the magic art, belongs in a typical oriental Jewish community to the domain of religion, the "medicine man" administering occult advice being often none other than the rabbi, or *ḥakham*, of the community. The recipes themselves often follow medieval or even talmudic patterns, while occasionally charms are prescribed the use of which was forbidden in ancient Jewish sources. In a Damascene Hebrew-Arabic manuscript book of charms for instance, which I have but recently had occasion to study, I found several prescriptions recommending precisely such charms as were expressly forbidden by talmudic sages some fifteen hundred years ago, and which the famous Hasidic rabbi of the eighteenth century, Nahman of Bratzlav, also was guilty of using.

Next to the rites of individual life, the other great set of customs is that clustering around the daily rituals and the weekly, monthly, quarterly, yearly, or septennially recurring feasts, fasts, significant days, or other dates. In any Jewish community, oriental or European, these belong in their entirety to the sphere of religion. It happens, though, on a few occasions that the religious feast is made use of for the arrangement of a veritable folk festival, such as on Purim or LaG ba'Omer. Of outstanding significance for historical-ethnological study are the rare cases in which it would seem as though traces of ancient biblical folk festivals had been preserved. A striking case in point is the dancing, singing, and merrymaking of the maidens with more or less active participation by the youths on the Day of Atonement, which I found scantily reported as taking place in two communities, one in the Caucasus and one in North Africa. Only investigation on the spot—which may or may not prove to be too late—could show how far one is justified in correlating this feast of maidens and youths with a similar feast which took place on the tenth of Tishri, the date of the Day of Atonement, in the days of the Judges in Israel.

The belief in the one and only almighty God who governs all the created beings and who knows all the actions and thoughts of man was always the cornerstone of Jewish religion. When logically carried to the end, such a belief would permit superhuman beings, and especially the evil ones, only the most restricted and precarious sort of existence. Notwithstanding this, Jewish popular belief, similarly to that of other peoples, filled the world with all kinds of spirits and demons, ghouls and ghosts, of whom man must always beware and who are at large especially in the dark hours of the night. Occult practices, such as those just mentioned, are partly based on a belief in the efficacy of the magic act or object itself, and partly presuppose the existence of such sinister beings, whose biblical or talmudic names and characters are sufficient to place them in the periphery of the realm of religion. Popular beliefs relating to the earth and the sky, as well as to this world and the world to come, are, in Jewish communities, permeated by ideas deriving from age-old religious doctrines. To illustrate with a single example: it is customary in Palestine as in all oriental communities, Jewish and Arab alike, to paint a broad blue frame around the doors and windows of the houses for the avowed purpose of averting the evil eye. When once I enquired from a Yemenite Jew why it was that they employed blue for this purpose, his reply was, "God, wishing to be secure from the evil eye, made his abode, the heavens, blue, so we too employ blue to avert the evil eye from our abodes." If we discount the clumsy naiveté of ascribing to God a dread of the evil eye, there remains the explanation that the blue color is an imitation of the color of the sky, an explanation already applied in the Talmud to the ritual use of this color.

The last subdivision of cultural anthropology, that of folk literature, requires as a rule so much printed space that in many cases it would be difficult to include it in a monograph dealing with a given community. Accordingly, collections of stories, songs, sayings, and the like are often published separately; even one of these categories alone often yields sufficient material to fill a bulky volume.

No attempt has as yet been made to collect the entire folk literature of any Jewish community, but if one be permitted to draw a conclusion from partial collections made at random here and there, it would appear that Jewish communities, even those numbering but a few members, possess a store of folk literature which compares favorably with that of any other community on a similar cultural level.

The scope of the first category of folk literature, that of the stories, is in itself so wide, colorful, and many-sided that no general characterization of their types and their topics in Jewish communities can be attempted as long as we do not possess even the scantiest survey upon which to base such an attempt. The meager material which is already available may, however, justify the assumption that one of the characteristics of Jewish traditional folk stories in general will be a certain religious coloring, though "religious" must here too be understood in that wide and not too strict sense in which we had to use it in connection with popular beliefs. A considerable proportion of the stories, both among East European and oriental Jewish communities, will, no doubt, be found to focus on the fabulous figures of wonder-working rabbis, of pious and righteous men, who already in talmudic times stood in the center of popular interest and enthusiasm. The popular institution of the pilgrimage to the shrines of such men of wonder-working fame in the hope of deriving benefits from the contact with their earthly remains is also echoed in stories which tell of the miraculous aid rendered by the saints in cases both of disease and distress.

Folk poetry and sayings, though they have a more concise form than folk prose, and are therefore easier to collect and record, have been but little better investigated in Jewish communities than the stories. In this province too the main work still remains to be done, and a great, extensive, and prolonged work it will be.

VIII.

Thus we arrive at the end of our cursory survey of the problems and tasks of Jewish folklore and ethnology. I have touched, it is true, only on that part of these studies which draws its material from the living communities, from what can be seen, heard, and experienced in their midst, or heard about them. I have entirely neglected even to mention those vast storehouses of Jewish literature out of which invaluable information can be gathered concerning Jewish popular life during the millennia of Jewish history. Though I have done so on purpose, this does not mean that I attach to the literary study of Jewish popular life only a secondary scientific importance as compared to the collection of oral information and living material. Should my present preoccupation with the living communities evoke such an impression, I may perhaps be permitted to call upon the contrary evidence of my printed works, which deal mainly with Jewish customs, beliefs, and legends of past ages collected from literary sources. If, nevertheless, I have herein dwelt exclusively on the study of present-day Jewish popular life, I had a very special reason for doing so. The study of Jewish historial folklore can wait. The books from which it has to be gleaned are safely kept in great libraries all over the world. If we do not accomplish the task, students in future generations will be in the same, and in some respects even in a better, position to accomplish it. But just the contrary is the case regarding the folklore and the ethnology of the Jewish communities of today. Living customs and oral traditions, as I have pointed out earlier, wherever they still exist, exist under the most unfavorable circumstances. The old people, the last living repositories of age-old lore and tradition, pass away, and with them vanishes their knowledge, their way of looking at things, their way of doing things, with them passes once and for all their world. The younger generation, lured by modern civilization, has only a faint interest in the doings of its elders, and looking down upon them as old-fashioned retains but a fraction of the traditional folklore and folkways. Thus the passing of every single year means irretrievable loss.

In World War II all of us learned the meaning and the necessity of establishing priority lists. From military actions through industrial production down to items of clothing, food, and travel, everything was arranged according to lists of priority. Were we to follow this example in the provinces of Jewish learning, the folklore and ethnology of the present-day Jewish communities would have to receive the highest priority in urgency and importance alike.

Notes

"Problems and Tasks of Jewish Folklore and Ethnology" originally was published in Hebrew in *Edoth* 1 (Oct. 1945):1–12, and subsequently in English in *JAF* 59 (1946): 25–39.

1. Bronislaw Malinowski, in *Encyclopaedia Britannica*, 13th ed., s.v. Anthropology.
2. Franz Boas, in *Encyclopaedia of Social Sciences*, 2:73, s.v. Anthropology.
3. According to Arthur Ruppin, *Soziologie der Juden*, 2 vols. (Berlin, 1930), 1:34, up to 15 percent.
4. Franz Boas, *Changes in Bodily Form of Descendants of Immigrants* (Washington, D.C., 1912).

2. Jewish Folklore and Jewish Tradition

I.

Fifteen years ago in a programmatic paper, "Problems and Tasks of Jewish Folklore and Ethnology," [1] I expressed the hope that the study of the folklore of present-day Jewish communities would receive the highest priority within the general field of Jewish learning. The years which have elapsed since then have brought no realization of this hope. While the great ethnic upheavals in the life of the post-Nazi remnant of the Jewish people hastened the oblivion of the living folklore of the Jewish communities, the study of Jewish folklore progressed at a snail's pace. In Israel itself, after five years of struggling for existence in the face of overwhelming odds, the Palestine (later Israel) Institute of Folklore and Ethnology and its journal *Edoth* became war casualties. Thus the few students of folklore in the new state remained without the stimulus of a scientific forum. Outside Israel, no periodical publication devoted to Jewish folklore has existed since 1925, when Max Grunwald's *Jahrbuch für jüdische Volkskunde* was suspended. In regional and general folklore journals, Jewish folklore has figured very meagerly.

Only two articles dealing with Jewish folklore have appeared in the

Journal of American Folklore since the publishing of "Problems and Tasks of
Jewish Folklore and Ethnology."[2] "Folklore Research in North America"[3]
contained individual reports on studies in American regional, German-
American, Spanish-American, Afro-American, and American-Indian folklore, but there was no report on Jewish folklore, in spite of the fact that a
great deal of the activity of the Yiddish Scientific Institute (YIVO) was
devoted to these studies. With whomever the fault lies—and it seems that
lack of interest on the part of Jewish folklorists is to a great extent responsible—the facts are that Jewish folklore has not figured so prominently in
American folklore research as have several other bodies of folklore, and that
the study of American Jewish folklore has not been so integral a part of
American folklore research as the study of the folklore of other nationalities
in this country.

II.

The great ethnic upheavals referred to above, including the establishment of the state of Israel and the large-scale "ingathering of the exiles,"
have brought about in the objective circumstances of the Jewish people a
number of significant changes which are not only limiting but also contributing factors in the study of Jewish folklore. These changed circumstances,
coupled with the recent advances in the worldwide effort of systematic
folkloristic study, call for a reexamination and restatement of the scope of
Jewish folklore. Let us begin with a glance at the reasons given in the
Standard Dictionary of Folklore, Mythology, and Legend[4] for excluding
Jewish folklore from its series of excellent survey articles which outline the
folklore of several important culture groups in the world.[5] Theodore
Gaster's article on Semitic folklore states, "modern Semitic folklore, including especially that of the Arabs and Jews, has been excluded, on the
grounds that much of it is due to direct borrowings from other peoples and
can therefore not be described as distinctive."[6]

This statement raises two immediate questions concerning Jewish
folklore. First, is it justifiable to include the folklore of the Jews under
"modern Semitic folklore"? The only legitimate definition of "Semitic
folklore" is the one correctly given in Gaster's article: "the folklores of the
peoples who spoke (or speak) Semitic languages." While this definition
enables us to include under "modern Semitic folklore" the folklore of those
Jewish communities whose colloquial speech belongs to the Semitic language family (such as the Jews of the Arab lands, of Kurdistan, and of
Ethiopia), it excludes the folklore of the great majority of the Jews whose
speech has until very recently been Yiddish—that is, Judeo-German—and

whose folklore by the same token would have to be included in Germanic folklore. The same linguistic classification would commit us to including the folklore of the Persian, Afghan, and Bokharan Jews under Iranian rather than Semitic folklore. It thus becomes evident that contemporary Jewish folklore as a whole cannot be regarded as a subdivision of ''modern Semitic folklore.''

The second question is whether it was justifiable to omit from the *Dictionary* a survey article on Jewish folklore ''on the grounds that so much of it is due to direct borrowings from other peoples and can therefore not be described as distinctive.''

No one familiar with Jewish folklore would deny that ''much of it is due to direct borrowings from other peoples.'' This is true, however, of the folklore of practically every people, even of those who have lived until recently in relative isolation. A comparative study of the total folklore inventory of a culture (if such were available) would inevitably lead to the conclusion that only a very small part of it is, beyond any doubt, not ''due to direct borrowings.'' Incidentally, the instrumentality of the Jews in these processes of borrowing, and especially in the transmission of folklore from the East to the West, is being more and more clearly recognized.

It would seem, moreover, that the distinctiveness of a body of folklore is not contingent upon the amount of borrowing characterizing it. Consequently, it does not follow that a folklore much of which ''is due to direct borrowing from other peoples'' can on this count ''not be described as distinctive.'' The amount of borrowing is usually determined with the help of the prevalent methods of folklore research by a study of motifs. But in addition to the more easily discernible, definable, and classifiable motifs contained in a piece of narrative folklore, the latter is also characterized by such traits as mood, flavor, spirit, and atmosphere. These traits may account for its distinctiveness even though its motifs and structure (i.e., its concrete content) may be borrowed. As Bascom has recently emphasized, ''the problem of stylistic features of a body of folklore is regarded as of primary importance . . . as well as the analysis of tales in terms of plot, incident, conflict, climax, motivation, and character development.''[7] In fact, much of the specifically Jewish character of Jewish folklore can be found precisely in these elements to which the usual classificatory techniques of motif analysis are not applicable.

III.

In addition to vitiating the argument on which the exclusion of modern Jewish folklore from the *Dictionary* was based, the above considerations demonstrate something definite about Jewish folklore itself. We recognize that the prevalent classification of folklore into subdivisions characterized by a common language and by residence in contiguous geographical territories is not applicable to the folklore of the Jews. In this respect, even the folklore of the Gypsies can be regarded as closer typologically to the folklore of other nations than to Jewish folklore. When we speak of Gypsy folklore, the reference is to a folklore characterized by many local variants. Gypsies reflect the influence of several countries and adhere to different religions (there are Catholic and Protestant as well as Muslim Gypsies), but they use everywhere the same linguistic medium: the common and ancient Gypsy language, rooted in Sanskrit and closer to Hindustani than to any other living tongue.[8] In contrast, the unifying characteristic of Jewish folklore is not the language it uses, but the common religious tradition underlying it.

Another people whose culture is occasionally pointed out as manifesting certain analogies to the Jews are the Armenians. Like the Jews, the Armenians live in many different countries and cherish everywhere the traditions of their common origin and history. But the Armenians, unlike the Jews, have preserved until very recently their Armenian language. Again, unlike the Jews, the Armenians are split into two mutually intolerant religions, one represented by the Armenian Orthodox church and the other by the Armenian Catholic church.

IV.

Since Jewish folklore is obviously the folklore of the Jews, the temporal and spatial extent of its subject matter must be coextensive with the duration of Jewish history and the spatial dispersion of the Jewish people. This much is evident. But, in addition, the Jews were throughout their long history a literate people, who developed at an early date the habit of committing to writing whatever they regarded as important in their oral traditions. As a result, the history of Jewish folklore is characterized, in each epoch, by a continuous process of lifting out considerable bodies of folklore from the stream of oral tradition and freezing them in written form. This process started with the earliest documents incorporated in the Hebrew Bible, in which the narrative element is fascinating both in the uniqueness of its style and spirit and in the incomparable interest of its motifs and content. The process continued through the early postbiblical literature of the Apocrypha, in which, incidentally, the polyglot character of Jewish folklore—initially indicated in some of the late books of the biblical canon itself—is first fully manifested; it then branched off into the Greek writings of the Jewish Hellenists, of whom Philo of Alexandria and Josephus Flavius are the classical exponents; and it culminated—still in antiquity—in the "great sea" of talmudic literature which sprang up in Palestine and then flourished simultaneously there and in Babylonia.

With the spatial spread of the Diaspora from ancient times onward, the originally unified Jewish tradition branched out into more and more independent branches. Hebrew and Aramaic remained the principle languages of literary expression, but Arabic, Persian, Ladino, and Yiddish soon appeared. Everywhere, however, the same process continued: oral traditions found their way into writings which, irrespective of their main intent, became repositories of the folklore of their age without detracting from the stream of oral, living, folk tradition, which continued undiminished century after century. The history of Jewish folklore therefore illustrates in detail B. A. Botkin's generalization that "the transference of oral tradition to writing and print does not destroy its validity as folklore but rather, while freezing or fixing its form, helps to keep it alive and to define it among those to whom it is not native or fundamental."[9]

Consider as an example the rich harvest of books of customs, or, better, one of their subvarieties, the collections of magical or religio-magical prescriptions used in obtaining benefits and preventing or curing ills. The earliest example of these within Hebrew tradition is contained in the Book of Genesis (in the story of Rachel and the mandrakes). Talmudic literature contains many such examples, but even more are found in Jewish literature of the Middle Ages and in later periods down to the nineteenth century.

In spite of the many outside influences that it absorbed and the changes that it underwent in many localities and in the course of many centuries, the specifically Jewish component in the folk life of the Jews everywhere is ultimately based on talmudic or biblical origins. Single customs cannot in every instance be traced back to the Talmud or the Bible, but in biblical, and even more so in talmudic times, a tendency developed among the Jewish people to conduct their entire lives, from the cradle to the grave, and including all daily and periodic activities, in conformity with explicit or implicit rules (these latter contained either in the Writ or in oral tradition and known as *Halakha*, a term covering the normative part of all Jewish tradition). This religious oral tradition became the main molding force of Jewish life, with all its customs and usages.

With the passage of centuries, in posttalmudic times the reliance on rules not only continued but became more pronounced, creating the need for repeated recapitulations of the Law in a series of codes once every few generations.[10] Thus a considerable part of Jewish literature in the Middle Ages consisted of collections of rules of conduct, of do's and don't's, which, although extending into all walks of life, had an essentially religious character and derived their binding force from the Bible and the Talmud as the ultimate sources of authority. The number of these codes increased, and the latest one, the *Shulḥan 'Arukh*, was provided with commentaries. Handy compendia, based on the *Shulḥan 'Arukh* and giving its essential rulings in brief form, also were prepared. Thus the habit of looking for guidance in a handbook became widespread, and supplemental handbooks containing collections of customs (*minhagim*) and other handbooks containing remedies and prescriptions were compiled both in Europe and in the Orient, first in manuscript, then in print. So many of these collections were prepared that one would expect much or all of the oral traditions to have been absorbed into the written word, but instead the exact opposite seems to have been true. In fact, the more that is committed to writing in any age and place, the richer the oral tradition that continues to flow thereafter. Therefore, much as the student of Jewish folklore may be enthralled by the wealth of manuscript and printed collections of customs, remedies, and prescriptions dating from past centuries, he finds himself in a world of even greater unexplored riches when he turns to the living lore of any Jewish community still anchored in its traditions.

The quasi-religious character of these books of customs and remedies is attested to by the fact that they were compiled, copied, printed, and used by Jews whose entire life was dominated by religious tradition as embodied in the first place in the religious codes. Scrupulous fulfillment of all the most minute rules of the *Shulḥan 'Arukh* went hand in hand with unquestioning belief in the binding force of local custom and in the efficacy of the prescriptions collected in books of remedies. Law and lore were followed together for centuries, until, with the onset of the Enlightenment, they were both questioned and, in many places, both discarded.

In certain specific details, occasional contradictions can be discovered between the local tradition and the instructions contained in the remedy books, on the one hand, and the hard-and-fast rulings of the officially sanctioned codes of conduct on the other. In most cases these contradictions went unnoticed, but whether noticed or not, the old talmudic observation that custom is stronger than law was confirmed again and again.

V.

While living Jewish custom and its repositories are thus the outgrowth of the Halakha, Jewish tales, legends, fables, parables, and other types of folk literature go back to the narrative parts of the Bible and to the second main component of talmudic literature, the so-called Agada which also includes ethical teachings. In one of the varieties of the talmudic Agada a superstructure of legends and tales was built upon the concise biblical foundations. In posttalmudic times, the development of Jewish legend and tale shows a close parallel to that of Jewish custom and usage. On the one hand, the legend material was excerpted from the Talmud and the Midrashim and published in separate volumes, such as the *'Ein Ya'aqov* (ca. eleventh century) and the *Yalqut Shim'oni* (thirteenth century). On the other hand, an independent literature grew up, consisting of collections of tales and legends which either follow the narrative portions of the Bible (e.g., the *Sefer haYashar* in the twelfth century) or deal with nonbiblical themes and show traces of outside influences to varying degrees. An important variety in this latter category is the collections of fables (e.g., the *Mishle Shu'alim*, or "Fox Fables," of Berekhya ben Natronai Hanaqdan in the thirteenth century) which continue a trend found in the Talmud and even earlier in the Bible itself (e.g., Yotham's fable, Judg. 9:8–15).

Like Jewish folk custom, the Jewish folktale also retained its close affiliation with Jewish religion, both being regarded as manifestations of Jewish tradition, which in its totality has always remained inseparable from Jewish religion and its cornerstone, the Pentateuch. Again, as in the case of Jewish folk custom, however much of this originally unwritten literature was being put to writing, more of it remained to be orally transmitted down to the time when the Enlightenment began to make its inroads upon Jewish traditional life in Europe. In the Orient, both custom and oral literature remained intact for several additional generations, until in our day the "ingathering" of several oriental Jewish diasporas in Israel initiated the process of their assimilation to the secular, western culture of the modern Jewish state, with its inevitable concomitant—the disappearance of folk traditions.

VI.

Legends, myths, tales, and other types of unwritten literature function as sanctions of custom and belief. This general thesis is fully borne out by an examination of Jewish folklore. Indeed, the close interlacing of custom and legend, and their mutual interdependence, are characteristics of Jewish folklore that are found in all Jewish literary sources from the most ancient times down to the present day. The story of Jacob's fight with the angel at the Ford of Jabbok (Gen. 32) explains the origin of the name Israel and of the prohibition of eating the sinew of the thigh vein. The story of the levity committed by the men and women in the Temple of Jerusalem (talmudic sources) explains the custom of separating the sexes during services.[11] The legend of the medieval martyr Rabbi Amnon explains the origin and the

significance of the moving prayer *Un'tane Toqef*, recited on the New Year
and on the Day of Atonement. The innumerable stories about the piety,
wisdom, and miracles of hasidic rabbis from the eighteenth century on
explain and motivate the veneration of their followers. And the equally
colorful tales told to this day by oriental Jews about their own miracle-
working rabbis (*ḥakhams* or *moris*) motivate and sanction the custom of
visiting the shrines of these holy men and of performing certain rites at their
tombs.

As long as the customs and beliefs were part of the reality of the life of
Jewish communities in the West or in the East, the survival of legends and
tales was assured, for by providing a sanction for customs and beliefs, the
legends and tales, too, constituted an integral part of the living religious
culture of each community. Once the beliefs crumble under the influences of
a modern, western, secular atmosphere, and once the customs are no longer
practiced for the same reason, or cannot be practiced because of the migra-
tion of the community into a new country (e.g., from Morocco, Yemen, or
Iraq to Israel), the unwritten literature, having lost its function, is bound to
be forgotten soon after.

VII.

Several conclusions can be drawn from the foregoing remarks on folk
custom and folk literature as the two main categories of Jewish folklore.

First, it seems evident that in the study of Jewish folklore it is possible
to an even lesser degree than in other folklores to deal separately with folk
custom on the one hand and with folk literature on the other. As an
anthropologist, one agrees with the anthropological definition of folklore as
"dependent on oral transmission" and thus including "myths, legends,
tales, proverbs, riddles, the texts of ballads and other songs, and other forms
of lesser importance, but not folk art, folk dance, folk music, folk costume,
folk medicine, folk custom or folk belief."[12] But as a student of Jewish
culture, one knows that Jewish legends and tales can be studied only in the
context of Jewish folk custom. If the scholarly consensus is that folk custom
is not a legitimate object of study for the folklorist because it belongs to the
realm of anthropology, then the Jewish folklorist must be an anthropologist
as well in order to be able to study fully the inseparable oral and behavioral
components of Jewish tradition.

Second, it has been found that modern Jewish folklore everwhere, as
expressed in this two-in-one manifestation of the oral and the behavioral, is
merely the surface appearance of an ore that goes deep down into the
bedrock of Jewish tradition. No Jewish custom, or belief, or piece of

unwritten literature can be fully understood and adequately studied without a thorough search of that vast accumulation of written literature in which so much of the Jewish tradition of past centuries has received a fixed form. A student of Australian folklore may have nothing to build on but the actually existing oral tradition of the tribe he studies. Methods developed for studying such "historyless" human groups are inadequate for the purpose of studying the folklore of the Jews, who have been the "people of the book" for millennia.

Third, a few conclusions can be reached about the outside influences on Jewish folklore, of which there have been many in every age and in every place. The tradition-bound and religion-dominated character of Jewish life everywhere up to the Enlightenment provided it with an extraordinary capacity for absorbing elements of foreign cultures. The life of a Jewish community under the aegis of its own religious tradition was one and indivisible. Religion was always ready, soon after something new appeared on the horizon, with its decisive reaction: whether to reject it as *huqqat hagoy* (the law or custom of gentiles) or to accept it, digest it, and make it part of the Jewish tradition. If the decision fell in the latter direction, a very short time later the non-Jewish origin of the trait was forgotten, and it acquired the same binding force, the same traditional sanction, as any traditional Jewish *minhag*. Or, if it was a tale or a fable or a legend, its acceptance meant that it had come to be regarded as a legitimate addition to the old Jewish storehouse of oral literature, and in this case, too, its non-Jewish origin was soon completely forgotten.

This tendency to incorporate foreign elements constitutes an additional challenge for the student of Jewish folklore. He must always be familiar with the results of general folklore studies, for Jewish folklore always contains non-Jewish elements and must be studied in its relation to them.

Finally—a warning. Israel the state and Israel the people have to be made aware of the acute danger of the total submergence of the folklore of the surviving Jewish communities in the new, nascent culture of Israel. In 1945 only the folklore of the European Jewish remnant seemed to be threatened with oblivion, while the folklore of the oriental Jews, who in those days still lived in relative peace in their tradition-favoring Muslim environment, seemed to be safe for generations to come. Now, only fifteen years later, the danger of extinction is greater for the folk traditions of the oriental Jews than for those of the European Jews. There are no more Jewish communities left in Yemen and Iraq; in other oriental countries their number has been drastically reduced and their communal life broken down. In Israel, which in the last ten years has absorbed close to a half-million oriental Jews, the dominant atmosphere of western society and culture is more unfavorable for the continued survival of oriental Jewish folk traditions than it is for the continued existence of western Jewish folklore.

Notes

"Jewish Folklore and Jewish Tradition" originally was published in Raphael Patai, Francis L. Utley, and Dov Noy, eds., *Studies in Biblical and Jewish Folklore* (Bloomington, Ind.: Indiana University Press, 1960), pp. 11–24.

1. Published in Hebrew as the introductory article of *Edoth* 1 (Oct. 1945): 1–12, and subsequently in English translation in *JAF* 59 (1946): 25–39.
2. L. R. C. Yoffie, "Songs of the '12 Numbers' and the Hebrew Chant of Echod Mi Yodea," *JAF* 62 (1949): 382–411; Ruth Rubin, "19th Century Yiddish Folksongs of Children in Eastern Europe," *JAF* 65 (1952): 227–54.
3. See *JAF* 60 (1947): 350–416.
4. Maria Leach, ed., *Standard Dictionary of Folklore, Mythology, and Legend*, 2 vols. (New York, 1949–50).
5. Europe and America are most fully covered, the former by survey articles dealing with Basque, Celtic, Estonian, European, Finnish, French, Germanic, Latvian, Lithuanian, Romany, Slavic, and Spanish folklore; the latter by articles on African and New World Negro, American, Mexican and Central American Indian, North American Indian, Pennsylvania Dutch, South American Indian, and Spanish folklore (which includes Spanish America). Although even this coverage is far from complete (we miss, e.g., Hungarian and Balkan folklore), it is unquestionably much more adequate than the spotty coverage of the rest of the world. Asia is represented only by articles on Chinese folklore, Indian and Persian folklore and mythology, Japanese folklore, and Semitic folklore (the latter confined to a discussion of the ancient Near East). Oceania and Australia are discussed in four articles, while Africa is summarily dealt with in an article which includes also New World Negro folklore. The folklore of the contemporary Middle East (which comprises the rich, though insufficiently explored, folklore of Iran, Turkey, and the Arab lands) is excluded altogether, as is Jewish folklore.
6. Cf. *Standard Dictionary of Folklore*, 2: 981.
7. William R. Bascom, "Folklore and Anthropology," *JAF* 66 (1953): 289.
8. Cf. *Standard Dictionary of Folklore*, 2: 953.
9. Ibid., 1:398.
10. The Mishna (ca. A.D. 200); the Babylonian Talmud (ca. 500); the code of Yitzḥaq Alfasi (1013–1103); the code of Maimonides (1135–1204); the code of Jacob ben Asher (ca. 1269–1343); the *Shulḥan 'Arukh* of Joseph Caro (1488–1575).
11. Cf. Raphael Patai, *Man and Temple in Ancient Jewish Myth and Ritual* (Edinburgh, 1947).
12. Bascom, "Folklore and Anthropology," p. 285. Cf. also Bascom's subsequent discussion of the scope of folklore in his paper, "Verbal Art," *JAF* 68 (1955): 245–52.

3.   What Is Hebrew Mythology?

It would be tempting to survey, as an introduction to this lecture, the manifold attempts at defining myth made by philosophers, historians, linguists, anthropologists, folklorists, and last but not least, mythologists, and then examine which of these definitions fit the Hebrew myths, and to what extent the study of Hebrew mythical material can throw light on the conceptual clarification of the nature of myths.

There is, however, so much to clarify about Hebrew mythology itself—a relatively new and hitherto largely unexplored field—that it seems preferable to skip such preliminaries and begin directly with a brief statement of my own understanding of the nature of myths. I shall then enumerate the sources of Hebrew mythology, go on to a series of examples illustrating how the Hebrew mythological material bears out the component segments of our definition of myth, and, finally, focus attention on the major characteristics of Hebrew mythology as compared with the mythologies of the other peoples of antiquity.

I.

Myth, as I understand it, is a traditional religious charter, which

45

operates by validating laws, customs, rites, institutions, and beliefs, or by explaining sociocultural situations and natural phenomena, and taking the form of stories, believed to be true, about divine beings and heroes.

Each part of this definition could be expanded, but, for reasons of economy, we shall pass directly on to the second of our tasks: describing and characterizing the sources of Hebrew mythology.

II.

The primary source is, of course, the Bible. A careful and unbiased reading indicates that much of the text goes back to, and retains the characteristics of, a period in the development of Hebrew religion which was transitional between polytheism and monotheism. Good and evil divine entities still abound, as do dragons, monsters, giants, demigods, and larger-than-life heroes; although the supremacy of the one and only God is already well on its way to assuming that unshakable form in which it was soon thereafter to become the cornerstone of Judaism and its daughter religions.

Surprisingly—and as an eloquent testimony to their almost incredible staying power—these old mythical traditions survived not only in Genesis, early chapters of which deal with the initial periods of the world, but also in the writings of the great poets and prophets, side-by-side and interwoven with their lofty teachings of universal, ethical monotheism. And, what is perhaps even more remarkable, they form an important element in the Palestinian and Babylonian Talmuds (completed ca. A.D. 400 and 500 respectively), and in the rich midrashic and early mystical literature, which encompasses roughly the twelve hundred years from the second to the thirteenth centuries, and originated in Palestine, other parts of the Middle East, Spain, and even in medieval Europe.

These, then, are the primary sources of Hebrew mythology: the Hebrew Bible, the two Talmuds, the midrashic literature and the *Zohar*, to which must be added the Apocrypha, the New Testament, the recently discovered Dead Sea Scrolls, and some other palaeographic material, written in Hebrew, Aramaic, Greek, and occasionally in other tongues, but all bearing the unmistakable stamp of Judaism.

III.

Before passing on to a series of illustrative examples, let us dwell for a moment on the "traditional religious charter" aspect of Hebrew mythology. This can easily be established: all the sources in which Hebrew myths are embedded are traditional and religious, in the sense that they were transmitted in most cases for many generations in oral form and were in all cases cherished as precious depositories of ancient teachings after they had been fixed in written form. The degree of holiness attributed to them varied, in direct relation to their age, from the oldest and most sacrosanct books of the Bible to the latest and least sacred medieval Midrash; but even in the case of the latter, its venerable character was unquestioned and its perusal was considered a devotional act. As to the charter aspect of this entire literature, suffice it to say that the Bible, Talmud, and Midrash are among the most important sources of Jewish religious creed and conduct. In some cases the charter character of a myth is explicit in spelling out the lesson which the myth intends to drive home, in the form of a didactic "therefore." For instance, the fourth commandment, after enjoining the Children of Israel to refrain from all work on the seventh day, validates the Sabbath rest by referring to the account in Genesis of how God rested after completing the work of creation. "For in six days Yahweh made the heaven and the earth, the sea and all that is in them, and He rested on the seventh day; therefore Yahweh blessed the Sabbath and hallowed it" (Exod. 21:11; cf. Gen. 2:2–3). Thus, the general scheme of the creation myth is made into the source, the cause, and the explanation of the basic Hebrew law of Sabbath rest. Similarly, following the mythical narrative of Jacob's nocturnal encounter with the man who turned out to be God at the Ford of Jabbok, in the course of which the divinity touched and thereby injured Jacob's thigh, the account concludes, "Therefore the Children of Israel eat not the sinew of the thigh vein . . . because He [i.e., God] touched the hollow of Jacob's thigh" (Gen. 32:33). These two examples, incidentally, also illustrate the specifications contained in the last part of my definition, that the traditional religious charter which is the myth takes "the form of stories, believed to be true, about divine beings and heroes." One may refine this part of the definition by adding that as long as the myth is believed to be true, it is alive and functions as a motive force in the society; once the belief in its truth wanes, the myth ceases to have any function and dies. It follows also that for the outsider, the myths of other cultures are dead myths, from which, by study, dissection, and analysis, he can draw certain conclusions about the way in which they functioned when they were alive within their own cultural context, but which can no more come alive for him than a cadaver can for students of anatomy. I find it necessary to emphasize the truth value of the myth within the culture of which it forms a part, because, if we follow some students of mythology into the fallacy of considering myths as *untrue* stories, we get caught in a logical trap and are unable to proceed toward an understanding of either myth in general or Hebrew myth in particular.

Now we can consider our examples illustrating the validatory or ex-

planatory character of Hebrew myths. Several validate the high prized
custom of hospitality, not explicity—that is, without the appended "therefore"—but implicitly, and yet with unmistakable clarity. The biblical account of Abraham's hospitable reception of the three men who turned out to
be God's messengers or Yahweh himself is well known, as is the sequel to
the story, the annunciation of Isaac's birth by the divine visitors (Gen.
18:1–15). Less known, perhaps, is the myth contained in the Hebrew heroic
Midrash *Sefer haYashar* (compiled in Spain in the twelfth century), which
tells of the inhospitable reception of Abraham by Meribah, Ishmael's wife.
According to this story, the message to Ishmael left with Meribah by
Abraham, "Cast away your tent-peg, and cut yourself another!" resulted in
her consequent divorce by Ishmael, who had no difficulty in interpreting the
cryptic words. Neither the biblical nor the midrashic myth contains the
lesson "Therefore, be hospitable!" Nevertheless, the impact of these myths
on people who believed them to be true must have been unequivocal. By
adducing the powerful example of one of the greatest of Hebrew heroes, the
two myths validated the custom of hospitality, and held out, in the first case,
the promise of reward for hospitable conduct, and, in the second case, the
threat of punishment for its opposite.

The mythical validation of a rite, or of a complex ritual, can be
illustrated by the much discussed *'Aqeda* narrative, the story of the "binding," the near sacrifice, of Isaac by his father Abraham. Human sacrifice in
general, and child sacrifice in particular, were rituals practiced in ancient
Palestine, and there are some indications of their existence also among the
early Hebrews (cf. Exod. 22:28–29). The deuteronomic legislation (Deut.
12:31), however, as well as the writings of the prophets Micah (6:7),
Jeremiah (7:31; 19:5–6; 32:35) and Ezekiel (16:20; 20:26), and the Levitical
code (Lev. 18:21; 20:2–5), all thunder against this rite, and Leviticus (12:6)
commands that the firstborn, instead of being sacrificed to God, be redeemed
by the offering up of a lamb as a burnt offering in his place (cf. also Exod.
34:20). As though prophetic warnings and legal injunctions were considered
insufficient to break the hold of an age-old ritual, the story of the binding of
Isaac recapitulates in a mythical, and therefore most effective, form the
abolishment of child sacrifice and the substitution of animal sacrifice in its
stead. For those who believe in the literal truth of this myth, it still has a most
powerful, gripping immediacy. But even those for whom it is a dead myth
cannot entirely escape its impact.

An institution validated by a myth was the desert tabernacle which,
whether it had had historical reality or not, was taken as the prototype of the
Solomonic Temple. The validation of all the details of the tabernacle's
construction, the various services performed in it, the personnel connected

with it, and the role it played in the life of the people as a whole takes the form of a lengthy, and, to our taste, dull narrative which recounts God's instructions to Moses about how to build, furnish, dedicate, staff, and operate the national sanctuary of Israel (cf. Exod. 24–31). The mythical aspect of all this is enhanced by making the top of Mount Sinai the locale of the divine instruction, with God speaking amid thunder and lightning and hidden by a dense cloud; by letting Moses abide with God for forty days and forty nights without food or water; and by adding the postscript that, as a result of this prolonged encounter with God, the face of Moses shone with such dangerous radiance that he had to be masked, lest those who glimpsed him come to harm (Exod. 34:29–35). It is a most eloquent testimony to the importance of the tabernacle (and its successor, the Jerusalem Temple) as the central institution of ancient Israel that on the single occasion when its greatest religious leader of all times is represented as having spent forty days in almost face-to-face confrontation with God, the only subject in which he is said to have been instructed by the deity was the temple ritual. Even the Ten Commandments, inscribed by God upon two stone tablets, are said to have been given by Him to Moses almost as an afterthought, at the conclusion of the forty days' oral instruction (Exod. 31:19).

Let us now pass on to two examples illustrating how Hebrew myths validate beliefs. Upon their penetration into Canaan, the Hebrews were struck by the numerous megalithic monuments which they found there, and they assumed that these huge, primitive stone structures were the work of primeval giants. Such attributions of gigantic origin were found also in ancient Greece, where the huge stones that form the walls of Tiryns, Mycenae, and other ancient cities were said to have been lifted into place by the monstrous Cyclopes. Biblical myth supplies the details of the provenance of the giants and thereby validates the belief that they were responsible for the Canaanite megaliths. The sons of God, we read in the fragmentary version in which this old myth managed to survive in the Book of Genesis, saw that the daughters of man were fair, went in unto them, and fathered on them the mighty men that were of old, the men of great fame, known as Nephilim (Gen. 6:1–4). It was, incidentally, the wickedness, and primarily the sexual immorality, of this generation of demigods that, we are told, caused Yahweh to bring the great flood upon the earth.

In another myth, preserved in much greater detail in talmudic, midrashic, and especially kabbalistic sources, we learn many details about a nocturnal she-demon named Lilith, who, among other exploits, was believed to enjoy strangling newborn babes and seducing men sleeping alone in a house. These beliefs are validated in the same sources by an entire cycle of myths, recounting in considerable detail the birth and life history of Lilith, who reached the zenith of her fantastic career when she became God's spouse. Without myth, a belief pertaining to the supernatural may be tenuous; with it, belief rests on the solidest of foundations available to the nonscientific aspect of the human mind.

How does myth explain a sociocultural situation? The example illustrating this is somewhat complicated, for it spans several centuries. You know the story of blind Isaac's blessing, which his firstborn, Esau, should have received, but which instead was "stolen" by Jacob. The political situation (which for present purposes can be taken as a subvariety of the sociocultural) validated by this myth was the one that obtained in the days of King David, when the sons of Edom (or Esau) became vassals of the Hebrews. The Edomites, closely related to the Israelites, but older than they in the area, were wild, seminomadic hunters, dangerous as individuals, but nevertheless subjugated by David's forces. This generated a certain confusion, which the myth resolves. Edom, we read, had foolishly sold his birthright to Jacob; then Isaac, unknowingly, put his stamp of approval on the situation thus created by giving Jacob-Israel the blessing he intended for his firstborn, and condemning Esau-Edom to dwelling far from "the fat places of the earth," i.e., in the desert, and to serving his brother.

But this is merely the opening phase of both the myth and the political situation. About a thousand years later, Judea found herself under Roman rule, a most perplexing development to a people convinced that they occupied a very special position in the divine scheme. How could the servants of the Lord be reduced to near slavery by a nation of idolaters? Note that the problem had nothing to do with the relative strength of armies or with political ramifications. It was viewed on a purely spiritual level, and the main agent was neither Rome nor Judea, but God. It is on this level, too, that the myth supplies the answer. Rome, by a process too lengthy to elaborate here, had become identified with Edom, that is, Esau. Esau, says the talmudic myth, had acquired one great merit, whatever his other faults: during the twenty years that Jacob spent in Aram building up his own family and fortune, and forgetful of his blind old father, Esau remained at home, supplied his father's table with venison, came day after day, dressed in his best clothes, to inquire after Isaac's health, and fulfilled in all other respects as well the commandment of honoring father and mother. It was, the myth concludes, this superiority of Esau over Jacob in filial piety that, after a long delay, secured the ascendancy of his children over those of Jacob. What this myth achieves is much more, of course, than merely explaining the subservience of Judea to Rome; it makes a spiritually intolerable situation acceptable. It reveals, so to speak, the deeper significance of the Roman overlordship in Judea, and, most important, it assigns the entire issue to its proper niche in the great divine scheme of things, in which everything happens according to the laws of a higher causality, a slow, inexorable heavenly justice, to which only myth provides the key.

Another example from this large, multifaceted area, this one again taken from among the talmudic and midrashic myths, deals with the question of the origin of evil in man. After Samael, the devil—who was none other than the fallen angel Lucifer in the shape of a serpent—persuaded Eve, and through her, Adam, to eat from the fruit of the forbidden tree, Adam fell asleep. Samael utilized this moment to violate Eve and imbue her with his impurity. The child born of this union was Cain, whose countenance shone at his birth with a radiance which betrayed his heavenly origin. However, Abel, Eve's second son, was fathered by Adam, and so was Seth and the other children of "the mother of all living." This myth is not didactic; it does not point a definite moral in either the early or the contemporary world; but its meaning is nevertheless clear. It answers the great question as to the origin of evil in man, which to the Jews of the talmudic period, for whom the stories of Genesis were literal truths, must have been most painful. If God, the quintessence of goodness, created Adam and Eve from whom all mankind is descended, how can there be evil in man? Here is the answer of the myth. Mankind goes back to three parents: Adam, Eve, and Samael. Hence, the evil of Samael slumbers in the heart of every man, as the *yetzer hara'*, the "evil inclination," and it is the duty of all to help the "good inclination" in him to triumph over the evil.

Lastly, as to the mythical explanations of natural phenomena in Hebrew mythology, the creation story, with its explanation of the origin of day and night, sun, moon, and the stars, the sea and the dry land, and the story of Noah and the rainbow, are two of innumerable examples. The sum total of myths of this type constitutes a veritable natural history, which most of the western world accepted up to the time of the Renaissance.

IV.

A few general remarks may be helpful in characterizing Hebrew mythology, with an occasional comparison between it and the mythologies of other ancient peoples. First, it should be pointed out that, as a rule, Hebrew myths are preserved in much more obscure form than is the case with ancient Near Eastern or Greek myths. The reason is that the latter were committed to writing by individuals who believed in their truth, or who gave unblemished accounts of myths, even if they no longer believed them. Hebrew myths, on the other hand, are almost invariable preserved in thoroughly revised, expurgated, and abridged versions. Although Hebrew myths date back to a premonotheistic age, all the sources in which they have reached us were either written or edited by monotheists. Thus, the original tone of the myths has been changed, offending passages excised, or both. The myth of Helel ben Shahar (Lucifer, son of Dawn), for instance, in the fragmentary four verses contained in Isaiah 14:12–15, tells only about the resolve of Lucifer to ascend to heaven and "be like unto the Most High," after which, following an obvious lacuna, all we are told is that Helel was brought down to Sheol, to the bottomless abyss. What happened in between is anybody's guess, although ancient Near Eastern parallels point to a theomachy, a combat between Helel and El, in which Helel was defeated by El before he was cast down into the abyss.

Or, consider the story of Noah's curse of Ham. The biblical version, evidently truncated because of the prudery of a later age, recounts only that Ham inadvertently saw the nakedness of his father sleeping in drunken torpor, and that when Noah awoke and "knew" (what he knew or found out we are not told), he cursed Canaan, Ham's son, and sentenced him and his descendants to slavery in the service of the Semites and Japhethites (Gen. 9:20–28). Surely this is much too severe a punishment for an unintentional glimpse, and the original full version of the myth must have contained the description of a heinous crime committed by Ham. Fortunately, in this case we not only have the parallel Greek myths of the castration of Uranus by his son Cronus, and of Cronus by his son Zeus, and the Hittite-Hurrian myth of the same outrage perpetrated by Kumarbi on his father, the supreme god Anu, but the full versions of the Hebrew myth itself, preserved in fourth- and fifth-century sources, which contain all the details of Noah's castration by Ham, including the instrument, a string, with which the impious son perpetrated the outrage. This example shows clearly that the biblical account of Ham and Noah is but the expurgated remains of an older and much more complete myth, which survived in full in oral tradition until it was finally fixed in written form in the Midrash. Incidentally, in the Hebrew context, this myth of Noah's castration explains the slave status of the Negroes—assumed to be the descendants of Ham—in the ancient Mediterranean world.

A second characteristic of Hebrew mythology is its preoccupation with creation to an extent unparalleled in other ancient Near Eastern, and certainly in Greek, mythologies. As in the case of the Ham myth, the older and fuller versions of the great creation myth cycle are preserved, not in the oldest, most sacred, and therefore most scrupulously selective literary depository, the Bible, but in the later talmudic and midrashic literature, in which, because it was considered less sacred, greater latitude was allowed. In Genesis, for instance, the only act which God is said to have performed in the six days of creation was *speaking*; from "Let there be light" to "Let us make man," He spoke and it came about. The atmosphere of creation by word of mouth is so pervasive in Genesis that even when the text refers, as it does on several occasions, to God having performed a physical act, such as "separating" or "making," one gains the impression that these verbs are used elliptically, and what they actually mean is that God "separated" or "made" by oral fiat alone. One begins to suspect that all this is merely residual from an earlier and more muscular myth cycle, upon encountering, in the poetic and prophetic books of the Bible, numerous brief allusions to heroic deeds performed by Yahweh in the course of creation. It becomes a certainty when one reads the talmudic and midrashic creation myths, which do not shy away from telling explicitly that certain personalized primordial entities, such as the "Prince of Darkness," the "Prince of the Sea," the Male and Female Waters, dragons or monsters, actually resisted God when He set out to transform chaos into cosmos, that a fight ensued between Him and them, and that, when He at last vanquished them, He killed them, or cast them into the abyss, or imprisoned them, or castrated them, or froze them, and thus secured for Himself enduring supremacy. In Genesis, the impression the narrative wishes to convey, and almost succeeds in achieving, is that of *creatio ex nihilo*; in the later documents, God, when He sets out to create the present world, encounters preexisting and inimical personalized entities, who, not having been created by Him, dare to oppose and fight Him. It is on the basis of a scrutiny of this type of mythical material that one gains the impression, referred to above, that much of Hebrew mythology stems from a transitional period between a premonotheistic world view and a monotheistic one.

A third characteristic of Hebrew mythology, directly related to the second, is its henotheism. This means the absence of that element which endows ancient Near Eastern and Greek myths with so much of their fascination, namely, the element of uncertainty regarding the ultimate outcome of all events involving a conflict between opposing deities. In Hebrew myths, it is a foregone conclusion that God will win, however powerful, frightening, gigantic, or monstrous His opponents may be. He is the chief and the head, the champion, often challenged but never defeated, who remains enthroned high above the other divine figures peopling the Hebrew pantheon. It would, however, be erroneous to assume that this type of henotheistic myth cannot evoke the tension that, together with its subsequent resolution, is necessary to make the myth effective in the human realm. The difference between it and the polytheistic myths of other cultures is rather like that between a one-shot adventure story and a television serial: the outcome of the former is in doubt; that of the latter is a foregone conclusion. We know that the hero will win and, a week later, face a new challenge. Yet such is the working of the human mind that it puts aside its knowledge of the outcome and goes along wholly with the excitement of the moment. Likewise, the knowledge that in all Hebrew divine conflict stories God must win does not detract from their tension-creating and tension-resolving cathartic effect.

A fourth characteristic of Hebrew myth is that it often postulates, expresses, and validates an all-pervading belief in the lasting effect of ancestral deeds upon descendants. This belief must not be confused with the historic insight which recognizes chain reactions set in motion by significant acts in former generations. Mythical causality differs essentially from historical causality, in that it moves along a nonrealistic plane propelled by moral or religious forces. The example of the Jacob and Esau myth can be referred to again here: the acts of those ancestral heroes determined, according to Hebrew mythological thinking, the fate of their descendants for all futurity.

A fifth characteristic is the complete disregard for the time element. Heroes who, according to historical tradition, lived many generations or centuries apart meet and interact on the mythical plane. One Hebrew myth, for instance, has Isaac spending three years in the house of study headed by Shem, son of Noah, who lived ten generations before him, delving into the law of Moses, who lived several centuries after him. (Incidentally, the point of this myth is to underline the timeless validity of the Law.) Another tells how Og, the giant king of Bashan, who escaped death in Noah's flood by hanging onto the ark from the outside, became Abraham's servant ten generations later, and was finally killed another ten generations later by Moses.

Connected with this cavalier treatment of time is the sixth and last characteristic of Hebrew mythology that we can discuss here: the assumption that not only do the acts of ancestors influence the fate of their descendants, but that the process can operate in the reverse direction; that is to say, the acts of an individual or a group influence the fate of their ancestors who lived many centuries earlier. In the abstract, it is somewhat difficult to grasp the principle underlying this kind of thinking. An example may help clarify it to some extent. When Abraham fought the four kings who had invaded Canaan, he defeated them and pursued them as far as Dan, the northernmost town in the country. At that point, however, Abraham's strength suddenly failed him, and the enemy escaped to the north. The cause of Abraham's weakness was not physical: he was a giant of a man who knew no fatigue. It was purely mythical; a thousand years later, an Israelite king, Jeroboam, set up a golden calf at Dan for idolatrous worship. It was the retroactive effect of this sin that weakened Abraham, although we are told nothing of the mechanism which enables a deed to have a retroactive influence extending back a thousand years.

This last mentioned feature greatly reinforces the moral character of later Hebrew mythology. The moral imperatives, untiringly reiterated by the prophets, pervade talmudic and midrashic mythological thought to the extent that they occasionally motivate a reinterpretation of the original intent of a biblical myth. The naive, uninhibited biblical accounts of the great deeds of early heroes, irrespective of all moral content or intent, became unacceptable to the rabbinic world view, in which every good deed had to reap its reward sooner or later, and every evil act its punishment. And, as if constantly harping on this theme were not enough, the supreme importance of the moral posture was driven home by the mythical frame of reference in which man's every act became a primary cause, radiating its effect not only into the contemporary environment, but also into the future, and even into the past. To one saturated with this mythical mentality, the commission of a sin became a truly unthinkable act, not so much because of the individual punishment it inevitably entailed, as because of the devastating effects it might have on one's society, descendants, and antecedents.

Notes

"What Is Hebrew Mythology?" originally was presented as a paper at the 26 October 1964 meeting of the Division of Anthropology of the New York Academy of Sciences and published in *Transactions of the New York Academy of Sciences*, ser. 2, vol. 27, no. 1 (Nov. 1964): 73–81.

4. The Goddess Cult in the Hebrew-Jewish Religion

I. The Canaanite and Israelite Pantheon

Before embarking upon a rapid survey of the history of a female deity in the Hebrew-Jewish religion—spanning almost three thousand years—it should be pointed out that from the Israelite settlement in Canaan (thirteenth century B.C.) to well after the capture of Judah by the Babylonians (586 B.C.), there existed side-by-side two different types of Hebrew religion. One was the Yahwistic religion fought for by some early Hebrew leaders (the so-called Judges), taught by the prophets, and embraced by the authors and editors of all the books which make up the Hebrew Bible. Within this religion a definite theological progress can be discerned, from the relatively primitive tribal Yahwism of the patriarchs to the lofty, universal, ethical monotheism of Isaiah or Jeremiah. However, this doctrinal development was not paralleled by a growth in popular acceptance. On the contrary, exclusive Yahwism remained the religion of a minority, so that the Yahwist point of view represented in the biblical books could rightly be termed "a minority report."[1]

The majority of the Hebrew people followed not this prophetic religion, but a different one, which can be termed popular and which either did not include the worship of Yahweh or consisted of his worship together with that of a number of other deities. As a critical perusal of the biblical sources will readily show, in villages and cities the simple folk and their leaders (often including the kings and their entourages) persisted in serving gods and goddesses, i.e., in following a religion which did not differ substantially from that of the neighboring Canaanites.[2]

In the Canaanite pantheon, as well as in the religions of other ancient Near Eastern peoples, there were four central deities who formed something like a tetrad, at least in the sense of intensively interacting with one another.[3] In Ugarit in the fourth century B.C., the four most prominent deities were El, the father god, called the Begetter of Creatures or Bull El; his wife Athirat (Asherah), whose full name was Lady Athirat of the Sea, and who was also called *Qudshu* (Holiness), the Maid Athirat, or She Who Gives Birth to the Gods;[4] their son Baal; and their daughter Anath. Baal is an appellative meaning "Lord"; the son-god's personal name was Hadad, and he was also termed Prince, King, Rider of Clouds, *Aliyan* (Triumphant), and Majesty, Lord of the Earth. He was the god of the storm and rain and of fertility, who periodically died and then came back to life.[5]

Anath, the sister and consort of Baal, was known as the Maiden Anath, the Virgin, the Girl, Mistress of Kingship, Mistress of Dominion, Mistress of High Heaven, and, at least in Ascalon, as *Derketo* (Dominion); in Carthage she was styled Radiance of the Presence of Baal.[6] She was the goddess of war and the hunt, and of female fecundity, and loved gods, men, and animals. On one occasion, while she assumed the shape of a heifer, Baal lay with her "seventy-seven—even eighty-eight times."[7] Yet Anath remained the Virgin. She thus united in herself the contrasting features of virginity and promiscuity, of motherliness and bloodthirstiness.

The Hebrew Bible speaks of El, or in its fuller form, Eloah or Elohim. In Israeli tradition Elohim had early become identified with Yahweh (shorter forms: Yahu, Yah), who consequently was often called Yahweh-Elohim. Occasionally the two names appear in parallelism.[8] In the Song of Moses, dating from the thirteenth century B.C., the names Yahweh, Yah, El, and Elohim appear together (Exod. 15:1–2). Other ancient names for God were Shaddai (Num. 24:4) and Elyon (Isa. 14:14). The worship of this male god had been well established among the Israelite tribes by the time they settled in Canaan. When they became acquainted with the Canaanite Baal, it was inevitable that they should identify the two deities. How the relationship between Yahweh and Baal developed is a crucial issue in the early history of Hebrew religion. The two gods may have been combined, they may have competed for the loyalty of the Hebrews, or they may have been served alternately. As far as we can judge from the biblical sources, the separate identity of Baal and El in Canaan went unnoticed by the Israelites, who by their own desert traditions were predisposed to consider El (Elohim) as the appellative of Yahweh.

Following their settlement in Canaan the Israelites acquired agricultural skills from their indigenous neighbors. This also meant that they came under the influence of the Canaanite goddesses who were in control of vegetation as well as animal and human fertility. Since their own nomadic religion included no female deity, when the Hebrews adopted the worship of the Canaanite goddesses they retained their Canaanite names. The result of this syncretistic development was that from the time of the Judges the religion of the Hebrews centered on a modest pantheon which consisted of Yahweh-Elohim and/or Baal, and the goddesses Asherah and Anath. Astarte was but an appellative of Anath, just as Elath was of Asherah, and Baal of Hadad in the Canaanite pantheon, and Elohim of Yahweh in the Israelite religion.

II. Asherah

Of the three Canaanite names of goddesses—Asherah, Anath, and Astarte—Asherah is most frequently mentioned in the Bible. Occasionally, especially when used in the masculine plural, *Asherim*, the term seems to refer to trees or groves sacred to Asherah. The other Canaanite name of Asherah, Elath, appears in the Bible only in the sense of *elah* (terebinth).[9] Thus in the Israelite environment both names of this Canaanite goddess assumed a dendritic connotation.

The historical basis for the frequent mention of Asherah in the Bible is the rapid spread of her worship among the Israelites. No sooner did they settle in Canaan than "the children of Israel . . . served the Baals and the Asherahs" (Judg. 3:5–7) and studded the countryside with *bamoth* (high places) or, as Albright argues, *stelae*, or standing stones.[10] At the time this happened the worship of Asherah had been largely replaced among the Canaanites by that of her daughter Anath (Astarte), so that the spread of Asherah's worship among the Israelites can be regarded as a cultural lag. The archaeological evidence is clear on this point. In numerous sites excavated in Palestine, the layers dating from the Middle and Late Bronze Ages (ca. twenty-first to thirteenth centuries B.C.), when the sites were inhabited by Canaanites, abound in Anath (Astarte) statuettes. From the beginning of the Iron Age (twelfth century B.C.) to the destruction of Judah in 586 B.C., when many of the same sites were settled by Israelites, the equally large number of statuettes found show Asherah. The two goddesses are represented in two types of figurines which differ so markedly that confusion between them is impossible.

The Asherah figurines show the goddess with a horizontal hairline across her forehead and a hairdo that hugs her head tightly all around. She has protruding breasts, often pushed upward by her two hands. From the waist down her body is not shown; instead, a cylindrical column with a flaring base is substituted. The frequency with which these Asherah figurines turned up in excavations of Hebrew sites in Iron Age Palestine indicate that the worship of Asherah played a role in Israelite houses corresponding to that of the *lares et penates* in ancient Rome. Her role as giver of fertility and facilitator of childbirth assured her a primary place in the home cult. A seventh-century B.C. Hebrew incantation text found in Arslan Tash in Syria invokes the help of the goddess for a woman in delivery.[11]

Just as Asherah was city goddess of Tyre and Sidon,[12] so she became a publicly venerated goddess in Israel. As early as in the twelfth century B.C., the town of Ophrah had a public sanctuary in which there was an altar of Baal and a wooden statue of Asherah, both attended by a priest, Joash. When Joash's son, Gideon (Jerubbaal), under the influence of a vision of the Lord Yahweh, destroyed this holy place, the townspeople wanted to put him to death and he was saved only by his father's plea (Judg. 6:25–32).

Three centuries later, soon after the death of Solomon, the Yahwist prophet Ahijah of Shiloh reproaches Israel for serving other gods, but the only ones he mentions by name are the "Asherahs" (1 Kings 14:15). Some fifty years after the secession of Israel from the Davidic dynasty, King Ahab (873–852 B.C.) of Israel "made an Asherah" (1 Kings 16:33) and thus incorporated her worship into the royal court ritual. The biblical historian notes that "450 prophets of the Baal and 400 prophets of the Asherah ate at the table of Jezebel" (1 Kings 18:19), the wife of Ahab who was the daughter of Ethbaal, king of Sidon. After the miraculous victory of Elijah over this legion of prophets, he had the 450 Baal prophets slaughtered, but, remarkably, no harm befell the Asherah prophets—at least the biblical account does not mention them. Subsequent halfhearted reforms carried out by Ahab's successors also only proceeded against the worship of Baal, who was regarded by that time as a competitor of Yahweh, but not against Asherah, who was considered his consort and complement.[13] The worship of Asherah continued in the kingdom of Israel until the Assyrians put an end to it in 721 B.C. The southernmost outpost of Asherah worship in Israel was Beth-el (some ten miles north of Jerusalem), which contained a *bamah* dedicated to her. Here her worship continued for another hundred years, until King Josiah of Judah (639–609 B.C.) took the city and put an end to her reign.

In Judah, the worship of Asherah was introduced into the Jerusalem Temple itself by Maacah, the wife of Solomon's son Rehoboam (928–911

B.C.), who wielded great influence over her husband (2 Chron. 11:21–22). She, we are told rather enigmatically, made a *mifletzet* (obscene object) for Asherah (1 Kings 15:13; 2 Chron. 15:16). From this time on, as the Book of Kings shows, the worship of Asherah remained part of the cult of the Jerusalem Temple for 236 years, or almost two-thirds of the 370 years during which the Solomonic Temple functioned in the capital of Judah. Only three times in those 370 years did a Yahwist king remove the Asherah figure from the Temple, but each time the goddess was soon restored to her place at the side of Yahweh by one of the king's successors.[14]

III. Anath-Astarte

The Bible does not contain a single direct reference to the worship of the goddess Anath. Only in place names, such as Beth Anath and Anatoth (the plural of Anath), and in personal names such as Shamgar, son of Anath, Anatoth, and Antothiya, did her name survive.[15] However, the reason for this silence is not the absence of the worship of Anath in Israel and Judah, but the fact that this name of the goddess was supplanted by her appellative, Astarte, just as Hadad was by Baal. In the entire fourteenth-century Ugaritic literature the name Athtart (Astarte) appears very rarely and, when it does, the context makes it probable that it was the appellative of Anath.[16] Between the fourteenth and the twelfth centuries, the use of the name Anath declined and the use of Astarte increased. In any case, in the days of the Hebrew Judges (twelfth to eleventh centuries B.C.), Astarte simply meant "Lady," in the sense of "the Goddess," just as Baal meant "Lord" or "the God."

The nature of the biblical references to non-Yahwistic worship is such that it is almost impossible to establish whether the two goddesses Asherah and Astarte were served simultaneously or whether Asherah was supplanted by Astarte, as she had been among the Canaanites.[17] The two phrases "the Baals and the Asherahs" and "the Baals and the Astartes"—both denoting foreign gods in general terms—appear in turn in the historical books of the Bible.[18]

Archaeological evidence indicates that the cult of Asherah was more popular than that of Astarte; compared to the abundance of Asherah figurines, Astarte statuettes are relatively rare from the Israelite period. Those found show a naked woman with two large spiral locks framing her face and neck (occasionally also two horns adorn her head) and with the breasts and pubic area strongly emphasized.

Another appellative of Anath, by which she was known at the latest from the Late Bronze Age on, was Queen of Heaven. Several Egyptian inscriptions, among them a stele erected in the twelfth century B.C. in Beth

Shean, Palestine, refer to Anath as Lady of Heaven. Similarly, Assyrian inscriptions call Ishtar, Anath's Mesopotamian equivalent, Queen of Heaven, and other documents attest to the use of this appellative elsewhere.[19] The Israelites adopted this appellative only in the seventh century, perhaps during the reign of Manasseh (698–642 B.C.). At any rate, the only biblical book referring to the Queen of Heaven is Jeremiah, from whom we learn that prior to the great Yahwist reform of King Josiah in 621, the people of Jerusalem and other Judean cities, led by their kings and princes, worshiped the Queen of Heaven by burning incense, pouring out libations, and offering her cakes (Jer. 7:17–18; 44:15–19). The last-named rite was performed in Babylonia as well, in honor of the Mesopotamian Queen of Heaven. The sacrificial cakes offered to her were called *kamanu*, possibly the origin of their Hebrew name *kawwan*.[20]

The Judaean exiles who found refuge in Egypt in 586 B.C. continued to worship the Queen of Heaven (Jer. 44:15–19), and their descendants persisted in this practice in the Jewish military colony in Hermopolis (160 miles south of modern Cairo) at least until the fifth century B.C. In another Jewish military colony, on the island of Elephantine (Yeb) in Upper Egypt, the worship of the goddess under the combined name of Anath-Yaho or Anath-Bethel continued to the end of the fifth century B.C.[21]

Outside of the Jewish communities, Anath survived into hellenistic times, when she was called Qudshu-Astarte-Anath (Her Holiness Astarte-Anath), and became known under the composite name Atargatis, that is, Astarte-Anath, the *dea Syria* of Lucian.[22] Among the Jews in the talmudic period, some of her features became incorporated into the image of the Shekhina, the "Presence" of God.

IV. The Cherubim

In the Solomonic Temple the goddess Asherah, as represented by her statue, was physically present, but no attempt was made to introduce her into the Second Temple, which was completed by Judaeans returned from Babylonian exile in 516 B.C. and remained the center of Jewish worship until it was destroyed by the Romans in A.D. 70. However, a representation of the feminine element was not lacking in the Second Temple. The only statuary to which even the strictest antiiconic Yahwist never took exception was that of the two cherubim, winged human figures, placed in the Holy of Holies, as the innermost sanctuary was called. According to biblical tradition, the cherubim in both the desert tabernacle and the Temple of Solomon stood on both sides of the holy ark, which was shielded by their outstretched wings. While no mention is made in the Bible of the sex of the cherubim, small ivory plaques from Egypt, Israel, and Syria, dating from the fifteenth to the ninth centuries B.C., show them in the form of winged feminine genii. From this evidence it can be concluded that the cherubim in the Temple were also female figures, and that when the Second Temple was built the new cherubim placed in it were of similar appearance. However, there is some circumstantial evidence that in the first half of the third century B.C. they were replaced by statuary which depicted a male and female cherub in sexual embrace.[23] The festive crowds which thronged the Temple courtyard on the pilgrimage festivals would be allowed to catch a glimpse of these cherubim and were told, ''Behold, your love before God is like the love of male and female!'' When Antiochus Epiphanes, king of Syria (175–164 B.C.), sacked the Temple, his henchmen dragged the sacred statuary out into the market-place of Jerusalem and derided the Jews as pornographers: they ''occupy themselves with such things!''[24]

The sources which refer to the embracing cherubim date from several centuries after the events they report. We thus have no contemporary interpretations of them. In the talmudic and midrashic passages describing the embracing cherubim, dating from the third and fourth centuries A.D., the idea of erotic statuary in the Holy of Holies of the Jerusalem Temple was so foreign that it verged on sacrilege. The least doubt concerning the authenticity of this tradition would therefore have induced the sages to suppress it; that it was reported means that it existed. We can likewise accept as authentic the rabbinic interpretation: the male cherub symbolized God, and the female the community of Israel.

There is some circumstantial but contemporary evidence concerning the presence of male and female cherub statuary in the Second Temple. The Alexandrian Jewish philosopher Philo (ca. 15 B.C. to A.D. 45) interpreted them as representing the two aspects of God: one cherub symbolized God (Elohim) as father, husband, begetter, and creator, with the qualities of reason, goodness, peacefulness, gentleness, and beneficence; the other cherub symbolized the Lord (Yahweh) as mother, wife, bearer, and nurturer, with the qualities of wisdom and sovereignty and the power to legislate, chastise, and correct. These two groups of divine powers, says Philo, were ''mingled and united''—perhaps a reminiscence of the intertwined male and female cherubim whom he may have seen if he had made the pilgrimage to Jerusalem.[25] The view that one cherub was male and the other female became a basic tenet of the Kabbala.

V. The Shekhina

In Babylonia, where a large Jewish community developed after 586

B.C., the worship of the goddess apparently disappeared. At least no traces of it were left in the meager historical sources relating to the early postexile period. Before long, however, a remarkable development occurred, which ultimately resulted in a return of the female divine principle to the Jewish religion. This process originated in the growing feeling that the numerous biblical anthropomorphisms and anthropopathisms conveyed a much too physical and humanlike picture of God. This resulted in a number of hypostases, i.e., conceptualized agencies or agents, acting as intermediaries between God and the human perception of His manifestation. Actually, this tendency emerged as early as 400 B.C., when the latest biblical books, Proverbs and Job, were written. In them *Hokhma* (Wisdom) appears as such a hypostasis, a personage separate and distinct from God. About the same time, the Targums, or Aramaic translation-paraphrases of the Bible, began to use with considerable consistency the term *Shekhina* whenever the original Hebrew text was felt to be too anthropomorphic. Shekhina means literally "act of dwelling," but can best be translated into English as "presence." Like many abstract nouns in Hebrew, it has the feminine gender. To mention a single example, the biblical verse "I will dwell among the Children of Israel" (Exod. 29:45) is rendered in the Targum of Onkelos, "I will let my Shekhina dwell among the Children of Israel."

Gradually the Shekhina assumed a more and more physical or tangible character. The end result of this process can be seen in those talmudic passages (dating from A.D. 200 to 500) which describe the Shekhina as, for example, keeping the infant Moses company while he lay in the ark of bulrushes, being carried in a casket by the Children of Israel in the desert, and dwelling in the desert tabernacle, the Temple of Jerusalem, and certain synagogues in Babylonia. She is said to have announced her presence by producing a tinkling sound like a bell, shown herself to humans and animals, walked with the brokenhearted, and rested between husband and wife. At the same time her radiance was said to have been such that even the angels had to shield themselves with their wings so as not to see her.[26]

In the talmudic period the Shekhina and the related concept of the Holy Spirit were used synonymously.[27] From about A.D. 300 on, we have testimony to the effect that the Holy Spirit was considered an independent entity that could confront and even admonish God.[28]

The femininity of the Shekhina is implicit in all the statements about her simply because the noun is of the feminine gender in contrast to the divine names Elohim, Yahweh, Elyon, Shaddai, and so on, all of which are masculine. In addition, however, the Shekhina assumed an unmistakably feminine role in her relationship to both men and God. Thus we read that when Moses died, the Shekhina carried him on her wings to his distant burial place, which act of kindness duplicates what Anath did for her brother-husband Baal. The Shekhina caressed and kissed the walls and columns of the Temple. When the patriarchs died, she took their souls in a kiss. She is the love aspect of God, but also represents the divine punitive power,[29] which again is reminiscent of the same two contrasting roles of Anath some two thousand years earlier.

VI. The Matronit

With the emergence of the Kabbala, the great mystical trend in Judaism, in the thirteenth century, the Shekhina was given a new name, Matronit (from the Latina *matrona*), and became both the sister and the wife of God who, in relation to her, was styled the King. The *Zohar* (Splendor), the most important book of the Kabbala, written around 1286 by Moses de Leon in Castile, Spain, contains an almost incredibly sensuous myth cycle about these two divinities.

Their origin can be traced to an earlier divine pair. The divine Father brought forth the Supernal Mother, or the Female. "She spread out from her place and adhered to the side of the Male (the Father), until he moved away, and she came to unite with him face to face. And when they united they appeared as veritably one body" (*Zohar*, 3:296a). The union between the Male and the Female is both complete and ceaseless. Thus when his "seed is about to be ejaculated, he does not have to seek the Female, for she abides with him, never leaves him, and is always in readiness for him. His seed flows not save when the Female is ready, and when they both desire each other; and they unite in a single embrace, and never separate" (*Zohar*, 1:162a–b).

Out of this union were born the Son, also known as the King, and the Daughter, or Matronit. The Father and Mother loved their children exceedingly, adorned their heads with many crowns, and showered blessings upon them. However, the Father loved the Daughter more, while the Mother's favorite was the Son. In fact, the Father constantly kissed and fondled the Daughter, until the Mother suffered pangs of jealousy and demanded of the Daughter that she cease beguiling the Father (*Zohar*, 1:156b, Sitre Torah). As to the Mother's love of the Son, she expressed it by giving him her breast most generously and continuing to suckle him even after he grew up and married his sister, the Daughter or Matronit (*Zohar*, 3:17a).

The marriage between the Son (the King) and the Daughter (the Matronit) was licit, because "above on high there is no incest"[30]—an archaic concept that again reminds us of the absence of incest in Ugaritic and other ancient Near Eastern myths.

The Temple of Jerusalem, built by King Solomon, served as the wedding chamber of the King and the Matronit, and as their bedroom thereafter. However, the marriage was marked by many quarrels, bitter separations, and tempestuous reunions. The reason for these vicissitudes was that the Matronit became closely associated with the people of Israel (this is why she is often referred to by the name *Kneset Yisrael* [Community of Israel]), and whenever Israel sinned the marriage of the King and the Matronit was disrupted. Otherwise, the sacred union between them took place in the Temple-bedchamber every midnight, or, according to another version, once a week, on the night between Friday and Saturday. This intensive lovelife of the King and the Matronit is reminiscent of the heightened sexuality of the ancient Canaanite gods, King Baal and the Maiden Anath. The issue of the union between the King and the Matronit are the human souls and the angels. When Israel sins, Samael (Satan), who in the form of a serpent or riding a serpent lurks at all times near the private parts of the Matronit, gains power, glues himself to her body, and defiles her. When this happens, the King departs from her and withdraws into the solitude of his heavenly abode. This unhappy state continues until the Day of Atonement, when the scapegoat is offered to Azazel (Satan). Attracted by the offering, Satan lets go of the Matronit and she then can reunite with her husband the King (*Zohar*, 3:79a; 1:64a).

The destruction of the Temple of Jerusalem was the ultimate tragedy for the King and the Matronit. The Matronit remained homeless and accompanied her children, the people of Israel, into their exile, where she is constantly being violated by other gods. The issue of these involuntary submissions are the souls of the gentiles, who are able to suck from the Matronit, just as the Children of Israel did while the Temple still stood (*Zohar*, 1:84b). The Matronit suckling her children is an image reminiscent of Asherah and Anath suckling their offspring in Ugaritic mythology.

The King, unable to endure the solitude, let a slave goddess, Lilith, take the place of his true queen, and thus it is now Lilith who rules over the Holy Land. This act, more than anything else, caused the King to lose his honor (*Zohar*, 3:69a).

VII. Mysticism and Mythology

As a rule, the kabbalistic authors represent the nature of God and the various persons comprised in Him in the form of mystical interpretations of passages, expressions, or single words contained in the Bible. Thus the four persons in the deity, the Father, the Mother, the Son (the King), and the Daughter (the Matronit), are derived from the Tetragrammaton, the most sacred four-letter name of God, YHWH (Yahweh). The letter *Y* is called the Father and stands for Wisdom; the first *H* is the Supernal Mother, called Understanding; the *W* is the Son; and the second *H* the Daughter (*Zohar*, 3:290a–b; 65b). However, even if we accept these statements at face value, three considerations indicate that much in kabbalistic theology is not the result of mystical speculation, but belongs to the realm of mythology. One is the striking similarity between the kabbalistic tetrad and several ancient Near Eastern tetrads. These similarities are so numerous and detailed that they can only be explained by borrowing, despite the considerable time lag between them.[31]

The second consideration is that, quite apart from these affinities, the concrete details given about the four persons in the deity and the relationships among them are unmistakably mythological. The kabbalistic authors stress that the Father, Mother, Son, and Daughter are but four attributes, aspects or *Sefirot* (as the Kabbalists term the divine emanations) of the one God, and are mystical symbols of his wisdom, understanding, beauty, and sovereignty. However, the stories about the four divine persons, their loves (couched in most explicitly sexual terms), jealousies, joys, sorrows, extra-marital unions, and separations are myths and must have been perceived as such by all readers, with the possible exception of a few with rigorously mystical minds and an unusual capacity for rigidly controlled abstract-symbolic thought.

The third factor is the specific power relationship the Kabbala assumed to exist between human actions and the vicissitudes that befell the divine Son-King and Daughter-Matronit. When the pious of Israel copulate with their wives on Friday night, this, it was taught, brings about a joyous union between the King and the Matronit. In fact, the human sexual act causes the King to emit his seminal fluid from his divine male genital and to fertilize the Matronit, who thereupon gives birth to angels and human souls (*Zohar*, 1:12b). When the same pious and learned men keep apart from their wives during the six days of the week, the Matronit joins them and couples with them (*Zohar*, 1:49b–50a). When there is strife in the world, the male cherub and the female cherub, representing the King and the Matronit, turn away from each other and thus their nakedness is revealed (*Zohar*, 2:176a; 3:59a).

Such a close correspondence between human and divine acts would only make sense to the followers of the Kabbala (the majority of Jews from the fifteenth to the eighteenth centuries) if it was based on a solid mythical belief in actual humanlike sexual relations between the King and the Matronit. Even if the kabbalistic authors originally understood them to be abstract-mystical symbols of two "emanations" of God, by the time their explications reached the average Kabbalist the mystical concept had turned into concrete mythical image. The spread of this popular-mythical, as opposed to the scholarly-mystical, view of the Matronit and her relationship to the King and to men was facilitated among the Jews who lived in Christian countries by the presence of a popular Mariolatry.

In any case, in the kabbalistic development of Judaism, the female deity, who was tenaciously worshiped by the Israelites in biblical times, again came to occupy an important place in popular Jewish religious consciousness. In the old days Yahweh had his female counterpart or consort[32] in either Asherah or Anath-Astarte-Queen of Heaven; in the later Middle Ages he—now styled the Son, the King, or the Holy One, blessed be He—has his wife, mate, or consort in the Matronit-Shekhina. Of course, in biblical times the goddess was worshiped with elaborate rites, none of which were carried over or revived for her later successor, the Matronit. From the days of the Second Temple of Jerusalem, God monopolized all ritual expression of worship in both private and public. Since the sixteenth century, however, on Friday nights, homage was paid in home and synagogue to Queen Sabbath, in whose tenderly erotic image one can detect but a faint echo of the more passionate Matronit.

This lack of ritualism for the Matronit contrasts strangely with the important role she played in the mythical belief system. Unlike the *deus absconditus*, she remained on earth, accompanied her children into exile, and continued to be keenly and emotionally concerned with their welfare. She thus supplied the psychologically important divine mother-and-wife figure in Judaism, just as her predecessors Asherah and Anath had in biblical times. Her essential identity with Asherah was recognized, in a remarkable flash of insight, by one of the greatest sixteenth-century Kabbalists, Moses Cordovero of Safed.[33]

Notes

"The Goddess Cult in the Hebrew-Jewish Religion" originally was published in Agehananda Bharati, ed., *The Realm of the Extra-Human* (The Hague: Mouton, 1976), pp. 197–210.

1. Frank E. Eakin, Jr., *The Religion and Culture of Israel* (Boston, 1971), p. 209.
2. William F. Albright, *Yahweh and the Gods of Canaan* (New York: 1968), p. 199.
3. Raphael Patai, *The Hebrew Goddess* (New York: 1967), pp. 164–70.
4. Marvin H. Pope and Wolfgang Röllig, "Syrien: Die Mythologie der Ugariter und Phönizier," in *Wörterbuch der Mythologie*, ed. Hans Wilhelm Haussig (Stuttgart, 1965), 1:246–49, 279–83; Albright, *Yahweh*, pp. 121–22.
5. Pope and Röllig, "Syrien," pp. 253–64; Albright, *Yahweh*, pp. 124–26.
6. Pope and Röllig, "Syrien," pp. 235–41; Albright, *Yahweh*, pp. 128–30.

7. Patai, *Hebrew Goddess*, pp. 61–62; Albright, *Yahweh*, p. 128.
8. Albright, *Yahweh*, p. 171.
9. Ibid., p. 189.
10. Ibid., p. 205.
11. William L. Reed, *The Asherah in the Old Testament* (Fort Worth, Tex., 1949), pp. 80–81, 87.
12. Pope and Röllig, "Syrien," p. 247.
13. Patai, *Hebrew Goddess*, pp. 40ff.
14. Ibid., pp. 45–50.
15. Albright proposed that the Hebrew text of Psalm 68:24 be slightly amended to read, "Why, O Anath, dost thou wash thy feet in blood, the tongues of thy dogs in the blood of the foes?" Cf. William F. Albright, "A Catalogue of Early Hebrew Lyric Poems," *HUCA* 23 (1950–51):28–29. See also Albright, *Yahweh*, pp. 187–88.
16. One point should be mentioned concerning the identification of Astarte with Anath. In the Ugaritic epic of Keret, all the gods are typically referred to by both of their current names in strict parallelism. Thus when Anath and Astarte are mentioned in the same manner, the two names almost certainly refer to the same goddess. In any case, whether Anath and Astarte were identical makes no appreciable difference in our understanding of the worship of Astarte among the Israelites.
17. *Encyclopedia Miqrait* (Jerusalem, 1971–), 6:407.
18. Pope and Röllig, "Syrien," p. 250; *Encyclopedia Miqrait*, 6:408.
19. Patai, *Hebrew Goddess*, p. 98; Albright, *Yahweh*, p. 272; *Encyclopedia Miqrait*, 6:316.
20. Eberhard Schrader, *Die Keilinschriften und das Alte Testament*, 3d ed. revised by H. Zimmern and H. Winkler (Berlin, 1902–3), pp. 441–42, 425.
21. Patai, *Hebrew Goddess*, p. 99; Albright, "Catalogue," pp. 18–19; Albright, *Yahweh*, pp. 138–39, 143, 187, 248, finds the traces of one more feminine deity in the Bible: he considers *Kosharot* of Psalm 68:7 a reference to the midwife goddesses called in Ugaritic, as well as in Canaanitic, by this name. The singular form in Canaanitic, *Koshart*, designated the goddess of childbirth.
22. Pope and Röllig, "Syrien," pp. 236, 244–45.
23. Patai, *Hebrew Goddess*, pp. 126–31.
24. Ibid., p. 123.
25. Ibid., pp. 111–16.
26. Ibid., pp. 140–47.
27. A. Marmorstein, *Studies in Jewish Theology* (Oxford, 1950), pp. 130–31.
28. Patai, *Hebrew Goddess*, p. 148.
29. Ibid., pp. 152–53.
30. Isaiah Tishbi, *Mishnat haZohar*, 2 vols. (Jerusalem, 1961), 2:623.
31. This subject is discussed in some detail in Patai, *Hebrew Goddess*, pp. 164ff.
32. This was argued by Hugo Gressman, *Die Lade Jahwes* (Berlin, 1920), pp. 64–65, and Julian Morgenstern, "Amos Studies III," *HUCA* 15 (1940):121n98; Julian Morgenstern, *The Ark, the Ephod and the "Tent of Meeting,"* (Cincinnati, Ohio, 1945), pp. 95, 96, 107, 111.
33. Moses Cordovero, *Pardes Rimmonim* (Koretz, 1780), p. 120c, says: "It is explained in the *Zohar* that Sovereignty, i.e., the Matronit, is called Asherah, since she sucks from Beauty (the King) who is her husband, inasmuch as he is called Asher. He is Asher and she Asherah." In fact, the passage of the *Zohar* (1:49a) referred to by Cordovero, while it speaks of Asher and Asherah, does not identify the latter with the Matronit. Thus this identification is original with Cordovero.

II.
Biblical
and
Talmudic

5.   The Rainbow

After the waters of the great flood dried from the face of the earth and the ark came to rest on the summit of Mount Ararat, Noah built an altar and offered sacrifices to God, who had saved him and his family from the deluge. ''And the Lord smelled the sweet savor'' (Gen. 8:21) and said to Noah,

> This is the token of the covenant which I make between Me and you and every living creature that is with you, for perpetual generations: I have set My bow in the cloud, and it shall be for a token of a covenant between Me and the earth. And it shall come to pass when I bring clouds over the earth, and the bow is seen in the cloud, that I will remember My covenant which is between Me and you and every living creature of all flesh; and the waters shall no more become a flood to destroy all flesh. And the bow shall be in the cloud; and I will look upon it that I may remember the everlasting covenant between God and every living creature of all flesh that is upon the earth'' [Gen. 9:12–16].

According to this passage the rainbow is the token of the covenant between God and man, the pledge of God's promise not to bring again a flood upon the earth. The folk belief underlying this myth is that if heavy rain clouds cover the sky and the rainbow appears among them, it is a sign that the rains will not be so voluminous as to threaten the life of man and beast. The belief is given mythical validation in the biblical story of the flood and in God's promise to Noah. This is how Philo, the Alexandrian Jewish philosopher (first century B.C.E.–first century C.E.) understood the function of the rainbow. He saw in it a symbol of the divine power: the rainbow is stretched across the clouds and does not allow all of them to burst and send a flood upon the earth.[1]

Let us attempt to find the bases of this ancient folk belief. Why did the ancient Hebrews and Jews believe that the rainbow prevents excessive rainfall? Was this belief confined to them, or was it also found among other peoples? And can the other peoples' beliefs shed some light on that of the ancient Jews?

In his *Folklore in the Old Testament*, Sir James George Frazer collected a huge amount of folkloristic material paralleling the biblical flood story. However, the rainbow appears only in two traditions. According to a Lithuanian story, only one couple escaped the flood. But these two people were old, and, under the influence of the horrible events, they were weak, broken, and exhausted. In order to comfort them, God sent the rainbow, and the rainbow advised them that they should jump nine times over the bones— that is, the stones—of the earth. The old couple did so, and when they jumped over the stones, nine other couples came into being, and from these descended the nine tribes of the Lithuanians.[2] As far as the rainbow is concerned, this story does not teach us anything new except for the fact that the rainbow here too serves the benefit of mankind, as in the Genesis story.

The second flood tradition in which the rainbow plays a role comes from India. North of Singbhum, in the Chota Nagpur area, lives the Mundari or Munda tribe, which is a branch of the Kols. They have a folktale according to which the god created man from the dust of the earth. But mankind quickly became corrupted, refusing to wash and to work. When the god Sing-Bonga saw this, he repented of having created man, and decided to destroy him with a flood. He sent down a stream of fire-water (*Sengle-Daa*) from the sky, and all men died. Only two, a brother and a sister, saved themselves by hiding under the *tiril* tree. (This is why the *tiril* tree is black and charred to this day.) When the god saw this, he reconsidered, and, in order to stop the stream of fire from the sky, he created the snake Lurbing, which inflated himself into the shape of the rainbow, thereby holding up the showers. To this day, when the Mundari see the rainbow, they say that no more rain will fall. Lurbing destroyed the rain.[3]

These folk beliefs present in a more primitive, but also clearer, form than the biblical story the connection between the rainbow and the cessation or prevention of rain. The rainbow is actually a big snake which stretches across the sky and thus keeps the rain from falling.

The rainbow is viewed as a serpent by other peoples as well. In the *Iliad*, Homer compares the snake-shaped ornaments on the shield of Agamemnon to the rainbow.[4] The Algonquin Indians call the lightning "great serpent."[5] In the Yoruba tribe, the rainbow is venerated as "the great serpent of the abyss," which rises up from time to time to drink water from the sky.[6] In the Anula tribe of northern Australia, the rain is identified with the dollar bird, which is called the rain bird.[7] A man whose totem is this bird can cause rain to fall near a certain pool. He catches a snake, puts it into the lake, takes it out, and then kills it and leaves it on the lakeshore. Then, out of grass stalks he makes an arched bundle in imitation of the rainbow, puts it on the body of the snake, and begins to sing while bending over it.[8] Either instantly or some time later, rain will fall as a result of this performance, which is explained with the following tale. Once, a long time ago, the dollar bird was a friend of the snake in this very place. The snake used to make the rain fall by spitting upwards towards the sky until the rainbow appeared and rain commenced.[9]

This tale, of course, does not supply the full explanation of the magic rite described above. It only adds some legendary features to it, such as the friendship between the snake and the bird. The tradition that the snake once caused rain to fall does not explain why it is necessary to kill the snake today in order to make the rain fall. On the contrary, the rite and the myth contain a definite contradiction. The basis of the rite seems to be that the dollar bird symbolizes the rain and the snake the rainbow. The bird cannot endure the snake. If one wants the bird (i.e., rain) to come down to the earth, one must first of all kill its enemy, the snake (i.e., the rainbow). Therefore the snake is killed in a magical rite. However, since in the course of time the identity of the snake and the rainbow has become less clear, a rainbow made of grass is placed upon the snake's body in order to emphasize the identity of the rainbow and the snake. Only thus can we understand why the man first immerses the snake in the lake. This is a sympathetic-magical act whose meaning is: just as I immerse the snake in water so that it should be destroyed (according to the principle of *post hoc, ergo propter hoc*), thus let the rains drown the rainbow and destroy it.

The beliefs and customs of the Central Australian Kaitish tribe confirm this explanation. This tribe believes that the rainbow is the son of the rain and that the feelings between the two are those of father and son. The rainbow therefore wants to prevent his father, the rain, from falling to earth.[10] If the rainbow appears in the sky when rain is desired, the Kaitish sing and adjure the rainbow to drive it away. If the head of the rain-totem clan wants to make rain fall, he goes to the sacred storehouse of the clan, paints the stones kept there with red ocher, and sings over them while sprinkling water from a vessel on the stones and on himself. Then he paints three rainbows in red ocher, one on the ground, one on his own body, and the third on a shield, which he also decorates with zigzag lines in white clay to represent lightning. Only men who belong to the same exogamous moiety as himself are allowed to see this shield. Should men from the other moiety see it, the magic would be annulled. Then he takes the shield from the sacred place and hides it in his own tent until rain falls. After rain has fallen, he destroys the drawings of the rainbow.[11]

There can be no doubt that the purpose of this rite is to imprison the rainbow and thus prevent its appearance until the clouds burst and rain falls. As a further act to bring about rainfall, the rainmaker keeps a vessel full of water next to himself all the time after his return from the sacred storehouse, and scatters about white down. They believe that these acts will hasten the coming of rain. In the meantime, the men who accompanied him to the sacred place go away to a separate place, for neither they nor the rainmaker may have any intercourse with women. The head of the tribe is not allowed even to speak to his wife, who goes away from the camp at the time her husband returns there. When, later on, the woman comes back, she imitates the voice of the plover, which they always identify with the rainy season.[12] Early next morning, the rainmaker returns to the sacred storehouse and covers the stones with bushes. Another night passes in silence, and then the head of the tribe, the other men, and the womenb as well, leave the camp and go out in different directions to search for food. When, after their return, they meet in the camp, they all imitate the cry of the plover, then touch the lips of the rainmaker with food they have brought, and thus they break the ban of silence. If rain falls, they attribute it to the magical virtue of the ritual. If not, they resort to the usual explanation that somebody prevented the rain by a more powerful magic.[13]

As we see, according to the Kaitish, in contrast to the views of the Munda and Anula, the relationship between the rain and the rainbow is not hatred, but friendship, or even a first-degree kinship. Nevertheless, despite the disparate motivation, the conclusion is the same: if the rainbow appears, there will be no rain. If one wants rain to fall, one must first remove the rainbow. For this purpose they hide the rainbow painted on the stone and the shield, in accordance with the principles of sympathetic magic. But they try to make rain fall not only by this negative measure, but also by positive acts. Therefore the rainmaker sprinkles water on the earth, in imitation of rain, and scatters down in imitation of the clouds.

A rite with a similar intent is reported from France. In the Ille et Vilaine, when the children see a rainbow, one of them who has never seen one before plucks a hair from his head, puts it into his left palm, spits on it, and recites an incantation. When he utters the last syllable, he hits the spittle with his right hand, thereby making it splatter about in all directions.[14] The hair stands here for the rainbow, the spittle for rain. The child spits on the hair just as the Yoruba magician immerses the snake in the lake. Then the child makes the spittle splash about, just as the Kaitish rainmaker sprinkles water in order to cause the rain to fall.

The belief that the rainbow and the rain are contrary forces and loathe each other is expressed among many peoples in the form of myths about the rainbow which drinks or sucks the waters of the earth and the rain. Thus Virgil says, "the great rainbow drinks."[15] Ovid states, "Iris [i.e., the rainbow] sucks the water and nourishes the clouds with it."[16] Pseudo-Plutarch (actually Aetius) writes, "Some people pretended to believe that ox-headed Iris sucked water from the rivers."[17] Hesiod comments, "Iris went down to Hades in order to draw water from the Styx."[18] Propertius says, "The crimson rainbow drinks the waters of the rain."[19] And Plautus puts these words into the mouth of somebody who sees an old man drink with great gusto: "Behold, the rainbow drinks; I think it will rain today."[20]

The same image recurs in places other than ancient Rome. Aleksandr N. Afanasiev quotes a Slovak saying about a man who drinks much: "He drinks like the rainbow."[21] In the upper Loire area, there is a belief that if the rainbow drinks from a stream, one can find in it a spoon and a vessel. The Swabians believe that in the places where the two ends of the rainbow touch the earth it draws up water from a golden plate and ewer. In Volhynia, in the Lutzk province, the rainbow is called *Cmok*, that is, "sucker," he who sucks. (*Smok* in Polish is "snake.") The people of Lutzk believe that the rainbow is a tube which sucks up the water of the rivers and the seas and pours it into the clouds. In the Litin district of Podolia, they believe that the color of the rainbow is blue and red when it is drinking, and all red when it is not. In the Grubeshov district (Lublin), the rainbow is considered a path on which the angels come down from heaven to draw water. Then they pour the water into a sieve, and thus rain falls. In Pleternica, Slavonia, they believe that the rainbow sucks up water. According to the Finns, the rainbow is a monster which swallows great quantities of water. When the rainbow appears, they say, "The rainbow is drinking." The Hungarian word for rainbow, *szivár-vány*, is derived from the verb *szipál-cibál-szivár*, which means "to pull" or "to suck."[22] In Jörg Wickram's *Kunst zu trinken*, one finds these similes: "saufen wie der Regenbogen," i.e., "to swill like the rainbow," or "saugt wie der Regenbogen geschwind," "he sucks like the rainbow, quickly."[23]

In sum, we find the belief that the rainbow prevents the rain from falling, or sucks up the water from the earth, among many peoples in both ancient and modern times. The belief is expressed in various fantasies and legends. The basis in nature of these fantasies and legends seems to be the observation that the rainbow appears mostly after the cessation of the rain, which was taken to mean that the rainbow made the rain stop.

As to whether we have to do here with the diffusion of one myth to many places or with the multiple independent origin of parallel concepts, I am inclined to the latter alternative. There seems to be no point in seeking a connection between the New Zealand belief according to which the rainbow is a ladder on which the souls go up into the sky and the German folk tradition to the effect that the moon went up into the sky on a rainbow. [24] Nor can one assume any connection between the Indian, pre-Islamic Arab, and Finnish beliefs, according to which the rainbow is the weapon of the storm god, from which he shoots his arrows, the lightnings. In a like manner we can assume that in ancient Israel also, the story about the rainbow and its significance developed independently.

So far we have not pointed out a basic linguistic fact which has played an important role in the modern scholarly interpretation of the meaning of the biblical rainbow. In Hebrew one and the same word, *qeshet*, means both a rainbow and the bow used by warriors to shoot arrows. This double, albeit undoubtedly related, meaning of *qeshet* led Julius Wellhausen to conclude that

> the rainbow was originally the instrument of the god who shot arrows, and was thus a symbol of his enmity. But he puts it down from his hand as a sign that his wrath has subsided, and that he has become reconciled and kind. When it stormed, so that one could fear a new flood, the rainbow appeared in the sky when the sun and the mercy again broke through. The Old Testament does not have the concept of the arch itself. In the Bible, the meaning of the word *qeshet* is always *tóxon*, even if the intention is to speak of the bow in heaven (e.g., in Ben Sira 43:11; 50:7; Sap. Sol. 5:21). [25] And what is most important is that also, according to the Arab view, the *iris* was always conceived as the war bow of God. Kuzah shoots arrows from his bow, and then hangs it in the clouds. Among the Jews and Judaizers, the rainbow retained a remarkably close relationship to the deity until well into Christian times. [26]

Hermann Gunkel follows in Wellhausen's footsteps and likewise interprets Genesis 9:12–16 to mean that when God got tired of shooting His arrows—this, more or less, is how they put it in the beginning—He set his bow aside. This is why the rainbow appears in the sky after the storm, and at its sight ancient man rejoiced because he saw that God's wrath had subsided. [27]

Let us quote in full the passages from the Apocrypha referred to by Wellhausen. Ben Sira 43:11 reads:

See the rainbow [*qeshet*] and bless its Maker,
For it is very magnificent in glory.
Splendor surrounds it in majesty,
And the hand of God stretched it in exaltation.

There is here no hint to the concept of the rainbow as a bow of war. On the contrary, the rainbow is presented as a creation of God, which He "stretched" just as He stretched the rivers (Isa. 66:12).[28]

Ben Sira 50:7 compares the high priest Shim'on ben Yohanan to the rainbow. When the high priest comes out of the Temple his appearance is like that of a star, the sun, the moon, "and like the rainbow which appears in the cloud."[29] Ben Sira here was influenced by Ezekiel 1:28.[30] There is no allusion here to *tóxon*.

The third passage (Sap. Sol. 5:21) is a mere poetic simile. "Shafts of lightning shall fly with true aim — And from the clouds, as from a well-drawn bow, shall they leap to the mark." The author here compares the *clouds*, and not the rainbow, to the weapons from which arrows of lightning are shot. In the verses preceding this one, he describes how God protects the pious: " . . . the righteous . . . shall receive a glorious kingdom . . . with His arm shall He shield them" (5:16). When describing the destruction of the wicked, the author continues to use the same poetic simile. "He shall take His jealousy as a complete armor— And shall make the whole creation His weapons of vengeance on his enemies— He shall put on righteousness as a breastplate . . . and shall sharpen stern wrath for a sword" (9:17–20). After comparing the acts of God to instruments of war, the author compares the way God fights to the phenomena of the storm. His arrows—that is, the lightnings—go forth from His clouds as if from a well drawn bow (9:21). "He hurls hailstones as from an engine of war" (9:22).

Such similes not infrequently are found in biblical poetry and are but poetic comparisons. Psalm 18:15, too, compares the lightning to arrows, and so on. Poetic imagination puts into God's hand not only arrows, but also all kinds of other weapons. Deuteronomy 32:41 speaks of the sword of God, v. 42 of His arrows and sword. Psalm 7:13 speaks of the sword and bow of God; Lamentations 2:4 describes God who "hath bent His bow like an enemy"; Habakkuk 3:9 refers to the bow of God, and v. 11 to His arrows and spear.[31] But all these, including the verses referred to by Wellhausen, are but poetic similes, and do not prove that the rainbow was ever actually considered a war bow.

We shall gain a better understanding of Genesis 9:13–14 with the help of the Indian and Australian views. In a comparison of the Genesis story and these legends, the important point is not the nature of the rainbow. The rainbow is viewed or interpreted in different ways by different peoples. The common feature which we wish to emphasize is that according to these peoples the rainbow is not a phenomenon which indicates the cessation of rain, but a sign that there will be no rain in the near future. And this is close to what the Genesis story tells: the rainbow, even if it does not indicate a complete absence of rain, is a sign of a similar thing. The rains will be moderate and will not cause destruction to man and beast.[32]

The subject of Genesis 9:12–16 proved of considerable interest to several talmudic sages. In their eyes the rainbow served as a token, or a pledge, to sinful generations that, despite their sins, there would be no new flood to destroy the earth. Hence, they thought, in those generations which were free of sin the rainbow did not appear, because they had no reason to fear a flood. Such generations were, according to R. Yudan, those of King Hezekiah and of the men of the Great Assembly.[33] Such beliefs were found in medieval Germany: for forty years prior to the day of Last Judgment the rainbow will not appear.[34] In England they believed that for 1,600 years prior to the great flood, the rainbow never appeared.[35]

According to the talmudic view, it is not necessary that the entire generation should be free of sin for the rainbow not to appear. It is sufficient if there be one completely saintly man in a generation; he serves as a guarantee that no flood will be visited upon the earth.[36] Such a saint was R. Shim‘on ben Yoḥai, during whose entire lifetime no rainbow was seen.[37] Once the sages visited him and asked, "Why has the rainbow not appeared in your days?" He said to them, "Is the rainbow not a sign of punishment? I am sufficient to ward off the punishment." When the sages heard this, one of them rose and said, " 'I have set My bow in the cloud' (Gen. 9:13)—this is R. Shim‘on ben Yoḥai, who is the sign of the world."[38]

In the Jerusalem Talmud, the statement that in the days of R. Shim‘on ben Yoḥai the rainbow never appeared is directly followed by this passage: "R. Shim‘on ben Yoḥai used to say, 'Valley, valley, be filled with golden denars.' And it became filled."[39] The connection between the two passages is puzzling. What has R. Shim‘on's function as the guarantor of the safety of the generation to do with a valley full of gold? Traditions of other peoples supply the connection. According to modern Greek belief, Byzantine gold ("Constantine's gold") is hidden in the spot where the rainbow touches the earth. In Germany they believe that a golden key can be found in that spot. In Carinthia there is a belief that if one throws a hat at the rainbow it will fall to earth full of gold.[40] It appears that a similar belief was found among the Jews in talmudic times. The connection between the rainbow and gold would then explain that R. Shim'on ben Yoḥai was believed to share this feature with the rainbow. He too could fill the valley with gold.

The belief that the rainbow was absent during the lifetime of a true saint became so entrenched that the presence or absence of the rainbow came to serve as a touchstone of the saintliness of leading rabbis. One of the stories told about R. Y'hoshu'a ben Levi was to the effect that Elijah of blessed memory used to study Tora with him, and when they came to a teaching of R. Shim'on ben Yoḥai, R. Y'hoshu'a had difficulty in understanding it. Elijah said, "Do you wish to ask R. Shim'on ben Yoḥai? Come, and I shall raise him up [from the dead] for you." They went, and Elijah called R. Shim'on ben Yoḥai. He instantly answered. Elijah said, "R. Y'hoshu'a ben Levi has come to ask you a *halakha* [a legal matter]." But R. Shim'on ben Yoḥai did not want to answer him. Elijah then said, "R. Y'hoshu'a ben Levi is worthy of seeing you. He is a *tzaddiq* [a saintly man]." R. Shim'on ben Yoḥai said, "Were he a *tzaddiq*, the rainbow would not have appeared in his days."[41]

R. Y'hoshu'a ben Levi gave some advice in connection with the rainbow which is interesting because of the contrast between it and a Slavonian custom. R. Alexandri quoted this saying of R. Y'hoshu'a: "He who sees the rainbow in the cloud must fall on his face, for it is said, 'As the appearance of the bow that is in the cloud. . . . and when I saw it I fell upon my face' (Ezek. 1:28). In the West [i.e., in Palestine] they cursed him who did thus, because it seemed as if he had prostrated himself to the rainbow. But, in any case, he should recite a benediction. What benediction? 'Blessed be He who remembers the covenant.' "[42] As against this, in Pleternica, Slavonia, when the first rainbow appears in the spring, everybody must go outside, lift his hands to the sky, and say, "God help you!" At that time the sick must not remain lying in their beds lest they die.[43]

Among many peoples the belief is that when the rainbow appears one must make some bodily move. In the Ukraine the children call to one another, "Run, lest the rainbow swallow you!" This custom is, of course, based on the belief that the rainbow, while it sucks up water from the sea or the rivers, also swallows everything found in the water: pebbles, frogs, fishes, etc. Therefore there is a danger that it also will swallow children.[44] A similar belief is reported from Finland. In Pleternica the children sing and dance when they see the rainbow. Walter Scott writes:

> As wilder's children leave their home
> After the rainbow's arch to roam.[45]

In a Mishna we find the statement, "He who has no regard for the honor of his Creator, it is better for him were he not born.''[46] This saying is explained by R. Abba. "This refers to him who looks at the rainbow. . . . as it is written, 'As the appearance of the bow that is in the cloud.' ''[47] This is again further explained by R. Y'huda ben R. Naḥman. "He who looks at three things, his eyes become dim: at the rainbow, at women, and at the Kohens [the priests].'' In another, midrashic, source, the view is expressed that the rainbow symbolizes God, or at least stands in a close relationship to Him. "I have set My bow [*qashti*] in the cloud. . . . My likeness [*qishuti*], a thing that is likened to me. . . . However, this is impossible [for nothing can visually be like God], therefore [what *qashti* means is that] it is like the straw [*qashin*] of the fruit."[48] That is, God said that the rainbow was the straw, the least of His works.

The view that the rainbow has some kind of relationship to God is found among the Kamchadales of Siberia. They see in the rainbow the hem of the garment of the god Biliukai.[49] The Karaib believe that the rainbow is the plume of the god Juluka.[50] In Zante the rainbow is called the girdle or bow of the virgin.[51]

Early indications of the view that the bow was a symbol of strength and majesty are contained in the Bible. In Jacob's blessing, kept throughout in highly poetic language, the power of Joseph is described by the words "his bow abode firm" (Gen. 49:24). Jeremiah refers to the destruction of a people's might by saying, "I will break the bow of Elam" (Jer. 49:35); Hosea says, "I will break the bow of Israel" (Hos. 1:5). In these passages *qeshet* means the war bow.

An interesting parallel to the belief that it is forbidden to look at the rainbow is found among the Teton Dakota, who hold that one must not point at it with one's finger.[52] The same prohibition exists in Bohemia: were one to do so, one's finger would be torn off, or great thunder would come, or the culprit would be struck by lightning.[53] In Amiens, in the Somme, it is forbidden to point at the rainbow, and he who does so has his finger cut off.[54] In Pleternica, they believe that if somebody sticks out his tongue at the rainbow, the rainbow will instantly make his tongue dry and wither. In India, in the Harz, in Bohemia, and in the Amicus *arrondissement*, it is forbidden to point at the rainbow, lest one's finger be cut off.[55]

The poetic concept that the rainbow is God's war bow is found in the Midrash. "The Holy One, blessed be He, punished the world with the *qeshet*, as is written, 'Thy bow [*qeshet*] is made quite bare, sworn are the rods of the world, Selah. Thou dost cleave the earth with rivers' (Hab. 3:9), and with it He settles the world, as it is written, 'I have set My bow [*qeshet*] in the cloud, '' (Gen. 9:13).[56] Another Midrash states, '' 'And the bow shall be in the cloud and I will look upon it' (Gen. 9:16), for I bent my bow and brought a flood upon the earth, but henceforth I shall see it not bent, to remember not to destroy the world again.''[57] Similarly, according to a pre-Islamic Arab view, the rainbow is the weapon of the wrathful god of war.[58] The Turks call the rainbow the bow of Kuzah, the angel of the clouds.[59] Kuzah is, of course, the ancient Arab war god, reduced to the status of an angel within monotheistic Islam. The rainbow as the bow of the storm god appears also among the Finns.[60] They call the rainbow Ukkonkaari, that is, "the bow of [the god] Ukko." Among the Indians, it is the bow of Indra. Among the Anakua and neighboring tribes in Mozambique, the rainbow is the bow of Malula, the good spirit.

The Alexandrian Jewish philosopher Philo saw in the rainbow "symbolically the invisible power of God."[61] Nahmanides in his commentary to Genesis 9:12 presents a similar view.

> And they said concerning the meaning of this sign that He did not make the rainbow so that its feet [i.e., the two ends] should point upward, for then it would seem as if they would shoot with it from heaven at the earth . . . but made it in reverse position, to show thereby that they will not shoot with it from heaven. And this is the way of the fighters, to turn it thusly in their hand when they call for peace with their opponents, and also [to show] that the bow has no more arrows to point at them.

Nahmanides himself saw in the rainbow nothing but a natural phenomenon. "And we, willy-nilly, adhere to the words of the Greeks that the rainbow is produced by the heat of the sun upon the wet air."

Philo refers to several views which were current in his days among Jews or gentiles. He himself thought that the biblical story of the rainbow "perhaps . . . indicates something else by the bow [namely that] in the laxness and force of earthly things there will not take place a dissolution by their being completely loosened to [the point of] incongruity nor [will there be] force up to [the point of] reaching a break.''[62] What Philo seems to mean is that the rainbow is an assurance to the world that no major calamity will occur.

The opposite view can be found among several peoples. The belief that the rainbow causes weakness and even illness is found in Bolivia. The rainbow harms people in the view of the Burmese also, who see in it an evil demon which eats souls. In the Bas Quercy, in Lot, France, they believe that where the rainbow touches the earth, it burns and destroys the crops. In the Ukraine they believe that the rainbow eats children, and in Estonia that it eats even adults. According to the Karaib, the rainbow brings illness and kills people. The Makka of Washington state believe that the rainbow has long fingernails with which it can grab anybody.[63] According to the *Iliad* (P 544), the rainbow is an omen of war or storm.

Philo's view that the rainbow helps man, or is an assurance that no ill will befall the world, also has its parallels among other peoples. The Cypriotes believe that the prevalence of certain colors in the rainbow presages the success of various crops.[64] In Greece and Germany, they believe that gold can be found in the place where the rainbow touches the earth. In Estonia the rainbow is the scythe of the thunder, with which it pursues evil spirits.[65] According to the Karaib, the rainbow accompanies seafarers and protects them.[66] In the Philippines and the Dutch East Indies, they believe that the rainbow carries people to the land of happiness. Philo goes on to explain that the rainbow is a sign showing that no new flood will come to destroy the whole earth, for just as the arrow shot from the bow does not strike everything, but only that which is far away, and does not harm that which is near, so the future floods will not cover the whole earth, but only part of it.[67]

The Midrash attempts to reconcile the famous pronouncement of Ecclesiastes 1:9, "There is nothing new under the sun," with the appearance of the rainbow the first time after the flood. It lists the rainbow among those ten things which were created on Friday at dusk. The rainbow "arose in the thought [of God]" at the creation, and when its time came it appeared in the clouds.[68]

According to the interpretation of Saadia Gaon, quoted in David Qimhi's commentary to Genesis 9:12, "Always when the rain stops the rainbow appears. But in the days of the flood the rainbow did not appear, for the rain did not stop for forty days and forty nights. And God promised them that they will always see the rainbow in the cloud, and this will be for them a sign that there will be no flood to destroy the earth." That is, according to Saadia Gaon the rainbow appears after the cessation of the rain.[69]

The numerous parallels adduced, and especially those from primitive peoples, show clearly that there is no basis for seeking a duplication of the pre-Islamic Arab view in the biblical view of the rainbow. The biblical story of the rainbow could be based on a simpler, and, it would seem, older view, according to which the rainbow announces moderate rainfall and is a visible guarantee that no excessive rain will fall. The parallels quoted indicate that the basis of this view is the belief that the rainbow prevents rain from falling.

From the abundance of similar and dissimilar legends about the rainbow found among many peoples in all parts of the world, one definite conclusion can be drawn. It is a general, almost natural, idea to see a connection, a mutual influence, between the rainbow and the rain. This idea is based partly on actual observation; however, the same observation can lead to different, and even opposite, conclusions. Thus one people considers the rainbow an impediment to rain; another thinks that it facilitates rainfall. Nevertheless, there is one common feature in all these legends. No people considers the rainbow a mere optical phenomenon, but all regard it as a force which can influence the life of the earth and of man. They see in it either a mythical being or an object, and endow it with fantastic, imaginary features.

Notes

"The Rainbow" originally was published in Hebrew in the *Jubilee Volume in Honor of Samuel Krauss* (Jerusalem, 1937), pp. 311–25.

1. Philo of Alexandria, *Questiones in Gen.*, 2:64.
2. Sir James George Frazer, *Folk-Lore in the Old Testament*, 3 vols. (London, 1919), 1:176–77. The Ukranians call the rainbow *vecelka* (cheerer), because when it appears, the cloud-covered sky makes a merrier impression (*Mélusine: Recueil de mythologie, littérature populaire, traditions et usages* 2 [1884–85]:42). *Mélusine* contains a rich collection of beliefs and practices connected with the rainbow from all over the world. See, for example, *Mélusine* 2 (1884–85):9ff., 38ff., 70ff., 108ff., 127ff., 401–2, 454; 3 (1886–87):128–29, 233–34, 310, 575–76; 4 (1888–89):561. The jumping over the bones of the earth is of course reminiscent of what Deucalion and Pyrrha were advised to do: to throw the bones of their mother—that is, stones—behind their backs (Ovid, *Metamorphoses*, 1 383ff.).
3. Frazer, *Folk-Lore*, 1:196, quoting Richard Andrée, *Die Flutsagen* (Brunswick, 1891), pp. 25–26, and L. Nottrott, *Die Gossnersche Mission unter den Kohls*, 2 vols. (Halle, 1874–88), 1:59. Frazer also quotes T. Dalton, *Descriptive Ethnology of Bengal* (Calcutta, 1872), pp. 188–89, according to whom the Karen, the Munda, and the Hos have no flood traditions, but only the belief that the snake Lurbeng (that is, the rainbow) causes the rain to cease.
4. *Iliad* A 24.
5. Cf. Ignacz Goldziher, *Mythology among the Hebrews* (London, 1877), p. 185, quoting *Zeitschrift für Völkerpsychologie* 7 (1871):307.
6. A. B. Ellis, *The Yoruba-Speaking Peoples* (London, 1894), p. 81, as quoted in *ERE*, 10:391–92.
7. The dollar bird belongs to the genus *Eurystomus*; its name comes from the big yellow spot on its wings.
8. In Stratfordshire, England, they make a cross out of grass stalks in order to cause the rainbow to disappear. In the Lorient area they make a cross out of two twigs and say, "Ditreyet ditfreyet truet locht er bley," "Hurry, hurry, cut off the wolf's tails." This will make the rainbow disappear (*Mélusine* 2[1884–85]:17, 110).
9. Cf. Sir James George Frazer, *The Golden Bough*, 3d ed., 1:287, quoting Baldwin Spencer and F. J. Gillen, *The Northern Tribes of Central Australia* (London, 1904), pp. 314–15.
10. According to the Tahitians, the rainbow is the son of the god Taaroa and his wife, the air (*Mélusine* 2[1884–85]:10). According to Pindar, *Olympia*, 11.2.3, the rain is the child of the cloud. Thus also in *Kitāb al-Aghānī* (Būlāq, 1285 H. [1868–69]), 20:54, 16; cf. Goldziher, *Mythology*, p. 167.
11. Frazer, *Golden Bough*, 1:258; quoting Spencer and Gillen, *Northern Tribes*, pp. 296–99, 530–31.
12. We have already met with the identification of a bird with rain in the Anula tribe.
13. Frazer, *Golden Bough*, 1:259.
14. *Mélusine* 2(1884–85):111.
15. Virgil, *Georgics*, 1.380.
16. Ovid, *Metamorphoses*, 1.271.

17. Plutarch, *De placitis philosophorum* (actually written by Aetius).
18. Hesiod, *Theogony*, 5.780–81.
19. Propertius, 3.5, 32.
20. Plautus, *Curculio*, act 1, sc. 2. All of the above quotations from Roman authors are presented in *Mélusine* 2(1884–85):9. Cf. also Wilhelm H. Roscher, *Ausführliches Lexicon der griechischen und römischen Mythologie*, 6 vols. in 9 (Leipzig, 1884–1937), s.v. Iris.
21. Aleksandr N. Afanasiev, *Poetical Pictures*.
22. *Magyar Nyelvör*, 7:4.
23. Jörg Wickram (sixteenth century), *Kunst zu trinken*, E4a and F3a, as quoted in Jacob Grimm, *Deutsches Wörterbuch*, s.v. Regenbogen.
24. Cf. also the Japanese belief that the rainbow is a "heavenly bridge" (Pierre Daniel Chantepie de la Saussaye, *Lehrbuch der Religionsgeschichte*, 4th ed., 2 vols. [Freiburg i. B., (1887–89), 1:274]).
25. John Skinner, in his *A Critical . . . Commentary on Genesis* (New York, 1925), p. 172, bases himself on this statement when he says that Wellhausen and others have "proved" that the meaning of the word *qeshet* is always the bow as weapon.
26. Julius Wellhausen, *Prolegomena zur Geschichte Israels*, 6th ed. (Berlin, 1905), p. 311, n. 1. This is not the place to show in detail the untenability of Wellhausen's view, but let me point to one biblical passage which he would have difficulty explaining along his lines. In the great throne vision of Ezekiel we read: "As the appearance of the bow [*qeshet*] that is in the cloud in the day of rain, so was the appearance of the brightness round about" [Ezek. 1:28]. It is crystal clear that here the reference is to the rainbow, that not even a residual image of the war bow is retained, and that it is the *brightness* of the rainbow and nothing else to which the prophet compares the luminous appearance which, in his vision, surrounded God. *Note added in 1980.*
27. Hermann Gunkel, *Genesis*, p. 150. Similarly Patrick, in Hastings, *Dictionary of the Bible*, 4:196, s.v. Rainbow.
28. Cf. Raphael Patai, *HaMayim* (Tel Aviv, 1936), p. 111.
29. The rainbow here is one of four heavenly phenomena or bodies to which the high priest is compared. It is clearly nothing but another heavenly sight, like the stars, the sun, and the moon. *Note added in 1980.*
30. This passage seems to have influenced Rev. 4:3 also: "And there was a rainbow round about the throne, in sight like unto an emerald," and also Rev. 10:1, "And I saw another mighty angel come down from heaven, clothed with a cloud: and a rainbow was upon his head, and his face was as it were the sun, and his feet as pillars of fire." The image re-echoed in Germany until the late Middle Ages. Grimm, *Deutsches Wörterbuch*, s.v. Regenbogen, quotes two poems: "Da kommt der liebe Gott gezogen / Auf einem guldnen Regenbogen" (Spruch: Wenn der jüngste Tag soll kommen); "Darnach wird Christus hocherwogen / Auf einem guldnen Regenbogen / In einer Wolke voller Blitzen / Mit grosser Kraft Gerichte sitzen" (Bartholomäus Ringwaldt, *Speculum Mundi*, 1590).
31. The Midrash develops the comparison of God to a man of war; cf. Mekh. Beshallaḥ 4:30 (14:16); Mekh. of R. Shim'on ben Yoai 47–48. Cf. Patai, *HaMayim*, p. 129.
32. Cf. Y. Ta'anit 81c: "R. Yudan the father of R. Matna said: 'God makes rain fall in measure, as it is said, "He meteth out the waters by measure" '[Job 28:25].'' This also is the significance of the rainbow according to Abrabanel, in his comments on Gen. 30:13: "God put His bow in the clouds . . . so that they should melt easily and have little rain . . . and should no longer be able to let a pouring rain fall to the earth."
33. Gen. Rab. 35:2, ed. Theodor-Albeck, 1:328; Mid. haGadol, ed. Schechter, p. 173.
34. Hastings, *Dictionary of the Bible*, 4:196, s.v. Rainbow.
35. Thomas Brown, *Study of Popular Superstition*, as quoted in *Mélusine* 2(1884–85):134.
36. Actually the idea is more complicated. The rainbow's appearance tells the people that they are sinful and that, were it not for God's covenant with Noah not to bring another deluge on the world, the sins of the generation would be sufficient to provoke Him to send another flood. The presence of a saintly man in the generation makes it unnecessary for the rainbow to appear because he himself is a guarantee of his generation's safety. *Note added in 1980.*

37. Y. Ber. 13d bot.
38. Mid. haGadol, ed. Schechter, p. 174.
39. Ibid., Gen. Rab. 35:2–3, ed. Theodor-Albeck, 1:329.
40. *Mélusine* 2 (1884–85):40.
41. Mid. Tehillim, ed. Buber, p. 252. In other sources with small variations: B. Ket. 77b; Gen. Rab. 35:2.
42. B. Ber. 59a; cf. Mid. haGadol, ed. Schechter, p. 173.
43. *Mélusine* 2 (1884–85):42.
44. Ibid.
45. Sir Walter Scott, *The Bridal of Triermain*, 2.3.
46. M. Ḥag. 2:1.
47. B. Ḥag. 16a.
48. Gen. Rab. 35, ed. Theodor-Albeck, 1:330.
49. *Mélusine* 2 (1884–85):109.
50. Ibid.
51. Hastings, *Dictionary of the Bible*, 4:195.
52. *ERE*, 10:371–72.
53. *Mélusine* 2 (1884–85):110.
54. Ibid., after Carnoy.
55. Ibid., pp. 43, 110.
56. Mid. haGadol, ed. Schechter, p. 171.
57. Mid. Leqaḥ Tov, ed. Buber, pp. 48, 17.
58. Wellhausen, *Prolegomena*, p. 311, n. 1.
59. Hermann (Armin) Vámbéry, *Die primitive Kultur des Turco-Tatarischen Volkes* (Leipzig, 1879), p. 168.
60. *Die Religion in Geschichte und Gegenwart*, 4:1811.
61. Philo, *Questiones*, 2.64.
62. Ibid.
63. *Mélusine* 2(1884–85):15, 43, 110.
64. Ibid., p. 110.
65. Ibid., pp. 40, 109, 110.
66. Ibid., p. 110.
67. Philo, *Questiones*, 2.64.
68. Mid. haGadol, ed. Schechter, p. 173.
69. This is how Lord Byron understood the story of the rainbow when he wrote, "Be thou the rainbow to the storms of life" (*The Bride of Abydos*, 2.20).

6.　*T'khelet*—Blue

In memory of my revered teacher and master, Professor
Ludwig Blau.

I.

   If one walks along the streets of Jerusalem in the Old
City, or outside it in the old quarters inhabited by oriental Jews, one cannot
fail to notice that the doors and windows of many houses are surrounded by a
light blue frame painted on the wall above and on both sides of the opening.
The same sky blue color also is met in other places and forms. Arabs hang
blue glass or beads on the doors of their houses and on their horses, donkeys,
bicycles, and automobiles. Their women prefer blue jewelry above all other
colors. The men, as they saunter along the streets, play with strings of blue
beads (the so-called worry beads). The fellah women decorate their faces
with blue tattooed dots on their foreheads, around their lips, and on their
chins. The Bedouins, both men and women, paint a blue frame around their
eyes with kohl. If one inquires from these people about the meaning of any of
these uses of the blue color, one invariably gets the answer that it serves as a
protection from the evil eye.

  The evil eye, and the dangers it represents to everybody and everything, are well known and widespread. The evil eye is feared by European
peoples as well. Witches, sorcerers, demons, spirits, and occasionally even

simple and innocent people, and especially pregnant women, have the power of harming others with their evil eye.[1] As for its victims, it is especially individuals possessing some good trait who are in danger of being harmed by the evil eye. Therefore, if reference is made to someone's good feature, such as beauty, one must add the words *unbeshrien* or *unberufen*, or, in Hebrew, *b'li 'ayin hara'*, "without the evil eye." Such words also served as protection against the evil eye among the ancient Egyptians.[2]

In the Middle East, where ancient ideas have survived and remained influential to a much greater extent than in the West, people were often not satisfied with such protective exclamations, but felt the need to protect themselves against the evil eye by more potent measures. Among these, in the first place, is the sky blue color.

Several outstanding Orientalists have investigated the views of the Middle Eastern peoples about the evil eye, the methods they used to protect themselves against it, and the sources of the belief that the blue color is a potent, or perhaps the most potent, apotropaic measure. According to Hugo Gressmann, fear of the evil eye was in its original form a fear of the blue eye, which seemed to the dark-eyed Orientals to be mysterious and threatening. In their fear of the blue eye they tried to protect themselves against it with the help of the blue color; that is, they resorted to homeopathic magic and attempted to combat like with like.[3] This explanation seems to me insufficient and unlikely. In the world of the Semitic peoples, the apotropaic measures, including the amulets whose special task is to protect their wearers from the evil eye, are based on entirely different principles. In most cases they try to protect themselves against demons and evil spirits by employing magical means whose basic effect lies in their ability to frighten away and drive off those evil forces. For example, they attach holy objects to their bodies so that the demons or the evil eye should not be able to approach them.[4] Another method requires that something unclean be hung around the neck of the individual wishing to be protected, e.g., a human bone, or the dead body of a "creeping thing," so that the demons are frightened off.[5] Such magic methods of protection also were found in ancient Egypt.[6] As against this, homeopathic or sympathetic magic intends to achieve a positive purpose: one pours water upon the earth in order to bring about rainfall.[7]

It would therefore seem that we must look elsewhere for the basis of the belief in the power of blue to ward off the evil eye. A discussion with a Yemenite rabbi in Jerusalem made me aware of the view of the Yemenite Jews as to the meaning of the blue frames around the doors and windows of their houses. "We paint our houses blue," he said, "against the evil eye, because the Holy One, blessed be He, also painted His dwelling place, heaven, with the sky blue color.[8] If we want to protect ourselves from the evil eye, we do as God did, and paint our houses blue.''

This explanation, of course, is secondary. The idea that the blue color of the sky is a protection against the evil eye could only have arisen after the practice of using blue door and window frames was already in vogue among the Yemenite Jews as an apotropaic measure. But the basis of the comparison, or, more precisely, the interpretation of the blue color as an imitation of the color of the sky, seems to contain the correct explanation: blue protects against demons and evil spirits because it is the color of the sky. The sky (or heaven) is the symbol of purity, the place of the ''upper waters'' whose purity is fixed and permanent. The dwelling place of the demons and evil spirits and all the sources of the evil eye is on the earth or beneath it. They can never reach the heights of heaven. Even the lower waters can expel demons and annul their evil influences.[9] How much more effective against them are the powers of the upper waters, of heaven, which are represented by the blue color around the doors and windows of the houses.

II.

Let us now look at the role the blue color and blue dye played in biblical and talmudic times.

According to Exodus and Numbers, blue was abundant in the building and furnishings of the ''Tent of Meeting,'' the desert tabernacle erected by the Children of Israel. While the curtains of the tabernacle had three colors—blue, purple, and scarlet (Exod. 26:1)—the loops from which the curtains hung were blue (v. 4). The Ark of the Covenant, the most holy object in the tabernacle, which contained the two stone tablets inscribed with the Ten Commandments, was covered with ''a cloth of all blue'' (Num. 4:6). ''The table of the showbread'' was covered with a cloth of blue (v. 7), as were ''the candlesticks of the light'' (v. 9), and the golden altar (v. 11), while ''all the vessels of ministry'' were put into a cloth of blue (v. 12). The veil in the Temple of Solomon was blue and purple and crimson (2 Chron. 3:14). The hangings in the tabernacle were woven in blue, purple, and scarlet, the work of skillful workmen headed by Bezalel and Oholiab (Exod. 35:35; 38:23). It seems that this weaving and coloring skill was lost in the course of time, so that when Solomon built the Temple he had to import from Tyre ''a man skillful to work . . . in purple and crimson and blue'' (2 Chron. 2:6).

Blue predominated not only in the furnishings of the tabernacle, but also in the garments of Aaron the priest. In general, ''the plaited garments for ministering in the holy place" were blue, purple, and scarlet (Exod. 39:1). The ephod, too, was blue, purple, and scarlet (Exod. 28:6,8). The "breastplate of judgment" had the same three colors (Exod. 28:15; 39:8). The ephod and the breastplate were connected to each other with threads of blue (28:28; 39:21). The robe of the ephod was all of blue (28:31; 39:22). About the lower edge of this robe there were "pomegranates" (probably pompons) of blue, purple, and scarlet (28:32; 39:24). The girdle had the same three colors (39:29). The mitre displayed "a thread of blue" (29:37; 39:31).

Blue was no less prominent in the life of the people in general. One of the most important commandments required that a "cord of blue" be appended to the four corners of every garment worn by a man.[10] The function of these fringes was to remind their wearer of "all the commandments of the Lord" (Num. 15:39). The question of how the fringes reminded one of God's commandments was dealt with by the greatest commentators on the Bible. Rashi explains, "The numerical value [*gimatria*] of the letters in the word *tzitzit* is 600; add the eight threads and the five knots and you have 613," i.e., the number of biblical commandments (Rashi, ad Num. 15:39). According to Maimonides, "Our rabbis explained that the blue is like the sea, and the sea is like the firmament, and the firmament is like God's Throne of Glory" (cf. n. 23).

If we want to understand the true meaning of the commandment of "the cord of blue," we must, first of all, clarify which are "all the commandments of the Lord" of which the looking at the blue cords must remind the Children of Israel. The second half of the verse in question defines these commandments more precisely: "and remember all the commandments of the Lord and do them; and that ye go not about after your own heart and your own eyes, after which ye use to go astray." That is, the blue cord serves as a reminder of those commandments which prevent a son of Israel from going astray after his heart and his eyes. The expression "go astray" is in Hebrew *zonim*, literally "fornicate," or "go awhoring," which both the Pentateuch and the prophets frequently use as a figurative expression for idolatry, which is conceived as a huge communal fornication.[11] If so, the commandments one must remember in order not to "go awhoring" after other gods are undoubtedly those which relate to the service of God, that is, the commandments of the service in the tabernacle. And if we remember how prominently blue figured in the tabernacle—in its structure, furnishing, vessels, and the clothing of the priest—we shall understand that looking at the blue cord of the tzitzit would indeed inevitably remind one of the rich display of blue in the tabernacle and of the divine service performed in it. The progress of associations is direct and logical: the blue cord of the tzitzit leads to the blue color display in the tabernacle leads to the service in the tabernacle leads to the turning away from idolatry.

III.

The use of blue as a favorite color was not confined to the people of Israel in the ancient Near East. The Bible itself contains some information in this respect. The prophet Ezekiel (early sixth century B.C.E.) knew that the blue and the purple dye and cloth were imported to Tyre from the isles of Elishah, and that the Tyrians used them for making awnings (Ezek. 27:7). They also wore blue garments (''wrappings of blue'') and traded them with several countries to the east and south (vv. 23–24).

Since it was especially persons of high status or of outstanding qualities who were exposed to the dangers of the evil eye, such individuals wore all-blue garments. Ezekiel states that ''the choicest men of Assyria,'' ''warriors . . . governors and rulers, handsome young men all of them'' were ''clothed in blue'' (Ezek. 23:5–7).[12] The royal robes of King Ahasuerus of Persia and Media were blue and white (Esther 8:15), and the hangings of his palace in Shushan were ''of white, fine cotton, and blue'' (Esther 1:6).

According to Jeremiah, a contemporary of Ezekiel, who witnessed the destruction of the Temple of Jerusalem in 586 B.C.E., the idols of the nations were bedecked with blue and purple clothing (Jer. 10:9)—which information supplies an unexpected parallel to the Yemenite Jewish view that even God has to protect himself with the blue of the sky from the evil eye.

IV.

Although in the days of the first, Solomonic, Temple of Jerusalem the Hebrew people had no reliable tradition as to the preparation of the blue dye, their descendants in talmudic times had mastered the technique of its manufacture. This is clearly attested in several statements in the Talmud. ''Abbaye said to Rav Sh'muel bar Rav Y'huda, 'This *t'khilta* [''blue''], how do you dye it?' Rav Sh'muel answered him: 'We take the blood of the *ḥilazon* [the murex, the shellfish which yields the dye] and spices [i.e., other ingredients], and pour it into a kettle, and boil it, and then we take an egg[shell] full of it and we try it out on a piece of skin. Then we throw away that egg[shell] and burn the skin' '' (B. Men. 42b). The talmudic tradition according to which the *t'khelet* was manufactured in the city of Luz (B. Sota 46b) seems to be based on the similarity between the name Luz and the word *ḥilazon*.

The fact that the talmudic sages invariably speak of the *t'khelet* as being made of the blood of the murex indicates that this was a fixed tradition. They, moreover, opined that the tzitzit was ritually acceptable (*kosher*) only if it was dyed blue with the murex-derived *t'khelet*. If it was dyed with another blue dye, called *q'la ilan* or *q'lailan* (indigo), a dye of vegetable origin, it was considered ritually unfit (*pasul*).[13]

The murex was hard to find. "This *hilazon*, its body is like the sea and its nature is like a fish, and it rises once in seventy years, and therefore its price is high" (B. Men. 44a).[14] According to a talmudic legend, when Zebulon complained that his share in the Land of Promise was all seas and rivers, God said to him, "By your life, all will be in need of you, due to the murex, as it is said, *And the hidden treasures of the sand*" (Deut. 33:19), and R. Yosef taught, "This is the murex" (B. Meg. 6a). The murex, it is stated, was caught along the shores of the Mediterranean, from Tyre to Haifa, by specialized fishermen called *yogvim*, i.e., "cultivators." After having caught the murex, they pressed it so as to extract its blood (B. Shab. 26a, 75a). Several kinds of murex were known.[15]

Although they knew a kind of *q'lailan* whose color was permanent (B. Bab. Qam. 93b), it was still considered unfit for dyeing the fringes. "Rava said, 'Why is the exodus from Egypt described next to [the commandment of] the tzitzit?' The Holy One, blessed be He, said . . . 'I shall punish him who hangs [fringes dyed with] *q'lailan* on his garment and says it is *t'khelet*.' "[16] The objection of the talmudic rabbis to the use of *q'lailan* was so strong that they forbade its use on the body (i.e., not on the fringes) of a tallit all of which was blue, although the use of other colors was permitted. Their reasoning was that another person, who did not know that the cloth was dyed with *q'lailan* and not with murex, might mistake it for the real thing and use it as such for fringes on another garment.[17] It would seem that a "tallit [i.e., garment] all of which was *t'khelet*" was nothing unusual. In fact, all kinds of all-blue garments were worn. It is related in the Talmud that once Rav and Rabba bar Bar Hana sat together when a man dressed in an all-blue garment passed by them, and Rav found that garment becoming.[18]

Talmudic opinion had it that it was not possible to recognize whether threads were dyed with *t'khelet* or with *q'lailan*, and that therefore it was permitted to purchase blue threads only from a reliable seller who knew that the use of *q'lailan* was forbidden.[19] However, Rav Yitzhaq, the son of Rav Y'huda, was of the opinion that it was possible to apply the following test. One should take alum and "snail water" (or "clover water"), and forty-day-old urine, and let the dyed threads soak in them from the evening until the morning. If the color changed, it was not *t'khelet*, but if its color did not change, it was *kosher*.[20] Rav Ada recommended another method: to take hard rye dough and bake the material to be tested in it. If this improved its color, it was *kosher*; if the color deteriorated, it was unfit.[21] Following this, it is related that once they made the test as recommended by Rav Yitzhaq and the color changed, showing that it was not dyed with *t'khelet*; then they carried out a second test as suggested by Rav Ada, and the color improved, which showed that it was not *q'lailan*. Thereupon it was decided that one must first test it with Rav Yitzhaq's method; if the color did not change, it was *t'khelet*; if it did change, then one applied Rav Ada's test; if the color improved, this proved that, after all, it was *t'khelet*; if not, it was not *kosher*.[22] Actually, Rav Yitzhaq's method is a base test, while that of Rav Ada is an acid test.[23]

V.

The idea that the color of *t'khelet* is an imitation of the color of the sky goes back to Tannaitic times. A Baraita states in the name of R. Meir,

> What is the difference between *t'khelet* and all other colors? It is this: *t'khelet* is like unto the sea, and the sea is like the firmament, and the firmament like the Throne of Glory, for it is said, "And there was under His feet the like of a paved work of sapphire stone, and the like of the very heaven for clearness" (Exod. 24:10), and it is written, "the likeness of the throne was as the appearance of a sapphire stone" (Ezek. 1:26).[24]

Rashi attempts to explain this fantastic comparison in a logical manner. "The *t'khelet* is like the sea, for the *hilazon* comes up out of the sea once in seventy years, and the appearance of its blood is like that of the sea, and the sea, we can see that it is like the firmament, and the firmament is like the sapphire, and the sapphire is like the throne of glory."[25]

The number of the joints in the tzitzit symbolize, represent, or refer to the structure of heaven. The upper part of the tzitzit is wound around by one of the threads and is divided into several parts by knots. "The number of these parts must be at least seven and at most thirteen. Not less than seven as against the seven firmaments, and not more than thirteen as against the seven firmaments, plus the six air spaces between them."[26] To which Rashi adds, "Their arrangement is compared to the structure of the firmaments."

The *t'khelet* is one of the things on which the living pride themselves and thus arouse the envy of the dead. "R. Hiyya and R. Yonatan were conversing while they strolled in the cemetery. A thread of R. Yonatan's tzitzit fell off. R. Hiyya said to him, 'Pick it up lest [the dead] say, "Tomorrow they will come to us, and today they deride us." ' "[27] It seems that the *t'khelet* also constituted a symbol of life, and therefore some sages commanded that it be removed from their garments when they died. "Abba Shaul used to tell his sons: 'Bury me under the feet of my father, and loosen the *t'khelet* from my cloak.' "[28]

VI.

The distance from the belief that the blue color can protect a person against the evil eye to the belief that it possesses actual curative powers is not great. The latter belief was also found among the Jews in talmudic times. There was a type of blue color called *z'horit* (literally, "crimson") to which such powers were attributed. A talmudic passage advises that against kidney stones one should take "a thread of *z'horit* which was woven by a harlot who is the daughter of a harlot, and hang it on the penis of a man or on the breasts of a woman."[29] A *z'horit* thread was also hung between the eyes of a horse,[30] just as the Arabs of Palestine still hang blue beads between its eyes as a protection against demons.

Since so many good qualities were attributed to the *t'khelet*, it is easy to understand that the term got the meaning of "the best." E.g., "[The people of] Havel Yama [the Sea District] are the *t'khelet* [i.e., the choice of purity of descent] of Babylonia and Tzor Tziyyer [a township] is the *t'khelet* of Havel Yama."[31] *T'khelta* was also the name of a garment which was not square.[32]

VII.

Immanual Löw quotes a scholar according to whom the *t'khelet* of the ancients had a blackish-blue color and was not very attractive.[33] Maimonides says that the color of the indigo (Arabic *nīlaj*) is black.[34] In his discussion of the ritual laws pertaining to the tzitzit, Maimonides identifies the talmudic *q'lailan* (whose appearance, as we have seen, was identical with that of the *t'khelet*) with black.[35] The talmudic sources definitely contradict this view. On the one hand, these sources show that there was no discernible difference in the color of the *t'khelet* and of the *q'lailan*; on the other, the color of the *t'khelet* is unmistakably described, in numerous passages, to be like the sea and the firmament, i.e., sky blue. A talmudic law states that one can recite the morning *Sh'ma'* prayer as soon as it is light enough to distinguish between *t'khelet* and white.[36] This too shows that these two colors were quite similar in tone. Between black and white one can distinguish at night, in moonlight, or even by starlight. There can thus be no doubt that the folk tradition of the oriental Jews and of the other Middle Eastern peoples preserved the color of the *t'khelet* accurately: it was and is sky blue.[37]

Notes

"T'khelet—Blue" originally was published in *Tanulmányok Dr. Blau Lajos . . . emlékére*
[Ludwig Blau memorial volume] (Budapest, 1938), pp. 174–81.

1. Cf. Pierre Daniel Chantepie de la Saussaye, *Lehrbuch der Religionsgeschichte*, 4th ed., 2
   vols. (Freiburg i. B., 1887–89), 1:56.
2. Cf. L. F. Chabas, *Le papyrus magique Harris* (Chalon-sur-Saône, 1861); Chantepie,
   Lehrbuch, 1:435.
3. Hugo Gressman, *Palästinas Erdgeruch in der israelitischen Religion* (Berlin, 1904), p. 9.
4. Cf. W. Robertson Smith, *Religion of the Semites*, 2d ed. (London, 1907), pp. 336, 381,
   382, 383, 453.
5. Ibid, p. 448.
6. Chantepie, *Lehrbuch*, 1:488.
7. Sir James George Frazer, *The Golden Bough*, 3d ed., 12 vols. (London, 1911–20),
   1:247ff; Raphael Patai, *HaMayim* (Tel Aviv, 1936), pp. 48–49.
8. It should be noted that in Hebrew *shamayim* means both "heaven" and "sky." *Note added
   in 1980.*
9. E.g., B. Yoma 77b; cf. Patai, *HaMayim*, pp. 31–32.
10. The fringes seem to have been an amulet or charm among the Hebrews in early patriarchal
    times; cf. Gen. 38:18. In talmudic times the tzitzit had a similar significance: "One is not
    allowed to sell a *tallit* which has fringes to a non-Jew, except if first one unties its fringes.
    Why? Because the non-Jew may give it as the fee of a harlot" (B. Meg. 43a and Rashi,
    ibid.). Cf. also Julius Wellhausen, *Reste arabischen Heidentums*, 2d ed., (Berlin, 1897),
    pp. 165–66; Robertson Smith, *Religon of the Semites*, pp. 437, 674; Heinrich Holzinger,
    Numeri, in Karl Marti, ed., *Kurzer Hand-Commentar zum Alten Testament* (Tübingen and
    Leipzig, 1903), pp. 64–65.
11. Cf. Deut. 31:15; Isa. 23:17; Hos. 4:15; 9:1; Judg. 2:17; Ezek. 6:9; Lev. 17:6.
12. In Assyrian the blue is *takiltu* (cf. Friedrich Delitzsch, *Assyrisches Handwörterbuch*
    [Leipzig, 1896] p. 706), which is, of course, a cognate of Hebrew *t'khelet*.
13. The talmudic term *q'la'ilan* is an adaptation of the Greek *kallainos*; cf. Immanuel Löw,
    Die Flora der Juden, 4 vols. in 5 (Vienna, 1924–34), 1:498–99.
14. Seventy years were something like a fixed period of maturation of rare animals or plants.
    Thus the carob tree was believed to mature in seventy years; cf. B. Bekhorot 8a; B. Ta'anit
    23a; cf. Patai, *HaMayim*, p. 151.
15. Cf. *'Arukh haShalem*, 3:398–99.
16. B. Bab. Metz. 61b. See also *Sh'iltot waEra*, no. 43; Yalqut Shim'oni 194; Mid. Leqah
    Tov, Num., ed. Buber, 113a.
17. B. Men. 41b, and Rashi on B. Bab. Metz. 61b.
18. B. Men. 39a–b.
19. Ibid., 42b.
20. Ibid., 42b–43a.
21. Ibid., 43a.
22. Ibid., 43b.
23. Cf. Löw, *Flora*, 2:478.
24. B. Men. 43b; B. Sota 17a; B. Ḥul. 89a; Y. Ber. 3a.
25. Rashi on B. Ḥulin 89a, cf. also Rashi on Sota 17a.
26. B. Men. 39a.
27. B. Ber. 18a.
28. Massekhet S'mahot, chap. 12; cf. Tosafot on B. Ber. 18a.
29. B. Git. 69b.
30. B. Shab. 53a.
31. Gen. Rab., chap. 37 end; cf. B. Qid. 72a; Y. Qid. 65d top.
32. Sifre, Ki Tetze, par. 234.
33. Löw, *Flora*, 1:499.

34. Maimonides, *Guide*, ed. S. Munk (Paris, 1856), 1:392 and n.
35. Maimonides, *Yad haHazaqa*, Hilkhot tzitzit, 2:8.
36. B. Ber. 9b.
37. For additional literature on *t'khelet*, see Abraham Epstein, "HaHilazon v'haT'khelet," in J. H. Weiss, ed., *Bet Talmud* (Vienna, 1886), 5:299–305; Samuel Krauss, *Talmudische Archaeologie*, 3 vols. (Leipzig, 1910–12), 1:146–47.

7. Some Hebrew Legends of the Sea

To my dear master and teacher, Professor Eduard Mahler

It has been repeatedly pointed out by modern biblical and talmudic scholars that there are many passages in ancient Jewish literature which can be fully understood only if one has a thorough familiarity with the geographical and topographical features of the landscape which surrounded, and impressed, their authors. This statement came to my mind when, in 1933, I drove for the first time along the highway leading from the hills of Jerusalem to the Tel Aviv seashore. As I left Kubeiba and approached the place where the Saris pumping station of the Jerusalem waterworks is situated, suddenly the mountains divided to the left and to the right, and between them, far below, appeared the *Sh'fela*, the lowland. Behind it, in the misty distance, one could see two thin bands—the golden one of the coastal sands and the greenish one of the sea itself.[1] And as I stood there and gazed at the sight, one of the most beautiful in Palestine, I suddenly remembered that I had read somewhere something about that green band. Then it came to me. In a talmudic passage it is stated that the biblical term *tohu* (Gen. 1:2) signifies "a green band which surrounds the world,"[2] while a later Midrash says that the circles of heaven are inserted into the waters of Okeanos which lie between the ends of the earth and of the sky, and that the ends of heaven are spread upon the waters of Okeanos,[3] the Great Sea encompassing the whole earth.[4]

I was transported in my imagination back to early biblical times, when the Children of Israel were confined to the hill country and the seashore was inaccessible to them because the Philistines held sway over it, and Israel "could not drive out the inhabitants of the valley because they had chariots of iron."[5] And I felt that just as I was standing there on the spot the Arabs of Palestine called *Bāb al-hawā*, "gate of the wind," and was enchanted with the view, so the ancient Hebrews must have stood and looked at the sea they could not reach, the sea whose sands in the days of their first forefathers already had become a symbol of fertility and blessing, and remained so in the vivid imagery of the great Hebrew prophets.[6]

Both in times when they were cut off from the sea and in times when they did control its shores, the sea agitated the fantasy of the biblical Hebrews and their heirs, the Jews of the talmudic period. The proof of the matter is in the numerous legends about the sea which are found in talmudic and midrashic literature.

To the author of the Book of Job the sea was a mystery: the cloud was its garment, and thick darkness a swaddling band for it.[7] Nobody could walk in the recesses of *Tehom*, the abyss.[8] Somewhat later, Ben Sira imagined that Wisdom, and only she, was able to descend to the place from whence come all the waters of Tehom[9] and walk safely on the waves of the stormy sea.[10] The size and extent of the sea remain known only to the Creator Himself— thus according to the Tossefta, a talmudic work dating from second-century C.E. Palestine.[11] Later Midrashim elaborate the idea that it is impossible to measure the depth of the sea. Hadrianus Caesar—thus the legend runs— wanted to measure the depth of the Adriatic Sea. What did he do? He took ropes and unrolled them into the depth of the sea for three and a half years. Then he heard a heavenly voice saying: "Hadrianus is annihilated."[12]

According to one of the legends of Rabba bar Bar Ḥana, an expert on problems of the sea and of navigation, and a man of unlimited imagination, there are places in the sea where the water is so deep that a carpenter's axe which was dropped into it did not reach the bottom in seven years.[13]

The author of the Book Kohelet wondered that "all the rivers run into the sea yet the sea is not full."[14] The Agada knows the reason of this strange phenomenon. There is a certain place in the Great Sea where the waters are in a state of eternal immobility. In this place the waters of the sea swallow all the other waters which flow there. The name of this place is *be b'li'e*, i.e., the Place of Swallowing. And once it happened to Rabbi Eliezer and Rabbi Y'hoshu'a that their ship came on this place. Then R. Eliezer said to R.

Y'hoshu'a: "Why have we come to this place but for an experiment?" And they took a barrel full of water from there. When they arrived at Rome, Hadrianus Caesar asked them, "What is the nature of the waters of Okeanos?" They answered, "Waters swallow waters." He said to them, "Give me of them!" They gave him a jug full and then they poured into it other water, and all the waters were swallowed in it. [15]

The waves of the ocean also appear in a wonderful size in the mirror of the Agada. There is a distance of 300 parasangs between one wave and the other and the height of the waves is also 300 parasangs. But this is only the regular size of the waves. There also exist waves of extraordinary height, which lift up the ships so high that the inmates may see "the resting place of the smallest star." [16] And in those dizzy heights the voice of the talk of the waves can be heard. One wave casts its voice to its mate and asks, "My friend, hast thou left anything in the world that thou didst not wash away? I will go and destroy it!" But the other wave replies, "Go and see the almighty power of thy Lord. I must not pass the sand of the shore even as much as the breadth of a thread, as it is written: 'Fear ye not me? saith the Lord, Will ye not tremble at my presence? Who have placed the sand for the bound of the sea, an everlasting ordinance which it cannot pass.' "[17]

But the waves not only speak and converse with each other; they feel and are kindly inclined. Thus runs the tale of a Hasid who used to do good deeds: once, when he was traveling in a boat, the wind broke and sank his boat in the sea. "When I sank into the depths, I heard voices of great noise coming from the waves of the sea, and they told each other, 'Run and lift up this man out of the sea, because he did good all the days of his life.' "[18]

The *Nehute yama,* "the descenders of the sea" (i.e., seafarers), in particular, told many wonderful things that happened to them while they were traveling on the high seas. The most greatly feared phenomenon was the angry wave. The "descenders of the sea" had a special sign by which to recognize whether a wave approaching the ship wanted to sink it. Such a wave appeared with a white fringe of fire on its head, and the experienced seaman, when he saw that such a wave approached his ship, took a club on which the words "I am that I am, [19] Yah the Lord of Hosts, Amen, Amen, Selah" were engraved and hit the wave with this club until it was forced to flee. [20] But as not all the seamen knew this sure means of escaping the wrath of the fiery waves, the waves often succeeded in sinking ships and boats and even breaking them into small pieces.

The Great Sea has a special depository into which it throws all the silver and golden packets and all the pieces of the ships wrecked in the sea. This depository of the Great Sea is, according to the Agada, the Sea of Haifa, that is Haifa Bay. [21] In accordance with the enormous extent of the sea, there are in it mighty treasuries of gigantic jewels and precious stones. Once a pupil of Rabbi Yohanan took a sea journey and saw the ministering angels cutting pearls and precious stones, each thirty cubits long and thirty cubits high. He said unto them, ''For what are these?'' The answer which is put into the mouth of angels is characteristic of the great love the talmudic sages had for Jerusalem, the Holy City: ''The Holy One, blessed be He, will set them up as the gates of Jerusalem.''[22]

Very important is the task of the Sea Okeanos in connection with the sun and the rain. Every evening the sun turns to rest in the waters of Okeanos and its candles are extinguished. Just as a man puts out fire with water, so the waters of Okeanos put out the flames of the sun, that it should have no light during the night, until it comes to the east and takes a bath in a fiery river which is called Nahar diNur.[23] Thus Okeanos serves as the resting place for the sun, but at the same time it is a source of new strength for the clouds which come down once every month to drink of its waters. Once it happened, so the legend tells, that the clouds swallowed, together with the water, a ship full of corn, and after that corn fell from heaven mixed into the rain.[24]

Although the water of the ocean is salty, it becomes sweet when penetrating the clouds. This phenomenon is called ''the qualification of the rains.''[25]

According to another view, the earth drinks the water of the ocean in a far more direct way. Okeanos is higher than all the earth, and thus it can supply water for the whole earth.[26]

These legends are built upon the view generally held by all the peoples of ancient times, that the earth is like a flat disk which swims over the water, and the water surrounds it. But the other view—that the earth has the shape of a ball—was also familiar to our forefathers. Thus they state that the earth is a ball swimming in the ocean, and the ocean has the shape of a vessel.[27] This is how Alexander the Great of Macedonia once saw the earth: in the likeness of a ball and the sea like a vessel.[28] And as if the sages of Israel had known, or rather felt, that the earth was in permanent movement, they spoke of ''the earth which is thrown from one hand into the other as a ball.''[29] Evidently the hands referred to here are not the hands of Alexander, but the hands of the Holy One, blessed be He.

A late legend describes the prophet Jonah as the first diver. While he was in the stomach of the fish, it served him as a kind of submarine. He even had a searchlight to light up the depths of the sea, a great pearl which hung in the stomach of the fish. In this way Jonah traveled in the stomach of the fish and all the secret places of the sea became known to him. He saw and even spoke to Leviathan, who dwells in the ''Heart of the Sea,'' rules over all the inhabitants of the sea, and every day eats a great fish to appease his hunger. Leviathan wanted to eat the fish in whose stomach Jonah was, but the prophet saved it from its fate. As a reward the fish showed Jonah all that exists in the deep. It showed him the great river of the waters of Okeanos, the Red Sea which was crossed by the Children of Israel, the Valley of Hinnom, the lowest Hell, the fundaments of the Holy Temple which rest upon the bottom of the sea, and the Even Shetiyyah, the Stone of the Foundation, which is sunk into the Tehom beneath the altar of God. While he was resting underneath the Temple, Jonah began to pray to God, who heard his prayers and saved him from the stomach of the fish.[30]

These few legends presented here are but a small fraction of the material which can be found in talmudic literature about the sea and Tehom. In addition to them, there is in these ancient sources a rich material concerning the practical aspect of the sea, the role it played and the importance it had in the economic life of ancient Israel.[31]

Notes

"Some Hebrew Legends of the Sea" originally was published in *Dissertationes in Honorem Dr. Eduardi Mahler* (Budapest, 1937), pp. 488–93). It is reprinted here with some stylistic changes.

1. Cf. B. Hag. 12a: "Heaven and earth seem to kiss each other."
2. B. Bab. Bat. 74a.
3. Pirke R. Eliezer, chap. 3.
4. B. 'Er. 22b.
5. Judg. 1:19; cf. Josh. 17:18.
6. Gen. 32:13. Cf. also Isa. 10:22; Hos. 2:1.
7. Job 38:9.
8. Job 38:16.
9. Ben Sira 24:5–6.
10. Ibid.
11. Tos. Hag. 12:1.
12. Mid. Shoher Tov, and Yalqut Teh., ed. Buber, p. 208.
13. B. Bab. Bat. 73a.
14. Eccles. 1:7.
15. Gen. Rab. 13:6; B. Bekh. 9a. Cf. the legend of Charybdis, which sips in the waters of the sea (Homer, *Odyssey,* 12.10ff., 235ff.; August F. Pauly and Georg Wissowa, eds., *Realencyclopädie der classischen Altertumswissenschaft* [Stuttgart, 1894–1978], s.v. Charybdis; Wilhelm Bacher, *Die Agada der Tannaiten,* 2 vols. [Strassburg, 1890–1903], 1:130ff.; Raphael Patai, *HaMayim* [Tel Aviv, 1936], p. 148). The legend of the Place of Swallowing is found also in Mid. HaGadol 1:9, p. 30, and Eccles. Rab. to 1:7 and 11:1. The end of the legend as related in B. Bekh. 9a is reminiscent of the Greek legend about the barrel of the Danaids.
16. B. Bab. Bat. 73a.
17. Ibid., quoting Jer. 5:22.
18. Avot diR. Nathan, ed. Schechter, vers. A, 9a.

19. Exod. 3:14.
20. B. Bab. Bat. 73a.
21. Mid. Tan. Deut. 33:19–21, 219, 3–7.
22. B. San. 100a.
23. Yalqut Shim'oni Isa. (66), 513.
24. B. Men. 69b, and Rashi, ibid.
25. B. Ta'an. 9b. The Hebrew phrase is *hakhsharat g' shamim*.
26. Gen. Rab. 5:2.
27. Num. Rab. 13.
28. Ibid.
29. Ibid.
30. Pirke R. Eliezer, chap. 10.
31. Cf. Raphael Patai, *HaSappanut ha'Ivrit bIme Qedem* [Jewish seafaring in ancient times] (Jerusalem, 1938).

8. The *'Egla 'Arufa,* or the Expiation of the Polluted Land

The rather strange ceremony of the *'Egla 'Arufa,* the breaking of the heifer's neck, which serves for the expiation of an untraced murder, is described in Deuteronomy 21.1–9. The text runs as follows:

> If one be found slain in the land which the Lord thy God giveth thee to possess it, lying in the field, and it be not known who hath smitten him; then thy elders and thy judges shall come forth, and they shall measure unto the cities which are round about him that is slain. And it shall be, that the city which is nearest unto the slain man, even the elders of that city shall take a heifer of the herd, which hath not been wrought with, and which hath not drawn in the yoke. And the elders of that city shall bring down the heifer unto a rough valley, with running water,[1] which may neither be plowed nor sown, and shall break the heifer's neck there in the valley. And the priests the sons of Levi shall come near—for them the Lord thy God hath chosen to minister unto Him, and to bless in the name of the Lord; and according to their word shall every controversy and every stroke be. And all the elders of that city, who are nearest unto the slain man, shall wash their hands over the heifer whose neck was broken in the valley. And they shall speak and say: "Our hands have not shed this blood, neither have our eyes seen it. Forgive, O Lord, Thy people Israel, whom Thou hast redeemed, and suffer not innocent blood to remain in the midst of Thy people Israel." And the blood shall be forgiven them. So shalt

thou put away the innocent blood from the midst of thee, when thou shalt do
that which is right in the eyes of the Lord.

The passage contains a number of problematic prescriptions. Why is
the nearest city, represented by its elders and judges, responsible for the
murder? Why has the heifer to be an animal "which hath not been wrought
with," etc.? Why has the ceremony to be performed in the desert valley, and
why is the presence of a perennial brook essential? What is the reason for the
unusual way of killing the heifer? What is the significance of the washing of
the elders' hands?

R. Yohanan ben Saul has tried to explain the prescriptions which are
peculiar to this ceremony: "Let the heifer which has never produced fruit
(i.e., which has never been set to do any work) be killed in a spot which has
never produced fruit (i.e., in rough, uncultivated ground) to atone for the
death of a man who was debarred (through being prematurely made to die)
from producing fruit."[2] This attempt at explanation which is based on mere
similarity of the expression *'asa perot* shows only the fact that the real
significance of the ceremony was not understood even by the rabbis of the
talmudic period.

If we now try to give a satisfactory explanation of the whole ceremony,
we have to examine the above passage of the Scriptures step by step. The
ceremony of the breaking of the heifer's neck has to be performed "if one be
found slain in the land . . . lying in the field." If the blood of an innocent
person is shed on the ground, the latter shall not henceforth yield unto the
murderer her strength.[3] Also, according to the prophets, the punishment of
bloodshed is famine, caused by a crop failure: "When the house of Israel
dwelt in their own land, they defiled it. . . . Wherefore I poured out My fury
upon them for the blood that they had shed upon the land."[4] Therefore,
according to this conception, famine is not a mere natural catastrophe, but it
is a "shame of famine,"[5] caused by the sins of the people and especially by
their shedding of innocent blood upon the ground. Jeremiah has the same
conception of drought: it is caused by the iniquities of the inhabitants of the
land. Therefore "are the plowmen ashamed," and therefore "they cover
their heads," seeing that "the ground is cracked" and that "there was no
rain in the land."[6] According to our conception, the natural reaction that
famine or drought should awake would be no shame and confusion, but
rather despair or hopelessness.[7]

An historical statement of that elementary conception concerning the
inmost connection between bloodshed and drought or famine is given in 2
Sam. 21.1ff. "Then there was a famine in the days of David three years,
year after year; and David inquired of the Lord. And the Lord answered, 'It

is for Saul, and for his bloody house, because he slew the Gibeonites.' "[8]
After the bloody revenge of the Gibeonites, the killing of seven of the
descendants of Saul, "God was entreated for the land."[9]

Thus, as the necessary consequence of bloodshed, the ground does not
further give her strength unto the murderer or the murderers.[10] This is the
way the land demonstrates that it was polluted by bloodshed.[11] If, however,
bloodshed was committed and innocent blood was poured upon the ground,
it has to be expiated,[12] and "the land cannot be atoned[13] for the blood that is
shed therein, but by the blood of him that shed it."[14]

This is the original significance of the sin of bloodshed: the earth opens
her mouth to receive the innocent blood and becomes defiled (polluted) by
it.[15] In mishnaic times this was still felt, and, therefore, according to the
mishnaic definitions, an *'Egla* has to be brought only when the blood of the
slain man was actually poured upon the earth; but, on the other hand, if the
dead was choked and thrown in the field, or killed and hanged on a tree, or he
was found covered by a heap of stones or swimming on the surface of water,
no heifer has to be brought.[16]

Consequently, when a slain man whose blood was poured upon the
ground is found in the field, and the murderer is not known, the town nearest
to the body is responsible for the murder. This conception is not restricted to
ancient Israel. It is a general notion both of the ancient and modern Orient. In
Arabia, when a slain man was found the inhabitants of the nearest place were
obliged to swear that they were not the murderers.[17] According to *Kitāb
al-aghāni*, the nearest house (*dār*) is responsible for the murder.[18] The Code
of Hammurabi, on the other hand, prescribes, "If a person is robbed the
town and the heads of the elders have to pay a manah silver to his family."[19]
The matter being such, the people of the nearest town have every reason to
apprehend that the ground will not give "her strength unto them" unless
they propitiate her. The expiation ceremony is the breaking of the heifer's
neck, as a substitute for the unknown murderer.

That the animal offering has to be female[20] is in accordance with all
other substituting sacrifices: if one person commits a sin, he has to offer a
female animal,[21] and only if the whole congregation or a "ruler" sins do
they have to offer a male.[22]

But in spite of this analogy to the atoning sin offerings, the *'Egla* is no
sacrifice. The very method of killing the heifer, the breaking of her neck,
which is the only case of such a proceeding, shows that this animal is not a
sacrificial one.[23] On the other hand, the prescription that the heifer has to be
one "which hath not been wrought with and which hath not drawn in the
yoke"[24] is found in connection with no sacrifice elsewhere. The only other
occurrence of this rule is in the ritual of the red heifer,[25] and the story about

the Philistines sending back the ark of the Lord on a new cart drawn by "two milch kine on which there hath come no yoke"[26] proves that this was originally a pagan ritual requirement. Neither the *'Egla* nor the red heifer is a sacrifice.[27] The purpose of the killing of the *'Egla* is only to expiate the ground.[28]

Blood vengeance was taken on the very spot where the innocent blood was shed. In the same place where Ahab killed the innocent Naboth will he also be killed, according to the prophecy of Elijah.[29] In the Valley of Jezreel, where Jehu killed his lord, will God avenge "the blood of Jezreel upon his house."[30] Similarly, the obvious way to expiate an untraced murder would be to break the heifer's neck on the same spot where the slain man was found.[31]

But it is known to us that the blood of animals has to be covered.[32] Moreover, when somebody killed an ox, lamb, or goat outside of the tabernacle, this act was considered a grave sin, as if he had killed a man: "blood shall be imputed unto that man; he hath shed blood; and that man shall be cut off from among his people."[33] Thus it is quite evident that, regarding the sin of bloodshed and its punishment, no difference was made between the blood of a man and the blood of an animal. Therefore it is very probable that by killing the heifer on the same spot where the slain man was found, they would have offended the ground—according to their conception—with this new "murder," and nothing would have been gained.[34]

Now the elders of the town are found to be in a real dilemma. If they do not cleanse the land of the blood that was shed thereon, the ground will be polluted by the innocent blood and will not yield unto them her strength, her crop. And, if they cleanse her—which could be done only by shedding the blood of the innocent heifer, replacing the blood of the unknown murderer—the ground will be polluted anew, because of this second bloodshed. The only solution is to bring the heifer into a valley (with perennially running water) which is neither plowed nor sown and to break the heifer's neck there. In that place there is no danger that the ground will become sterile.[35] This is also the reason why it is forever forbidden to plow or sow the spot where a heifer was killed.[36] The ground should have no opportunity to retaliate on the person who shed the heifer's blood.[37] The prescription that the water into which the blood of the heifer is poured should perennially be running[38] is a similar precaution; it should not happen that by the drying up of the water the blood of the heifer poured into it should become uncovered.[39]

A separate question is why do the elders wash their hands over the heifer whose neck was broken in the valley? The solution is given in verse 7: "Our hands have not shed this blood, neither have our eyes seen it." The rabbis of the Mishna felt that there was a certain difficulty in this sentence:

"Could it possibly occur to anyone to suspect the elders of murder? No! By this avowal the elders of the town declare, 'He did not come to us hungry and we failed to feed him; he did not come to us friendless and we failed to befriend him.' "[40]

This answer evidently does not give the real sense of the above verse. But anyhow the question is right. Nobody suspected the elders of murder; they have only to bear the moral responsibility for it. Why, then, do they accent their innocence? And a second difficulty: the body of the slain man is lying in the cornfield, whereas the elders speak these words in the desert valley, evidently far away from him. If they intend to refer to the blood of the slain man, can they say the words "Our hands have not shed *this blood*"? These words evidently aim at the blood which is actually before them while speaking, the blood of the heifer.[41] And the real intention of their words is: our hands have not shed this blood, the blood of the heifer, but the unknown murderer shed it—he is responsible for this bloodshed.

If this is so, what was attained by the whole ceremony of the breaking of the heifer's neck? They achieved thereby that they cleansed the field of the blood that was shed thereon and transferred the whole act of murder into the valley which is neither plowed nor sown. The cornfield may now yield its crop unto the inhabitants of the town, and the unknown murderer has become responsible for a murder that was committed in the desert valley and that cannot endanger the crop of the field.

The washing of the elders' hands aims at their purification from the sin of murder.[42] This act becomes necessary because, after all, even if the unknown murderer is guilty in the killing of the heifer and he has to bear this sin, the elders' hands executed the ceremonial killing, and therefore they have to cleanse them. The washing of the elders' hands may be compared to the purificatory ceremonies to which the persons who prepared the red heifer's ashes were submitted.[43] On the other hand, in mishnaic times, even the Bet Din was considered to be in need of atonement for the scapegoat which was sent out to atone for the Bet Din's death sentences.[44] We find a similar custom in the Greek world: the judges had to purify themselves by water in cases where they meted out capital punishment.[45]

The closing act of the ceremony of the *'Egla* was, according to mishnaic tradition, to bury the heifer's body.[46]

Thus, the ceremony of the breaking of the heifer's neck reveals a section of old Israelite and partly Canaanite religious usages which originated in the reverence for the soil.

Verse 5 of the passage shows the effort made by the priests to subordinate the whole ceremony to their authority. Anyhow, their presence is regarded even by the redactor of the passage as having no obvious necessity, and therefore he adds the argument in the second half of the verse: "for them the Lord thy God hath chosen," etc.

The closing verses, 8 and 9, show how these old customs became a part of the higher ideas of the Israelite religion, and how they tried to obscure the original significance of the rite by a final appeal to the forgiveness of the Lord God.[47]

Notes

"The *'Egla 'Arufa*, or the Expiation of the Polluted Land" originally was published in the *Jewish Quarterly Review*, n.s. 30, no. 1 (1939):59–69.

1. *Naḥal etan* has to be rendered literally: "perennial brook." See Raphael Patai, *HaMayim* (Tel Aviv, 1936), p. 194.
2. Cf. B. Sota 46a.
3. Cf. Gen. 4:12.
4. Ezek. 36:17–18.
5. Ezek. 36:30. The Revised Version renders "reproach of famine." I would rather suggest rendering the phrase *ḥerpat ra' av* by "shame of famine."
6. Jer. 14:3–4, 7.
7. On the connection between the moral conduct of the people and rain, see Patai, *HaMayim*, pp. 48ff., 68ff.
8. The further course of the narrative shows that the form and extent of the blood vengeance was decided by the family of the descendants of the murdered person. David asks the Gibeonites wherewith to make the atonement, and they demand seven of Saul's sons to "hang them up unto the Lord in Gibeah of Saul." "They were put to death in the days of harvest" and they remained hanged "until water dropped upon them out of heaven" (2 Sam. 21:1–14). Sir James George Frazer, in *The Golden Bough*, 3d ed., 12 vols. (London, 1911–20), 1:284ff. and 5:21ff., explains the hanging of the bodies of Saul's sons as an independent magical ceremony of rain making; see also Gustaf H. Dalman, *Arbeit und Sitte in Palaestina*, 7 vols. (Gutersloh, 1928–31), 1:147. The above context shows that not the mere hanging of the bones had to produce rain; Saul's sons were killed in order to propitiate the offended land, and their bones were hanged for the purpose of a demonstration toward heaven and earth. The blood vengeance was executed; rain now had to fall and the famine to be over. On *qil'lat Elohim taluy*, see Julian Morgenstern, "The Book of the Covenant, Part VII," *HUCA* 7 (1930):193–96.
9. Cf. 2 Sam. 21:14.
10. Cf. Sir James George Frazer, *Folk Lore in the Old Testament*, 3 vols. (London, 1919), 1:82ff.
11. Cf. Num. 35:33–34; also Isa. 26:21; Ezek. 24:7; Job 16:18.
12. According to the legend, the earth would not receive the body of Abel, and therefore the angels put him on a rock (*Apocalysis Mosis*, in R. H. Charles, ed., *The Apocrypha and Pseudepigrapha*, 2 vols. [Oxford, 1913], 2:152. Cf. 1 Enoch 22:7; Book of Jub. 4:29. According to Ezek. 24:7–8, the wrath of God is aroused even by the uncovered blood on the rock. Cf. also the legend about the bodies of the Egyptians who died in the sea (Mekh. R. Shim'on ben Yoḥai, p. 68).
13. The Revised Version renders "expiated." "Atone" is the precise English equivalent for Hebrew *kipper*.
14. Num. 35:33. Cf. the legend about the blood of Zakariya (B. Git. 57b; B. Sanh. 95b; Deut. Rab. 2:25; Lam. Rab. 1; Pesiqta Rabbati 25). See Bernhard Heller, "Notes de Folk-lore

Juif,'' *Revue des études juifs* 82 (1926):315–16; Bernhard Heller, *Encyclopaedia of Islam*, old ed., s.v. Zakariya; Leo Baeck, ''Secharja ben Berechja,'' *MGWJ* 76 (1932):313–19; Louis Ginzberg, *Legends of the Jews*, 7 vols. (Philadelphia, 1909–46), 6:396; B. Murmelstein, ''The Legend of the Blood of Zechariah (in Hebrew), in *Samuel Krauss Jubilee Volume* (Jerusalem, 1937), pp. 161–68. On the question of biblical blood vengeance, see Erwin Merz, *Die Blutrache bei den Israeliten*, Beiträge zur Wissenschaft vom Alten Testament, no. 20 (Leipzig, 1916). See also Julian Morgenstern, *HUCA* 7 (1930):56–101; 8 (1931):79–121.

15. Cf. Gen. 4:11.
16. M. Sota 9.2; Tos. Sota 9.6.
17. Cf. William Robertson Smith, *Kinship and Marriage in Early Arabia*, 2d. ed. (London, 1894), p. 263.
18. *Kitāb al-Aghānī* (Būlāq, 1285 H. [1868–69]), 9.78.25ff.
19. Code of Hammurabi, sec. 24; see other parallels in I. Scheftelowitz, ''Die Sündentilgung durch Wasser,'' *ARW* 17 (1914):382–83.
20. *'Egla* is the feminine form of *'egel*.
21. Lev. 4:28,32; 5:6.
22. Lev. 4:14,23.
23. Cf. Exod. 13:13, where breaking the neck is given as the way of killing the firstborn of the unclean animal. See also the *m'liga* at the birds (Lev. 1:15; 5:8); also Morgenstern, *HUCA* 7 (1930):90–91.
24. On the other hand, bodily defect does not unfit the heifer for the ceremony (Sota 9.5).
25. Num. 19:2.
26. 1 Sam. 6:7.
27. Contra Karl Marti in Emil Friedrich Kautzsch, *Die Heilige Schrift des Alten Testaments* (Tübingen, 1922–23), 1:297. According to R. Press's view in ''Das Ordeal im alten Israel,'' *ZATW* 51 (1933):240, the purpose of killing the *'Egla* is not to expiate the sin of the unknown murderer, but to expiate the uncleanness of the environment which he caused.
28. In a similar way did the Greeks turn down toward the earth the heads of the animals which were to be offered to the chthonian gods and killed them in this position. See P. Stengel, ''Die griechischen Kultusaltertümer,'' reprint from *Handbuch der klassischen Altertums-Wissenschaft*, (Munich, 1887–), 5:101; A. Bertholet, in Karl Marti, *Kurzer Hand-Commentar zum Alten Testament*, p. 65.
29. 1 Kings 21:19.
30. Hos. 1:4–5.
31. Evidently there is no reason to suppose that in the beginning the order was actually to kill the heifer where the slain man was found; contra Merz, *Blutrache*, p. 55.
32. Lev. 17:13.
33. Lev. 17:4.
34. Even in mishnaic times, the rabbis still regarded the heifer as a being whose value was the same as that of man. They speak about ''false witnesses'' in connection with the heifer, just as in the case of a murder (Tos. Keri. 4.3) and, according to Tos. Sanh. 3.4, the consent of a Bet Din of seventy-one members is necessary for the killing of a heifer (contra B. Sanh. 1.3: the killing of a heifer by three judges); cf. also B. Ket. 38a and parallels.
35. It is quite evident that breaking the heifer's neck is no atonement for the murderer, for even if he is found after the neck-breaking, he has to be killed (M. Sota 9.7; cf. B. Sota 47b; Ket. 37b; Sifre and Sifre Zuta to the end of Numbers).
36. M. Sota 9.5.
37. According to the legend, the spot where Cain killed Abel remains waste forever (''Agadath Shir Hashirim,'' ed. S. Schechter, *JQR* 7 [1895]:160).
38. But cf. M. Sota 9.5 and Sifre Deut. 207: ''even if it is not perennial, it is *kosher*.'' See Jacob Z. Lauterbach, ''Tashlik,'' *HUCA* 11 (1936):218–19.
39. In a similar way the Romans killed a ram and let his blood drip into the well Bandusia in

order that the water should carry away the blood; see Heino Pfannenschmid, *Das Weih-wasser im heidnischen und christlichen Kultus* (Hannover, 1869), p. 29.
40. See Sifre Num. 209; Midrash Tann., p. 125; B. Sota 46a, b; see also Rashi to this verse.
41. This is the simple sense of the verse. When I once read the respective passage of the Bible with my eleven- to twelve-year-old pupils, they interrupted me and asked, "How can the elders say that their hands have not shed this blood, whereas they actually broke the heifer's neck?"
42. Purification by washing the hands was in vogue not only in the Orient, but also in ancient Rome. On the day of the Pales festivities the herdsmen atoned for their sins by washing their hands and jumping over fire (see Ovid, *Fasti*, 4.778ff.).
43. Num. 19:7ff.; cf. Patai, *HaMayim*, p. 20.
44. M. Shevuot 1.7.
45. Cf. Scheftelowitz, "Sündentilgung," *ARW* 17 (1914):362. Thus the washing of the hands is not a symbolic action to establish innocence (contra Marti in Kautzsch, *Heilige Schrift*, 1:247), neither in the case of the elders nor in Ps. 26:6; 73:13. In the latter place, handwashing serves only to attain ritual purity in order that the person cleansing himself may pass around the altar.
46. M. Temura 7.4.
47. I herewith express my thanks to Professor Bernhard Heller of Budapest, who had the kindness to look over this study and make some supplementary remarks.

9. Hebrew Installation Rites

A Contribution to the Study
of Ancient Near Eastern-
African Culture Contact

The penetration of cultural influences from the ancient Near East into Negro Africa is being more and more generally recognized. One of the culture complexes well attested in both the ancient Near East and Negro Africa is the divine kingship, of which a hitherto relatively neglected trait is the royal installation ritual. It is with this ritual that I propose to deal in the following pages, attempting to show how far the African pattern can be related to the ancient Hebrew installation ritual, which in itself has yet to be gleaned from biblical passages and allusions.

I.

In a highly suggestive chapter of his book *Kingship*, A. M. Hocart established a general pattern of the coronation ceremony as practiced by a number of peoples in Asia, Africa, and Europe. The center of the area Hocart dealt with roughly corresponds to what we are used to call the ancient Near East, and it is this area which may have been, according to Hocart, "the original home of all consecration rites."[1] In the years following the publication of Hocart's study, more attention was paid than previously to the ceremonies accompanying the installation of kings or chiefs in countries within the area of the Near East and bordering upon it.

C. K. Meek has repeatedly described the installation ceremonies of kings and chiefs among a number of West African tribes and unhesitatingly ascribed them to Egyptian influence.[2] C. G. and Brenda Z. Seligman pointed out the prevalence of similar installation ceremonies in a territory much nearer to Egypt, namely the Nilotic Sudan,[3] and though they did not attribute precisely these ceremonies to ancient Egyptian influence, they commented, "that the country was influenced by her great neighbour seems a mere truism."[4] A year later, in his Frazer lecture, Seligman pointed to the correspondence between the "divine kingship" of the ancient Egyptians and that of the Nilotic tribes as expressed in ceremonies such as installation, "re-investiture," and the ritual killing of the king. He added, however, that chronological factors made the idea of direct Egyptian influence untenable, and he was inclined to recognize in the divine kingship of the Nilotic Sudan and West Africa an old and widespread Hamitic belief.[5]

A German ethnologist, W. Schilde, maintained that the divine kingship originated in the Near East, whence it spread over Arabia to Abyssinia, and from there to the rest of Africa.[6] The same opinion is held by H. Baumann[7] and endorsed in a recent dissertation by Tor Irstam, who has collected much relevant material pertaining to "the institutions of sacral kingship in Africa."[8] His data show very clearly that a basically homogeneous pattern of sacral kingship—and this, naturally, comprises also the enthronement ritual—exists throughout a wide area of Africa, largely coextensive with, but often extending beyond, the territory occupied by Sudanic-speaking peoples, or the grassland and savanna belt bordered by the desert in the north and the tropical forests in the south, and stretching from Abyssinia in the east to Senegal in the west.[9] The special features which lead Irstam "to think precisely of the Near East [as the place of origin of the African sacral kingship] are for example the notions of the scapegoat, the substitute king, the water of life and the life tree, and the identification of the king's life with the life of the country."[10]

Concurrently with these ethnological and anthropological studies, the theme of the divine kingship was taken up also by students of the ancient Near East. S. H. Hooke edited two volumes of essays dealing with the myth and ritual pattern of the ancient Near East in which the contributors devoted considerable space to the role played by the king in the great seasonal festivals,[11] while Hooke himself reverted to the subject in his Schweich lectures of 1935.[12] The enthronement proper, however, has been only touched upon in these three studies.[13] The same can be said of the excellent studies of Julian Morgenstern, who has shown that in the preexilic period it was the king, both the Judean and the Israelite, who performed the chief role in the celebrations of the New Year festival in his capacity as chief priest of the nation.[14]

In a recent dissertation Ivan Engnell has exhaustively dealt with the manifestations of divine kingship among the peoples of the ancient Near East (with the exclusion of the biblical material, to which Engnell intends to devote a special volume), but even here the installation ceremonies are only casually referred to, and Engnell contents himself with a reference to Widengren's article in the *Uppsala Universitets Arsskrift*[15] as dealing "with the enthronement as divinization and the appertaining ideological importance of these things with regard to Phoenicia, Ras Shamra, Palestine, and particularly the pre-Israelite Jerusalem."[16] This paper is, unfortunately, not available in Jerusalem, and so I have to content myself with the short summary of Widengren's findings concerning the Canaanite enthronement ritual as recapitulated by Engnell in a short footnote:[17] "The items are, as worked out by Prof. Widengren: the ascension of the throne (after an oracle promise), the handing over of the sceptre (the king's triumph), bringing of gifts, the epiphany of the king-god (after his investment with the holy insignia), the promise sworn by the father-god." Engnell himself intends in his forthcoming volume to touch upon the question of the coronation and enthronement "arguing 2 Samuel 7 as an historicized coronation liturgy (adducing Egyptian and Sumerian parallels): a dialogue between the god and the king comprising the god's promise (through a prophet—cf. Ps. 2, 110 etc.) vv. 8–16: selection victory, enthronement among 'the great ones that are in the land' (= 'the holy ones that are in the land' Ps. 16.3 q. v. Nyberg, Studien zum Hoseabuche, p. 121, ZDMG, 1938, p. 336) i.e. divinization, the existence of the dynasty etc.; followed by the king's psalm of thanksgiving (vv. 18b–22, cf. Ps. 132) culminating in a prayer of fulfilment."[18]

As to the connection between the African and the ancient Hebrew installation rituals, it is clear that the ritual must have passed from the ancient Near East to Africa, and not vice versa. It follows, however, from the very nature of the two sets of data we wish to collate, that the African will appear fuller and more complete than the biblical, even though the ancient Hebrew (as in general the ancient Near Eastern) installation ritual must have been richer both in structure and detail than its present-day African counterpart. It lies in the very nature of ceremonial patterns that they tend to disintegrate when transmitted either from one generation to the next or from one people to another. Thus, while supposing in theory that the ancient Hebrew installation ritual was the fuller and richer of the two, we shall nevertheless take as our point of departure the ritual pattern of the African installation ceremonies of which we possess a far more complete picture, and shall investigate point after point whether descriptions of, or at least allusions to, corresponding ritual features can be found in ancient Hebrew literature.

The pattern of the African coronation ritual, as worked out by Irstam from the study of accounts of sixty-two coronation ceremonies in various parts of Africa, is as follows:[19]

1. Ceremonies that symbolized the king's death and rebirth
2. The king was dressed in special robes
3. The king received a new name
4. Entrance dialogue and proclamation
5. Ritual fight
6. The king went into retirement for a certain period
7. Communion
8. The king was baptized
9. The king mounted a hill
10. The king planted his life tree
11. Admonitions and promises
12. The king was anointed with oil
13. The king put on shoes
14. The king received certain regalia
15. The king sat on the throne
16. The king was crowned
17. Fires were extinguished and rekindled
18. The king scattered beans, etc. among the people
19. Not all were allowed to be present at the most important ceremonies
20. After the coronation the king traveled around his domain and received homage
21. Festivities were held
22. The king was made the butt of the people
23. Those taking part dressed themselves as gods
24. Human sacrifices
25. The king's brothers were killed
26. Substitute king
27. The queen was crowned at the same time as the king

Naturally, one must not suppose that all the twenty-seven rites contained in this list occur at the coronation ceremonies of each and every one of the sixty-two African peoples referred to above. The contrary is the case: there is not a single people whose coronation ceremony contains all the twenty-seven points. The most complete coronation ceremonies were held in Ganda (eighteen), Nyoro (seventeen), Jukun (fifteen), Shilluk (thirteen), and Abyssinia (thirteen). In many cases the number of the rites observed does not exceed five or six. The list thus details a hypothetical coronation ceremony compounded from the individual rites which are to be found among a great number of peoples. In many cases, moreover, certain deviations from the items of the pattern are to be found, the various forms of occurrence of a given rite often bearing only a faint resemblance to each other. Neither is the order of the individual rites necessarily that of Irstam's list. These facts must be borne in mind when we come to reconstruct the coronation ceremony of the ancient Hebrews.

After these introductory remarks, let us now examine what descriptions of, or allusions to, acts of a ritual nature can be found in biblical literature. Most of these will pertain to the installation of Saul, first king of Israel. We shall, however, be able to complete the pattern of Hebrew coronation rites with data drawn from the accounts of other Hebrew kings and—in some cases at least—from the account of the consecration of priests.

II.

Let us now begin with the method of choosing the king from among the eligible candidates. Kingship was both in Judah and in Israel a hereditary office. But the first two kings, Saul and David, as well as some of the later kings in the Northern Kingdom, were chosen by seers or prophets.[20] The seer or the prophet, as the spiritual leader of the people, wielded authority enough for his choice to be unquestioningly accepted by the people when it fell on a recognized hero, such as Jeroboam or Jehu. But when the seer chose an unknown youth, such as Saul or David, his choice had to be made acceptable for the people either by the king-elect's proving his mettle, as it happened in the case of David, or by a perceptible manifestation of the will of God, namely by the oracle, as in the case of Saul. First we hear that when Samuel saw Saul, the Lord said unto him, "Behold the man whom I spake to thee of! This same shall reign over my people,"[21] whereupon Samuel told Saul of his election as king and anointed him.[22] With the anointing of Saul his election became a fait accompli; nevertheless, when Samuel called the people together to Mizpah to perform the public election of the king, he let the king be chosen out of the whole of the people by oracle.[23] He said to the people, "Now, therefore, present yourselves before the Lord by your tribes and by your clans.[24] And Samuel caused all the tribes of Israel to come near, and the tribe of Benjamin was taken [by the oracle] and he caused the tribe of Benjamin to come near by its families, and the family of Matri was taken;

[and he caused the family of Matri to come near man by man[25]] and Saul the son of Kish was taken."[26]

The whole procedure is identical with that adopted by Joshua to find out who had taken "of the accursed thing."[27] But the identity is only formal. As to the content and purpose there is a fundamental difference: Joshua did not know who had committed the trespass; he knew only that somebody had "taken of the accursed thing"[28] and, following the instruction of God, he cast lots to find out who the sinner was. Samuel, on the other hand, knew well whom the lot would choose; in fact, he had already anointed the chosen king and consecrated him by a number of other installation rites,[29] so that while the casting of lots was for the people in general the first indication of the identity of their future king, for Samuel it was a mere formality by which he could avoid any questioning of his choice on the part of the people or of disappointed pretenders.

Much the same procedure is adopted by the electors of African kings. Among the Jukun in Nigeria, the following is the procedure of the election of the Aku (the king) of Wukari, one of the principal towns of the country. The official known as Kinda Cheku "ascertains the wishes of all of the senior officials. There is necessarily a great deal of preliminary intrigue and bribery, and the final choice remains a secret until the day of the election. It is said that the person chosen must have received the formal approval of the gods as declared by the divining apparatus."[30] Among the Roba of northern Nigeria, "if there are several candidates from qualified families, resort is usually had to divination. A diviner, or Ed Gambo, as he is called, is to be seen in most villages. He has a shrine of his own in the middle of the village—a circle of stone covered with a conical thatch. The floor is covered with gravel, on which rest a large number of pottery figurines. If the diviner is called on to declare who shall be chief, the figures are arranged to represent the various eligible candidates." The diviner performs diverse manipulations with broken pieces of calabash, shells, and so on. "After chanting for three or four minutes, he suddenly stops and indicates a particular pottery figure—the person chosen as chief by the occult powers."[31] It is clear that the role played by the Roba diviner in the choice of the chief closely corresponds to that played by the Kinda Cheku of Wukari. He, probably after consultation of the influential persons, decides on the selection of a certain candidate and proceeds to let the divinity have its choice.

A third example can be found among the Konde who live in Nyasa land and Tanganyika territory. After the death of Chungu, their ruler, the chiefs and their men, fully armed, gather to the mourning, and the councillors meet to select a successor from among the Bakerenge, a group of families who alone can provide a new Chungu. Who this shall be is determined by divination. At a great feast Mulwa, one of the hereditary councillors, prays to the spirits that their choice be confirmed. "Mulwa, carrying in his hands the 'rod of lordship,' stands out and looks around on the assembled chiefs. Suddenly he throws the rod at the man selected. Immediately he is seized with a shout of triumph."[32] The common feature of both the Roba and the Konde procedures is that in both cases the premeditated choice of the councillors is given the appearance of a spontaneous divine decision. The same procedure, though in a somewhat different form, is observed among the Shilluk of the Nilotic Sudan, on the banks of the While Nile. Here the selection of a new king is in the hands of the chiefs of the districts into which the Shilluk territory is divided. In a secret meeting the chiefs decide who among the pretenders may run for the election. Each of the candidates admitted gets a stone, which he in turn submits to those conducting the ceremony, as the candidates themselves are not present at the proceedings. The stones are thrown into a fire and the stone of the chosen candidate remains after the others have burst out of the fire, or, according to another account, the kingship is determined by the color one of the stones assumes in the fire. Hofmayr, the author of this account, remarks, "As each of the princes admitted to the elections had been assigned his stone, by clever manipulation of the stones it is always the favourite of the electors who is thus chosen king."[33]

From certain remarks of Diodorus on the royal election in pre- Christian Abyssinia, it would appear that the method of both secretly electing the king and publicly choosing him by lots was practiced in Africa some two thousand years ago.[34]

The choice of the true king by means of a miraculous oracle recurs as a legendary motive among both Jews and Africans (as well as elsewhere). According to Jewish tradition, the oracle by which Saul was chosen was the Urim and Tummim.[35] According to a talmudic legend, when Samuel tried to pour the holy oil on David's brothers, it remained in the horn, but at David's approach it flowed of its own accord and poured itself over him. The drops on his garments changed into diamonds and pearls, and after the act of anointing him the horn was as full as before.[36]

With this we may compare the following African story. "When Dagara, the king of Karagwe, on the western shore of Lake Victoria Nyanza, died, he left behind him three sons, each of whom was eligible to the throne. The officers of state put before them a small mystic drum. It was of trifling weight, but being loaded with charms, no one could lift it, save him to whom the ancestral spirits were inclined as the successor."[37]

According to another talmudic legend, the crown of David[38] possessed the mystical power of being able to distinguish between a lawful and an unlawful heir to the throne. According to 2 Sam. 12:30 (= 1 Chron. 20:2), the golden crown taken by David from the king of Rabbath Ammon weighed one talent. The first question raised in the Talmud in connection with this verse is how could David wear such a weight? The answer given by R. Yose ben Ḥanina is "A magnet was in it which lifted it up." Then follows a remark of R. Y'huda in the name of Rav. "The crown was a testimony for the house of David: whosoever was worthy of the kingship—it fitted him; and whosoever was unworthy of the kingship—it fitted him not."[39] According to another source, the precious stone on the crown was too heavy for a non-Davidic king, so that a king who was able to wear the crown was thereby attested as a true Davidic king.[40]

A similar means of miraculous choice was the rod of Moses. This rod was, according to talmudic legends, in the successive possession of Adam, Enoch, Noah, Shem, Abraham, Isaac, Jacob, Joseph, and Jethro. When Jethro stuck the rod in the ground it sprouted, and the suitors of Jethro's daughters, who had to stand the test of being able to pull it out, were all killed as soon as they touched the rod. Moses, however, uprooted the rod easily, and this rod became the one with which he wrought numerous miracles.[41]

Another kind of miraculous choice by means of a rod is related in Numbers. It is the well-known story of the rod of Aaron, which alone among all the twelve rods placed in the tabernacle blossomed, thus proving in the eyes of all Israel that it was Aaron who was chosen by God to function as His priest.[42] Later Jewish legend identified Aaron's rod both with the rod of Moses and with the staff of kings, "so that the blossoming of this rod proved not only the justice of Aaron's claim to the priesthood, but also established David's claim to the kingdom."[43]

As a conclusion to the theme of the oracular choice, let us point to the correspondence between the story of Saul's election and that of the revelation of Jesus as described in the Gospels. Both Samuel and John recognized the chosen person one day after the divine revelation.[44] When Samuel saw Saul coming to him, God said unto him, "Behold the man whom I spake to thee of! This same shall reign over my people!"[45] When John saw Jesus coming to him, he said, "Behold the Lamb of God. . . . This is he of whom I said, 'After me cometh a man which is preferred before me.' "[46] In the case of Saul, his public proclamation as king followed his choice by means of the oracle.[47] In the case of Jesus, his public proclamation followed his choice by means of the descent of the dove upon him.[48] Gunkel emphasized that "the descent of the dove upon Jesus serves the purpose of proclaiming him publicly as the Christ" and that this narrative is based upon the *Märchen* motive of the choice of the new king by the descent of a bird upon him.[49] Two more coronation traits can be discerned in the story of Jesus' baptism: the entering of the Spirit into him, and his consequent turning into the "son of God," both of which we shall deal with in due course.

As to the person of king-elect, there seems to be in Africa, and to have been in ancient Israel, certain requirements concerning his physique. These requirements follow from the basic concept of the dependence of the country's and the people's welfare on the well-being of the king.[50] We shall yet have occasion to refer to the probation time of the king of Konde, during which he is kept under observation "lest, being a weakling he should be a menace to the land."[51] Among the Jukun of Nigeria, the king "being a god it may never be said of him that he is ill."[52] As far south as among the Varozwe (a Shona tribe), "absence of bodily blemishes was considered absolutely necessary in the occupant of the throne."[53]

A reminiscence of the demand of bodily excellence in the king lingered also in ancient Israel. Of Saul we are told that "he was higher than any of the people from his shoulders and upward. And Samuel said to all the people, 'See ye him whom the Lord hath chosen, that there is none like him among all the people?' "[54] Again, when sent by God to the house of Jesse, Samuel believed that Eliab was the chosen one of God, on account of "his countenance and the height of his stature."[55] And even when Samuel's first choice was repudiated by God because whereas "man looketh on the outward appearance but the Lord looketh on the heart,"[56] the youngest son of Jesse who was finally chosen is again described as "ruddy and withal of a beautiful countenance."[57] Absalom the son of David and first pretender to the throne was the most beautiful man in all Israel, and, moreover, "from the sole of his foot even to the crown of his head there was no blemish in him."[58] In the royal wedding hymn, Psalm 45, the king is addressed as follows: "Thou art the fairest of all men, grace is poured into thy lips."[59] The beauty of the king was proverbial. "Thine eyes shall see the king in his beauty," we read in Isaiah.[60]

When Uzziah-Azariah was smitten with leprosy he was deposed, and his son Jotham reigned in his stead.[61] Hebrew priests, who took over in postexilic days ritual functions performed in the days of the first Temple by the kings,[62] had to be of an unblemished body, for "whatsoever man that has a blemish" was not allowed to perform the priestly functions.[63]

A further correspondence between the African kings on the one hand, and the Hebrew kings and high priests on the other, lies in the interdiction to defile themselves by coming in contact with a dead body.[64] According to later Jewish tradition, neither kings nor high priests were permitted to defile themselves with a dead body. If a near relative of theirs died, they had to stay within the sanctuary or the royal palace.[65]

III.

Turning now to the installation proper, we find that after Samuel announced to Saul that he would be king of Israel, he led him up to the *bamah* (the high place), invited him to the chamber where some thirty persons were present, bid him to sit in "the chiefest place," and gave him to eat certain portions of a slaughtered animal.[66] The narrative as it stands seems at first glance to relate a series of chance happenings. At the time the narrative was put to writing it was, no doubt, regarded as the account of a historic event, which occurred once, and once only, in the past and consisted of a number of unpremeditated actions and exchange of words. A closer scrutiny of the context, however, is apt to make us at least suspect that Samuel, who played the active role in this scene, had planned each of his movements and actions, as well as those of Saul—in other words, had in reality performed what we shall recognize as a number of rites belonging to an installation ritual.

According to 1 Samuel 9:15–16, Samuel was advised by God of the coming of Saul twenty-four hours in advance. Thereupon (early on the next day) Samuel betook himself to Ramah[67] and called the people to a sacrifice on the *bamah*,[68] just as later he went to Bethlehem and called Jesse and his sons and the elders of the town to a sacrifice.[69] A further correspondence between the two events may be seen in the circumstance that in both cases the king-elect came late to the sacrifice; in fact, he came as the last one, after the sacrificial animal had been slaughtered and prepared.[70] This repetition allows us to suppose the existence of an ancient installation ritual which opened with the following ceremony. The person who conducted the ceremony came to the place where the installation of the king was to occur. He convoked the people (or a number of persons determined beforehand) to partake of a sacrificial meal. The meal was begun before the king-elect arrived, or else the participants waited for him.

Similar to this is the procedure followed at the installation of a number of African kings. We have already seen that among the Shilluk the king-elect was not present at the election ceremony. Only at a later stage does the elected king come (with or without an escort) and join the assembly of electors.[71]

In the case of Saul it was Samuel himself who conducted him up the hill, from the gate of the town,[72] and, after the sacrificial meal, accompanied him back, down from the *bamah* to the town where his house was.[73] To "mount a hill" is, as we have seen, one of the rites in African coronation ceremonies. The size of the hill to be mounted by the king-elect varies considerably, from a veritable hillock up which he has to climb, to a small mound of sand or a white-ant hill or a rock or a stone.[74] In the Hebrew rite the *bamah* seems to have been replaced later by a pillar, for in connection with the coronation of Joash we read that he "stood on the pillar as was the rule."[75] The only other occasion we hear of a king standing on the "pillar" is in connection with the covenant Josiah made after the "book of the covenant" was found in the Temple. "And the king went up into the house of the Lord and all the men of Judah and all the inhabitants of Jerusalem with him, and the priests and the prophets and all the people both small and great; and he read in their ears all the words of the book of the covenant which was found in the house of the Lord. And the king stood on the pillar[76] and made a covenant before the Lord."[77]

Many hundred years later we again hear of a king ascending an elevated place in the Temple. It is Archelaus the son of Herod, who seven days after his father's death "put on a white garment and went up to the Temple, where the people accosted him with acclamations. He also spoke kindly to the multitude from an elevated seat and a throne of gold.[78]

Of more concern to us is a mishnaic tradition relating to approximately the same period, according to which the king had an important function to fulfill on the Feast of Tabernacles every seventh year: he had to read out in public certain passages of Deuteronomy.[79] It is worthwhile to quote in full the Mishna which shows that down to the last days of the Second Temple the king retained the ritual role first assumed by Josiah, that of reading out the Tora in the Temple.

> At the conclusion of the first day of the Feast [of Tabernacles], in the eighth [year], at the expiring of the seventh [year], they make him [i.e., the king] a wooden platform in the courtyard [of the Temple] and he sits on it; as it is written, "At the end of every seven years at the time," etc.[80] The warden of the congregation took a Torah scroll and gave it to the head of the congregation. The head of the congregation gave it to the deputy [priest], and the deputy [priest] gave it to the high priest, and the high priest gave it to the king. The king received it standing and read it sitting.[81]

The next point we wish to consider is the "entrance dialogue and proclamation" forming among African peoples the opening of the installation ceremony.[82] Traces of such an initial dialogue and proclamation may be found in the words exchanged between Samuel and Saul,[83] Samuel and Jesse,[84] Ahijah and Jeroboam,[85] and the young prophet (the disciple of Elisha) and Jehu.[86] These passages may be regarded as "historicized" records of what was originally a ritual dialogue.

Now we come to the sacrificial meal itself. The scene is the chamber, or, to use the expression of Robertson Smith, the "banqueting hall for the communal sacrifice,"[87] which seems to have been a stereotyped feature attached to holy places among the ancient Hebrews, Phoenicians, and Greeks alike.[88] In this chamber there were assembled the men invited by Samuel, "and they were about thirty men."[89] The number thirty, though given here only approximately, may have well been the exact number of the persons invited by Samuel to witness the first sacrificial meal, the communion, of the king-elect. The numbers thirty, thirty-one, and thirty-two appear constantly in Hebrew tradition in connection with kingship and national or tribal leadership. According to an old Hebrew tradition, the number of the petty kings of Canaan vanquished by Joshua was thirty-one.[90] In David's time the thirty electors seem to have constituted a sort of permanent council or body of chieftains around the king, known as "the mighty men of David."[91] The "mighty men" had a special house of assembly in the "city of David," known even centuries later as "the house of the mighty men."[92] The context in 1 Chron. 11:10 even suggests that it was actually these "mighty men" who helped David in some way to become king over Israel. Thirty was only the traditional number of the "mighty men," for in reality the number varied.[93] Ben-Hadad, king of Syria, had "thirty-two kings who helped him."[94] These thirty-two royal "helpers" of the king of Syria are called in another place simply "thirty-two captains of chariots.[95]

Moreover, it would seem that the attendance of thirty men upon the leader already had been in vogue among the Hebrews in predynastic times. Of the Transjordanian judge, Jair, we read that "he had thirty sons that rode thirty ass-colts [cf. the thirty-two charioteers of Ben Hadad!] and they had thirty cities which are called Havoth-Jair [the "farms" of Jair] unto this day, which are in the land of Gilead."[96] Again, Judge Ibzan of Bethlehem had "thirty sons,"[97] and Judge Abdon the Pirathonite had "forty sons and thirty grandsons who rode on seventy ass-colts."[98] I think we shall interpret these traditions rightly if then we take the word "sons" not in its literal sense but in the sense of followers, just as, e.g., *b'ne n'vi'im* means "the followers of the prophets." Also an occasional group of followers consisted of thirty men,[99] while in the wedding ceremony in which royal state was accorded to the bride and bridegroom,[100] the bridegroom was given thirty companions—at least so we find recorded in the report of the wedding of Samson.[101] These companions were called "the sons of the bridal chamber."[102] In view of the evidence adduced above, it seems certain that the "about thirty men" gathered by Samuel to be present at the first installation ceremony of Saul were an official body of electors or councillors,[103] in conformity with the general Canaanite-Syrian, and the special Hebrew, tradition and usage.

It is difficult to determine the number of the officials taking part in the election and installation ceremonies in Africa. The number of persons taking part in, or being present at, a ceremony is such a minor detail that unless the attention of the observer is specially drawn to it, he will in all probability omit to record it. Thus the fact that I am unable at present to give African examples as to the presence of thirty officials at the election and installation ceremonies does by no means indicate that no such arrangement exists in Africa.[104] On the other hand, the unequivocal evidence of the communion received by a number of African kings in the course of the installation ceremony makes it seem very probable that the sacrificial meal of which Saul partook is to be regarded as one of the rites of the installation ritual. To mention only one African example: "Ganda's new king spent his first night in the house Buganda on Budo hill. There *Semanobe* served him a meal consisting of a roasted goat and plantains roasted in their skins."[105] In the case of Saul we are not told what animal was sacrificed for the "communion," but besides this we hear quite a number of instructive details. After having ushered Saul and his servant into the "chamber," Samuel "gave them a place at the head of the invited men." Then he said to the cook, " 'Bring the portion which I gave thee of which I said unto thee, Set it by thee.' And the cook lifted the thigh and the fat tail[106] and set it before Saul. And [Samuel] said, 'Behold that which is left! Set it before thee and eat, for it has been kept for thee for this time [since I] said, "I have invited the people." ' And Saul ate with Samuel that day."[107]

Both pieces of the sacrificial animal which were specially kept for Saul play an important role in Hebrew sacrificial ritual. The thigh or leg, called "the thigh of the heave offering," was the piece of "the ram of consecration" which was allotted to Aaron and his sons.[108] According to Leviticus, it was the right leg which was given to the officiating priests.[109] The extensive use of the right front leg of a sacrificial animal already was characteristic of the Canaanite ritual in the thirteenth century B.C.[110] According to Exodus 29:22–25, the leg, together with the fat tail and some other parts of "the ram of consecration," had to be burned upon the altar as a burnt offering. In a number of other sacrifices only the fat tail had to be burned in a similar manner.[111]

The terminology used in connection with the leg and the fat tail in Exodus and in Leviticus is the same as that appearing in the narrative of Saul's installation. In the sacrificial ritual the leg is called "the leg of the heave offering"; it is "heaved up," that is, lifted. The right leg becomes the "portion" of the priest who offers up the blood and the fat.[112] Similarly Samuel demands of the cook the "portion" set aside for Saul, and the cook "lifts up" the leg and the fat tail when setting them before Saul.[113]

Our conclusion is that the sacrificial meal partaken of by Saul was part of his installation ritual, and this contention is strengthened by the parallel offered by the Bible itself in the narrative of the consecration of Aaron, in which both the leg and fat tail of a sacrificial animal play an important part.[114]

IV.

The next scene took place on a roof. After the sacrificial meal was finished, Samuel accompanied Saul down from the *bamah* to the town, "and he spoke to Saul on the roof."[115] The next verse, "And they arose early, and about the coming of dawn Samuel called to Saul on the roof, saying, 'Get up that I may send thee away' " implies that Saul spent the night on the roof of the house. This may be compared to an episode told of Absalom, the son of David. When Absalom usurped the kingdom in the lifetime of his father, Ahitophel, the famous councillor of David, advised him that, in order to make his accession to the throne manifest in the eyes of the people, he should "go in unto" the few concubines David left behind in the palace. "So they spread Absalom a tent on the roof and Absalom went in unto his father's concubines in the sight of all Israel."[116] That taking possession of a king's wives was regarded as equivalent to taking possession of the kingdom we can infer from the words of Solomon in which he refused to grant his brother Adonijah's request for Abishag, a concubine of David. "And why dost thou ask Abishag the Shunamite for Adonijah? Ask for him the kingdom also."[117] David himself married the widows of Saul.[118] In ancient Egypt it was common for the founder of a new dynasty to marry the widow of the last king.[119] In modern Africa among the Jukun, this ceremonial marriage is part of the installation ritual. The king-elect sleeps two nights with a widow of the late king in a specially erected enclosure. This woman subsequently becomes head of the women of the palace.[120]

The roof was in preexilic days a place of sacrifice and worship[121] on which altars were erected,[122] while in postexilic times the booths were erected on the roofs.[123] The roofs were the place both for joy[124] and for mourning.[125] As in the case of Saul, there was no special reason, such as in the case of the two spies in Jericho,[126] to let him spend the night on the roof; the inference seems plausible that both Saul and Absalom spent a night on the roof in the course of their respective installation ceremonies in accordance with a rite. This inference is strengthened by the fact that the great New Year ritual of the ancient Near East—which was also the reenthronement festival—contained a ceremonial sacred marriage which, in one case at least, was celebrated in a special room on the top of the temple building.[127] Also to the Hittite spring enthronement festival belonged a tent ceremony (*za-lam-gar*)[128] while in the Ras Shamra texts we hear of a ritual for the king in a roof rite during a seven days' festival which was, according to Gaster, "part of the ritual of the winter-festival when the king was formally re-instated."[129] Moreover, certain biblical scholars hold that the "booths" which the Bible prescribed as a dwelling place for the period of the seven days of the Tabernacles "originally represented the sacred grove in which the divine marriage was consummated."[130]

The next rite, the anointing of the king-elect with oil, is the best attested among all the Hebrew installation rites. In addition to the anointing of Saul,[131] we are informed of the anointing of David, Absalom, Solomon, Jehu, Joash, and Joahas.[132] The king is called the messiah, i.e. "the anointed," of God. Prophets and priests also were anointed with oil[133] and the chief priest was called "anointed."[134]

The origin of the use of the sacred anointing oil has been repeatedly investigated.[135] The use of oil has certainly something to do with the belief in the vital properties of oil, such as its nourishing, conserving, and healing powers. In the Hebrew ritual of the anointing of kings, the special sanctity of the oil used in the ceremony was added to these properties. Zadok the priest, when anointing Solomon, took "the horn of oil out of the tabernacle and anointed Solomon."[136] David also was anointed with the holy oil.[137]

A talmudic tradition has it that the Hebrew kings were anointed with the oil of anointing made by Moses in the wilderness. The same oil was used for anointing the tabernacle and its vessels, Aaron and his sons, and the successive high priests. This could be accomplished with the small amount of oil prepared by Moses only thanks to a miracle of self-multiplication.[138] The oil was prepared out of the following "principal spices": liquid myrrh, 500 shekels; sweet cinnamon, 250 shekels; sweet calamus, 250 shekels; cassia, 500 shekels; and one *hin* of olive oil.[139] It is interesting to note that according to one talmudic tradition the Davidic kings were anointed but the Israelite kings were not, while according to another tradition both in Judah and Israel, only those kings were anointed who were either the founders of a new dynasty or in whose case the succession was contested by a rival pretendent.[140] Talmudic tradition also tells of the exact way in which kings and priests were anointed. In the case of kings the oil was applied to their heads in the form of a wreath (i.e., around the head), while in the case of priests it was applied in the form of the Greek letter X.[141] The anointing of kings also is well attested in Africa and other places.[142] The baptism of the king-elect should be mentioned in connection with the anointing. In Africa the king-elect was baptized or had to drink water ceremonially.[143] Ceremonial lustration of the pharaoh before the coronation as well as during the ritual itself was apparently customary in ancient Egypt.[144] Reference to the baptism of Hebrew kings can be seen in the taking down of the king-elect to the spring of Gihon and his anointing "in Gihon."[145] According to talmudic tradition attached to the verse telling of Solomon's anointing in Gihon, all the kings had to be anointed at a spring, and this for a sympathetic-magical reason: "that their reign might be long drawn out" (namely, like the waters of the spring).[146] Also Solomon's rival, Adonijah, when he wished to be acknowledged as the successor of his father, "slew sheep and oxen and fat cattle by the stone Zoheleth which is by the spring of Rogel."[147]

The rite of anointing was accompanied by a short proclamation on the part of the person performing the ceremony and was followed by the acclamation of the king by the people. Samuel said to Saul, "Is it not that the Lord hath anointed thee to be captain over his inheritance?"[148] In the case of Saul, where we have a detailed description of the installation proceedings, this proclamation is distinct from the so-called entrance dialogue. In the case of other kings, more summarily dealt with, we hear only of one meeting between them and the person performing the anointing, and, consequently, the entrance dialogue is merged with the proclamation, as is the case with many an African king.[149]

That the acclamation was not a spontaneous outbreak of enthusiasm on the part of the people, but a veritable rite, we can learn from the instructions given by David to Zadok the priest, Nathan the prophet, and Benaiah as to the performance of the coronation of Solomon: "and let Zadok the priest and Nathan the prophet anoint him there king over Israel, and blow ye with the trumpet and say, '[Long] live king Solomon!' " The old king's instructions were carried out to the letter. Only one significant difference can be noted in the narrative relating the actual ceremony when compared with David's instructions: it was not only the servants of the king, but "all the people" who acclaimed, "[Long] live king Solomon!"[150] The same acclamation, "[Long] live king so and so!" is repeatedly reported, first of all in connection with the coronation of Saul, then with that of Adonijah, Absalom, and Joash.[151] It should be noted that this form of acclamation also became the usual way of greeting a king.[152]

Hocart has noted that the entering of the spirit of God into the newly anointed king,[153] in consequence of which he "turns into another man,"[154] closely corresponds to other peoples' ceremonies symbolizing the death and rebirth of the king.[155] According to Hocart, the general theory of the installation ritual is that "the king (1) dies; (2) is reborn, (3) as a god."[156] Traces of the existence of this theory in the Hebrew installation ritual can be found in Psalm 2, which puts these words in the mouth of God: "I have set up my king upon Zion, my sacred mountain." This statement is answered by the king: "I will declare the statute(?), the Lord hath said unto me, 'Thou art my son, this day have I born thee.''[157] To quote only one African example in which the rebirth of the king on the day of his enthronement, referred to in this psalm, is most strikingly enacted, let me mention the following detail from the coronation ceremonies of the Atah (the king) of Idah, a state lying in the angle formed by the Niger and the Benue. "Two officers, the Onobe Ogbo, 'the oldest man in the world,' and the Oneda, the 'birth giver,' sport together as man and wife; then the Oneda mimics child-birth, and after a diviner has prophesied that the child will be a 'boy . . . lord of the earth,' the Atah appears from beneath the skirts of the Onede.''[158] While noting the parallelism between the African enactment and the Hebrew reference, one must not lose sight of the difference between the African king's ritual rebirth by a court official and the Hebrew king's rebirth by God, though in the African installation rite the theory also seems to be that the king is "reborn as a son of the gods.''[159]

As to the ancient Hebrew concept that the Davidic king is the son of God, there is ample evidence to this effect in addition to Psalm 2, in the Psalter and in other biblical writings.[160] According to later Jewish tradition, the king becomes on the day of his coronation "like a one-year-old babe who has not known the taste of sin,''[161] while the concept that the spirit of God enters into the anointed one so that he becomes the son of God reappears in the Gospels in the baptism story of Jesus.[162]

It would be tempting also to relate the closing verses of Psalm 2 to the coronation ritual, and, by retaining the Massoretic Text of verse 12, translate it, "Kiss the son," i.e., the king-elect who on the day of his coronation became the newborn son of God.[163] This would be in accordance with the narrative of the installation of Saul where we read, "Then Samuel took a vial of oil and poured it upon his [Saul's] head and kissed him.''[164] In the Babylonian New Year reenthronement festival, a ritual kissing of a person and of objects was one of the regular rites.[165]

V.

Before going on with our investigations into the installation ritual performed in connection with Saul, we shall have to make an attempt to establish the proper order of the passages contained in 1 Sam. 10–13. That the present sequence of the narrative is out of order will be evident at first sight. It is impossible, to mention only one of the numerous difficulties, that all the events related in 10:10–13:7 should have taken place within seven days, as indicated by 10:8 and 13.8. This and other incongruities in the Masoretic Text (MT) have induced biblical scholars to put forward a great number of proposals as to the reconstruction of the original form of the narrative. It is not up to us to view or recapitulate all that has been said in this connection; let us mention only that one of the favorite methods of eliminating such difficulties is to try to discern in the present MT the traces of heterogenous sources. The majority of biblical scholars finds two parallel versions in the narrative,[166] others discern three,[167] and again others four or even five.[168]

We need not go as far as any one of these scholars, and will be able to content ourselves with applying to the chapters in question the principle of the famous talmudic sage of the second century A.D., Rabbi Meir, "there is no time sequence in the Bible,"[169] which means that there is no need to accept the sequence of the narrative in the MT as being chronologically exact. We would, therefore, tentatively suggest the following time sequence, which would seem to follow logically from the interrelation of the different scenes described in chapters 10–13.

When the people saw that Nahash, king of Ammon, made preparations to attack them, they applied to Samuel for a king.[170] Samuel, first reluctant, finally complied with their wish and anointed Saul to be king over Israel.[171] On the same day[172] three signs came to Saul as foretold by Samuel.[173] When Saul was thus convinced of his calling, he returned to the *bamah*, to Samuel,[174] whereupon, probably the following day, his public installation took place in nearby Mizpah, where Samuel's and the thirty electors' choice was confirmed by the choice of the oracle.[175] At the end of this ceremony Samuel sent the people home (v. 25) and ordered Saul to meet him seven days later in the Gilgal (v. 8). Saul was ridiculed by some people (v. 27), just as he had been a day earlier when he joined the group of prophets (v. 11). But again, as on the previous occasions, he bore the derision patiently,[176] and retired to his house in Gibeah together with a small band of men who joined him immediately after his public election (v. 26).

In the meantime Nahash, king of Ammon, started his campaign, and he "encamped against Jabesh-Gilead" (11:1). Now it was up to Saul to show that he was able to perform the task for which he had been chosen king of Israel, namely to defeat Ammon. The elders of Jabesh-Gilead asked Nahash for a seven days' respite, which was granted to them,[177] and sent messengers to Gibeah, to Saul (11:4). When hearing the message, Saul became possessed of the spirit of God—the first indication of the success with which his campaign would be crowned; he rallied the people and next day he destroyed the Ammonite army (11:5–11). Now that Saul had proved his mettle, his kingship could be confirmed, made definitive (v. 14). The people now proposed to Saul[178] to kill those who said, "Shall Saul reign over us?" (cf. 10:27), but Saul answered to them, "No man shall be put to death this day"

(vv. 12–13). Saul, now confident in his strength and success, proposed to go to Gilgal in order to "renew the kingship" (v. 14), whereupon "all the people went to Gilgal, and they made there Saul king before the Lord in Gilgal, and they sacrificed there *shelamim* sacrifices before the Lord and Saul, and all the men of Israel rejoiced there greatly" (v. 15).

It is this scene in Gilgal which is described in more detail in 13:7–15. Saul was still in Gilgal and all the people, namely those who were not taking part in the battle of Jabesh-Gilead, came quickly there after him (v. 7).[179] Saul waited until the seven days' term set by Samuel expired,[180] and when Samuel did not arrive and Saul saw that the people got tired of waiting and began to disperse, he ordered the burnt offering and the *shelamim* to be brought before him and performed the sacrificial rite himself (vv. 8–9).[181] Only now, after both sets of offerings ordered by Samuel seven days earlier were carried out in his absence, did Samuel appear on the scene, and there followed the humiliation of the young king on the very day of his first triumph.[182]

VI.

It is to this point that we need at present follow the traditional history of Saul, and after having thus established an approximate chronological order of events, we may now continue the analysis of the Hebrew royal installation ritual as reflected in this narrative.

Samuel, then, after having anointed and kissed Saul, instructed him to make a round in the countryside so that three signs might come to pass which would convince Saul of his being the chosen one of God. Saul had to go to three holy places: to the tomb of Rachel, the mother of his tribe (Benjamin), to the terebinth of Tabor, and to the Gibeah (the hill) of God (10:2–5). At each place a certain event occurred exactly as foretold by Samuel. The events showed a progressive importance:[183] the first one was a simple encounter with two people known to Saul, probably servants of his father, who told him that the lost asses had been found; in the second three unknown people showed him kingly honor;[184] and in the third, in the encounter with the group of prophets, Saul himself turned "into another man." Without entering into a discussion of the exact significance of these signs, let us only note one thing, that the newly appointed king went round in his country, as he again did at a later time. "Saul came to the Carmel[185] and, behold, he set him up a monument and is gone about and passed on and gone down to Gilgal."[186] Saul made this second round at the close of his victorious battle with Amalek; it was followed by an encounter in the Gilgal between him and Samuel in many details similar to their first meeting at the same place. But of this later.

Saul's double round may be compared to point 20 in the installation ceremonies of African kings ("After the coronation the king travelled around his domains and received homage")[187] or to the corresponding point in the coronation ceremony as established by Hocart ("At the conclusion of the ceremonies he goes the round of his dominions and receives the homage of the vassals").[188] It should be noted that although in their schematized forms both Hocart and, after him, Irstam speak of the round as made after the coronation or at its close, in fact there exist wide variations in the performance of this rite. Thus—again to confine our examples to Africa—among the Umundri the king made a tour of his domain both at the beginning and at the end of the coronation ceremonies.[189] This closely corresponds to Saul's two rounds.[190]

Among other African peoples, this rite took a form which parallels a Hebrew coronation rite recorded not in connection with Saul, but with later Hebrew kings. Among the Igara the king rode three times round a small circular hut.[191] In Abyssinia and among the Jukun the king rode around receiving the people's homage.[192] When Solomon was crowned, "they have caused him to ride upon the king's mule."[193] According to Jeremiah, the kings are "riding in chariots and on horses,"[194] while in postexilic days the prophet Zechariah thus describes the triumphal procession of the king: "Rejoice greatly, O daughter of Zion, shout, O daughter of Jerusalem. Behold, thy king cometh unto thee; he is just and having salvation, lowly and riding upon an ass and upon a colt, the foal of an ass."[195] Thus we see that the riding upon a colt, which we discerned as a sign of rulership in the days of the Judges, remained a symbol of kingship down to postexilic days, and thence right down to the times of Jesus. In talmudic literature the usual mount associated with kings is again the horse.[196]

Before resuming the discussion of the Hebrew coronation rites in their chronological order, a few words should be said about the "pillar" or "monument" (*yad*) which Saul set up for himself in Carmel.[197] In the present state of the narrative it is difficult to determine whether the round made by Saul in his domain after his victory over Amalek and the feast held by him subsequently in the Gilgal[198] may be regarded as belonging to the installation rites proper or not. We know, however, from Hocart's investigations that "a king may be consecrated several times, going up each time one step in the scale of kingship."[199] Such repeated consecrations may even assume more or less fixed forms, as was the case in Egypt, where the periodic jubilee festival, the Sed festival, was performed with a view to the rejuvenation of the ageing king.[200] The Sed festival was not the only feast of this kind in ancient Egypt. At Edfu an annual religious drama was performed, professedly in commemoration of Horus's wars with Seth, his final victory, his coronation as king of a united Egypt, the dismemberment of his foe, and his "triumph" or "justification" before the tribunal of the gods, but in fact in order to make the reigning king victorious over his foes, secure him a prosperous reign, and obtain for him the same "triumph" as was won by his divine prototype. [201]

To return now to Saul, the numerous parallel details between Saul's second feast in Gilgal and the first one[202] show that we have to do here with a repetitive coronation or rejuvenation festival not unlike, in character and intent, the Egyptian festivals mentioned above. [203] If this be so, one may perhaps be permitted to compare the erection of the *yad* by Saul previous to his festival in Gilgal with the raising of the *Dd* column which was "a ceremony closely associated with the Sed-festival and performed on the eve of that celebration by the king."[204] Let us add to this that in Africa the original version of this ceremony has been preserved to this day, inasmuch as the African kings do not set up columns in the course of their coronation ceremony, but plant a tree, their own life tree. [205] The life tree in Africa, it is believed, is of ancient Near East origin. [206]

The main point in the next scene, the identification of the chosen king by the oracle, has already been discussed above. We saw that the choice of the king by public oracle after his election has been agreed upon by the electors is a not uncommon procedure in Africa. African parallels enable us to interpret 1 Sam. 10:21–23 also as a rite. There we read,

> and Saul the son of Kish was taken [by the oracle] and they sought him but he could not be found. Therefore they enquired of the Lord further, "Will [the] man still come thither?" And the Lord said, "Behold, he hath hid himself among the stuff." And they ran and fetched him thence, and he stood among the people and he was higher than any of the people from his shoulders and upward. [207]

With this narrative we may compare the following account given by Meek on the installation of a chief among the Fali of Wuba district in northern Nigeria.

> After an interval of a year the chief's successor is chosen by the official known as the Mazu, who ties a turban round the new chief's head, and then takes him to his own house for a period of five nights. The sixth night is spent in the house of another official, and the seventh in the house of a third. In the early morning of the eighth day this third official takes the chief out to the bush where he leaves him. Returning himself to the town he shouts out: "My slave has run away, and is lost in the bush." At this all the male members of the community seize their arms and set off to search the bush. When they find the new chief they bring him back with acclamations.

"This custom," continues Meek, "is paralleled among the Jukun; for at a certain stage of his chieftainship the Jukun king has to undergo rites in the course of which he is lost in the bush and found again by his people."[208] These African ceremonies, which resemble the Hebrew installation rites in more than one point, make it, I believe, probable that Saul's hiding and subsequent being found and fetched by the people was not a chance happening, but a rite.

The same can be stated as to the frequent admonitions directed by Samuel both to Saul and to the people, and the subsequent promises on their part.[209] In the Hebrew installation rites the admonition was at times administered by a prophet,[210] at times by the people,[211] at times by God,[212] or even by the king's predecessor.[213] The admonition was at times included in a covenant.[214]

The admonitions themselves were intended to impress upon the king the necessity of keeping the laws,[215] of ruling in a just manner,[216] and of conducting victorious campaigns against the enemies of the people.[217] With this we may compare the African admonitions and promises, which were practically the same everywhere.[218] In Dahomey two officials conducted the newly enthroned king into a building, where they showed him sacks filled with pebbles which represented the population of Dahomey. For every succeeding king there was a separate chamber containing such sacks.

> As the two old men led their royal master through the rooms, they pointed out how the size of the sacks for each reign was greater than those which represented the population of Dahomey during the preceding King's tenure. They recounted to him the conquests of each of his ancestors, and impressed him with the manner in which these had increased the number of people in the kingdom. When they reached the room which contained the sacks of pebbles that represented the population of Dahomey during the reign of his father, the two elders said to the new King: "Young man, kneel!" and as he knelt there, they continued, "Young man, all your life you have heard 'Dahomey, Dahomey,' but you have never until today seen the true Dahomey; for Dahomey is its people, and here they are." Then . . . they said, " . . . You must never allow the contents of these sacks to diminish; you must see to it that these pebbles increase in number. . . . Every year we will come here with you to count the pebbles, and to see if you have increased the number, or reduced it. Young man, rise! We did not give you this thought to discourage you!" They gave him a very old gun—tradition has it that in the time of Hwegbadja they gave him a hoe-handle, the weapon with which the Dahomeans are said to have fought in early times—and said, "Fight with this. But take care, that you are not vanquished." Then they sang for him songs which might not be sung outside this place and told him to meet them there again the following year.[219]

As we see, the admonition of the king was in this case accompanied by his humiliation, while the repetition of this rite year after year may be compared to the annual humiliation of the king which was part and parcel of the ancient Near Eastern New Year ritual. [220]

In connection with the scene in Mizpah we are told that "the sons of Belial [i.e. the good-for-nothings] said: 'How shall this one [i.e., Saul] help us?' And they despised him and brought him no presents. But he held his peace.'' [221] Though this passage looks very much like a genuine piece of historical tradition, comparison with Africa makes us again suspect that we have here a misrepresented or misunderstood ("historicized") record of another installation rite. The humiliation of the king figures among the installation rites of several other African peoples in addition to those of Dahomey. "Among the Shilluk," to quote Irstam,

> the new king had to be prepared during a certain period before the actual coronation to be treated very badly by the people. He was obliged patiently to tolerate [222] everything—practical joking, sneers and derision. This was to teach him humility. Among the Kpelle everyone had the right on the day of the coronation, before the coronation, to throw stones at the new king, indeed, to give expression in general to repugnance towards him. The intention here was (according to Westermann) to get at the evil spirits that might conceivably exist in the king's body and drive them out before he received the good spirits of his predecessor. Among the Pangwe similar ceremonies were performed. [223]

Our "ritualistic" interpretation of the incident between Saul and the "sons of Belial" would seem to be confirmed by a parallel contained in the story of David. When David fled before his son Absalom, a man from the house of Saul, Shimei ben Gera by name, came forth, cursed David and cast stones and dust at him and at his servants, and called him "a man of Belial"—and all this the presence of the "mighty men" of David notwithstanding. When Abishai ben Zeruyah, one of these "mighty men," offered to kill Shimei, David did not let him do so, saying that it was God's will that Shimei should curse him and that "God will requite him good for his cursing this day." [224] David's behavior here is exactly the same as that of Saul towards those who derided him. The occurrence of the name "Belial" in both cases also may be significant.

Some time later, when David returned from Transjordan, after he had defeated Absalom, he was met by the people of Judah at Gilgal, [225] the traditional place of coronation, and there a sort of reinstallation of David in his reign took place. [226] Again Shimei appears on the scene, now downcast and asking for forgiveness. Again Abishai offers to kill Shimei, and again David refuses to grant this permission, saying, "What have I to do with you, ye sons of Zeruyah, that ye should this day be adversaries unto me? Shall

there any man be put to death this day in Israel?[227] These are almost literally
the words said by Saul, when after his return from his victorious battle
against Nahash the people proposed to kill those who had ridiculed him. Saul
had answered, "There shall not be a man put to death this day."[228]

VII.

We now come to the instruction given by Samuel to Saul, according to
which Saul should wait seven days until Samuel would come to him to
Gilgal.[229] Later we are told that Saul followed these instructions literally
(13:8). According to our reconstruction of the original order of events,
Samuel must have issued these instructions at the end of the ceremonies at
Mizpah, when he "sent all the people away, every man to his house"
(10:25), and when "also Saul went home to Gibeah" (v. 26). It was at this
juncture, when one series of rites had been completed and everyone repaired
home, that it was appropriate to issue instructions as to the time when the
ceremonies should be resumed.

The wording of Samuel's instructions in their present form is far from
clear. For though Saul is bidden to wait in Gilgal seven days, it is not stated
from what date the counting of these days should begin. The seven days
cannot be meant from the date on which the instructions were given in
Mizpah, for it is expressly stated that after the ceremonies in Mizpah Saul
repaired to his home. Any other date would, however, require to be explicitly stated. As no such statement is contained in the context, we are led to
the conclusion that the seven days were indeed to be counted from the day on
which the instructions were given, but their intention was not that Saul
should spend all the seven days in waiting, but that he should be in Gilgal in
seven days' time, and then, on the seventh day, wait until Samuel himself
should arrive. We do not intend to propose a revised reading of 10:8 and 13:8
to make them express this meaning—though this could easily be done—as
we do not think the MT to be a corrupt version of an older, correct text. What
we believe is that the MT is based on an oral version which itself no longer
understood the full implication of the orally traditioned original passage. Be
this as it may, it seems quite clear that Samuel ordered a week's interruption
in the installation ceremonies, which week, thus at least it seems to us, he
intended Saul to spend in his home[230] in the company of a few persons
"whose hearts God had touched."

In the African installation ceremonies, it is a regular feature that "the
king goes into retirement for a certain period,"[231] this period being more
often seven days than any other number of days, weeks, or months.[232]
Under "retirement" not solitude is understood, but rather a cessation of the

installation festivities and a period of transition for the new king, during which he leads a sort of semiofficial existence. A typical example of this is found in Dar Fur, where after the coronation the king retired "for one week into his home without giving either orders or interdictions; during this time no affair was brought before him."[233] A similar seven days' period of retirement was observed by the chief-elect in the Fundj, Wadai, among the Babur, the Kilba, the Mbum, in the Hausa states, and in various Jukun communities.[234] Among other tribes the length of the period of retirement varies from two to ten days, or it extends over a fortnight, a month, three months, or even longer.[235] In a number of cases, for example among the Jukun, the king-elect undergoes during the period of seclusion a process of divinization, learns to receive his food in ritual fashion, is shown the secret amulets, etc.[236] Among other peoples, for instance in Uganda, among the Pangwe, and in Ziba, the point in the retirement seems to be the spending by the king of a certain period of time in a temporary dwelling place while he attends to many affairs of state.[237] Among the Konde the seclusion, lasting three months, serves as a test period, during which the health of the king-elect is carefully noted, lest being a weakling he should be a menace to the land.[238]

These cases enable us to interpret Saul's retirement as conditioned by some ritual rule.[239] This ritual retirement during which Saul continued to pursue his domestic occupations (11:5), was, however, interrupted by the call for help of Jabesh Gilead. I would not go as far as to contend that the report of Saul's campaign against the king of Ammon is a "historicized" account of a ritual combat, similar to that which formed in the ancient Near East[240]—just as it still forms today in Africa[241]—an integral part of the coronation ritual. Such an interpretation, though, would at once eliminate some of the difficulties noted, for instance, by Lods, when he stated that the account contains "de bien graves invraisemblances: est-il croyable que Nahach ait accordé aux assiégés un délai de sept jours avant de capituler, pour leur permettre d'envoyer demander du secours dans tout le territoire d'Israel?"[242] Neither shall we try to solve the other difficulties in which this chapter abounds. I should only like to advance a theory which, I believe, will prove helpful when applied to passages such as 1 Sam. 11. If we suppose that biblical traditions preserve a recollection of historical events, and this is by now a generally accepted view, we may postulate, in the case of an event such as Saul's installation, the existence of a double set of traditions corresponding to a double set of events, the one covering the successive stages and rites of the protracted installation ritual, and the other recording the historic events taking place at the same time. In the course of time details of the one set of traditions might have got mixed up with the other set of traditions.

The seven days' grace, asked for by the men of Jabesh Gilead in order to send for help and implicitly granted to them by Nahash, king of Ammon (11:3), could thus be explained as a detail taken over from the tradition of the seven days' interruption in the installation ritual of Saul. In its original version the tradition may have contained a story of the siege of Jabesh Gilead without this detail. The messengers could have stolen out of the town even while Nahash was making his preparations for the siege or for the attack. The words said by the men of Jabesh Gilead to Nahash *after* they knew that help was coming, "Tomorrow we will come out unto you and ye shall do with us all that seemeth good in your eyes,"[243] show that they were intent upon concealing from the enemy the fact that the relieving army was approaching. These words thus stand in direct contradiction to the wording of their first message to Nahash, "Give us seven days' respite that we may send messengers unto all the boundaries of Israel, and then if there be no man to save us, we will come out to thee" (11:3). It is evident that of these two contradictory messages, it is only the second which can be genuinely historic.

But, to return to the question of the ritual combat in the Hebrew installation ceremony, even if we do not hold that traces of it may be discovered in the fight of Saul against Nahash, we have reason to suppose that it had its role among the rites of installation. Psalm 2, of which we have already quoted a passage referring to the rebirth of the king on the day of his coronation, contains a rich description of the rebellion of the peoples, kings, and rulers of the earth against God and his "anointed," of God's derision at the sight of their vain struggle, and of His promise to His newly enthroned king on Zion, "Thou shalt break them with a rod of iron, thou shalt dash them in pieces like a potter's vessel" (v. 9). Psalm 89, which again refers to the covenant entered by God with His chosen, with David His servant to establish his seed forever (namely as kings in Zion),[244] describes God's primeval victory over the forces of the dark, the sea, Rahab, and in general his "enemies" (vv. 10–11), and the help he extends to the king to become victorious over his enemies (vv. 23–24), whereupon the king will call God "My father art thou" and God will make the king His "first-born."[245] In Psalm 45, a royal marriage hymn, the king is addressed as follows: "Thine arrows are sharpened, peoples fall under thee, in the heart of the king's enemies" (v. 6).

But in addition to these liturgical references, I believe that traces of the ritual combat executed by the Hebrew kings can be found in a historical narrative. Of Joash, king of Israel, the following incident is related in the

Book of Kings, closely following the short stereotyped notice on his accession to the throne, his evilness, and his death:[246]

> Now Elisha was fallen sick of the sickness whereof he died. And Joash the king
> of Israel came down unto him and wept over his face and said, "O my father,
> my father, the chariot and horsemen of Israel!" And Elisha said unto him,
> "Take bow and arrows." And he took unto him bow and arrows. And he said
> to the king of Israel, "Put thine hand upon the bow." And he put his hand upon
> it, and Elisha put his hands upon the king's hands. And he said, "Open the
> window eastward!" and he opened it. Then Elisha said, "Shoot!" And he
> shot. And he [Elisha] said, "The arrow of the Lord's deliverance and the arrow
> of deliverance from Syria! For thou shalt smite the Syrians in Aphek till thou
> have consumed them." And he said, "Take the arrows," and he took them.
> And he said unto the king of Israel, "Smite upon the ground!" And he smote
> thrice and stayed. And the man of God was wroth with him and said, "Thou
> shouldest have smitten five or six times, then hadst thou smitten Syria till thou
> hadst consumed it; whereas now thou shalt smite Syria but thrice."[247]

It is clear at first sight that we have here an almost unique description of a magical act performed by a Hebrew king following the instructions of a Hebrew prophet for the avowed purpose of securing him victory over his enemies. But it is this purpose precisely which was and still is aimed at by the participation of the kings of other peoples (ancient Near East, Africa) in the ritual combat. We have, it is true, no evidence whatsoever that the shooting of the arrow by Joash took place in conjunction with his installation as king of Israel. We can, however, suppose that the meeting between Joash and Elisha took place on some festive occasion. The sequel of the context seems to indicate that the meeting took place on New Year's Day, for the next verse recounts a miracle which occurred at the burial of Elisha, which took place "at the beginning of the year."[248] The opening words of the whole scene (v. 14) indicate that the death of Elisha must have followed immediately, or at least very shortly, after Joash's visit, and he must have been brought to burial, as was usual among the Hebrews, on the same day. The burial of the other man, who revived when, thrown into the grave of Elisha, he touched the "bones," i.e., the dead body of the prophet (v. 21), must have taken place on the same day at a time when the grave of Elisha was not yet covered. We may thus conclude that the meeting between Joash and Elisha took place on New Year's Day. This inference, if we keep in mind the repetition of the installation ritual of Saul in the Gilgal, enables us to suppose that in the passage about the shooting of the arrow by Joash a rite has been preserved which was originally a part of the installation ritual of Hebrew kings, itself taking place on, or about, New Year's Day.

A very similar rite also has been preserved in ancient Egyptian pictorial representations, and, as if to make the correspondence more striking, there too the records refer not to the coronation ceremony proper, but to its ritual repetition, the Sed festival. One of the characteristic features of this festival was the discharge by the pharaoh of arrows towards the four cardinal points, a scene which is repeatedly depicted on monuments. A scene from Karnak, for instance,[249] which shows Thotmes III shooting the arrows, impresses one almost as if it were an illustration to 2 Kings 13:16. We see the king holding the bow and arrow in his hands, while a god places his own hands upon the arms of the king.

The same rite was observed elsewhere. The story of the king of the Indian tribe of Kurus describes how every three years he held a festival at which he stood in the presence of the demon Citraraja and shot an arrow towards each of the four quarters.[250] Again, in Africa we find the same ceremony taking place annually "about the beginning of the year."[251] The rite was performed by the king of Kitara (Unyoro) at his "coronation" and was "described as 'shooting the nations.' This was done with the royal bow, Nyapogo, restrung with human sinews at each succession. "When it had been restrung it was handed to the king with four arrows and he shot these, one towards each of the four quarters of the globe, saying *'Ndasere amahan-ga kugasinga'* (I shoot the nations to overcome them), and mentioning as he shot each arrow the names of the nations in that direction."[252] In the case of Joash, it is true, we hear of the shooting of one arrow only, against Syria, which actually lies east of Israel, the direction in which the arrow was shot. From a later period, however, that of the Second Temple, we have knowledge of an annual ceremony[253] in which the nations of the world were symbolically overcome by the Lulav, shaken towards the four quarters, and figuratively-ritually referred to as an "arrow."[254]

But to return to the installation of Saul. We saw that the narrative does not contain any reference to a ritual combat, but instead, as it were, an account is given of a real fight which took place between Nahash and Saul, and at the victorious conclusion of which the installation ceremonies were continued and Saul was definitively confirmed in his reign. It is interesting to note that while among various African peoples actual battles between the aspirants to the throne had to preceed the coronation of a king,[255] there is at least one instance of the ritual battle being altogether omitted in case there was a real fight going on in some part of the realm. In Uganda the morning after the day in which the new king first entered his newly built dwelling, a sham battle took place. "Kasuju (the minister who had charge of, and responsibility for, the princes and princesses) came and engaged in battle with the king. Both were armed with a shield and a spear, and each was to thrust at the other's shield with the spear. This battle took place to confirm the king in his kingdom, and to show that there was no fear of rebellion. If there was any appearance of a rebellion, the Kasuju did not come.''[256] Thus it would seem that in the case of Saul also, the ritual combat was omitted as there was a real fight to be fought.

After the victory over Nahash, Saul and his following again went down to Gilgal, and he was there reaffirmed in his reign. This part of the ritual comprised the offering up of sacrifices ''and there Saul and all the men of Israel rejoiced greatly.''[257] Rejoicing and acclamations were a recurrent ceremonial feature of the Hebrew installation ritual,[258] as well as of the African installation of kings and chiefs.[259]

VIII.

One of the most frequent features of the African installation ritual is the conferring of certain regalia on the king.[260] In the great majority of cases the regalia given to African kings at their installation are a spear (or spears), a sword, or a shield.[261] Now, in connection with Saul, though we are not told that he received any regalia at his installation, we hear that at a time when ''neither spear nor sword were found in the hand of any of the people'' such weapons were nevertheless provided for Saul and his son Jonathan.[262] This report in itself would give the impression that the spear and the sword were given to Saul and Jonathan simply as arms to be used in their battles. But, at least concerning Saul's spear, this was not the case, as we learn from several other passages which repeatedly speak of the ''spear of Saul.'' When he is sitting on his royal seat in Gibeah under a tree[263] and all his servants are standing around him, he ''has his spear in his hand.'' When sitting in his house, again he has ''his spear in his hand.''[264] When in battle, he ''is leaning upon his spear,''[265] and at night while sleeping ''his spear is stuck in the ground at his bolster.''[266] These passages suggest that the spear was one of the regalia of Saul.[267] A spear figured also among the regalia of the Davidic kings and was even used in connection with the coronation ceremony. When Jehoiada the priest made the preparations for the coronation of Joash, he gave to the captains over the hundreds ''the spear[268] and the shields of King David which were in the Temple of the Lord.''[269] The ''spear of David'' referred to in this passage seems to be identical with the spear of Goliath, the Philistine of Gath. This spear of gigantic dimensions[270] must have been deposited, together with Goliath's sword, first in the tent of David[271] and then in the sanctuary of Nob,[272] and later transferred thence to the Temple built by Solomon.[273]

Swords and spears belonged also to the paraphernalia of the Baal prophets,[274] while according to Numbers 25:7 the Hebrew priests in the desert also were armed with spears. A similar weapon, the *kidon*, also translated by the Authorized Version's "spear," belonged to the insignia of Joshua, and was, moreover, used by him as a magic wand. He stretched out the spear which he had in his hand towards the city of Ai and held it so until complete victory was won over its inhabitants.[275]

With this we may compare the role of the royal spear among the Kam in northern Nigeria. The royal spear, known as Rum, is given to the king-elect. "In time of war, if the Kam were attacked, he would hold up this spear and say: 'If I have done these people [his assailants] any evil, may they overthrow me, but if I had done them no evil, may all that they do be brought to naught.' He would then plant the spear in the ground, and it was believed that the arrows of the enemy would be diverted or break in pieces before reaching their object."[276]

But to return to the Hebrew regalia, we have seen that in addition to the spear the sword also is mentioned as a weapon used by Saul. The sword is a royal weapon. Besides the sword of Saul,[277] mention is made of the sword of pharaoh (Exod. 18.4), the sword of Hazael, and the sword of Jehu (1 Kings 19:17). In a prophecy of Ezekiel God gives his own sword into the hands of the king of Babylon.[278]

We have also seen that in addition to "the spear of David," "the shields of David" also were kept in the temple (2 Kings 11:10). Also the shield as a royal emblem in Israel can be traced back to Saul. David, in his lament over Saul and Jonathan, refers to the "shield of Saul"[279] as to a sacred weapon. The association of the "shield" with the house of David is well known. The Davidic king may be described as the "shield" of his people.[280] Psalm 18 which was, it would seem, composed for the Davidic king and describes the king's deliverance from his enemies—pictured as "death"—by God, his justification, and his ultimate victory over his enemies, the nations, contains, I believe, a reference to the mythical concept of "David's shield." "Thou [God] hast given me the shield of thy succour and thy right hand hath holden me up."[281] When David smote Hadadezer, king of Sobah, he "took the shields of gold that were on the servants of Hadadezer and brought them to Jerusalem"[282] in order to dedicate them to God together with all the other silver and gold which he took from all the nations which he subdued (vv. 11–12). It was presumably in imitation of these golden shields that Solomon made an additional two hundred golden "targets" and three hundred golden shields, which he put in his "house of the forest of Lebanon."[283]

Of the use of these shields in the royal ritual we are informed in a later passage. In the fifth year of king Rehoboam, the son of Solomon, Shishak, king of Egypt, came up against Jerusalem and looted the treasures of the

Temple and of the king's house. Curiously enough, of all the treasures taken away by Shishak, we are informed precisely only of the replacement of the three hundred shields. Rehoboam made in their stead brazen shields, in order presumably to be able to continue the royal ritual in which these shields played an indispensable role. The shields were entrusted to the hands of the captains of the royal guard and kept in the guard chamber. When the king entered the Temple, the guards carried the shields before him, and when he returned to his house, the shields too were returned into the guard chamber. [284] Elsewhere I have adduced evidence to show that in rabbinic tradition cosmic significance was attributed to these shields, of which it is related that they were used in a race once a year. [285] If we accept this as a historic reminiscence, we may find in it a strengthening of the impression we gain from the biblical account itself, namely that these processions of the king into the Temple took place once a year only, presumably on New Year's Day, as a commemoration of the king's installation festival, in the course of which too the king was taken in procession from the palace to the Temple and back "by the way of the gate of the guards" (2 Kings 11:19). This "gate of the guards" is, of course, the gate next to which was situated the "chamber of the guards."

Thus we have already found evidence as to the existence of two royal insignia, originally introduced into Hebrew kingship by Saul and renewed by David. It seems to have been David's policy to adopt the insignia of foreign heroes or kings conquered by him. A third royal emblem, the crown (2 Sam. 1:10), already was possessed by Saul, but, as in the case of the spear and the shield, David did not take it over from him but, as befitted the founder of a new dynasty, took it—again just as he took the spear and the shield—from a conquered king. After David took Rabbah of the children of Ammon, "he took their king's crown from off his head, the weight thereof was a talent of gold and a precious stone [was set into it], and it was put on David's head" (2 Sam. 12:30).

Crowning with a crown was one of the integral rites of the installation of Hebrew kings. [286] In later times Josephus records that Herod had both a diadem (*diádēma*) and a crown (*stéphanos*). [287] Saul possessed yet another royal emblem, the traces of which in later times are as good as lost. This was the bracelet worn on the king's arm. [288] Only in the Book of the Maccabees do we again hear of a similar emblem of rank. There it is said that Alexander sent a golden *pórpē*, a brooch or clasp, to Jonathan as a royal emblem. Another such clasp was sent to Jonathan by the young Antiochus. [289]

On the other hand, no reference is made in connection with Saul to the throne which was introduced by David. Saul sat, as we have seen, under a tree, but "David's throne" soon became a symbol of Hebrew kingship and remained such down to the days of the exile.[290] The royal throne was also called "the throne of the kingdom,"[291] or "the throne of kings,"[292] or "the throne of Israel,"[293] or even "the throne of God."[294] During the installation ritual the king ceremonially took his seat on the throne.[295] Where no throne was available, for instance in an army camp, garments were put under the king (Jehu: 2 Kings 9:13). A description of Solomon's throne is found in 1 Kings 10;18–20, while the throne of Herod is referred to by Josephus (*Wars* 2.11).

There is another royal emblem the identity of which is difficult to determine. When Joash was made king by the priest Jehoiada, "he put the crown and the 'testimony' upon him" (2 Kings 11:12; 2 Chron. 23:11). The word *'ēdūt* may be derived from *'adi* = jewels, thus David Kimhi, Abr. b. Ezra, Metzudath Zion ad loc., or it may be a misspelling of *hatz'adot* (cf. Isa. 3:20) which, in the singular, is mentioned together with the crown as constituting the regalia of Saul. It seems improbable that this *'ēdūth* should have anything to do with the *'ēdūth*, the "testimony," which was contained in the Ark of the Covenant, also called "Ark of the Testimony."[296]

As to the royal robes, it was remarked by Robertson Smith that "from Ps. 45.8 (E. V. 7) compared with Isa. 61.3, we may conclude that the anointing of kings at their coronation is part of the ceremony of investing them in the festal dress and ornaments appropriate to their dignity on that joyous day (cf. Cant. 3.11)."[297] It would seem that from the day of coronation onwards, the kings were always dressed in their royal robes, and "in accordance with the current practice among contemporary societies were accustomed to wear their royal robes even in battle."[298] From a later period we have ample testimony to the purple being the royal vestment.[299] Once, however, we hear that an heir to the throne put on white garments on the occasion of his informal accession.[300] We shall have occasion to return to the role played by the vestments in Hebrew installation rites in connection with the consecration of priests.

Another royal emblem associated with Hebrew kings, as well as with the older, uncrowned leaders of the Hebrew people, was the scepter.[301]

Reverence towards the regalia and the person of the king persisted in Judaism long after the cessation of kingship. In a mishnah we read, "It is forbidden to ride upon his [the king's] horse, to sit on his throne, to use his scepter, to look at him while his hair is being cut, or when he is naked, or when he is in the bath."[302]

IX.

Before entering upon the interpretation and classification of further points in the Hebrew installation rites, it will be necessary to familiarize ourselves with a number of additional features of the African installation ritual. We shall have, first of all, to bear in mind that the installation of a king or a chief is a very protracted affair, extending over a period of many months (in some cases even lasting for two full years), during which special rules of conduct have to be observed. During this time long periods of quiescence intervene between shorter times of ceremonial activity. Among the Pabir of northern Nigeria, for instance, the new chief is installed by being given the royal spear and being taken to a village to reside for seven days. After one year, during which he must not enter the royal palace, he is taken to the river Surakumi and ceremonially washed on a rock in the middle of the water, blessed, invested with his royal robes, and formally conducted to the palace. At the conclusion of a further year, during which the only restriction retained from the first is the interdiction of shaving, the king "goes to the house of Yemta-ra-Waba at Limbir and is there shaven."[303]

Nor is the royal ritual ended with the discharge of even the most protracted series of installation ceremonies. In accordance with the central role played by the "divine" king in all aspects of his country's life, he is constantly kept busy with ceremonial observances on which depend the well-being of his people. In many cases these routine rituals show a certain periodicity, being performed monthly, annually,[304] or at larger intervals, and they often serve the all-important purpose of reinvigorating the king, renewing his powers. In the Egyptian Sed festival we have already become acquainted with such a ritual, and we have also seen that at least two of its rites, the "shooting of the nations" and the setting up of the *Dd* column, have their parallels both in modern Africa and among the ancient Hebrews. We have also pointed out that the functioning of the Hebrew kings in the sanctuary on every New Year's Day as the chief priests of their people constituted a partial annual repetition of the installation ritual.

Another rite connected with the African installation ritual, but in many cases taking place only after a certain length of time had elapsed, is the killing of a human victim.[305] When this rite is performed at a later date, it frequently takes the form of spearing a slave. Among the Baganda, within a short time of his accession the king ceremonially speared men in order "to invigorate himself." He slightly wounded these men with a spear, where-upon they were taken away and killed.[306] After the king had reigned three years or so, a much more important ceremony took place, in the course of which a son of Nankere, a chief of the Lung-fish clan, after having been fed, clothed, and treated in all respects as a king for the duration of a month, was presented to the king and then killed—again in order to prolong the life of the king.[307] Among the Jukun, sometime after the king had been in office he . . . carried out a rite . . . by which he attained a new name, was reinvigorated and reconfirmed in his kingdom. . . . The rite consisted, it is said, in the spearing of a slave by the king in person. According to another account, the king himself merely wounded the slave, or made a pretence of wounding him, the actual killing being carried out by the Ta ko atyu (the priest under whose supervision the whole rite was performed) who used for the purpose the royal spear and knife, of which he was the custodian.[308]

The ceremonial spearing of a youth by the king in order to reinvigorate himself may have a bearing upon the attempted spearing of David by Saul (1 Sam. 18:10–12; 19:9–10). It is difficult to imagine that had Saul's wish originally been simply to remove David, he should have been unable to achieve his purpose and have him killed in one way or another while David still lived in his proximity. If, however, it had to be a "ceremonial spearing," things were different. In this case Saul could not simply dispatch a couple of his servants to finish David off; the killing, or at least the first wounding, of David had to be done by him personally. This may explain why Saul sent messengers not to kill David straight away, but to bring him to him alive that he personally might slay him (1 Sam. 19:14–15).

This inference is strengthened by another narrative which tells of an actual human sacrifice carried out in close connection with the installation of Saul. We have already drawn attention to the fact that Saul's installation ritual consisted of several stages. To recapitulate: the first stage was that in Ramah on the *bamah* and at the house of Samuel (1 Sam. 9:15–10:7), closely followed by the round made by Saul, in the course of which the three "signs" were encountered by him (10:9–13), and by the oracle and the acclamation in Mizpah (10:17–26). This is followed by the interval of seven days during which the battle against Nahash takes place (10:8, 26; 11:1–12). Then comes the second stage, the "renewal" of the kingship at Gilgal with sacrifices and general rejoicing (11:14–15; 13:7b–15). Immediately after this the battle against the Philistines begins, the victorious outcome of which is followed by the building of an altar and the offering up of sacrifices at an unspecified place, but presumably again in Gilgal (13:1–7a, 16–23; 14:1–45). This episode, which closes with the remark that "Saul captured the kingship over Israel" (14:47), should be regarded as the third stage. Now follows an exhortation of Samuel addressed to Saul, announcing, "It is I whom the Lord sent to anoint thee to be king over his people Israel" (15:1), and demanding that Saul wage a war of destruction against Amalek, the traditional foe of Israel, in obedience to the command of God (15:2–3). Saul obeys and routs the Amalekites, then again repairs to Gilgal to sacrifice (15:4–34). This development can be regarded as the fourth stage.

We have thus an opening stage followed by a threefold repetition of the same general pattern, with only slight deviations.[309] This in itself strongly smacks of a ritual pattern,[310] the basic features of which may have been:

1. The king is sent by the prophet into battle against a specified enemy.
2. The battle is fought and won by the king.
3. The king repairs to the sacred place (Gilgal), where
4. He builds an altar and offers up sacrifices from the spoil, as well as
5. A human sacrifice, and
6. Is reaffirmed in his reign amidst the acclamation and rejoicing of the people
7. The prophet who also is present at the triumphal feast shows a certain animosity towards the king

Out of the seven points of this ritual pattern, five (1, 2, 3, 4, 6) are self-evident after what has been said in the previous pages. Two (5 and 7), however, still require substantiation. Before doing this, I should like again to emphasize that we do not possess in the biblical narratives about Saul accurate records of rituals, but reminiscences of rituals mixed with traditions of historical occurrences. Thus we will not expect to find more than a mere basic agreement between the various repetitions of the ritual pattern, made almost unrecognizable by the overlaid historical coloring. Keeping this in mind, we shall find that the narrative of each one of Saul's three victorious campaigns contains an account of, or at least a reference to, a human sacrifice.

The clearest instance is the third one. After Saul's triumph over Amalek, Samuel, who took part in the sacrificial feast at the urgent request of Saul, "hewed Agag [the captured king of Amalek] in pieces before the Lord in Gilgal" (15:33). On the previous occasion, after his victory over the Philistines, Saul consulted the oracle, and, finding that his son Jonathan "sinned," wished to kill him, but "the people redeemed Jonathan [as contended by the majority of scholars, by giving the life of another man in his stead] and he died not." (14:15).[311] Finally, after the first battle, that against Nahash, when the people proposed to put to death those who had mockingly opposed and derided Saul in Mizpah (11:12; cf. 10:27), Saul answered, "There shall not a man be put to death this day, for today the Lord hath wrought salvation in Israel" (11:13). The double emphasis on "today" shows that it was only that same day on which Saul did not desire the man or men to be put to death, the implication being that the putting to death was carried out on another, probably the following, day.[312]

The other point, the animosity of the prophet towards the king, seems at first sight to be genuinely historical. After all, one will be inclined to argue, the animosity of the prophet towards the king whom he himself had anointed can be nothing else but a piece of actual history. I would by no means deny that in the case of Samuel and Saul there may have been a special, historically conditioned, dissent. All I wish to suggest is that this dissent was a special, overemphasized case of a ritual hostility, or rather incompatibility, between the king, on the one hand, and the prophet, priest, or official who installed him, on the other. Numerous examples of such a ritual incompatibility are to be found in Africa. Thus among the Baganda, Nankere, of whose role in connection with the coronation and reinvigoration ceremonies we have already heard, was not permitted to see the king except when he performed the rite for the prolongation of the king's life, in the course of which he had to sacrifice one of his sons.[313] Among the Jukun, the Ku Vi, the head of the Ba Vi kindred, who exercises priestly functions and has a court of his own, and whose role in the installation of the king is in many a detail comparable to that played by Samuel at the installation of Saul,[314] "must never again meet the king face to face. . . . It is not uncommon in Jukun communities that the chief and certain priests must never meet."[315] During the installation ceremony itself, ritual demands that the Ku Vi treat the king-elect rudely. The king-elect "is made to run round a mound three times and in doing so is well buffeted by the Ku Vi and his followers."[316] Among the Kona and Gwana Jukun, "the chief and the chief priest may not meet face to face. The power of the chief priest is so great that he can threaten to bring illness or even death on the chief if the chief fails to treat him with proper respect or to supply the necessary sacrificial gifts."[317]

A scrutiny of the meetings which took place between Samuel and Saul will show that such meetings occurred only in connection with the various stages of Saul's installation: first in Ramah, then in Mizpah, then in Gilgal (13:10–15), then before the battle against Amalek (15:1), and lastly again in Gilgal (15:12–34), after which we are expressly informed that "Samuel did no more see Saul until the day of his death" (15:35). Similarly, after Samuel anointed David to be king (16:13), he left him never to see him again.[318] The same relationship seems to have existed between Ahijah and Jeroboam, whom he made king over Israel (2 Kings 11:29–39). When, years later, the son of Jeroboam fell ill and he wished to consult the prophet, he did not go himself, and even his wife, whom he sent, he bade disguise herself that Ahijah should not know that she was the king's wife (1 Kings 14:1ff.). The same relationship between the anointing prophet and the anointed king persisted also in later times, when one of the "sons of the prophets," at the bidding of his master, Elisha, "fled" immediately after he had anointed

Jehu to be king over Israel (2 Kings 9:3, 10). We cannot fail to grasp the basic identity of the relationship not only of the three different Hebrew prophets to the four Hebrew kings, but also of the pattern underlying this relationship and of the African priest-king pattern.

The inference that the inimical behavior of Samuel towards Saul was in conformity with ritual requirements is strengthened by a rite which was performed in the course of the Babylonian New Year festival. On the fifth day of this festival the king entered Nebo's chapel and stood alone before the statue.

> Soon the high-priest appeared and took away from him his regalia, his sceptre, ring and crooked weapon and his crown, which he placed upon a stool before Marduk. Next he struck the king a blow on the cheek, pulled his ears, and forced him to kneel before the god. In this humiliation the king had to recite a sort of ''negative confession,'' ''I have not sinned, O lord of the lands, I have not been unregardful of thy godhead . . . '' etc.[319] To this the chief priest replied with a message of comfort and blessing from the god. . . . Once more, however, the priest was to strike him upon the cheek and that not softly, for a sign was to follow—if tears came into his eyes, Bel was gracious, if not, Bel was wroth.[320]

X.

The next points we come to consider are based on the inference that the annual functioning of the Hebrew king in the New Year ritual was of a commemorative, or rather repetitive, character, insofar as it consisted of the performing on the king's part of rites which he first performed in the course of his installation ritual. This inference is clearly implied in the results of Morgenstern's studies, in which he has shown not only that it was on New Year's Day that the preexilic Hebrew king functioned in the sanctuary in his capacity as chief priest of the nation, but also that both the installation of kings (as well as of priests) and the dedication of temples—in Israel as well as in other countries of the ancient Near East—took place on the same day.[321] Morgenstern has also shown that originally the New Year's Day was immediately preceeded by a seven days' festival, the Asif-Sukkot festival, which was only in a later calendar system transferred to VII/15–21.[322] This being so, it would seem that the seven days of the Asif festival are identical with the seven days which had to pass between the first (the opening) and the second stage of the installation of kings. In fact, in the African sphere, with the royal ritual of which we have constantly compared the ancient Hebrew installation ritual, the annual feast of ingathering is up to this date also a festival of the renewal by the people of their allegiance to the king. The examples in point are found among two peoples of Nigeria, the Arago and the Jukun.[323]

Among the Arago, about harvest time the chief of Keana

> goes into retreat for a period of seven days during which there is silence throughout the town, no sound of axe or hammer being heard. . . . On the conclusion of the seven days' retirement, after much blowing of horns in the early morning, the chief appears in public mounted on a horse and adorned with marabout feathers. At a tree near the compound he dismounts, a lamb and fowl are killed, and the blood sprinkled on the branches of the tree. The chief then re-enters his o-pu-nu, or sacred enclosure. On the eighth day he again comes forth in the moonlight and visits the graves of his ancestors. On the ninth day at daybreak the people carry out calabashes of food and pots of beer to the former site of Keana and in the afternoon the chief himself rides out. He is preceded by young men dressed in various coloured cloths round their waists and each carrying a freshly peeled stick, and all proceed to a shrine. [These young men had for several days previously been parading the town with their sticks and spears. Cf. Lev. 23:40.] On concluding the business at the shrine the chief returns to his enclosure and the whole town gives itself up to feasting and merriment. The chief reappears clad in his adornments of marabout feathers and is carried on the shoulders of a man, with two assistants at the side.[324]

More complete is the account of the corresponding ritual among the Jukun of Wukari. "The Puje festival is held in booths outside Wukari at the close of the harvest, and lasts seven days [Deut. 16:13; Exod. 23:16; Lev. 23:34, 39]. It is open to women and strangers [Deut. 16:14], unlike all other religious ceremonies of the Jukun. Puje means 'booths of menstruation,'[325] and no explanation is given of the term beyond the rationalization that women are permitted to attend the ceremony." The Puje festival cannot be held without the presence of a number of priestly and other high officials. For the festival plenty of beer is prepared, which is both drunk and used for libations. While the beer is being prepared, booths or pavilions made of grass (Lev. 23:34, 42; Neh. 8:15–17) are erected at Puje, which is situated two miles east of Wukari, for the king and the principal officials. In former times the king slept at Puje the night before the festival, and it was customary to sacrifice a black cow or bull. Lately the king leaves Wukari for Puje early in the morning in a procession which is headed by a woman called She Who Runs in Front, without whose participation the festival could not be held. The king rides on a horse escorted by an attendant, who runs beside him holding up the circular tray of woven grass in order to shield the king's eyes from the sight of the former Jukun capital known as Bioka, lest he die in consequence of perceiving it. The king is also escorted by the royal drummer and fiddler and is surrounded by grooms known as Ba-tovi. Behind the king is carried the couch on which he will rest during the afternoon. Young men carrying peeled sticks (Lev. 23:40) drive off, and may even severely beat, curious onlookers. When arriving at Puje the king performs the daily morning ritual of ceremonial beer drinking.

At about eleven A.M., the two senior officials visit the site of the former capital Bioka, which is close to Puje. Here a mound of sand raised at the basis of a *kirya* tree (*prosopis oblonga*) marks the spot where the former king of Wukari used to reside. One of the officials stands beside the mound and calls each former king by name, saying, "The king has come to Puje to observe the custom of his predecessors. We have been sent to bear witness of this to you and we bow down before you. Grant that our millets, ground-nuts, and beans may provide us with an abundance of food. Let not hunger invade the land. Do you care for our people that all may live their lives in health and prosperity [Deut. 16:15]. Ward off disease and increase our numbers. Close the mouths of all wild animals. May the kings sit on a seat of iron and not of stone" (for iron endures, but stone crumbles away). When the officials return, the king withdraws in order to perform the daily midday rite of ceremonial beer drinking. On the conclusion of these rites, beer and food are freely distributed, and the younger people engage in dancing. In the afternoon the king receives the Angwu Tsi (the chief wife or queen) who, on her dismissal, leads the royal procession back to Wukari. At Wukari, pending the arrival of the king, the people assembled at the capital give themselves up to various forms of amusement (Deut. 16:14; Lev. 23:40). Bands of young men, fully armed, sing and dance the old war dances; women devotees of various ecstatic cults begin those dances of their order which result in a state of dissociation and ecstasy. About five P.M. the royal procession arrives, headed by the Angwu Tsi and her courtiers. She is greeted by the people with shouts of "Our corn!" and "Our beans!" expressions applied only to the king and herself. Behind various groups of attendants, dishbearers, etc. follow the senior officials riding in at a gallop, then turning swiftly and galloping back to meet the king as he enters the eastern gate amidst loud shouts of welcome from his people. The drummers announce the king's arrival by playing two chants. For the triumphal entrance into the capital, the king and his officials wear special gowns or coats. After visiting the north and south gates of the capital, the king returns to the palace and there dismisses the people, saying, "I thank you all. I have performed the custom of our forefathers." Feasting and dancing are kept up in the town for seven days.[326]

Here we have, among a people whose religious life has in all probability been influenced by the ancient Near East, a typical New Year's festival, containing all the characteristic features of the ritual pattern of the ancient Near Eastern New Year's festival,[327] and showing in particular great resemblance to the Hebrew Asif-Sukkot festival.[328] This festival in which the king played the central role is, moreover, also a feast of repetition or commemoration of the coronation rites.[329]

The analogy is instructive indeed. It leads us to the inference that not only did the Hebrew king play the central role in the ritual of the Asif-New Year's festival (as shown by Morgenstern), but that this festival in its entirety may have served a double purpose: to render certain the agricultural blessings of the ensuing year and to reinstall the king in his office by the repetition or commemoration of his installation ritual, thereby also reinvigorating him and ensuring for him the spiritual-magical properties he must possess in order to make his country fruitful, his people prosperous, and his armies victorious.[330] This consideration in its turn lends additional support to Morgenstern's inference that "the participation in these all-important rites of the king himself was seemingly indispensable."[331] If the purpose of the feast was also the reinstallation of the king in his reign, it is clear that the rites could be carried out only with the participation of the king himself.

Keeping this in mind, we shall be able to discern in the ritual of the sacred fire a rite which must have originally figured also in the installation ritual of Hebrew kings. The extant texts, it is true, do not mention the ceremonial extinguishing and rekindling of the sacred fire in connection with the installation ritual, but we have ample evidence to show that this rite was part and parcel of the New Year's ritual.[332] This in itself would, after all that has been said above, enable us to draw the inference that the ritual of the king's installation also must have contained the fire rite.[333] In addition, in the description of the priestly consecration there is a statement to the effect that "there came a fire out from before the Lord and consumed upon the altar the burnt offering and the fat, which when all the people saw, they shouted and fell on their faces."[334] As the priestly consecration ritual was patterned after the installation ritual of kings,[335] we have here a confirmation of our inference that the extinguishing and subsequent ceremonial rekindling of fire originally constituted a part of the installation ritual of Hebrew kings.

This inference is further strengthened by reference to the African installation ritual, the correspondence with which is already overwhelming. In Africa the fire ritual has been preserved in what would seem to be an older, fuller version. Here too we find the custom of extinguishing all the old fires every year and receiving new fire given by the king.[336] Among the Nyamwezi this rite was carried out every year at the harvest feast.[337] In the great majority of cases, however, the king's fire was kept going as long as the king lived. When the king died, it was extinguished, as were the fires in his entire domain. In connection with his coronation the new king lit a new fire,[338] frequently by drilling (which was understood to be symbolic of the sexual act), and from the new fire were then rekindled all the fires of the country.[339] The possible or even probable connection of these African fire rites with those of the ancient Near East is indicated by a legend of the Hungwe, according to which their forefathers who introduced the custom of having a new fire kindled by each new king came from the north,[340] and by an Egyptian representation of a Sed festival of Amenhotep III at Soleib, south of Wadi Halfa, in which the sacred fire is shown being passed from one priest to another ''and possibly lit by the Pharaoh himself.''[341] In the light of these data, the existence of the fire rite in the ancient Hebrew installation ritual may be regarded as probable.

The same considerations and the same chain of reasoning will make it very likely that a substitute king, who functioned during the eight days of the Asif-New Year festival, figured at the installation ritual. What precisely the tasks were of this substitute king we do not know, but Morgenstern has shown reason to suppose that he was of a saturnalian character, in accordance with the general freedom from authority and wide license which seem to have been the order of the day during this festive period.[342]

XI.

One of the few remaining rites of the African installation ritual the presence of which in the corresponding Hebrew ritual we have not yet investigated is no. 18, ''The king scattered beans, grains or the like among the people.''[343]

We have no direct evidence as to the existence of this rite in the ancient Hebrew coronation ritual. It can, however, be inferred in much the same manner in which we have arrived at the conclusion that the fire rite in all probability constituted a part of the installation ritual. Thanks to such evidence as has survived in the Bible and elsewhere, Morgenstern was able to conclude that in the eating of raisin cakes ''was a part of the celebration of the main annual agricultural festivals of the Northern Semitic peoples, and particularly of the Maṣṣōt and Asif festival in ancient Israel and the corresponding festivals among their neighbours.''[344] Moreover, from 2 Sam. 6:19 = 1 Chron 16:3, Morgenstern also deduced that it was presumably on New Year's Day that David brought up the ark to Jerusalem and installed it in his tent sanctuary there. The verse in question tells that David ''distributed among all the people, even among the whole multitude of Israel, to men as well as to women, to every one a cake of bread, an *ešpar*, and a raisin cake.'' This is not the place to enter into the question of the exact meaning of *ešpar*, but in view of the fact that the other two gifts distributed by David were articles of food made of grain, we may accept the Septuagint's translation (in

1 Chron. 16:3) of this word as ''sweet cake.'' We have thus the description of a New Year's rite in which the king distributed certainly two and possibly three sorts of cakes among the people. In the parallel narrative in 1 Chron. 16:3 there is a slight variation: instead of ''cake of bread'' the text has ''loaf of bread.''

We argued above that rites carried out by the king on New Year's Day are in all probability repetitions of corresponding rites belonging to the installation ritual, and we would contend that the argument holds good in this case too. This inference is strengthened by the following considerations. In the ritual of the priestly consecration (which, as repeatedly indicated above and as shown in detail below, was formed after the ritual of the king's installation), there figured a rite carried out with three kinds of baker's ware. Aaron and his sons had to ''wave before God'' these three kinds of bread, the names of which are given in somewhat different versions. They are an unleavened bread, an unleavened cake tempered with oil, and an unleavened wafer anointed with oil. Thus in Exodus 29:2. In the same chapter in verse 23, we read, one loaf of bread, one cake of oiled bread, and one wafer. Again, in Leviticus 8:26 we read, one unleavened cake, a cake of oiled bread, and one wafer. Though the nomenclature differs, it seems clear that all the three verses designate the same three kinds of baker's ware: a bread, a cake, and a wafer. Of the three kinds of baker's ware distributed by David, two, the *ešpar* and the raisin cake, are not mentioned among the baker's ware used in the consecration of Aaron and his sons. But the third, or rather the first, is mentioned, in both the versions of Samuel and of Chronicles (cf. Exod. 29:23). We thus see that three kinds of baker's ware had their special role in connection with the consecration of priests. Above we referred to the two loaves of bread given to Saul by a man carrying three sacrificial breads (1 Sam. 10:3–4). This happened in the course of Saul's installation. While these instances clearly show the role played by bread given to the person being installed, the distribution of baker's ware by David at a New Year's festival, when taken together with the African installation ceremony of scattering beans and other cereals among the people, strongly suggest that this too was a Hebrew installation rite.

The African kings often have a special connection with the moon.[345] One of the outstanding features of this connection is the performance of rites and the arranging of festivities by the king every new moon.[346] Among the Zumu (a Bata-speaking tribe of northern Nigeria), each month the day after the new moon is sighted, the king repairs with his family to the shrine, where he says, ''We are now about to perform the monthly custom which has been handed down to us by our forefathers.'' Then the chief and all members of his family, including females and children who are old enough, partake of a draught of sweet beer. ''No member of the royal kindred may absent himself from these rites unless he is prevented from attending by illness.''[347] ''Every month king Rumanika in Karagwe held new moon festivities. These included beating on many drums and dancing, as well as—and this was the most important feature—a declaration of allegiance on the part of chiefs, officials and other subjects, to the king.''[348] Among the Baganda, at each new moon a ceremony is performed which seems to be intended to ensure the king's life and health throughout the ensuing month.[349]

Of special interest for us is the following account of a ceremony repeated every new moon in Monomotapa, as reported by the *Asia Portugesa* of Manual de Faria e Sousa (pp. 24ff) and quoted after Frazer by Irstam. ''On the day the new moon appears, the king with two javelins runs about in his house as if he were fighting. The great men are present at this pastime. . . . The greatest holy day is the first day of the moon of May. . . . On this day all the great men . . . resort to court, and there with javelins in their hands run about representing a fight.'' Eight days later the king ''orders the nobleman he has the least affection for to be killed; this is in the nature of a sacrifice to his . . . ancestors.''[350]

These African new moon rituals naturally remind us of the new moon meals of Saul (1 Sam. 20:5, 18, 24–34). These meals were held regularly (cf. v. 25) at every new moon at the king's table (v. 29) for two successive days, on the first and second day of the new moon (v. 27). The king himself sat on his special seat at the wall, i.e., at the head of the table, and each one of the king's family and the court had his fixed place, so that when anyone was missing his place was left empty (vv. 25, 27). Only persons ritually impure were excused from being present at these meals (v. 26); probably they were even forbidden to partake of them. If somebody was absent without such a valid reason, this could be interpreted by the king as treason (vv. 27–31).[351]

Let us now summarize the features we have found in the installation ritual of Hebrew kings, in the order set forth by Irstam in his study of the African sacral kingship. (The individual rites will be numbered by the numbers appearing in Irstam's list.)

1. The Hebrew king was conceived of as being reborn at the time of his installation as the son of God
2. He was dressed in purple royal robes
4. The prophet or the person functioning as his anointer addressed him. The king answered. He was proclaimed as king
5. A real fight preceded the king's final installation. The king's (ritual) victory over his enemies was often alluded to

6. After the initial stage the installation ritual was interrupted for a week
7. The king received communion by partaking of a sacrificial meal
8. He was baptized
9. He mounted a hill, the *bamah*, or the "pillar"
10. The king set up for himself a memorial pillar
11. He was admonished by the prophet and promised to follow the divine instructions
12. The king was anointed with oil
14. The king received as his regalia a spear, a shield, etc.
15. The king sat on the throne
16. The king was crowned
17. A fire rite took place
18. The king distributed baker's ware among the people
20. He made the round of his domain
21. Festivities were held
22. The king was made the butt of the people
24. Human sacrifices
26. Substitute king

We have thus found twenty-one points of the twenty-seven listed by Irstam. This is three points more than the maximum number found in the most complete ritual of a single African people (the Ganda) and much higher than the average number to be found among the majority of the sixty-two peoples Irstam studied. This exceptionally high number justifies the assumption made at the beginning of this paper that the ancient Hebrew installation ritual, being nearer to the original pattern than its African counterpart, must have been the richer of the two both in structure and in detail.

The correspondence of the patterns, however, does not end with the points included in the list. In the course of our investigations we have found quite a number of additional ritual features of the ancient Hebrew kingship which also have their counterpart in Africa. These can be subsumed under the following fifteen headings.

1. The king is chosen by both electors and oracle
2. A high official (priest, prophet) functions at the election as well as at the installation
3. Animosity or incompatibility exists between this official and the king
4. The king must be of unblemished body, healthy, strong, and beautiful

5. The king must not defile himself with a dead body
6. Ceremonial marriage in a special hut
7. The king marries the widow of his predecessor
8. The king rides on a mount
9. The king hides, is sought, and found
10. The "shooting of the nations"
11. Ritual combat omitted in case real fighting goes on
12. Installation ritual very protracted
13. Periodical (annual, on New Year's Day) repetition of installation rites
14. Monthly new moon festivals
15. The king is the chief priest of his people

The above treatment of the ritual features in the Hebrew royal installation in general, and in the installation of Saul in particular, may seem to overemphasize the typical, that is, the ritual side, while neglecting or even taking no account of the unique historic character of the installation of each Hebrew king, and especially that of Saul, first king of Israel.[352] I wish, therefore, to stress that I am fully aware both of the historicity of the biblical Saul traditions and of the fact that a comprehensive scientific treatment of them should aim in the first place at a full historic grasp of the particular chain of events which brought about Saul's election and installation. Leaving this greater task aside, however, I confined my investigations—as far as they touch upon Saul—to a lesser problem which may be formulated as follows: on what ritual precedents did the actors in the historic drama of Saul draw when performing the various rites of the installation ritual; and, further, which of the historic events and actions recorded in our sources were consciously planned so as to conform with a preexisting ritual pattern?

There is, however, in my opinion no sufficient justification for setting ritual performance and historical occurrence opposite each other as mutually exclusive concepts. After all, even a ritual takes place somewhere and sometime in history. A ritual is performed within a given historical setting, and it has a direct bearing on events preceding and following it, and this is particularly true of a ritual such as a coronation ceremony, which is a political ritual par excellence. Saul's installation ritual, being the first of its kind in Hebrew history, was surely an event of great moment. Nothing is detracted from the historicity of such an event when it is pointed out that certain actions performed in its course were not conditioned by a unique historical constellation, but by a preexisting ritual pattern—in this case the royal installation. The very demand for a king, though unquestionably born out of a particular historical situation, nevertheless implies a knowledge of what kingship is. In our case the people expressly clamored for kingship as known to them from their neighbors: "Give us a king to judge us like all the nations" (1 Sam. 8:5). Again, when they or their leaders came to install their king, they drew upon installation rites known to them. Thus it should be clearly understood that even though a ritual was performed in full accordance with a preexisting pattern, the performance itself was nevertheless a historical event.

XII.

It remains to follow the Hebrew installation ritual into postexilic times, when the greatest part of the king's ritual functions was transferred to the high priest.

Morgenstern has drawn attention to the fact that in Zechariah 3:1–8a and 4:11, 14, we have a vision of the installation of Joshua as high priest, and that the prophet's account of the anointing of Joshua and his symbolic clothing with the robes of his new office is the forerunner of the much more elaborate account of the anointing of Aaron and his sons and their clothing in official robes in Leviticus 8:1 ff.[353] He has also pointed out that the two men figuring in Zechariah's vision "are consecrated and inducted into their holy office by anointing with the sacred oil, precisely as was the king in the preexilic period. It was this ceremony of anointing with the holy oil which established this chief priest, with his new office and peculiar duties, as the successor of the preexilic kings as the recognized head of the theocracy of Judah."[354] The "anointed priest" (Lev. 4:3, 16; 6:15) "had taken the place in the cult formerly held only by the king."[355] At a later period the place of the "anointed priest" was taken by the "high priest," and he too was "inducted into his high and sacred office by the rite of anointing with the holy oil."[356] Again, Morgenstern has shown that the consecration of the priests, the "anointed priests" as well as the "high priests," took place on New Year's Day, and that the original account of the ordination and installation of Aaron told that this was celebrated upon the New Year's Day as the culmination of the ceremonies of the dedication of the tabernacle in the wilderness, which on its part was modeled after the account of the dedication of Solomon's Temple in 1 Kings 8.[357]

We may thus distinguish three stages in the history of high priesthood: in the first, the preexilic stage, the king functioned as chief priest; in the second, the early postexilic stage, it was the "anointed priest"; while in the third, the later postexilic stage, reflected in Leviticus, it was the "high priest."[358] African peoples, to whose parallel customs and institutions we have constantly referred in this study, are still in the first stage. Among them it is the king who functions as chief priest of his people, who performs (in some places only once a year) the most important ceremonies intended to bring prosperity and fertility, to procure rich harvests and large herds of cattle for his people.[359]

But to return to the Hebrew priesthood, it now remains to be seen whether in the two successive postexilic periods we can discern the installation rites, or rather ordination rites, as we have done concerning the preexilic installation of kings, and if yes, whether these rites will more or less conform to the pattern of the royal installation.

The material covering the second period is unfortunately very meager. It is contained only in the vision of Zechariah referred to above, and in a prophetic vision we shall, evidently, not expect to find even so much information as to details of a ritual as in a historical narrative. Nevertheless, it would seem that the following features of the originally royal installation ritual may be discerned (the numbers again refer to Irstam's list):

2. The priest is divested of his ordinary clothes (here referred to as "filthy garments" in order to heighten the contrast between them and the priestly robes) and dressed in official robes[360]

1. The consecrated priest is freed from all sin that hitherto attached to him, the implication being that he is reborn (v. 4) in a divine character (v. 7)

16. He is crowned with a "pure mitre" (v. 5) and a golden and silver crown (6:11)

11. He is admonished to fulfil his duties in a just manner (vv. 6–7)

12. He is anointed with oil[361]

One additional point: the number seven, characteristic of the Hebrew royal ritual, appears here too (v. 9)

Incomparably richer are the data pertaining to the third stage. Here at last we have a full description of a ritual, extending to every detail.

10. We have already pointed out that just as the first king was chosen by an oracle, the (traditionally) first high priest, Aaron, also was chosen by the oracle of the budding rod.[362] In the rod of Aaron we may also see a reference to the life tree[363]

2. Aaron was invested with the priestly vestments (Exod. 28:4–5, 34; 29:5; Lev. 8:7)

6. Aaron and his sons retired for seven days and seven nights into the Tabernacle (Exod. 29:35; Lev. 8:33, 35–36)

7. Aaron and his sons received communion at the door of the Tabernacle: holy meat and bread (Exod. 29:31–34; Lev. 8:31)

8. They were washed with water (Exod. 29:4; Lev. 8:6)
11. They were admonished by Moses to keep the commandments of God, and they "did all the things which the Lord commanded by the hand of Moses" (Lev. 8:31–36)
12. Aaron was anointed with oil (Exod. 29:7; 30:30; Lev. 8:12)
14. He was given the priestly "regalia" (Exod. 28; 29:5; Lev. 8:8)
16. He was crowned with the mitre and the crown (Exod. 29:6; Lev. 8:9)[364]
17. The fire rite was performed (Lev. 9:24)[365]
24. On the same day two of the sons of Aaron were killed by the fire of the Lord (Lev. 10:1–2). But "Aaron kept quiet" (v. 3)[366]

To a number of additional rites of the priestly consecration which may be compared to similar rites of the royal installation ritual, reference has repeatedly been made above.

The immediate continuation of the narrative of Aaron's consecration is found in Leviticus 16.[367] This chapter contains, in the form of divine instruction given to Aaron through Moses, a detailed description of the ritual to be performed on the tenth day of the seventh month, that is, on the day on which in preexilic times the New Year ritual was performed by the king. A close scrutiny of this ritual will show that it is but a shortened version (with a few insignificant additions) of the consecration ritual of Aaron and his sons, which reached its peak on this very day. The ritual deals with the preparation of the priest and with the sacrifices to be offered. The first can be summed up in the following points:

2. The priest was dressed in "holy garments" (Lev. 16:4, cf. v. 32)
8. He had to "wash his flesh in water" (vv. 4, 24; cf. 26, 28)
16. On his head he was attired with a linen mitre (v. 4)

I did not detail the sacrificial ritual when dealing with the consecration of Aaron. It seems, however, worthwhile to place the two sets of sacrifices side-by-side, that of the consecration of the priest (Aaron) and that of the tenth day of the seventh month, to make thus the correspondence of the two clear.

It is clear that the two rituals are much more than basically identical. The identity extends, in fact, to every detail, so much so that there can be no doubt as to one of them being modeled after the other. It follows, moreover, from the very nature of things that it is the annual recurrent ritual which must have been patterned after the consecration ritual, and not vice versa. In this conclusion we are strengthened by comparing the sacrifices offered at these

Lev. 9 *The Consecration of Aaron*	Lev. 16 *The Ritual of VII/10.*
vv.	vv.
2 A young calf for sin offering	3 A young bullock for sin offering
2 A ram for burnt offering	3 A ram for burnt offering
3 For Israel: a he-goat for sin offering	5 For Israel: two he-goats for sin offering
3 For Israel: a calf and a lamb for a burnt offering	5 For Israel: A ram for a burnt offering
4 For Israel: an ox and a ram for *shelamim*	
4 For Israel: *minha* with oil	
7 Moses said to Aaron, ''offer thy sin offering and thy burnt offering and atone for thyself''	6, 11 The priest shall offer his bullock of the sin offering and atone for himself and his house
8 and for the people . . . Aaron . . . slew . . .	
9 Aaron dipped his finger in the blood of the calf of sin offering and put it upon the horns of the altar and poured out the blood at the bottom of the altar	14 The priest shall take of the blood of the bullock of sin offering and sprinkle it with his finger upon the mercy seat [*kapporet*] eastward; and before the mercy seat [i.e., on the ground] he shall sprinkle of the blood seven times
12 He slew the burnt offering and sprinkled its blood round about the altar	15 The same rite to be repeated once with the blood of the he-goat of sin offering within the Veil
15 The people's offering: ditto	
18 The ox and the ram: ditto	18 He shall take of the blood of both the bullock and the he-goat, put it upon the horns of the altar round about, and shall sprinkle of
	19 the blood upon the altar with his finger seven times[368]
10 The fat and other parts of the sin offering are burnt upon the altar	25 The fat of the sin offering he shall burn upon the altar
19–20 The fat of the ox and the ram, etc.: ditto	

11 The flesh and the hide of the calf of sin offering he burnt with fire without the camp	27 The bullock and the he-goat of sin offering shall burn in the fire, their skins and their flesh and their dung without the camp
23 Moses and Aaron entered the tabernacle with censers on which they burned incense[369]	12–13 A censer with incense shall be brought by the priest before God within the Veil
23 The glory of God appeared to all the people (cf. 4:6)	13, 17 Not even the officiating priest might see the "mercy seat"
21 The waving	
	7–10, 21–22, 26 The scapegoat
22–23 The blessing of the people	
7 *Purpose of the ritual:* to atone for Aaron and the people	11, 16, 20, 24, 30, 32–34 *Purpose of the ritual:* an annual atonement for the sanctuary, the priests, and the people

two occasions with the earlier sacrifices offered at the dedication of the temple of Solomon, and with the still earlier ones of Saul on the occasion of his installation as king. In the annual atonement ritual we found two types of offerings: sin offerings and burnt offerings. In the priestly consecration, which was at one and the same time also the (traditional) consecration of the tabernacle, there figured in addition to these two *shelamim* and *minha*. At the dedication of Solomon's Temple he offered burnt offerings, *shelamim* and *minha* (1 Kings 8:63–64). Saul at his installation offered only burnt offerings and *shelamim* (1 Sam. 10:8; 11:15; 13:9–10). Thus the two original types of sacrifice, the burnt offerings and the *shelamim*, persisted from Saul's days down to the postexilic description of the consecration of the priest and the dedication of the tabernacle. When Solomon dedicated his temple, he added the *minha*. At the priestly consecration another addition was made, that of the sin offering. Finally, in the annual atonement ritual the *shelamim* and the *minha* were omitted.

The conclusion that the annual atonement ritual was patterned after the ritual of the priestly consecration and the dedication of the tabernacle closes the circles of both our argument and our present investigation. For in this conclusion, the final proof may be seen of our contention that the preexilic New Year's ritual also was modeled after the installation ritual of kings. The all-important role played by the preexilic king in the New Year's ritual thus appears in a new light. It was not merely as the chief priest of his nation that the king functioned on this fateful day; it was also in his capacity as a magic king in whom superhuman powers dwell[370] that he had to perform a partial or abridged repetition of his installation ritual in order to reinvigorate himself for the duration of the ensuing year with the divine power and spirit which was first allotted to him on the day of his coronation.

In Israel this magical-ritualistic aspect of kingship declined and as good as disappeared in postexilic times. The king gave place to the high priest, who on his part retained the "magical control of nature," not institutionally, but only in popular imagination. Magical kingship in Africa, on the other hand, deriving from the same ancient Near Eastern source, showed an opposite trend. The magical powers of the king were there on the increase, and though the king had to delegate many of his functions to priestly sorcerers, he nevertheless retained power enough to remain in the center of the magical world view of his people. That in spite of these divergent developments African and Hebrew installation rites can be shown to possess such a surprising similarity is due to two facts: to the extraordinary powers of persistence and tenacity of ritual in general and of royal ritual in particular, thanks to which African installation rites survived during uncounted centuries practically unchanged; and to the lucky accident that in Hebrew literary pieces of nearly three millennia so much material has been preserved, in the form of either plain statement or interpretable allusion, pertaining to the royal and priestly installation ritual. The African material helped to elucidate quite a number of scriptural passages which would otherwise have remained obscure; on the other hand, the similarity between the Hebrew and the African rituals is significant when regarded in connection with the dependence on the ancient Near East of many a feature in the African cultural configuration.

Notes

"Hebrew Installation Rites" originally was published in the *Hebrew Union College Annual* 20 (1947):143–225.

1. A. M. Hocart, *Kingship* (London, 1927), p. 98; the chapter referred to above is chap. 8, "The Coronation Ceremony," pp. 70–98.
2. C. K. Meek, *A Sudanese Kingdom* (London, 1931), pp. 120ff., esp. 129, 134, 136, 138, 139, 141, 143; C. K. Meek, *Tribal Studies in Northern Nigeria*, 2 vols. (London, 1931), 1:3ff., 110, 159, 184, 302; 2:292ff., 442. Meek also uses for comparison material drawn from John Roscoe, *The Baganda* (London, 1911).
3. Charles G. and Brenda Z. Seligman, *Pagan Tribes of the Nilotic Sudan* (London, 1932), pp. 90ff., 110, 541ff.
4. Ibid., p. 34.

5. C. G. Seligman, *Egypt and Negro Africa: A Study in Divine Kingship* (London, 1934), pp. 58–60.
6. Willy Schilde, *Ost-westliche Kulturbeziehungen im Sudan* (Leipzig, 1929), p. 160; Willy Schilde, "Die afrikanischen Hoheitszeichen," *ZE* 61 (1929):137.
7. H. Baumann, *Völkerkunde von Afrika* (Essen, 1940), pp. 56ff., 62, 65.
8. Tor Irstam, *The King of Ganda: Studies in the Institutions of Sacral Kingship in Africa*, The Ethnographical Museum of Sweden, Stockholm, n.s., no. 8 (Stockholm, 1944), pp. 192ff.
9. In fact the sacral kingship extends southward through the Bantu line, mainly in the vicinity of the western shores of Lake Victoria, but this is immaterial for our present purpose.
10. Irstam, *King of Ganda*, p. 193.
11. S. H. Hooke, ed., *Myth and Ritual* (London, 1933); S. H. Hooke, ed., *The Labyrinth* (London, 1935).
12. S. H. Hooke, *The Origins of Early Semitic Ritual* (London, 1938).
13. See their respective indices, s.vv. Coronation, King, Kingship.
14. Julian Morgenstern, "Amos Studies," *HUCA* 12–13 (1937–38):1–34; Julian Morgenstern, "A Chapter in the History of the High Priesthood," *AJSL* 55 (1938):1–24, 183–97, 360–77.
15. *Uppsala Universitets Arsskrift* 7, no. 1 (1941):6ff., 12ff.
16. Ivan Engnell, *Studies in Divine Kingship in the Ancient Near East* (Uppsala, 1943), p. 79.
17. Ibid., n. 8.
18. Ibid., p. 175, n. 7.
19. Irstam, *King of Ganda*, p. 26. This pattern agrees nearly on all points with that arrived at by Hocart, who based his pattern mainly on non-African material, namely Fijian, Brahmanic Indian, modern Cambodian, ancient Egyptian, Hebrew, Roman (the triumphal procession), Byzantine, Abyssinian, and European Christian coronation ceremonies (*Kingship*, pp. 70–98). Hocart's material, however, has been drawn from a great variety of peoples distant from each other, and precisely those rituals which are derived from the ancient Near East proper—the Egyptian and the Hebrew—are very poorly attested, and it is evident that they did not contribute anything to the construction of Hocart's pattern, which is based mainly on the Fijian, Brahmanic, and Cambodian material. Irstam's list, on the other hand, is based on largely homogeneous material drawn from a single continent, Africa, and as pointed out above, mainly from the central belt of Africa at that.
20. Saul: 1 Sam. 9:17ff.; David: 1 Sam. 16:1ff.; Jeroboam: 1 Kings 11:29ff.; Jehu: 1 Kings 19:16, 2 Kings 9:1ff. Also Hazael, king of Syria, 1 Kings 19:15, 2 Kings 8:13.
21. 1 Sam. 9:17, cf. vv. 15–16.
22. 1 Sam. 9:19ff., 10:1ff.
23. As to the choice of kings by oracle, see Adolphe Lods, "Le rôle des oracles dans la nomination des rois," *Memoirs de l'Institut français* 66 (1934):91ff., as quoted by Martin Buber, *Das Kommende*, vol. 2, p. 160, n. 62. This volume of Buber's book was partly typeset in Germany in 1937 but could not be printed. Professor Buber kindly put at my disposal the proofs in his possession.
24. *Alafēkhem*, literally: "your thousands."
25. So to complete according to the Septuagint. Cf. Josh. 7:17.
26. 1 Sam. 10:19–21.
27. Josh. 7:16–18.
28. Josh. 7:11.
29. See below.
30. Meek, *Sudanese Kingdom*, p. 135.
31. Meek, *Tribal Studies*, 2:441–42.
32. Duncan R. MacKenzie, *The Spirit-Ridden Konde* (Philadelphia, 1925), pp. 69–73, as quoted by Seligman, *Egypt and Negro Africa*, p. 29.
33. W. Hofmayr, "Die Schilluck," *Anthropos* 2, no. 5 (1925):145, as quoted in Irstam, *King of Ganda*, p. 45. Cf. Diedrich Westermann, *The Shilluk People* (Berlin, 1922), p. 122; C.

W. Domville Fife, *Savage Life in the Black Sudan* (London, 1927), p. 110; Seligman and Seligman, *Pagan Tribes*, p. 93.

34. Leo Frobenius, *Und Afrika sprach* (Berlin, 1912–13), 3:57–58, as quoted by Irstam, *King of Ganda*, p. 45.
35. Louis Ginzberg, *The Legends of the Jews*, 7 vols. (Philadelphia, 1909–46), 4:65; vol. 6, n. 52.
36. Ibid., 4:84; vol. 6, nn. 22, 23.
37. Edwin Sidney Hartland, *Ritual and Belief* (London, 1914), p. 317, as quoted in *ERE*, 10:634b.
38. See below.
39. B. 'Av. Zara 44a; B. Sanh. 21b.
40. Targum to 2 Chron. 23:11 and to 1 Chron. 20:2. Cf. D. Klosterman to 2 Kings 11:12 in Hermann L. Strack and O. Zoeckler, *Kurzgefasster Kommentar zu den heiligen Schriften* (Munich, 1887); Ginzberg, *Legends of the Jews*, 6:359, n. 9.
41. Ginzberg, *Legends of the Jews*, 2:291ff.
42. Num. 17:16–28.
43. Ginzberg, *Legends of the Jews*, 6:106.
44. 1 Sam. 9:15–16; John 1:19ff., 29. Cf. Matt. 3:7ff., 13; Mark 1:7, 9.
45. 1 Sam. 9:17.
46. John 1:29–30.
47. 1 Sam. 10:20ff.
48. John 1:32–33; cf. Matt 3:16; Mark 1:10; Luke 3:22.
49. Hermann Gunkel, *Das Märchen im Alten Testament* (Tübingen, 1917), p. 150. Gunkel is, however, not right in saying in connection with the choice of Saul by oracle that "the choice of kings by the lot is a feature so distant from reality that we can with certainty derive it from the *Märchen*" (p. 147). Rudolph Kittel, *Geschichte des Volkes Israel*, 2 vols. (Stuttgart-Gotha, 1925), 2:151, also points to the improbability of the choice by lot. The African and other examples mentioned above show that many peoples actually practiced and practice to this day the—at least apparent—choice of their kings by lots and oracles.
50. Cf. Hocart, *Kingship*, passim.
51. See below.
52. Meek, *Sudanese Kingdom*, p. 127.
53. S. S. Doran, "The Killing of the Divine King in South Africa," *South African Journal of Science* 15 (1918):397, as quoted by Seligman, *Egypt and Negro Africa*, p. 31.
54. 1 Sam. 10:23–24.
55. Ibid., 16:6–7.
56. Ibid., v. 7.
57. Ibid., v. 12.
58. 2 Sam. 14:25.
59. Ps. 45:3.
60. Isa. 33:17.
61. 2 Kings 15:5; 2 Chron. 26:19–21.
62. See below.
63. Lev. 21:16–23.
64. Jukun kings: Meek, *Sudanese Kingdom*, p. 129. The king of Idah: Seligman, *Egypt and Negro Africa*, p. 47. Hebrew high priest: Lev. 21:11.
65. According to R. Y'huda, M. Sanh. 2:1, 3.
66. 1 Sam. 9:19–24.
67. The city of Ramah was the permanent abode of Samuel. From there he set out on his annual rounds visiting a number of neighboring places. It was on such a round that the divine announcement came to him, whereupon he immediately returned to Ramah.
68. 1 Sam. 9:12.
69. Ibid., 16:3–5.
70. Saul: 1 Sam. 9:22–24; David: ibid., 16:11.

71. Seligman and Seligman, *Pagan Tribes*, p. 93; Irstam, *King of Ganda*, pp. 58–59.
72. 1 Sam. 9:18–19.
73. Ibid., v. 25.
74. Irstam, *King of Ganda*, p. 66.
75. 2 Kings 11:14. According to 2 Chron. 23:13, this pillar was at the entrance of the Temple.
76. Cf. 2 Chron. 34:31.
77. 2 Kings 23:2–3. Julian Morgenstern, "The Mythological Background of Ps. 82," *HUCA* 14 (1939):46n, suggests that the word *ha'amud* in 2 Kings 11:14 and 23:3 was substituted "by late P editors for an original *hamizbeah* in order to escape the otherwise inevitable conclusion that in both cases the king was functioning at the altar in priestly capacity." This view is, however, contradicted by the parallel passage 2 Chron. 23:13, "the king stood on his pillar at the entering."
78. Josephus Flavius, *Wars of the Jews*, 2.1.1. In Madagascar a new ruler mounted a sacred stone (Arnold Van Gennep, *Tabou et totémisme à Madagascar* [Paris, 1904], p. 17).
79. Deut. 1:1–6, 9; 11:13–21; 14:22–29; 26:12–19; 17:14–20; 28:1–69.
80. Ibid., 31:10. The sequel of the verse is: "at the time of the year of release [*shmitta*, sabbatical year] on the Feast of Tabernacles . . . thou shalt read this Torah before all Israel." Originally the Sukkot festival was celebrated at the end of the year so that the Sukkot of the sabbatical year was the closing period of the seventh year. After the calendar reform this Sukkot festival fell to the beginning of the eighth year, as stated in the Mishna. See Julian Morgenstern, "The Three Calendars of Ancient Israel," *HUCA* 1 (1924):33.
81. M. Sota 7:8; in the sequel an incident is related which took place when King Agrippa read the Tora in conformity with this ritual.
82. No. 4 of Irstam's list.
83. 1 Sam. 9:18–21.
84. Only partly recorded, 1 Sam. 16:4–12.
85. Also only partly recorded, 1 Kings 11:29ff.
86. 2 Kings 9:5ff.
87. William Robertson Smith, *The Religion of the Semites*, 3d ed. (London, 1927), p. 254, n. 6.
88. As to *lishka*, ibid. and the note of S. A. Cook on p. 587. As to the later function of the chambers (*l'shakhot*) in the Temple, see 2 Kings 23:11; Jer. 35:2; 36:12; Ezek. 40:17, 45; 42:1ff.; M. Middot 2:5; 5:3–4; M. Yoma 1:5, etc.
89. 1 Sam. 9:22.
90. Josh. 12:9–24.
91. 2 Sam. 23:8, 13, 23, 24.
92. Neh. 3:16. Cf. Samuel Klein, "David's Mighty Men" [in Hebrew], *Bulletin of the Jewish Palestine Exploration Society* (1940), pp. 95ff.
93. 2 Sam. 23:39: thirty-seven. 1 Chron. 11:11ff., even more than that. See also Cant. 3:7: sixty! See also 1 Chron. 11:15, 25; 12:4; 27:6.
94. 1 Kings 20:1, 16.
95. Ibid., 22:31.
96. Judg. 10:4.
97. Ibid., 12:9.
98. Ibid., v. 14.
99. Jer. 38:10.
100. Cf. Johann Gottfried Wetzstein, "Die syrische Dreschtafel," *ZE* 5 (1873):270ff.
101. Judg. 14:10.
102. Matt. 9:15. Though the passage is of much later date, the expression itself is but a translation of the Hebrew *b'ne huppa*; thus again *ben* in the sense of "follower," "companion," as above.
103. This was also recognized by Buber, *Kommende*, 2:47. Buber is reminded by the number of the councillors of the Spartan constitution.
104. Seligman and Seligman, *Pagan Tribes*, p. 93, mention that the election of the Shilluk

king is, theoretically at least, in the hands of the chiefs of the ten districts into which the Shilluk territory is divided.

105. Irstam, *King of Ganda*, p. 64.
106. Reading *v'ha'alya* instead of *v'he'aleha* of the Massoretic Text, with Rabbi Yoḥanan in B. 'Av. Zarah 25a; Abraham Geiger, *Urschrift und Übersetzungen der Bibel*, 2d ed. (Frankfurt am Main, 1928), p. 380; and the majority of modern commentators. Buber, *Kommende*, 2:48, would retain a *hif'il* form of the *'ala* root and compare the expression with 2 Kings 17:4, where an offering (*he'ela minḥa*) to a king is mentioned.
107. 1 Sam. 9:22–24. Verse 24 is evidently corrupt, and many scholars have tried their hands at its emendation, but without satisfactory results.
108. Exod. 29:27.
109. Lev. 7:32–34.
110. William F. Albright, *From the Stone Age to Christianity* (Baltimore, 1940), pp. 179, 226.
111. Lev. 3:9; 7:3; 8:25; 9:19. As to the modern Palestine-Arab use of the fat tail, the *liyeh*, see F. A. Klein, "Mittheilungen über Leben, Sitten und Gebräuche der Fellachen in Palästina," *ZDPV* 6 (1883):98; Abraham Geiger, "Die gesetzlichen Differenzen zwischen Samaritanern und Juden," *ZMDG* 20 (1866):547–50.
112. Exod. 29:27; Lev. 7:34.
113. 1 Sam. 9:23–24. Josephus Flavius, *Antiquities of the Jews* 6.4.1 calls the portion set before Saul "the royal portion." The identity of the terminology in 1 Sam. 9:23–24 and in Exod. 29:26ff., Lev. 7:32ff., was pointed out by Buber, *Kommende*, 2:48.
114. Lev. 8:25. I shall deal with the similarity between the priestly consecration and the royal installation in sec. XII, below.
115. 1 Sam 9:26.
116. 2 Sam. 16:20–21.
117. 1 Kings 2:22.
118. 2 Sam. 12:8.
119. Meek, *Sudanese Kingdom*, p. 139.
120. Ibid., pp. 138, 139.
121. Zeph. 1:15; Jer. 19:13; 32:29.
122. 2 Kings 23:12. Cf. Robertson Smith, *Religion of the Semites*, pp. 230, n. 4, 544, 580.
123. Neh. 8:16.
124. Isa. 22:5.
125. Jer. 48:38; Isa. 15:3.
126. Josh. 2:6, 8.
127. In Babylonia, where according to Herodotus 1.181 the sacred marriage between Marduk and a woman was celebrated in a sacred room at the top of the ziggurat. See Morris Jastrow, *The Religion of Babylonia and Assyria* (Boston, 1898), pp. 678–79; Morris Jastrow, "Sumerian Myths of the Beginning," *AJSL* 33 (1916–17):118–19; see also C. J. Gadd, "Babylonian Myth and Ritual," in Hooke, ed., *Myth and Ritual*, pp. 56–57. On the "bedroom" in the Mesopotamian temple, see also A. Leo Oppenheim, "The Mesopotamian Temple," *Biblical Archaeologist* 7, no. 3 (Sept. 1944):55; Raphael Patai, *Man and Temple in Ancient Jewish Myth and Ritual* (Edinburgh, 1947), pp. 88–89, 141.
128. Maurice Vieyra, "Rites de purification hittites," *Revue de l'histoire des religions* 119 (1939):139–40, and literature, ibid., p. 140, n. 1. Cf. Engnell, *Studies*, p. 64. As to the role of the ritual tent in Hittite and Babylonian purification, see Albrecht Goetze and E. H. Sturtevant, *The Hittite Ritual of Tunnawi*, American Oriental Series, vol. 14 (New Haven, Conn., 1938), p. 98.
129. Theodor H. Gaster, "Notes on Ras Shamra Texts, II," *OLZ* 39 (1936), col. 405; cf. Charles Virolleaud, "Les Inscriptions Cuneiformes des Ras Shamra," *Syria* 10 (1929): 304–10. Endorsed by Engnell, *Studies*, p. 154, n. 2; cf. pp. 153–54. Engnell also refers to 2 Sam. 16:20.
130. W. O. E. Oesterley in Hooke, ed., *Myth and Ritual*, p. 140; endorsed by Hooke, *Origins*, p. 54.
131. 1 Sam. 10:1. According to the Septuagint, also 11:11–15.

132. David: 1 Sam. 16:1, 13; 2 Sam. 2:4; 5:3. Absalom: 2 Sam. 19:11. Solomon: 1 Kings 1:39, 45. Jehu: 2 Kings 9:3, 6. Joash: 2 Kings 11:12. Joahas: 2 Kings 23:30.
133. 1 Kings 19:16; Lev. 4:5, 16; Num. 35:35; cf. Zech. 4:14.
134. Of this later, in connection with the consecration of priests.
135. Robertson Smith, *Religion of the Semites*, pp. 232–33, and Cook's note, ibid., pp. 582–83, with references to literature; Ernest Crawley, *ERE* 1:549ff.
136. 1 Kings 1:39.
137. Ps. 89:21.
138. Y. Sota 22c mid.; Jer. Horayot 47c mid.; B. Horayot 11b; B. Ker 5a–b.
139. Y. Sota 22c mid.; B. Ker. 5a, basing on Exod. 30:22–25.
140. Y. Sota 22c mid.; Y. Horayot 47c mid; B. Horayot 11b; B. Ker. 5b. This observation was repeated some fifteen hundred years later by C. R. North ("The Religious Aspects of Hebrew Kingship," *ZATW* 50 [1932]:14), who, however, was not aware that he had been preceded by the Talmud.
141. B. Horayot 12a; B. Keretot 5b.
142. Irstam, *King of Ganda*, p. 57, no. 12; p. 70; Hocart, *Kingship*, p. 71, etc.
143. Irstam, *King of Ganda*, p. 56, no. 8; pp. 64ff.; Meek, *Sudanese Kingdom*, p. 136.
144. Cf. James H. Breasted, *Ancient Records of Egypt*, 5 vols. (Chicago, 1906), 2:99, 222.
145. 1 Kings 1:45; cf. vv. 33, 38. As to the spring Gihon, see 2 Chron. 32:30; 33:14.
146. Tos. Sanh. 4:10; Y. Sota 22c mid.; Y. Horayot 47c mid.; B. Horayot 12a; B. Keretot 5b. Cf. Raphael Patai, *HaMayim* (Tel Aviv, 1936), p. 11.
147. 1 Kings 1:9.
148. 1 Sam. 10:1.
149. See Irstam, *King of Ganda*, pp. 58–60.
150. 1 Kings 1:34, 39.
151. Saul: 1 Sam. 10:24. Absalom: 2 Sam. 16:16. Adonijah: 1 Kings 1:25. Joash: 2 Kings 11:12; 2 Chron. 23:11.
152. E.g., 1 Kings 1:31.
153. Saul: 1 Sam. 10:6, 9. David: 1 Sam. 16:13.
154. Saul: 1 Sam. 10:6; cf. v. 9.
155. Hocart, *Kingship*, p. 86.
156. Ibid., p. 70.
157. Ps. 2:6–7. In Hebrew *y'lidtikha*, i.e., "begotten," "fathered," but literally, "born."
158. Seligman, *Egypt and Negro Africa*, p. 44, basing on accounts of Miles Clifford (unpublished) and R. S. Seton, "Installation of an Attah of Idah," *JRAI* 48 (1928):255ff.
159. Meek, *Sudanese Kingdom*, p. 137.
160. E.g., 2 Sam. 7:14; 1 Chron. 17:13; Ps. 89:27–28. Cf. Aubrey R. Johnson, "The Role of the King in the Jerus. Cultus," in Hooke, ed., *Labyrinth*, pp. 78ff., 108ff. As to the father-son concept in ancient Canaan, see John Hastings Patton, *Canaanite Parallels in the Book of Psalms* (Baltimore, 1944), p. 15. As to the divinity of Hebrew kings, cf. North, "Religious Aspects of Hebrew Kingship," pp. 21ff.
161. Midrash Samuel, 17. Cf. B. Yoma 22b; Y. Bikkurim 65d top.
162. John 1:32–34; Matt. 3:16–17; Mark 1:10–11; Luke 3:21–22.
163. V. 7. Reference to this verse has been made by Ibn Ezra ad loc., who also mentions that among some people, such as the Indians, it is customary to salute the king by kissing him.
164. 1 Sam. 10:1. We know from 1 Kings 19:18 and Hos. 13:2 that kissing was also a form of Baal worship, though it naturally can be seen as an expression of filial devotion (cf. Gen. 27:26; cf. also Buber, *Kommende*, 2:157, n. 35: "Der Kuss ist hier . . . eine sakrale Gebärde des machtübergebenden Menschen."
165. Stephen Herbert Langdon, *Semitic* (Boston, 1931) (vol. 5 of John A. MacCulloch, ed., *The Mythology of all Races*, 13 vols.), pp. 320–21.
166. Friedrich Bleek and Julius Wellhausen, *Einleitung in das Alte Testament*, 4th ed. (1878), sec. 104; Carl Heinrich Cornill, "Ein Elohistischer Bericht über die Entstehung des Israelitischen Königtums in 1 Samuelis 1–15 aufgezeigt," *Zeitschrift für kirchliche Wissenschaft und kirchliches Leben* 6 (1885):114ff.; Abraham Kuenen, *Historisch-*

kritische Einleitung in die Bücher des Alten Testaments, 2 vols. (Leipzig, 1887–92), sec.
21.7; Julius Wellhausen, *Die Composition des Hexateuchs*, 3d ed. (Berlin, 1899), pp.
240ff.; Kittel, *Geschichte des Volkes Israel*, 2:26ff. Cf. also the biblical commentaries to
the passage.

167. Ch. Bruston, *Revue de théologie et de philosophie* (1885), pp. 511ff.; Rudolph Kittel,
in Emil F. Kautzsch, *Die heilige Schrift des Alten Testaments*, 4th ed. (Tübingen,
1922); Edouard Louis Montet, *Histoire du peuple d'Israël* (Paris, 1926), pp.
70–71; Adolphe Lods, "Les sources des recits du premier livre de Samuel sur l'institution de la
royauté," *Etudes de théologie et d'histoire* (1901), pp. 257ff; Adolphe Lods, *Israël*
(Paris, 1932), pp. 408ff.; Richard Press, "Der Prophet Samuel," *ZATW* 56 (1938):
177–225.

168. Ivar Hylander, *Der literarische Samuel-Saul-Komplex* (Uppsala, 1932), passim, esp. pp.
309ff.; Otto Thenius, *Die Bücher Samuel* (Leipzig, 1864), pp. xiff., in *Kurzgefasstes
exegetisches Handbuch zum Alten Testament*, 17 vols. in 10 (Leipzig, 1850–97), W. A.
Irwin, "Samuel and the Rise of the Monarchy," *AJSL* 58 (1941):121.

169. Y. Sota 22d mid.

170. 1 Sam. 12:12.

171. Ibid., 10:1.

172. V. 9. As to the date of the event, see Julian Morgenstern, "The New Year of Kings," in
Occident and Orient (Moses Gaster Anniversary Volume) (London, 1936), pp. 449ff.;
Julian Morgenstern, "The Mythological Background of Ps. 82," *HUCA* 14 (1939):44–
45n., where it is argued that the anointing of Saul, similarly to the installation of kings in
general, was performed on New Year's Day.

173. Vv. 2–9.

174. V. 13; cf. 9:12, 13, 14, 19, 25.

175. 1 Sam. 10:17–25.

176. Ibid., v. 27: "but he bore silently." *Haḥresh* is used many times in the Bible in the sense
of bearing something silently, patiently; cf. Ps. 50:21; Gen. 24:21; 2 Sam. 19:11, etc.

177. As to the problematical points in this part of the story, see below.

178. In verse 12, instead of "Samuel" one ought apparently to read "Saul." It must be Saul
whom the people address, as it is he who answers them. Similarly in verse 14, again
"Saul" has apparently to be read instead of "Samuel." This would seem to be confirmed
by v. 15, in which only the people and Saul are mentioned. Thus the picture becomes
clear, and Samuel has no place in it. It is Saul alone, victoriously returning from his first
battle, who calls the people—in accordance, however, with the previously issued directions of Samuel (10:8)—to Gilgal to confirm him in his kingship.

179. *Ḥarad* in the sense of coming quickly to somebody or after somebody, in 1 Sam. 16:4;
20:2.

180. This would seem to be the sense of v. 8, which is defective in the MT.

181. It may be argued also from a comparison of the advice of 1 Sam. 10:8 with the above
passages that 11:15 and 13:7b–15 belong together. In 10:8 Samuel ordered Saul to go
down before him to Gilgal and to wait there for him seven days, "and behold I will come
down unto thee to offer burnt offerings [and] to sacrifice *shelamim* sacrifices." We have
here a double set of offerings: *'olot*, burnt offerings, and *shelamim*, "peace offerings."
Now, in 11:15 we are told of the performance of one part only of this order: the sacrificing
of the *shelamim*, presumably by Saul, while in 13:9–10, though Saul commands both the
'ola and the *shelamim* to be brought before him, he offers only the *'ola*. To complete the
narrative, 11:15 should, therefore, be merged into 13:9–10.

182. Through the taking out of vv. 7b–15 from their present context in chap. 13, the remainder
of the chapter becomes more compact and uniform. Moreover, a hitherto puzzling
contradiction within the MT is thus eliminated: according to vv. 7b–15, Saul is in Gilgal,
but according to v. 16, he and his son Jonathan "abode in Geba Benjamin." That 10:8
and 13:7–15 cannot originally have belonged to their present context was recognized by
Julius Wellhausen in *Die Composition des Hexateuchs*, 3d ed. (Berlin, 1899), pp.
245–46 and *Prolegomena*, 6th ed. (Berlin, 1905), pp. 254–55, though he naturally drew

quite different conclusions from this finding. Incidentally, David Kimchi recognized that 10:8 does not stand in its proper place (ReDaK, ad loc.).

183. So Heinrich Ewald, *Geschichte des Volkes Israel*, 3d ed., 3 vols. (Göttingen, 1866), 3:30.

184. As to the bread, cf. Gen. 14:18; Hylander, *Samuel-Saul-Komplex*, p. 137. Erwin R. Goodenough, "Kingship in Early Israel," *JBL* 48 (1929):186, remarks in connection with the two loaves given to Saul, "apparently this was to represent the divine nourishment of kings."

185. A place in Judah; cf. Josh. 15:55; today El-Kurmul, some thirteen kilometers south of Hebron. Cf. the biblical commentaries of Nowack, Schulz, etc., ad loc.

186. 1 Sam. 15:12. As to the *yad*, see below.

187. Irstam, *King of Ganda*, pp. 56, 72. In Dahomey, after the enthronement of a new king was achieved, he made a tour of the grounds within the palace walls (M. J. Herskovits, *Dahomey* [New York, 1938], 2:72).

188. Hocart, *Kingship*, p. 71.

189. Irstam, *King of Ganda*, p. 72.

190. Let us mention only in passing that Samuel himself made an annual round to Beth-el, Gilgal, and Mizpah, while his permanent house was at Ramah (1 Sam. 7:16). Cf. John Garstang, *The Heritage of Solomon* (London, 1934), p. 288.

191. Seligman, *Egypt and Negro Africa*, p. 46.

192. Irstram, *King of Ganda*, p. 72; Meek, *Sudanese Kingdom*, pp. 137, 138.

193. 1 Kings 1:44.

194. Jer. 17:25.

195. Zech. 9:9.

196. Sifre Deut. 17:15; B. Sanh., chap. 2.

197. 1 Sam. 15:12. Cf. *Yad Abshalom*, 2 Sam. 18:18. The expression is, however, ambiguous; cf. 1 Chron. 18:13, *l'hatziv yado* (to set up his rule) and 2 Sam. 8:3, *l'hashiv yado* (to recover his rule). In connection with the significance of the Gilgal, Goodenough, "Kingship in Early Israel," p. 186, suggests that "the twelve stones which Joshua had piled up there after the crossing of the Jordan (Josh. 4:20) may have been in the form of a pillar or column and that here is another association of the king with a pillar."

198. 1 Sam. 15:1ff.

199. Hocart, *Kingship*, p. 71, point Z.

200. A. M. Blackman, "Myth and Ritual in Ancient Egypt," in Hooke, ed., *Myth and Ritual*, p. 22; Hocart, *Kingship*, pp. 83ff.; Seligman, *Egypt and Negro Africa*, pp. 15, 52; Engnell, *Studies*, pp. 5, 10ff., 64, 200.

201. A. M. Blackman and H. W. Fairman, "The Myth of Horus at Edfu II," *Journal of Egyptian Archaeology* 28 (1942):32, 37.

202. 1 Sam. 15 and 11:14–15; 13:7b–15.

203. Morgenstern has shown that the Hebrew kings in preexilic times functioned as the chief priests of their nation in the central sanctuary once each year, on New Year's Day ("A Chapter in the History of the High-Priesthood," *AJSL* 55 [1938]:5ff.). As this functioning was the first time fulfilled by the king in the course of his installation ritual (cf. above at n. 181), the New Year's officiation in itself constitutes an annual repetition of a part, probably a very important part, of the installation ritual.

204. Blackman in Hooke, ed., *Myth and Ritual*, p. 22; cf. pp. 20ff.

205. Irstam, *King of Ganda*, pp. 22, 68.

206. Ibid., p. 193; Engnell, *Studies*, pp. 25–26; Hooke, *Origins*, p. 14.

207. The traditional interpretation of this passage—namely, that Saul hid himself out of modesty (cf. Rashi, Kimchi, Metzudat David, ad loc.)—does not seem at all convincing in view of the preceding and following events, chaps. 9–10, 13, and 10:23b–11, which show Saul as a man of strong character, quick decisions, and self-confidence.

208. Meek, *Tribal Studies*, 1:302; cf. Meek, *Sudanese Kingdom*, p. 140.

209. 1 Sam. 8:11–21; 10:7–8, 18–19, 24–25; 12:1–25; 13:13–14; 15:1–3, 17–30.

210. Ahija-Jeroboam; 1 Kings 11:38–39.

211. David: 2 Sam. 5:1–2. Rehoboam: 1 Kings 12:3ff.
212. Solomon: 1 Kings 9:2ff.
213. David-Solomon: 1 Kings 2:1ff.
214. David: 2 Sam. 5:3. Joash: 2 Kings 11:17.
215. 1 Kings 2:1ff.; 9:4; 11:38–39.
216. Ibid., 12:3ff.
217. 2 Sam. 15:1–3, 17ff.
218. Irstam, *King of Ganda*, p. 56, point 11, p. 68; Hocart, *Kingship*, p. 71, point F: "The king is admonished to rule justly and promises to do so."
219. Herskovits, *Dahomey*, 2:73.
220. See below.
221. 1 Sam. 10:27; cf. n. 176 above and see also below on the similar silent bearing of Aaron.
222. Cf. *vay'hi k'maharish*, the emendation of which, according to the Septuagint and Josephus Flavius, *Antiquities* 6.5.1, into *vay'hi k'mehodesh* ("and it happened after about a month") thus becoming unnecessary.
223. Irstam, *King of Ganda*, p. 74.
224. 2 Sam. 16:5–13.
225. Ibid., 19:15–16.
226. Cf. v. 23; cf. also the reinstallation of Saul in the Gilgal, below.
227. 2 Sam. 19:23; cf. vv. 16–24.
228. 1 Sam. 11:13. In the original Hebrew the similarity of the two sayings is still greater. As to the final fate of the men who derided Saul, see below. Shimei was killed by Solomon at the express advice of David (1 Kings 2:8, 36–46).
229. 1 Sam. 10:8.
230. 10:26, perhaps his new home, as previously we only hear of Saul as living in his father's house (9:1–3).
231. Irstam, *King of Ganda*, p. 56, point 6.
232. Ibid., pp. 62–63.
233. Mohammed Ebn-Omar el-Tounsy, *Voyage au Darfour* (Paris, 1845), pp. 159ff., as quoted by Irstam, *King of Ganda*, p. 63.
234. Irstam, *King of Ganda*, pp. 62–63; Meek, *Sudanese Kingdom*, pp. 133–34.
235. Irstam, *King of Ganda*, pp. 62–63.
236. Meek, *Sudanese Kingdom*, p. 133.
237. Irstam, *King of Ganda*, pp. 62–64.
238. Mackenzie, *Spirit-Ridden Konde*, pp. 72ff., as quoted by Seligman, *Egypt and Negro Africa*, p. 29.
239. As to David, it was remarked by W. A. Irwin, "Samuel and the Rise of the Monarchy," *AJSL* 58 (1941):126, that the implication of the narrative is that after he had been anointed "he also returned undisturbed to simple pastoral tasks." In n. 35, Irwin comments upon the "parallel, apparent or real, to the supposed delay of Saul and David after their anointing" found in the story of Jesus, who after his baptism "went into the wilderness for his forty days' temptation. . . . This period of solitary meditation was apparently a part of Jesus' career as a teacher . . . but for the early fighting men (i.e. Saul and David) no such interval was required." I think I have shown above that, ritually at least, such an interval was indeed required.
240. Hooke, ed., *Myth and Ritual*, pp. 8, 22ff., 84; Engnell, *Studies*, pp. 11, 36, 64–65, 111, 128–29, 150, 153, 162–63, 168, 212–13.
241. Irstam, *King of Ganda*, pp. 60ff.
242. Lods, *Israël*, p. 411.
243. 11:10.
244. Vv. 4–5, 20–21, 29–30, 36–37.
245. Vv. 27–28; cf. above.
246. 2 Kings 13:10–13.
247. Ibid., 13:14–19.
248. V. 20: MT *ba shana*, read with Septuagint and Targum *b'va shana*.

249. Cf. Karl Richard Lepsius, *Denkmäler aus Aegypten* . . . , 12 vols. (Berlin, 1849–59), vol. 3, pl. 36b; also reproduced in Alexandre Moret, *Du caractère religieux de la royauté pharaonique* (Paris, 1902), fig. 21; Seligman, *Egypt and Negro Africa*, p. 17, fig. 2.
250. Hocart, *Kingship*, p. 86.
251. Cf. 2 Kings 13:20.
252. John Roscoe, *The Bakitara or Banyoro* (Cambridge, 1923), p. 134, as quoted by Seligman, *Egypt and Negro Africa*, p. 15. We have seen above that the Dahomean king, when enthroned, was given an old gun (in ancient times, a hoe handle, the traditional weapon of Dahomey) and was exhorted to conquer his enemies with this weapon.
253. That Sukkot was originally a New Year's festival is shown by Julian Morgenstern, "The Three Calendars of Ancient Israel," *HUCA* 1 (1924):22ff.
254. Cf. Raphael Patai, *Man and Earth in Hebrew Custom, Belief, and Legend*, vol. 2 (Jerusalem, 1943), p. 186 [in Hebrew]; Raphael Patai, *Man and Temple* (Edinburgh, 1947).
255. Irstam, *King of Ganda*, pp. 60ff.
256. Ibid., p. 21, quoting Roscoe, *Baganda*, p. 204.
257. 1 Sam. 11:15.
258. Saul: 1 Sam. 10:24. Solomon: 1 Kings 1:40, 45. Jehu: 2 Kings 9:13. Joash: 2 Kings 11:12, 14; 2 Chron. 23:11.
259. Irstam, *King of Ganda*, pp. 56, 74.
260. Ibid., p. 56, point 14.
261. Ibid., pp. 70–71, 91–98; Meek, *Tribal Studies*, 2:544; cf. Schilde, "Die afrikanischen Hoheitszeichen."
262. 1 Sam. 13:22. It may be significant in this connection that later Jewish tradition has it that the spear and the sword were given to Saul by an angel or by God Himself (Midrash Samuel 17).
263. 1 Sam. 22:6; cf. 14:2.
264. 19:9; cf. 18:10–11; 20:33.
265. 2 Sam. 1:6.
266. 1 Sam. 26:7; cf. vv. 8, 11, 16, 22.
267. Similarly Garstang, *Heritage of Solomon*, p. 290.
268. *Haḥanit* in the singular; in the parallel passage, 2 Chron. 23:9, in the plural.
269. 2 Kings 11:10.
270. 1 Sam. 17:7.
271. Ibid., v. 54.
272. Ibid., 21:9–10. The slaying of Goliath was a legendary deed variously attributed to David and to another Bethlehemite hero, 2 Sam. 21:19.
273. The assumption that "the spear of David" was none other than the spear taken by David from the vanquished Goliath is based on a comparison of the passages quoted above with 2 Sam. 8:7 = 1 Chron. 18:7. Similarly the Philistines, after they had taken Saul's arms from his dead body, placed them in the "house of Ashtoret" (1 Sam. 31:9).
274. Cf. 1 Kings 18:28.
275. Josh. 8:18, 26. Cf. Moses lifting up the "rod of God" to secure victory for the Israelites over Amalek (Exod. 17:9–13).
276. Meek, *Tribal Studies*, 1:159; 2:541; cf. Irstam, *King of Ganda*, pp. 91–98.
277. 1 Sam. 31:4 = 1 Chron. 10:4; 2 Sam. 1:22.
278. Exod. 30:25; cf. ibid., 21:24; 32:11.
279. 2 Sam. 1:21.
280. Ps. 84:10; 89:19; cf. 47:10. Cf. Aubrey R. Johnson, "The Role of the King," in Hooke, ed., *Labyrinth*, p. 76.
281. Ps. 18:36; cf. 2 Sam. 22:36.
282. 2 Sam. 8:7 = 1 Chron. 18:7.
283. 1 Kings 10:16–17 = 2 Chron. 9:16–17.
284. 1 Kings 14:25–28 = 2 Chron. 12:9–11.
285. Cf. Patai, *Man and Temple*, pp. 74, 99.

286. 2 Kings 11:12 = 2 Chron. 23:11. Cf. Ps. 21:4. A third term for "crown," *keter*, is found only in Esther 1:11; 2:17; 6:8.
287. Josephus, *Wars* 1.33.9. As to the relation of these two, cf. Leopold Löw, "Kranz und Krone," in his *Gesammelte Schriften*, 5 vols. (Szegedin, 1889–90), 3:407–37.
288. 2 Sam. 1:10; cf. Num. 31:50; Isa. 3:20. Goodenough, "Kingship in Early Israel," p. 190, attaches special importance to the bracelet in view of the royal bracelet of the Assyrians and Babylonians.
289. 1 Macc. 10:89; 11:58; cf. 14:43. Bracelets were also worn as regalia in Persia; see *ERE*, 10:637a.
290. 2 Sam. 3:10; 1 Kings 2:12, 24, 45; Isa. 9:6; Jer. 17:25; 22:2, 30; 29:16; 36:30.
291. Deut. 17:18; 2 Sam. 7:13; 1 Kings 1:46; 9:5.
292. 2 Kings 11:19.
293. 1 Kings 2:4; 8:20, 25; 9:5; 2 Kings 10:30; 15:12.
294. 1 Chron. 29:23; cf. the intermediary expression, "the throne of the kingdom of God" (1 Chron. 28:5).
295. Solomon: 1 Kings 1:46; 2:12. Zimri: 1 Kings 16:11. Joash: 2 Kings 11:19. Jeroboam: 2 Kings 13:13.
296. As to the significance of this second *'ēdūt* and its role in the sanctuary, see Julian Morgenstern, "The Book of the Covenant," *HUCA* 5 (1928):34ff., n. 41. According to Goodenough, "Kingship in Early Israel," *JBL* 48 (1929):190, *hatz'adot* should be read with Codices A and B of the Septuagint.
297. Robertson Smith, *Religion of the Semites*, pp. 232–33.
298. Garstang, *Heritage of Solomon*, pp. 290–91, referring to 1 Kings 22:30.
299. 1 Macc. 8:14; 10:20, 62, 64; 14:43; Josephus, *Wars* 1.33.9.
300. Josephus, *Wars* 2.1.1.
301. *Shevet*, Gen. 49:10; Num. 24:17; Isa. 14:5; Ezek. 19:11–14; Amos 1:5, 9; Ps. 2:9; 45:7, etc. *Sharvit* of gold only in Esther 4:11; 5:2; 8:4; cf. Josephus, *Wars* 1.33.9. Let us mention only in passing that among the regalia of Herod Agrippa I there figured an umbrella which is shown on one of his coins (see Mordechai Narkiss, *Coins of Palestine* [in Hebrew], vol. 1 [Jerusalem, 1936], p. 136 and pl. 4, no. 9; cf. *ERE*, 10:637b).
302. M. Sanh. 2, 5; cf. Tos. Sanh. 4, 2, ed. Zuckermandel, p. 420. As to the reverence toward kings in general, see Eccles. 8:2; Prov. 24:21; Gen. Rab. 94, 9, ed. Theodor-Albeck, p. 1183; B. Berakh. 58a; B. Zeb. 102a; Num. Rab. 8, 6.
303. Meek, *Tribal Studies*, 1:159.
304. As pointed out above, certain rites of the Dahomean installation ritual were repeated every year, among them the admonition and humiliation of the king and his presentation with arms. To these may be added the annual military campaigns led by the king, which, though serving practical ends, had an emphatically ritual character (see Herskovits, *Dahomey*, 2:79–98).
305. Irstam, *King of Ganda*, p. 56, point 24 and p. 74; Hocart, *Kingship*, p. 71, point L.
306. Roscoe, *Baganda*, pp. 209–10.
307. Ibid., pp. 210–11, as quoted by Seligman, *Egypt and Negro Africa*, pp. 53–54; Irstam, *King of Ganda*, pp. 21–22.
308. Meek, *Sudanese Kingdom*, pp. 139–40.
309. David and Solomon also, it would seem, were installed in their reigns more than once. David was 1) anointed by Samuel (1 Sam. 16:13); 2) recognized by 400 followers as their prince (ibid., 22:2); 3) recognized by Saul as the future king (ibid., 24:20; 26:25); 4) anointed by the tribe of Judah (2 Sam. 2:7); and 5) anointed by all Israel (ibid. 5:3). Solomon's second installation is referred to in 1 Chron. 29:22.
310. Irwin, "Samuel and the Rise of the Monarchy," p. 130, recognizing the similarity between 1 Sam. 15 and Num. 31:1–20, comments, "Clearly it has become a dogmatic or theological vogue to represent an Israelite force as setting forth on punitive expedition, with ecclesiastical sanction and blessing, which in the sequel was forfeited and the triumph turned into consternation because of the failure of the victors to observe some ritual regulation." It is difficult to see how various "punitive expeditions" could be

represented according to such a scheme, unless there existed a ritual frame for the launching of an attack and for its ceremonial aftermath.

311. From the context it may be deduced that it was Saul's premeditated intention to kill Jonathan. The sequence of the events was as follows. Jonathan went into the Philistine camp and began slaughtering the Philistines (vv. 4–16). Saul numbered his men and found that Jonathan was missing (v. 17). In Jonathan's absence Saul pronounced a curse upon anybody who would eat any food until the evening (v. 24), a prohibition which must needs be transgressed by a person who did not hear it pronounced. After Jonathan ate of the honey he found in the wood, he was informed by somebody of his father's curse (vv. 27–30). When Saul got no answer from God—via the oracle—whether he should continue to fight the Philistines, he said, "Though it [namely the sin] be in Jonathan my son, he shall surely die" (v. 39). These words, pronounced by Saul before consulting the oracle on the point of the hidden guilt, clearly show that Saul at least suspected that it was Jonathan who "sinned." This is shown also by the irregular procedure of casting the lots, implying that the sinner expected to be pointed out was Jonathan (vv. 40–42). Moreover, 20:33 tells us that Saul tried to kill Jonathan in the same way he tried to kill David, by casting his spear at him.

312. There is no contradiction between this ceremonial killing of the mockers and the fact that the mocking itself was but a rite. It is a characteristic feature of the ritual to assign certain persons ritual tasks and then kill them for performing them. During the installation of the king of Ganda, when the king journeyed to Kababi, some boys were sent ahead with the vessels in which the sacred meal was prepared. When the king saw these boys, he asked, "What do you mean by carrying these vessels in front of me and dirtying my path with soot from the vessels?" The king's followers thereupon smashed the vessels on the ground and killed as many boys as they could catch (Irstam, *King of Ganda*, pp. 22–23). Such examples could easily be multiplied.

313. Roscoe, *Baganda*, pp. 210–11, as quoted by Seligman, *Egypt and Negro Africa*, p. 54.

314. E.g., the Ku Vi instructs the king-elect in the ritual which the king must observe and addresses him thus: "Follow in the footsteps of your forefathers and do evil to none, that your people may abide with you and that you may come to the end of your reign in health" (Meek, *Sudanese Kingdom*, pp. 136–37).

315. Ibid., p. 138.

316. Ibid., p. 136. Cf. also the humiliation of the king among the Shilluk and the Pangwe by the officials who conduct the installation ceremonies in Dahomey, above.

317. Ibid., p. 322.

318. 1 Sam. 19:18 24, telling of David's and later Saul's coming to Samuel and of the contagious prophetic-ecstatic atmosphere surrounding Samuel, cannot have formed part of the original narrative, which never speaks of Samuel as an ecstatic or an arouser of ecstasy. On the contrary, when Samuel wished Saul to be possessed by the spirit, he sent him away to a place where he would meet a group of ecstatic prophets (1 Sam. 10:5–6, 10–12). 1 Sam. 19:18–24 is regarded by W. O. E. Oesterley and T. H. Robinson, *Introduction to the Books of the Old Testament* (London, 1934), p. 85, n. 1, though on different grounds, as a "late midrash." Their view is endorsed by Irwin, "Samuel and the Rise of the Monarchy," pp. 128, 129.

319. Cf. Saul's words, "I have performed the commandment of the Lord" (1 Sam. 15:13).

320. Gadd, "Babylonian Myth and Ritual," in Hooke, ed., *Myth and Ritual*, pp. 53–54; Langdon, *Semitic*, pp. 318–19; cf. the literature on the humiliation of the king listed by Engnell, *Studies*, p. 35, n. 2.

321. Morgenstern, *HUCA* 1 (1924):36–58; *AJSL* 55 (1938):9, 190, 367; *HUCA* 14 (1939): 44ff. See also Hooke, ed., *Myth and Ritual*, p. 22, quoting Alan H. Gardiner, *The Tomb of Amenemhet* (London, 1915), p. 124; Kurt Heinrich Sethe, *Untersuchungen zur Geschichte und Altertumskunde Aegyptens* (Leipzig, 1903–5), 3:136.

322. Julian Morgenstern, "Two Ancient Israelite Agricultural Festivals," *JQR*, n.s. 8 (1917): 31–34; *HUCA* 1 (1924):22–58, 77; *HUCA* 10 (1935):72–148.

323. The Arago have long been closely associated with the Jukun; their city-states of Doma and

Keana were founded from Wukari, the main Jukun center. In accordance with the fashion prevailing among most of the more important West African tribes, Muslim or pagan, the Jukun too claim Arabia, more particularly Mecca, or east of Mecca, or the Yemen as their original home (Meek, *Sudanese Kingdom*, pp. 22, 23, 24). Meek himself noted the resemblance between the biblical Feast of the Ingathering and the African festivals he observed and described. The bracketed references are to the corresponding rites of the Hebrew Asif-Sukkot festivals as described in biblical passages.

324. Meek, *Sudanese Kingdom*, pp. 142–43, quoting A. S. Judd.

325. Menstruous women have to retire to a special hut until the period is over (ibid., p. 330).

326. Ibid., pp. 144–53.

327. Cf. Hooke, ed., *Myth and Ritual*, p. 8.

328. The correspondences and resemblances are indeed so clear that it seems unnecessary to work them out in detail. In the above much condensed account, I have restricted myself to referring to the biblical parallels by citing the corresponding passages. The resemblance between the Puje and the Sukkot as celebrated in the Second Temple, the so-called Joy of the House of Water-Drawing, is still greater. This festival is described in detail in Patai, *Man and Earth*, 2:161–92, and *Man and Temple*, chap. 2. Attention should here be drawn in particular to one common feature of both festivals which is not obvious. Neither the biblical references to the Asif-Sukkot festival (with the exception of Zech. 14:16–19) nor Meek's description of the Jukun Puje contains any statement about the securing of seasonal rains being one (or the chief) purpose of the celebration. That this was nevertheless the case with the Hebrew festival is shown in my *Man and Earth*, 2:161ff., and the same can be inferred as to the Puje from a comparison of this festival with the Jukun rainmaking ritual performed in case of drought (Meek, *Sudanese Kingdom*, pp. 282–83).

329. Meek, *Sudanese Kingdom*, p. 139.

330. Cf. Patai, *Man and Temple*.

331. Morgenstern, "Chapter," p. 23, n. 63.

332. 1 Chron. 21:26 (2 Sam. 24:25); 2 Chron. 7:1 (1 Kings 8:1–11); 1 Kings 18:38. Ginzberg, *Legends of the Jews*, 3:244; cf. Morgenstern, "Amos Studies II," pp. 12–13; "Chapter," p. 9, n. 23; "Amos Studies III," *HUCA* 15 (1940):179.

333. As to the role of fire in the Sukkot celebrations in the Second Temple, see Patai, *Man and Temple*.

334. Lev. 9:24; cf. Morgenstern, "Chapter," pp. 15ff.

335. See below.

336. E.g., in Monomotapa (Irstam, *King of Ganda*, p. 139).

337. Ibid., p. 140.

338. Ibid., p. 56, point 17.

339. Ibid., p. 141.

340. Leo Frobenius, *Erythräa* (Berlin and Zurich, 1931), pp. 144ff., as quoted ibid., pp. 139, 141.

341. Seligman, *Egypt and Negro Africa*, p. 53.

342. Morgenstern, "Chapter," pp. 22ff.; "Amos Studies II," p. 50, n. 82, where he also refers to evidence showing the existence of the same practice in ancient Babylonia. Cf. Sir James George Frazer, *The Golden Bough*, 3d ed., 12 vols. (London, 1911–20), *The Scapegoat*, pp. 306–417; Vieyra, "Rites des purification Hittites," pp. 139ff.; Engnell, *Studies*, p. 17 with n. 6, pp. 59, 67 (Hittite), 129–30 (Ras Shamra). As to the African substitute king, see Irstam, *King of Ganda*, pp. 74–78.

343. Irstam, *King of Ganda*, pp. 56, 72. Beans are a staple food in Africa. The king is hailed as "Our beans!" (Meek, *Sudanese Kingdom*, pp. 151–52). In accordance with the prevailing money economy of Dahomey, on his enthronement the king distributed large quantities of cowries to his people (Herskovits, *Dahomey*, 1:80).

344. Morgenstern, "Chapter," pp. 7–8 with n. 22.

345. Cf. Irstam, *King of Ganda*, pp. 122ff.

346. Ibid., p. 128; Meek, *Tribal Studies*, 1:72–73, 547ff.; 2:494, 542–43; Meek, *Sudanese Kingdom*, pp. 123ff.

347. Meek, *Tribal Studies*, 1:72–73.

348. Irstam, *King of Ganda*, p. 128, quoting J. H. Speke, *Journal of Discovery of the Source of the Nile* (London, 1863), pp. 224–25, and E. Jonveaux, *Two Years in Africa* (London, 1875), pp. 366ff.

349. John Roscoe, *JRAI* 22 (1902):63, 75, as quoted by Frazer, *Golden Bough, Adonis*, p. 375.

350. Sir James George Frazer, *Anthologia Anthropologica: The Native Races of Africa and Madagascar* (London, 1938), pp. 14–15; Paul Schebesta, "Die Zimbabwe-Kultur in Africa," *Anthropos* 21 (1926):496, as quoted by Irstam, *King of Ganda*, pp. 126–27.

351. Cf. the comments of R. Levi ben Gershom ad v. 26. The king is likened to the moon in Ps. 89:38. "It [the throne of David; vv. 36–37] shall be established forever as the moon." According to the Talmud, B. Rosh Hash. 25a, "Rabbi [Y'huda the Patriarch] said to R. Ḥiyya, 'Go to 'Ein Tab and consecrate the new moon, and send me a sign: "David the king of Israel lives and exists!" ' " The medieval commentator Rashi connects this saying with Ps. 89:38. The words "David the king of Israel lives and exists" form to this day part of the Jewish liturgy recited once every month at nighttime to consecrate the new moon.

352. Martin Buber drew my attention to this point; the passage that follows was added by me by way of clarification.

353. Morgenstern, "Chapter," p. 192, n. 89; cf. pp. 188–92.

354. Ibid., p. 192.

355. Ibid., p. 187, with reference to the notes in North, "The Religious Aspects of Hebrew Kingship," *ZATW*, n.s. 9 (1932):13–17. Cf. also William F. Albright, *AJSL* 35 (1919): 185–86.

356. Morgenstern, "Chapter," p. 368.

357. Morgenstern, *HUCA* 1 (1924):44–48, esp. p. 46; "Chapter," pp. 15–16, 368; see also *HUCA* 17 (1944):126, n. 472.

358. Wellhausen, *Prolegomena*, pp. 143–44, argued that up to the exile the sanctuary was the property of the king and the priest was his servant; in postexilic times, on the other hand, the high priest stood at the head of the nation; he was invested with anointing, crowned with diadem and tiara, and clothed in purple, like a king.

359. Cf. Irstam, *King of Ganda*, pp. 30–31, 119ff. The same was the purpose of the Sukkot festival; see Patai, "The Control of Rain in Ancient Palestine," *HUCA* 14 (1939):258ff.; *Man and Earth*, pp. 161ff.; *Man and Temple*, pp. 24ff.

360. Cf. Morgenstern's note, *AJSL* 55 (1938):190, n. 82.

361. Implied by 4:11, 14; cf. ibid., pp. 191–92.

362. Num. 17:16–26.

363. Patai, *Man and Earth*, 1:231–39.

364. At the great Syrian monastery at Hierapolis the chief priest (who, incidentally, held office for only one year and was then succeeded by another chief priest) was clothed in purple robes of office and wore a golden tiara on his head; cf. Lucian, *De Dea Syria* 42, as quoted by Morgenstern, *AJSL* 55 (1938):368, n. 121.

365. Cf. Morgenstern, "Chapter"; "Amos Studies II"; *HUCA* 15 (1940).

366. This should be compared with Saul's keeping quiet (1 Sam. 10:27); see above. In both cases a newly anointed person—here the high priest, there the king—silently suffers an occurrence which under normal (i.e., nonritual) circumstances would evoke a most violent reaction. The parallelism of Aaron's silent bearing of his bereavement with Saul's silent bearing of the derision not only confirms our ritualistic interpretation of both Saul's and his derider's behavior, but also makes the death of Aaron's two sons appear to have a ritual coloring. Cf. Morgenstern, "Chapter," pp. 364ff.

367. Cf. Morgenstern, *HUCA* 1 (1924):25.

368. Cf. Exod. 30:10.

369. This can be concluded from 9:23–24 compared with 10:1–2; 16:12–13; Num. 16. Cf. also Julian Morgenstern, "On Lev. 10.3," in *Oriental Studies Published in Commemoration of the Fortieth Anniversary (1883–1923) of Paul Haupt . . .* (Baltimore, 1926), pp. 97–102.

370. Cf. Patai, *Man and Temple*.

10. Earth Eating

I. Introduction

In a short but important study, Berthold Laufer assembled a significant amount of material on the widespread custom of geophagy, or earth eating.[1] He showed that, although earth eating is by no means general, it is found in almost every part of the world. It is not tied to climate, race, sex, religion, or level of civilization. It exists among literate and illiterate peoples, in both subsistence economies and affluent societies. Where it does exist, it is found in all segments of the society: in every one there are individuals who eat earth and others who do not and even try to influence their neighbors to give it up. Nowhere is earth regularly eaten as a foodstuff, in a manner similar to victuals of animal or vegetable origin. This is to be expected since earth is, by and large, inorganic material which cannot be digested. But people have resorted to eating it, and in many places still eat it today, in times of drought and famine, as a food substitute, in order to allay hunger pains, which are alleviated as a result of the feeling that the stomach is full. Many peoples also ingest earth as a medicine for certain physical and psychic disorders, and earth eating plays a role in their ritual.

Laufer also touches upon the question of the global distribution of earth eating and points out that there are several peoples among whom it has never been practiced. He states that earth eating was totally unknown among the ancient Semites.[2] As we shall show below, this generalization is incorrect, for in talmudic sources there are clear references to the practice of earth eating, in most of its typical varieties, among the Jews in the first few centuries C.E.

I shall try to show that traces of earth eating also are found among the Jews outside talmudic sources, in the past and in modern times. I shall refer, in supplementation and elucidation of the Jewish custom, to parallels among other peoples. My intention in doing so will not be to seek connections between these customs among the Jews and the gentiles, but to show that the Jewish customs are not isolated phenomena, and that the customs of the other peoples, even if there is no connection between them and their Jewish counterparts, can shed light upon them, and especially upon old Jewish usages to which only unclear references are found in ancient Jewish literature.

II. As Food

Among many peoples it is customary in times of famine to try to assuage hunger pangs by eating earth. Laufer presents in detail the Chinese references to this custom.[3] His book and other studies contain data on the eating of earth as a food substitute among various peoples. From a passage in the Midrash Genesis Rabba and parallel sources, we learn that earth eating for the purpose of alleviating hunger was practiced, or at least occurred, among the Jews in Palestine in tannaitic times (i.e., ca. 100 B.C.E. to 200 C.E.). It is told of R. Eliezer ben Hyrcanos, a disciple of Rabban Yohanan ben Zakkai, that after he fled from his father's house he lived in great poverty and "used to eat lumps of earth, until his mouth became evil-smelling."[4]

Various authors give details about the harmful effect of protracted ingestion of earth: it caused diseases and even death.[5] Among Negro slaves and the Tupinamba Indians in Brazil, it has been known to happen that people who wanted to commit suicide did so by eating earth regularly.[6] In the Babylonian Talmud, a story is told about a man who died as a result of earth eating, albeit in somewhat peculiar circumstances. He ate earth and then ate cress; the latter began to grow in the earth in his stomach and "perforated his heart," so that he died.[7] It is known that among various peoples earth is eaten in order to counter or mitigate the sharpness of certain vegetables. Thus the Zuni Indians swallow a bit of white clay with the tubers of *Solanum fendleri*, and it has been suggested that they do this to counteract, or reduce, the acridity and astringency of the tuber. The Pomo of

California, in making bread, mix red earth with acorn meal, and "in a few wretched villages of Sardinia bread is still prepared from the meal of acorns" mixed with a ferruginous argillaceous earth to counteract the tannic acid of the acorn.[8] The Ainu of Japan boil the bulbs of the *Corydalis ambigua* with a certain kind of earth to remove its bitterness.[9] The difference between these customs and the event reported in the Talmud is that in the latter the earth was not eaten together with the vegetable, but before it. But the extraneous information nevertheless allows us to suspect that the purpose of the earth eating related in the talmudic story also was to counteract or reduce the sharpness of the cress.

The kind of earth eaten is called in the Talmud *gargishta* or *gargushta*, and Rashi, the great medieval commentator, explains this term by translating it into the French *arzila* or *ardalia*,[10] that is, *argile*, derived from the Latin *argilla* and meaning "clay."[11]

The opinion of the talmudic sages about eating earth was negative. When R. Y'huda haNasi asked, "How about eating earth on the Sabbath?" R. Yishma'el, son of R. Yose, answered him, "And on weekdays is it allowed? For I say, it is forbidden even on weekdays, because it is harmful."[12]

As against this Palestinian view, represented by R. Yishma'el, the Babylonian sages offered a different reason for objecting to earth eating. According to R. Ami, "He who eats of the dust of Babylonia is as if he ate of the flesh of his fathers," because Babylonia was full of old graves.[13] A third opinion had it that he who ate of the dust of Babylonia "is as if he ate unclean creatures and creeping things, as it is written, 'And He blotted out every living creature which was upon the face of the ground, from man to cattle, to creeping thing and to the fowl of the heaven.' "[14] Resh Laqish said, "Why was its [Babylonia's] name called Shinar? Because all the dead of the deluge were thrown [*nin'aru*] into it." R. Yohanan said, "Why was it called the Deep [*m'tzula*]? Because all the dead of the deluge sank into it."[15] That is, according to these sages, it was forbidden to eat of the earth of Babylonia because it contained the bodies of the men and animals who perished in the deluge. However, this view could not stand up against criticism. "And some say [one must not eat of the dust of Babylonia] because it is as if he ate unclean creatures and creeping things? But surely they disintegrated long ago?" That is, "they were blotted out and did not become dust."[16] Following this discussion, the Babylonian sages settled on the same reason given by their Palestinian colleagues: one comes to harm by eating earth and this is why the rabbis prohibited it.[17] As for the view that by eating of the dust of Babylonia one ingests the remains of unclean animals, let us remark that in various places all over the world people eat precisely that kind of earth which contains the petrified or calcified remains of small sea animals.[18] Is it possible that the sage who gave this as his reason for prohibiting earth eating actually observed the kind of earth eaten and found that it contained fossil remains?

But let us return from Babylonia to Palestine. One of the ancient peoples of Canaan were the Hivites.[19] Rav Papa, who agadically interpreted this name as being derived from the Aramaic word for snake (*ḥivya*), said that they were so called because they used to taste the earth like a snake, whose food, according to the Bible, was dust.[20] The Hivites' purpose in tasting the earth was to determine what kind of seeds to sow.[21] At first glance, this statement seems to be nothing but agadic fantasy, but we have information from other places as well about the ability of people to distinguish among various types of soil by tasting them.[22] Jakob Polak reports that the Persians are such experts in tasting the varieties of soil that they can distinguish among them without any difficulty.[23]

In the same talmudic source[24] the name Hori (Hurrite), another of the ancient peoples of Canaan,[25] is explained. "They smelled [*m'rihim*] the earth." Smelling the earth also was practiced in Palestine in talmudic times. It is related of the elders of Sepphoris that they used to smell the earth in order to know how much rain would fall in the coming year.[26] The smell of the earth has an important role in determining which kinds of earth are chosen for eating and in evaluating certain kinds of earth as delicacies.[27]

III. By Pregnant Women, Women in Childbed, and Nursing Mothers

Pregnant women can crave to eat earth. In many places, including Persia, India, Malaysia, and Melanesia;[28] in Sumatra; in several places in Africa and Mexico;[29] and in Arab lands such as Iraq, Syria, and Egypt, pregnant women are reported to have a special craving for eating a certain loam, called *ṭin* in Arabic, and occasionally also coals.[30] The same phenomenon was observed among the Arab women of Palestine. Pregnant women in sixteenth-century Europe also ate earth.[31] Among the Persian women the craving for earth is especially strong in the last two months of pregnancy. They take some earth into their mouths and chew it slowly.[32] Holding earth in the mouth for a long time is the typical way in which the North American Eskimo women eat it,[33] and this seems also to have been the manner in which Jewish women in talmudic times ate earth. Thus it could happen that at the time of the *ḥalitza* ceremony, when the widow was supposed to spit into the face of her brother-in-law as part of the ritual required to make it possible for her to marry someone else, she "was eating earth and spat it out of her mouth."[34]

It is reported from several peoples that pregnant women eat earth because they believe that this will have a good effect on the embryo. For example, in the Moluccas pregnant women eat a grayish white clay to ensure that the child they carry will be white of skin.[35] A belief of this kind was found among the Jewish women in talmudic times. In that period there were many beliefs about prenatal influences on the physical shape and mental quality of the child. They included the belief, subscribed to by the sages, that if a pregnant woman ate earth her child would become ugly.[36] A trace of this belief is found among oriental Jews. In a manuscript book of remedies and charms entitled "Sefer S'gullot w'Ḥiddot," written in Damascus in 1871 on the basis of older sources, we read, "In order to have ugly children, let her eat red dust, and her children will be ugly." Precisely the same warning was given by the midwives to pregnant women in ancient Mexico. There the belief was that if a woman ate earth, her child would be sick or disfigured.[37]

In various places pregnant women eat earth because they believe that this will help them in delivery. Thus expectant mothers in Java eat earth so that the embryo will take the proper position in the womb.[38] In Nigeria they eat white earth in the first three months of pregnancy so as to ensure successful delivery.[39] In various places women eat earth during the delivery itself in order to ease the pangs of childbirth.[40] In Andjra, Morocco, if a woman cannot be delivered of her child, a friend goes to a rock at the foot of which is buried Lalla Ta'bullat, a holy spinster, scratches off some grit, mixes it with hot water, and gives it to the woman to drink.[41] Among the Jews of the Caucasus a similar custom is practiced. If a woman cannot deliver, they take earth from the grave of a man who has died within the last forty days, put it into a glass of water, and give it to the woman to drink. If it does not help the first time, they again take earth, this time from deeper down in the grave, and give it to her in the same way.[42] One of the Caucasian Mountain Jews writes about this custom, "If the pangs of childbirth are too hard and too many, they send somebody to the cemetery to bring a handful of earth from the grave of So-and-so. . . . They mix it in water and give it to the suffering woman."[43]

Among several peoples it is customary for nursing mothers to eat earth or to drink a potion into which earth has been mixed in order to increase their milk. In ancient Greece, women drank for this purpose "milk stone" dissolved in honey water. On the islands of Crete and Melos, the women still use "milk stones."[44] In Palestine, both Muslim and Christian Arabs believe that a piece of limestone taken from the Milk Grotto in Bethlehem and dissolved in water increases a mother's milk. Legend has it that the Virgin Mary suckled Jesus in that grotto and that a drop of her milk was squirted on its walls; from that time on, a piece of rock from there augmented the milk of women and animals.[45]

In a Midrash we read, "The *kristallo* is one of the quarry stones, like unto precious stones, and it is white and bright, and its virture is to augment the milk in women." And again,

> The *galaritzidi*[?] is a stone similar to ashes, and it is found in Egypt in the Nile River, and it has the taste of milk, and if it is hung on the neck of a woman it increases her milk, and if it is put on her hips it is good for the woman who sits on the birth stool. And the shepherds in Egypt say that if they pulverize it and mix it in water and salt and let it flow in the place where the flock stands, it will fill the udders of the flock with milk.[46]

In contrast to these opinions, one talmudic sage, Rav Kahana, held that earth eating harmed the milk of a nursing mother.[47]

IV. By Children

Reports abound on small children who develop a craving for earth eating.[48] A popular Hebrew remedy book, written in Palestine in the nineteenth century, contains several prescriptions for ridding children of this harmful craving.

> If a child eats dust, take *al-katira* [acanthus gum] or leaven from the dough and soak it in sweet wine, pulverized, and give it to him to drink once and twice. Or take four leaves of the *al-sabas* herb, and in the foreign tongue it is called *finogio* [fennel], and grind them and extract their juice and mix it with wine, and bring it to a boil on the fire, and make it a *sharab* [drink], and give it to the child, and this will help anybody, even an adult. Or hang on him the hair of a goat, a male for a male, and from a female for a female. And if he vomits gall give him to drink cinammon and *mustaqa* [i.e., chewing gum], ground with a little water or another drink, and he will be healed with the help of God, blessed be He.[49]

According to R. Lasch, earth eating causes vomiting.[50] It seems that it was on account of this property that the ancient Romans used earth as a remedy for poisons and as one of the ingredients in their antitoxins.[51] About 1316, Peter of Abano mentioned the *terra sigillata*, the famous ingredient of which we shall have more to say below, stating that eating it causes vomiting if there is a poison in the stomach. Kings and princes in the lands of the west ate it with their meals as a precaution against being poisoned.[52] A similar belief is reported by a Jewish medical author, Abraham haRofe, in his book *Shilte haGibborim*, about the onyx. "Its virtue is that it preserves the eyes, and it helps against deadly poisons. If about eight grains of barley, well pounded until it becomes thin dust, is taken by him who has eaten a deadly poison, it will save the sick from death."[53] The author does not say how the powdered onyx helps against poison, but from the prescription of Peter of Abano we may conclude that it too was believed to be an emetic.

The above prescription can be compared with the customs found in Andjra, Morocco. "If a little child is fond of eating earth, the mother takes some earth from the fireplace and puts it at the place where the fowls spend the night, leaving it there for three days so that they shall make it dirty. She then puts the child on that earth in order that he may eat of it and, owing to its nasty taste, never again feel inclined to eat earth." Or, "some earth is brought from a *qbar mensi* [the grave of an unknown person] and put on the top of its feet; and it is believed that if the child itself takes a portion of it and eats it, but not if another person puts such earth into its mouth, it will get rid of the bad habit."[54] Among the Ait Waryager in Morocco, "if a child is fond of eating earth, a charm is written on a small loaf of bread and another one on a hard-boiled egg, after the shell has been removed; the loaf and the egg are then given to the child to eat, with the result that it loses its taste for earth."[55] Among the Indians of Carolina in the early eighteenth century, also, the children were "much addicted to eat dirt, and so are some of the Christians, but roast a bat on a skewer and make the child that eats dirt eat the roasted rearmouse (bat), and he will never eat dirt again."[56]

V. As a Remedy

I mentioned above eating earth as an emetic. On the other hand, various peoples—including the ancient Greeks, the Arabs, and the Sumatrans—used certain kinds of earth for the opposite purpose.[57] In ancient Rome, a patient who vomited blood was given earth from Lemnos mixed with vinegar. They used the same earth, and also the red earth of Sinope, for stopping the menstrual blood of women. For this purpose they administered the earth in dosages of the weight of one denarius.[58] In India they use for the same purpose Armenian earth, *bolus armena*, or *bole armenic*, which is brought from the Persian Gulf.[59] As late as the seventeenth century, Greek women drank earth from Lemnos mixed in water to facilitate delivery and to stop the flow of blood.[60] Among medieval German Jews, *oven lima* (oven clay) was used to help hemorrhaging women.[61]

The most famous medicinal earth was the *terra sigillata*, "sealed earth." In the Arab world this became famous under the name *ṭīn maḥtūm*. Ibn Sina (Avicenna) considered it an antitoxin, under whose influence the body eliminated poison, whether it was taken before or after ingesting the poison.[62] The sealed earth is often referred to in the Arabic medical literature. Maimonides mentions it in his book on *materia medica*.[63] The well-known Arab physician and botanist al-Baytar (1197–1248) mentions eight kinds of medicinal earths, among them sealed earth.[64] In the medical world of medieval Europe it became famous under its Latin name, *terra sigillata*.[65]

The Arabs in Egypt eat oblong and flat cakes made of grey earth as a remedy for several ailments. The cakes are about one inch long and are inscribed, ''In the name of Allah. The dust of our country, with the spittle of several of us.'' The earth for these cakes is taken from the tomb of the Prophet Muhammad. Occasionally they sew them into small leather satchels and wear them as amulets.[66] In the Arabian Peninsula they use a kind of yellow clay as both soap and medicine, ''for thus did the Prophet use it.''[67] In Morocco they take earth from the grave of a saint, mix it with water, and drink the potion as a remedy for various diseases.[68] In the Talmud (B. Gittin 69a) it is recommended that if one suffers from lesions in the throat after pustules burst open, one should take dust from the shadow of the latrine, mix it with honey, and eat it.

Two more uses of earth or dust are reported among the oriental Jews. Egyptian Jews use powder made by grinding a stone and mix it in a drink as a love potion. Abraham Halevi, in his reponsa *Ginat V'radim* (70b), writes, ''His wife made him witchcraft and gave him to drink certain potions made of powdered stone with water, in order to find favor and liking in his eyes.''[69] The other use is as an inebriating draught. ''If you put the ashes of a wick, or of the dust which is on the wheel of a cart, in wine and drink it, you will become drunk.''[70] Both of these charms are good examples of sympathetic magic. The ashes of a wick, produced by fire which moves back and forth, or the dust from the wheel which turns, produce similar phenomena in the person who ingests them. He will reel, shake, or turn in his drunkenness.

VI. As a Ritual

In many cases earth eating is connected with a ritual. Occasionally a religious feeling prompts people to eat the earth of a holy place. In ancient India, earth eating served to purify one of his sins. According to the Agnipurana, the pious ate earth and said, ''O Earth! I take thee, consecrated by Kasyapa; O Earth, take away the sins and misdeeds that I have committed!'' The custom of earth eating, or the addiction to it, has survived among many Indians in all parts of the country, in many cases as a ritual, a charm, or a medicine.[71]

In ancient Mexico, earth eating was an integral part of the worship of Mother Earth. On the tenth of May of every year, at the end of summer and the onset of the rains, the chief priest, dressed in the garments of the god

Tezcatlipoca, appeared as the god's representative, was called by the god's name, and took earth and swallowed it. This rite was the beginning of a complex ritual in which a youth was sacrificed in order to ensure the fertility of the earth.[72] At the conclusion of the annual feast celebrated in ancient Mexico in honor of the goddess known as Mother of the Gods, Grandmother, or Heart of the Earth, all those present lifted up a little earth with one of their fingers and swallowed it. Similar earth-eating rites were performed in all their feasts, and also when they "presented themselves" before the statues of the Christian saints, and in their honor. The act was considered an expression of humility and adoration.[73] When the ancient Mexicans rendered an oath, they called upon the earth, which also was named All-Mother, and ate some earth in a festive manner.

Among various peoples earth-eating confirms and accompanies oaths of fealty. Among the Loango in Africa, next to the king there ruled a queen who was independent of him and was considered the representative and symbol of Mother Earth. Her name was Makonda. When a stranger arrived and wanted Makonda to admit him into the tribe, he fell upon his face before her, beat the ground, and put some earth on his tongue. Then the queen lifted him up from the earth and he kissed her breasts, thereby becoming her property. From that moment on, he stood under her protection as a son of the earth.[75] In Togo, Africa, the earth has a similar role in connection with rendering an oath, but they only beat the earth with their hands when swearing.[76] "Among the Chin in Upper Burma it is customary to eat earth as a sign of swearing to tell the truth, and earth is administered to witnesses giving evidence in a criminal case." Similarly, it was "formerly customary among the Angami Naga tribe in rendering an oath to snatch up a handful of grass and earth, and after placing it on the head, to shove it into the mouth, chewing it and pretending to eat it."[77] Herodotus tells of the Nasamon tribe in Libya that when they wanted to demonstrate their faithfulness to each other, they drank water from each other's hands; if they could not obtain water, they lifted up some dust and licked it.[78] There are also peoples who do not eat earth, but are satisfied with touching it by way of giving confirmation to an oath.[79]

In the Middle Ages, the earth of a certain place in Hebron was considered a source of beneficial powers. It was either eaten or used in some other way. The location of this specifically efficacious earth was connected with the "transfer" in the Middle Ages of the traditional "navel of the earth" from Jerusalem to Hebron. Many legendary features originally associated with Jerusalem were transferred there, and at the same time all kinds of miraculous powers were attributed to the earth of Hebron. In the twelfth century, R. Ya'aqov b. R. N'tan'el wrote in his *Sefer Masa'ot*

"And there [in Hebron] is the place from which Adam the first man was created. And they take dust from it, and build houses, and it does not diminish, and at all times it is full."[80] R. M'shullam b. R. M'nahem of Volterra wrote in 1481 in his *Mikhtav Massa'*, "Hebron . . . is a goodly city, and a fat land. And I saw the cave of Machpela, which is the navel of the earth."[81]

The descriptions of the Christian travelers are more detailed. The first to report the specific use of Hebron earth is Fetellus, who visited Palestine ca. 1130. "In Hebron they show the field of whose dust, they say, Adam was created. Those who live nearby take from that earth in order to sell it in certain districts of Egypt and Arabia, where it is in demand, for they use it as *specie*."[82] What was the nature of this use as *specie*? John of Würzburg, who visited Palestine in 1160–70, tells us, "And there is a field in Hebron whose soil is red. They dig up that soil and sell it and export it, they eat it and send it to Egypt and sell it there for a high price. By God's providence, however much they dig up from this field, from its depth and width, at the end of every year everything is renewed as it was."[83] Theoderich, in his 1172 *Description of the Holy Places*, repeats this.[84] Ludolf von Suchem, too, refers to the field of Hebron in 1350 in his *Description of the Holy Land*.[85] According to Felix Fabri, who visited Palestine in 1481 and wrote a long travel book, this field in Hebron was called the Field of Damascus. He and his friends took along a little of this holy earth, which was very thick or viscous, because "they say that he who carries with him a little of this earth will never grow tired on his way, or, if he rides an animal, will not stumble or fall, and if the man or the animal nevertheless does fall, neither of them will come to any harm but will get up unscathed.[86]

An interesting parallel to the eating of earth from a place which is always replenished miraculously is found in a Chinese document.

During the period of Wan-Li (1573–1620) of the Ming dynasty, the district of Tse-yang (in the prefecture of Yen-chow, Shantung) was struck by a great famine. Suddenly there appeared a Taoist monk with a star-cap, gourd, and sword, and pointing to a lot of waste-land, said, "Beneath this spot there is earth-rice, which may serve as food." He vanished at once, and the crowd regarded him as a strange apparition. The people dug the soil more than a foot deep, and found earth of a bluish color, which somewhat had a flavor like grain. The famished people swallowed it eagerly, and as they greatly enjoyed it, quarrelled about the same piece. Several thousand men took so much of this earth away that it resulted in a pit several acres wide, and about twenty feet deep. All of a sudden it was full, and again people began to dig; however, they found nothing but sandy earth which could not be eaten; for the fairies are crafty and make such earth only to help men.[87]

As for eating earth from a holy place in order to secure blessings, this too is not unique for the Hebron field, but is found elsewhere, e.g., among the Mexican Indians and in India.[88]

From the descriptions of the medieval travelers, it appears that there was a belief in those days in Palestine according to which the Hebron earth had the same virtue as that which was attributed to a stone, called *t'quma* stone, in talmudic times.[89] Both were believed to protect man and beast, and even houses, from harm from falling. It can be assumed that similar or even greater virtues were attributed to the eating of the Hebron earth, which, according to the travelers, was practiced in neighboring lands as well.[90]

VII. As an Ordeal

When it is not possible to establish, with the help of witnesses or other evidence, the guilt or innocence of a person accused of a transgression, various peoples appeal to supernatural powers for a decision. Such a decision by extrahuman forces is elicited in an ordeal whose essential feature is that it exposes the accused, the accuser, or both to great physical danger, from which in the normal course of events they could not escape unharmed, or even alive.[91] For instance, they are thrown into a wild river, or are made to walk through fire, and the like. The underlying assumption in these ordeal procedures is that nobody can escape from these dangers except through the special intervention of superhuman powers, and that the latter will intervene in the affairs of men only for the sake of the person who is innocent. However, this thought process, although widespread, is not the original basis of the belief in the effectiveness of the ordeal. The intervention of "heavenly" powers is a highly developed idea which appears only in relatively complex and advanced cultures. In the simpler form of the ordeal, heavenly or divine powers do not appear, and it is the dangerous substance or element itself which is believed to kill the guilty person brought in touch with it, or into proximity to it, and to let the innocent emerge unharmed. This is the idea on which the ordeals in several African tribes are based.

The most frequent means used in African ordeals is poison, which the accused must drink. The poison, they believe, is a substance endowed with an inner intelligence, capable, upon entering the innards of a person, of recognizing there the signs of his innocence or guilt; it will kill the guilty and let the innocent live.[92] In practice, of course, what happens is that the life or death of those undergoing a poison ordeal depends on the medicine man or witch doctor, who prepares and administers the potion. If he makes it a potent poison, the accused will die; if not, he will live.

However, in one part of Africa the ordeal is administered in a form which is the opposite of the poison ordeal. Among several tribes in the former French Sudan and Senegal, and the former British Gold Coast, the substance mixed in the potion given to the person undergoing the ordeal is not poison, but a material which physically could do no damage. Therefore, if the person undergoing the ordeal nevertheless comes to harm, his reaction must have a psychological basis. The substance mixed into the ordeal potion in these tribes is earth. They believe that the guilty will die because the earth, considered by them to be a goddess, will kill him.

It is interesting that the two types of ordeal, which we could consider methodological opposites, are found in close proximity to one another, in neighboring villages. The information comes from the Mossi, a pagan tribe of mixed descent from the foreign conquerors and the natives they subjected, who are spread out over the wide plain of the great bend of the Niger river to the north of the Gold Coast. Their capital is Ouaghadoughou (or, in the English spelling, Wagadugu).

> At Dembo, in the district of Yatenga, when any young person died unexpectedly, it was customary to make the whole population swear by the Earth that they had not killed him or her by sorcery, and to attest their innocence they had to drink a draught of water mixed with a red powder, which was supposed to kill the guilty. The nature of this red powder is not mentioned, but we may conjecture that it was prepared from the pounded bark of the so-called sass or sassy wood (*Erythrophleum guinense*), which furnishes the poison employed in the ordeal over a great part of Africa. In other villages of the same district the draught which the accused must drink in order to refute a charge of witchcraft was tinctured, not with the red powder, but with earth taken from the sacrificial places. . . . All who refused to purge themselves by the ordeal were put to death.[93]

Ordeals based on swallowing some earth also are practiced in all the tribes of the Mossi-Gurunsi country. They believe that the earth is a just divinity who does good to the virtuous and punishes the wicked. An accused man swears by the earth to attest his innocence.

> When a man is charged with having caused the death of somebody by sorcery he is made to drink water in which is mixed a handful of earth taken from the place of sacrifice. Before he drinks he protests his innocence and calls upon the earth to kill him if he lies. Should he be guilty, it is thought that the Earth will take him at his word and slay him on the spot. . . . One way in which the earth slays a perjurer is by causing his belly to swell after he has drunk the water.[94]

In this part of the former French Sudan it is a widespread custom to make an accused drink water in which holy earth has been mixed. In the village of Pissié, belonging to the Kassounas-Frass tribe, any sudden death is attributed to witchcraft, and the chieftain, who is also the priest of the Earth, compels all the adults of that particular ward to go with him to the place where sacrifices are offered to Earth. There he takes earth from the holy spot, mixes it in water, and makes all drink of it and swear their innocence under pain of being killed by the Earth. Reports say that sometimes the guilty who denies his guilt is slain by the Earth. Similarly at Saveloo, a village of the Boura tribe of the Gold Coast, both the person accused of sorcery and his accuser have to drink the same kind of potion and pray that it might kill them if they are guilty. It is believed that one of the two will always fall victim to the holy dust. Again, among the Dagaris and the Zangas, partly in the French Sudan and partly in the British Gold Coast, the guilty one who drinks the draught and forswears himself "[will] sometimes swell up so that he die[s]"—killed by Earth for his crime.[95]

In Barbados, according to an eighteenth-century report, the ordeal had the following form. The man who had to prove his innocence took a clod of earth from the grave of his nearest relative—if possible, from the grave of his parents—mixed it with water, called down upon himself the punishment of heaven if he were guilty, and drank the potion. If he were guilty of the accusation, his body swelled up and his belly burst. The belief in the deadly outcome of the ordeal was so strong that only a man totally convinced of his innocence dared to undergo it.[96]

A trace of the role of earth in ordeals was preserved among the Greeks in Alexandria.

> When they want to find a thief, they gather all those suspect, and carry out a most impressive ceremony, under the supervision of the Caloires [a kind of priest] who whispers words of incantation in its course. They prepare unleavened dough and make of it small loaves of bread, about the size of an egg. Every suspected person must eat three of these loaves. He must swallow them whole, and must not drink water after it. Once we witnessed such an ordeal. The man who had committed the theft could not manage to swallow the third loaf, and when he tried to force it down he almost choked, and had to spit it out. The Greek Church keeps this ceremony secret. We have heard that it is performed with the help of the "eagle stone" [which is the same as the talmudic *t'quma* stone[97]], some of whose dust they mix into the loaves.[98]

Outside Africa, ordeals by earth eating are practiced in Java, Timur, and southern India. In Java, "when a dispute arises about a boundary, it is believed that a bit of the controversial earth swallowed will swell the wrongdoer or burst him." In Timor, in ordeals, "some earth was eaten while the Mistress of the Earth was invoked." In southern India also, a boundary dispute is settled by an ordeal of earth eating.[99].

These ordeals parallel the biblical ritual which decided whether a woman accused of adultery was guilty. We quote the biblical passage describing it in full.

> If any man's wife go aside and act unfaithfully against him, and a man lie with her carnally, and it be hid from the eyes of her husband, she being defiled secretly, and there be no witness against her, neither she be taken in the act, and the spirit of jealousy come upon him and he be jealous of his wife and she be defiled; or if the spirit of jealousy come upon him and he be jealous of his wife and she be not defiled; then the man shall bring his wife unto the priest, and shall bring her offering for her. . . . And the priest shall bring her near and set her before the Lord. And the priest shall take holy water in an earthen vessel; and of the dust that is on the floor of the Tabernacle the priest shall take, and put it into the water. And the priest shall set the woman before the Lord, and let the hair of the woman's head go loose, and put the meal-offering of memorial in her hands, which is the meal-offering of jealousy; and the priest shall have in his hand the water of bitterness [with the dust mixed in it] that causes the curse. And the priest shall cause her to swear . . . with the oath of cursing . . . and shall write these curses in a scroll, and he shall blot them out into the water of bitterness. And he shall make the woman drink the water of bitterness that causeth the curse, and the water . . . shall enter into her and become bitter. . . . And it shall come to pass, if she be defiled . . . that her belly shall swell, and her thigh shall fall away, and the woman shall be a curse among her people. And if the woman be not defiled, but be clean, then she shall be cleared, and shall conceive seed.[100]

The Mishna, written several centuries later, adds some details about the dust put into "the water of bitterness." "The priest entered the sanctuary and turned right, and there was a place there, one cubit by one cubit, a tablet of marble with a ring fixed into it, and when he lifted it up he took dust from under it, and put it into the water so that it be visible on it."[101] If no dust was found there, "he took it from outside and brought it into the sanctuary."[102] This last detail shows that the dust was believed to obtain its power to distinguish between the guilty and the innocent woman through contact with the earth in the sanctuary. In several of the African rituals adduced above, the earth had to be taken "from the place of the sacrifices."

The use of dust is explained symbolically by the Midrash. "Why did the Tora say, 'Bring dust for the *sota* [the woman suspected of adultery]? If she was innocent a son was to issue from her like unto our father Abraham, of whom it is written, 'I am but dust and ashes';[103] and if she was guilty, she would return to dust."[104] The effect of the water of bitterness was held to be direct and immediate. "The priest said to the woman, 'Let this water of bitterness enter your intestines so that it make your belly swell and your thighs fall away.' "[105] According to the view expressed in the Mishna, the water itself "investigated" the woman[106] and said to her, "My daughter, if you are pure, and it is clear to you that you are pure, stand fast, for this water is but as a dry poison which, if put upon sound flesh, does not harm it, but if there is a wound there, it penetrates and sinks into it.''[107] That is, only if the woman committed the sin of fornication could the water penetrate the wound that act left inside her and kill her; if not, it could do her no harm. The horrible effects of the water of bitterness on the sinful woman are described in much detail in the Talmud,[108] but we don't have to dwell upon them here. However, let us point out that the most gruesome effect of the ordeal on the guilty woman, the swelling of her belly, was considered also among the African peoples as the most visible result of the ordeal.

As against the punishment meted out by the water of bitterness to the guilty woman, its beneficial effect on the innocent woman was that she would become pregnant.[109] This positive outcome, too, preoccupied the talmudic sages. "We have learned, 'She shall be cleared and shall conceive seed.' That is, if she was barren, she would conceive, thus the words of R. Akiba. R. Yishma'el said to him, 'If so, could not all the barren women hide [from their husbands so that the latter suspect them of adultery, and drink the water of bitterness] and conceive? And a woman who did not hide would be the loser. What then is the meaning of ''and she shall conceive seed''? That if she used to deliver in much pain, she will thenceforward deliver easily; if she bore females, she will bear males; short ones, will bear long ones; black ones, will bear white ones.' ''[110] The same view is transmitted in greater detail in the name of R. Y'huda quoting R. El'azar ben Matya. "If she gave birth in pain, she will bear easily; if she bore females, she will bear males; if ugly ones, she will bear good-looking ones; black ones, she will bear white ones; short ones, she will bear long ones; one at a time, she will bear twins."[111] The sages attributed such importance to this possible beneficial effect that they decreed that a woman who cannot bear children, due to her age or to some physical defect, is not given the water of bitterness to drink.[112]

Elsewhere I discussed the custom of drinking water as a charm against barrenness.[113] Here I wish to comment only on the other ingredient in the potion, the dust from beneath the floor of the sanctuary. The belief that the earth can make barren women fertile finds expression in the rites of various peoples. Let us begin with an African example in which the belief in the fructifying power of the earth, considered a goddess, does not lead to earth eating. As in the sota ritual, so among the Ewe of southern Togo water and earth (or, more precisely, pebbles) are the elements which kill the sinful woman and give pregnancy to the innocent. If a Ewe woman is childless, her husband goes with her to the priest of the Earth with some gifts and asks him to pray to the goddess to cause his wife to conceive. The priest says, addressing the goddess, "This woman says she would like to have a child, and if she gets one, she will come again and thank thee." Then the priest instructs the husband to inquire of his wife at home whether she has been guilty of any secret sin, for should she have sinned and not confess it before putting her hand into the sacrificial vessel of the goddess, she will surely die. If the wife agrees, she draws water the next morning, and she and her husband go with the water to the priest, to whom the woman then confesses her secret sins. If she hides anything, she will surely die. Then the priest pours holy water into a vessel of the goddess in which there are palm kernels and pebbles which consecrate the water, causes the woman to kneel down, and pours the water over her. [114]

In other cases earth eating gives fertility to women without being connected with an ordeal. In the Armenian version of the life of Saint Nino, it is related about a childless couple that a "man of light" told Nino to go to the garden, take earth from the roots of a cedar next to the roses, and give it to the couple to eat it in the name of God, and He would give them offspring. [115] In Egypt, women who want to have children go to an ancient Egyptian monument, scrape off a little of the sandstone of which it is made, and drink it mixed in water. [116] In Sumatra, there is a tomb covered with a protective roof. The barren women go there, offer up a sacrifice, and eat a little of the earth of the grave. What is buried in the grave is the male member of a man, which had been cut off by his wife. [117] In southern India, barren Tamil women eat a little earth taken from an ant heap in which a snake dwells, in the belief that this is an infallible method of obtaining offspring. [118]

The legend of Ardshi Bordshi tells of a barren queen who receives a handful of earth from a monk, who tells her to cook it in sesame oil in an earthenware vessel. She does as advised, and behold, the dish becomes a porridge of barley. The queen eats it and becomes pregnant. The queen's handmaid eats the leftover porridge and she, too, gives birth to a son. A cosmological story from Thailand tells that after the gradual degeneration of the human race the sea will dry out and the land will be destroyed by fire. The wind will cleanse the dust and the ashes and remove all traces of the conflagration. A sweet savor will rise up from the purified earth and will attract a female angel from heaven, who will take a little of the sweet-smelling earth and eat it. She will, however, have to pay dearly for her indulgence, for she will not be able to rise again and return to her dwelling place. From eating of the strange food she will conceive and bear twelve sons and daughters, who then will repopulate the earth. [119]

VIII. Conclusion

We have not touched upon the connection between earth eating and the other customs in which the idea complex of "man and earth" finds its expression. In spite of Laufer's statement that the worship of the earth has nowhere led to earth eating[120]—which he bases primarily on Chinese sources—it seems reasonable to assume that such a connection does exist. The earth has an important role in birth, marriage, and death customs. At the crucial and fateful stations of the human life cycle, man seeks refuge in the eternal powers contained in the earth. Earth eating is expressive of the human desire to draw strength in this most immediate manner from the tellurian storehouse of power. We have seen that in ancient Mexico earth eating was part of a ritual of the adoration of the earth. The customs of certain peoples of India who eat earth shaped into small human and animal figures[121] point in the same direction. The belief in Mother Earth is found all over India. Man, whose origin is from the earth, can obtain new strength by eating a miniature man who also has been taken from the earth. In various places in the world, including Europe, earth is eaten as a medicament, to regain health. One of the sources of the use of earth as medicine is the ancient belief in the general powers of the earth. In the Middle Ages, as we have seen, there was in Hebron an important center from which red earth was exported to be eaten. The field from which this earth was taken was the place from which God, according to tradition, took the raw material for fashioning the body of Adam. That field in Hebron preserved its miraculous powers from the day Adam was taken from it, and until the Middle Ages pilgrims sang the praises of its wondrous qualities; it regenerated and replenished itself year after year. Thereby that earth proved its powers and confirmed the belief that eating of it had blessed results.

A Tahitian legend to the effect that the first men were created from red clay and that their first food was red clay[122] expresses in a simple form the original connection between the creation of man from the earth and earth eating. Man, who was created from the earth, must ingest the same material in order to renew his strength for his laborious existence upon the earth.

Notes

"Earth Eating" was written in 1946 and originally published in Hebrew in *Metsudah* [London] 5–6 (1948): 330–47.

1. Berthold Laufer, *Geophagy*, Field Museum of Natural History Anthropological Series vol. 18, no. 2 (Chicago, 1930).
2. Ibid., p. 103.
3. Ibid., pp. 120–21.
4. Gen. Rab. 41 (42): 1, ed. Theodor Albeck, p. 398; cf. Yalqut Shim'oni, no. 72; Yalqut Makhiri ad Ps. 37, no. 20; Avot diR. Nathan, version A, chap. 6, version B, chap. 13; Tanh. Buber 63; Pirqe R. Eliezer 1 and 2.

5. Laufer, *Geophagy,* pp. 105, 157, 176, 190.
6. Ibid., pp. 160, 185.
7. B. Shab. 113b.
8. Laufer, *Geophagy,* pp. 108, 167, 173.
9. Ibid., p. 149.
10. B. Yeb. 106b; B. Bab. Metz. 40a.
11. A. Darmesteter and D. S. Blondheim, *Les gloses françaises dans le commentaires talmudiques de Rashi* (Paris, 1909), 1:9, no. 71.
12. B. Shab. 113b and Rashi ibid.
13. Ibid.
14. Gen. 7:23.
15. B. Shab. 113b.
16. Ibid. and Rashi, ibid.
17. Ibid.
18. Laufer, *Geophagy,* pp. 102, 138, 178.
19. Gen. 36:2.
20. Isa. 65:25.
21. B. Shab. 85a.
22. Laufer, *Geophagy,* pp. 102, 185, 187.
23. Jakob Eduard Polak, *Persien, das Land und seine Bewohner,* 2 vols. (Leipzig, 1865), 2:273.
24. B. Shab. 85a.
25. Gen. 36:21.
26. Y. Ta'anit 68b top; cf. Raphael Patai, "The 'Control of Rain' in Ancient Palestine," *HUCA* 14 (1939):282–83.
27. Laufer, *Geophagy,* pp. 102, 183, 185, 191.
28. Ibid., pp. 104, 136, 137, 140, 141.
29. Ibid., pp. 109, 157, 159, 161, 179.
30. Oral communication from Yahya Ahmed Shahin of Iraq, and 'Abdallah Muhlis of Jerusalem. Cf. O. Hovorka and A. Kronfeld, *Vergleichende Volksmedizin,* 2 vols. (Stuttgart, 1908–9), 2:578–79.
31. Laufer, *Geophagy,* pp. 163ff.
32. B. Stern, *Medizin, Aberglaube, und Geschlechtsleben in der Türkei,* 2 vols. (Berlin, 1903), 2:297ff.
33. Laufer, *Geophagy,* p. 175.
34. B. Yeb. 106b.
35. Laufer, *Geophagy,* p. 133.
36. B. Ket. 60b.
37. Laufer, *Geophagy,* p. 179.
38. Hovorka and Kronfeld, *Volksmedizin,* 2:579.
39. Laufer, *Geophagy,* p. 162.
40. Ibid., p. 165; Hovorka and Kronfeld, *Volksmedizin,* 2:578.
41. Edward Westermarck, *Ritual and Belief in Morocco,* 2 vols. (London, 1926), 1:69.
42. Juda Tscherny (Chorny), "Die kaukasischen Juden," *Globus* 36 (1880):200; Richard Andrée, *Volkskunde der Juden* (Bielefeld and Leipzig, 1881), p. 182; Hovorka and Kronfeld, *Volksmedizin,* 2:578; Albrecht Dieterich, *Mutter Erde* (Leipzig and Berlin, 1925), p. 125; Heinrich Ploss, Max and Paul Bartels, and Ferdinand Reitzenstein, *Das Weib,* 11th ed., 3 vols. (Berlin, 1927), 3:21.
43. Y. Elzet (Y. L. Zlotnik), "MiMinhage Yisrael," *R'shumot* 1 (1918): 366, quoting Jacon Anisimov, "The Caucasian Mountain Jews" [in Russian], *Sbornik materialov po etnografii,* 3d issue (Moscow, 1888).
44. Sir James George Frazer, *The Golden Bough,* 3d ed., 12 vols. (London, 1911–20), 1:165; Raphael Patai, *Adam va'Adama,* 2 vols. (Jerusalem, 1942–43), 2:32ff.
45. T. Canaan, *Aberglaube und Volksmedizin in Lande der Bibel* (Hamburg, 1914), p. 89; T. Canaan, "Mohammedan Saints and Sanctuaries in Palestine," *Journal of the Palestine*

Oriental Society 5 (1925):188. Cf. Hovorka and Kronfeld, *Volksmedizin* 2:578; Laufer, *Geophagy*, p. 154.

46. *Mid. Talpiyot*, s.v. Avanim Tovot, 17a–b.
47. B. Ket. 60b.
48. Laufer, *Geophagy*, pp. 157, 159, 171, 176, 181, 182, 184, 187, 188, 189, 190.
49. R'fa'el Ohana, *Sefer Mar'e haY'ladim* (Jerusalem, 1908), 49a, quoting "a manuscript book of his honor Y. Z. Almehdevi of blessed memory."
50. R. Lasch, "Über Geophagie," *Mitteilungen der Anthropologischen Gesellschaft in Wien* 28 (1898): 219.
51. Pliny, *Historia Naturalis* 35.14.
52. Peter of Abano, *Tractatus de veneris*.
53. *Sefer Shilte haGibborim* (Mantua, 1612), pp. 45ff. Cf. *Mid. Talpiyot*, s.v. Ephod, 64aff.
54. Westermarck, *Ritual and Belief*, 2:311, 557.
55. Ibid., 1:212.
56. Laufer, *Geophagy*, p. 176.
57. Ibid., pp. 109, 151–52.
58. Pliny, *Historia Naturalis* 35.13, 14.
59. Laufer, *Geophagy*, p. 151.
60. Ibid., p. 165.
61. A manuscript entitled "Asufot," 89a, as quoted in Moritz Güdemann, *Geschichte des Erziehungswesens und der Cultur der Juden in Frankreich und Deutschlands* (Vienna, 1880), 1:216.
62. Laufer, *Geophagy*, p. 150.
63. Max Meyerhof, *Glossaire de matière médicale de Maimonides* (Cairo, 1940), p. 85.
64. Laufer, *Geophagy*, p. 150.
65. David Hooper and Harold H. Mann, "Earth Eating and the Earth Eating Habit in India," *Memoirs of the Asiatic Society of Bengal* [Calcutta] 1, no. 12 (1906):249–70; Laufer, *Geophagy*, pp. 164ff.
66. Edward W. Lane, *Manners and Customs of the Modern Egyptians*, Everyman's Library ed. (London, n.d.), p. 262.
67. Richard Burton, *Pilgrimage to Almadinah and Mecca* (London, 1898), 1:415.
68. Françoise Legey, *The Folklore of Morocco* (London, 1935), p. 31.
69. Joseph Perles, in *Jubelschrift zum 70. Geburtstage . . . H. Graetz* (Breslau, 1877), p. 31.
70. "Sefer S'gullot v'Hiddot," 59a; cf. *Sefer Sh'vile Emuna*.
71. Hooper and Mann, "Earth Eating," pp. 251–70; the quotation is from p. 252.
72. Wilhelm Mannhardt, *Wald und Feldkulte*, 3 vols. (Berlin, 1904), 1:362.
73. Sir James George Frazer, *The Worship of Nature* (London, 1926), 1:434, 438.
74. *ERE*, s.v. Earth; Laufer, *Geophagy*, p. 181.
75. Bernhard Struck, "Nochmals Mutter Erde in Afrika," ARW 11 (1908):402–5.
76. Ibid., pp. 403–4.
77. Laufer, *Geophagy*, p. 143.
78. Herodotus 4.172.
79. E. g., among the Romans (Macrobius 1.10.21); among the Greeks (*Iliad* 14.272); cf. Ludwig Preller, *Römische Mythologie* (Berlin, 1865), p. 417, etc.
80. Y'huda David Eisenstein, *Otzar Massa'ot* (New York, 1927), p. 61.
81. Ibid., p. 98.
82. *Palestine Pilgrims' Texts Society*, 13 vols. (London, 1889–97), vol. 5, *Fetellus* (London, 1896), pp. 9–10. The exportation of this earth to eastern countries continued for several centuries due to the persistent belief in its magical and curative powers (cf. Johann Zuallardo [Zuallart], *Il devotissimo viaggio di Gerusalemme* [Rome, 1587], pp. 262–63).
83. *Palestine Pilgrims' Texts Society*, 5:59–60.
84. Ibid., p. 52.
85. Ibid. 12:92.

86. Ibid. 10:412. Medieval Jews attributed similar powers to the agate: "Riders wear it constantly, for it fixes the rider onto the saddle and makes him succeed in the riding business all his days" (Baḥya ben Asher's commentary on the Bible, Exod. 28:17–18. According to the Syrian Arabs, if a menstruating woman puts a little earth under the saddle, she will not be hurt by riding (Eijub Abela, "Beiträge zur Kenntnis abergläubischer Gebräuche in Syrien (Saida)," *ZDPV* 7 [1884]:110–11).

87. Laufer, *Geophagy*, p. 113.

88. Hooper and Mann, "Earth Eating," p. 259; Laufer, *Geophagy*, p. 182.

89. Cf. Patai, *Adam va'Adama*, 2:28–29.

90. According to an Oldenburg belief, if some earth is put into cattle's mouths before leading them to pasture, it will protect them against witchery (Siegfried Seligmann, *Der böse Blick*, 2 vols. [Berlin, 1910], 2:39).

91. On ordeals in general, see Edward Westermarck, *Origin and Development of the Moral Ideas*, 2 vols. (London, 1926), 2:687–90: *ERE*, s.v. Ordeal. On the poison ordeal, cf. Sir James George Frazer, *Folk-Lore in the Old Testament*, 3 vols (London, 1919), 3:304ff. On ordeals among the Semites, see Julian Morgenstern, "Trial by Ordeal among the Semites and in Ancient Israel," in *HUCA Jubilee Volume*. (1925):113–43; Hans Schmidt and Paul Kahle, *Volkserzählungen aud Palästina* (Göttingen, 1918), p. 16, n. 6.

92. Frazer, *Folk-Lore*, 3:304ff.; cf. Raphael Patai, *HaMayim* (Tel Aviv, 1936), p. 67.

93. Frazer, *Folk-Lore*, 3:319, quoting Louis Tauxier, *Le Noir de Sudan* (Paris, 1912), pp. 580ff.

94. Sir James George Frazer, *The Worship of Nature* (London, 1926), pp. 399ff.

95. Frazer, *Folk-Lore*, 3:320–21, quoting Tauxier, *Noir de Sudan*, pp. 225, 292, 375.

96. Griffith Hughes, *The Natural History of Barbados* (London, 1750), p. 15, as quoted in Laufer, *Geophagy*, p. 160.

97. Cf. Patai, *Adam va'Adama*, 2:28–29.

98. Morgenstern, "Trial by Ordeal," p. 122, quoting Paulus, *Sammlung der merkwürdigsten Reisen im Orient*, 4:149.

99. Laufer, *Geophagy*, pp. 131, 142.

100. Num. 5:12–28. An interesting parallel to the powers of discernment attributed to the water is found in Philostratus, *The Life of Apollonius of Tiana*, who describes a well near Tiana in Asia Minor called the Well of Asbama. Its waters are good and sweet for those who fulfill their oaths, but mete out dire punishment to those who swear falsely, causing them all kinds of painful diseases and rendering them incapable of moving away from the place (bk. 1, chap. 6).

101. M. Sota 2:2. Cf. Num. Rab. Naso 9:32; Sifre Zuta Num. 5:17; Sifre Num. 10; Yalqut Shim'oni, par. 704.

102. B. Sota 15b; Y. Sota 18a. As for Philo's statements, cf. Isaak Heinemann, *Die Werke Philons von Alexandria*, 6 vols (Breslau, 1909–38), 2:198–202; Isaak Heinemann, *Philons griechische und jüdische Bildung*, (Breslau, 1929), pp. 23ff. Cf. also Josephus Flavius, *Antiquities of the Jews* 3.11.6.

103. Gen. 18:27.

104. Num. Rab. 9:15.

105. Num. 5:22, 27.

106. M. Sota 5:1; Y. Sota 19a bot. f.

107. Tos. Sota 1:6, ed. Zuckermandel, p. 293; cf. B. Sota 7b, etc.

108. The material has been presented in N. Wahrmann, *Untersuchungen über die Stellung der Frau im Judentum*, vol. 1, *Das Ermittlungsverfahren gegen eine des Ehebruchs Verdächtigte* (Breslau, 1933), pp. 43ff.

109. Num. 5:28.

110. B. Sota 26a; cf. B. Ber. 31a; Sifre Num. 19; Num. Rab. 40–41; Yalqut Shim'oni, par. 704. Philo and Josephus state that the innocent woman would become pregnant. Cf. also Patai, *HaMayim*, pp. 67ff.

111. Tos. Sota 2:3, ed. Zuckermandel, pp. 294–95.

112. M. Sota 4:3; Y. Sota 19c mid.; B. Sota 25b.

113. Patai, *Adam va'Adama*, 1:200.
114. Frazer, *Worship of Nature*, 1:415–16.
115. R. Campbell Thompson, *Semitic Magic* (London, 1908), p. 33.
116. W. Robertson Smith, *Religion of the Semites*, 3d ed. (London, 1927), pp. 568–69 (Cook).
117. Ploss, Bartels, and Reitzenstein, *Weib*, 2:330.
118. Hovorka and Kronfeld, *Volksmedizin*, 2:520.
119. Edward S. Hartland, *The Legend of Perseus* (London, 1894–96), 1:113–14.
120. Laufer, *Geophagy*, pp. 110, 125.
121. Hovorka and Kronfeld, *Volksmedizin*, 2:579.
122. Frazer, *Folk-Lore,* 1:9; Wilhelm Wundt, *Völkerpsychologie* (Stuttgart, 1914–21), 5:237.

III.
The Marranos
of Meshhed

11. Folk Traditions about the History of the Meshhedi Jews

The following notes on the folk history and customs of the Jews of Meshhed, the capital of the Khorasan province of Iran and the most holy city of Iranian Shi'ite Islam, are based primarily on information supplied in 1944–45 by Farajullah Nasrullayoff, head of the Meshhed Jews in Jerusalem, and Yitzhaq Gohari, a member of the same community. Some details were elicited in the course of interviews with other Meshhedi Jews in Jerusalem. In general, the information supplied by one informant confirmed that given by the second or the third. On several points one of them added details forgotten or omitted by the other. In the few cases where the statements were contradictory, I have explicitly noted this fact.

All informants knew that their ancestors had come to Meshhed from the city of Kazvin, located some 140 kilometers northwest of Teheran. According to the seventeenth-century Persian Jewish poet-chroniclers Babai ben Lutf and Babai ben Farhad, there was a Jewish community in Kazvin in that century.[1] The old Jewish cemetery in Kazvin also testifies to the existence of an old Jewish community in the city.[2] Gohari told me that he once saw, in the home in Meshhed of one of his Jewish acquaintances, a manuscript book which contained the Persian translation of the Koran and a brief history of Persia until the rule of Reza Shah (1925–41). In that book there were several derogatory remarks about the Jews of Persia, and, incidentally, its author stated that the Jews had settled in Kazvin in the year which was the Muslim equivalent of the Christian year 1483.

According to the tradition known to Nasrullayoff, the settlement of the Jews in Meshhed was connected with Nadir Shah. The death year of this despotic ruler was remembered from a saying coined on the occasion of his death: "Nadir b'derek raft," that is, "Nadir went to hell." The letters of the three words have the numerical value of 1161, the year of his death according to the Muslim calendar. The *Encyclopaedia of Islam* gives 1160 as the year of Nadir's death, corresponding to 1747 c.e.[3]

According to Nasrullayoff, the circumstances of the settlement of the Jews by Nadir Shah in Meshhed were as follows.

When Nadir returned from his victorious campaign in India, he brought with him a hoard of jewels and precious stones and chose the fortress of Kalat to serve as his treasure house. This fortress, located in the vicinity of Meshhed, was thereafter called Kalat Nadiri, that is, the Kalat of Nadir. It was surrounded by forbidding mountains, and wheeled vehicles could reach it only by two narrow roads. In addition, there were nine footpaths which could be negotiated only by people good at mountaineering. Nadir wanted to place Jews in charge of guarding the fortress, because the Jews were beholden to him. He instructed the city of Kazvin to send forty Jewish families, chosen from among the leaders of the community, to Kalat and its environs. Because of difficulties in travel, not all the forty families could leave Kazvin at the same time, so that when Nadir was killed, only seventeen had arrived in Kalat, sixteen had reached Meshhed, and seven had got only as far as Shabzevar, which is located on the way from Kazvin to Meshhed.

Once Nadir Shah was dead, the people of Meshhed did not want to allow the sixteen Jewish families to settle inside the city and allocated them rooms in houses by the city walls—something they would never have dared to do while Nadir was alive. Three years later, the seven families who had stopped in Shabzevar also reached Meshhed, and within a few more years several of the Jewish families from Kalat moved to the city as well. Thirteen or fourteen years after the first Jews arrived in Meshhed, they were able to purchase parts of the gardens which were just inside the city walls, and they built themselves houses on these plots. This is how the Jews settled in Meshhed.

Meshhed is an important place of pilgrimage for Shi'ite Muslims because in it is located the tomb of the eighth Imam, 'Ali al-Riḍa ibn Musa ibn Ja'far (768–818), known among Muslims and Jews alike as Imam Reza. His tomb gave its name to Meshhed (sanctuary) and made it the most holy city of Iranian Islam, and the seventh most holy city for the entire Muslim world.[4]

Because of the intense religious fanaticism of the inhabitants of Meshhed, the position of the Jews in the city was very difficult. They could observe many of their own religious commandments only in secret. On the other hand, as a reaction to the enmity of the Muslims, the internal ties among the members of the Jewish community became very strong, and they helped and supported one another in every way possible.

After the forty Jewish families had left Kazvin, the Jewish community in that city decayed and, before long, disappeared altogether. According to Nasrullayoff, there were a hundred Jewish families in Kazvin before the exodus of the forty. The sixty families which remained suffered persecutions and a generally harsh attitude on the part of the people of Kazvin, and consequently they too gradually left the city within a few years. By the end of the eighteenth century, no more Jews remained in Kazvin. Their houses and synagogue decayed and became ruins. The Muslims did not touch the Jewish houses and plots of land because they considered them unclean. Finally, in the early 1900s, the mufti of the city, Sayyid Ḥusayn by name, found a way for the Muslims to take possession of the abandoned real estate. He declared that the power of uncleanness of the buildings and plots had expired after three generations. And since the plots were ownerless property, the mufti himself took possession of them under the rule of finders, keepers, and sold them lot by lot for good money. On this formerly Jewish property the new city of Kazvin was built in the last generation, as Nasrullayoff himself had seen before his immigration to Jerusalem.

According to Nasrullayoff, the Jews had lived in Kazvin prior to the emigration of the forty families for about one hundred years, which would date their settlement in that city ca. 1647. Tradition still recalls that the Jews in Kazvin spoke the so-called Gilak dialect, so named after the Gilan district, located at the southwestern corner of the Caspian Sea. This dialect also is spoken in the city of Mazenderan, near the southern shore of the Caspian, and it was assumed that the Jews had come from there to Kazvin. Tradition also remembers that at the beginning of the settlement in Kazvin the number of the Jews was very small, which is also attested by several of their customs.

In brief, according to the folk history of the Meshhed Jews, their ancestors lived until about 1647 in Mazenderan, from about 1647 to 1747 in Kazvin, and from 1747 in Meshhed.

The scarcity of documents pertaining to the history of the Jews in Meshhed is matched by an equal dearth of details transmitted by their folk traditions. However, it would appear that the community thrived, for within two generations after their settlement in the city, the first Jewish cemetery had filled up, and the community purchased a large tract of land some five kilometers from the city and began to use it for the burial of their dead.

In 1830 a cholera epidemic struck Persia and many Jews in Meshhed fell victim to it. In those days the spiritual head of the community was Mullah Siman-Tov, a disciple of Mullah Abraham, who had died several years before the plague. (See below the story about how Mullah Siman-Tov stopped the cholera.)

In 1839, an event occurred which put an end to the existence of the Jewish community in Meshhed, at least officially. In the Muslim month of Ramadhan, when the masses of Shi'ite pilgrims were gathered in the city for the annual commemoration of the death by martyrdom of Husayn, the son of 'Ali and grandson of the prophet Muhammad, a libelous accusation was brought against the Jews.[5] They were accused of having desecrated the holy feast with the blood of a dog. The mob broke into the Jewish quarter, killed thirty-six Jews, and gave the others the choice between converting to Islam or making a run for their lives. Many of the Jews chose to escape. Leaving behind all their possessions, they trekked to Herat, across the Afghan border. Among the Meshhedi Jews who settled in Herat, the Gilaki dialect of Persian was preserved, while among those Jews who remained in Meshhed it was replaced, after the forced conversion, by the local Meshhedi dialect.

The converts, called Jadid al-Islam, or "New Muslims," continued to observe in secret their Jewish faith and customs, while outwardly they conformed to the local variety of Islam. For instance, they would buy meat from a Muslim butcher, but then give it to the dogs in their houses or to Muslim beggars. They gave their daughters in marriage at a very young age to the youths of their community, so as to make sure that Muslims did not come and ask for their hands when they reached maturity. They celebrated two wedding ceremonies; one, according to the Muslim rites with pomp and circumstance, and the other, a Jewish wedding in secret a few days later. On the Sabbath and the Jewish holidays they opened their stores and workshops, but if a customer came they asked exaggerated prices so that he should not wish to buy anything. If he nevertheless made a purchase, they donated its price to the synagogue or to the community, which was always in need of charity. On Fridays they would go to the mosque to attend the Muslim communal prayers, but on Friday evening they would gather in their synagogue, which they continued to maintain in secret. In order not to have to desecrate the Sabbath, they learned no craft at all, but engaged only in commerce.

In this manner they succeeded in observing the commandments of Judaism despite the very difficult circumstances. In general the Muslims were satisfied with an oral declaration by the Jews of their adherence to Islam, and did not investigate whether the Jadidim actually observed the Muslim rites in their private lives. For this reason it never happened that a

Jadid al-Islam was caught observing the Jewish religion. Nevertheless, they suffered much from the religious fanaticism of the people of Meshhed and from libelous accusations brought against them from time to time.

The double life the Jadidim were forced to lead left its mark on the entire community, its organization, the trades its members engaged in, their family life, and their secular and religious customs. The community had no official organization, but its mutual aid institutions were developed to an extent rarely found in other Jewish communities. The homes were arranged in such a way that a Muslim visitor was unable to notice that the family observed Judaism.

Notes

"Folk Tradition about the History of the Meshhedi Jews" originally was published in Hebrew in *Dappe Zikkaron liR'fael Aharonoff* (Jerusalem: Heshvan, 1945), pp. 35–38, and as an offprint, as part of *Historical Traditions and Mortuary Customs of the Jews of Meshhed* (Jerusalem: Palestine Institute of Folklore and Ethnology, 1945), pp. 5–8, with an English summary on pp. iv–vi.

1. Cf. Wilhelm Bacher, "Les Juifs de Perse au xviie et au xviiie siècles d'après les chroniques poétiques de Babaï b. Loutf et de Babaï b. Farhad," *Revue des études juives* 51 (1906):121–36, 265–79; 52 (1906):77–97, 234–71; 53 (1907):85–110; Walter J. Fischel, "Toldot Y'hude Paras bIme Shoshelet haSafavidim . . . " [History of the Jews of Persia under the Safavid dynasty . . .], *Zion* [Jerusalem] 2 (1937):273–93.
2. Cf. Fishchel, "Toldot Y'hude Paras."
3. According to Walter J. Fischel, "Q'hillat haAnusim b'Faras" [The Marrano community in Persia], *Zion* 1 (1936):50, the Jewish community in Meshhed was established by Nadir Shah in 1734, which date seems improbable since Nadir Shah came to power only in 1736 (*Encyclopaedia of Islam*, old ed., s.v. Nadir Shah).
4. Cf. *Encyclopaedia of Islam*, old ed., s.v. Mashhad; *Cambridge Modern History*, 13 vols. (Cambridge, 1902–11), 6:307, 524.
5. Cf. Fischel, "Q'hillat haAnusim b'Faras," pp. 53ff., on the legend concerning the libel.

12. Marriage among the Marranos of Meshhed

I. The Age of Marriage

In Persia, as in all the countries of the Middle East, boys and girls were married off at a very tender age. Especially in well-to-do families, where the considerable expenses involved constituted no obstacle, the weddings were celebrated well before the onset of puberty. Among the Jews of Meshhed, marriages were arranged at an even earlier age than among their Muslim neighbors. This especially was the case with a girl, out of fear lest a Muslim come and ask for her hand in marriage for his son. For this reason they arranged the engagement of their daughters at the age of four to six years, and when the girl reached the age of nine or ten, they celebrated the wedding (Persian *arusi,* or Hebrew *qiddush*).

Occasionally a father would engage his daughter on the very day of her birth, as was practiced in talmudic times.[1] The same custom was practiced in other Middle Eastern Jewish communities as well, e.g., among the Jews of Afghanistan,[2] as well as among the Arabs, e.g., the fellahin of Palestine.[3] It also was customary among the Muslims in Persia to engage children while they lay in their cradles, or even before birth.[4] Among the Jews of Meshhed, such an engagement of a girl on the day of her birth had no legal validity unless both the girl and the boy to whom she was betrothed consented in later years. Occasionally, if a father was downcast because a daughter instead of a son was born to him, a relative would comfort him, "Don't worry, she will be for my son." If the daughter objected after she grew up, the engagement was null and void, but usually the children did not refuse to follow their parents' wishes, and when the time came, they were duly wedded to one another. The father of one of my informants engaged his daughter in this manner on the day she was born. The boy who became her bridegroom was six years old at the time. After the children grew up, they married.

The general rule was to celebrate the wedding several years before the bride reached puberty, so that it did not signify the beginning of cohabitation, but had only legal and social significance. After the wedding the bride moved from her parents' house to that of the bridegroom's parents. The Jews of Meshhed believed that the girl must mature in the house of her husband's parents rather than in her own parents' home. If a girl reached puberty (ca. thirteen years of age) and was still in her parents' house, she was considered an old maid, a girl who "has remained in the house" (*khānah māndeh*).

It often happened that immediately after the wedding the young husband would embark on a lengthy commercial trip to other Persian cities or abroad (especially to Russia) and return only several years later, and only then did the couple begin to live together as man and wife. And even if the husband did not go on a voyage, regular sexual cohabitation began, in most cases, a few years after the wedding.

The arranging of a marriage (*numzad dāri* or *numzad kardan*) for a girl at the suitable age was a concern not only of the parents and close relatives, but of the community as a whole. Discussions with a Muslim who came to ask for the hand of a Jadidi girl could have caused unpleasantness and even brought danger for the whole community. Therefore, if the heads of the community saw that the parents procrastinated in arranging a marriage for their daughter, they would visit them, inquire into the situation, urge the father to arrange for the marriage as soon as possible, and, where needed, would give him financial aid. When the sister of one of my informants was about eight years old, the head of the community, Mullah 'Abdallah Aminoff, came one evening to his father's house and said to him, "You must have the wedding right away, lest the Muslims come and ask for your daughter for one of them!" Before the girl reached her ninth year, she was married. Her bridegroom was seventeen years old. This young woman gave birth the first time when she was sixteen. The passage of several years between engagement and marriage, and again between marriage and the first birth, was the general rule in the community.

II. The Choice of a Match

Marriages between close relatives, and especially between children of two brothers, which are customary among the Persian Muslims, as well as in the entire Middle East,[5] were practiced even more frequently among the Jews of Meshhed. The closest female relative (beyond, of course, the forbidden first degrees) was considered the natural match for a young man. A father who wanted to find a wife for his son would, first of all, look to a daughter of his other son, or the daughter of his own brother. The same factors which made for arranging the engagement and wedding at an early age induced them to choose a wife within the closest family. In the Marrano condition it was obligatory to maintain and strengthen the family ties so that the community constituted a strong, self-contained unit in the face of the constant dangers threatening it from the outside. In addition, the choice of marriage partners reflected the class differences which characterized not only the Meshhed Jews but Persian society in general: the rich people married only among themselves.

Housing conditions played a considerable role in these endogamous marriages. The young men remained living in their parents' houses after their marriages, so that paternal cousins and other paternal relatives who could become marriage partners grew up together. Moreover, members of the same extended family knew each other well, and the boy's parents were thoroughly familiar with the character and manners of the girl whom they considered as a match for their son. Financial arrangements also were easier for the parents of both the boy and the girl, for any assets that had to change hands as a result of the marriage would remain within the same extended family. In addition to all this, they subscribed to the view that a bride from the same family would be more devoted and faithful (*najīb*) to her husband than one from a strange family.

Several of my informants, when I asked them the reason for marriages between close relatives, replied with the same word which was their answer to my question concerning the reason for early marriage: *galut*—"exile." An old woman quoted a proverb in reply: "Home-baked bread is better than bread from the marketplace."

If the engaged couple lived in the same house, or, more precisely, in rooms opening into the same courtyard, certain modifications, albeit not significant ones, took place in the engagement and wedding ceremonies. These changes were due to the fact that the two families lived in close proximity.

III. The Engagement

In rich or well-to-do families, the mother began to prepare clothes and jewels for her daughter soon after she was born. A rich bride got from her parents a great number of dresses and other wearing apparel made of velvet and silk embroidered in gold and silver. The preparation of these embroidered dresses proceeded slowly, over the course of several years. It was generally held that the respect a woman would enjoy from her husband and his family was directly related to the amount of property she brought with her as dowry (*jehāz*; see below). For this reason, the women of the family busied themselves assiduously with the preparation of the dresses which constituted the main part of the *jehāz*.

The engagement among the Jews of Meshhed, as among the Jews and Muslims of Persia in general, was in fact a long series of ceremonies and rites, all of which had to be carried out before the engagement acquired legal validity and the couple was considered actually engaged to be married.

IV. *Zir dandāni:* Under the Tooth

When the parents of the boy found a girl whom they wanted to become their daughter-in-law, they would send one of their own relatives, either a man or a woman, to her parents in order to sound them out. This emissary was never a professional matchmaker, as was the *delāleh* among the Muslim Persians,[6] but always a member of the family, usually an old man who was used to doing good works, or an old and respected woman. With the first visit of this emissary began a long series of visits and ceremonies whose purpose was to bring the two families closer together. The first visit was supposed to find out how the girl's parents felt in general about her marriage, and whether they would reject the matter with some excuse, such as the tender age of their daughter. Only after several visits, with decent intervals between them, did the girl's parents finally give a definite answer about their willingness to give her to wife to the youth in whose name the emissary acted. As a token of his consent, the father of the girl gave the emissary a small lump of sugar; this custom provided the name for this phase of the engagement: *zir dandāni*, that is, the giving of a lump of sugar "under the tooth" of the emissary.

V. *Baleh giri:* Taking Yes

When the emissary came and informed the father of the boy that he had received the *zir dandāni*, the father got together a small group of people—

two, three, or more respected male relatives—and this delegation proceeded to the girl's parents in order to "obtain yes," that is, to get their explicit consent to the marriage. Only after this, too, had been accomplished did the task of the matchmaker (*khāzandeh*) begin. The *khāzandeh* was either a man or a woman who mediated between the two families the arrangements of all the details pertaining to the marriage.

VI. *Shirni girān* and *Shirni dādān:* Taking Sweets and Giving Sweets

One of the tasks of the *khāzandeh* was to set the date for the first meeting between the families of the bride and the bridegroom and to arrange all the particulars connected with this important event. This meeting took place in the bride's parents' home, and their name for it was *shirni dādān*, "giving sweets," while from the point of view of the groom's parents it was called *shirni girān*, "taking sweets." On the date set, ten or twenty men from the boy's family paid a group visit to the parents of the bride. The latter prepared a large quantity of candy and sweets, as well as a sugar cone (*kaleh qand*) for the occasion, keeping all this in an inner room so that when the guests arrived they saw no traces of any preparations made for their reception.

If the families involved were rich and respected, the heads of the community also participated in the *shirni dādān*. The master of the house received the guests in a friendly but dignified manner, and, first of all, greeted the head of the community with all of the respect due to his position. The initial conversation touched upon various subjects—for it would not have been seemly to broach the purpose of the visit right away—and then the head of the community would say to the father of the girl, "So-and-so, the son of so-and-so, sent us to ask for the hand of your daughter for his son." These words touched off a play of refusal whose form was firmly set by age-old custom. The expected first answer of the father was, "I cannot engage my daughter, she is too young." An additional request elicited the response, "I must, first of all, ask my father who is at present out of town," or "I must ask my uncle who lives in Teheran," or "my elder brother who is now in India," and the like. Each excuse of this kind had its proper answer delivered by the head of the community or another member of the delegation.

The opinion of the elder women also had to be heard in the *shirni dādān*. The bride's father, for instance, would say, "I must ask my mother." Then the old lady would be brought into the room and would be asked whether she consented that her granddaughter become engaged to so-and-so. Her usual answer was, "I do not know the young man." In a like manner all the relatives of the bride would be asked, and all gave a negative or non-committal answer. This gave the relatives of the groom ample opportunity to praise his looks, his fine nature, his intelligence and learning, and so on. At last the bride's father said yes, whereupon tablecloths were brought in and spread upon the rugs on the floor, and then the *shirni* was fetched and offered the guests. In addition to sweets there were various kinds of candied nuts, such as peeled and sugarcoated almonds (*noqlo badām*); round halvah with manna (*halva-i-gaz*),[7] and more of the like. The sugar cone was sent to the bridegroom's house.

Neither the bridegroom nor the bride were present at the *shirni dādān*. When the guests finished enjoying the sweets, the two families fixed the date for the official engagement ceremony, and then the guests took their leave.

VII. *Shirni khorān:* Eating Sweets

The official engagement ceremony was called *shirni khorān*, "eating sweets." This too took place in the house of the bride's parents, and the bride and groom were again absent. The period of time between the *shirni dādān* and *shirni khorān* was not fixed. They could take place one after the other, on the very next day, or several months could elapse between them. The latter was the case if the parents of the bridegroom needed time to prepare the presents, or if the father of the bride had to go out of town on a business trip.

On the morning of the day fixed for the *shirni khorān* the bridegroom, or, more precisely, his parents in his name, sent a *khancheh*, a square tray as big as a tabletop, laden with all kinds of gifts for the bride. The gifts, attractively arranged, comprised dresses, a coat, shoes, stockings, and the like, as well as gold and silver ornaments and the inevitable sweets. The parents of the bride, on their part, prepared a meal of sweets for the guests and also invited a group of musicians (*sāzendeh*). The musicians were Muslims, and their instruments consisted of drums (*dā'ireh*), tambourines (*danbaq*), flutes (*nay*), and six-stringed violins (*tār*).[8] The large orchestras were ten to fifteen men strong. The flutist occasionally played a solo piece.

The rejoicing at the *shirni khorān* reached its peak with the recitation of Psalm 121, "A Song of Ascents." "I will lift up mine eyes unto the mountains, from whence shall my help come?" The mullah was honored with the reading of this psalm, with which the engagement became a legally accomplished fact.

Although the engagement was also called by the Hebrew name *qinyan* (pronounced by them *gönyan*), no formal *qinyan*, a binding agreement between the parties by the handing over of an object, was made. Nor were *t'naim*, literally, "conditions"—a formal wedding agreement or nuptial contract—written.

The joyful company did not break up until late at night, when some of the sweets were sent to the bridegroom's house so that he too should be able to enjoy them. The party which took the sweets to the bridegroom was accompanied by lanterns (*shām lāleh*), which were candles within lily-shaped glass enclosures.

Most of the details of the *shirni khorān* as described above also were observed by the Muslim Persians, so that the Jadidis were able to celebrate it openly, without having to hide anything from the Muslim servants who worked in their houses, or from their Muslim neighbors. The main difference between the Muslim and the Jadidi *shirni khorān* lay in the sex of the participants. Among the Muslims only the women of both families participated in it,[9] while among the Jadidis both men and women took part, although they sat separately, as was the general custom on all festive occasions. In another version of the *shirni khorān*, found among the Jadid al-Islam, even this difference had disappeared, and only women participated in it, while for the menfolk a second *shirni khorān* was given on another day, at which the bridegroom and his friends also were present. In days past, a game of dolls was held at the *shirni khorān* in a women's room.

VIII. *Dāmād khān barān:* Invitation of the Bridegroom

Some time after the *shirni khorān*, the parents of the bride invited the bridegroom to their house. This was the first time that the bridegroom entered his bride's house. This visit too was the occasion for a festive meal attended by a large group of men from the bridegroom's side. The bride's parents gave the bridegroom a present, in most cases a tray laden with suits of clothes and a gold watch. There were some who, instead of suits, gave the bridegroom fine material, from which he had a suit custom made.

IX. From Engagement to Wedding

According to a custom observed all over the Middle East, the bridegroom was not allowed to see the bride until the day of the wedding. Among the Jadid al-Islam the bride was even forbidden to speak with any of the groom's male and female relations. The observance of this custom was considered a matter of honor for the bride. However, it presented some difficulties in the normal routine of life if the families of the bride and the groom were related and dwelt in one courtyard. If the bride sat in the courtyard and saw, for instance, that the groom's mother came out of her door, she had to hide, and in most cases she fled in confusion into her own house, to her mother's room.

It often happened that the bridegroom left for another city or went abroad in connection with his business immediately after the *shirni khorān* or the *dāmād khān barān*. In this case, of course, no incidental encounter could take place between him and his bride. One of my informants, for instance, went to Russia after his engagement (when he was fourteen years old!) and remained there, with short interruptions, until his wedding, which took place seven years later, when he was twenty-one and the bride fourteen. In the course of those seven years, he returned to Meshhed only once in a year or in two years for short visits.

Immediately after the *shirni khorān* the bride, even though still a child, had to begin to wear the veil (*maqna'ah*) with which the Meshhed women covered themselves while at home. However, modesty demanded that the bride should not show herself to the groom even when covered by the *maqna'ah*, and that she hide from him so that he should not see even the clothes she was wearing.

Custom also required that during the long years between engagement and wedding the bridegroom send the bride, for every holiday, and especially for Purim, Passover, and the fifteenth of Sh'vat, a large round tray (*majmu'eh*) with clothes, ornaments, and sweets.

X. *Otaq kardan* and *Numzad Bazi:* Making Room and Bride Play

On a few rare occasions between the engagement and the wedding, the bride and groom were given an opportunity to spend a few minutes together, and to do so without the presence of a third person. The parents of the bridegroom would invite the family of the bride once, and on that occasion they "made room" for the two young people. At other times one of the relatives invited both families and the bride and groom were enabled "to make room" in his house. The manner in which this brief ritualized togetherness took place was as follows. They put the bride and the groom in a room, locked the door, and left them alone in it for about a quarter of an hour. During that time the couple sat side-by-side, the groom gave the bride the present which he had brought for her (for each *otaq kardan* the groom had to bring a gift of jewels or gold coins), and he asked her to remove the veil which covered her face, or, if he had enough courage, he lifted it himself. Modesty and good manners required that the bride sit all the time without making any movement, with her eyes closed, and without uttering a single word. If the groom dared to kiss the bride, and she, in her childish innocence, later told it to her mother, no more *otaq kardan* was allowed, and the bride's parents did not let the groom even see her until the wedding day. But if the groom behaved properly, he could meet the bride in this way several times.

Occasionally the bridegroom would ask the bride to look at him and to answer his questions, but only rarely did he succeed in persuading her to behave contrary to custom. These first attempts at approach between bride and groom were called *numzad bāzi*, "bride play."

If the couple did not come out of the room on its own initiative after the fifteen minutes were over, the parents of the bride would knock on the door and say, "Come out, quickly!" The young couple then had to emerge from the room shamefacedly and in confusion, to the merriment of the assembled guests. Rich families also invited musicians for the *otaq kardan*.

Although the *otaq kardan* was an established custom, nevertheless the parents of the bride usually gave it the appearance of a special favor they did for the bridegroom. This being the case, the groom used to bring presents not only to the bride herself, but also to her parents. In most cases these were sweets, but occasionally some silver object, which he would give, for instance, to her grandmother as an inducement to let him meet the bride.

The practice of the *otaq kardan* among the Jews of Meshhed was symptomatic of the generally less stringent restrictions among them on contact between men and women in comparison with the rules obeyed by their Muslim neighbors. While among the Jews this custom enabled bride and bridegroom to meet at least occasionally in an approved fashion during the long period between the engagement and the wedding, no such possibility was available to Muslim engaged couples. For example, Nurullah Khan describes quite enthusiastically in his autobiographical notes that, after he became engaged in 1877, on one single occasion his mother made extraordinary arrangements to enable him to see his betrothed through a hole in a curtain.[10] Only in the very week of the wedding (when, according to the rules, the groom was still not allowed to see the bride) was he able, with her help, to sneak in to her occasionally. The Muslims called this *nāmzat bāzi*, that is, "play of the engaged (couple)."[11] Both the Jewish and the Muslim customs are reminiscent of the old Jewish custom which was practiced, according to the Talmud, in Judea but not in the Galilee in tannaitic times. Rabbi Y'huda said, "In Judea, at first they let groom and bride be together alone for a short while [prior to their entering the huppa, i.e., prior to the wedding ceremony], so that he should not be shy toward her, but in the Galilee this was not practiced."[12]

XI. *Bāshlaq barān:* Sending the Bride Price

When the parents of the bridegroom decided that the time had come for celebrating the wedding, they informed the bride's parents by sending them a special present. This was done one or two months before the wedding. This present was called *bāshlaq*, "gift" or "donation."[13] The *bāshlaq* was, in fact, the bride price which the groom paid to the bride's parents. According to my informants, this custom was adopted by the Jadidim from the Muslims after the forced conversion of 1839. Among the Muslims the *bāshlaq* was considered a payment rendered to the bride's mother for having suckled her as an infant. In accordance with this view, the Muslim Persians termed the bride price *shīr bahā*, "milk price."[14]

Soon after the custom of *bāshlaq barān* became established among the Jadidim, the heads of the community issued a decree limiting to 150 qarān the amount the parents of the bridegroom, whether rich or poor, could send to the parents of the bride.[15] The regulation was, in general, obeyed, and if it nevertheless happened that a rich bridegroom sent a larger amount, the family of the bride considered it an insult, as if it would indicate that they were poor and needed the money. In the late 1890s, when an elder brother of one of my informants got married, his parents sent 250 qarān instead of the 150. The bride's parents became angry, for they looked at this as a slight on their honor, and the quarrel over the matter lasted several months. After World War I, however, the regulated *bāshlaq* fell into disuse, and every family sent as much as it wanted.

On the other hand, if the parents of the bridegroom sent no *bāshlaq* to the parents of the bride, the latter refused to celebrate the wedding. They would say, "You sent us no *bāshlaq*; how can we have a wedding?"

The gold wedding ring which was part of the *bāshlaq* was wrapped into a thin silk handkerchief (*dastmāl kasari*) made in Yezd. The little bundle was placed into the middle of a large copper plate (*b'shqāb*). Around it were arranged sweets, and especially candied sugar and a sugar cone, as well as other sweets and fruits. All these were covered by a tray cover (*khancheh pūsh*), and thus the tray was sent to the bride's house. According to one of my informants, they sent four plates full of candy, cookies, tea, and other things.

In the richest families the mother would distribute the *bāshlaq* money, or part of it, among the poor. The less well-to-do used it to defray the expenses of the wedding, such as payment to the seamstresses who sewed dresses for the bride from the materials sent by the groom, the purchase of jewelry for the bride, and the like. From part of the money the bride's father used to buy a suit, or material for a suit, for the bridegroom. He would invite the groom to go with him to the bazaar to choose a piece of material he liked, and then bought it for him and gave it to a tailor to sew it up.

XII. *Salāḥ binān:* Consultation

A week or two before the wedding, the father of the bride would invite several of his relatives, as well as relatives of the bride, for a consultation (*salāḥ binān*) concerning all the particulars of the wedding. Since several hundreds of guests were invited to the wedding feast, the house of the family was not always suited to accommodate such a large-scale banquet. Therefore, the first thing to be decided at the *salāḥ binān* was where the banquet was to be held. In most cases the solution was to decide on the house or the courtyard of one of the rich relatives. It was also necessary to prepare a list of those to be invited. The list was written with black ink (*murakkab*), and hence its name, *si'ī,* from si'ah, "black." The list would occasionally comprise two hundred or even more names.

At the same time, the women would hold a consultation concerning the invitation of women. Since the women were unable to write, they called in an old woman of the family and asked her to be the inviter—*adam talk,* literally, "people inviter." If the woman accepted the task, she brought along with her yellow peas (*nokhōd*) tied in her veil. The women of the house called out names to her, saying, "Invite So-and-so, her daughter, her sister, etc." After listening to each name, the inviter would transfer one pea to another place in her veil, or, temporarily, to her hand. When all the names were enumerated, the woman would repeat them, returning one pea with each name. In this manner she knew that she remembered all the names. When she went from house to house to deliver the invitations, she took the peas along with her, and after each invitation she put one pea into a different part of her veil. When all the peas were thus transferred, she knew that she had delivered all the invitations without forgetting any of them.

A third important matter which had to be decided in the men's consultation was the date of the wedding. Not at any time and any hour could a wedding be celebrated. First of all, there were certain periods in the year in which Jewish law did not allow weddings, such as the 'Omer days between Passover and Pentecost (with the exception of the new moon of Sivan and the thirty-third day of 'Omer), and the days of mourning from the seventeenth of Tammuz to the ninth of Av. In addition, no weddings could take place, according to Muslim law, during the whole two months of Ramadhan and Muḥarram. If no suitable place could be secured for the wedding, one also had to take the weather into account: in the summer, weddings could be celebrated in a courtyard in the open air, but in the winter the tables had to be set inside the house. For this reason the poor people preferred to have weddings in the summer, while the rich, whose houses were spacious enough, had weddings in the winter as well. Finally, it was customary to have the wedding in the middle of the week, on a Tuesday or a Wednesday, but not on a Friday or on the eve of a holiday. In the following description, in order not to confuse the days, we shall assume that the wedding ceremony was held on a Tuesday. It must also be mentioned that, in contrast both to the Muslim custom and to that of the Kurdish Jews in the past,[16] it was not customary among the Jews of Meshhed to consult an astrologer for choosing a lucky day for a wedding, or for any other undertaking for that matter.

XIII. *'Aqd bandān:* Gentile Wedding

The family conference also had to decide on the manner in which the Muslim wedding, the *'aqd*, would be celebrated. In general, rich families invited the *mushtahed* (spelled *mujtahid*), the Muslim clergyman, as well as several *shaykhs* and other Muslim religious functionaries, to officiate at the wedding. The poor went to the mosque of Imam Reza and had the wedding there. The date for the Muslim wedding was, as a rule, three days before the Jewish wedding. (In this connection it is interesting to recall that among the Spanish Marranos in the Middle Ages the order was reversed: first they had the Jewish wedding and then went to the Christian church to celebrate the Christian nuptial.) For the Muslim wedding both the bride and the groom appointed a *vakīl*, a representative, and these two persons took care of the wedding formalities for and in the name of the couple. The Muslim wedding ritual was considered a ridiculous thing by the Jadidim, and when they described it to me they did so amid much laughter and merriment.[17] The witnesses, who of course were of the Jadidi community, signed their names on the Muslim marriage contract in Hebrew letters.

From the days of Reza Shah (r. 1925–41) the authorities were no longer satisfied with a Muslim religious wedding, but required the couple to appear before a notary in the marriage bureau (*maḥzar izdavāj*).

XIV. *Dīm vardārān:* Taking of Face

Two days before the wedding—that is, on Sunday if the wedding was set for a Tuesday—the women of both families gathered in the bride's house in order to carry out the *dīm vardārān*, "taking of face." This ritual involved beautifying of the bride by the removal of all hair, even the faintest and thinnest, from all over her body, and especially from her face and forehead. The women who came over from the bridegroom's house brought along the bath tray (*khancheh hamām*), which was a present of the bridegroom to the bride, to be used by her the next day when she went to the bath. The bath tray contained about fifty pieces of fragrant soap, for the bride and for all the women who accompanied her to the bathhouse; a large quantity of henna; perfumes; face powder; a richly decorated comb; a pair of wooden shoes; all kinds of utensils for the beautification of the body; and money for the expenses of the bath. All this, as well as sweets, was beautifully arranged on the bath tray and tied with a large kerchief (*khāncheh pūsh*).

The process of *dīm vardārān* was carried out by the *dīm vardār*, the "face taker," a woman who had this as her profession. In the Meshhed Jadidi community there were some four or five such women. They took care not only of the preparation of the bride on that day, but also of her beautification after the wedding, by removing the hair from her face, forehead, and body once a month, after her menses and before she went to immerse herself in the bathhouse.

To begin with, the *dīm vardār* tied a kerchief around the bride's head, pulling it tight over her hair. Then she took a small knife and with it she scraped downward the thin and short strands of hair which grow over the forehead just at the hairline. Then the groom's mother stepped up to the bride with a gold coin in her hand, pinched one of the short hairs between her nail and the coin, and thus plucked it out. Then she threw the coin into the lap of the bride and kissed her on the forehead. The coin then was given to the *dīm vardār*. The same act was performed by the other women after the groom's mother, and only after they all had their turn came the time for the *dīm vardār* to get to work seriously on the removal of the superfluous hair from the bride's body. She did this with the help of a thin thread. She first wetted it with water and then made of it a large loop which she twisted around several times. Next she pulled it along the bride's face, so that all the hairs which got caught between the two sides of the loop were plucked out. After the forehead and the face came the rest of the body, from which all hairs were thus removed, except, of course, the hair of the head, which was covered by the kerchief. Lucky was the bride who at the time of this operation had not yet reached puberty, for otherwise the *dīm vardārān* would have caused her considerably more pain.

In order to make the procedure easier for the bride, they gave her candy to eat, while the assembled women performed dances in front of her so as to entertain her.

The removal of all of the bride's body hair was practiced by the Muslim Persians as well. The account of it given by Nurullah Khan also apprises us of the belief underlying the custom: the bride was taken to the bath and there they painted her hair, hands, and feet with henna, and removed all her body hair very meticulously, because they believed that there was one single hair of the Angel of Death on the body of the woman, and if that hair remained in its place bad luck would come upon the whole family.[18]

XV. *Harzeh vazān:* Rude Things

The same day (Sunday) in the evening, they gave a meal in the house of the bride in which only women participated, especially the young friends of the bride. This meal was called *harzeh vazān*, "rude things," because there was great merriment as they cheered up the bride with all kinds of games and pranks, and there was no lack of licentious language. The latter, however, was more in evidence at the *harzeh vazān*, which was given at the same time in the bridegroom's house for men and his young friends. In the course of this gathering the more experienced relatives of the bridegroom made him understand, with hints and joking comments, the meaning of married life. The bride's relatives did the same for her at her meal.

XVI. *Arūsi hamām:* Bath of the Bride

Next day, Monday, at two or three o'clock in the afternoon, the bride was taken to the bathhouse for the ritual immersion. Before she left her parents' house her fingernails were carefully cleaned.

Until Hajji Y'hezq'el built them a bathhouse in the Jewish quarter, the Jadidim used one of the Muslim baths which were suitable as a *miqve* (ritual bath; also called *khazīneh*) from the Jewish halakhic point of view. Rich Jadidim would rent the whole bathhouse for the special use of the bride and her entourage, so that they should be able to perform all the rites of the immersion without being disturbed by the presence of strangers. This renting of the bathhouse was called *qoroq*, "special." The poor Jadidim who could not afford a *qoroq* sent the bride with her women companions to the bathhouse at a time when it was open for other women as well. Of course, in such a situation the Jadidi women had to be more careful about how they acted and what they said than in the presence of the female bath attendants alone, for the latter could be relied upon to keep quiet against the payment of sizable baksheesh.

The bride was taken to the bathhouse in a festive procession accompanied by musicians, and especially by players on a *danbaq*, or tambourine, and a *dā'ireh*, a round drum. Many women from the families of both the bride and the groom were invited to participate in this ritual procession. The women of the bride's family prepared and brought along all kinds of sweets, fruits, cakes, and milk dishes, as well as *kōkō sabzī*, a vegetable omelette, and *sherbet*, sweet drinks. The women's company spent at least three to four hours at the bathhouse, eating, drinking, and bathing, and returned home after sunset.

The bathing itself comprised several phases. The first was to wash in a tub full of warm water. Then came the immersion in a pool of cold water, which was the ritual *kasher miqve*. The water in the pool was very cold (in the winter it was even frozen over), and it was necessary to break the layer of ice in order to be able to submerge oneself in the water.

After this submersion, the *kīseh māl* went to work on the bride. She used a small bag (*kīseh*), with which she smeared a fragrant pasty cream called *lakhlakheh*, made of a powder mixed with water, all over the body of the bride. This rubdown took some fifteen or twenty minutes, after which the bride again entered the tub to remove the paste. As a result of this treatment, her whole body became clean, soft, and sweet-smelling. The fragrance of the *lakhlakheh* remained and enveloped her body for several days. (It should be mentioned here that the men, when they went to the bathhouse, were similarly treated by a male *kīseh māl*. This treatment, and the *mushtu māl* which followed it, were integral parts of every thorough bathing.) After this bath, the bride proceeded to the other room in the bathhouse in which she had left her clothes, and there, before she could get dressed, she had to undergo a treatment by the *mushtu māl* (masseuse).

After the massage, too, was finished, they painted the soles and the feet of the bride with henna, as a kind of preliminary to the elaborate painting with henna to which the whole night following that day was devoted.

Apart from this visit to the *hamām*, which was obligatory for the bride from the point of view of her ritual purity, there was a custom of taking her to the bath (*hamām barān*) about a month prior to the wedding. This was a way in which the groom's mother honored the bride. She invited the bride and several women from both families to the *hamām* for a joint bath. This ritual was observed only by the rich, who would rent the whole bathhouse for the occasion as a *qoroq*.

According to one of my informants, the bride went twice to the *hamām*: once on the day before the wedding (i.e., on Monday) when she was washed thoroughly, as described, and a second time on the wedding day itself (Tuesday), in the morning, for a simple immersion.

For comparison let us describe briefly the customs attendant to the bathing of the bride among the Muslim Persians. They made the bride sit on a saddle in the bathhouse, with her face turned toward Mecca, and with all the knots in her clothes loosened. In front of the bride they placed a mirror and a comb, and before the mirror they put and lighted two candles. A white sheet was draped over her head, sweets were put into her mouth, and two lumps of sugar were rubbed together over her head so that the powder should fall on it. In order to increase her luck, they performed yet another rite: a woman would take a needle and thread it with a thread made of seven thin colored threads twisted together, and with this thread she would sew back and forth several times through the sheet with which the bride's head was covered. Spices were strewn into the fire which was lit in the *hamām* in order to fill the place with a good fragrance.[19]

XVII. *Dāmādi hamām:* Immersion of the Bridegroom

On Tuesday, in the morning, the bridegroom would go to the *hamām* in the company of his friends. The men too were given sweets, and the bridegroom underwent a treatment by a male *kīseh māl* and a male *mushtu māl*, in a manner similar to that of the bride.

XVIII. *Hanā bandān:* Henna Tying

The night before the wedding day (i.e., the night between Monday and Tuesday) was the night of the henna, or *Hanā bandān*, "henna tying." The long and dark corridor which led from the street to the courtyard of the houses of the Jadidim was lighted up for that occasion with many candles and lamps. A watchman was seated before the gate of the house on a low chair, with a lamp in his hands in order to show the way to the approaching guests. Men and women did not mingle in this festivity either, and the father of the bride arranged for suitable places for men and women to gather in separate groups. The whole courtyard was illuminated with lamps (*lāleh*). Musicians, too, were invited, as well as a group of two or three comedians or actors (*mōghallad* or *lūtī*), who occasionally would bring along a monkey, to the greater merriment of the people. These musicians and actor-comedians were Muslims. In past times they also had a performance of a puppet theater, in a manner similar to that of the engagement night.

The henna was brought by the women from the house of the bridegroom to that of the bride on the previous day, together with the bath tray. Red henna was used (the henna came in various shadings), and the fingertips of the bride were painted with it all around. Then white bandages were tied around her fingers—hence the name "henna tying"—and left there until the morning of the next day. Occasionally the bridegroom would send a round tray filled with small bags containing henna and candy to the bride's house on the very night of the henna. This gift was called *tabaq barān*, "sending of a tray."

On the other hand, on the night of the henna the family of the bride would send a large number of plates with sweets and candy to the groom, as well as material for a suit of clothes, and a pair of shoes. This gift was accompanied by some henna. The young man who carried the trays to the groom's house would dance with them. While this was going on, the bridegroom sat in a place of honor, surrounded by the elders of the community. He was considered a king. The gift-bearers also danced before him in the house. The middle of the bridegroom's palms were painted with henna. The festivities of the *hanā bandān* lasted at least until midnight.

XIX. The Clothes of Bride and Groom

No special clothes were worn for the wedding. Only the fact that both the bride and the groom wore new and luxurious clothes, made especially for the wedding, indicated that this was indeed a great day in their lives. However, the same clothes were worn thereafter on the holidays of the Jewish year.

The bride wore a *yāl*, a short jacket made of dark blue or red velvet (these two colors were the favorites in velvet clothes), with sleeves decorated with gold *gulduzi* (embroidery) with flowery patterns, and with beautiful buttons called *dogmeh*. From the hips down she wore a *shelvār*, a short skirt, also of velvet, which reached to the knees. From the knees to the ankles the *nezūmi* (trousers) were visible, likewise made of velvet and richly embroidered in gold around the legs. On her feet she wore *qorjeh sa‘rī* (shagreen shoes), in the Gruzinian (Gurji) fashion, made of green, rough, granular leather and shaped like slippers. They covered only the front part of the feet, had high tapering heels, and pointed toes bent up and back in a semi-circle. These were the best and most expensive shoes, the like of which are no longer produced today (1945). The head of the bride was covered with a golden kerchief, (*charqad zari*), to which were sewn small, round, and shiny sequins called *pulak* (literally, "fish scales"). Over all her clothes the bride wore the "prayer wrap" (*chādor numāz* or *maqna‘ah*), which covered her body from the top of the head to her feet.

Of all the clothes worn by the bridegroom, only the hat, the coats, and the shoes were visible. The hat (*kulāh*) was tall and conical, made of the black fur of unborn lambs. Under the *kulāh* he wore a sweat cap (*‘araqchin*). At his neck the shirt (*pirāhan*; pronounced *pirhan*) could be seen. A sleeveless cloak (*‘abā*) descended from his shoulders, open in front, or a cloak with sleeves (*chukhā*). Under this the bridegroom wore a long kaftan (*qabā*), also open in the front. Under the *qabā* he had on a smooth undershirt (*alkholoq*; literally, *alkhāleq*), with a broad and many-colored linen or silk hip belt (*shāli kamar*). On cold days the bridegroom (and men in general) worc also a *labādeh*, a long overcoat with sleeves, lined with cotton wool and quilted. The *labādeh* was worn under the '*abā* or the *chukhā*, but over the *qabā*. At the bottom, under these coats, one could see the trousers (*tombān*; pronounced *tanbān*). The bridegroom too was shod in *qorjeh sa'ri*.

XX. *Arūsi:* The Marriage

On the wedding day both the bride and the groom fasted until after the ceremony under the wedding canopy, the huppa. In the morning they removed the bandages which were tied on the evening before around the bride's henna-colored fingers. Then the bride was dressed in her festive red and blue velvet clothes with the rich embroidery. (After World War II they began to use, instead of these traditional clothes, a white dress.) The bride's hair was braided into thirty to forty thin braids, around which colored papers were tied. On her forehead they pasted small, round, shiny, confettilike metal disks (*zarak*) of various colors and sizes. They were to remain in place for several days. These disks were fixed to her forehead with wood glue (*zönj*) and were left until they fell off by themselves. Often they caused small irritations on the bride's sensitive skin. The application of the *zarak* was carried out by an old woman, who undertook it as a special task.

The huppa was set up in the house of the bride about the time of the *minḥa* (afternoon prayer). Since the huppa was the most visible *Jewish* ritual in all the wedding festivities, they conducted it in secret, in the presence of only a few invited guests. Until the guests assembled, the bride and the groom sat side-by-side. One of the guests approached them, held out a mirror in front of the bridegroom, and said to him, ''Look, what do you see in the mirror?'' or words to this effect. The bridegroom looked into the mirror and saw in it his veiled bride.

After a minyan (ten adult men) gathered, they locked the door so that no non-Jew should be able to witness the proceedings, and spread a tallit (prayer shawl) over the heads of the bride and the groom. When the couple stood under the huppa, they threw coins (*shābash*) at them. These coins were later given to the musicians. Four to six men held the corners of the tallit over the head of the couple. The mullah, i.e., the person who functioned as a rabbi, recited the traditional Seven Benedictions and the blessing over the wine. Then the groom and the bride each took a sip of the wine, after which the wineglass was wrapped in a kerchief and the groom threw it to the floor and thus broke it. Since in many cases the floor of the room was covered with rich rugs, the groom did not throw the glass on the rugs, but hurled it through the window into the courtyard. But if a non-Jewish serving woman happened to be in the courtyard, the bridegroom did not throw the glass there, but

Hebrew marriage contract from Meshhed, 1784. 60 × 69 cm. Courtesy of Farajullah
Aminoff, Jerusalem

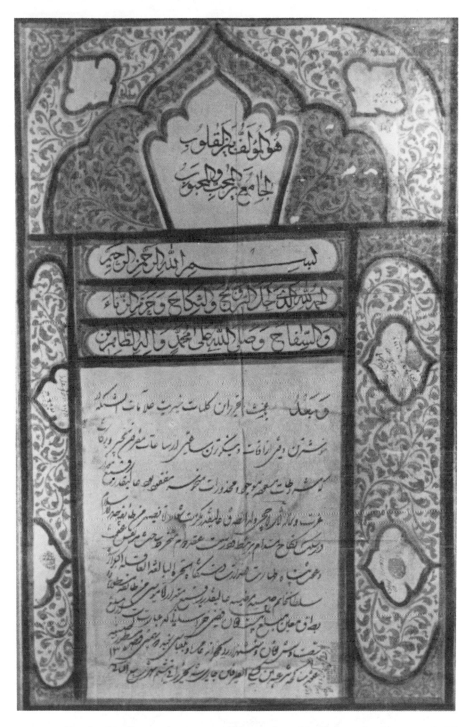

Persian Muslim marriage contract of a member of the Marrano Jewish community of Meshhed, 1306 H (1888/89). Witnesses' signatures in Hebrew. 43 × 66 cm. From the author's collection; gift of the family of Farajullah Nasrullayoff, Jerusalem

Hebrew marriage contract from Meshhed, 1902. 67 × 23 cm. Courtesy of Farajullah Yakuboff, Jerusalem

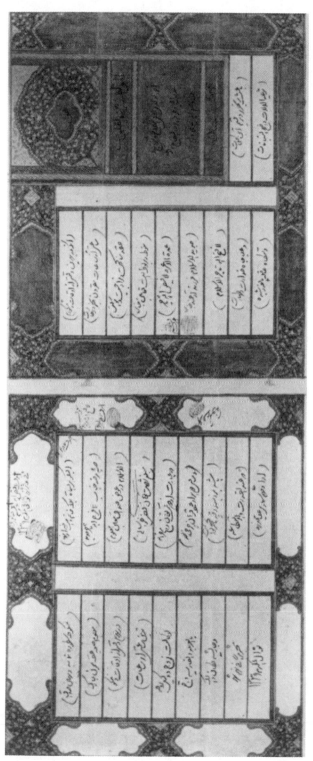

Persian Muslim marriage contract of a member of the Marrano Jewish community of Meshhed, 1339 H (1920/21). Witnesses' signatures in Persian. 58 × 24 cm. Courtesy of Farajullah Yakuboff, Jerusalem

broke it in the room, near the wall, next to the broom. The moment the glass broke the people present cried, *Mazal tov*—"Good luck!" Some of them added, "Thus should break your enemies and the enemies of Israel!"

After the breaking of the glass, the mullah read out the text of the *ketubba*, the marriage contract.[20]

The tallit under which the wedding ceremony was held was a present from the bride to the groom. The bride embroidered its four corners with a gold thread. When the couple moved out from under the huppa, those present showered them with candy and sweets. Then the bride and groom, who had fasted up to that time, had a meal consisting of chicken and meatballs, and then part of the assembled guests accompanied the groom to his house.

Immediately after the wedding ceremony, they brought a printed copy of the Five Books of Moses to the bridegroom's house on a tray which also held a jar full of water, candy, and a mirror. At the same time they also sent, from the bride's house to that of the groom, the bedding which the young couple was to use in the first night of their married life.

XXI. *Majles:* Banquet

Now came the main banquets of the wedding, one in the bride's house for the women, and one in the groom's for the men. If the wedding took place in the summer, they spread rugs on the brick-paved courtyard of each house, and upon them placed mattresses as seats. In front of the mattresses was spread a long white piece of linen, measuring thirty or more meters long and one meter wide, taking up practically the whole length of the courtyard. This linen, called *sufreh* (long tablecloth) served as both table and table-cloth. If the number of guests was great—and there were Jewish weddings in Meshhed in which several hundred guests were invited to the banquet—they either set up two rows of mattresses with a *sufreh* in front of each or arranged two rows of mattresses with one *sufreh* between them, with one row of mattresses along the wall. In this case the elders and honored members of the community would be seated next to the wall so that they could lean against it, while the youths and children sat opposite them on the other side of the *sufreh*. Along the whole length of the tablecloth they placed large numbers of colored candles, both for light and for decoration. Above the heads of the guests they stretched a long rope across the courtyard, from which they hung glass-enclosed lamps and paper-covered lanterns.

The preparation of a sumptuous meal for a hundred or more guests required careful planning. For several days before the banquet, large-scale food purchases were made by the two parental couples, each for its own banquet. They bought meat, rice, vegetables, fruits, sugar, and many more ingredients needed for the dishes and the sweet drinks. A task of considerable difficulty was to collect enough pots, pans, plates, and tableware from relatives and friends for the large number of guests invited. The serving, too, had to be organized. The cooking itself was entrusted to expert cooks (*āshpaz*), who labored for several days. The *āshpaz* were non-Jewish men, and their number, for a large banquet, reached ten to fifteen. In the large houses of the Meshhed Jews there was no lack of space—the entire ground floor was taken up by kitchens and storerooms—so that there was enough room for the cooks and for a requisite number of servant girls, also non-Jewish, whose task it was in the main to wash the used dishes while the meal was going on and to do other cleanup jobs. The vegetable dishes were prepared in their entirety by the non-Jewish cooks, but the meat reached their hands only after the women of the house rendered it *kosher* in the traditional Jewish manner.

A large group of young men from both families undertook the important task of serving the food to the guests in the groom's house and of removing the used plates from the tablecloth to the kitchen. In the bride's house, the same tasks were taken care of by young girls. Thus both banquets were strictly one-sex affairs. The groom's father directed the voluntary waiters, assisted by five or six men from among his closest friends, issuing an incessant flow of instructions as to whom and what to serve. When the waiters saw that the plate in front of a guest was empty, they instantly filled it again with a large perforated ladle (*kafgir*) In the bride's house, her mother and her friends managed the banquet in a similar manner.

The food was taken from the kitchen to the tablecloth on large copper trays. In front of every two guests a joint plate (*da'uri*) was placed. It was filled with a mixture of cooked rice and chicken meat (*pelau; pilau*), with half a chicken per *da'uri*, as well as mutton. The *pelau* was eaten with the fingers, without any utensils. After the *pelau*, the waiters served the *sherbet*, a cold drink made with sugar, *hel* (cardamom seeds), which gave it a pleasant aroma, various fruits, such as lemon and melons, saffron, and so on. In the summer they put also pieces of ice into the *sherbet*, which was served in wide and deep cups (*tās*), from which it was spooned up with wooden ladles (*qāshaq chūbī*), two of which were provided for each *tās*. They also served *arak*, a strong drink made of raisins. After the *sherbet* they served seven *khoroshi*, which were dishes of vegetable with meat—whence the name of the wedding banquet menu, *pelau hafkhoroshi*, i.e., *pelau* with seven *khoroshi*. The *hafkhoroshi* were served as seven separate dishes, each of which consisted of meat and a different kind of vegetable or fruit.

1. *Khorosh nokhod*, with peas
2. *Khorosh qormeh sabzi*, small pieces of fried meat with fried vegetables and onions
3. *Khorosh bāden jān*, eggplant
4. *Khorosh beh*, quinces
5. *Khorosh sib*, apples
6. *Khorosh ālu*, plums
7. *Korosh livās* (literally, *rivās*), a kind of rhubarb which was described as ''juicy and sour; sweet at the bottom near the roots and sour at the top, and very widespread in Iran''

Occasionally, instead of the *khorosh livās*, they served *khorosh kangar* (artichokes). These were described as ''similar to lettuce, have thorns, and only the thick central part is eaten.''

If the seven *khoroshi* were served, no mutton was added to the *pelau*, but only the half of a chicken for each *da'uri*. The same dishes were served at weddings among the rich Muslims, except that they used butter and *leben* (a kind of sour milk) for cooking.

Musicians were invited to this banquet, too, and in an even greater number than to all the preceding rites. Usually they hired a drum band (*sāzeh balabān*) consisting of at least twelve men. Accompanied by this band, the young friends of the bridegroom executed dances in one corner of the courtyard in order to cheer him up. The adult men and the elders said words of moral instruction and delivered homilies, and alternatingly the whole company sang wedding songs. Only after this had been going on for quite a while did the groom's father announce that the serving of the meal was about to begin, and at that time the last-minute preparations for serving the *pelau* were made in the kitchen. These preparations took, in general, about half an hour, after which the servers began by bringing jars of water with large bowls and towels, holding them for each guest to enable him to wash his hands. Then the *pelau* was brought out, and the meal began.

XXII. *Arūs kashān:* Bringing the Bride
(or *Lāleh kashi*—Bringing the Lamp)

When the banquet was finished at about midnight, the father of the bridegroom sent the musicians, together with twenty to thirty young men, to the house of the bride to fetch her. As this deputation was arriving at the bride's house, the members of her family brought her out, surrounded by a crowd of women. Then the procession set out with many lamps and torches, especially around the bride. When the sound of music indicated that the procession was approaching the bridegroom's house, he too left his house in the company of his family and friends, so as to meet the bridal procession in the street.

When the two processions had approached to a distance of about a hundred meters, they seated the bride and the groom on chairs in the middle of the street, while the guests lined up along the two sides. The bridegroom's parents then said to the bride's group, "Bring the bride a little nearer!" The answer was, "No, you bring the bridegroom nearer!" One side pushed the chair with the bride a step forward, and the other side did the same with the chair on which the bridegroom sat, and so the bridal couple was gradually brought nearer, step-by-step. Suddenly, when they were quite near, the company of the bride (or of the groom) would say, "You did not bring the bridegroom (or the bride) near enough," and thereupon they would move the bride (or the bridegroom) back a little distance. When the company of the bridegroom (or the bride) saw this, they too took him (or her) back, until the distance between the couple was again as great as in the beginning. This game was repeated several times, until finally they let the bride and groom approach each other. Then both would get up from their chairs, and at that moment the guests, and especially the young men and the children, began to fire toy guns, send up firecrackers, and let go colored balloons under which there were lamps with cotton wool, and more of the like.

Now the father of the bridegroom stepped up to the young couple, took the bride's hand, put it into the hand of the groom, and pronounced a blessing, "Be happy, be good, have much luck." And since it was always possible that Muslims were nearby, since Muslims lived even in the *'ēdgāh*, the Jewish quarter itself, one of those present would remember and say, "Recite a *Ṣalāt*," a brief Muslim prayer. Also, when they passed by the house of a Muslim they would say in a loud voice, "He who loves the religion of Muhammad should mention his name."

The bride and groom kissed the hands of their parents, and then the groom again took the bride's hand in his and led her into the house, followed by the guests. At the moment when the couple reached the door of the house, a lamb or chicken was slaughtered as a *kappara* (atonement) for the bride who entered the bridegroom's house for the first time. The blood of the animal was allowed to flow to the floor so as to make a line in front of the threshold, and the couple stepped over the line as it entered the house. This sacrifice was called *qodom* (foot), for it served as an atonement for the foot of the bride, i.e., the entrance of the bride into the groom's house. The meat was distributed among the poor.

There were some who, for fear of the Muslims, carried out the game of approach and withdrawal not in the street, but in the courtyard of the bridegroom's house, after the procession bringing the bride had arrived there. In any case, it was customary to shoot with toy guns and to let fly fireworks similar to bombs at the moment the procession arrived at the groom's house. They also set off *aftau māhtau* (literally, "sunlight moonlight"), which were firecrackers of various colors and shapes, and let several *fānūsi franji* (European lamps) rise up slowly into the air over the guests' heads. These "lamps" were paper globes under which they lighted a candle, so that as the air in them warmed up they rose up, like miniature hot-air balloons. All these fireworks were tended to by a special expert. In the courtyard they also lighted a *hizam* (bonfire) of dry twigs and danced around it. The groom's party stood on one side and the bride's on the other, with the bonfire in between. Here too they took the bride and the groom back and forth, to and from each other, with many jocular requests and refusals. Many of the young men would leap across the fire in their exuberance.

As a comparison to the Jewish custom, let us again refer to Nurullah Khan's description of the Muslim wedding procession. The men gathered in a hall in the bride's house, and the women in the women's rooms. Sherbet was served, and then tea and a *narghilah* (water pipe). When the bride was ready to go, the men formed a procession, after which came a second procession of the women of both families, who surrounded the bride seated on a richly caparisoned Bahrein donkey. However, the bride's father and mother remained at home. The moment the bride left the house her youngest brother gave her some bread, salt, and cheese tied in a kerchief. Before the bride walked a man who held a mirror turned toward her face in his hands. On the way, women of her family repeatedly held up the procession demanding presents, which had to be given to them by the groom's family. When the bride approached the groom's house, the women in her entourage stopped and declared that they would not go on until the bridegroom appeared. The groom, upon hearing the approaching sound of music and the noise of the fireworks, would leave his house and go to receive his bride. When the women saw him they cried, "We have received you! You have made great exertions!" Then the bridegroom turned around and thus led the bridal procession back to his house. When the procession reached the street in which the groom's house was located, his family sacrificed five lambs in order to avert the evil eye, and the procession passed between the lambs' bodies on one side and their heads on the other. The meat was distributed among the watchmen, the musicians, and others.[21]

XXIII. The Union

But to return to the marriage customs of the Meshhed Jews: when the bride and the groom entered the room in which their union and first cohabitation was to take place, the groom tried to step on the foot of the bride. If he succeeded, it was believed he would realize the words of the Bible, "and he shall rule over thee" (Gen. 3:16). But the bride, who was warned in advance by her mother and older girl friends, tried to prevent him from doing so. Nurullah relates that his bride tried to step on his foot, but he avoided her and managed to step on her foot, so as to rule over her all his life.[22]

In the wedding chamber the groom and the veiled bride sat down side-by-side, but they were still not alone. Several of the family members entered with them; they took the mirror which was brought to the groom's house, together with the cup of water and the printed copy of the Tora, and held up the mirror before the couple. Then it was time for the bride to lift her veil, and she and the groom looked at each other for the first time in the mirror—so that their lives might be as bright and shining as the mirror. This custom was called *ayneh Tora*, "mirror Tora."

The groom's father then opened the Tora at random and read a few lines from the top of the page. Next the groom's mother opened the book the same way, and since women in general could not read, again the groom's father read a few lines for her at the top of the page. This rite was a kind of augury, in order to know what kind of life awaited the young couple. But almost every passage in the Tora could be given a favorable meaning.[25]

This was followed by a presentation of various sweets, especially sugared almonds, to the bride. She took the sweets into the palm of her hand, and the groom picked one candy directly out of her hand with his mouth and ate it. Then the mother of the groom took a candy in the same fashion from the bride's hand, and, following her, the other relatives of the groom did likewise. This custom was called *kaf dasi nabāt* (sugar from the palm of the hand), and its purpose was to make sure that the bride would bring sweetness into the house of the bridegroom. From the moment the groom's relatives ate the sweets from the hand of the bride, she was again allowed to speak to them. Then the bridegroom, too, took sweets into his hand, and the bride ate one candy from his hand. Everybody stood up while this eating went on. A few minutes later, all those present would leave the room, and bride and groom were finally left alone.

Some ten or twenty experienced women from both families, however, would sit down in front of the closed door of the wedding chamber. They were termed *yengeh* (witnesses), and they incessantly emitted the high trilling sound of *lu-lu-lu-lu-lu*, the typical Middle Eastern sound of female jubilation, produced by the rapid vibration of the tongue or the uvula. The stated purpose of this noisemaking was to prevent any sound from the wedding chamber from being heard outside. The women also had a popular tradition according to which the women had uttered this sound—or, more precisely, *Leah-Leah-Leah-Leah*—ever since Laban brought Leah, instead of Rachel, into the tent of Jacob. On that occasion the women wanted to warn Jacob by trilling *Leah-Leah-Leah-Leah*, but he did not understand them.

Since, in general, the bridegroom was a young boy without any sexual experience—even though both he and the bride received some jocular instruction at the *harzeh vazān* meal—the women witnesses had, in most cases, to wait until the morning for the bridegroom to emerge from the wedding chamber. Thereupon they would enter in order to see whether any blood was visible on the sheet or on the bride's gown. Often it happened, especially in times past, that because the bride was so young the first intercourse did not take place in the wedding night, but only much later, even several years later. Because of the very early marriages and the extremely strict supervision of the daughters it never happened—according to the unanimous testimony of all the informants—that a bride should be found not a virgin. The bloodstained sheet or gown was shown by the women to all the guests, and then the bride's parents would keep it. [24]

The custom of placing a mirror before the bridal couple was practiced among the Muslim Persians as well, and it is possible that the Jews of Meshhed adopted it from them. Nurullah Khan describes how he and his bride saw each other in the mirror which was placed before the bride. However, before she let him see her visage in the mirror he first had to give her an expensive present, a ring with a pearl set into it. [25] The same custom was followed by the Muslims in Meshhed: on both sides of the mirror in which the bride and groom caught the first glimpse of each other, there were burning candles, and in front of the mirror was placed a copy of the Koran with dishes of sweets around it. [26]

XXIV. The Day after the Wedding

Next morning (Wednesday), two or three friends of the bridegroom came to his house and took him first to the bath and then to the synagogue. In the synagogue all those present rose when the bridegroom entered, and they sang special songs in his honor. In general, they treated him as if he were a king, for the bridegroom was considered a king, a shah. If he knew how to pray, he functioned as the prayer leader both on that morning and at the services on the Sabbath three days later. If he were not versed in the art of the prayers, each of which had its own special melody, then his father or another relative took his place. On the Sabbath he was also called up as third to the reading of the Tora (after the Kohen and the Levite, who always have the first two places), and as he went up to the reading desk the people threw candy and sweets at him.

On the day after the wedding, the dowry was sent from the bride's house to that of the bridegroom. This was done in a procession, with as much pomp and circumstance as the family could manage. Many porters carried the bride's belongings and the dowry she received from her parents. This was an occasion for the bride's parents to parade the riches and variety of presents they gave their daughter and to show them demonstratively to the bridegroom and his family. For this reason they employed a large number of porters, each of whom carried much less than what he would have been capable of. At the head of the *jehāz* procession they sent the bride's clothes which had been prepared in the course of many years, and the clothes which they sewed for her from the fabrics given her by the bridegroom. Gold and silver jewelry was, of course, an integral part of the *jehāz*, which also contained all kinds of kitchenware, cooking utensils, tableware, and bedding (in addition to the set of bedding which was sent in advance for the wedding night). Furniture and furnishings, rugs, boxes to keep the clothes in, and so on also were sent. The porters usually were Muslims whose wives worked in the Jewish houses as maids, cooks, and servants. They were mostly from Seistan, for the people of Seistan were known to be good, quiet, and patient.

Among the Muslim Persians the *jehāz* was sent to the bridegroom's house on the very day of the wedding, before the arrival of the bride herself. Nurullah Khan relates that this was done on the afternoon of his wedding day. The procession of porters passed all the major streets of the town, so that everybody should see the riches of the presents. There were many pieces of furniture, such as cushions and featherbeds, gold-embroidered velvet curtains, lamps, candlesticks, copper and china vessels, cups and saucers for tea and coffee, and many other objects of utility and of luxury. All this was carried by the porters on large trays. The rugs and boxes full of the bride's clothes were carried by richly caparisoned mules, with bells hanging from both sides of their necks.[27] Jakob Polak, who spent several years in Persia in the 1850s, describes the *jehāz* in great detail. He remarks that these things remained the property of the wife, and the husband could in no way dispose of them. He comments also on the artificial lengthening of the procession of porters, by, e.g., loading empty boxes on the backs of the mules.[28]

XXV. *Shab-sūb:* The Night of the Repast

This day (Wednesday) too came to a close with a *majles* (festive meal) in the groom's house. This meal was called *shab-sūr* (night of the repast), and the main course was *slau nokhodau*, a rice and vegetable soup. In the course of this meal took place the *jehāz numai* (exhibition of the dowry). In a separate room they would set out everything sent from the bride's house, lifting up each object in turn to show it to the guests, and the groom's parents and other relatives would come to view each piece and to estimate its monetary value.

XXVI. The Seven Days of the Feast

Among the Muslim Persians it was customary for the bridegroom to refrain from touching the bride for three days after the first cohabitation. When the three days were up, the bride went to the *hamām* to immerse herself, and then she was again permitted to the bridegroom. In the beginning of their Marrano existence the Jadidim adopted this custom and considered the bride unclean for three days only. Only occasionally did it happen that the bridegroom's mother warned him on his wedding day, "For seven days you are not allowed to touch the bride!" During World War I a *hakham* (a learned man, rabbi) came to Meshhed from Samarkand in Turkestan, one Mullah Hezki by name (he died in 1944 in Jerusalem), and he introduced a very strict rule, prohibiting the bridegroom from touching the bride for fourteen days after the first cohabitation; that is, there were seven days of uncleanness and seven days of purification, exactly as observed at the time of the regular menses. The Jadidim, who always set store by family purity, accepted this stricture.

For seven days after the wedding, the bride and groom were not allowed to leave the house without a retinue. In general, they rarely went out of the house during that week, and if they did, a group of relatives and friends would accompany them. According to the Meshhedi view, the reason for this was the fear of demons.

During those seven days the bride and groom also were forbidden to do any work. Every day they put on new clothes, and the clothes which they wore they did not return to the *boqcheh*, the bundle tied in a large kerchief in which clothes were usually kept, but hung them from a rope in the room, because to fold up the garments and to tie them in the *boqche* was considered work.

After the festive week was over, workaday life began for the young couple, and the bridegroom often left immediately thereafter on a long business trip to another city or abroad. Nevertheless, for a whole year after the wedding the young wife was referred to as a "bride." During that year she wore the festive dresses in which she was clad during the wedding ceremony.

XXVII. Polygyny

Although polygyny was permitted according to both Muslim and Jewish law, only a very few Jews in Meshhed had more than one wife simultaneously. Only if the first wife was barren, or sick and bedridden for a long time, did the heads of the community occasionally give their consent to a man to marry a second wife. In those instances, each of the two wives had to have a separate room of her own.

One of my informants told me that, having had no children from his first wife, he wanted to marry a second one, but the leaders of the community did not permit it. And, although this lack of consent had only a moral force, it was strong enough to keep him from marrying a second wife despite his strong desire to have children.

XXVIII. Divorce

While polygynous marriages were very rare, divorce did not exist at all in the community. For more than a hundred years which were remembered firsthand or known secondhand by the old people in the community, there was not a single case of divorce. Mullah Hazqi of Samarkand wanted to allow divorce, but a veritable storm of protest arose, and the mullah had to back down. Nevertheless, his attempt to permit divorce was held against him, and he had to leave Meshhed, which he did by moving to Jerusalem.

XXIX. A Jewish Wedding Song from Meshhed

The language of the song below is typical of the Judeo-Persian spoken by the Jews of Meshhed. The italicized words are Hebrew terms and expressions, several of them taken from the Hebrew liturgy. The spelling of these words in the Meshhedi Jadidi script is entirely phonetic in the manuscript I had at my disposal; e.g., *ḥtn* (bridegroom) is spelled *ḥātān*; *Ysral* (Israel) is spelled *Yṣrā'īl*, etc. The expression *Ya'qub nabi* (or *navi*: "the prophet Jacob") shows Muslim influence; in Jewish sources Jacob does not have the title "prophet."

Wedding Song

Shadi *hātān*, mubārak bād,	You became a bridegroom, be blessed,
Hashem pushtu panāhat bād,	God behind you be your shield,
Tavīle omr hamrāhad bād,	Long life be with you,
Benik nāmi dar *Yisrael*	With a good name in Israel.
Shlah go' el shlah go' el!	Send the Redeemer, send the Redeemer!
Z' khut ne' eman Y' qutiel.	The merit of faithful Y'qutiel.
Hashem bāshad b'tō yāvar,	God be your helper,
Shavand khosh nūd pedar mādar,	Let father, mother rejoice,
Modām bāshi saro sarvar	Be always head, prince
Miane qom *Yisrael*.	In the people of Israel.
Shlah . . .	Send . . .
Nedā āmad ke yā Musa:	A vision came, O, to Moses:
B'gīr dar dast to in asa,	Take the staff in your hand,
Boro dar Mesr b'kon *nēs*-hā	Go to Egypt, make miracles
Barai qom *Yisrael*.	For the people of Israel.
Shlah . . .	Send . . .
Alām vāri bolandam kon,	Like a flag raise me up,
Agar zeshtam pasandam kon,	If I am ugly, choose me,
Agar talkhem cho qandam kon,	If I am bitter, make me like sugar,
Miane jāme *Yisrael*.	In the people of Israel.
Shlah . . .	Send . . .
Qadat chon sarv āzādast,	Your stature like a free cedar,
Rukhat chon mah khoda dādast,	Your face like the moon which God gave,
Choh Yusef shākh shemshādast,	Like Joseph, a cypress branch,
Shavi jabbār dar *Yisrael*.	Be a hero in Israel.
Shlah . . .	Send . . .
Khoda bāshad nigāh dārat,	God be your guardian,
Dehad pirūz dar har kārat,	Let Him give success in all your deeds
Bovad mādām sar dārat,	Let Him always watch your head,
V'ham bar qom Yisrael.	And also the people of Israel.
Shlah . . .	Send . . .
Shavad omrat choh *Ben Amram*,	Let your life be like the son of Amram,
Shavi del shād zefarzandan	Let your heart rejoice in sons
Choh Yaqub *navi* pordān,	Wise like Jacob the prophet,
Bekām(e) del dar *Yisrael*.	With heart's desire in Israel.
Shlah . . .	Send . . .

Hame yāran qam khārān,
Bebazm āyid sar dārān,
Sarūd khanīd sad hazārān,
Jamī qom *Yisrael*.

Shlah . . .

Z'khut Moshe uSh'mu'el,
Dar ayāmat shavad *go'el*,
Dar *bet hamiqdāsh shirā hādāsh*
Dar *Yisrael shlah go'el*.
Shlah . . .

B'siman tov shodī *hātān*,

Shavad yāvar tura sultān,
Shavi qaleb tovar shaytān,
Qavi bar din(e) *Yisrael*.
Shlah . . .

Besho khosh (nūd) behamzādat,
Nesībat in khodā dādeh
Tura hamrāh, feresdādeh
Hamān sultān *Yisrael*.
Shlah . . .

Dar in haft rūz to āzādi,
Ba bazm eysh bepardāzi,
Valī khod ra nayandāzi
Zerasme din(e) *Yisrael*.
Shlah . . .

Zahokme qadere yaktā
Ke tā yek sāl bā hamtā
Shavīd mashqūl bai eysh'hā,
Bebīnīd khēr dar *Yisrael*.
Shlah . . .

Khoda bāshād nazīre to,
Behamrāhe vazīre to
Shavad dōlat asīre to,
Shavī nām dār dar *Yisrael*.
Shlah . . .

Ayā *hātān*, toi qābel,
Omīd hāyat shavad hāsel,
Dar ayāmat shavad vāsel

All my friends and well-wishers,
The banquet guests and the princes,
Sing a hundred thousand songs,
The community of the people of
Israel.

Send . . .

The merit of Moses and Samuel,
In your days let the Redeemer be,
In the Temple a new song
To Israel send the Redeemer.
Send . . .

In a good sign you become a bride-
groom,
May the Sultan [God] be your shield,
Be victorious over Satan,
Strong in the religion of Israel.
Send . . .

Rejoice in your spouse,
The noble one, whom God gave
To be your spouse: she was sent
By the Sultan [God] of Israel.
Send . . .

In those seven days you are free,
Them you shall spend in joy,
But let yourself not fall away
From the law of the religion of Israel.
Send . . .

At the command of the only God
For one year with your spouse
Be busy with rejoicings,
See the good of Israel
Send . . .

God be your guard,
With your vezir [i.e., wife]
Let riches be captive to you,
Be a man of name in Israel.
Send . . .

O bridegroom, be capable,
May what you hope come to you,
In your days let there be and received

Daru *shefa b'Yisrael*.
  Shlah . . .

A gate of plenty in Israel.
  Send . . .

Arūsat kām dārat bād,
Shavad az qam delat āzād,
Khānahat rā konad ābād,
Benik nāmī dar *Yisrael*.
  Shlah . . .

May your bride give you satisfaction,
Let your heart be free of sorrow,
She will build your house,
With a good name in Israel.
  Send . . .

Hameh kāmi ziyek digar
Bebīnītān dar barābar,
Eysh(u) eshrat ham sarāsar;
Hunar mandān dar *Yisrael*.
  Shlah . . .

All the wishes of one from the other
May you see [fulfilled] in each other,
Joy and happiness all the time;
Be nimble in Israel.
  Send . . .

Shavid lāyek befarzāndān
Khoda tarsān vehūsh mandān;
Bebārad bar to chun bārān
Nemate hak dar *Yisrael*.
  Shlah . . .

Be worthy of sons
Who will fear God and will be wise;
May descend upon you like rain
The blessing of the God of Israel.
  Send . . .

Agar mā khod gonah kārīm
Shafā'at khāh basī dārim,
Choh Musā pishe haq dārim,
Nemitarsim zehij *mamzer*.
  Shlah . . .

If we commit sins
We have many mediators,
Like Moses before God we have,
We shall not fear any bastard.
  Send . . .

Daran ayām keh ū āyad,

In that time, when he [the Messiah]
                will come,

Dar(e) *shefa* begushāyad,
Digar *gālūt* nafarmāyad,
Kesi bar qom(e) *Yisrael*.
  Shlah . . .

The door of plenty will be opened,
Exile will not be decreed again,
By anybody upon the people of Israel.
  Send . . .

Bet hamiqdāsh shavād ābād,
Azen *gālūt* shavim āzād,
Ravim khāne shavim del shād,
Zenūreh khāse *Yisrael*.
  Shlah . . .

The Temple will be rebuilt,
Of this exile we shall be free,
We shall go home with a joyful heart,
From a special light of Israel.
  Send . . .

Hame āyim bedel khāhi,
Bedō cheshmāne bīnāī,
Shekhīna ra biyāvarāni,
Tamāme qom(e) *Yisrael*.
  Shlah . . .

We shall come with a willing heart,
With two eyes [we shall] see,
Bring the Shekhina for us,
All the people of Israel.
  Send . . .

Hame khānīm khudū lāhu,
Hazaq barukh. Anjām shūd.

We all say thanks to Him,
Be strong and blessed. Finished.[29]

Notes

"Marriage among the Marranos of Meshhed" originally was published in Hebrew in *Edoth* 2 (Apr.–July 1947):165–92.

1. M. Qid. 3:5; B. Qid. 62b; cf. Maimonides, *Mishne Tora*, Hilkhot Ishut 7:16.
2. Cf. Erich Brauer, "The Jews of Afghanistan," *Jewish Social Studies* 4 (1942):127.
3. Cf. Yosef M'yuḥas, *HaFallaḥim* (Jerusalem, 1937), p. 57; Moshe Stavsky, *HaK'far ha'Aravi* (Tel Aviv, 1946), pp. 237–38; Klein, *ZDPV* 6:81ff.
4. Jakob E. Polak, *Persien, das Land und seine Bewohner*, 2 vols. (Leipzig, 1865), 1:200; B. A. Donaldson, *The Wild Rue* (London, 1938), p. 49.
5. Polak, *Persien*; Raphael Patai, *Golden River to Golden Road: Society, Culture, and Change in the Middle East*, 3d ed. (Philadelphia: University of Pennsylvania Press, 1969), pp. 135–76.
6. Cf. Polak, *Persien*, 1:206; Nurullah Khan, *The Glory of the Shia World*, translated and edited by P. M. Sykes (London, 1910), p. 66. Nurullah Khan was a Persian nobleman born in 1859, and his book contains autobiographical material. His own engagement was arranged in 1877, when he was eighteen.
7. The *gaz* is the manna tree and also candy made of manna. According to Farajullah Nasrullayoff, *gaz* can be found only in Isfahan. *Halvah* is made of wheat flour, oil, and sugar, and various substances to improve the taste.
8. Cf. Polak, *Persien*, 1:221.
9. Nurullah Khan, *Glory of the Shia World*, p. 70.
10. Ibid., pp. 67–68.
11. Polak, *Persien*, 1:211.
12. Tos. Ketubbot 1:4, ed. Zuckermandel, p. 261; Y. Ket. 25a mid. The words in brackets are added in B. Ket. 12a.
13. Farajullah Nasrullayoff explained to me that *bāshlaq* is a Turkish word which literally means "for the head," that is, a payment through which the head of the bride is acquired.
14. Polak, *Persien*, 1:200.
15. In 1880 this sum still sufficed for the living expenses of an average family for at least a year. A similar decree limiting the bride price to 130 qarān plus jewelry was issued in 'Amadiyya, in Kurdistan, about 1890 (Erich Brauer, *Y'hude Kurdistan: Meḥqar Ethnologi*, translated and completed by Raphael Patai [Jerusalem, 1947], p. 91).
16. Ibid., p. 98; Nurullah Khan, *Glory of the Shia World*, p. 71.
17. On the Persian wedding ritual, see Polak, *Persien*, 1:210ff.; Nurullah Khan, *Glory of the Shia World*, p. 75; Donaldson, *Wild Rue*. pp. 48ff.
18. Nurullah Khan, *Glory of the Shia World*, p. 79.
19. Ibid., pp. 72–75.
20. Several *ketubbot* from Meshhed were published by Y. Yoel in *Kiriath Sefer* 21 (1944–45):302, 303, 306.
21. Nurullah Khan, *Glory of the Shia World*, pp. 78–80.
22. Ibid., p. 76.
23. The same rite also was performed before entering a new house or setting out on a trip.
24. Similar customs were practiced in many other places in the traditional Middle East.
25. Nurullah Khan, *Glory of the Shia World*, p. 76.
26. Donaldson, *Wild Rue*, p. 50.
27. Nurullah Khan, *Glory of the Shia World*, pp. 77ff.
28. Polak, *Persien*, 1:212.
29. I wish to thank Nassim Bassalian, a member of the Meshhedi Jewish community in Kew Gardens, New York, for his help in transliterating this wedding song. *Note added in 1980.*

13. Jewish Burial Customs in Kazvin and Meshhed

The following study is based on oral information supplied by Farajullah Nasrullayoff, head of the Meshhedi Jewish community in Jerusalem, and by M. Gohari, a member of the same community.

I. In Kazvin

In the city of Kazvin, the previous hometown of the Jews of Meshhed, it was the custom that as soon as a person died they laid him on the floor with his feet pointing to the west, the direction of *Hekhal Zion* (the Temple of Zion). Although the direction was westward, toward Jerusalem, they called it *Mizrah* (East), just as later, until the very end of their sojourn in Meshhed, the Jews used to hang *Mizrah* tablets (indicating the direction of prayer) on the west side. At the head of the deceased they put an oil lamp and watched it carefully lest it go out. They covered the body with a white sheet, on top of which they put all his possessions, including his silver and gold and the legal documents pertaining to any immovable property he owned.

All members of the family, young and old, would sit down on the floor around the body. The richer the deceased, and the more important the family to which he belonged, the greater were the wailing, mourning, and crying over his death. Each of those present would hold two pebbles in his hand and beat them together according to the rhythm of the dirges. This was a custom which, according to their tradition, the Jews of Kazvin had brought with them from Babylonia.[1] When a visitor entered the house, they began the wailing anew. This order of wailing and reciting dirges was continued until the deceased was taken to the cemetery and the mourners returned to their home.

The ceremonial washing of the dead was performed as follows. Next to the spring outside the city they pitched a tent,[2] into which they placed the box or casket on which the body was laid for the washing. The deceased was brought into the tent and then they washed the body with pure water taken from the spring. They used a special soap, called "Zion" because it was made of pure olive oil imported for this specific purpose from the holy city of Jerusalem, which they referred to as Zion. With this soap and the spring water they washed the body seven times. After the last thorough rinsing of the body, they plugged all of its orifices with clean cotton wool. They did not shave the hair of his head,[3] nor did they pare his fingernails.[4] If the deceased was a woman, they did not even comb her hair.

The shroud was made of fine and expensive white linen.[5] It consisted of a shirt, long trousers, a vest in the shape of a small tallit (prayer shawl), and over all this a long coat. The head of the deceased was covered with a cap and wrapped in a turban. When all this was done, the body was wrapped in a sheet tied over his head, at his hip, and at his feet.

The coffin was made of polished nut-tree wood. They made sure that the coffin should not become wet, because any wetness would again render the body unfit after the *tahara* (ritual washing) was completed. However, if the coffin became wet from rain, this was not considered to cause impurity.[6] The deceased was eulogized in the tent, and then they took him in a procession to the cemetery.

In the cemetery a two-cubit deep grave was dug. Since the Persian cubit was a double cubit, it corresponded to ca. one meter; the depth of the grave therefore was about two meters. The grave was referred to as *serdabeh* (cold room). It actually was given the shape of a room, into which the body was introduced from the side, and not from the top, through an antechamber, a ramp which slanted downward from the ground level. In order to be ready for any eventuality, they always had ten to fifty such "cold rooms" prepared in advance. After the body was placed in the grave, they closed its side entrance with bricks. On top of the grave they set a large tombstone, which also was prepared in advance. After the burial they chiseled into the tombstone a brief elegy in Hebrew Rashi script.

Thus far Gohari's account. According to Nasrullayoff, the custom of

burial in the *serdabeh* continued in Meshhed until the middle of the nineteenth century. He explained that the *serdabeh* was a sort of artificial cave
dug into the slope of a mountain, or in a place where the ground was slanting,
and it served as a family tomb. The dead were laid one beside the other on the
floor of the cave, which then was closed up. The cave remained closed until
the next death in the family, when it was opened to receive the new body.
According to him, this was a Muslim custom, and in the courtyard of Imam
Reza's tomb there were several such caves.

To return to Gohari's description of burials in Kazvin: as long as the
Jewish community was small, not only the members of the deceased's
immediate family, but all those who accompanied the dead to the cemetery
would perform the rite of *q'ri'ah*, making a cut or a tear in their outer
garment as a sign of mourning upon their return from the interment. Then
they all sat in mourning until the following day. [7]

The mourners sat on the floor, and over their heads they spread a black
linen covering. A bowl full of food was placed before them, which was
replaced by a new one for every meal. The black covering was called
"mourning screen," and the mourners sat under it from morning to evening
for seven days. This screen prevented the mourners from seeing anybody,
and the visitors who came to comfort them could neither see them nor hear
their wailing and crying. Only the mourning children were exempt from
sitting under this screen. All the visitors who entered the house of mourning
would themselves wail and cry, and in the course of the seven days of
mourning all the members of the community would come to participate in
the sorrow of the mourners.

Since the visitors had to be offered a meal, the mourning family had to
bear great expenses during the seven days of mourning. For this reason, if
the bereaved family were poor, the members of the community, each
according to his means, participated in the expenses. Also, on the thirtieth
day after the burial and on its anniversary, meals were given in the mourners'
house for all members of the community. However, two or three generations
later, when the number of the Jews in Kazvin had grown, the custom of
tearing the garments of all the participants in the burial was confined to the
mourners themselves. A change was also introduced in connection with the
mourning screen. Although the mourners continued to sit under it, it was
arranged so that they could see the faces of those who came to comfort them.
They were also allowed to raise their voices in wailing and crying.

A short time prior to the transfer of the Jews from Kazvin to Meshhed, a
great change took place in the mourning customs: the screen was abolished
altogether, and the shiny, polished nut-wood coffin was replaced by a simple
one made of rough eucalyptus planks. Opposition to the participation of

nonfamily members in the mourning rites grew, and the tearing of garments and the sitting on the floor by outsiders came to be considered a sin which would bring about a death in the families of those who performed them. Because of the growth of the community, all members were no longer invited to the mourning meals, but only the rich and the leaders. On the other hand, the custom developed of purchasing 100 cubits of linen, from which they made the shroud for the deceased as well as mourning shirts for the relatives and acquaintances who wore them on the day of the burial. Those who came to comfort the mourners would take some ashes from a bowl prepared for this purpose and put it on their foreheads. They would be given a cup of black coffee without sugar. The visitor would read a few chapters from the Book of Psalms, and then leave without the customary greeting.

II. In Meshhed

When somebody died, all the members of the community participated in the traditional death rites. They washed the body in the cellar of the house. Except for this change and for the abolition of the use of Zion soap, the washing and the burial continued according to the old customs. However, the shroud was no longer made of expensive fine linen, but rather of simple "Arab cloth." The dead were buried in the Jewish cemetery, the land for which was acquired by the Jews soon after their arrival in Meshhed. The cemetery was located within the city, near the Jewish houses. Since the cemetery was small, they reduced the size of the graves to the minimum, ca. two meters long and three-quarters of a meter wide. In place of the mourning shirt which they used in Kazvin, they gave a kerchief to each of those who accompanied the dead to the cemetery.[8] The old tombstone inscriptions, which can be seen to the present day (1944) in Meshhed, were in most cases written in faulty Hebrew.

During the decades after 1839, when the Jews of Meshhed lived as Muslim Marranos, as Jadid al-Islam, the death customs they observed were partly of Jewish and partly of Muslim origin. When they saw that a person was about to die, they were careful lest he or she notice anything that could be interpreted as a preparation for his or her demise. Only in the very last minute did the nearest relative put his hand over the eyes of the dying person, and the latter, if he was able to, would recite the *Sh'ma' Yisrael*, "Hear, O Israel, the Lord our God, the Lord is One."[9] Immediately after the dying person gave up his soul, they lifted him from the mattress and blankets on which he lay and placed him on the floor, with his head under the niche which was in the eastern wall of the room, so that his feet pointed to the west, toward Jerusalem. On the ledge of the niche, above the head of the deceased, they put a lighted oil lamp. Placing a second candle at the feet of the deceased was discontinued in the years prior to 1944.[10] Then a white sheet was placed over the body, including the face. All the water found in the house, in any jar, pot, or vessel, was poured out, because it had become defiled. But if there was water in the *miqve* (ritual bath) one did not have to pour it out, for it remained pure.[11]

It was customary to provide oneself well in advance with white linen so that it be available in case of death for sewing the shroud. When death occurred, one member of the family immediately notified those people in the community who made it their voluntary task to take care of the burial rites. While these were busy washing the body, women volunteers began to sew the shroud.

The body was washed in the courtyard of the house. The community had in its possession a tent and a box for washing the dead. The tent was set up in the courtyard, the box placed in it, and the body was laid out on top of the box. There it was washed three times with warm water and soap from Jerusalem and then rinsed with cold water. (In the Persian Jewish community in Jerusalem the use of soap had been given up.) With the help of a tube, the body was cleansed on the inside as well. Burning candles were placed at its head and feet. According to Gohari, a custom taken over from the Muslims was to sprinkle the washed body with clear water, with water mixed with *sadr v'kafur* powder, a kind of lemon salt, or to strew this powder on it in a dry form. The property of this powder is that he who eats of it loses his sexual desire. They besprinkled the dead with it so that his heart should be able to tear itself away from this world and that he should not yearn for his family. According to Nasrullayoff, *sadr* is a white powder similar to salt, which they put into the water with which they wash the body. This *sadr* is not identical with *sedr*, which is an unguent made of lotus leaves and similar to henna, with which the Persians used to anoint themselves after bathing.[12] *Kafur* is, of course, camphor. According to Nasrullayoff, they used to sprinkle *kafur* powder—which is a very cold substance and a remedy for a hot nature—upon the body of the dead after it was washed.[13] Plugging the orifices of the body was practiced by both Jews and Muslims. Contrary to their former custom, the Jadid al-Islam used to pare the nails and cut the hair of the dead.[14]

After the washing, the rabbi of the community circumambulated the body seven times. Each round was accompanied by the breaking of a small earthenware jar full of water, which had been placed for this purpose upon the box next to the body.[15] At each round, moreover, one of those present would throw a coin into the air so that it should fall outside the tent. If a Muslim happened to be nearby, they omitted the rounds altogether. But if there was no fear of being observed, others participated in the round walk in addition to the rabbi. After the washing, the sons of the deceased sprinkled some dust into his eyes, which it was believed would cause the eyes, which had been open until that moment, to close by themselves. This was in accordance with the saying which was frequently quoted by both Jews and Muslims, "Only earth satisfies the eyes of men."[16] Thereafter, pads of cotton wool were placed upon the eyes of the deceased.

If there were Muslim houses near enough to the courtyard in which they set up the tent that the Muslims could see what went on, they clothed the deceased in the shroud inside the tent. If there was no such danger, they carried the body out of the tent, put him on a rug, and then dressed him.

The shroud was made of cotton cloth which the deceased had purchased for himself while still alive. Part consisted of a pair of long trousers which reached below the soles of the feet. Each leg of the trousers was tied in a knot under the feet, like a sack. Another part was a long shirt which reached to the feet, made of a square of cotton cloth of about two by two meters. In its middle they made an opening, and thus it was draped over the head of the deceased. This shirt was called "the dress of Adam, the first man." Over the shirt they put on a coat about as long as the body; this coat opened in the front, and its two sides were folded over the chest. The hands of the deceased were placed over his belly, so that one palm rested on the other. The head was covered with a turban. The mouth, nose, and ears were wrapped in a white veil. On the chest they put a seal made of clay brought from one of the Muslim holy places. They also placed upon the body the beads which he used during his lifetime in order to know whether his endeavors would succeed or were doomed to failure. These two rites were executed in accordance with the Muslim custom. Under each armpit they put a staff, which was to serve him as a support in the hour of the resurrection of the dead. This, too, was adapted from the customs of the Muslims, who put two green willow twigs under the armpits of their dead.[17] Over the entire shroud came a white sheet, tied above the head and under the feet and fastened with a belt tied over the navel.

The men who washed and dressed the dead were allowed to look into his face. The relatives of the deceased who wished that he would appear to them in a dream did not look at his face. If they did not want him to appear, and in order that they should not yearn for him too much, they uncovered his face and looked at it.[18]

When all the preparations were finished, the deceased was placed in a coffin which was wider at the head and narrower at the feet. This coffin, in which the dead rested only on the way from his house to the cemetery, had four or six legs. It was carried on the shoulders,[19] and the bearers often changed places on the way. Sons, too, accompanied their dead father to the cemetery.

The coffin was wrapped in a white cloth, and on top of it they placed an embroidered blanket of varying colors. If the deceased were a man, they put a turban on the middle of the coffin and tied it on; if it were a woman, they wrapped her coffin in a large woman's veil. All this was in accordance with the Muslim custom, since the coffin had to be carried through streets inhabited by Muslims. If the deceased were a greatly respected man, a rabbi, or a scion of a leading family, they covered his body with a tallit inside the coffin, but not on the outside, lest it be recognized that he was a Jew.

After the Jews of Meshhed became Marranos, for about fifty years (from 1839 to about 1890) they had to follow the Muslim custom in the public-religious part of the burial. They washed the body in the house, in secret, and put the shroud on it according to the Jewish custom, but from the moment they left the house until the actual interment, they had to observe the Muslim burial customs. Following the Muslim custom, if the deceased were an important person, they organized a great procession in which large crowds participated. A group of men would beat their chests according to the rhythm of the dirge; another group would take up iron chains tied to the ends of sticks and whip their own backs with them, over the right and left shoulders alternatingly, with this too according to the rhythm. In the funeral procession of a woman they would lead a white horse covered with beautiful cloths and colored shawls, with two swords hanging on its two flanks. For the funeral of a man they would place a turban and two swords on the back of the horse which was led in front of the coffin, while the people participating in the procession followed the bier. In this manner the procession went from the house of the deceased to a *ziyara* (visitation) at the shrine of the Imam Reza. There the deceased was eulogized, and parts of the Koran were read for him. Finally, they moved on to the cemetery (after a number of years the Jadid al-Islam were again able to purchase a separate cemetery for themselves). But even in the grave they were forced to orient the body toward Mecca, that is, to the south of the direction of Jerusalem.

The shape of the grave and of the tombstone was like those in Kazvin. On the sixth day after the funeral, both the Muslims and the Jadidim would go to the cemetery, to take a meal and stay there until the evening.

III. The Story of the Woman Johar

About 1890, an event occurred in consequence of which the Jews of Meshhed were freed from the duty of imitating some of the Muslim funeral customs. At that time a Jewish woman died. They washed her body in her house and sewed her shroud according to the Jewish custom. While they were busy doing this, one woman asked the other, "Have you finished sewing the shroud?" This was overheard by Muslim women who were sitting on the roofs of their houses nearby and watching. They went and told their husbands, "See these Jews, to this very day they have misled us!" (The main difference between the Jewish and the Muslim shrouds was that the Jews sewed the shroud, while the Muslims did not.)

After the preparations were completed, ten men carried the woman's coffin to the mosque. In the meantime the rumor had spread, and a large group of Muslims had gathered at the mosque and received the Jews with angry shouts: "You are Jews, and you will now die!"

"No, for we are Muslims," answered the Jews. The Muslims demanded that a Muslim woman examine the shroud, to see whether they were sewn according to the Jewish custom or followed the Muslim custom. But none of the Muslim women dared to go near the body, and the men were, of course, forbidden by their religion to touch the body of a woman.

Among the Jewish women there was one who had accepted Islam, not only outwardly but wholeheartedly. There were such, although not many, among the Jews of Meshhed. This woman, named Johar, was a widow who had not remarried. She was neat in her garb, good to look at, and pleasant in her speech, so that she was known and liked among the Muslims of Meshhed. When Johar heard of the evil the Muslims were planning to do to the Jadid al-Islam, she ran to the mosque, and when she arrived there she started to shriek and shout, saying, "You despicable Jews, you have cheated us all these days. Now we shall kill all of you!"

While carrying on in this manner she approached the coffin and said, "Let us see how the Jews did sew the shroud!" She reached in under the top sheet which covered the whole body and quickly pulled apart the sewing in the shroud until it was exactly like a Muslim shroud. Then she said, "Behold, she is a Muslim! Come and see!" Then others also stepped up to the coffin and saw that, in fact, the woman's shroud conformed to the Muslim custom. So they buried the woman in peace.

In this manner the woman Johar saved the whole Jewish community of Meshhed. And more than that: after this event the Jews went to the mufti, complaining of the troubles and harassment they had to endure from the Muslims when bringing their dead to the tomb of the Imam Reza. They got permission from the mufti not to have to fulfill this duty any longer, except in the case of the burial of an important person, such as a hajji, a man who had made the pilgrimage to Mecca and Medina. (Under pressure from the Muslims, every year several of the rich Jadidim had to go on such pilgrimages.)

As for the woman Johar, a few years later she immigrated to Jerusalem, where she settled in the Bohkaran quarter and lived in one of the rooms in the courtyard of the synagogue named after Hajji Adoniya Kohen Aharonoff. In Jerusalem, too, Johar continued her good works, in charity and aid to the poor, until her death in 1911. The informant who reported the event described above still remembered the day of her burial. It was on a Friday, on a cold winter day, when a heavy blanket of snow covered the whole city. A large crowd attended the funeral; before her coffin walked the pupils of the Talmud Tora school, and after it all the people of the quarter.[20] Thus they took her to the cemetery on the Mount of Olives, walking on foot back and forth.[21]

IV. In the Cemetery and the House of Mourning

Let us return now to the death customs of the Jadid al-Islam of Meshhed.

In their cemetery there was a spacious house, and in it was a table upon which they would place the body. Next to him they put seven coins, and, accompanied by prayers, they threw the coins one by one to the outside.[22] In some cases it was only in the cemetery that they sprinkled dust into the eyes of the deceased; for this purpose they opened the topmost sheet which covered his face after they had placed him in the grave.

The body was put in the grave without the coffin. Over the body they left a space, and somewhat higher, upon a ledge in the grave, they placed stone slabs which effectively closed the grave. Over these slabs they poured earth, until the grave was completely filled up.

On the way to the cemetery and back they recited Muslim prayers. If no Muslim were present at the interment, they recited the *Kaddish*, the Jewish prayer for the dead, over the grave. If a Muslim were present, they omitted it, and recited it after they returned to the house of the mourners. The Muslim custom demanded that the mourners make a rent in their shirts, mourn for the dead three days, and then sew up the rent shirts; therewith the mourning ritual was actually finished. Not so among the Jadidim. When the company returned from the cemetery, they washed their hands at the entrance to the house,[23] but they did not dry them with a towel. Instead they held them out in the air and wind until the hands dried of themselves. After entering the house, each mourner performed the "rending" for himself.[24] The rending was done by hand (that is, not with a razor, knife, or scissors), at the neck opening of the shirt which they wore next to their skins. If somebody were unable to make a rent with his hands, he used scissors to make a cut. They wore this same torn shirt during all the seven days of mourning. Thereafter they sewed up the rent and continued to wear the shirt until the end of the thirty-day mourning period. After the thirtieth day they gave the shirt to an indigent. The first meal after the return from the cemetery comprised a hardboiled egg and some bread. For thirty days after the burial, the mourners did not go to the bathhouse, cut their hair, nor pare their nails.[25]

During the first seven days of mourning the mourners sat on the floor on rugs, in the very room in which the departed breathed his last.[26] There they would recite the afternoon (*minha*) and evening (*ma'ariv*) prayers in a minyan, i.e., in the company of ten adult males. However, for the morning prayer (*shaharit*), part of which on Mondays and Thursdays is a reading from the Tora, they would repair to the synagogue in the company of friends, for the mourners were not allowed to go out alone during those seven days.[27]

However, relatives came to comfort them every day, although friends and acquaintances came only once. The comforters read before the mourners chapters from the Book of Psalms, and the bereaved family served them tea or coffee (a Muslim custom). When the visitors left, they did so without saying good-bye.

During these seven days, day and night, many people were invited to meals in the mourners' house.[28] The food was cooked and prepared by the relatives, and the expenses were borne by the community. Since it was considered a great mitzva, a religious commandment and good deed, to participate in these expenses, there was never any lack of means to defray them. Meals were given on the thirtieth day and on the day of the anniversary, but the mourners had to bear the expenses for these.

The mourners wore dark garments.[29] They had a candle lighted in the house of mourning for thirty days. At the end of the year, the mourners' relatives gave them new clothes. The members of the family did not use the clothes of the deceased, but gave them to the poor. On the seventh, thirtieth, and anniversary days, it was customary to visit the grave of a deceased father or mother. Each time somebody visited the grave he put a stone on the tombstone. They also would visit the graves of the parents before leaving the city for a long voyage. On the anniversary day of a father's or a mother's death they would fast until the evening meal.[30]

If parents lost a second child within thirty days after the death of the first one, they slaughtered a cock (for a son) or a hen (for a daughter), and buried the bird together with the deceased child. This was believed to prevent a third death in the family.[31]

The tombstone was inscribed with a few lines in accordance with the age and character of the deceased. There were always some people in the community who knew how to write poetry, and they undertook the task of composing these brief elegies, as well as longer dirges which were recited in the house of the mourners.[32] Thus according to Gohari. According to Nasrullayoff, the tombstones were divided into two parts: the upper part was inscribed in Persian with the Persian name of the deceased, and the lower part with his Hebrew name in Hebrew characters.

Notes

"Jewish Burial Customs in Kazvin and Meshhed" originally was published in Hebrew in *Dappe Zikkaron liR'fael Aharonoff* (Jerusalem: Heshvan, 1945), pp. 39–54, and as an offprint, part of *Historical Traditions and Mortuary Customs of the Jews of Meshhed* (Jerusalem: Palestine Institute of Folklore and Ethnology, 1945), pp. 9–24.

1. In other communities it was the custom to leave a pebble in the house of the mourners. Thus, e.g., among the Jews of Kutais in the Caucasus, who considered the stone "a symbol of lifelessness, since the body had become lifeless" (Yosef Y'huda Chorny, *Sefer haMassa'ot b'Eretz Qavqaz* [Saint Petersburg, 1884], p. 188.

2. Ibid., p. 117, about the Jews of Mogo in the Caucasus: "They took him [the deceased] to the field, where they pitched a tent *fun layvint* [of linen] and placed the deceased into it." Cf. S'mahot 8:2, ed. Higger, p. 149, and the term "the *huppa* [canopy] of the dead" in the *Baraitot of Evel Rabbati*, ed. Higger, p. 231, and parallel passages there.

3. In contrast to B. Mo'ed Qatan 8b, where it says, "They cut his hair." Cf. Maimonides, *Mishne Tora*, Hilkhot Evel 4:1. The Yemenite Jews shave the hair of the deceased (Erich Brauer, *Ethnologie der jemenitischen Juden* [Heidelberg, 1934], p. 222).

4. Eighteenth-century German Jews used to pare the nails of the dead (Johann C. G. Bodenschatz, *Kirchliche Verfassung der heutigen Juden*, 4 vols. [Erlangen and Coburg, 1748], 4:171).

5. Shroud of white linen: B. Mo'ed Qatan 27b; cf. Tos Nid. 9:17, ed. Zuckermandel, p. 651; B. Ket. 8b; *Sefer Maharil* (1858), p. 240. This is the general Jewish custom to this day; cf. *Sefer Z'khira v'Iny'ne S'gullot* (Wilmersdorf, 1729), p. 53b: "The *s'gulla* [virtue] of white linen for the dead and the quick."

6. Cf. B. Sanh. 47a: "If rain streams down upon his bier, this is a good sign for the dead."

7. The same custom was observed in medieval Germany; see *Kol Bo* (Lvov, 1860), p. 88a [*Hilkhot Evel*]: "And the comforters likewise sit on the floor."

8. Cf. Rabbi David Ibn Abi Zimra [RaDBaZ], pt. 2, par. 94. Similarly among the Jews of Calcutta, India; see Ya'qov Sapir, *Even Sapir*, pt. 2 (Mainz, 1874), p. 101: "In the days of their mourning they wear a white kerchief around their necks hanging down to the chest."

9. According to one of my Meshhedi informants, not a relative, but an old man would close the eyes of a dead man, and an old woman the eyes of a dead woman.

10. Among the Jews of Kutais, Caucasus, the custom of placing a candle at the head and the feet of the deceased was observed by Chorny, *Sefer haMassa'ot*, p. 188.

11. The Bene Israel of India poured water upon the body of the deceased from seven clay vessels, one after the other, and then broke the empty vessels (Haeem Samuel Kehimkar, *The History of the Bene Israel of India* [Tel Aviv, 1937], p. 154). The breaking of vessels is performed when the body is removed from the house in various Jewish communities; see Abraham M. Luncz, *Y'rushalayim* (Vienna, 1882), 1:13; Y'huda Bergmann, *HaYahadut, Nishmatah v'Hayyehah* (Jerusalem, 1938), pp. 76, 83; Johannes Buxtorf, *Synagoga Judaica* (Basel, 1643), p. 630; Bodenschatz, *Kirchliche Verfassung*, 4:173; Paul C.

Kirchner, *Jüdisches Zeremoniell . . .* (Nürnberg, 1724), p. 217; Max Grunwald, "Aus Hausapotheke und Hexenküche," *Jahrbuch für jüdische Volkskunde* (1923), p. 219.

12. Nevertheless, one should not exclude the possibility that originally it was the lotus which was used in connection with washing the dead, since in Egypt they used to wash the dead with water in which lotus leaves (*nabq* or *sidr*) had been boiled (Edward W. Lane, *Manners and Customs of the Modern Egyptians*, Everyman's Library ed. [London, n.d.], p. 518).

13. The belief that camphor diminishes the sexual desire is found among many peoples; see Hovorka and Kronfeld, *Vergleichende Volksmedizin*, 2 vols. (Stuttgart, 1909), 2:166.

14. Thus according to Gohari. According to Nasrullayoff, they pared the nails but did not touch the hair.

15. One cannot fail to notice the similarity between these burial rites and the bride's circumambulation of the bridegroom, the breaking of a glass at the wedding, between the tent and the huppa (*note added in 1980*).

16. Similarly among the Bene Israel of India: they sprinkle earth from Jerusalem into the eyes and mouth of the dead (Kehimkar, *History of the Bene Israel*, p. 155).

17. However, there are similar customs also among the Ashkenazi Jews. They put a wooden fork in the hand of the deceased (Bodenschatz, *Kirchliche Verfassung*, 4:174) or into his coffin, to serve him as a support on his way to Jerusalem in the days of the resurrection (A. M. Spoer, *Folk-Lore* [London], 42 [1931]:73). According to Luncz, *Y'rushalayim*, 1:12, "The custom of putting branches into the hands of the dead . . . is not practiced here [in Jerusalem]." The Jews of India put a branch into the deceased's right hand (Kehimkar, *History of the Bene Israel*, p. 155).

18. However, cf. *Sefer Maharil*, p. 241: "He warned his sons that they should not look into the coffin when they opened it in order to lay the dead into it in a proper manner." Among the Jews of Morocco also it was forbidden to look at the face of the dead (Lancelot Addison, *The Present State of the Jews . . .* [London, 1675], p. 223).

19. In accordance with the old custom: "The deceased is carried on the shoulders" (*Baraitot of Evel Rabbati*, ed. Higger, p. 246).

20. This is a Jerusalem custom which I observed numerous times. See also Luncz, *Y'rushalayim*, 1:13.

21. Another informant told me the story of the woman Johar with slight variations.

22. Thus according to Gohari. According to Nasrullayoff, this rite was performed in the tent set up in the deceased's house. The custom continued to be observed among the Meshhedi immigrants in Jerusalem. Similar customs with coins were found also among other communities in Jerusalem (Bergmann, *HaYahadut*, p. 76). Among the Jews of Basra, Iraq, see Grunwald, "Aus Hausapotheke," p. 219.

23. Cf. the Ashkenazi custom of medieval times: "They should wash their hands prior to entering their houses" (*Kol Bo*, Hilkhot Evel, chap. 10, p. 2). The general Jewish custom is to wash the hands when leaving the cemetery.

24. Thus according to Gohari. According to Nasrullayoff and a third informant, they made the tear after washing the body but before they took it to the cemetery. Cf. also S'mahot 9:8, ed. Higger, p. 171; and in general, S'mahot, chap. 9 on the rules of the *q'ri 'a* (rending).

25. This conforms to the general Jewish custom; see S'mahot 6:1, ed. Higger, pp. 130–31; 6:11, pp. 140–41, and other sources there; also 9:11. See also R. Abraham ben Natan haYarhi, *Sefer haManhig* (Warsaw, 1885), pp. 174, 178.

26. In Germany the mourners used to sit in the place where the deceased lay (Kirchner, *Jüdisches Ceremonial*, p. 220).

27. Cf. Gen Rab. 96:5; haYarhi, *Sefer haManhig*, p. 178; *Kol Bo*, Hilkhot Evel, 88a. Similarly among seventeenth-century Moroccan Jews: Addison, *Present State of the Jews*, p. 218. In Jerusalem: *Sefer Taqqanot* (Jerusalem, 5602 [1842]), p. 68a, par. 83.

28. Similarly among the Jews of Calcutta: Sapir, *Even Sapir*, 2:100. "The mourners spend a lot of money in the days of mourning, for every day during the seven days of mourning they give ample repasts to the poor and the rich, like the meals at circumcisions and weddings,

with many desserts and all kinds of fruits, so as to give occasion to many benedictions. This is done to honor the dead, for the exaltation of the soul of the deceased. And thus they do on the thirtieth day, and again on the first anniversary. And the expenses of mourning are as high as those of the weddings, except that at the mourning meals the invited guests do not sit on chairs at tables, but sheets are spread for them on the floor, and so they eat.'' Also among the Caucasian Jews: Chorny, *Sefer haMass'ot*, p. 117; also Leon de Modena, who says in his *History of the Present Jews* (London, 1707), p. 229, that in the east and in many other places the relatives and friends have the custom of sending, in the evening and in the morning of the seven days of mourning, grand and sumptuous repasts to the deceased's relatives, and to eat with them in order to comfort them. As for banquets after the conclusion of the seven days of mourning, see Josephus Flavius, *Wars of the Jews* 2.1.1. Among the Yemenite Jews: Brauer, *Ethnologie*, p. 227.

29. On the mourners' garments: Joseph Perles, ''Die Leichenfeierlichkeiten im nachbiblischen Judenthume,'' *MGWJ* 10 (1861):393; A. Marmorstein, ''Beiträge zur Religionsge- schichte und Volkskunde, II,'' *Jahrbuch für jüdische Volkskunde* 2 (1924–25):257, n. 1.

30. This custom is attested elsewhere as well: see *Sefer haTashbetz* (Lemberg, 1858), par. 427; *Sefer Maharil*, p. 238. Among seventeenth-century Moroccan Jews: Addison, *Present State of the Jews*, pp. 223–24.

31. Similarly in Jerusalem: ''If two should die in one courtyard, they will slaughter a cock for a man and a hen for a woman. They bury the head and the feet of the birds and distribute the meat among the poor'' (Moshe Reischer, *Sefer Sha'are Y'rushalayim* [Warsaw, 1879], p. 91).

32. Likewise among the Jews of North Africa: cf. Benjamin II (Israel Joseph Benjamin), *Sefer Massa'e Yisrael* [The book of travels of Israel] (Lyck, 1859), p. 129: ''The dirge contains those things which are befitting the value and works of the deceased, and they compose new dirges for almost every person who dies.''

14. Three Meshhed Tales of Mullah Siman-Tov

The Jews of Meshhed, the capital of the province of Khorasan, Iran, were forced in 1839 to adopt Islam, and have lived ever since as Marranos, or, as they were called, Jadid al-Islam, "Newcomers to Islam," outwardly professing the Muslim faith but in secret remaining faithful to the religion of their fathers.[1] Mullah[2] Siman-Tov, who was the religious and spiritual leader of the community in the beginning of the nineteenth century, died in 1830. The three tales which follow were told to me by Farajullah Nasrullayoff, the head of the community of Meshhed Jews in Jerusalem, as "true stories" which he had heard some fifty-five years ago from old men, who in their turn remembered the events as taking place another sixty or so years earlier.

I.

In the days of Mullah Siman-Tov, peace be upon him, the rule of Meshhed was in the hands of a descendant of Imam Reza,[3] who was the Imam Jumah[4] of Meshhed, a truth-loving and just man. When the Imam Jumah heard of the great wisdom of Mullah Siman-Tov, peace be upon him, he wished to talk to him and to discuss with him matters of religion. But the

Jews were regarded as impure by the Muslims, and so it was impossible for the Imam Jumah either to invite Mullah Siman-Tov, peace be upon him, to his house, or to go and visit him. So the Imam Jumah had a small *madraseh*[5] built in the Jewish quarter, consisting of only three rooms, and in the innermost room of this *madraseh* he would meet in secret Mullah Siman-Tov, peace be upon him, once or twice a week, with no one present to witness their meetings. The Imam Jumah would ask all manner of questions, especially concerning religious prescriptions in which the Muslim faith differed from the Jewish, and Mullah Siman-Tov, peace be upon him, would answer the questions by referring to the Bible,[6] and thus showing that the Jewish precept is the right one. Finally the Imam Jumah felt that not knowing the Bible he was unable to argue with Mullah Siman-Tov, peace be upon him, or to catch him in making a mistake.

At that time there came to Meshhed on pilgimage[7] two converted Jews from Teheran, two brothers, Yitzḥaq and Moshe[8] by name. These two were learned men, well versed in the traditional Jewish lore, and they brought with them a letter of recommendation from the mujtahid[9] of Teheran, in which he asked the Imam Jumah of Meshhed to give all honor to the two converted mullahs, who were great scholars in the Bible, so that all the Jews might see it, and following their example might embrace Islam. The Imam Jumah rejoiced greatly at their arrival, for he thought, ''These precisely are the people I need for my discussions with Mullah Siman-Tov, peace be upon him.'' So he took them into his house and they were his guests of honor for six months.

After a time the Imam Jumah began to take his two guests àlong with him to his secret meetings with Mullah Siman-Tov, peace be upon him, that they might see whether the answers Mullah Siman-Tov, peace be upon him, would give to his questions were correct. On these occasions the Imam Jumah and Mullah Siman-Tov, peace be upon him, would sit side-by-side on a *dushak* (mattress) at the upper end of the room, while the two brothers would sit opposite them, near the door, holding between them a Hebrew Bible. Whenever Mullah Siman-Tov, peace be upon him, would answer one of the questions put by the Imam Jumah, the latter would turn to the two brothers. They would consult their Bible and reluctantly pronounce the answer correct.

Thus passed many weeks, and when the two brothers already had stayed with him for about six months, and the Imam Jumah saw that all *his* questions were always answered with the utmost precision by Mullah Siman-Tov, peace be upon him, he decided to let the two brothers question Mullah Siman-Tov, peace be upon him, and he said to them, ''You know the Bible; therefore, next time you ask him a question which he cannot answer.''

They agreed only too eagerly, and at the next meeting they said to Mullah Siman-Tov, peace be upon him, "You Jews believe that all that God has created or ordained from the first day to the last day of the world is hinted at in the Song of Moses."[10] Said Mullah Siman-Tov, peace be upon him, "That is true." Then the two brothers said, "We two were Jews, learned persons, mullahs, and we left the Jewish faith and converted to Islam. Tell us, where in the Song of Moses is there any hint of that?" Mullah Siman-Tov, peace be upon him, answered without a moment's hesitation, "This is hinted at by the fifth verse of the Song of Moses, which reads, 'Corrupted are those who are not His children; it is their blemish, a perverse and crooked generation.'[11] The third letter of the word *banaw* [His children, spelled *bnyw*] is a *yod*, which is the first letter of the name Yitzhaq, and you are called Yitzhaq, while the third letter of the word *mumam* [their blemish, spelled *mwmm*] is a *mim*, which is the first letter of the name Moshe, and you are called Moshe."

When the two brothers heard this, they became exceedingly angry, took hold of the Bible which lay before them, and threw the heavy book at the head of Mullah Siman-Tov, peace be upon him. Thereupon the Imam Jumah cried out wrathfully and commanded the two brothers, "Come here immediately and kiss the feet of Mullah Siman-Tov, peace be upon him, and ask for his forgiveness. You asked him a question and he truthfully answered it; you should be thankful to him for the answer. And now that you have thus behaved, you will have to leave Meshhed within twenty-four hours, for one minute after the twenty-four hours have elapsed I shall give orders to kill you."

II.

In the days of Mullah Siman-Tov, peace be upon him, there lived in Meshhed a Jewish *zargar* [goldsmith]. One day a Muslim came to this goldsmith and gave him five *miskal*[12] of gold, saying, "I am going to marry and should like you to make of this gold *gushwareh* [earrings] for my betrothed." At the time no one was present in the workshop of the goldsmith excepting him and the Muslim. A few days later the man came again to fetch the earrings and said, "Did you finish them? Give them to me!" But the goldsmith answered, "Who are you? I have never seen you! You never gave me anything to do for you!"

When the Muslim saw that he could not persuade the Jew to return his gold, he went to the Imam Jumah and brought his complaint before him. The Imam Jumah let the Jewish goldsmith come, but neither could he extract from him an admission. The deliberations lasted for six months,[13] and the goldsmith stuck to his denial. When six months had elapsed and the Imam Jumah saw that he was unable to bring a judgment, he decided to let his friend, Mullah Siman-Tov, peace be upon him, show his wisdom in this case, and sent the two litigants, accompanied by an official of his court, to Mullah Siman-Tov, peace be upon him, to present the case to him.

When the three men came before Mullah Siman-Tov, peace be upon him, the official began to relate to him the case in all detail, repeating what the Muslim said and what the Jew said, and not forgetting to stress that the case had already lasted for full six months. When Mullah Siman-Tov, peace be upon him, perceived how things stood, he said—while the official was still talking—to the Jew in the Lo-Torai language,[14] *Nagāle, ālilā bemen!* [Do not be afraid! Deny!] And the Jew answered him back, quickly, *Menidam* [I have denied]. Immediately Mullah Siman-Tov, peace be upon him, interrupted the official and said to him, "Take these two men back to the Imam Jumah and tell him that the Jew has confessed his guilt before me. He is now ready to give back the gold to the Muslim."

When the official told the Imam Jumah how things happened and how Mullah Siman-Tov, peace be upon him, had decreed the guilt of the Jew even before he, the official, had finished explaining the case, the Imam Jumah was very much astonished and could not understand the matter. So when he met Mullah Siman-Tov, peace be upon him, the next time in the *madraseh*, he asked him, "Was it not out of fear that you pronounced the Jew guilty? Why did you do this, all I wanted was a true judgment!" Mullah Siman-Tov, peace be upon him, answered, "No, I did not fear you. When I am sitting on the chair of judgment, I cannot do aught but judge the case according to its merits." And then he proceeded to explain to the Imam Jumah how he was able to make what seemed to be a lightning judgment.

III.

In the days when Abbas Mirza was governor of Meshhed,[15] there lived in the town some hundred Jewish families. In those days a devastating *wabā* [cholera] swept over Meshhed and carried away within six months one third of the population, Jews and Muslims alike. The old Jewish cemetery, situated within the *'ēdgāh*,[16] the Jewish quarter, was already disused at that time. This old cemetery was actually nothing more than a small courtyard surrounded by the houses of the Jews. No entrance door was left from any of these houses to the cemetery; only two cellars of two houses had small windows opening onto it. In the very middle of this old cemetery was the grave of Mullah Abraham, who had been many years previously the teacher of Mullah Siman-Tov, peace be upon him. As the Jews got no permission to establish another cemetery near the town, they had to bury their dead at a cemetery at a distance of some three miles from the city.

In the days of the plague, every day one, two, or three people of the Jewish community succumbed to the cholera. The dead were placed in wooden coffins, fastened to the back of donkeys or horses, and so, with great difficulty, transported to the distant cemetery. One day twenty-seven Jews died of the cholera. Each one of the hundred families was already many times bereaved, and they were by then in such despair because of the plague that they did not find the courage to bring these dead to burial, not knowing whether they themselves would live to reach the cemetery. Some twenty to twenty-five people assembled, among them the heads of the community, and they decided to approach Mullah Siman-Tov, peace be upon him, and ask him to do something that the plague should cease. They came to the house of Mullah Siman-Tov, peace be upon him, and said to him, "Do something, if you can, that the plague should cease." He said to them, "Come with me, all of you." He led them to one of the cellars next to the old cemetery, opened the window, and remained there standing, facing the grave of Mullah Abraham which was visible from the window. All the people stood behind Mullah Siman-Tov, peace be upon him, waiting silently.[17] Suddenly Mullah Siman-Tov, peace be upon him, said in a loud, clear voice, "Mullah Abraham! Go beneath the Seat of Glory and annul this *gezērah!*"[18] The people behind him listened but could hear no answer. A little later Mullah Siman-Tov, peace be upon him, again cried out, this time still louder, "Mullah Abraham! Go beneath the Seat of Glory and annul this *gezērah!*" But still no answer was heard. Then Mullah Siman-Tov, peace be upon him, cried, "Mullah Abraham! If you cannot, I shall come!" And again there was neither a sound nor an answer.

Finally, Mullah Siman-Tov, peace be upon him, turned back to the people and said, "Let us go." When they left the cellar and stood in the street, he said, "Have no fear. From now on no one will die of the plague. Go and gather your dead and bring them to burial. The plague has ceased." So the people went, and he returned to his house and said to his wife, "I am going up to my room. Do not let anybody come to me within one hour. Neither should you yourself disturb me. But after an hour come and visit me."

Mullah Siman-Tov, peace be upon him, had his study on the second floor of his house, a room full of holy books, where he used to sit and learn. He now retired to this room, spread out a white linen sheet on the floor in the middle of the room, took off his clothes so that he remained clad only in his white linen shirt and underwear, neatly folded his clothes, and lay down on the sheet. With another sheet he covered himself entirely, then stretched out his feet, stretched out his hands, closed his mouth, closed his eyes . . .

An hour later his wife came and entered the room. She saw Mullah Siman-Tov, peace be upon him, lying under the sheet. She called to him, but he answered not. She approached him, lifted up the sheet, saw that his eyes were closed, and touched his forehead. His forehead was cold like that of a man dead for an hour. She lifted up her voice and cried out, and the people came and saw that Mullah Siman-Tov, peace be upon him, was dead. Only then did they understand what he had meant when he said that he himself would come, that he himself would go to the Seat of Glory and annul the *gezērah*. For the cholera had really ceased, and from the moment that Mullah Siman-Tov, peace be upon him, died, no one, neither Jew nor Muslim, died of the plague.

Mullah Siman-Tov, peace be upon him, was buried in the old cemetery beside his teacher, Mullah Abraham. Both graves can still be seen in Meshhed.

Notes

"Three Meshhed Tales of Mullah Siman-Tov" originally was published in *Folk-Lore* [London] 57 (Dec. 1946):179–84.

1. See Raphael Patai, *Historical Traditions and Mortuary Customs of the Jews of Meshhed* (Jerusalem, 1945) [in Hebrew, with English summary].
2. *Mullah*, i.e., "teacher," "master," is the title of religious personages among both the Muslims and the Jews in Persia.
3. 'Alī al-Ridā ibn Mūsā ibn Ja'far, popularly called Imam Reza, was the eighth of the twelve imams. He died in Tūs in 818. Because he was buried there, the town, renamed Meshhed, became the most holy place of Shi'ite Islam. See *Encyclopaedia of Islam*, new ed. (Leiden and London, 1960), 1:399–40, s.v. 'Alī al-Ridā.
4. Imam Jumah=the Imam of the Congregation.
5. A *madraseh*, "school," is a religious college for studious adults, as distinguished from the *maktab*, the Muslim religious school for children. See Raphael Patai, "The Hebrew Education of the Jews of Meshhed" [in Hebrew], *Edoth* 1 (July 1946): 213–26.
6. This took place at a time when no Persian translation of the Bible was yet current. The translation by the Persian savant Fazil Khan was published by the British Bible Society in 1856, and became popular among the Jews of Meshhed who could not read the Hebrew Bible because they were ignorant of the Hebrew alphabet and language.
7. The pilgrims who today come to Meshhed to visit the shrine of Imam Reza number about sixty thousand annually. A man who has made the pilgrimage to Meshhed assumes the title *Meshhedi*, just as a pilgrim to Mecca and Medina receives the title *hajji*.
8. Or Ishāq and Mūsā in Persian.
9. The Persian equivalent of mufti.
10. Deut. 32. This belief still prevails among the Jews of Meshhed.
11. The text of the verse evidently is corrupt in the original Hebrew and defies all attempts at translation.

12. *Miskal* is the smallest measure of weight, equivalent to twenty-four *nakhud* (peas). See Jakob E. Polak, *Persien, das Land und seine Bewohner*, 2 vols. (Leipzig, 1865), 2:157.
13. Note the recurrence of six months as the duration of anything critical; see above and also below, in the third tale.
14. The Lo-Torai, i.e., not Toraic, is a secret language of the Jews of Meshhed, containing Hebrew, Persian, anagrammatical, and other elements.
15. It is characteristic of the reliability of the historical traditions as remembered by my informant that all the data which can be verified by historical sources are corroborated by them. My informant knew that 'Abbās Mīrzā was the governor of Meshhed, that he was the crown prince, the son of Fatḥ 'Alī Shāh, and that he did not succeed his father to the throne, as he died before him. All of these are correct historical facts, as is the occurrence of a severe cholera plague in Meshhed (as well as in all Persia) in 1830. Cf. *Encyclopaedia of Islam*, old ed., s.v. Meshhed; George Fowler, *Three Years in Persia* (London, 1841), 1:31.
16. *'Ēdgāh* = "place of festival." This was the original name of the gardens just within the city walls, where the Jews bought land and built their houses in the middle of the eighteenth century.
17. When he reached this point in his narrative, my informant, overcome by emotion, had to interrupt his account.
18. *Gezērah* is an evil decree, a natural or social catastrophe ordained by God.

15. A Popular "Life of Nadir"

The history of Nadir Shah (1688–1747), king of Persia, whom Armin Vámbéry justly called "the last great Asiatic conqueror," is well known thanks to a number of contemporary biographies and accounts written by both oriental and European authorities. The Persian authors either stood directly in Nadir's service or at least were eyewitnesses of much of what they recorded. Some of the western sources too are either eyewitness accounts or are based on information derived from persons who witnessed many phases of Nadir's career. In the two hundred years which have passed since Nadir's death, hundreds of authors have studied his life and published books or articles concerning his history. Dr. Laurence Lockhart published in 1938 a careful and detailed critical study of Nadir's life based mainly upon contemporary sources.[1] Nadir's career is thus as fully documented as could be wished.

This circumstance gives additional interest to the study of the folk traditions about Nadir which still live in that district of Khurasan which witnessed his birth, childhood, and early career. When viewed against the background of historical fact, the particulars handed down in the popular "Life of Nadir" throw a sharp light on the working of folk tradition. We see events which in reality took place at a distance of many years from each other thrown into one by the legend; we find that different persons are fused into one and geographical features confused; we find that great and important happenings left no trace at all in the folk story, while on the other hand we find in it recounted incidents which lack any historical foundation. Stories already told of Cyrus in Herodotus' time become attached to Nadir. The emphasis too is quite different in the folk tale from that in the historical narrative. A gigantic military operation, such as Nadir's invasion of India, is remembered only in the form of two anecdotes telling what had happened on the way there and back. An insignificant accident, on the other hand, like the jokingly made promise of Nadir's former master that he would conquer Baghdad for him, becomes a weighty event, pregnant with "historical" consequences, for owing to it does Nadir finally succeed—according to the folk story—in taking Baghdad. Nothing is remembered in folk tradition of the misery, famine, illness, and death Nadir's constant wars brought upon the great masses of Persia's peoples, almost no word of the enormous loss in life suffered and caused by his armies, but it is meticulously recorded that he took seven rotl (that is, ca. 46 lbs.) of eyes from his own army, and that he wished to make a tower out of a million skulls. Of the later phases of Nadir's life, well documented in history, the folk tale has comparatively little to tell. But his early life, of which history knows practically nothing, is described in great detail. It is thus the humble birth, the simple childhood—which could have been that of any one of those who loved to tell this tale or hear it—the early steps which gradually led him to the throne, on which the popular tale dwells with special interest everywhere when it comes to tell of a hero. In Nadir's later life it is the colorful or the terrible, the picturesque or the extraordinary happenings, which remain alive in folk memory, or rather which folk fantasy attaches to the figure of its hero.

In the following pages I give an almost verbatim translation of the popular "Life of Nadir" as it was told to me, partly in Persian and partly in Hebrew, by Farajullah Nasrullayoff, aged seventy-seven, in Jerusalem. The notes point to some of the main discrepancies between his story and the historical data of the life of Nadir. The lower-case letters *a* through *m* refer to the notes appended to the end of the article. These were written by Dr. Lockhart, who was good enough to go over the manuscript. Nasrullayoff told the story in the course of several meetings in the early summer of 1946. In March 1947, I asked him to repeat parts of the story in order to check the precision of his memory and narration, and I can state that the repetitions corresponded to the first version down to the minutest details. Nasrullayoff is a merchant and is the head of the community of Meshhed Jews in Jerusalem. He was born and spent his youth in Meshhed as a member of the Marrano Jewish community, the so-called Jadid al-Islam. He lived from

1895 to 1920 in the town of Muhammadabad, the chief town of the district of Darragaz in northern Khurasan, some 130 kilometers northwest of Meshhed. This town is generally referred to as Deregez—that is, it is called by the name of the district of which it is the capital. It was in this district that Nadir was born and that he spent his early youth. Thus, the first part of the story, which in fact is the richest, falls into the category of local tradition. Nasrullayoff heard the story from the elders of Muhammadabad, among them the "governor" of the town and a certain Mohammad Husain Beg, a member of the Turkish Afshar family (or, better, tribe), to which also Nadir belonged.

The little town of Kona Gale (Kohnah Qal'ah, i.e., Old Fort)[2] in which Nadir was born, Nasrullayoff told me, was situated about half a farsang (i.e., 3 km.) from Muhammadabad. At the time of Nadir's birth, Kona Gale was the chief town of the district of Deregez (Darragaz). It was surrounded by a city wall with three gates, corresponding to the three roads which led through the mountains into the city. Round about Kona Gale and very near to it there were high mountains. Outside the city wall there were wells, the water of which was conducted around the city and used to irrigate the gardens. The water was, however, not allowed to run into the town, for the town was situated in a depression, lower than the surrounding countryside. The stream was bordered by numerous watermills; some houses also stood there. This outer part of Kona Gale was called Dastgird, "hand-girdle." Kona Gale suffered much from the attacks of robbers who could easily direct their shots into the city from the surrounding mountains. Some one hundred and thirty years ago, when Nasrullayoff's great-great-grandfather died, he was buried in the Jewish cemetery of Kona Gale. At about the same time, all the inhabitants of the town decided to leave it and to settle at a new point which lay in the midst of open country, where they would not be exposed to the attacks of robbers. This new town is Muhammadabad, the new capital of the district. Kona Gale is today a ruin; only the city walls can still be seen.

It was in Kona Gale that Nadir was born. His father was a poor man, the shepherd and the cowherd of the town. Each inhabitant had a few sheep and a few cows. He would gather these in the morning, take them into the pastures, and bring them home in the evening.[3] In the early days of her pregnancy, Nadir's mother dreamed a dream: she saw herself standing on a high mountain. She began to urinate, and the urine turned into a flood that rose and engulfed the whole land. The flood rose and covered the mountain on which she stood, until it reached her own feet, and yet it continued to rise. Then she awoke with terror. She was much frightened by her dream and went to ask its meaning from a mullah.[4] The mullah listened to the woman's story and then, although as yet no signs of her pregnancy were visible, he asked her, "Are you pregnant?" She answered, "Yes." Thereupon the mullah said, "Know you then, that if you give birth to a son, he will become a king and will conquer all the lands; and if it be a girl that you give birth to, she will become a queen, the wife of the greatest king on the earth."[5]

Despite this prediction, no unusual attention was paid to the child when it was born. He was brought up in the Turk mother tongue. When Nadir was seven years old, he was attacked by an illness which left him bald.[a] It was about this time that his parents began to send him with the other boys of his age to gather brushwood and grass for heating. Every day the children would set out together, carrying their food with them. Before long Nadir had become the leader of his band. When six months had gone by in this manner,[6] Nadir said to the boys, "Let us not eat until we have gathered the brushwood and thorns for heating. When we have done our work, let us sit down together and share the food we have received from home. If there is in our midst a boy who is poor and has no food, we shall give him from ours." All the boys agreed, and thenceforth they did as he had said. One day it happened that one of the boys sat down to eat his food alone, before the brushwood and the thorns had been gathered. When all the other boys sat down together to eat, it was found that this boy had already eaten his food. Nadir ordered the boys to get up and beat the one who had disobeyed. The boys beat him until he died. They then sat down again and ate their food. When they had finished they rose, each boy took his bundle of brushwood, and they returned to the town. The dead boy remained lying where he had fallen, near his pile of brushwood. All the children returned home and Nadir too went to his mother. He said to her, "Such and such a thing did we do today, and the boy died. The boys will tell it to the family and to the *hakem* [the head of the town], and they will come and catch me. I want to escape. Give me two or three loaves of bread and I shall go to another place."[7]

So Nadir left his town and fled to Chapushli, a big village at a distance of one farsang (ca. six km. from Kona Gale). When he arrived at Chapushli, he went straightaway to the *hakem* of the place and said to him, "Such and such a thing has happened, and I have come to you to place myself under your protection." The *hakem*, who chanced to be the brother of the *hakem* of Kona Gale, accepted him. In the meantime, the news of the boy's death had spread through Kona Gale, and the *hakem* arrested Nadir's parents for interrogation. They said, "We know not where the boy is." Before long, however, it became known that Nadir was in the nearby village of Chapushli. So the *hakem* of Kona Gale sent messengers to his brother, the *hakem* of Chapushli, to demand that he deliver the boy and thus enable the kinsmen of the murdered boy to avenge his death upon Nadir. The *hakem* of Chapushli, however, answered to the messengers, "Go and tell my brother that the boy came to me and honestly told me what had happened and asked my protection. I accepted him, and therefore so long as he is under my protection, I cannot give him up. If it be possible to persuade the dead boy's family to accept blood money, I am willing to put up the amount myself.'' The messengers went to and fro a number of times, and nothing could be settled. Both sides became angry and obdurate, and things reached such a point that a fight broke out between the followers of the two. The skirmishes between the contending sides lasted a year, and sixty of the men of Chapushli lost their lives. At last the *hakem* of Chapushli called Nadir to him and said, ''You are under my protection and, as you know, we have fought for you and I have lost many of my fighting men. Should my brother, the *hakem* of Kona Gale, send fresh forces against us, we may find ourselves unable to face them. And if I should be taken prisoner, you too will be in his power. Therefore it is my advice to you that you leave us and go to Abivard.[8,b] I have there a friend with whom you will be safe.''

So Nadir left the village of Chapushli, escorted by the *hakem* himself at the head of a band of his fighting men. The *hakem* entrusted Nadir to his friend in Abivard, and then returned with his men to Chapushli.

This friend of the *hakem* was the richest man in Abivard.[9] He possessed large herds of sheep. He took the eight-year-old Nadir to his chief shepherd to teach the boy to become a shepherd. Nadir would go out with the other shepherds to tend the flocks, and thus did he live for five years. When Nadir had attained the age of thirteen, the *hakem*'s friend gave into his care a flock of four or five hundred sheep. Now it was the wont of the shepherds in winter to let their sheep graze on the *gheshlagh* (winter grassland) near Abivard. As summer drew near, the *gheshlagh* became exhausted and the flocks would be taken to the *yeylagh*[c] (summer quarters), where the grazing was good. The *yeylagh* was situated some two or three farsang from Abivard. Every two or three days food and drink was sent from Abivard for the shepherds and their donkeys and dogs. Every month or two the master himself would make the rounds of his flocks in their summer pastures to see if all was well. It was upon one such visit that the master, approaching the field where Nadir was pasturing his flocks, saw from afar that the sheep were scattered unwatched all over the countryside. In surprise he hurried forward and soon came upon Nadir. Nadir stood perfectly still in the open field, with his eyes closed, his face turned upwards, and his chin resting on the back of his hands, which lay clasped over his long shepherd's staff.[10] He stood there oblivious of everything about him, lost in reverie. ''Some wild animal can attack the flock!'' thought the master to himself, and he drew up to Nadir. Nadir did not hear him come. ''What do you think you are doing!'' shouted the master. ''What do you mean by allowing the flock to scatter unwatched!?'' Nadir started, stared at his master, and then cried out in Turkic, *Even yükhülsun!*—''May your house be destroyed! In my thoughts I had conquered the whole of Persia, and just as I was about to take Baghdad, you came and disturbed me!'' "Never mind," said his master derisively, "when you have conquered all of Persia and only Baghdad will be left, call me and I shall come and take it for you." Nadir looked at him for a moment and said to him solemnly, "Do not forget what you have just said!"

Some months elapsed and Nadir returned with the flocks to Abivard. His master began to notice strange things about Nadir which are not seen in other people. He would always get lost in thought and seem preoccupied with plans of his own. His master, watching him, began to fear him. One day he said to Nadir, "I would like you to think well of me. Name what you wish and I shall give it to you." Nadir said, "Give me a horse, a saddle, and a sword." His master said, "Choose any horse you wish." Nadir said, "Give me a good horse and a good sword." So his master brought him a fine horse, a good sword, and two saddlebags. Nadir filled the bags with bread and fodder. His master asked him, "Do you think well of me now?" Nadir said, "Yes, I do."

Nadir was eighteen when he thus left his master's service. What did he do now? He rode out into the fields, far away, came to a village, and stole two or three camels. He brought the camels back to Abivard and sold them there, and with the money thus acquired he bought himself another horse. This horse he gave to one of his friends who was willing to join him in his adventures. However, he made one condition, that half of anything his friend should bring back was to belong to Nadir in payment for the horse. With this first follower Nadir set out and once more carried off a number of camels. These he again sold in Abivard and for the money he got he bought horses. Then he made known that anyone who wanted to join him would receive a horse, for which he would have to give him half of his loot. Within twenty days he had a following of ten riders. Nadir continued to receive half of anything they plundered in return for his horses. When he had twelve men he raided Khivah,[d] the capital of the territory of Khorazm (Khwarizm), a big Turkoman town.[11] There they drove off two big herds of sheep. The sheep, however, could not be hurried, and hampered the speedy retreat of the band. So what did Nadir do? He slaughtered one sheep, bound a rope around its legs, and gave the end of the rope into the hands of one of his horsemen. The rider dragged the slaughtered animal behind him and the flowing blood formed a trail as he rode. All the sheep hurried after the trail and ran as fast as the riders rode.[12] So they all arrived back to Abivard, where Nadir sold the sheep and bought horses for the money. And once more he let it be known, as before, that whosoever would join him would receive a horse and in return would have to share his booty. Soon the number of his band reached fifty.

When Nadir saw that he had fifty riders, he said to himself, "The time has come for me to take Kona Gale, Chapushli, and all the land of Deregez!" So one day he set out with his fifty horsemen, rode to Kona Gale, took the town, and then subjugated Chapushli also and all the land of Deregez. All this he accomplished with his band of fifty riders.[13] He appointed his former benefactor, the *hakem* of Chapushli, ruler of Kona Gale in place of his brother. Nadir himself set up his court in Chapushli and lived there like a king. When he had secured all Deregez, Nadir thought the time had come to be confirmed in his rule by the shah. At that time Shah Sultan Husein sat on the throne of Persia,[14] holding court at Isfahan, and he had a *vezir* in whose hands the real power lay. It was to this *vezir* that Nadir now wrote, or rather had a letter written in his name, for he himself could neither read nor write. In the letter Nadir said, "I am not a rebel. I shall do what you tell me to do. The government in Deregez was not good, and therefore have I done what I have done." The letter was accompanied by appropriate presents to the *vezir*, and Nadir was duly confirmed in his governorship.[15]

For three months Nadir remained in Deregez, and in this time he gathered round him a cavalry a thousand strong. Every day he went raiding the surrounding country. One day he led his men against Quchan, situated eight farsang from Chapushli. Quchan was a town eight times the size of Kona Gale. They set out, all the thousand horsemen, in the afternoon. By nightfall they had ridden three farsangs, and they rode throughout the night, so that they reached Quchan with the dawn and quickly overpowered the city. In the six months that followed, Nadir's headquarters were at Quchan. From there he organized his predatory expeditions, and in these six months he subjected to his rule Shirvan,[16] Böjnurt (Bujnurd), and Radkon (Radkan)—in fact, the whole area surrounding Quchan. Shah Sultan Husein's rule was weak, so many towns revolted against him and declared themselves independent. Nadir occupied these towns, and he could always say that he only restored in them the rule of the shah.

In Quchan Nadir's army grew apace, until it reached the formidable number of 5,000 horsemen. Nadir at that time was no more than twenty years of age. One day he led his 5,000 horsemen to Radkon which, as mentioned before, he had already conquered, and stayed there with them for a few days. One evening he set out with his troops, rode through the night, and towards dawn reached Meshhed.[17] He easily overran the town, occupied it, captured and killed its rulers and the heads of its army, and established his headquarters in the famous capital of Khorassan (Khurasan).[18] From there he again sent a letter to the *vezir*, saying, "I am not a rebel. The government in Meshhed was not good and for this reason I conquered the town." The letter was accompanied by presents which surpassed everything he had sent to the *vezir* up till then, and in due course the answer of the *vezir* came, saying, "You have done well. You are to be from now the governor of Meshhed." So Nadir stayed in Meshhed for about five years.

The *vezir* in the meantime plotted against the shah, for he himself wished to be king. He could, however, do nothing, for he was always near the shah, and though he had many adherents, many others in the court were faithful to the shah. At that time it happened that the city of Merv (today inhabited by Turkomans and belonging to Soviet Russia), which was at that time a part of Persia, rebelled against the shah's rule. So the *vezir* said to the shah, "Let us organize an army, go to Meshhed, and from there we shall attack Merv and punish the rebels. But you yourself must lead the army, otherwise we shall not succeed." The shah agreed, and some time later he arrived with the army and the *vezir* at Meshhed, and camped one farsang from the town.

Every morning the great ones of Meshhed, led by Nadir, came to the royal camp to pay homage to the shah. The camp, however, was full of the adherents of the *vezir*, so that anything the *vezir* wished to do he could do. The *vezir* made plans to kill the shah and to proclaim himself king in his stead. One day when Nadir was received by the shah in his tent, the shah wanted to tell something to the *vezir*. He said to a servant, "Go and call the *vezir*." The servant went and returned, saying, "The *vezir* said he is busy now, and he will come when he has finished his work." The shah became exceedingly angry, seeing that his *vezir* did not obey him, and he said to Nadir with great wrath, "I do not know what to do with this *vezir*!" Nadir said, "Give me your permission, and I shall be able to arrange things with the *vezir*." The king said, "Good." Some time later the *vezir* entered, and the shah immediately addressed him in wrath. "Why did you not come at the time I sent for you?!" The *vezir* answered, "I had work to do. I cannot come any minute." Nadir then cried, "You wicked man! Is this how one speaks to the king?!" And he drew his sword and cut off the man's head.[e]

Seeing this, the shah became very frightened, for the *vezir* had many servants and adherents in the camp. Nadir said to him, "Give me three hours and the guns." The king agreed. Nadir immediately ordered his men to take the guns to the nearby mountains and to direct them against the army. In the camp there were some six thousand soldiers. They knew nothing of what had happened, and when they saw the big guns turned on them, they came to the shah and asked, "What happened?" The shah said, "The *vezir* has been killed, and this was done so that the army should not be able to do anything against the shah." Whereupon all said, "We are your faithful servants." Then Nadir gave orders to bring before him all the adherents of the *vezir*.

They were brought, and Nadir killed many of them, while others he let go free. Then Nadir said to the shah, "It is not necessary that you should go yourself to Merv. Return to Isfahan and I shall go with the army to Merv and capture it." So the shah returned to Isfahan and Nadir took Merv and put it again under Persian rule.

Before Nadir left Merv, he said, "If any one of you will do violence to anybody else, I shall come back and punish him." Some time later, when Nadir camped with his army at a distance of many days' riding from Merv, a man came to him and told him that there was an old woman in Merv whose husband had died, and now one of the inhabitants of Merv had taken seven or eight of her sheep from her by sheer force. Nadir thereupon said to his officers, "I want to go somewhere, and shall be back in about two weeks' time. Stay here in the meantime with the army and take care that I should find everything in order upon my return." No one of the officers dared to ask him, "Where are you going?" At midnight, when the whole of the army was asleep, Nadir set out on his horse, accompanied only by two or three riders. He rode with them to Merv, entered the house of the widow, and asked her, "Is it true that so-and-so took from you by force seven or eight sheep?" The old woman said, "Yes, it is true." Nadir then went to the man's house and took the sheep and returned them to the widow. Then he punished the man; he put him to death. Seeing this, all the inhabitants of Merv were very much afraid and did not dare again to do any violence. Nadir rode back, and a fortnight after he had set out from his camp, he came back there, again in the dead of the night.[19]

Again a number of years passed, and seventeen towns in the Caucasus rebelled against Persia. The shah wrote to Nadir to come and conquer the seventeen towns. Nadir came with his army from Meshhed and reached Isfahan. There the shah gave him an additional army, and thus reinforced, Nadir marched through Azerbaijan to the Caucasus. His conquest of the whole of the Caucasus was effected in about two and a half or three years. But some months after Nadir had set out for the Caucasus, or, at the utmost, after a year, the Afghans rebelled against Persia.[f] One of the great Afghan leaders collected an army 20,000 men strong. He entered Persia from the east and proceeded, conquering and destroying everything on his way, until he reached the neighborhood of the capital, Isfahan. Shah Sultan Husein sent his son with an army of about five or six thousand men against him. The prince's army met the Afghan invader at a distance of some six farsangs from Isfahan, and there suffered utter defeat. The whole Persian army was scattered and the prince himself was killed. The Afghans marched up to the city, surrounded it, and began to besiege it. The siege lasted for about forty days.[g] In the meantime the shah sent a letter to Nadir, saying, "Leave the

Caucasus and come quickly to rescue Isfahan!" But Nadir did not obey the shah and answered, "First I want to finish the conquest of the Caucasus; then I shall come and retake Persia."

When the forty days were up, the Afghans captured Isfahan. Within Isfahan there was the *ark*, the citadel, the fortified palace of the shah. The shah withdrew into it with the remnants of his men. A few days later the *ark* also was taken by the Afghans. The shah fled to the harem, where his own mother also lived, and he said to her, "Where shall I now go, where shall I flee?" His mother scornfully parted her legs, pointed to her privy parts, and said, "Go to the place from where you came! What sort of a king are you?!" The Afghans entered and killed the shah and all his family. Only one of the shah's wives escaped. She was then pregnant. The Afghans remained in Isfahan about eight months.[20]

Six months after the Afghans killed the shah, Nadir completed his conquest of the Caucasus and returned to Azerbaijan. He then proceeded into Persia and fought the Afghans. He conquered town after town until he reached Isfahan. The Afghans fled from Isfahan also, and Nadir pursued them, so that they had to flee the very way they came, until they reached the eastern borders of Persia. Nadir killed them all. He entered even into Afghanistan and conquered it, just as he had conquered the whole of Persia proper.

Then Nadir said, "Persia must have a king, and he must be from the royal family, the family of the Safavi." A man came and said, "There is a woman from among the wives of the late shah who was pregnant and escaped death. She has in the meantime given birth to a son. This is the only one of the shah's sons who has remained alive." The child was then about six months old. Nadir said, "This child must be the king!" So Nadir sent messengers to all parts of Persia to invite the nobles and the rulers of the people to come and elect the king. They all came. Nadir gave orders to bring in the child in his cradle, and they put the cradle on the *takht* (royal throne). Above the child's head they hung the crown on a string. Nadir then turned to the great ones of the country present and said to them, "This child shall be our king!" And he fell upon his knees before the child and bid all the others do the same. Then he said, "Until the child grows up, I shall be the *naib sultani* (regent)." So all the rulers present fell on their knees, and then Nadir gave leave to them to return everyone to his place, and he himself stayed in Isfahan and was regent.[21]

Six months later the child-king died. Who knows how this happened? He died. So all the great ones of Persia came and said to Nadir, "You must be Shah!" Nadir consented, and he was crowned shah of Persia. He knew neither how to read nor how to write, and did not learn before he died.[22]

A year or two later Nadir decided to go against Baghdad and to conquer it. He went with his army and fought against the Babylonians.[23] He reached the shore of the river Euphrates,[24] but the town was on the farther side of the river and he was unable to cross in face of strong opposition on the part of the Babylonian army. Six months passed like this, and Nadir still could not cross the river. Suddenly he remembered how he had dreamed, when he was still a simple shepherd in Abivard, that he had conquered all Persia, and how his former master came up to him and disturbed him in his dreams just as he was about to conquer Baghdad in his imagination. And he remembered what his former master had jokingly promised him: "When you shall have conquered the whole of Persia and only Baghdad will be left, call me and I shall conquer it for you!" So Nadir sent quick messengers to ride to Abivard and to call his former master to him. The man came; Nadir showed him some honor and said to him, "Do you remember what you promised me when I was your shepherd? Now I have conquered the whole of Persia and only Baghdad is left. Now you must conquer Baghdad for me!" The man said, "Good, I will do it." And he stayed with the army. He said to Nadir, "We must do this by deceit. Give orders to bring 5,000 big goats, 10,000 candles, and 10,000 big earthenware jars." Nadir did as he told him and prepared everything he wanted. The man said, "Good. How many soldiers have you got here?" Nadir said, "About forty thousand men."[25] The man said, "Order the five thousand best horsemen to leave the camp in the dead of the night quietly and ride along the bank of the river to a distance of about two or three farsangs. But let them do it so that nothing should be noticed from the other side." This was done at after midnight or one o'clock. Then the goats were brought and two candles were tied to the horns of each. The candles were lit and the goats were driven into the water by five thousand specially appointed men. The military bands also were brought up and ordered to play at full force. The men shouted and broke the jars, thus creating a terrible din.[26] When the Babylonian army from over the river saw the lights and heard the noise, they believed that the Persians were attempting a general attack by crossing the river at that point, and they concentrated all their strength opposite the goats. At the same time word was given to the five thousand horsemen waiting two or three farsangs away to swim over on their horses. Horses can swim far better than men. The horsemen crossed, gained the other shore without any opposition, and attacked the unsuspecting enemy from an entirely unexpected quarter. In the confusion thus created, the rest of the Persian army could cross the river, and soon they were the lords of Baghdad.[27,h] After the conquest of Baghdad, Nadir conquered all the outer boundaries of Persia, from the Caspian Sea in the north to the Persian Gulf in the south.

In earlier days India also formed a part of the Persian empire, as it is written, "From India to Ethiopia."[28] So Nadir decided to reconquer this country. He set out on his expedition against India with 10,000 camels carrying ammunition, mainly lead cannonballs. After leaving Peshawar, between Afghanistan and India, behind, they reached a mountain pass[29] so narrow that the heavy guns could not get through. The leaders of the army said, "What is to be done? It is impossible to pass." Nadir said, "Bombard the mountain with the cannons until it will be possible to pass." They did so and spent more than half the ammunition on it.[30] When the high officers saw this, they said to Nadir, "What are you doing? We are on our way to fight India, a mighty empire, and you waste all our ammunition on this mountain?" Nadir said, "You are fools! Do you think these cannonballs are aimed at the mountain? They are aimed straight at the heart of the king of India. When he hears that we are wasting so much ammunition on the mountain, he will think we have enormous reserves of ammunition, and he will not dare oppose us." And so indeed it came to pass.

On his way to India, Nadir reached a bridge. While crossing the bridge, Nadir suddenly turned to his learned *vezir*, Mīrzā Mahdī Khān,[31] and asked him, "What is the best food which in one bite gives the most strength?" Mīrzā Mahdī Khān answered, "An egg." Many months later, when on their way back from India they again reached the bridge, Nadir remembered what he had asked Mīrzā Mahdī Khān on the same spot, and queried, "With what?" Without a moment's hesitation, Mīrzā Mahdī Khān answered, "With salt."[32]

From India Nadir brought back rich treasures. Among them was a great diamond, round as a hill, which was called *Kuh-i-Blur*, that is, "crystal mountain."[i] Another great brick-shaped diamond brought back by Nadir from India was called *Deria-i-Nur*, "sea of light."[33] When Nadir returned from India he was so mighty and rich that he hung the Deria-i-Nur at the back of his saddle to serve as an ornament, so that it dangled over the hind legs of his horse. The kings who ruled Persia after Nadir were no longer so mighty, and they set the Deria-i-Nur in an armband (*bazu-band*). The dynasty which followed, that of the Kajars, sat it in their crown—that is, they were even less rich. Fath-Ali Shah had the Fatiha, the opening chapter of the Koran, engraved upon the diamond. In doing so he lowered the diamond's value, so that it was worth only 50,000 pounds sterling. The kings who followed him no longer had the honor to wear the diamond and kept it in their treasure house under lock and key.

When Nadir returned from India, he fortified his old castle, Kalat Nadiri (Qal'at Nadiri), which lies north of Meshhed, with enormous blocks of hewn stones brought there from a great distance. He paid special attention to reinforcing the natural caves which were in the mountain. He wanted to convert these caves into a treasury. Kalat is a natural fortress built by God. It is surrounded by a range of very high mountains in the form of an unbroken chain, the length of which attains twenty-four farsangs. There are but two mountain paths over which camels, horses, and carts can pass. Nine further paths can be traversed only on foot. Nadir did not trust the Persians, and therefore he wished to settle Jews in Kalat to serve as the guardians of his treasures. Accordingly, he gave orders to the town of Kazvin (Qazvin) to send forty Jewish families to Kalat.j Owing to the difficulties of the way, the forty families could not travel together and divided into three groups. At the time of Nadir's death, only seventeen of the Jewish families had arrived in Kalat, and sixteen had got as far as Meshhed, while the remaining seven only reached Sabzavar. This, incidentally, was the beginning of the Jewish community of Meshhed, which exists there to this day.[34]

Nadir's trust in the Jews may have been connected with the following occurrence. One day Nadir invited to him two Shi'a *mushtahids* (*mujtahid*, a Muslim priest), two popes (i.e., Christian priests), and two Jewish rabbis. He wanted to know which is the true religion, for he was a Sunni, and not a Shi'a.[35] He said to them, "Sit down in one place and prepare yourselves to answer my questions." Then he asked them which of the books was the real one. First he asked the *mushtahids*, "What is written in the Koran?" They read out to him, and he saw that it spoke of Moses, Abraham, and others. Then he turned to the Christians and asked them, "What is written in the *Injil*?"[36] They read out to him, and he saw that their book too was built on what had happened to the Jews previously. Then he asked the rabbis, "What is written in the *Taurat*?"[37] They read out to him from the beginning, and he saw that the book of the Jews begins from the creation of the world and goes on explaining what happened after then. So Nadir said, "This is the true book; this is the real book of God."[38]

When Nadir came back from India, he found that his son had collected an army around himself. This army consisted of ten thousand horsemen. A thousand had white garments and white horses, a thousand had black garments and black horses, a thousand grey garments and grey horses, a thousand yellow garments and yellow horses, a thousand brown garments and brown horses, and so on to ten thousand, according to each of the colors horses have. It was whispered to Nadir, "Maybe your son plans to revolt against you and wants to be king." Once his son came to him, and Nadir asked, "Who are you that you have made yourself all these horsemen, a thousand of each color?" His son answered him haughtily, "I am the son of Nadir Shah!" Then Nadir said, "But Nadir himself did not do the like!" His son said, "And whose son is Nadir?" To this question Nadir could not answer, so he became very angry and gave orders to deprive his son of his two eyes. Mīrzā Mahdī Khān came and begged, "Do not do this; do not blind your son." Thereupon Nadir answered, "First your own eyes will be taken out, then the eyes of my son." And so it came to pass.[39]

Some years later it happened that a letter came to Nadir from Europe, from one of the kings there. But nobody could read the letter. It was very shameful for the Persian government to admit that they could not read the letter. So they went to Mīrzā Mahdī Khān and asked, "Do you know if there is a man in Persia who can read the letter and understand it?" He answered, "No." They said, "What shall we do? The shah must give an answer to the letter; he must know what is written in it." Thereupon Mīrzā Mahdī Khān said, "I can read the letter and translate it. Take me to the hot bath and bring there ice, and draw the forms of the letters on my naked back with ice, and in this manner I shall be able to translate the letter." This was done, and when the translation of the letter was presented to Nadir, he felt great regret for having blinded Mīrzā Mahdī Khān.[40,k]

Nadir was so mighty and powerful that each time before he attacked a town, he let the inhabitants know, "If you do not submit, I shall conquer the town, make slaves out of you, and take away all you have; the gold, the silver, and even the dust of your town I shall take away." So each time after he conquered a town, he said to his soldiers, "Take the dust of this town to Meshhed." Whereupon the soldiers took the sacks in which they used to give fodder to their horses, filled them with earth, and took them away with them. When they reached the neighborhood of Meshhed, they emptied their sacks so that large hills rose up. Such hills are to be found all over Persia. Between Meshhed and Quchan there are two such hills at a distance of two farsangs from each other. These hills are called *tas tappe*, that is, "bowl hills." In Deregez there are six or seven such hills. Other kings also used to build such hills, but the greatest number of them was made by Nadir.

After Nadir came back from India, he became very cruel. Once he said, "Tomorrow I shall take the eyes of my army until I have seven rotls of them." And he fulfilled his threat.[l]

It was his cruelty which made Nadir's commanders decide to kill him. Nadir camped with his army in Radkon, at a distance of eight farsangs from Meshhed. From Radkon it was just barely possible to see the upper edge of the golden dome of the shrine of Imam Reza in Meshhed. The dome was covered with gold from before Nadir's time, paid for by foundations which had been established for the purpose of maintaining and embellishing the shrine. One evening Nadir said, "Tomorrow I shall have the heads of so many soldiers cut off that from the top of the hill made of the heads I shall be able to see the whole of the golden dome."[41] When his commanders heard this, they knew that Nadir had become mad, and they were afraid that he might kill a million in order to make a hill out of their heads, and, should he still not see the dome well enough, he might kill another million. So the nine commanders, among them the brother of Nadir's wife, decided to kill him the same night.

Nadir used to sleep in a tent within the camp. He would tell his wife to cross her legs and he would rest his head in her lap, while in his hand he grasped a naked sword. As long as Nadir slept, his wife had to keep awake. He knew that in this position he would be awakened by the slightest movement made by his wife, be it of fright or of anything else. In the dead of the night the nine men set out jointly for Nadir's tent. But on the way there they dropped off one by one, so afraid were they of Nadir. They were afraid even of his name. Finally only the brother of Nadir's wife reached his tent. When he saw that he was alone, he was very much afraid. He slowly lifted the curtain covering the entrance to the tent. His sister, Nadir's wife, when she suddenly perceived her brother standing in the tent opening with a drawn sword in his hand, started, and Nadir woke up. Nadir jumped to his feet and his brother-in-law took to flight. Nadir ran after him with the sword in his hand, but his foot got caught by the rope of the tent and he fell. Thereupon his brother-in-law ran up to him and killed him with his sword.[42]

Nadir had had a beautiful garden laid out in Meshhed. This garden already was called the Garden of Nadir in his lifetime. He also gave expression to his wish to be buried in Meshhed. So after his assassination they took his body to Meshhed and buried it in the Garden of Nadir.[43]

When Nadir was killed, a chronogram was composed, the numerical value of the letters of which give 1160, the date of his death by the Muslim year, 1747.

Nadir b' derek raft—"Nadir went to hell."[44,m]

Notes

"A Popular 'Life of Nadir' " originally was published in *Edoth* 3, nos. 3–4 (1948):1–20.

1. Laurence Lockhart, *Nadir Shah* (London, 1938).
2. Here and in the following pages I give the phonetic form of place names. On first mention, I give the correct spelling in parentheses.
3. Cf. Lockhart, *Nadir Shah*, pp. 18, 20.
4. *Mullah*, i.e., "master," "teacher," is the title of religious personages in Persia.
5. Herodotus reports the same to have occurred in connection with the birth of one of the remote predecessors of Nadir on Persia's throne, Cyrus. Astyages dreamed that his daughter Mandane urinated and the water filled not only his town, but the whole of Asia. Again, when his daughter was pregnant with Cyrus, he dreamed that a vine grew out of her womb and covered all of Asia. The dreams were interpreted by the magi: his daughter's son would reign in his stead (Herodotus 1.107–8).

6. The period of six months recurs frequently in the narrative; cf. "Three Meshhed Tales of Mullah Siman-Tov," above.

7. Again we are reminded of what Herodotus tells about the childhood of Cyrus. When Cyrus had reached the age of ten in the house of the poor shepherd, his foster father, he played with the children in the streets of the village and they chose him to be their king. One of the children disobeyed him, and he commanded the others to beat him with whips. The beaten child complained to his father, and in consequence Cyrus' identity was discovered (Herodotus 1.114–16).

8. Abivard, according to my informant, lies six farsang (thirty-six km.) east of Chapushli.

9. This is the first instance where we are able to check the veracity of the folktale. It does seem to be a historical fact that in his youth Nadir entered the service of Baba 'Ali Beg Kusa Ahmadu, chief of the Afghans of the town of Abivard (Lockhart, *Nadir Shah*, p. 21).

10. Upon reaching this point in his narrative, my informant got up from his chair and went through Nadir's movements in the scene he was describing.

11. East of the Caspian Sea, near the Oxus River. Today the whole territory is called Khiva. It is of course impossible that Nadir should have raided Khiva, at a distance of 500 km. from Deregez, with twelve horsemen. We may perhaps attribute this story to a muddled reminiscence of Nadir's Turkistan expedition in 1740, when he took Khiva with a force many tens of thousands strong (Lockhart, *Nadir Shah*, pp. 193–95).

12. According to my informant, this method is used even today, and it is in the nature of sheep to behave like this.

13. It is a fact that Nadir, after having first served and then opposed Malik Mahmud of Meshhed, fled back to Abivard, where he raised a force of horsemen with which he raided the Deregez district (Lockhart, *Nadir Shah*, pp. 22–23).

14. My informant knew only of Shah Sultan Huscin as having been the king of Persia during the whole period of Nadir's ascent. According to him, Shah Sultan Husein was followed on the throne by the infant king, and then by Nadir himself. Actually, however, Shah Sultan Husein ruled only from 1694 to 1722, when he was deposed; he was finally put to death in 1726. In 1722 his third son, Tahmasp, proclaimed himself shah. Tahmasp was crowned in 1729 and was deposed by Nadir in 1732. From 1732 to 1736, nominally at least, the infant Abbas III, son of Tahmasp, was shah.

15. In 1726 Hasan Ali Beg, the "assayer of the kingdom," appointed Nadir deputy governor of Abivard on Tahmasp's behalf (Lockhart, *Nadir Shah*, p. 24).

16. The town of Shirvan lies between Radkon and Bujnurd. All three towns lie southwest of the district of Deregez.

17. The actual distance between Radkon and Meshhed is 75 km.

18. In fact Nadir took Meshhed in 1726, when he was thirty-eight (Lockhart, *Nadir Shah*, p. 27).

19. A raid on Merv actually figures among Nadir's early exploits (ibid., p. 23).

20. The whole story is legend. Isfahan was besieged by the Afghans in 1722, and Tahmasp, after having been elected crown prince, escaped. Some months later his father surrendered the city. In 1729, Nadir recovered Isfahan for Tahmasp, who was then and there crowned shah. Nadir's Caucasian campaign did not take place until 1741 to 1743, that is, even after the invasion of India (ibid., pp. 39, 197–211).

21. In 1732 Nadir arranged for the deposition of Shah Tahmasp and for the investiture of the shah's eight-month-old son as Abbas III. A chronicler in Nadir's service, Muhammad Muhsin, relates that the infant's cradle was brought forward and Nadir laid the *jiqa*, the aigrette of sovereignty, by his head and placed a shield and sword beside him. Nadir was made regent on the same occasion (ibid., p. 63).

22. Actually Nadir's coronation took place in 1736, four years after the coronation of Abbas III. Nadir sent the child-king to Khurasan to join his father, Tahmasp. Both father and son were put to death in 1740 by Reza Quli, the eldest son of Nadir Shah, during the latter's absence in India (ibid., pp. 104, 176–77).

23. The Hebrew name of both Iraq and Baghdad is *Bavel*, Babylon. Actually Nadir's opponents in this campaign were the Turks who ruled Iraq.

24. Actually, of course, Baghdad lies on the banks of the Tigris, not the Euphrates.
25. In this point the folk story falls behind reality. The number of Nadir's army was much greater than 40,000 (ibid., pp. 69–70).
26. One can feel in this story a clear reminiscence of the biblical story of Gideon's tactics with the pitchers and torches against the Midianites (Judg. 7:16ff.).
27. Nadir's Baghdad campaign took place in December 1732. He crossed the Tigris over a floating bridge with 2,500 men, was followed the next day by another 1,500, and thus blockaded Baghdad. The city suffered from famine, but a Turkish army was sent to relieve it, and Nadir's forces were defeated in July 1733. Nadir reorganized his army, again besieged Baghdad, and in December 1733, he signed a treaty with Ahmad Pasha, the Turkish governor of Baghdad—which did not, however, include the surrender of the city (ibid., pp. 65–75). It is thus only in the folktale that Nadir conquered Baghdad.
28. Esther 1:1. This, of course, is a personal addition by my informant; the Persian peasants of Mohammadabad are most unlikely to have quoted the Bible.
29. Actually Peshawar lies some eighty km. west of the Indus River, that is, beyond the mountain passes leading from Afghanistan into India.
30. This was the only part of the story in which my informant's second version differed from his first. The second time he said, "They came to a very steep hill. They could not draw up the guns. There was no way around the hill. So Nadir commanded that the hill be leveled by artillery fire."
31. Mīrzā Muḥammad Mahdī Kaukabī Astarābādhī was appointed by Nadir at his coronation in 1736 to serve as official historiographer. His Taarīkh-i-Nādirī is judged by Lockhart to be the most important contemporary source of the history of Nadir. Mīrzā Mahdī actually accompanied Nadir to India. His title was Munshī al-Mamālik, "secretary of the kingdoms" (ibid., pp. 292, 293).
32. This anecdote has been attributed to many historical figures.
33. Lockhart, Nadir Shah, p. 152, mentions only the famous Kohinor diamond as having been brought back by Nadir from India.
34. Historical sources do not refer to this order. However, M. Truilhier, who was in Meshhed in 1807, reported that there were about a hundred Jewish families there whom Nadir Shah had gathered with a view to activating commerce, and whose situation had deteriorated greatly after Nadir's death ("Mémoire descriptif de la route de Tehran à Meched . . . ," Bulletin de la Société de Géographie [Paris], 2d ser., 9 (May 1838):273). Lockhart wrote to me on 19 June, 1946, "In view of Nadir's habit of transferring large numbers of tribesmen from one place to another for purposes of defence, I think that it is quite probable that he did in fact give orders for these Qazvini Jews to be moved to Kalat." See "Folk Traditions about the History of the Meshhedi Jews," above; Raphael Patai, "The Hebrew Education in the Marrano Community of Meshhed," [in Hebrew], Edoth 1, no. 4 (1946):213ff.
35. See Lockhart, Nadir Shah, pp. 278–81.
36. I.e., the Evangelion, the Gospel.
37. I.e., the Tora, the Pentateuch.
38. This legend, of course, has a distinctly Jewish coloring. However, it seems to be a fact that Nadir ordered the Old and New Testaments as well as the Koran to be translated into Persian, and that he assembled the priests of the respective religions to make the translations (Lockhart, Nadir Shah, p. 280).
39. Actually Nadir's eldest son, Reza Quli, was made viceroy of Persia by his father when the latter set out on his Indian campaign. Reza Quli "formed a special corps, 12,000 strong, of Khurasani jazayirchis, whom he equipped with gorgeous uniforms of cloth of gold and silver." When Reza Quli met his father on his return from India in 1740, the latter ordered his son's fancy troops disbanded. The blinding of Reza Quli took place in 1742, more than two years later. Nadir suspected his son of having hired an assassin who tried to kill him, and it was for that reason that he blinded him. History knows nothing of the blinding of Mīrzā Mahdī. On the contrary, it is said that Nadir put to death many of his nobles who were present when the sentence was carried out for not having offered to undergo the punishment in place of his son (ibid., pp. 126, 174, 180, 207–9).

40. It is a fact that Mīrzā Mahdī drafted several letters, manifestos, and treaties for Nadir. He was well versed in Persian, Turkish, and Arabic (ibid., pp. 60, 293, 295, 296).
41. This has a legendary flavor. It is, however, a fact that in 1747 "wherever he halted he had many people tortured and put to death, and had towers of their heads erected" (ibid., 259).
42. This account of Nadir's assassination largely corresponds to that given ibid., p. 262.
43. Actually Nadir had built himself tombs in Kalat and in Meshhed in the Khiaban-i-Bala, the Upper Avenue (ibid., p. 198).
44. The chronogram is not quite correct, for it gives 1161, while Nadir was assassinated in 1160. If, however, we take Nadir's name written, not in its full form (with an alif after the *N*), which was assumed only at his coronation, but in its original form without the alif, we reduce the number by one and thus get 1160. It is very possible that the hatred felt toward Nadir was expressed in the original form of the chronogram not only in the words, but also by referring to him by his original humble name, Nadr.

Notes by Laurence Lockhart (27 May 1947)

It is unfortunate that so little authentic information has been preserved regarding Nadir's early life. It is possible that, if ever the missing first volume of Muhammad Kazim's work is found, we may learn a good deal more, but that is mere conjecture. I must regret that I have, so far, been unable to visit the Darragaz-Abivard country, so as to collect for myself any local tradition that may still be current.

a. Nadir's baldness. I have not seen any reference elsewhere to Nadir's baldness and regard this statement as improbable.
b. Abivard. For position, see map on p. 19 of my book on Nadir.
c. "Gheshlagh" and "Yeylagh." I suggest that the spellings "Qishlaq" and "Yailaq" are preferable.
d. Raid on Khiva. There is confusion here with the early raid on Merv, as stated in n. 11.
e. There seems to be some confusion here between 1) Fath Ali Khan Daghistani, who was disgraced and blinded for his alleged plot to deprive Shah Sultan Husain of his throne, and 2) Fath Ali Khan Qajar of Astrabad. There seems, however, to be very little doubt that Nadir was responsible for the death of his rival Fath Ali Khan Qajar.
f. The Afghan invasion. The chronology here is, of course, faulty, as the Afghan invasion took place in 1722. As stated in n. 20, Nadir's Caucasian campaigns took place nearly twenty years later.
g. Siege of Isfahan. Shah Sultan Husain sent word to Vakhtang, the viceroy of Georgia, asking him to march to the relief of the capital, but Vakhtang refused.
h. The story of the capture of Baghdad is pure fantasy.
i. Kuh-i-Blur. Kuh-i-Bulur, "mountain of crystal."
j. Sending of Jewish families to Kalat. This is certainly very probable. It will be recalled that Shah Abbas the Great moved many Armenians from Julfa on the Aras to 'New' Julfa, just south of Isfahan, in order to foster trade in his capital. Nadir may well have decided to imitate him. He had often transferred tribesmen from one district to another for purposes of defence.
k. There is no truth in the statement that Nadir blinded Mirza Mahdi.
l. Wholesale blinding of people and the towers of skulls. There is no doubt whatever about Nadir's terrible cruelties in his later years, but the story of the eyes reminds me of Agha Muhammad's wholesale blinding of the people of Kirman after his capture of that city in 1794.
m. I agree that, in order to make this chronogram correct, the alif in Nadir's name should be dropped, causing it to revert to its original form.

IV.
Sephardim and Oriental Jews

16. Sephardi Folklore

The more tradition-bound a society, the greater the role folklore plays in the life of its members. Accordingly, in the case of an ethnic group as traditional as the Sephardim up to one or two generations ago, we will expect to find a society steeped in folklore, folk custom, and folk tradition. And this, in fact, was the case wherever Sephardi Jewish communities lived in environments favorable to the preservation of old ways of life, and especially in Greece, Turkey, Turkish Palestine, and other countries of the Turkish Empire.

One of the most important factors in the preservation of folklore in general is language. The Sephardi Jews retained medieval Spanish (Ladino) as their everyday language. There is a marked similarity in the function of Ladino, on one hand, and of Yiddish, on the other. But there is also a difference between the two. The Hebrew element in Yiddish is richer than in Ladino. If we count the Hebrew words in the famous *romances* of the Sephardi Jews, we find only a very few—something completely unthinkable in a Yiddish poem or folk song.

The similarity between Ladino and Yiddish is found in the facts that both are written in Hebrew characters and both have retained medieval forms of the language. German in Germany and Spanish in Spain have developed since the fifteenth or sixteenth century. They became modernized. But the languages retained by the Jews, Yiddish by the Ashkenazim and Ladino by the Sephardim, did not develop in the same way. Ladino remained frozen in the form in which it existed at the time when the Jews left Spain. Like Yiddish, in time Ladino became endowed with a certain traditional quality, almost sanctity, second only to the "holy tongue" itself. Even certain prayers were composed and recited in it. There is, for instance, a very interesting bedtime *Sh'ma'* prayer which exists in many versions from Salonica and from other parts of the Sephardi world, recited in Ladino. Its first lines are as follows:

> Quatro cantonadas
> Ay en esta casa,
> Quatro malakhim,
> Que mos acompanian
> Y mos guadrin.

> Four corners
> Are in this house,
> Four angels,
> Who accompany us
> And protect us.[1]

The greatest and most joyous ceremony known to folk societies is the wedding. Accordingly, we find that much folklore material is concentrated around the wedding among the Sephardi Jews, as is the case in practically all folk societies. The wedding ceremony is surrounded by innumerable customs. It is not a single ceremony, as in our own society, but a prolonged period in the life of the two young people and the two families concerned. In Salonica, a "town and mother" in Sephardi Israel, preparations for a wedding began many months in advance. The bride, her mother, and sisters were busy assembling and sewing the *asugar* (trousseau). Mattresses were made for the bride on a special day, called the "wool washing," in which women friends of the family participated, all working together to the accompaniment of music. On Saturday night preceding the wedding, the actual festivities opened with the night of *almusama*, during which the bride was expected to sit, silent, serious, and motionless, in the midst of the singing, dancing, and merrymaking of all her friends. On the following day, Sunday, the *el preciado* (evaluation) of the *asugar* took place, after which the entire trousseau was transported in a festive, musical procession from the bride's to the bridegroom's house. The bridegroom, in return, sent his *bogcha* (literally, "cloth") with the returning procession. This consisted of bathing utensils and sweets, all wrapped in a silk cloth—hence the name—

and placed on a large brass tray or in a basket. On the following day, the bride went to the Turkish bath, accompanied by a large group of women. On the way to and from the bathhouse, as well as in the bath itself, the women sang and danced around the bride. In the bath they all partook of a rich repast.

Then followed Tuesday, the day of the wedding. Again a festive and gay procession took the bride from the house of her own parents to that of the bridegroom. The groom, standing on top of the stairs, threw rice, sweets, and coins at the bride. The *huppa*, the canopy under which the wedding ceremony proper took place, was made of the embroidered velvet curtains of the holy ark. It was set up in a room or in the hallway of the house, and under it the bride and the groom were united in the traditional way, with the Seven Benedictions, the pronouncement of the wedding formula, the breaking of the glass, and the shower of sweets and *mazal tov* cries. In olden days, following this ceremony, the *el fablar*, the "speaking" or "advice," took place, in which the bride and groom separately received detailed advice as to how to behave during the *noce del enciero* (wedding night).

Next morning, the bride donned the *cofia*, the traditional dress of the married Sephardi women in Salonica. For seven days following the wedding neither the bride nor the groom left the house. They were always in the company of relatives and friends, as a precaution against evil spirits who were believed to try to harm people, especially on such festive occasions as a wedding. On the eighth day the groom went to the market to buy a big live fish. The fish was placed in a copper tub in the middle of the room and the bride jumped over it three times. Each jump was followed by the loudly pronounced good wishes of the attending women. They said, "Be blessed by many children as the fish of the sea."

At these ceremonies, music was played all the time and much singing used to go on. It was at these ceremonies that the famous *romances*, or ballads, were sung. These ballads are the Sephardi variety of the famous Spanish *romancero*, which go back to the old Spanish epics of the eleventh and twelfth centuries. Those epics were originally very long, and nobody could remember their entire text. They were shortened, or cut up into pieces, and in this way these *romances* came into being. Most of them assumed their final shape in the fifteenth and sixteenth centuries. These ballads, as befits weddings, were in most cases of an erotic character. Here is one which was sung in Salonica.

> Una ija tiene el reyes,
> Una ija regalada.
> Mitiola en altas tores,
> Por tenerla bien guardada. . . .

The king has a daughter,
A delicate daughter.
He placed her in a high tower,
To keep her well guarded.
One day, in the heat of the day,
She looked down from her window
And saw a "reaper" pass by,
Reaping wheat and rye.
Quickly she sent to call him
One of her slave girls:
Come here, you reaper,
My mistress calls you!
What does your mistress want of me,
What does she want and demand?
She wants you to sow wheat,
To cut and reap the rye.
The spade is of gold
And the ploughshare of fine silver.
Where shall I sow the wheat?
Where shall I reap the rye?
In her body sow the wheat,
And in her lap the rye.[2]

In another ballad the bridegroom is addressed as a horse.

The beautiful maiden
Saddled up her horse,
Saddled it, bridled it,
Led it to the water.
        With love, my bride, with pleasure.
The water was troubled,
The horse became hot,
The maiden got angry,
And threw him into the lake.
        With love my bride, with pleasure.
"What is my sin, O maiden,
That you throw me into the lake?
Ever since you were little
I have been your pure lover."
        With love, my bride, with pleasure.
She kissed him and embraced him,
Took him to the palace.
They set tables for her
Seated her to eat.
        With love, my bride, with pleasure.
They made the bed for her,
Carried her to lie down on it.
Finally, in the middle of the night,

> They discovered a new game.
>> With love, my bride, with pleasure.
> The groom won the bride,
> For a hundred and twenty years.
>> With love, my bride, with pleasure.[3]

One can easily imagine the merry atmosphere created by these songs and by the lively music accompanying them.

If within a few months after the wedding the bride did not become pregnant, this was regarded as a cause for worry. The young wife then was advised to take recourse to all kinds of magical means and remedies. One of these was the *indulco*. The *indulco* was made of many ingredients from the animal and vegetable world, but the most important substance in it was a piece of a mummy. The *indulco* was given to the woman to eat in the firm belief that it would cause her to become pregnant. Of course, the rabbis of the Sephardi communities disapproved of this remedy, just as they frowned upon many folk customs and folk beliefs, and they issued a stern warning against it. But, needless to say, this warning, like many others, was useless against the force of established folk custom.

There are many interesting folk customs in connection with childbirth itself. Most of these customs are based on sympathetic magic, that is to say, on the belief that by enacting symbolically what one expects to happen, one can bring about the desired event. If a woman has difficulty in labor, this is caused by her womb's refusal to open up. To induce it to open, one has to open all kinds of household objects, such as drawers, doors, windows, or the door of the *aron*, the holy ark in the synagogue. An alternative method is to have the woman look into a cup filled with oil and then take the oil to the synagogue and burn it in a lamp; or to blow the shofar at the bed of the woman; or to give donations to the synagogue, and so forth.

Eight days after the birth of a boy came the great event of circumcision, of introducing the child into the Covenant of Abraham. There was a very interesting custom of the Sephardi *mohelim*, the ritual circumcisers: they used to collect the foreskins from all the circumcision ceremonies they performed and to preserve them in a box. When a *mohel* died, a necklace was made of these foreskins and hung around his neck. This was done because of the belief that by demonstrating in this manner that the *mohel* had performed this great mitzva so many times, he would gain immediate entrance to heaven.[4]

Many songs were sung in connection with childbirth and circumcision, some of them quite lengthy. One of these, containing the story of the birth of Abraham, was very popular in Salonica.

Quando el rey Nimrod, el campo salia,
Miraba en el ceilo y en la istriaria.
Vido luz santa en la judiria.
Que avia de nacir *Abraham avinu*. . . .

When Nimrod the king went out to the field,
He looked to the sky and to the stars.
He saw a sacred light among the Jews,
For our father Abraham was about to be born.

He sent for the midwives and commanded them
That every man's wife, when she becomes pregnant,
The moment she gives birth, the child be killed,
For our father Abraham was about to be born.

And the wife of Terah became pregnant.
Day after day he asked her:
Why has the expression of your face changed so much?
But she knew the good she was carrying.

At the end of nine months she wanted to give birth,
Went walking into the fields and vineyards,
To her husband she said nothing.
She found a cave, there she gave birth to him.

In that hour the newborn child spoke:
—Go, O my mother, from the cave,
I shall find somebody to suckle me,
An angel from heaven will accompany me,
For I am a creation of the blessed God.

At the end of twenty days she came to visit him,
She saw him before her, a jumping boy.
He was looking carefully at the heaven
In order to know the God of truth.

—Mother, my mother, what do you want here?
—Here I gave birth to a son,
I came to search, whether he is here,
If he is still alive, I shall be comforted with him.

—My dear Mother, what are you talking?
How could you leave such a precious son?
How could you come to visit him after twenty days?
I am the dear son of yours.

See, O Mother, God is one,
He created the Heavens one by one.
Go tell Nimrod that he is lost
Because he does not know the God of truth.

To Nimrod the king the thing became known,
He commanded that they bring him quickly . . .

Abraham said: *Rasha'* [Evil One]! Why do you revolt against God!?
Why do you deny the God of Truth?

—Light the furnace, light it well!
Hurry, throw him in, for he knows,
Carry him in chains, for he understands.
If God saves him here, he is the true one!

They threw him into the furnace. He was walking
With the angels, he was pacing . . .
Hence we knew the true God.
Great is the *z'khut* [merit] of Señor Abraham
Thanks to him we know the God of Truth.

Great is the *z'khut* [merit] of the father
Who fulfills the *mitzva* of *Abraham avinu*.
Let us congratulate the señor father
That the newborn be in *siman tov* for him,
That *Eliyahu hanavi* should appear to us.

Let us give thanks to the God of truth
Let us greet the *sandaq* [godfather] and the *mohel*
Because of their *z'khut* [merit] let the *goel* [redeemer] come
Let him redeem all Israel.
Let us give praise to the God of truth. [5]

One notices that only a very few typically Jewish concepts are expressed by Hebrew words: *mohel, sandaq, goel, z'khut, mitzva, siman tov, Abraham avinu,* and *Eliyahu hanavi*. All the rest is in good Castilian.

Another important field of Sephardi folklore is that of the proverbs. There are tens of thousand of Spanish proverbs collected in great and rich collections, and the Sephardi Jews made significant contributions of their own to them. Let me quote only three examples.

Le gusta el asno su gritar
Como al bilbil su cantar

The donkey likes its braying
Like the nightingale its singing.

Quando sube el asno de la escalera
Se pasan el muera y esfuegra

When the donkey goes up the ladder,
Will daughter-in-law and mother-in-law make peace.

Una golondrina venida temprano
No anuncia el enverano

One swallow come early
Does not announce the spring. [6]

The Sephardim also have created much and transmitted much in the realm of the folk tale. Often we find folk tales known from other areas, such as central or eastern Europe, in a Sephardi version containing interesting variations. The well-known Cinderella story, for instance, has the following variant in a Sephardi folk tale.

A girl washes linens in the Vardar river. The prince passes by and falls in love with her. The girl turns into a lamb and goes to the palace. The king and queen beat her with a rag used for cleaning the stove. Once, when the queen goes to a ball, the lamb-girl pulls out one of her hairs and turns it into a beautiful dress and jewels. She puts on the dress, goes to the ball, and sits down next to the queen. The queen asks her, "Who are you, my daughter?" And she answers, "I am from the race of the oven-rag." The girl returns home and is about to put the lamb's skin on again when the prince enters and burns the skin, and then he marries the girl. [7]

Another Sephardi folk tale, which contains several well-known motifs, tells of two men who find a purse full of gold in the street. They begin to quarrel over it, and finally bring the disputed purse to the king. The king's decision is that the one who can solve three riddles is the rightful owner of the purse. The three riddles are: What is the fastest thing in the world? What the fattest? And what the sweetest? One of the two men has a clever daughter, and she says to her father, "What is faster than the eyes? What is fatter than the soil? What is sweeter than the human soul?" The king gives the gold to her father and asks him, "Who told you these answers?" The man admits that it was his daughter, and the king commands him to bring his daughter to him when she is hungry and yet not hungry, dressed and yet undressed, riding and yet not riding. The girl fasts until the evening and then eats a few melon seeds; she puts on a transparent dress and comes to the king, walking with one foot and leaning on a lamb with her other. The king marries her, but makes it a condition that she must never interfere in the affairs of the government. Once two peasants come to the king. One of them had been leading a pregnant she-ass on the road and met the other, who led a calf. The latter asked him for permission to tie his calf to the she-ass. The first peasant agreed, and after a while the she-ass stumbled and fell and gave birth to a dead donkey. The owner of the she-ass now asks for damages, and the king holds the owner of the calf responsible. But the poor peasant has no money and cannot pay. Next Friday, while the king is in the mosque attending the prayers, he goes to the palace and asks the queen for help. She advises him, "Go to the brook to a place where there are no fish and where the king is wont to pass by. There do as if you were fishing. The king will ask you, 'What sense does it make to fish in a spot where there are no fish?' You answer him, 'And what sense does it make to hold a calf responsible for a dead donkey?' And so it happens. The king knows immediately that the peasant acted upon the advice of the queen, and sends her away. But he permits her to take along from his palace whatever is most precious in her eyes. The queen lulls the king to sleep and carries him on her back to the house of her father. This impresses the king so much that he takes her back.[8]

Sephardi folklore often constitutes a connecting link between Arab Middle Eastern folklore and European western folklore. The historical and geographical position of the Sephardi communities was such as to predestine them to play the role of mediators and transmitters in this respect, as well as in many other fields of cultural creativity.

Today in Israel the Sephardi Jews are but a small group, numerically insignificant, between the two great sections of the population, the Ashkenazim and the oriental Jews. But they again can, and undoubtedly will, play an important role as cultural mediators between those two groups, whose cultures are so different from each other.

Notes

"Sephardi Folklore" originally was published in *Herzl Institute Pamphlet No. 15* (New York, 1960), pp. 22–36; this reprinting is somewhat abridged.

1. Moshe Attias, "The Bedtime *Shema* in Ladino" [in Hebrew], *Edoth* 2 (Apr.-July 1947): 213.
2. Moshe Attias, "Marriage Customs in Salonica" [in Hebrew], *Edoth* 1 (Oct. 1945):33.
3. Ibid., p. 34.
4. I can still clearly remember when I first learned of this custom. It was the late Rabbi David Prato who told me about it and showed me a sizable wooden box which he kept on top of one of his bookcases in his Tel Aviv apartment. It contained, as he put it, his "passport to paradise."
5. Moshe Attias, "Songs on the Birth of a Child in Salonica" [in Hebrew], *Edoth* 2 (Apr.-July 1947):275–76.
6. Menahem Azuz, "Judaeo-Spaniolic Proverbs" [in Hebrew], *Edoth* 1 (Jan. 1946):101–2.
7. M. Grunwald, "Spaniolic-Jewish Folk-Tales and Their Motifs" [in Hebrew], *Edoth* 2 (Apr.-July 1947):230.
8. Ibid., p. 231.

17. Collectanea

I. Birth Customs among the Jews of Morocco

Among the Jews of Morocco the following *s'gullot* (charms or remedies) are used for barrenness. On the Day of Atonement, the barren woman drinks a glassful of the water in which the *kohanim* (the descendants of Aaron) washed their hands; or she swallows a small fish in whose insides there is another fish; or she drinks a glass of wine mixed with saffron on the eve of her submersion in the *miqve* (ritual bath). On the other hand, a woman who does not want to become pregnant resorts to the following *s'gullot*. She takes one or more bees, makes small bundles of them, and swallows them. She then will not conceive for as many years as the number of bees she swallowed. Or she makes a ring from the eye of an animal called *har*(?), and as long as she wears the ring she will not conceive. A woman who wishes never (or never again) to conceive takes a little gold, pounds or grinds it, mixes it in water, and drinks the potion.

A woman who loses her children uses the following *s'gullot*. She drinks, early in the morning, a mixture of vinegar and oil; or she takes an ounce of honey, an ounce of sugar, seven nuts, and seven dates, mixes all this together and fries it in olive oil, and eats the concoction every morning on an empty stomach. Or an unmarried young man ties a belt around the belly of the pregnant woman who is afraid of miscarriage and locks it with a small lock. As long as the lock remains locked, the womb of the woman also will be locked, and she will not miscarry. When the nine months of pregnancy are up, the same young man opens the lock, and delivery will take place.

At the time of delivery the woman is laid on a mattress on the floor. Those attending her paste sheets of paper with "names" (of angels) on the curtains of the room, or on the dress of the woman, as a protection against the evil eye. The moment the head of the child emerges, somebody pours water on the threshold of the house. Over the head of the woman they hang a small mirror.

If several children of a woman have died soon after their birth, and she is about to give birth again, they take an earthenware jar and break open its bottom. As soon as the child is born, they pull him through the vessel three times, back and forth. The vessel is then preserved until the child grows up and marries, when it is thrown away. The name of this vessel is *tasur* (barrel), and the child who was pulled through it is called *Tasur* if a boy, and *Tasura* if a girl. Another custom practiced in case a woman has had several children die in infancy and she gives birth again is to bury the afterbirth in a field in a place where no one walks, so that the child should live and the afterbirth be its *kappara* (atonement).

Three days after the birth of a child, they rub oil on his body and sprinkle powdered henna on him.

It is forbidden to dress a male child in female clothes, or a girl child in male clothes, lest they become immoral upon growing up ("immoral" in this connection means sexual immorality). Each newborn child must be wrapped in a new blanket.

Every night between the birth of a male and the circumcision, family members stay awake. At midnight they take a big knife and make slashing movements with it along all the walls of the room; this is done so as to protect mother and child against demons. They recite the *Vihi no'am* and *HaMal'akh hago'el* prayers. In the evening preceding the day of circumcision, the barber comes to the house and cuts the hair of the young father and all the relatives.

The foreskin and the umbilical cord are kept and put into the pillow upon which the child sleeps during the first year of his life. If the child's eyes become diseased, they take the umbilical cord, put it into perfumed water, and wash his eyes with it.

II. Birth and Marriage Customs among the Jews of Egypt

Birth Customs

Various charms are used against barrenness among the simple folk in our country. Among them are 1) to swallow the foreskin of a newly circumcised child; 2) to go to the public bath and drink a potion made of ground beans and ground pomegranates mixed in water; and 3) to hang a hare's foot on the neck of the woman.

If a woman has borne children and then cannot conceive again, let her sit for half an hour on the birth stool of another woman who has finished delivering her child. It is also customary to place a tub of water under the birth stool or under the bed.

Effective *s'gullot* for a woman who has difficult labor are 1) to write the name of the woman on a silver coin and put it under her tongue; 2) to wash her in wine; 3) to give her water from seven cisterns; 4) to give her a little milk from the breast of a nursing mother; 5) to burn incense under her so that the smoke enters her body; 6) to blow the shofar, the ram's horn which is blown on the High Holy Days, and to whisper in her ear; "Go out, you and all the people who are at your feet!''; and 7) to go to the synagogue, open the door of the holy ark, and recite psalms.

When the child emerges from its mother's body, they wash it in warm water, but they do not salt it. They make sure to dress a male child in male clothes and a female child in female clothes. Often the child is wrapped in a new sheet when it is born. If the afterbirth is not ejected, they fumigate the woman with the excrement of a cat. They bury the afterbirth. It is customary to hang a *sh'mira* (literally, "watching" or "guard," but meaning a written amulet with the names of angels) over the bed of the woman so as to protect her and the newborn from demons.

The night before circumcision is called "night of watching"; during it they remain awake all night lest the child be harmed by Satan, whose intention is to hurt him, as it is written, "And thou shalt keep my covenant" (Gen. 17:9). The child needs protection from Satan, and therefore the custom is to study all night.

The circumcision meal is given on the day following the circumcision, but some people have it the night preceding the circumcision.

The people who pray in the synagogue of the child's father come on the Sabbath after the prayers to visit him in his house.

The *sandaqit* (godmother) brings the child to the synagogue for the circumcision and hands him to the *sandaq* (godfather). The *mohel* (circumciser) puts the child on the Chair of Elijah, saying, "This chair belongs to the prophet Elijah, the angel of the covenant, of blessed memory.'' Then the *sandaq* sits on the chair and holds the child on his knees. The father recites the *Sh'ma' Yisrael* (''Hear, O Israel''), and ''We beseech Thee, O Lord, save now! We beseech Thee, O Lord, make us now prosper!'' (Ps. 118:25), and the whole congregation repeats the words after him. Then he recites the blessing, ''Blessed art Thou, O Lord, our God . . . who hast commanded us to enter him into the covenant of Abraham our father.'' The *sandaq* and the father are each wrapped in a tallit (prayer shawl).

In general, a newborn is given the name of a deceased relative. However, some call the child by the name of a living ancestor, such as the grandfather or grandmother.

Marriage Customs

The *qiddushin* (betrothal) ceremony is held in the bridegroom's home. On the eve of the wedding they prepare the huppa (wedding canopy), decorated with the embroidered curtains from the holy ark in the synagogue and with flowers. The huppa remains standing for the seven days of the wedding feast. Under it are the seats of the bride and groom. The bride is brought from her home to that of the bridegroom in a festive procession, accompanied by her parents, relatives, and invited guests, to the tune of musical instruments. The groom receives her at the door of his house. He tries to step on her foot, so that the biblical verse, ''and he shall rule over thee'' (Gen. 3:16), shall be fulfilled in the marriage. The bride, however, usually manages to avoid being stepped on.

The bride and groom are then led under the huppa, and two candles are held on their two sides. The *hakham* (rabbi) who officiates spreads a tallit over their heads and says, ''So God give thee of the dew of heaven, and of the fat places of the earth, and plenty of corn and wine'' (Gen. 27:28–29), and then recites the Seven Benedictions. The groom puts the wedding ring, which must not contain any precious stone, into the hand of the bride, and the *hakham* recites for him the words which are the essence of the Jewish wedding ceremony: ''Behold thou art betrothed to me according to the laws of Moses and Israel.'' The bridegroom repeats the words after him, one at a time.

The bride and groom fast on the wedding day so as to atone for their sins, and break their fast by drinking wine from the wedding cup. After this ceremony there is much music and dancing until late into the night.

Weddings are held on the first to the fifteenth days of the Hebrew month, when the moon is on the increase, and not in the second half of the month when it is on the decrease.

It is the custom to break a vessel or a glass after the wedding ceremony in memory of the destruction of Jerusalem.

The bridegroom must be watched over during the seven days of the feast, lest demons or witches harm him.

On the Sabbath after the wedding, special songs are sung in the synagogue in honor of the bridegroom. He is also honored with a special Tora scroll which is opened at "And Abraham became old, well stricken in age" (Gen. 24:1). The bridegroom takes his seat holding the scroll. When the readings of the weekly portion from the Pentateuch and of the Haftara (the section from the Prophets) are finished, the bridegroom goes up to the lectern with his Tora, and the cantor reads from it the verses mentioned above. After each verse, the singers sing it in its Aramaic translation from the Targum of Onkelos, and thus they proceed until the end of the verse "He will send his angel before thee, and thou shalt take a wife for my son thence" (Gen. 24:7). After the service, all the people go to the house of the bridegroom to bless him with *Mazal tov*, "Good luck."

III. Birth and Marriage Customs among the Sephardi Jews in Jerusalem

Birth Customs

Among the Sephardim in Jerusalem, the following *s'gullot* are used against barrenness. The barren woman eats mandrakes, or she rubs oil on her body. (According to Mrs. Danon of Tel Aviv, they also practice the custom of seating the woman on the afterbirth while it is still warm, as a *s'gulla* against barrenness.)

Among the rich people, a few days before the woman is expected to give birth, they prepare a cradle for the child. At the time of delivery all the female relatives and friends are invited to the house. Several blankets are spread over a mat on the floor, and the expectant mother lies on them, in most cases in the window bay, which has a ledge about a foot higher than the floor of the room. Candles are lit as a protection against demons, and the names of angels are written on slips of paper.

After delivery the woman is laid in the bed, on whose four posts hang heavy curtains so that she cannot be seen by those in the room. For eight days the woman must never be left alone. All day and night visitors sit with her in relays. Men sit in the room with her at night. This night watch is called *velen* in Ladino. Occasionally jesters come to visit the woman and to entertain the guests, in a manner similar to their function at weddings. The afterbirth is preserved for two or three days after the birth, until the mother recovers her strength, and then it is buried in the earth.

Circumcision is a great festivity among the Sephardim. On the eve of the eighth day they light a seven-branched menora, called *tara*, after which that night is called "the *tara* night." Songs are sung and drums are beaten: the *pandero*, a small wooden wheel over which a skin is stretched and which is hung with bells all around; and the *darbukka*, an earthenware jar having the shape of half a globe, with a skin stretched over its wide opening.

In preparation for the day of circumcision, special cakes are baked in the shape of a sickle and distributed among the children during a meal. Early in the morning of the day, people gather in the house of the new parents and form a festive procession to accompany the child and his father to the synagogue. On the way they sing and make music.

The Sephardi Jews in Jerusalem believe that if a barren woman swallows a foreskin, she will conceive and bear a child. The *mohel* often is asked in advance by a barren woman's husband to keep the foreskin of the child he is about to circumcise for her. Occasionally they even give the *mohel* a baksheesh for this favor.

In order to protect the life of a newborn child, they put a kabbalistic book under his head during his first year, or they take the hand of a small child who has died, dry it, and put it under the newborn's pillow.

Marriage Customs

The favorite times for weddings are the half-holidays of Sukkot and Passover. A week before the wedding, all the members of the family are invited to accompany the bride to the bath. On the night before the bath the bride is painted with henna. She gets seven dresses: one of them, which she wears under the *huppa*, is white. Some two or three days before the wedding, the bridegroom's relatives go to the bride's house and evaluate her dresses. The bride also gets a *bogo* which contains all the things required for the visit to the *miqve*, such as a comb, soap, towels, high wooden shoes, anklets, a copper *tasa* (bowl), and so on. The night preceding the day of the visit to the bath is called *la noce del banio* (night of the bath). On that night the hands of the bride are painted with red and black (i.e., dark brown) henna. The girl friends of the bride, who help in the preparations for the wedding, also paint their hands with henna. The bride sends to the bridegroom a gift consisting of a *tarbūsh* (the red fez), a girdle, a shirt, and a collar.

On the day of the huppa the bride wears her white dress, and on her head she has a white crown made of white drops of wax. The bride's face is covered with a veil under the huppa. The bridegroom wears no special garb for the huppa (such as the *kitl* worn by the Ashkenazim), but merely a good suit of clothes.

After the Seven Benedictions, the bridegroom steps on a glass placed before him on the floor. After the ceremony, when the bride enters the house of the groom, the latter steps on her foot because of ''and he shall rule over thee'' (Gen. 3:16). At the same time, they break open a cake over the bride's head as a symbol of blessing, so that she and her family shall never go hungry. The people throw wheat and other grain on the bride and the groom so that they shall ''be fruitful and multiply'' (Gen. 1:28).

At the meal after the wedding, the bride and groom eat fish, which is a reference to ''let them multiply like fish'' (Gen. 48:16). They also eat pigeons, because pigeons love each other. The plate on which the pigeons are served to the couple is called *plato*, and it is considered a symbol of love.

The wedding festivities last seven days, during which the bridegroom is considered a king. He does not step outside his house alone, and especially not at night, for fear of coming to harm from demons. In the house, a canopy made of a curtain of the holy ark is set up with a podium under it, and the bride and the groom sit there. The bride also sits on a podium under a canopy on the day preceding the wedding. Every day during the seven days of the wedding feast new guests are invited. On one of the days musicians come to play, sing, dance, and make merry. (According to Mrs. Danon of Tel Aviv, it is customary on the night of the wedding to light torches and parade the bride and groom in all the streets of the city, and to dance before them with a drawn sword to the accompaniment of a band.)

On the Sabbath following the wedding, the bridegroom sits under a special canopy in the synagogue, set up in a special place. Wedding songs are sung; rose water is sprinkled about; the bridegroom is called up to the reading of the Tora, and at that moment he is pelted with candy and sweets.

IV. Marriage Customs among the Jews of Morocco

Ten days before the huppa, on a Monday, the mother of the bridegroom goes to the mother of the bride and tells her that the bride should begin to count her seven days of purification from that day.

On the following Monday, the bride's father is host to all the members of the community, and they spend all night singing and dancing. A woman singer with her choir entertains the guests, each of whom gives her some money. At the end of the night, after all the feasting, they paint the bride with henna. They paint red lines on her fingers, palms, and feet. Each of the guests participates. While she is being painted, the bride sits motionless. The bridegroom paints his own little finger, and so do his friends.

On Tuesday they bring a cow to the bride's house, dress it in a sheet, and then slaughter it. The meat is eaten at the wedding feast. On that day the bridegroom's parents go to the bride's house and look over all the things she has received from her parents. If they find that something is missing, they demand that it should be added. Quite often quarrels break out in this connection.

That night the barber comes to the bridegroom's house; the bride's mother also comes and brings a present to the bridegroom. The bridegroom, his parents, relatives, and friends have their hair cut. A male singer (Hebrew *paytan*) sings merry songs in which he makes fun of each of those present, and he receives some money from them. When the hair-cutting is finished, the bridegroom's parents go to the bride's house and accompany her to the bath, in a procession with a band, burning candles, dances, and much hand-clapping. After she has her bath, old women comb the bride's hair. The bridegroom goes to the bath on the same day, but without any festive ceremony. If the bridegroom's father is not alive, the bridegroom fasts.

On Wednesday people go to the bride's house early in the morning and pray there. After the prayers they set up the huppa. The bridegroom recites the words of the betrothal, and then he and the bride drink the wedding wine and the bridegroom breaks the wineglass on the floor. The bride's mother invites the groom to her home and gives him presents, as do other relatives of the bride. Small children go with the bride to the roof of the house and dishevel her hair. Musicians come and play and sing. After the huppa they seat the bride on a chair, and then a man picks it up with the bride sitting on it, and carries it on his head to the bridegroom's house. The man who does this is the one who also calls people to funerals. He also has other women sit on the chair and dances with them.

Before leaving her parents' house, the bride weeps over having to part with them. A procession with musicians accompanies the bride. When she arrives at the door of the bridegroom's house, he takes her into his arms and gives her an egg. The bride throws the egg against the wall over the door. The bride's father leads her to a special canopy set up in the bridegroom's room. This canopy is made of silk or linen, with curtains closed all around. The bride is covered with a white veil and wears all her golden ornaments and all the presents she has received from the beginning until the day of the huppa.

For seven days after the huppa the bride and groom are not allowed to go out of the house, and they are feasted every day.

A Charm against the Evil Eye

The Jews of Morocco take a small black rag, put into it *shabb* (alum), a kind of stone which men rub over their faces after shaving, as well as blue beads, *ḥarmal* (wild rue), and a golden or silver ''hand'' with five fingers. They make two such bundles and tie one to the hand and the other to the foot of a child smitten by the evil eye. They leave them there for forty days. This is done only for a male child.

V. Death and Burial Customs among the Jews of Egypt

Many among the Jews of Egypt prepare the shrouds in which they are to be buried well in advance. Some of them give a banquet for the members of their family on the day on which the shroud is tailored.

When a man is dying, they call a *ḥakham*, who recites with him the *Sh'ma'* prayer. If the dying man is conscious, he recites the *vidduy*, the confession of sins. After a person has breathed his last, they pull the pillow from under his head and then lay him on the floor.

They try to have the funeral as quickly as possible. The body is prepared for burial by washing it with cold water and soap and putting the shroud on it. In times past it was customary to wash the dead at home, in the house in which he died. Today (1942) the washing takes place in the cemetery, where there is a special room for this purpose. While the body is being washed, a *ḥakham* sits in the neighboring room and recites psalms. They do not cut the hair of the dead nor pare his nails. When the deceased has been dressed in the shroud, they straighten out his hands and place them on his thighs. They put one candle at his head and another at his feet. If a mirror hangs in the room, they turn it toward the wall. All the water in the house at the moment of death is poured out. The neighbors, too, pour out the water in their houses.

If the deceased was a great and respected man, they circumambulate his body several times. Some people include instructions in their wills that the four traditional capital punishments—stoning, burning, decapitating, and strangling—should be carried out symbolically on their bodies.

When the body is being carried from the house, and again at the actual interment, it is customary to ask for the deceased's forgiveness. They throw earth into the grave, and upon it they place dust from the land of Israel. The sons do not accompany the body of their father to the cemetery.

When the burial party leaves the cemetery, all wash their hands but do not dry them with towels. Some throw grass behind them as they leave.

Immediately upon returning from the burial they have the ''recovery meal,'' for which the costs are borne by the Ḥevra Qadisha or some other pious society, and not by the bereaved family. The meal comprises bread and boiled eggs. They drink no wine. After the meal, the mourners rend the gowns they are wearing next to their bodies and recite the benediction, ''Blessed is the True Judge.''

On the anniversary of the death, the sons of the deceased fast, go to the cemetery, and recite the *Kaddish*, the prayer for the dead.

It is customary for people to place pebbles on the grave each time they go to visit it. This seems to be a symbol of atoning for those sins of the deceased for which the punishment would be stoning.

Aborted fetuses and children who died before their eighth day are circumcised, given a name, and buried next to an existing grave.

VI. Jewish Customs and Charms from Italy, Egypt, and Tripoli

Among the Jews of Italy it is customary to cover the bride and groom with a tallit at the time of the *qiddushin* (betrothal). At the meal after the betrothal, the bride and groom each eat half of a pigeon. They eat it with their fingers, without using knives and forks, because the tableware is made of iron and iron is a sign of war.

The breaking of the glass under the huppa, which is the custom of the Italian Jews, is explained in two ways. One is the traditional explanation that it serves as a reminder of death, of the fragility of life. The other is that it is forbidden that anyone else should drink from the glass after the bride and groom.

During the wedding children stand around holding burning candles.

Among Egyptian Jews there is a belief that a barren woman will be able to conceive and give birth if she crosses the channel between France and England. Once a Jew came to the rabbinical court and said that he had been married for ten years and had no children, and therefore he wanted to divorce his wife. The wife, however, refused to accept the *get* (letter of divorce). She argued, ''I did everything to give children to my husband. I even traveled to England and crossed the *Manica*'' (La Manche; English Channel).

In Tripoli it is customary among both the Jews and the Muslims for barren women to swallow a foreskin or to drink water in which a dead body has been washed.

The general belief that the night before the day of circumcision is dangerous for the child's life is found among Egyptian and Italian Jews. They believe that Satan comes to the house then to steal him. Therefore they sit up all night in order to protect the child. They pray, they study, they read the Zohar, and they sing, and always in a minyan, a quorum of ten adult males. Next to the mother's bed they hang amulets—*Sh'ma' Yisrael*, names of angels.

Among the Jews of Egypt it is customary to put the foreskin into sand. Among the Jews of Italy the *mohel* keeps the foreskins in a box until his death. When he dies, they make a chain of them and hang it around his neck, and so he is buried. (At this point Rabbi Prato pointed to a wooden box which stood on top of the bookcase in his study and said, "There are the foreskins of the children I circumcised.")

In recent times (1942) the custom has spread among the Jews in Italy of burying the dead not in a shroud, but in fine holiday clothes, such as dinner jackets.

If a deceased has left sons or grandsons behind, they measure the height of each of them with strings and then bury the strings in his coffin with him. The meaning of this custom is that thereby the deceased brings along something of his children.

The custom of eating an egg at the "recovery meal" after the burial is observed in Florence, but not in Leghorn.

When a rabbi is buried, they bury a *pasul* (unfit) Tora scroll with him.

Among Egyptian Jews it is customary that, if a bachelor or a virgin die, they throw sweets from the windows at his or her coffin—the same sweets which custom requires must be thrown at the bride and groom at the wedding—because the deceased did not merit being married.

In Egypt they are very meticulous about washing the dead. They wash him internally as well. Before taking the body out of the house, they slaughter a bird at the door. Sons do not go with their father's body to the cemetery. They believe that demons come into being from a man's involuntary nocturnal emissions and that these demons accompany him to the cemetery. The sons do not want to encounter their demonic brothers. Professional mourning women participate in the funeral.

VII. The Dancing of Maidens on the Day of Atonement

In Judges 21:19–20, we read, "Behold, there is a feast of the Lord ever since olden times in Shiloh, which is on the north of Beth-el. . . . and behold, if the daughters of Shiloh come out to dance in the dances, then come ye out of the vineyards, and catch you every man his wife of the daughters of Shiloh." Although this passage reports a single event, in which the Children of Benjamin who, because of their misconduct, were denied wives by the other tribes of Israel (cf. Judg. 21:1ff.), made use of the annual dance of the maidens at Shiloh to seize and abduct them, it seems more than probable that the selection of brides by young men from among the dancing maidens was a regular feature of the "feast of the Lord at Shiloh." It is also probable that this merry feast was held in Shiloh precisely because the tabernacle was located there in the days of the Judges.

Many centuries later, Rabban Shim'on ben Gamliel referred to this feast in a Mishna. "There were no feasts in Israel like unto the fifteenth of Av and Yom Kippur [Day of Atonement], on both of which the daughters of Jerusalem went out in white garments (which were borrowed, so as not to shame those who had none) . . . and danced in the vineyards," and with songs and merry calls encouraged the young men who looked on to choose wives from among them.[1] A reference to the same folk festival is found in the Targum to Lamentations 1:4. The Hebrew text reads, "Her virgins are afflicted, and she herself is in bitterness." This is elaborated in the Aramaic of the Targum. "Her virgins mourn because they ceased going out on the fifteenth of Av and on Yom Kippur, which is the tenth of Tishri, to dance in feasts."[2]

Something of this original character of Yom Kippur was preserved until the twentieth century among the Jews of Derbent in the Caucasus, of whom the Jewish traveler Yosef Y'huda Chorny reports, "On Yom Kippur they pray according to their custom, without any *niggun* [melody] or weeping, as on other days, but all of them fast. Only the maidens gather in groups and take a stroll in the streets with drums, and play music with *harmonikim* [harmonicas]. And there are those among the young men who occasionally also mingle with the maidens in their rejoicing."[3]

Three decades after Chorny, another Jewish traveler, Zvi Kasdai, gave a more detailed description of this Yom Kippur folk festival which was still observed among the Jews of Derbent. He says that the music with drums and pipes was made by non-Jews who accompanied the maidens in the market-place and streets,[4] and that the maidens themselves "sing love songs in their language, but they do not dance; and from all sides the young men rush to join them, and help them in their songs. . . . Thus they make the rounds of the town together for about two hours, and then, when it becomes dark, they return home when the fathers have already returned from the synagogue." Kasdai also reports that the Jews of the Caucasus celebrate on the fifteenth of Av "with drums and dances in the vineyards which are near their towns and villages. The young men dance with the maidens, and the old men make a small heap of wood and light a fire."[5]

The same old custom also was preserved among the Jews of Tripoli until the early twentieth century. "On the morning of Yom Kippur, the boys aged nine to eleven, dressed in festive clothes, gather around the great synagogue and dance and sing marriage songs."[6]

A third Jewish community in which the same custom has survived is that of the Falashas, the Jews of Abyssinia. On Yom Kippur, "All of them, men, women, and children, became most enthusiastic. From sunrise to the evening they sang hymns which were—peculiarly—joyous, and after the songs come dances which were carried out separately by the men and youths, the women and the maidens."[7]

It is remarkable, to say the least, that the ancient folk character of Yom Kippur has been preserved, or, rather, combined with the later biblical Day of Atonement ritual of repentance and self-mortification, in three remote Jewish communities.

VIII. A Demon Wedding in Jerusalem

This happened in the Old City of Jerusalem about thirty years ago (i.e., ca. 1916). For three nights the demons hurled black stones into a courtyard, and then the people who lived there knew that the demons wanted to celebrate a wedding in that courtyard, and that they would have to vacate it for them. The stones, even if they hit someone, did not wound him. The people set up tables with candles, plates, dishes, and tableware, and opened wide all the doors. Then they went out and locked the gate after them. For a full month nobody entered that courtyard. After a month they opened the gate, went in, and said, "We caused you no harm; you, too, cause us no harm." Then they took ashes from the hearth and sprinkled them on the earth, poured oil on the floor and scattered sugar on it, and said, "Peace be unto you, peace be unto you!" Only then did they reenter their rooms.[8]

Notes

Section I, "Birth Customs among the Jews of Morocco," is based on interviews with a Moroccan Jewish woman in Jerusalem. It originally was published in Hebrew in the Tel Aviv daily, *HaTzofe*, 9 Oct. 1942. Section II, "Birth and Marriage Customs among the Jews of Egypt," is based on information supplied by Ben-Zion Taragan of Alexandria. It originally was published in Hebrew in *HaTzofe*, 16 Oct. 1942. Section III, "Birth and Marriage Customs among the Sephardi Jews in Jerusalem," is based on interviews with Yosef M'yuhas of Jerusalem. It originally was published in Hebrew in *HaTzofe*, 23 Oct. 1942. Section IV, "Marriage Customs among the Jews of Morocco," is based on interviews with a Moroccan Jewish woman in Jerusalem. It originally was published in Hebrew in *HaTzofe*, 30 Oct. 1942. Section V, "Death and Burial Customs among the Jews of Egypt," is based on information supplied by Ben-Zion Taragan of Alexandria. It originally was published in Hebrew in *HaTzofe*, 20 Nov. 1942. Section VI, "Jewish Customs and Charms from Italy, Egypt, and Tripoli," is based on interviews with Rabbi David Prato in Tel Aviv. It originally was published in Hebrew in *HaTzofe*, 20 Nov. 1942. Section VII, "The Dancing of Maidens on the Day of Atonement," originally was published in Hebrew in *Edoth* 1, no. 1 (1945):55; 1, no. 2 (1946):112–13; 1, no. 3 (1946):186; 1, no. 4 (1946):252–53. Section VIII, "A Demon Wedding in Jerusalem," is based on an oral communication by Moshe Ḥai Neḥama of Jerusalem. It was originally published in Hebrew in *Edoth* 2, nos. 3–4 (1947):285.

1. M. Ta'anit 4:8; cf. Y. Ta'anit 89c, B. Ta'anit 30b–31a. Cf. also Julian Morgenstern, *JQR*, n.s. 8 (1917):42–46; and Morgenstern, "Supplementary Studies in the Calendars of Ancient Israel," *HUCA* 10 (1935):136–37. Morgenstern sees a reminiscence of the original Saturnalian character of the ten days between New Year and Yom Kippur in the talmudic statement, "From New Year to Yom Kippur [in the Jubilee year] the slaves did not go back to their homes, nor were they enslaved to their masters, but they ate and drank and made merry with wreaths on their heads. When Yom Kippur arrived, the Law Court had the shofar blown, and the slaves returned to their homes." Cf. Morgenstern, *HUCA* 3 (1926):107. As for the dances in the vineyard, cf. also Morgenstern, "The Three Calendars of Ancient Israel," *HUCA* 1 (1924):23; A. Marmorstein, "Comparisons between Greek and Jewish Religious Customs and Popular Usages," in *Occident and Orient (Moses Gaster Anniversary Volume)*, (London, 1936), pp. 409–14. Saturnalian features also survived in the "Joy of the House of Water Drawing," which was celebrated in the Temple of Jerusalem twelve days after Yom Kippur (Raphael Patai, *Man and Temple in Ancient Jewish Myth and Ritual* [Edinburgh, 1947], pp. 24ff.).
2. My attention was called to this passage by Dr. Jacob Nacht of Tel Aviv; cf. *Edoth* 1, no. 2 (1946):112–13.
3. Yosef Y'huda Chorny, *Sefer haMassa'ot* (Saint Petersburg, 1884), p. 303.
4. This detail, the participation of gentile musicians in this "Yom Kippur dance" of the Jewish maidens and youths, indicates that the dance was not a spontaneous expression of youthful exuberance, but a celebration planned well in advance and with the consent of the elders. The gentile musicians certainly had to be booked or hired in advance of the holy day, and it was surely the fathers and not the teenagers who had the money to pay them for their services (*Note added in 1980*).
5. Zvi Kasdai, *Mamlekhet Ararat* (Odessa, 1912), pp. 38, 40, 95–96.
6. Nahum Slouschz, *Massa'i b'Eretz Luv*, 2 vols. (Tel Aviv and Jerusalem, 1943), 2:85.
7. Jacques Faitlovich, *Quer durch Abyssinien* (Berlin, 1910), pp. 96–97; and following him also Hildegard and Julis Lewy, "The Origin of the Week and the Oldest West Asiatic Calendar," *HUCA* 17 (1942–43):137, n. 404; A. Z. Aescoli, *Sefer huFalashim* (Jerusalem, 1943), p. 67.
8. A more detailed story about a demon wedding in Gallipoli has been published in Hebrew in *Edoth* 2, nos. 3–4 (1947):283–84.

18. *Indulco* and *Mumia*

I. *Indulco*

Melvin M. Firestone's article, "Sephardic Folk-Curing in Seattle,"[1] is a welcome contribution to the neglected field of Sephardi folklore studies. The following comments are intended to supplement the information gathered by Firestone with some additional detail, pertaining mainly to its acted part, as practiced in the eastern Mediterranean area in particular.

The sources familiar to me agree with my old friend Michael Molho.[2] The usual form of the name of the magic cure is (or was) *indulco*.[3] Whatever the actual linguistic derivation of the name, the Sephardi Jews took it to mean "sweet" or "sweetening," i.e., a ritual intended to give something sweet to the demons and thereby propitiate them. This conforms to the principle employed throughout the ritual: everything sacred or holy is removed from the house in which it is performed, the patient himself (or herself) must refrain from uttering any word of prayer, from reciting any biblical passage, and from going to the synagogue during the period of his "cure."

The intention of the ritual is thus clear: to propitiate, appease, the demons who are believed to have caused the disability, to appeal to their goodwill, sympathy, pity. The *indulco* therefore stands in sharp contrast to the customary methods of protecting a person against the demons or of exorcising them; there the method is to erect a barrier of sanctity around the person which the demons cannot penetrate, or to expel them by bringing sacred influences to bear upon them before which they must flee. Hence the amulets containing the names of God and other holy names, the placing of the patient before the open doors of the holy ark, and so on. The evil power of the demons is, in all these methods, broken by the forces of holiness marshaled against them. In the case of the *indulco*, the demons are treated gingerly; they are almost cuddled; everything unpleasant (such as words or emblems of holiness) are carefully removed from their way. The effort is directed, not toward keeping them out or expelling them, but toward inviting them, making their temporary stay as "sweet" as possible, and then, groveling before them, imploring them to return whatever they have stolen from the patient. It is, in a word, a treatment of demons in exactly the same manner in which orthodox religion treats God. No wonder that rabbis found the *indulco* more abhorrent than any other "superstitious" practice prevalent in their flock, and that they saw in it something akin to idolatry, against which the biblical prophets had fought with such vehemence.

A detailed description of the *indulco* is contained in a small Hebrew volume entitled *K'nesiya l'Shem Shamayim* [Gathering for the sake of heaven], written by Manasseh Matlub Sithon and printed in Jerusalem in 1874. In it the *indulco* is referred to by the Hebrew word *matuq* "sweet" (or, possibly, *mittuq*, "sweetening"). It is stated to be of two kinds: a "great" one and a "small" one. The custom of administering the *indulco*, the author states in a lengthy description in rhymed prose, prevails among the Jews of all Muslim lands, as a remedy or preventive against sickness, barrenness of women, spontaneous abortion, death of one's children in infancy, eye diseases, idiocy, "and all kinds of painful illnesses." Its effectiveness is based on giving something "sweet" to the demons who cause these diseases and misfortunes, and thereby propitiating them.

The procedure is described as follows (my translation from the Hebrew).

> They take a vessel full of wheat or barley, and three or four eggs, and water and salt, and honey made of grapes and dates or bee honey. And some take milk or sugar and other kinds of sweets. The entire house is thoroughly swept and cleaned, and all its rooms are emptied of people, as well as the neighboring houses and the courtyard, so that nobody remains in it, or near it. Also, all the holy books are taken out from the house, and some go so far as to remove even the mezuzot [doorpost scrolls] from the doors, so that there be no

hindrance there to prevent the demons from entering the house. Thereafter, the sick person, or barren woman, or whoever it may be, is led into the house and left there alone overnight together with the woman who administers the Sweetening. And the patient is warned and doubly warned to say neither the *Sh'ma'* nor any other prayer, to recite neither a long nor a short benediction, not even the after-meal grace, to say which is a biblical commandment, nor to utter the name of God, nor any other holy thing, from neither the written nor the oral Torah, neither aloud nor in a whisper, so that the demons should enter the house and join him and appear to him in his dream. The woman takes a fistful of the wheat or barley, mixes it with the honey, and pours it around the bed of the patient, and into the four corners of the house, and on the threshold and next to the door and its hinges; then she does likewise with the water and the salt or the sugar and the milk and the *mumia* in all the places mentioned. And she begs and implores, and prostrates herself and pours out her soul in requesting the *shedim* [demons] and the *s'irim* [hairy demons] and speaks to them thus:

"I beg of you, you who are our masters, to have pity and compassion on the soul of your slave, the patient, So-and-so, son of So-and-so, your hand-maid, and take away his guilt and if he sinned and did you any wrong, have pity on him and forgive him his sin, and give him his soul, his strength, and his health." (And for a barren woman they say, "Open her womb and return to her the fruit of her belly and loosen her ties"; and for women who abort they say, "Cause the souls of her sons and daughters to live.") "And behold, here is this honey [or sugar] for you to sweeten with it your mouth and palate, and here is wheat or barley for food for your cattle and sheep, and the water and the salt to maintain the love, and the brotherhood and the peace and the friendship as an eternal salt-covenant between us and you."

Thereafter she breaks the eggs before them and says, " . . . here is this sacrifice for you, a soul for a soul (for the egg out of which the chick is about to grow is regarded as a thing in which there is a living soul and spirit), so that you return to us the soul of this patient and his thoughts, or loosen the bonds of her pregnancy, and open the doors of her belly, or open their blindness, and heal their madness." And she pours the fluid of the eggs to the ground, and bows down before them, kneeling and prostrating herself, kissing the floor several times, in order thus to avert their wrath from the frightened patients.

All this is done three times, and then repeated for three nights, for each patient. Some, however, insist that it has to be done as often as seven or even nine times, as well as at noontime on Friday . . . Also on certain other nights of the week, which are the fixed time for this procedure, because in them many Liliths and demons are abroad, and go up and down, and in particular on Wednesday nights . . . .[4]

Some perform the Sweet in bath houses, or near pits and latrines in which the demons like to sojourn.

Sometimes they have to make a channel for the remedies, a Great Sweet and a great banquet, and in addition to all the things mentioned above they prepare a great table for the demons, load it with all kinds of sweets and candies, and all kinds of spices, camphors, and nards . . . and the patient exchanges his clothes for white festive clothes, and they light many wax candles in their honor, and they break forty or fifty eggs, and they bring kinds of spices made of grasses and trees, and incense and cassia and cinnamon and a sheaf of nard and others from among the eleven spices, and they burn for them all these kinds as a sweet savor, so that they cease being angry at the smitten and suffering patients.

And in some cities in certain countries they also slaughter a black cock for them to supplicate and entreat, and in some places they slaughter a lamb for them. Some repeat their folly several nights and days, and sometimes as often as forty days and forty nights. In some countries it is customary to set the table for them [the demons] on the New Year's holiday; this they call *Mesa de Rosh Hashana* [New Year's Table], and they forbid the patient to go to the syna- gogue lest he pray or utter a request, and lest he hear the voice of the shofar, which confuses Satan.

And some are unable to empty the house and the courtyard of all people, because non-Jews live next to them, or because the patients are poor and cannot afford the expenses; these have to be satisfied with a little, with going to pits and tanners, and with pouring water and salt for the demons. And this, being easy to perform, is found so frequently, every day, that there is no day in which this would not be performed several times. And some throw sugar and *mumia* and spices. And this libation is the slightest of all the works of Satan, and it is called in several places "the Small Sweet." And some pour water and salt on the door of the store of a poor man so that the demons loosen the ties of his livelihood and make him successful in all his undertakings.

The wide prevalence of the *indulco* is attested by the fact that the above "unmasking" of its superstitious practices was approved of by the rabbis of all the Sephardi and Ashkenazi communities in Palestine (Jerusalem, Safed, Hebron, Tiberius, Jaffa, and Haifa), as well as the Sephardi rabbis of Smyrna, Damascus, and Beirut, and the chief rabbi of Egypt. Their *haska- mot* (approvals) are printed in Manasseh Sithon's book.

Eight years after the publication of Rabbi Sithon's book, another attack was made on the *indulco*, this time by Abraham Moshe Luncz (1854–1918), a member of the small Ashkenazi community in Jerusalem and a pioneer of Palestinian studies.[5] He based his description of the *indulco* ceremony primarily on Sithon, but added several details which show that he had personally observed the ritual, which does not seem to have been given up by the people in spite of the stern rabbinical warnings against it. First of all, Luncz adduces a variant to the name *indulco: indulcado*. His explanation of these names is that they were originally applied to abandoned and desolate houses and then transferred to the ritual for whose duration the patient's house must be abandoned by all the other residents.

The afflictions for which the *indulco* is resorted to are, according to Luncz, "only impermanent diseases such as lunacy, blindness, sudden fright, barrenness of women, difficulty in childbirth, loss of children, epilepsy, and the like." Luncz's description of the ritual itself is an almost verbatim repetition of Sithon's account, but he adds that "the amount of honey mixture which they scatter in the house every night is about half a rotl'' (ca. 3 pounds), and that the mixing together of the various ingredients is performed by the women at midnight.

Luncz also makes a tantalizingly brief mention of a repeated dream experience reported to him by a Jerusalemite woman for whom the *indulco* had been performed. ''In the first and second night she dreamed that armed soldiers and many horsemen entered the house, but she was afraid and did not dare to cry out. On the third night the soldiers came again and rubbed all parts of her body with their hands.''

Luncz reports, in agreement with Sithon, that the *indulco* is performed either in a vacated house or in a place of impurity. Then, still quoting Sithon, he adds, ''Sometimes, on the contrary, they perform this thing in holy places, such as in a synagogue, or in the cave of the prophet Elijah on Mount Carmel, or in the house of study which is over the tomb of Ezra the Scribe in Baghdad. The patient is left lying alone in that place. And when the purpose of the ritual is to give children to childless couples, the man and woman will stay alone overnight in the sacred place, while the woman who performs the ceremony for them leaves the place upon its conclusion and locks them in.''

Although both Sithon and Luncz regard this ritual as a variety of the *indulco*, it is evident that—whatever the formal similarity of the performance itself—the two are based on completely different, in fact contrasting, motivations. While the true *indulco* aims at propitiating the demons, the varient ritual brings the patient into close contact with the holiness of a sacred site in order thereby to rid him of their baneful influence.

However, the second variety too was and remained known under the name *indulco*. Michael Molho describes this second type, which was practiced in Salonica. Although in this ritual too everybody must leave the house, three or four women remain with the patient ''to guard him against the evil spirits who might attack him.''[6] Moreover, and more importantly, in the Salonica *indulco*, the *indulcadera* (the old woman who administers the *indulco*) invokes Abraham, Isaac, Jacob, and other saints to intercede with God.[7]

That the *indulco* is merely the special East Mediterranean Sephardi variant of a much more widely prevalent method of ridding patients of demonic possession is attested by the following report of a propitiation ritual coming from Fez, Morocco.

> If the disease is of a diabolic origin, that is to say caused by the *jenun* [demons], one takes, in order to combat it, a mixture of cumin and coriander and makes an offering of oil and of grains to the demons.
> The following are some of the cases in which these magic ingredients are used.

An old woman goes to the patient. She takes a handful of cumin and coriander seeds, and she passes these around his head while addressing the following sentences to the demons.

"I enter under your protection, under the protection of the great ones and the small ones among you. Under the protection of our lord Semdayn, of our lord Jebrayn, of our lord Semharos and of Lalla Kona bent Elkon [Dame Kona, daughter of Elkon], the daughter of the sultan of the demons. If So-and-So [name of the patient], daughter of [father's name] and of [mother's name], has caused you any offense, if she has conducted herself unjustly toward you, if she has become angry at you, or if she has run after you, seek out the one among you who has been wronged and beg him to deliver her."

Thereafter the old woman chews the cumin and the coriander seeds and wets the patient's hand with her saliva. It seems that this rite is regarded as both an offering and a conjuratory performance. The cumin and the coriander seeds are undoubtedly as much a present as they are a prophylactic.

If, as a result of a quarrel, somebody goes home angry, one sends a woman to throw a little oil on the spot where the argument took place. With this oil, which has appeased the demons whom the man has offended, the woman anoints the head of the patient, saying to him meanwhile, "May this oil be efficacious to you and to *Qrinek* [your *Qarina*, demonic double]." One recognizes the belief in accordance with which, at the precise moment when a human being is born, a double in the world of the spirits is born with him. This, however, is called his Qrine [*qarina*], or his brother, or more exactly, his companion who is inseparable from him.

In Rabat, if the harm is attributed to the *jenun* [demons], a woman takes charge of casting oil into the sea, while saying to the devils, "Here is your feast."

In this city, according to an Arab custom reported by M. Brunot in *La Mer dans les traditions et industries indigènes à Rabat-Salé*, the oil is placed in a glass and it is cast, during the course of three days at the same hour, either into the sea or into the slaughterhouse.

In Fez, when a patient cannot recover in spite of all the drugs prescribed, people believe that he has been hurt by demons. In order to placate the demons one offers them a *diyafa* [meal]. The person charged with performing this brings some oil, and, without saying a word, goes to fetch the grain from the house of a woman married for the first time to a man who is neither a widower nor was divorced. Still without speaking a word, she mixes this grain with the oil and at night spreads it around the demons' favorite spots, corners of the bedroom and doors of the house and of the rooms. While doing this she pronounces the following invocation: "We beg of you for the love of those among you who are powerful and those among you who are humble. For the love of our lord Simday, your sultan, we come to you as strangers. Have pity on us and be merciful. Console us while doing good unto us."[8]

Although these Moroccan rituals differ in many details from the East Mediterranean one described earlier, they belong to the same category, inasmuch as they too aim at the propitiation of the demons. Remarkable in this context is the manner in which several individual male and female demons are addressed as "our lord." The underlying psychology is identical: the sick and the ailing, the desperate and the troubled, are willing, in exchange for a cure, to sell their souls to the powers of darkness.

II. *Mumia*

In Manasseh Matlub Sithon's description of the *indulco* ceremony, reference is made to *mumia*, which is placed, together with the other substances, in various places around the patient. Firestone also reports the use of *mumia* among the Sephardim in Seattle. He states that his informants asserted that foreskins removed at circumcision were used in making *mumia*, and that, according to one informant, the *mumia* was made of flesh taken from a corpse before the funeral service.[9] The available evidence—and it is plentiful—contradicts both of these derivations of the *mumia*, and one must assume that these statements reflect a relatively recent folk belief which developed among the Seattle Sephardim or their parents after the actual origin of the *mumia* had been forgotten.

A concise recapitulation of the history of the *mumia* is given by Warren R. Dawson,[10] who shows that the word *mumia* is of Persian origin (*mūm*), that it originally meant "wax" and also natural bitumen derived from the "Mummy Mountain" in Fars. In Syriac medical books also, bitumen is sometimes called *mumia*.[11] Bitumen was regarded in antiquity as a potent drug; its power was believed to vary with the place of its origin.[12] The bitumen found in the Dead Sea in Palestine, called *bitumen judaicum*, was believed to be especially efficacious.[13] The bitumen of the Dead Sea was called *mumia* by the Arabs, who borrowed the term from the Persians. They used the same term also to denote the material which was used by the ancient Egyptians for embalming the dead, although this material was in reality not bitumen but resin. The erroneous belief that the substance used for embalming was bitumen gave rise to the transference of the term *mumia* to the embalmed bodies themselves.

Arab and Jewish physicians in the Middle Ages continued to use and recommend *mumia*, i.e., bitumen, as a drug for many and varied ailments.

By the twelfth century, Jews of Alexandria were engaged in breaking up embalmed bodies of ancient Egyptians in order to obtain what they believed was bitumen, but what in reality was resin. In the course of time the belief developed that *mumia* was efficacious only if it was taken from an embalmed human body. When the supply of Egyptian mummies dwindled, new ones were manufactured in order to meet the unabating demand. Guy de la Fontaine, physician to the king of Navarre, visited Alexandria in 1564, and a local Jewish mummy supplier told him that his practice was to buy the bodies of dead slaves and other persons, open them, fill them with bitumen, then bandage them and let them dry in the sun. The trader showed de la Fontaine some forty such "mummies" in various states of preparation.[14]

"Mummy"—i.e., *mumia*—became a very popular drug in Europe, as evidenced by British, French, German, and other medical books of the sixteenth to the eighteenth centuries. In them the mummy is described as deriving from the bodies of men or women, the best being taken from embalmed Egyptians. Desiccated bodies found in the Lybian sands were also much in demand, and other sources too were found.

From the seventeenth century on, the term "mummy" was applied to any medicated flesh taken from the bodies of jays, owls, and so on. Finally, the word became a cookery term, denoting any dish cooked to a dry and tough consistency, even if it contained only vegetables. Nevertheless, as late as the middle of the eighteenth century, "mummy" still appeared in British pharmacologies.[15] In Upper Bavaria, Germany, "Mumie" or "wild human flesh" was sold in pharmacies as late as the nineteenth century, as a remedy against consumption.[16]

Jews being so closely involved in the mummy trade, it was inevitable that they should also become its avid customers. Hence the concern shown by rabbis from the sixteenth century on in the question of whether eating *mumia* for medical purposes and trading in it were permissible from a religious point of view.

The matter was taken up by Rabbi David ben Zimra (ca. 1479–1573), the famous Sephardi Talmudist and Kabbalist who was born in Spain, educated in Safed, Palestine, and was chief rabbi of Egypt from 1517 to 1557. One of his responsa[17] was written in answer to the question, "On what basis do people use the flesh of dead persons, called *mumia*, as a drug, even when there is no mortal danger involved, and by swallowing it; and moreover, it is being traded, and bought and sold, even though it is our established law that it is forbidden to eat the flesh of a dead person."[18] David ben Zimra's answer is very lengthy. Its gist, however, is contained in these sentences.

> It is allowed, because its form has changed, and it has reverted to dust. For the *mumia* is the flesh of embalmed bodies which had been embalmed with all kinds of spices in order to preserve their form and their bodies. But it [the body thus treated] has become again similar to bitumen, and it is not forbidden to eat it. . . . Moreover, it is taken not for the sake of the flesh, but of the spices that are in it, for it is well known that the flesh of the other dead, which are not embalmed, has no medicinal value at all.[19]

One generation later, Jacob Castro (died 1610), another Egyptian rabbinical authority, referred to this decision and approved of it. [20]

Late in the seventeenth century, yet another Egyptian rabbi, Abraham Halevi, returns to the question of the *mumia*, and, while deciding against its permissibility (except to use it externally), gives us a description of the manner in which the *mumia* was obtained in his days.

> The *mumia* is made with spices and salves, and the corpse is wrapped in bandages and clothes, and then it is placed in a coffin made of sycamore wood, which withstands rot. The bandages and clothes, since they have not turned into dust, are removed from the mummy. And even if some of the bandages become like thin, polluted clothes, they nevertheless do not get mixed up with the flesh of the corpse, which is as hard as a stone. All one has to do is to blow on these clothes and they fall away. As to the wood of the coffin, even if there be some rot in the sycamore wood, it certainly does not mingle with the flesh of the corpse. The spices and salves do not cause the flesh to endure, but merely remove from it the harmful substances which would otherwise attack it. . . . One takes pieces from the upper limbs; from below its hips it is worthless. . . . And, although it is said that the mummy is now nothing but dust, and all its medicinal value is contained in the spices and salves, in any case there is an enjoyment and usefulness in the mummy itself [and it is therefore forbidden]. [21]

Yet, in spite of this prohibition, the use of *mumia* continued among the Sephardi Jews. In 1870, Moshe Reischer described it.

> The Sephardim make to this day a remedy, *mumia*, which is prepared from the ground dry bones of dead people found in the desert in the sand. For along the road leading to Mecca there is a big desert, and there is a place full of sand which is called the Sand Sea. And when a storm arises, it lifts up the sand to a height of more than twenty cubits [about thirty feet] and covers everybody who happens to be on that road, for a distance of about one mile. And people go there and, searching diligently, they find these pieces in human form, black and dry as a stone, for even the biggest man who is left lying under the sand dries out and becomes as small as a finger. And they sell it to apothecaries, and they put it into remedies. And the Sephardim, when they have a patient sick for many days, God forbid, take it and grind it well and put a certain amount of it into honey water which the patient drinks from time to time during three nights. Before he drinks it, they wash him and clothe him into a white robe, and lay him on a bed covered with a white sheet. Menstruating women are not allowed to enter the house as long as the illness of the patient persists, lest this cause harm to the patient and to themselves. The patient lies alone, and nobody else is with him in the house, not even a hen. Moreover, he must beware of the smell of garlic and onions. The only food of the patient throughout the nine days is milk, bread, and butter. [22]

Additional details about the *mumia* as used by the Jews of Jerusalem in the late nineteenth century are given by Luncz.

> By this name (*mumia*) is called in Arabic a piece of bone which has become completely black. [Footnote:] According to what the children of the land of the east say, this bone can be found in the sandy desert of Arabia, and it is a part of the bodies of people who were buried among the waves of that sea of sand while on their way to Mecca or to the other cities of that country, and from the great and burning heat their bones hardened and became black and exceedingly small, like the form of embalmed bodies. The *mumia* is offered for sale in Arab pharmacies of medicines and charms. The price of a *dirham* [drachma] is about five piasters, and those who buy a large quantity of it can see in it the shape of the member from which it is derived [end of footnote]. Its power is such as to heal all illness and disease, and especially sudden and unusual ones.
>
> This drug is prepared in the following manner. A certain quantity of the *mumia*—or a part of the black bone—is pounded in a mortar to thin powder—and sometimes they mix some honey and spices into it—and a handful of it is placed on the roof for a night so that the dew descends upon it, or they put it in a coffee cup, and of this balsam of Gilead the patient drinks for nine successive nights. On the fifth and ninth day, before he drinks of it, they wash his body, wrap him from head to foot in white clothes, and a man or a woman sits next to him all night to watch him—for they believe that the two nights are most dangerous for the patient. The patient's food during this period consists of bread, butter, and milk only, and they also take care lest the patient inhale any strong smell, and especially the smell of garlic, onions, and fish. Women who are in their menses must not enter the house throughout that period, lest they cause damage to the patient and to themselves, and, in general, very few people will visit him.
>
> The neighbors who live in the same courtyard—and who believe this nonsense—are very much afraid lest the power of the *mumia* affect them adversely, and they therefore leave their houses for several days, or—if they do not care about the state of the patient and about the improvement of his health—they will draw on the door of his house the picture of a hand, which is a well-known amulet, and then the power of the *mumia* is broken, and it will neither help nor harm the patient. Therefore, if the patient is apprehensive lest his neighbors perform this contrary act, he will do everything in secret, unknown to anybody.[23]

The unanimous testimony of all the sources, therefore, from antiquity down to the nineteenth century, is that the *mumia* is the body or part of the body of old, preferably embalmed, but at least desiccated, corpses. It was this circumstance that enabled the rabbis to find a ritual basis for permitting its internal use. The swallowing of a piece of flesh taken from a fresh corpse, before the funeral, would never have had a chance of rabbinic approbation. In view of this, it would be most interesting to find out whether any of

Firestone's Seattle informants actually ever practiced or witnessed such a removal of a piece of flesh from a fresh corpse, or whether all they stated was that they believed that this was the source of the *mumia*.

As to the identification of the *mumia* with the foreskin removed at circumcision, again the evidence adduced above speaks against it. However, it is known that the swallowing of foreskins used to be practiced by barren Sephardi women in order to conceive. Possibly this custom was confused or conflated with the *mumia*. The question of actual observed practice versus oral tradition based on hearsay is important in this case too.

Another interesting deviation in Seattle from the centuries-old tradition is the surreptitious administering of the *mumia*. Throughout the two-thousand-year history of the *mumia* it was always given openly. The fact that it was thus taken, that it was a substance believed to be of a horrible, disgusting origin, that it was difficult and costly to obtain, provided it with an effectiveness on the psychological plane that it lacked physiologically. In the Seattle variant, if the patient did not know he was taking *mumia*, its psychological effect was confined to those who administered it to him and knew about it. This would seem to be a rather roundabout way of obtaining improvement in the patient. In view of these considerations, it would seem significant to establish precisely in what cases the *mumia* was given surreptitiously, and in what cases openly.

Notes

"*Indulco* and *Mumia*" originally was published in the *Journal of American Folklore* 77 (Jan.-Mar. 1964):3–11.

1. Melvin M. Firestone, "Sephardic Folk-Curing in Seattle," *JAF* 75 (1962):301–10.
2. Quoted ibid., pp. 303, 309.
3. See, e.g., M. D. Gaon, "The Fight of Sephardim and Ashkenazim against the 'Indulco' " [in Hebrew], *Edoth* 1 (1946):104–7.
4. I.e., the night between Tuesday and Wednesday.
5. Cf. Abraham Luncz, *Y'rushalayim*(Vienna, 1882), 1:21–23.
6. Michael Molho, *Usos y costumbres de los Sefardies de Salonica* (Madrid and Barcelona, 1950), p. 279.
7. Ibid, pp. 279–80.
8. Elie Malka, *Essai d'ethnographie traditionelle des Mellahs; ou Croyances, rites de passage, et vielles pratiques des israélites marocains* (Rabat, 1946), pp. 108–11.
9. Firestone, "Sephardic Folk-Curing," p. 306.
10. Cf. Warren R. Dawson, *The Bridle of Pegasus* (London, 1930), pp. 162–73.
11. See E. A. Wallis Budge, *Syrian Anatomy, Pathology, and Therapeutics: The Book of Medicines* (Oxford, 1913), index, s.v. Mumia.
12. Cf. Pliny, *Historia Naturalis* 5.15; 6.26; 35.51; Virgil, *Georgics*, 3.448–51; Diodorus Siculus, 2.12, 48; 19.99; Dioscorides, *De materia medica* 1.100, 101; Josephus Flavius, *Wars of the Jews* 4.8.4; Celsus, *De medicina* 3.27.2; 3.5.3, 11, etc.

13. Paulus Aegineta, 3.54, 78, 97, 130, etc.
14. Guy de la Fontaine, *Discours d'Ambroise Paré* (Paris, 1582), pp. 7–8.
15. End of my summary of Dawson, *Bridle of Pegasus*, pp. 162–73. To his sources should be added those quoted in Charles du Fresne Du Cange, *Glossarium ad Scriptores Mediae et infimae Latinitatis* (1678 and several eds.; e.g., Paris, 1845), s.v. Mumia, e.g., Constantinus Africanus, an eleventh-century Arab medical scholar who spent most of his life in the Benedictine monastery on Monte Cassino, and who held that the *mumia* was efficacious against broken skulls.
16. Adolf Wuttke, *Der deutsche Volksaberglaube der Gegenwart*, 2d ed. (Berlin, 1869), p. 126; 3d ed. (Berlin, 1900), p. 134.
17. Rabbi David Ibn Abi Zimra, Responsa III, no. 548 (various editions).
18. Ibid.
19. Ibid.
20. Cf. Jacob Castro, *Sefer Mahariqash Haniqra Erekh Leḥem* (Constantinople, 1718), ad Yore De'a 391.1: "In any case it is permitted to eat the *mumia* and trade it, because it is nothing but dust."
21. Abraham ben Mordecai Halevi, *Ginnat V'radim* (Responsa), Yore De'a 1.4 (Constantinople, 1717), 1:fol. 89b.
22. Moshe Reischer, *Sefer Sha'are Y'rushalayim* (Jerusalem, 1870), no pagination. The passage is found on fol. 50a.
23. Luncz, *Y'rushalayim*, pp. 20–21.

19. Exorcism and Xenoglossia among the Safed Kabbalists

In the sixteenth century the little Galilean town of Safed was the most important center of the Kabbala, the Jewish school of mysticism and esoteric speculation. The main preoccupation of the Safed Kabbalists was with mystical theory and quasi-mythology, but speculation inevitably spilled over into practices which can only be characterized as magical. A doctrine which presented a thousand details about God and his emanations; about angels, demons, spirits, and souls; about purity and impurity; contamination and restoration; fall and elevation; sin and piety; punishment and reward—such a doctrine perforce had to exercise a powerful influence not only on the psyches of those over whom it held sway, whether they were rabbis, teachers, and masters or their simple followers, but also on their behavior patterns.

In the following, I first summarize the kabbalistic beliefs about sin and the post mortem punishment which followed it; second, discuss the rituals and incantations performed for the purpose of exorcising spirits from the persons of whom they took possession in order to escape their punishment; and third, present a sample account of a case of spirit possession and exorcism written by an eyewitness and containing a rare instance of xenoglossia.

I.

Both the rabbinical leaders and their followers, who in the sixteenth century comprised the entire Jewish population of Safed, firmly believed that if a man became guilty of certain sins in his life, upon his death his soul was not allowed to enter Gehenna directly; for Gehenna was held to be, not a place of eternal damnation, but a place of purification, albeit horribly painful, in which the souls sojourned only for the brief span of twelve months before being allowed to rise into the Garden of Eden, as the heavenly paradise was termed.[1] Before the soul of a sinner was admitted into Gehenna, it first had to undergo preliminary punishment, often of a duration of hundreds of years, during which it was exposed to great suffering. According to an alternative theory, the order was reversed. The sinner was first punished in Gehenna and then had to suffer one or more reincarnations in the bodies of animals or birds.[2] As soon as such an evil man died and was buried, angels of destruction beat his grave, which burst open, whereupon the angels dragged out his soul, beat it cruelly, and then placed it in the hollow of a sling and hurled it back and forth across space many times. Even if his soul escaped this particular form of torture, it had to wander from mountain to mountain, and everywhere angels of destruction went with it and tortured it.

As for spirit possession, two alternative theories were current. According to one, the spirits of persons who committed certain sins were condemned to enter the bodies of animals or humans when they died. The most frequent sin for which a soul was sentenced to this kind of reincarnation was of a sexual nature. Many kabbalistic books are preoccupied with this subject and specify the correspondence between the sin and its punishment. The following excerpt, taken from the *Sefer haGilgulim* [Book of transmigrations] by Ḥayyim Vital (1542–1620), summarizes these beliefs.

> He who has intercourse with a male transmigrates into a hare or a rabbit (for they are males and females [?] and one year they mount him and one year he mounts others). He who has intercourse with a [domestic] animal transmigrates into a bat. . . . He who has intercourse with a wild animal or a bird transmigrates into a raven. He who has intercourse with a married woman transmigrates into a donkey. . . . He who has intercourse with a gentile woman transmigrates into a Jewish whore. He who has intercourse with a woman in her menstrual impurity transmigrates into a gentile woman who does copulate while menstrually unclean. . . . He who has intercourse with his sister transmigrates into a stork. . . . He who has intercourse with his mother transmigrates into a she-ass. He who has intercourse with his mother-in-law transmigrates into a female mule (and also he who has intercourse with his son's wife). He who looks at the sexual parts transmigrates into a *raah* [an unclean bird]. . . . He who has intercourse with his aunt, his end is that he will

be clothed [that is, transmigrates] into a gentile woman, and that woman will convert to Judaism. . . . And he who has intercourse with his brother's wife, his end will be that he will be clothed into a mule. . . . And he who has intercourse with his uncle's wife will be clothed into an Ashdodite woman. And he who has intercourse with two sisters will transmigrate into a gentile whore who will be mounted by two brothers. He who has intercourse with the wife of his father will transmigrate into a camel . . . because he was impudent in regard to forbidden intercourse, his end is that he will be bashful like a camel. And all this holds good only if he did not repent while still alive.[3]

According to the other theory, the spirit condemned to serve as a slingshot for angels of destruction tries to escape this torture by taking refuge in the body of a human or an animal. Once inside a living body, the angels cannot touch the soul and it can enjoy some rest. But to be inside an animal causes discomfort and pain to both the human soul and the soul of the animal, because the two are incompatible. Before long the animal goes mad and dies, and the soul of the sinner must leave the dead body, whereupon the evil angels again pounce upon it and resume their torture. Now only one thing remains for the tortured soul of the sinner: to try to enter the body of a human. This becomes possible if that human makes himself vulnerable by an inadvertent wrong move. For instance, if a person gets angry and cries out, "To the devil!" this is enough to enable the sinful soul to enter and take possession of his body.

In most cases the person into whom a spirit (as the sinful soul is generally referred to in this context) enters feels pain, thrashes about or faints, and remains unconscious. In the majority of cases the spirit is that of a man, but the person into whom he manages to enter is a woman. A sure sign of being possessed by such a spirit is that the sick or semiconscious woman utters words in a male voice.

II.

If the relatives of the persons who suddenly fall ill suspect that the trouble is caused by a spirit, they will hurriedly send for an expert exorcist, who is their only hope. In Safed the foremost kabbalistic luminaries had the reputation of being the most powerful exorcists. Among them were R. Yitzḥaq Luria (1534–72), who is generally recognized as the greatest kabbalistic genius of the period, and his foremost disciple, R. Ḥayyim Vital, whom we have already met and whose work consisted mainly in recording the teachings of his master. Ḥayyim Vital's son, Sh'muel Vital (1598–ca. 1678) followed in his father's footsteps both in contemplative studies and writings and in practical work as an exorcist.

The practice of exorcism developed its own ritual, which had to be followed scrupulously in order to be effective in removing the spirit. The main features were:

1. To question the spirit closely as to his name, the date of his birth and death, the nature of his sin or sins, the method of his entry into the body of the possessed, and so on. Often the spirit had to be forced to divulge his name by reciting mystical names of God and by various incantations, mostly verses from the Book of Psalms. Only after the exorcist learned the name of the spirit could he proceed to the next step.

2. To fumigate the patient with fire, smoke, and sulfur, making sure that he inhaled the smoke. This was believed to make it painful, or even impossible, for the spirit to remain in the body.

3. To promise the spirit that the exorcist and other scholarly and pious persons would pray for him, so as to enable him to enter Gehenna and thus commence the final stage of his purification.

4. To blow the shofar (ram's horn), preferably in the presence of ten scholarly and pious men, the traditional minyan (quorum) required for communal prayers.

5. To demand of the spirit that he leave the body through a toe. Otherwise he would leave through the throat of the possessed and choke him in the process.

6. To command the spirit to give a sign that he actually had left the body; for example, to blow out a candle or to say, "Peace be upon you."

7. To hang amulets around the neck of the patient immediately, thereby preventing the spirit from reentering his body.

In most cases the spirit would resist all attempts at exorcising it, and increasingly potent rites and incantations had to be resorted to in order to make him leave. Occasionally, however, the spirit would like to leave the body but would be unable to do so. Such a spirit would willingly submit to the rites of exorcism, even though these might be painful for him.

The ritual of the exorcism was usually concluded when the exorcist believed that the spirit had left the body. This, however, did not mean that the patient always recovered. The death of a patient, which was as likely to be the result of excessive administration of fire, smoke, and sulfur as of the trancelike seizure itself, was as a rule diagnosed as having been caused by the spirit that somehow managed to reenter the patient's body.

We must touch upon the attitude diplayed by the Kabbalists toward spirit possession. That such possession was a fact none of them doubted. Where they were skeptical was in concluding that the patient's ailment was indeed caused by spirit possession and not by other physical causes. Consequently the exorcist took great pains to ascertain, first of all, that the voice issuing from the patient's mouth was really that of a spirit, and second, that the self-proclaimed identity of the spirit was verified by the answers it gave to a long series of probing questions. The exorcist would ask the spirit many details about his life on earth, concentrating especially on matters which presumably only the spirit would know. The detailed account of the exorcism given below is a good example of this kind of skeptical inquiry.

However, the main reason I chose to present this particular account from among the many available in kabbalistic literature is the remarkable inquiry into the spirit's knowledge of several languages it contains. The spirit identified himself as that of a man who had lived in Safed and had died thirty-three years previously in Tripoli. It was known by those who still remembered him that, in addition to the Ladino colloquial of the Sephardi Jews of sixteenth-century Safed, the man also knew Hebrew, Arabic, and Turkish, but not Yiddish (which was the language of the small Ashkenazi contingent in Safed). Accordingly, the exorcist proceeded to address the spirit in each of the three languages in turn, and, as the account states, "the spirit answered in each language and spoke it clearly as he did when he was alive." When addressed in Yiddish, he answered that "he did not understand that language." If we accept at its face value the statement contained in the account, that "the woman [who was possessed] knew none of these languages," then we have here a remarkable case history of multilingual xenoglossia.[4]

The patient is referred to only as a "pure woman" (the Hebrew term used, *k'shera*, feminine of *kasher*, means a woman who scrupulously observes the ritual laws obligatory for women). She was engaged in sweeping the house when the spirit entered her; hence she must have been a housewife. The account mentions her father-in-law and her grandmother as being present at the exorcism; hence she must have been a young married woman. The likelihood is that such a person would know some Hebrew (since women also recited Hebrew prayers), as well as some Arabic (which women needed while shopping at local merchants, purchasing foodstuffs, and so on). She may also have known a few words of Turkish (the language required for contact with Turkish officials, with whom, however, women would have very little to do). These considerations introduce some doubt as to the categoric statement that the woman knew "none of these languges." On the other hand, given the skeptical frame of mind of the exorcists as to the identity of the spirit, one must assume that the spirit's display of mastery of the three languages was sufficient to convince them that it was indeed the spirit who was speaking, because it exceeded by far the rudimentary knowledge the woman could have had. That is to say, the account as it stands must be taken as prima facie evidence of an authentic multiple xenoglossia.

III.

The following text, presented in my literal translation from the Hebrew, is taken from the *Sefer haGilgulim*. I used the Przemyshla, 1875 edition, in which the account of the exorcism given here is contained on pages 10b–12a. It is signed by R. Elijah Falqen (or Falken, Folqen, Folken), about whom I could find no data, although we know of a Falken family in Breslau in the fourteenth century. One of the signatories who attested to the truth and accuracy of the account is well known. He is R. Sh'lomo haLevi (ben) Alqabetz (or Alkabez, 1505–84), a Kabbalist and mystical poet whose Sabbath hymn, *Lekha Dodi* ("Come, my friend") is sung to this day on Friday evenings in every synagogue. His book, *Shoresh Yishai*, mentioned in our text, was published in his lifetime. Sh'muel Bueno was a member of a large family, other members of which lived in Jerusalem, France, Italy, Holland, and England. Abraham Arueti too was a member of an important Sephardi family, also known as al-Rueti, Roti, and so on. I was not able to find any data about Abraham haLahmi. However, since the sole purpose of having witnesses sign such an account was to enhance its credibility, one must assume that the signatories were among the respected leaders of Safed Jewry.

> I am presenting herewith before you the letter which was sent from Safed. . . .
>
> A great event occurred in the holy community of Safed. . . . It is a fact that man is more inclined toward the pleasures of his body and his feelings rather than towards going after the advice of his soul and after the instructions and direction of the Tora. And even the believers and those who are punctilious in everything—because the matters of the world to come are not perceived by the intellect. And who can fix in his heart all the sides so as to make himself an impression to separate himself from the side of evil and sin, in speech as well as in thought and deed? Since not every man merits this, therefore I agreed to put this down in writing so as to let others profit from what I have experienced. Today, the eleventh of the First Adar, 5331 of the Creation [that is, A.D. 1571].
>
> It happened to a woman into whom the spirit of a man from Israel entered, as I shall put it before you. And the truth is that he who was there at that time and heard from the spirit what it said and what it revealed, and he who heard it from the mouth of those who heard it, must humble his heart toward heaven and fear and dread the day of judgment on account of their souls, for everything must be accounted for, and in Sheol [the underworld] there is no house of refuge. For it became known from one who came from that world and related what happened there. And it is possible that the Holy One, blessed be He, sent him so that they should be afraid of Him, as the sages of blessed memory have said, "God made them afraid of Him—this is a bad dream." But this [happened] not in a dream but while they were awake, in the clear sight of everybody.

I was in the midst of a large group of people who were there, close to a hundred people, among them scholars and heads of communities. And two men, who knew adjurations and many things, approached the woman to make the spirit which was in the woman speak to them, by means of the smoke of fire and sulfur which they made enter her nostrils. . . . ⁵

And the woman was as lifeless, in that she did not pull herself away, nor moved her head away, neither from the side of the fire nor from the side of the smoke. And as a result of the adjurations a voice began to be heard, a thick and sustained voice, like the roaring of a lion and the voice of a young lion, without any movement of the tongue or opening of the lips. And when this voice began to be heard, the two aforementioned men exerted themselves and warmed themselves up quickly and diligently to do what they did rapidly, and they argued and spoke against him [that is, the spirit] with a loud voice and said to him, "You evil one, speak and tell us who you are in a clear language." And then the voice revealed itself and appeared to all as the voice of a human. And they repeated and spoke to him in a loud voice and in the manner mentioned, "What is your name, you evil one?" And he answered, "So-and-so, and my last name is So-and-so." And they asked him, "How can we know that you are So-and-so?" And he replied that he had died in Tripoli, and that he had left behind a son whose name was So-and-so, and that he had had three wives, and the name of the first was So-and-so, and the name of the second was So-and-so, and the name of the third was So-and-so, and that he had died while he was married to the third, and that she was now married to So-and-so. And as to all the signs he gave he spoke the truth. And then all of us who were there recognized that it was the spirit who spoke. And they asked him, "For what sin do you have to wander about in the world in these transmigrations?" He answered, "For the many sins I committed in my life." And they again asked him, "Enumerate them." But he said that he did not want to, for what use would there be in it? And then they pressed him very much that he should mention at least the greatest sin he had committed, and he answered that he had been a heretic and had spoken against the Tora of our master Moses, peace be upon him.

And many people testified that he actually had spoken such things while he was alive. And they asked him, "And now, are you still of that opinion?" And he replied with a groan in a bitter voice, shouting and storming, and he said, "I recognize that I sinned, transgressed, and did evil." And he asked forgiveness from the Holy One, blessed be He, and from His perfect Tora for his many sins. And then the two men began to press him and to force him that he should go out from her and should go to a desolate desert place, and [did this] through all the [means] mentioned above, and [told him] that they would ask mercy for him and would blow the shofar so that he should not have to continue in this transmigration. And they said to him, "Do you want us to ask mercy and pray for you, and blow the shofar?" And he answered, "I do wish so." They asked him who should blow the shofar. He said, "The sage, his honor R. Sh'lomo Alqabetz." But that sage replied that he could not. They again said to him, "Ask for somebody else." He said, "Let it be the sage, his honor R. Abraham Lahmi." And they asked him, "Who should pray for you?" And he answered, "Let it be the rabbi Elijah Falqen." And then we recited three times *El melekh* [that is, the *Shema'* prayer] and *Waya'avor* [that is, Exod. 34:6] with the blowing of the shofar, and everything was done as he wanted.

Then we said to him once more that he should depart, since we fulfilled his wishes. He answered, "Let some time pass, and then I shall depart." And they asked him, "Do you wish that we recite a *tikkun* [a prayer for repair or healing] of your soul?" He answered that no *tikkun* would help. They said to him, "Do you want your son to say *Kaddish* [the prayer for the dead] or to study Tora [for the peace of your soul]?" He answered that nothing would help him, and that his son was unfit to study Tora. And I asked him about the beating [of the dead] in the grave.[6] And one of those who sat there answered, "This one certainly never entered his grave." Then the spirit contradicted his words and said, "I did enter my grave on the day of my burial, and during the night they took me out of it and I never again entered it. And since that time, which was thirty-three years ago, I have been going from mountain to mountain and from hill to hill, and nowhere could I find rest, except that during that time I found myself in Shekhem [Nablus], and there I entered into a woman, and she came here, and they exorcised me according to all that is stated above. But they immediately placed amulets upon her so that I could not enter her again." And all this was true, for we knew from the mouths of others that this is what happened.

And then he said, "I was wandering about in the city [trying] to enter synagogues; perhaps I shall find rest and respite for my soul, but they did not let me enter any synagogue." And they asked him, "Who prevented you?" He said, "The sages." And they continued to ask him, "Were they alive or were they dead?" He said, "Dead. And they trod on me and said to me, 'Get out of here, you evil one!' " And the questioner continued to ask him, "To which synagogue did you go first?" He said, "To my own congregation." And they asked him, "Which one is that?" He answered, "Beth Jacob." And they went on to ask him, "Who sits now in your place?" He answered, "Since they did not let me enter, how can I know who sits in my place?" And they continued to ask him, "Who used to sit next to you when you were alive?" He answered, "So-and-so." And everything he said was true.

Then they said to him, "And how did you enter into this woman? Is it not forbidden to you to harm her?" He said, "What could I do when I found no rest in any place, except in her, for she is a pure woman?" The two first men went on to ask him, "How could you enter this house which has a mezuza [ritual doorpost scroll]?" And he answered, "I entered from below [through the cellar], for that door had no mezuza." And they asked him, "And in what manner did you enter her, since she was a pure woman?" He said, "It was in the hour when she swept; she threw some mud upon my head, and thus I was able to enter into her. And all this was on the fifth day [Thursday] of the last week, towards evening." The spirit himself told all this, and so it was, for from that time on the woman herself felt [the pain].

And while they stood there and pressed him that he should leave, they said to him, "And why have you disregarded the ban put on you yesterday to leave and not to return into her? How could you transgress it?" He answered, "I did leave, but I could find nowhere a place of rest, until I saw that they did not put amulets upon her, and then I was able to enter into her a second time." And then they took strength and said to him, "Go out, and if not we shall put an all-inclusive ban on you so that you will have to go out." And they put an all-inclusive ban on him, and he swore by the Ten Commandments that he would leave at the end of one hour. And many people testified that this was his custom while he was still alive, to swear in this manner. And they waited around and in the meantime they reproached him and spoke harshly to him, "Are you not afraid of any ban, not even of your own oath, nor of an all-inclusive ban?" And he answered, "What shall I do? As I am lost, so I am lost."

And thereafter he [one of the exorcists] wanted to make a test to see whether it was really the spirit which spoke, and he addressed him in the holy tongue, and in Arabic, and in the language of Ishmael [that is, Turkish]. And the spirit answered in each language, and spoke it clearly, as he did when he was alive, as those who knew him testified, while the woman knew none of these languages. And then he [the exorcist] spoke to him in the Ashkenazi language [Yiddish], and he did not answer, but said that he did not know or understand that language. They also asked him what was his trade in life. He answered, "The work of *Saraflik* [money changing]." And so it was. And others asked him, "Who am I?" and he gave the name of each of them.

And they also asked him about Ben Musa, whether he saw him in a transmigration. And he answered that he had not seen him at all. And they pressed him with the aforementioned adjurations, and with the aforementioned smoke, and with the Names,[7] that he should go out through the nail of the great toe of one of her feet.[8] And then he showed us by movements that he was about to go out the way they had told him; he raised her legs and let them down one after the other, with great speed, again and again. And because of those movements which he made with great force, the blanket which was on her fell off her feet and thighs, and she uncovered and demeaned herself in full view of everybody. And they went near her to cover her thighs, and she felt nothing of all this. And those who were acquainted with her knew her to be a most modest woman, and now her modesty was lost to her, and all this because she was like dead, without consciousness, as we said above.

And they said to him, "The true sign by which we shall know that you indeed went out completely is that when you go out you should extinguish the candle hanging on the wall at a distance of about three cubits from her." And by those movements which we mentioned he wanted to extinguish the candle. But although he took strength and hurried and warmed himself up to show us that he was going out through the nail which we mentioned and [was ready] to extinguish the candle which hung on the wall, nevertheless he did not go out. For he did not want to go out, but wanted to mislead us, and many times he said, "Bring the candle nearer, to the place where it was yesterday," so that he should be able to extinguish it there. And they said to him, "If you extinguish the candle in the place in which it is, we shall know for sure that you did go out, but if not, then you are merely mocking us." And he again gathered strength to make movements and shakings with the legs, as mentioned, and he caused the air to move with those movements. And since he did not want to go out and abandon his dwelling in that place, he was unable to extinguish the candle from there. But had the candle been nearer he could have extinguished it, for the spirit was standing on top of her feet as he said. And both the adjurers and we did see that the spirit went out and was close to the feet. And they again adjured him and gave him smoke, fire, and sulfur into the nostrils, so that he should go out completely through the aforementioned nail, and should uproot himself with a total uprooting and should extinguish the aforementioned candle, which was at a distance of three cubits. He could extinguish it on his way out from there while going to the desolate desert place. And he said many times, "Let this poor Jewish woman be, and do not hurt her!" And they said to him, "It is you who hurts her; get out if you have pity on her." And he answered, "Do not continue to force me, for if you force me to go out I shall take out her soul with me." Nevertheless, the aforementioned adjurers decreed upon him that he should go out unfailingly. But he did not go out. They said to him, "Sit up on the bed and then go out, and if you do not want to, then we will force you with all [the things] mentioned." And he sat up on the bed without any help. And then, when he was seated, they said to him with a great voice, "Go out, you evil one, quickly, without delay." Then he himself touched the feet with the fingers as if he was pushing the spirit which was in the flesh through the nail by means of that touching. And then suddenly she began to speak. She was sitting and saying, "He has left."

And they did not believe her; perhaps the spirit himself was speaking. For they saw that he did not extinguish the candle. And she said, "It seems that he forgot to extinguish the candle because of the great confusion and the great hurry to go out." Nevertheless, they still did not believe her, and they wanted to torture her again as they had done before, and she cried to her father-in-law and her grandmother, "Why do you let them burn me, for he has already left, and they do not believe me!" And she said, "I know that it is true that he indeed has left." And they said to her, "What is the matter [that is, how do you know that he has left]?" And she answered, "Must I tell you?" And then they understood that it was a matter which cannot be told in public, and they said to a woman, "Go to her and she will reveal you the matter." And so it was done, and it became known that the spirit went out through that place [that is, the privy parts] and drew blood as he went out. And all these excuses made all of them accept that there was truth in her words. And they put upon her the amulets which had been prepared in the house, which were on loan, and she was assumed to have recovered.

And an hour later the sages came to her when the cry went out in the city, "Behold, the spirit of a man from Israel speaks in a woman." And when they saw her they said, "He certainly did not leave, and if he left he again returned." [They said so] because of the signs they saw, such as the eyes which were *invidriados* [glazed] and the breathing which seemed labored. And from these signs they knew that he was still in her. And then the voice [in the city] told about the ruination, a voice which did not cease, that the spirit was still in her. But the two adjurers told me that he surely had gone out, but thereafter he returned, because, for one thing, the amulets which they put on her were not written for her name,[9] and for another, because of the confusion, since the whole city, Jews and Turks, were coming one after the other to see the terrible thing which was astonishing to the eyes of every man. [But] they hushed up the matter because of the danger on the part of the nations who would have wanted to burn her, until it should be forgotten in a few days, and then the matter could be corrected. And eight days later the poor woman died because of the spirit which did not leave her, and they say that he choked her and went out with her soul.

Everything I wrote above, every detail, is written precisely as it was. And one must not doubt anything in it, because it is written accurately, and there is no addition in it nor any deletion, for I wrote exactly what I saw and heard. And I request the sages who were there that they too should put their signatures on this, for it is due to the merit of their faces that we live, that they verify my words through their signatures. And the eye which sees this writing of mine and the ear which hears it should believe with a complete faith, as if he had heard it from the mouth of the spirit, and should fear and be afraid and believe everything written in the Tora and in the words of our rabbis of blessed memory, and then he will rest on his couch in peace, and three groups of ministering angels will go out before him. One will say, "Peace, etc.," and no plague will go near his tent, and his soul will cleave to God and will return to the place whence it was hewn.

Thus says the writer, the young and the poor among the thousands [of Israel], the devoted servant of the fearers of the Lord, and of those who think of His name, ELIJAH FALKEN.

I was there and my eyes saw and my ears heard all this and more, what he saw testifies your servant SH'LOMO LEVI BEN ALQABETZ (he is the author of the book *Shoresh Yishai* on the Book of Ruth).

These words are words of truth which have no measure, so that every man should know about this event and leave his evil ways, and every man [should give up] the wrong of his thoughts before he goes [that is, dies] and is not, and he who knows will return, and repent, and come back, and will be healed. The youth ABRAHAM HALAHMI. SH'MUEL BUENO.

I too was called to see this matter and my eyes have seen and my ears have heard, and it is a miraculous thing, to teach us that we should turn back in repentance. Says ABRAHAM ARUETI.

Notes

"Exorcism and Xenoglossia among the Safed Kabbalists" originally was published in the *Journal of American Folklore* 91 (1978):823–33.

1. This belief is talmudic-midrashic; cf. *Nistarot R. Shim'on ben Yoḥai*, a twelfth-century Midrash fragment, in Adolph Jellinek, *Bet haMidrash*, vol. 3 (reprt. Jerusalem: Bamberger and Wahrmann, 1938), p. 81.
2. See Ḥayyim Vital, *Sefer haGilgulim* (Przemyshla, 1875), p. 15a.
3. Ibid., pp. 15a–b.
4. The literature on xenoglossia, that variety of glossolalia in which a person speaks a language he normally does not know, is meager. However, see L. Carlyle May, "The Dancing Religion: A Japanese Messianic Sect," *Southwestern Journal of Anthropology* 10 (1954): 130; "A Survey of Glossolalia and Related Phenomena in Non-Christian Religions," *American Anthropologist* 58 (1956):75, 77, 83–86; and Felicitas D. Goodman, *Speaking in Tongues: A Cross-Cultural Study of Glossolalia* (Chicago: University of Chicago Press, 1972), p. 5. I am indebted to Professor Erika Bourguignon of Ohio State University for her advice on the problem of xenoglossia.
5. At this point the editor of *Sefer haGilgulim* inserted in brackets a lengthy quotation from the letters of R. Moshe Zacuto (ca. 1620–97), the famous Venetian Kabbalist, about the methods of administering fumigations to exorcise spirits.

6. According to talmudic-midrashic and kabbalistic belief, the Angel of Death or the angel Duma beats the deceased with a fiery chain immediately after burial; cf. *Massekhet Ḥibbut haQever*, in Jellinek, *Bet haMidrash*, 1:150–52.
7. The Names are magic names of God and of angels used in incantations.
8. They tried to force the spirit to do so lest he go out through the woman's throat and choke her.
9. According to kabbalistic belief, each amulet must be written specially for the person who will wear it, and his or her name must be mentioned in it.

20. The Love Factor
   in a Hebrew-Arabic
   Conjuration

The tenor of Hebrew incantation texts is, as a rule, one of command, of overpowering influence, of mastery, of compulsion. The conjurer performs his magic acts and recites the magic formulae, and thereby forces the spirit or demon whom he adjures to do his bidding. The spirit or demon is regarded as basically antagonistic to the conjurer, just as he is to men in general. But the magical power wielded by the conjurer leaves the spirit no choice, and he is forced to obey. This is how, in talmudic legend, King Solomon and his emissary Benaiah subdued Ashmodai, the king of the demons, with Solomon's magic signet ring and forced him to fulfill Solomon's desire.[1] And this remained the basic relationship between conjurer and demon through the ages, as illustrated, e.g., by the late medieval *Sefer Mafteah Shelomoh* [Book of the key of Solomon], the Hebrew original of which was published in facsimile by Hermann Gollancz.[2]

Hebrew MS 214 in the Bavarian State Library in Munich contains on fol. 154a-58b a medieval incantation text which, while similar in its technical details to the run-of-the-mill adjurations, differs from them in one significant respect: in addition to prescribing the acts to be performed and the words to be recited in order to force the demon to appear, to answer, and to do the conjurer's bidding, it endeavors to establish an atmosphere of friendship and sympathy between the demon and the conjurer. This *captatio benevolentiae* almost imperceptibly assumes the characteristics of a quasi-love relationship between demon and conjurer, with faintly erotic overtones. Reading the repeated asseverations of the conjurer's love for the demon and the solicitations of the demon's love for the conjurer, one cannot help feeling that there is a certain analogy between the relationship the conjurer tries to establish with the demon and that of the Middle Eastern Muslim master with the object of his physical love, whether wife, concubine, or male lover. In each case the first step is to gain control over the love object's person, but for the relationship to be truly satisfactory for the master, he must be able to feel that his advances have met with a loving response.

This is precisely what the Munich incantation text prescribes as the proper procedure. At the very beginning of its instructions, it assures the conjurer that the demon Bilar, than whom there is none better among all the spirits, "is desirous to do marvels for the sons of Adam," that "he will deliver himself only into the hand of a strong and powerful man," and that he will do this "with love" (fol. 154a). The incantation itself repeatedly adjures the demon Ramrami, a seventh-generation descendant of Bilar, to whom it addresses itself in the sequel, that he should show himself and come to the conjurer "willingly and not under compulsion, joyfully and not in fear," "pleasantly and not wrathfully" (fol. 154b). It goes on to assure Ramrami that "I [the conjurer] indeed love you and have exerted myself in seeking your well-being" (ibid.). This is followed by a description in Arabic of the demon, who is expected to appear in the shape of "a young man, brown of color, with long hair, a golden crown on his head," etc. (fol. 155a). Ramrami is then asked to appear in his own (beautiful) shape and "not in an ugly shape," to come and sit with the conjurer, and to rest by his side. The conjurer then informs Ramrami that "I have made a seal of your hands" and "put it on my right finger, and I placed it among good scents," evidently in order to please the demon. After a repetition of the request that Ramrami show himself "pleasantly and not wrathfully, joyfully and not in fear, in your shape and not in an ugly shape," he is described as wearing a crown, dressed in white clothes, and having sevenfold(?) hair upon his head. While this last reference is not clear, repeated mentions of Ramrami's hair remind one that among the Jews a woman's hair was considered erotically exciting and was therefore to be kept hidden.[3] Somewhat later, the conjurer again asks Ramrami to speak to him "with a good heart" (fol. 155b) and to show himself in his own shape, "pleasantly and not wrathfully," and assures him that "if you show yourself to me it will be good for you and will add fame to your power" (ibid.).

In the concluding instructions, the conjurer is again reassured that "if he is strong, he [the spirit] will love him and will fulfill all his needs" (fol. 156a), and is advised to smile at Ramrami and whisper to him, "Are you not Ramrami, and is it not that your shape is the shape of a youth and pleasant, and your hair reaches down to your ankles, and you are beautiful and desirable? In that hour he will come in the shape of a youth, and you will see his backside" (ibid.).

Another interesting feature of this conjuration is that it refers repeatedly to demon pairs, each bearing the same name in a masculine and a feminine form. Among the "heroes" and "men of counsel" of Ramrami appear Rebel (m.) and Riblah (f.); Lahab (m.) and Lahabah (f.), both meaning "flame"; Esh (m. in form, although grammatically f.) and Eshtah (f.), both meaning "fire." There is also a reference to Ramrami's father, Ma'aqa, and mother, Barbahoṣa'ah,[4] whom he "esteems," and whose honor is invoked, in true Middle Eastern fashion, to persuade Ramrami to do the conjurer's bidding.

All in all, we have in this conjuration the use of a wide range of psychological motivations: the demon is described as desirous of doing wonders for the sons of Adam; as impressed by a show of strength; as compelled to obey the command of the owner of the magic signet ring; as attracted to a clean, well-swept, and pleasant place and the scent of burning spices. He is reminded of the honor of his father and mother; of his greatest and most remote ancestor, Ashmodai, who was king of the demons yet nevertheless had to obey King Solomon; of the angel Galgiel, who nourishes all spirits; and of course of the name and power of God, the Creator. But over and above all this, the conjuration makes sure that a relationship of friendship, sympathy, and love is established between the conjurer and the spirit, so that the latter will actually desire to satisfy the wishes of the former.

What follows is the full text of the conjuration in my literal translation from the Hebrew and Arabic original.

> In the name of the Knower of secrets.[5] This is the matter of Bilar,[6] king of the demons, the beginning of the knowledge of Bilar and the making of his seal and its perfection, and the mention of the names of all his servants who do all things of valor before him and [do] his will. Everyone whom the Holy One, blessed be He, loves and to whom He wishes to give a good present in this world, He lets him rule over and control the knowledge of the affairs of Bilar. And if he controls him, nothing of the good things which he seeks to come to his hand will be left out. And it is better than all merchandise, and more beautiful than all wisdom. And the beginning of his [Bilar's] genealogy goes back to Ashmodai, son of Shamdon,[7] who lived in the days of Solomon and with whom Solomon did everything he wanted, whether a great thing or a small thing. And this Bilar, there is among all the spirits none better than he.

And he is desirous of doing wonders for the sons of Adam, and he desires the Name.[8] But he will not deliver himself except into the hand of a strong and powerful soul.[9] For in the hour when a man conjures him up, he appears to him in peculiar shapes in order to frighten him and test him. And if he sees the conjurer strong of heart and mighty of strength, he is instantly reconciled with him and delivers himself into his hand with love, and does everything he wishes. And happy is he who merits to control him, for all the money in the world and all honor will come into his hands, and all creatures will be afraid of him, of the man who merits to do [this] and to control him, and they will fear the man who has this seal in his hand.

And this is the manner of his seal and the making of all his things to perfection. Take weights of burnished copper and go to the goldsmith, and let him make you of it a seal weighing two zūz.[10] And let the tablet of the seal which surrounds the eye of the ring be of pure silver, and let the eye of the ring be square. And if you make it, and [if] the Lord wishes to honor you and make you wise before the creatures, warn the goldsmith to make it in three nights, neither less nor more, and let him divide the work into three parts, and let him begin and make the first part on the night following the Sabbath, and the second on the night preceding Monday, and the third on the night preceding Tuesday.

And you should have a good and plain box into which you should put it [the seal]; and if you wish, on the night preceding Wednesday, to sit in a circle, do so; and if you cannot manage it, do not worry, for every night preceding Wednesday is good for engaging in these things.

And in the hour when you wish to sit in a circle, go to a house in which there are no women; go alone, so that no other man would enter it, and let it be a pleasant place, as provided for by the Book of the Qebiṣah.[11] And burn various kinds of spices or *quslulu'ah*.[12] And if you fear [fol. 154b] that you will come to harm, take four pieces from a deer's antlers, one piece out of each antler, and stick them into the ground around the circle, toward its four winds, one west, one north, one east, and one south, and start from the east; and then sit in the circle [and] begin to say these names—and the box with the seal should be in your hand, pen and paper before you—and sit in the circle and say:

"In the name of Yah Yah Yah Yah Weh Weh Weh Weh Ah Ah Ah Ah Weh Weh Yah. Fire consumes fire, and in the name of the fire which controls all fire, and in the name of the Ineffable Names which burn everything with fire and extinguish the flames of fire, I adjure you, Iramrami son of Ma'aqa son of Senir son of Danhash son of Saqli son of Sarqas son of Bilar son of Hanar son of Kishron son of Saluqa son of Mazqon son of Yarqon son of Sa'si'a son of Zahron son of Beṭel son of Bashbash son of 'Afrit[13] son of Meda son of Ashmon son of Shimron son of Ashmodai, who is the highest of the kings, who is mentioned before the great ones, who ruled in the days of Solomon and in the days of the prophets and excelled all of them, and you excelled all of them in the greatness of deeds. I adjure you, Ramrami son of Ma'aqa, by the spirit[14] of the mountain peaks where you and all your relatives dwell, and moreover, I adjure you by the honor of Ma'aqa your father and by the honor of Barba-hoṣa'ah your mother, who are esteemed before you, and by your white clothes, and by the crown which is upon your head, that you come to me now and show yourself to me, willingly and not under compulsion, joyfully and not in fear, in truth and not in deceit. And furthermore, I adjure you, Ramrami, by the name of the Name[15] whom you fear always, day and night, which is Yo'iyaḥ, Ṣa'fi'aron, Zo'iyah, Ṣa'ba, that anyone who is not afraid of this and does not fall down before me, woe is unto him, woe is unto him who will not be conjured for my needs by this name with which I conjured you and with which I decreed on your wings and on your face, O Ramrami, that you show yourself to me now, in your shape and not in the shape of another, pleasantly and not wrathfully, for I indeed love you, and I have exerted myself in seeking your well-being, and I took pains and sat before you to see you. And I adjure you [fol. 155a], and I adjure you by the name of the angel who nourishes all the spirits, whose name is Galgiel.''

And[16] if there appears to you a young man, brown of color, with long hair, on his head a golden crown studded with pearls and sapphires, sitting on a golden throne, in his hand a rod of fire, and around him his army, on his right and on his left, ask him, and he will return an answer to you.

And these are the names of the heroes who are around him.

"And I call upon your heroes and the men of your counsel who stand before you:

"Please Salqoron, please Robisar, please Mihumiyah, please Siqlar, please Helar, please Nazar, please Raḥas, please Riḥaruaḥ, please Manoah,[17] please Kusran, please Furqan, please Ḥathat, please Sigmar, please Yar'ab, please Ṭabṭībē, please 'Ubayd,[18] please Nukhayr, please Nubir, please Harot and Marot,[19] the two youths who go up every day unto the ice of heavens, please Rebel and Riblah, please Lahab and Lahabah, please Esh and Eshta, please the tall ones and the short ones, and please those of four faces[20] who are brought here now in the wink of an eye. And fulfill my petition and my request, by permission of Ramrami, your lord. And I adjure yóu, Ramrami, by the honor of the oath which is between you and your mother, that you come and show yourself to me in your shape and not in an ugly shape, and that you speak to me and stand before me and sit with me and rest by my side every time that I entreat you, and that you give me two of your servants to serve me in your stead, and let them be before me always, in every need and in everything that I want to do. For I have made a seal of your hands, and put it on my right finger, and I placed it among good scents. And I adjure you by these names of the angels of fire and hail, by the name of Ashashiel, Ra'ad, 'Adiel, L'habhabiel, Kedareriel, Naṣ'ṣiel, Nuriel,[21] that you show yourself to me, pleasantly and not wrathfully, joyfully and not in fear, in your shape and not in an ugly shape, quickly, rapidly,[22] and appear in an appearance, in your own name and with the crown which is upon your head, and in your white clothes, and with the sevenfold hair upon your head, and with the honor of your honored companions, and with the honor of these names with which[23] you eat and with which you drink: Marwān n''a[24] Maryān, the master of your sword, and Basilo,[25] the master of your troops, and Tricintu,[26] the master of your clothes, and Anarisi who is appointed [fol. 155b] over all your richess, and 'Arṭis, the master of your counsel. Show yourself to me now and look not forward and backward, answer me and speak to me with a good heart, in the name of A'abel Abiron and in the name of the two angels who rule over you, Qaḥriel Marmaniel, so that you answer me, and be not silent at this time and in this season, until I write the names of your servants and cast them into the fire. And, moreover, I adjure you by the names of your Creator which you fear always, in the name of

Dolfeyah, Rodfeyah, Horereyah, Hohneyah, Hotleyah, Hotenyah,[27] and fulfill my request, and delay not, for I shall not move hence until you come and show yourself to me and speak to me. And moreover, I adjure you, and I decree upon all your troops, and I seal upon your body, and I forbid all your deeds, so that you do not go, and do not move hence until you come and show yourself to me and fulfill all my wishes.[28] Appear, appear in an appearance, and beware of the sparks of fire and of the names which are like fire, and burn the tablets with flames of fire, and they are: Melahseyah, Mekhalseyah, Metarseyah, Menaseyah, Merakhreyah, Meshahdeyah;[29] fire male and female, flame male and female, shall come down and bring to me every spirit who hears my words and comes not and fulfills not my wish. And moreover, I adjure you, Ramrami, by what has been and by what will be, that you look at what is in front and what is behind, and that you see the power near you of the names which I have mentioned, and the power of my act; and beware lest you drop your visages and leave behind all your troops, and hurry and come and show yourself to me in your own good shape, pleasantly and not wrathfully, and I shall speak to you and request of you all my needs, and thereafter you shall return to your place in peace. And if you show yourself to me, it will be good for you, and you will add fame to your power. Do it, and delay not and stand not there [even] for one hour and imagine not in your soul that your coming . . . ''[30] [fol. 156a].

And make sure that you smile, so that he [the spirit] may see that you are not afraid of him, and he will fear you there. It is his custom to test every man who wants to control him, whether he is strong or weak. If he is strong, he [the spirit] will love him very much and will fill all his needs for him, and if he is weak and soft of heart, he will pay no attention to his words. And when you have finished your words, sit smiling and say in a whisper: "Is it not that you are standing [here], and you are Ramrami? And is it not that your shape is the shape of a youth and pleasant, and your hair reaches down to your ankles, and you are beautiful and desirable?'' In that hour he will come [in] the shape of a youth, and you will see his backside.[31] And do not look [at him] at once, but raise your eyes from the ground little by little until you see him. And when you see him take the ring out of the box and put it on your right little finger, and then tell him all your needs, and he will answer you and fill all your needs. And thereafter put the ring back into the box. And you should have wax, and when you want to do a small or a great thing, impress the seal of the ring upon the wax and [one word unclear] all your needs, and he will do [it] for you.

This is proven and tested. Act in wisdom and in purity, and you will succeed with the Creator's help.

[fol. 156b] And this is the aforementioned preparation from the Book of the Qebisah.[32] Go to a house in which there are no women, and sweep the house thoroughly, and make in it a circle, and open four openings in the circle toward the four winds of the world, and put spices in each opening with thorns of sycamore trees,[33] and leave this in the house all day and all night; and in the second night write down the twelve names of the prayer for rain,[34] and put it in your lap, and thereafter enter the circle, and let there be in your hand a knife of Indian iron, and the place of the hand of goat.[35] And cut three notches in the neck of the knife. And still in the same night burn *qasi lalu' i*[36] over coals, and at four o'clock of the night,[37] after the people have gone to bed, sit in the circle, with a strong and firm heart, like unto a brave man whose sword is drawn in his hand, and fear not. And [now] peace. And if you want to write an amulet or to mention sanctified names, let that which is written be upon you: Pofiel, Baqu, Zaftuel, Itiel, Shantiel, Shaftiel, whose name is Ṣebaot Yah[38] u''f.[39]

Finished. Thanks be to God.

Notes

"The Love Factor in a Hebrew-Arabic Conjuration" originally was published in the *Jewish Quarterly Review*, n.s. 70, no. 4 (1980):239–53. I wish to express my thanks to the Bavarian State Library for its kind permission to study and publish this text.

1. On the Solomon-Ashmodai legend, see L. Ginzberg, *Jewish Encyclopedia*, s.v. Asmodeus, and *Legends of the Jews*, 7 vols. (Philadelphia, 1909–46), 4:165ff.
2. *Sepher Maphteaḥ Shelomo (Book of the Key of Solomon): An Exact Facsimile of an Original Book of Magic in Hebrew* (Oxford, 1914).
3. E.g., "The hair of a woman is a shameful nakedness" (*'erva*) (B. Ber. 24a).
4. The origin and meaning of most of these demonic names can no longer be established.
5. I.e., God.
6. Bilar seems to be derived from the Arabic *Bulāz*, Satan. The Arabic letter *z* is the same as *r*, but has a dot over it.
7. According to midrashic sources, Ashmodai's father was Shamdon and his mother Na'amah; see Ginzberg, *Legends*, 1:150.
8. I.e., wants to do the will of God. God is often referred to in traditional Hebrew literature as "the Name."
9. I.e., person.
10. A zūz (pl. zūzīm) is a coin weighing one fourth of a shekel.
11. See the instructions at the end of the text and n. 32 below.
12. So spelled here in the Hebrew text; at the end of the text it is spelled *qasī lalū' ī*.
13. *'Afrīt* or *'Ifrīt* is the common Arabic name for a malevolent spirit, akin to the jinn.
14. *Yetzer* in the Hebrew original, which also means "instinct" or "inclination."
15. I.e., God.
16. This and the following paragraph are in Arabic in Hebrew characters.
17. The biblical name of Samson's father.
18. Arabic name meaning "little slave."
19. Hārūt and Mārūt are the Arabic names of the two angels (cf. Koran 2:102/96) who in Muslim folklore administer punishment to the dead.
20. The reference seems to be to the cherubim in Ezekiel's vision (1:6), who are described as having four faces.
21. All of these are typical Hebrew angelic names, ending (with the exception of Ra'ad) in *ēl*, i.e., God. Nuriel is an angel well known from the Midrash. Lehabhabiel can be interpreted as "my flame is God." Natzatziel as "my spark is God."
22. The next five words are in Arabic.
23. I.e., with the owners of these names.
24. Probably the abbreviation for *nusaḥ aḥer*, "another version."
25. Evidently from the Greek *basileus*, "king."
26. So vocalized in the Hebrew text; probably *trecento*, "three hundred."
27. These are again Hebrew angelic names ending in *yah*, i.e., God. Their meanings are not clear.
28. The next five words are in Arabic.
29. See n. 27 above.
30. Fol. 155b ends here; the sentence is left unfinished.

31. Cf. Exod. 33:23, where it is stated that Moses saw only the backside, not the face, of God.
32. *Qebitzah* means "collection." No "Book of Collection" is known to me.
33. *Ibrin* in the original; probably from the Arabic *ibrah*, "needle," "thorn," "sycamore tree."
34. Meaning unclear.
35. Probably meaning that the handle of the knife should be made of goat's horn.
36. See n. 12 above.
37. I.e., ca. 10 P.M.
38. I.e., "God of Hosts," the frequently used Hebrew name of God.
39. Meaning unclear.

V.
From the
Four Corners

21. Jewish Birth Customs

I. Introduction

The use of charms and amulets in various Jewish communities is, in most cases, based on the same general principles of magic which are found among many peoples all over the world. When saying "based on principles of magic," I do not mean that the folk, whether Jewish or gentile, which used or still uses certain charms and amulets had or has a conscious knowledge of the principles which underlie the almost infinite variety of magical acts performed and substances utilized. The folk mind which believes in the efficacy of magic is aware only of the specific effect attributed by tradition to the act performed. The common element to which the various magical acts conform had to be discovered by students of folk culture, who collected data on magical beliefs and practices from many peoples, classified and categorized them, and found that they can be explained by a relatively small number of common principles. It was the "magicologist," as he can be called, who established that in most cases there was a basic similarity between the magical act performed (or the magical object used) and the desired end, as well as in the beliefs upon which the practices were based.

In one type of magical acts this similarity is external and formal. The children in one of the New Hebrides, for example, use stones which are similar in their shape to a certain fruit in order to ensure the growth of that fruit. In another type of magic the similarity lies in the function. The libation of some liquid (water, wine, beer, blood) causes rainfall; the opening of a door or of a lock brings about the opening of the womb of the woman who has difficulty in delivery; the locking of a lock or the burying of a bone in the earth causes sterility. Sir James George Frazer termed this type of magic "sympathetic" or "homeopathic."

Next to the principle of similarity, magic uses the principle of the persistence of contact. If a bonfire is lit at midwinter in order to give the sun strength to overcome the cold and renew its warmth, this is a magical act based on the principle of similarity. But if a hair or a nail clipping of a person is burned with the intention of causing him to die in fire, then the principle of persistence of contact is added to that of similarity, and we are dealing with "contagious" magic (another Frazerian term), which is based on the belief that, even though actual physical contact between the person and the hair has long been severed, the magical contact between them persists. Consequently, whatever is done to part of the person's body will also happen to him.

When dealing with magical acts, the question arises: what is the relationship between efforts to achieve a goal by using practical ways and means and obtaining the desired end by magical methods? To put it differently: under what conditions will man turn to magic in order to achieve his desire? In very general terms this question can be answered by referring to Bronislaw Malinowski's well-known observation that the proclivity to magic arises when practical methods prove insufficient to obtain the desired end. The greater the uncertainty concerning the occurrence of the hoped-for event, the greater the inclination to resort to magic; the more evident it is that practical measures alone cannot consistently bring it about, the greater the use of magic. Malinowski gained this important insight while working among the Trobriand Islanders who did not use magic in lagoon fishing, in which an adequate catch and the safety of the fishermen was a matter of course, but did employ ample magic in open-sea fishing, where the catch was uncertain and the danger great.

An equally good example for the correlation of magic and uncertainty can be found in agricultural activities. Even the most primitive cultivators know that, in order to produce crops, they have to plough or otherwise prepare the soil, to sow or to plant, and to carry out a series of concrete and practical steps. But a good harvest depends not only on these routine measures, but also on factors over which man has no control, such as the time and amount of rainfall, the absence or presence of blight, locusts, and so on. No amount of agricultural know-how and experience can influence these factors. Here, then, a wide field opens for magical acts whose purpose is to exercise control precisely over these in practice uncontrollable factors, and to eliminate thereby the uncertainty and apprehension concerning the success of the crops. Therefore, magical fertility rites observed at certain phases of the growth cycle play an important role among agricultural peoples.

The situation was very similar with regard to human birth. The birth of a child has always been a dangerous thing. Despite all the practical precautions, despite the services of experienced midwives, it often happened that the child, the mother, or both died. This was a danger which practical measures, as far as they were known to "the folk," could not eliminate. Therefore, recourse was had to magical means to ensure successful delivery. However, nowhere was magic alone relied on. The traditions of every people contain much folk wisdom based on the experience of generations, and many of the steps taken to insure successful delivery belong to this category. Often, in fact, it is not easy to distinguish between the practical and the magical aspects of a given measure. Occasionally the two are combined, and a recommended procedure is both magical and practical.

The present study deals with Jewish folk traditions centering on childbirth. The material is organized chronologically, following the life of the woman from the time she hopes to or does become pregnant to the weeks after delivery. Section II deals with charms against barrenness, section III with charms against miscarriage. Then follows, in section IV, a treatment of the charms which have the opposite purpose, namely, to prevent conception and birth. Section V discusses charms against difficulties in labor. Section VI presents the widespread practice of delivery on the earth, or ground, or floor, section VII the laying of the newborn child on the earth. Section VIII discusses the comparison or parallel between the fruit of the womb and the fruit of the earth, which is drawn in many places. Section IX examines the salting of the child, which is a very widespread apotropaic measure among both Jews and gentiles. Section X speaks of the special treatment accorded to the afterbirth and the umbilical cord and the ideas connected with them. And, finally, section XI presents the numerous measures resorted to for the protection of the mother and the child in the days and weeks following delivery.

II. Charms against Barrenness

The desire for offspring has remained strong among traditionally oriented Jewish women. The search for efficacious substances, either to be taken internally or applied externally, to rid the woman of the ''curse of barrenness'' continued after the biblical period. The substances resorted to belong to several categories, of which I shall discuss those of mineral origin, of vegetable origin, of animal origin, and of human origin.

A. Of Mineral Origin

In another study I discussed several inanimate substances used to cure barrenness.[1] Hence I shall confine myself here to a discussion of the use of precious stones and certain metals for the purpose of making barren women fertile. Such customs and beliefs are found among both Jews and other peoples.[2]

In certain oriental Jewish communities, barren women take precious stones internally so as to become pregnant. The ruby is considered especially efficacious for this purpose, because an indication is found in the similarity between its Hebrew name, *odem*, and the Hebrew name of the mandrakes, *dudaim*, as well as between its foreign name *rubin* and the name of Reuben, the son of Leah, who found the mandrakes. Accordingly, the ruby was considered the stone of Reuben.[3] A typical recipe for the use of the ruby reads: ''For a barren woman. Let him take a ruby, grind it to dust, and mix it in food, and let the woman eat it, and she will conceive . . . since the ruby contains the charm of the mandrakes.''[4]

Abraham haRofe (i.e., the physician) whose book *Shilte haGibborim* was printed in Mantua in 1612, identifies the ruby with the ''carniol.'' ''Corniola or carniola [thus called] after the flesh, is a red stone similar to flesh and blood.''[5] In the Middle Ages the coral was identified with the ruby.

> This stone is called rubin and it grows in certain places in the sea, and it is a big rock, and its origin is like the origin of silver and the origin of gold. . . . and its virtue is that a woman who wears it will never have a miscarriage, and that it is good for a woman who has difficulties in childbirth, and if they pound it and mix it into food and drink, it helps very much for pregnancy, like the mandrakes which Reuben found, which have the shape of a man; and therefore it is called *odem*, and it is spelled without the *waw* [for the *o*], to point to man (*adam*), for the reading indicates that it is a stone, and the spelling without the *waw* indicates its effect [i.e., that it brings about the birth of a man].[6]

Another efficacious antibarrenness precious stone is the carbuncle (Hebrew *b'dolah*). ''Take one eighth of an ounce of carbuncle, and one eighth of an ounce of honey, and pound them all well and mix them together, and let the woman eat it with a finger in the night of her immersion, and she will conceive with the help of God, blessed be He, and it is proven.''[7]

Pearls, too, are considered effective antibarrenness stones.[8] According to a Hebrew book of charms, ''If the woman swallows three pearls, called *lulu*, she will conceive.''[9]

Among the metals which are efficacious against barrenness, gold and silver occupy an important place.[10] In certain cases the fertilizing power is attributed, not to the metal itself, but to its shape.[11] Among both European and Middle Eastern Jews this belief and attendant customs existed in various forms. R. Naḥman of Bratzlav writes, ''The letter *hē* made of silver is a charm for fertility.''[12] *Hē* stands for the name of God and is considered a charm for many purposes. Among both the Jews and the Muslims of the Middle East, the shape of a hand often takes the place of the letter *hē*, since the hand has five fingers and *hē* has the numerical value of five. Among the Muslims the hand amulet is called ''hand of Fatimah.''

Another charm in which silver figures advises,

> Take sixteen pieces of silver from sixteen women who have children of whom none has died, and the pieces must be given to you for nothing as an outright gift, in the name of *H* [God], the God of Israel. And give them to the silversmith that he make of the pieces a round disk, purified of all dross, and let him engrave the shape of a *hē* on one side of it, and on the other side he should engrave *Hē lakhem zera'* [Behold, seed for you], and it is better if it [the writing] protrudes. And then put the disk into three satchels and hang it around the neck of the woman.[13]

Other traditions recommend the use of tin for such a disk.

> Another amulet, and it must be on a tin disk without any admixture of another kind, neither lead nor any other kind, and engrave on it this drawing.

ד	יד	מו	א
מ	ז	ו	יב
ה	יא	י	ח
יי	כב	ג	יג

And the letters and the drawing must protrude on every side . . . and the engraving must be done on Thursday, when the star Jupiter rules. And after the name was made properly hang it around the neck of the woman, or above her bed, in a satchel.[14]

A third metal used is lead.

Another matter. Take pieces of lead according to the number [i.e., numerical value of the letters] of the man's name, and the number of the woman's name, and engrave on each piece the letter *ṭet*. And the letter *zayin* must be provided with crownlets. And take an iron spoon and put all the pieces into it over the fire, and when the lead begins to melt, say seven times, "There will be no miscarrying or barren woman in thy land, the number of thy day I will fulfil (Exod. 23:26). . . . And then take standing water from the well of a source, and take a cup and pour the water into it, and another man should hold the cup over the head of the person. And you pour the lead into the water, and then say, "Just as I have extinguished the lead, so shall all evil force, and evil affliction, and evil happening be extinguished."

At the end the water is poured out "under the millstones."[15]

The "magnet" (this is the word used in the Hebrew text), whose main virtue is to facilitate childbirth, also is a charm against barrenness.[16] Mercury, on the other hand, prevents pregnancy. "A barren woman should be very careful not to let any quicksilver fall on her, even a small amount, for this prevents pregnancy. Neither should she drink absinthol, which is called *wirmt oel* [wormwood oil], not even as part of a mixture."[17]

Mineral and vegetable substances together figure in the following charm. "Take for her [the barren woman] dust from seven roads, and ashes from seven ovens, and water from seven cisterns, and dust from seven graves, and some bunch of *kofer* [that is, henna in Arabic], and gather all of it and heat it in a fire, and let her wash herself with it in the night of her immersion."[18]

B. *Of Vegetable Origin*

Perhaps the most ancient Jewish folk cure is the use of the *dūdā'īm*,[19] which were identified by the Septuagint and by Josephus[20] with the "mandragora," the mandrake.[21] How the barren Rachel used the *dūdā'īm* is not specified in the biblical narrative, but, if it be permitted to draw a conclusion a posteriori from the way barren Jewish women subsequently used mandrakes, it would seem safe to say that Rachel either ate them or tied them around her body. These two alternative methods have been practiced until recently by barren Sephardi women[22] in Jerusalem.[23] A third method was practiced by Samaritan women in the seventeenth century: they placed the mandrakes beneath their beds.[24]

Among the Hasidic Jews in eastern Europe, the willow branches beaten against the synagogue benches on the seventh day of the Feast of Tabernacles serve as a remedy for barrenness or various kinds of pain or paralysis. The branches are boiled in water after beating, and the water is given to the childless woman or patient.[25] A charm for begetting sons is to boil willow leaves, for "willow" equals "seed."[26] We may note in passing that among the ancient Romans and Germans a beverage made of willow leaves or of leaves of other fruitless trees was believed to cause sterility in women by virtue of the rule of sympathy.[27] The Jewish belief in the fertilizing power of the willow is based on their use in the Lulav, a bundle consisting of a long, thin palm branch and some small branches of willow and myrtle tied together, and of a citron (*ethrog*). These four plants are used on the Feast of Tabernacles (Sukkot, which falls in the autumn) in the following way. Each morning of the seven days of this holiday they are taken to the synagogue, and there, after the appropriate benediction has been pronounced over them, they are held in both hands and shaken. The purpose of this rite, as recognized by the sages of the Talmud, is to induce rainfall and to confer life.[28] The willow, as closely associated with the beneficial functions of the Lulav, came to be regarded as a charm or remedy promoting conception in women, a belief which found a welcome support in the happy discovery that the numerical value of the words "willow" and "seed" is the same.

At least two more of the remaining three species composing the Lulav, namely the myrtle and the citron, rank high among the Jewish popular charms for obtaining an easy delivery. Moreover, according to Naḥman of Bratzlav, a Hasidic rabbi of the eighteenth century, "through [the use of] myrtle on Sabbath one obtains sons who will be learned in the Law." According to the same author, "thorns are also a charm for fertility."[29]

The eating of leaves of fruit-bearing trees by barren women is nearer to the direct working of sympathetic magic. In a Hebrew manuscript called "The Book of Charms and Riddles," which was compiled in Damascus in 1870 but contains copies of much older recipes,[30] we read:

> A charm for pregnancy. I found it written in an ancient manuscript book as follows: He [i.e., the husband of the barren woman or the person who wishes to administer the charm] should go to an orchard and take there five leaves, from each tree one leaf, and they must be [taken] from food trees [i.e., fruit trees]. And as you cut the leaves you must say over each leaf, "Behold, I cut this leaf in the name of so-and-so the daughter of so-and-so" [the name of the mother]. And also of the herbs [he should take] from each herb one leaf in her name and the name of her mother. And when coming home write upon each leaf the Holy

Name which is efficacious for pregnancy, and it is this: WHLH, which is composed of [the first letters of] the verse "Vayitten H [stands for the name of God] Lah Herayon" (The Lord gave her conception).[31] . . . Then place all the leaves one by one into a vessel, and if the mouth of it be narrow, so much the better. And pour over them water taken from seven wells. And also when you draw the water say, "In her name and the name of her mother." Then seal thoroughly the mouth of the vessel, and also stick the mouth of it with dough as is done with alcoholic drinks, so that no vapor whatsoever should escape from it. And boil it on fire and let her go to the bath [the ritual bath prescribed for Jewish women on the seventh day after menstruation ceases] and bathe and dip. After returning home, let her eat and drink and do all her work. Before the hour of the intercourse let her set everything [i.e., the aforementioned vessel] on the fire until it boils four or five boilings while it remains sealed. And she should invite herself to intercourse and take off her underclothing and cover her whole body with a covering reaching to the ground, then she should bring the vessel still sealed, and open it and place it against her privy parts as near as possible, that the vapor may enter her body, and let her remain thus about half an hour, and the longer she is able to sit on the vessel the better, and then he should quickly have intercourse with her. Afterwards she should pour off the water into another vessel and keep the leaves apart, because if, heaven forbid, it should not help the first time, she ought to add to them five leaves from five food-trees and pour over them water from seven wells [drawn] in her name and the name of her mother, and she should boil it on fire as mentioned above. And if, heaven forbid, it does not help the second time, she should do so also a third time as mentioned above. And the water which we said she should remove from the leaves, let her drink it during the seven days with a little sugar, in the morning before eating anything, each day one part of it, until seven days are completed. . . . And if she become pregnant she must not go to the bath until four or five months pass, until the child is noticeable. With the aid of God.[32]

Let us mention in passing that the eating of leaves, fruits, etc. as a means of inducing pregnancy is found in many parts of the world, either in practice or in legend.[33]

In other Jewish charms for pregnancy the use of a great number of "magical" plants is prescribed. Such charms are to be found, e.g., in a book written by Eliyahu Ba'al Shem, a wonder-working rabbi who lived in the seventeenth century in Chelm, Poland. He wrote in Hebrew, but the names of the plants are given in the German-Jewish vernacular of his time, sometimes derived from an original German, sometimes from a Latin or Greek name. (The names used by Eliyahu Ba'al Shem are given below in parentheses.)

Take nutmeg (muškit nus), mace (muškit blit), *alpinia*[34] (galgin neglih), ginger (ingber), zedoary (sit'pr), cubeb (kww'bin), *folia salviae* (zalpi bletlih), *semen primulae* (prim kerner), white incense (weišn weiarih),[35] anise ('anis), myrrh (mira), *semen betulae* (be'twil zamin), licorice (lakris), an equal amount of each kind, pound it well and let her eat it in bread when she is pure [i.e., after having taken the prescribed ritual bath].[36]

Another recipe prescribed by the same rabbi is "Take five almonds, five apricot pips, one nutmeg, and an equal amount of anise, and pound it all together and boil it in wine, and let her drink it at night when she is pure; let her do so several times."[37]

Further recipes from the same source recommend the external use of fruits or other parts of fruit trees.

> For a barren woman. Take a large walnut and put into it a small lizard, three flies, three fresh peppers, and a piece of natron which is called *kreit* [*Kreide*, "chalk"?], and write on the natron *HēLāZe* and wrap it in a piece of new linen, and seal the nut with new shoemaker's pitch which is called cobblers' wax, and it must be new pitch which has not yet been used, and hang it [the walnut] on the neck of the woman on a Friday which falls on the fourteenth of the [Jewish] month, or the eighth of the month, or on the eleventh of the month.[38]

> For a woman who has no children. Extract water from an apple tree while it is moist and green, and let the woman wash in this water her face and her hands. Thus should she do several times.[39]

The apple tree is rich in magical properties which can be put to use by barren women in several ways. In the manuscript mentioned above we read, "Take a piece of white linen and dip it into her menstrual blood and go and tie it to an apple tree. On the way do not cross water nor a river either. And the tree will become dry and the woman will become pregnant."[40] This is but a specimen of the well-known method by which an evil can be transferred to an object or a person in exchange for some positive quality possessed by that object or person. Methods of transferring barrenness from a woman to a fruit tree, similar to the one mentioned above, are found among many people.[41] According to another recipe contained in a Hebrew collection of folk cures, "Make out of wax the likeness of a pot and put in it some of her menstrual blood, and close the mouth of the pot and hide it under an apple tree—and then the woman will become pregnant and the tree will not bear fruit. It is proven and tried."[42] Another passage in the same book speaks not of an apple tree but of fruit trees in general.

> Take a long piece of paper and dip it into her menstrual blood and then let her go to a tree full of fruit and insert the paper into a hole or a crack in the tree, and should there be no hole or crack, let her make a hole and put into it the aforementioned paper, and say seven times: "Tree, tree, I give unto thee my ailment and thou give unto me thy fruits." And she should not approach that tree again.[43]

Various kinds of herbs and grasses also have a fertilizing power, according to popular belief. Rabbi Tuvya Katz, who was "professor of medicine" in Constantinople in the sixteenth century, advises the use of the following remedy in cases of barrenness.

> Leaves of the herb *salvia* with a little salt or ammi (*'amiws* or Indian *nahbi*)[44] seed, one drachma, in wine in the morning; and [let her drink] this three times in the week before she becomes pure for her husband, in order that she should not discharge the semen. And Rabbi Y'huda heḤasid[45] ordered the herb ox-tongue (*buglosa*) boiled in wine to be given her to drink in the night of her ritual bath; and this is proven.[46]

Eliyahu Ba'al Shem, whom we have already quoted above, writes, "Also the herb called lovage (*lib shtikl*) [is potent against barrenness]. Boil it in clear water taken from a well or a spring, and in the morning she should wash her face and hands [with the infusion]. And it must be boiled thoroughly so that the water should receive the taste of the herb."[47] Or: "To take a bath and to put into the bath herbs called ox-tongue (*oksen zung*), vervain (*eisen kroit*), *urtica*,[48] *buglosa, pasir* [?], and about three hours after the bath to fumigate her with these herbs. This should be done for three months, in each month three days."[49] Some of these as well as other herbs, are also efficacious when taken internally.

> A charm for pregnancy. Take the herb which is called *buglosa* among the sellers of spices and in the pharmacies, and boil it in good wine and give it to the woman to drink on the night of her bath, and take care that it should boil thoroughly in order that the wine should receive the taste of the herb buglosa.[50]

Or: "Let the herb called vervain be boiled in clear water and let her drink the water and eat the herb."[51] Or again: "A woman who cannot become pregnant as a result of sorcery, let her husband drink an herb called *'Inglah(?)*[52] in *psrin (?)*[53] beer, and let the woman drink an herb called *twrin* for ten consecutive days in the morning on an empty stomach, as well as in the evening."[54] The vervain is one of the ingredients used in the following dish, which is recommended by the same author as a charm against barrenness.

> Take wheat flour from the millstone, in secret precisely, that no man should notice that you are taking it, and take vervain, urtica, lovage, ox-tongue, and fourteen cloves (*neglich*) and three ergots (*mutter neglich*)[55] and some rue (*pizwm*).[56] Dry them thoroughly, grind them and rub them between the palms of your hands until they become powdery. And take good wine which should be very old, at least three years, and knead all the things mentioned above in the flour mentioned above with the wine mentioned above. The flour must be

cleansed of any grits previous to kneading. And bake it on a Friday into the Sabbath loaves, and after the baking let the woman eat the cake mentioned above in the days of her purity.[57]

Jewish popular belief also ascribes fertilizing properties to certain roots and grains.

Take the root of the herb called *shishili'og[?]* and make the root into the likeness of small nuts, and take of them four ounces. Take also the gall of a ram or a deer and three ounces of honey, and mix everything together in a glass vessel and let the man and woman drink of it at the time of intercourse with a little wine. And the woman should also take some of it and put it beneath her privy parts, and then he should have intercourse with her and she will conceive. . . . Or else: To conceive. A tradition from the Great Ones of past generations: Let her boil cotton seed in water or in wine two days previous to her menses. Let her drink it and immediately after the first [ritual] bath that follows she will become pregnant of a male child. This is a tried thing.[58]

The grass which grows between the big stones of the Wailing Wall in Jerusalem is believed to have a beneficial effect in promoting conception. "Barren women are wont to pluck grass from the slits of the Western Wall, growing there between the rows of the stones of the wall. This they boil and drink the infusion as a charm."[59]

A highly efficacious herb for the same purpose is rue, which is known among the oriental Jews by its Arabic name, *roda* (in Latin, *ruta*). "For pregnancy. If the woman should put some rue into her womb after the intercourse, and sleep lying on her back, she will conceive at once."[60] Saffron, which is known by its Arabic name of *za'frān*, also is drunk as a remedy against barrenness. Among the Jews of Morocco barren women drink saffron mixed with wine on the night before they take their ritual bath.[61] Similar practices also are found among the Sephardi Jews in the Near East. "She should take saffron and some musk and rose-water and should dip into them a piece of cloth and should place it in her womb, and then should sleep with her husband and she will conceive."[62] Or: "Whosoever wishes to conceive of a male child should take some saffron and pound it and she should drink it in water or wine on the night of her bath."[63]

Among the Egyptian Jews it is customary to this day for the barren woman, when going to the public ritual bath, to drink pounded beans and cumin mixed with water.[64] Written sources referring to the same custom also recommend mixing the beans and the cumin with beer or wine.[65]

Garlic, which is regarded in the Orient as a potent charm against the evil eye, is also used as a cure for barrenness both by Sephardi and Ashkenazi Jews. "Let him take white garlic and pound it with honey and make of it a pessary and put it in her womb, and let it remain there some two hours. Then steam her with good wine and let the vapor enter her womb, and then he should lie with her and she will conceive."[66] Or: "Take a head of garlic and peel it, and fry it in olive oil, and then take nutmeg and clove (*karnfwl*), marshmallow (*ngal*) and *wgh(?)*, and pound it all and make a clot of it, and let her put it into her womb every day during the days of her cleansing,[67] and when she returns from the bath, at night, let her do the aforementioned things. This is proven."[68] The use of such pessaries is age-old, and is found prescribed in the Hippocratic writings. Among the ingredients into which the pessary was to be dipped, according to these ancient Greek recipes, were natron, garlic, figs, honey, cinnamon, oil, and wine.[69]

C. Of Animal Origin

The number of charms the ingredients of which derive from the animal kingdom is much greater than that of those taken from the vegetable world. Let us begin our survey with the fishes, which are, with the Jews as well as with a number of other peoples, the animals par excellence used for the attainment of all kinds of sexual potencies in general, and pregnancy in particular. The fish is a symbol of the male organ of generation among various peoples.[70] In the folktales of many peoples we find the motif of pregnancy resulting from eating fish; so, for instance, in Slavonic, Serbo-Croatian, Czech, Russian, Indian, Brazilian, English, Nordic, Icelandic, and Breton tales.[71] The practice corresponding to these tales, namely that of eating fish in order to attain pregnancy, also is widespread. Hartland has collected several instances of it.[72] Among the Palestinian Arabs a woman who has only daughters will eat fish in order to bear male children.[73]

In popular Jewish thinking, too, the fish is perhaps the most prevalent sexual symbol. Jacob blessed Ephraim and Manasse, saying, "let them grow into a multitude in the midst of the earth."[74] The Hebrew verb *yidgu*, rendered here "let them grow," is derived from the noun *dag*, "fish," thus meaning precisely to be like fishes, to multiply like fish. The Messiah whose appearance will, according to Jewish legend, bring a wonderful fruitfulness to the whole world,[75] is called in one ancient collection of Jewish legends *Nun*, "fish."[76] The fish served as a symbol for the Messiahs of several peoples.[77] Concerning the meaning of the word *daga* in the verse "We remember the fish we did eat in Egypt freely,"[78] there is a controversy in the Talmud between "Rav and Sh'mu'el; one of them said [*daga* means] 'fish'; the other said 'sexual license.' "[79] To this the great medieval commentator Rashi remarks, "*Daga* (fish) is a name for sexual intercourse."[80] Elsewhere he explains in a similar fashion the name "Leviathan" (whale).[81] According to a talmudic passage, the eating of fish increases the blood, wherefore it should be eaten the day before and the day after the letting of blood.[82]

Oriental and occidental Jewish books of charms, remedies, and customs equally enjoin the eating of fish upon women who have ceased to bear children. The following advice, addressed to the husband, is found in quite a number of seventeenth- and eighteenth-century collections. "Take a fish which was found inside another fish and the stomach of a hare, and put them into a pan, and they should be fried until they become dry, whereupon grind them with flour and put into them water and mix them together, and let her drink it and she will conceive."[83] Another seemingly corrupt version of the same prescription says, "Take a fish which was found in the stomach of a hare, dry it," etc.[84] According to another book of charms, "A fish found within a fish, dried and pounded, has the same effect if taken for three nights in wine."[85] Among the Moroccan Jews it is customary for the childless woman to swallow a fish in which there is another fish.[86] The symbolism of the fish within another fish, indicating the desired position of the child in the womb of the mother, is obvious enough.

Eliyahu Ba'al Shem, whom we have already quoted twice, knows also of a third, more complicated recipe, one of the ingredients of which is the gall of a fish. "For pregnancy. Take the gall of a pike (*hecht*) and the gall of a wolf and enfold them into purple-blue woolen cloths, and let her put them into her womb, and at the time of intercourse let her remove them from there."[87]

The next magic animal which to popular imagination appears to be related in several respects to the fish is the snake. But as the snake derives its fertilizing powers in many cases from its connection with the tombs of the dead, it seems best to reserve its treatment, together with that of the tombs, for Section E of this study.

Another important group of magical animals is birds. The first place among them is occupied by the cock and the hen. According to the Talmud, "whosoever sees a cock in his dream should expect a male child; cocks, should expect male children."[88] Among the Jews of Turkey, a woman who had only daughters was given after her ritual bath a whole cock to eat, including its entrails and crest.[89] Both European and oriental books of charms suggest, "Take the bladder of a black hen which lays eggs and dry it and give it to her to drink on the night of her [ritual] bath; and this should be done three times, each time on the night of her bath."[90] Or: "Let him smear the [male] organ with the gall of a cock and she will conceive quickly."[91] Or: "If you take sesame and the blood of a black hen and mix them together and she smear with them her womb—it will be efficacious with the help of God, blessed be He."[92] In Algeria next to Constantine, there is a spring at which both Arab and Jewish barren women sacrifice a black hen in order to become fruitful.[93]

Another bird possessing magical virtues is the raven. The following recipe is contained in both a European and a Palestinian book of charms:

> For pregnancy. Take the tongue and the gall of a raven and dry them thoroughly and then pound them very fine, and the woman should drink them on the night of her bath, previous to intercourse, in the following way. The ashes are to be put into old wine and lukewarm water, and take care not to use too much of the wine lest the power of the dust become annihilated. This has two ways. The first time take the tongue and the gall from a male raven and another time from a female raven. And this thing he should do several times and it should be begun on the night previous to Tuesday precisely, and should the night of the bath be another night, one should not begin it.[94]

Or: "Take the brain of a raven and arsenic and saffron and mix them together and hang it upon her for forty days, and she will conceive."[95] Or: "Take the wings of two ravens and straighten them out at the time of intercourse, and she will conceive."[96] Still another part of the body of the raven is used by barren women in Aglu, Morocco. They drink its blood warm as it flows from the body.[97]

Next in the group of birds is the goose. "If he [i.e., the husband of the barren woman] eat two skins of geese and have intercourse with his wife on the same days, she will assuredly receive pregnancy."[98]

Of the dove, the efficacious parts are the brain and fat. "Let her take the brain of a white dove and wear it in her womb all day, and in the evening remove it and sleep with her husband, and she will become pregnant."[99] Or: "Let her take the fat of a dove and smear [with it] her privy parts for three days, and she will become pregnant."[100] Among other peoples barren women were wont to eat doves. In the Murray Islands, e.g., women eat male doves in order to conceive a male child, and female doves in order to bear daughters.[101]

It happens that the instructions contained in the books of charms do not specify what kind of a bird it is which should be used with a view to obtaining pregnancy, but only speak of a bird in general. "After the bath, let him take a male and a female bird and slaughter them and immediately extract their brains, and let her put them into her womb and sit in her bed without getting up, and an hour later she should have intercourse with her husband, and she will become pregnant."[102] Among other peoples too, unspecified birds are used to cure barrenness in women.[103]

Eggs also have magical properties.

Take from a white hen an egg which was laid on Friday or Sunday or on the night preceding Monday or on the night preceding Tuesday. And the egg must be taken from under the hen and there must be in it a chick. And open the egg and take the chick and put it into a new pot, and take a new cover and cover the pot, and smear dough over the cover and place it on the fire until the chick in the pot is burnt, and take the ashes and put them into a piece of new linen, and sew up the linen with silk threads, black and white and green and also the green which is called *gel* [*Gelb*, yellow], namely a little of black and a little of white and so on, and they [the threads] should not be twined together, and hang it round the woman's neck. And this should be done on a Friday.[104]

Until a couple of years ago it was customary among the Jewesses of Poland in the district of Warsaw to search in case of barrenness for an egg which contained another egg, and to drink the inner egg while standing in the water of the ritual bath.[105] Another Jewish egg charm used in Jerusalem as a cure for various ailments, among them barrenness, was communicated by A. Goodrich-Freer in a study some forty years ago.[106] Let us mention only in passing that eggs were and still are used by various peoples in a great many ways as a cure for barrenness, as well as for other ailments.[107]

To pass on from birds to four-legged animals, let us begin with the fox, which is known in Jewish folklore as the most cunning of animals, although he won this fame much later than the snake. In an ancient Hebrew collection of traditional material called *Tosefta 'Atiqta* we read,

What is written about the wife of Manoah [the mother of Samson]? She observed her impurity [I.e., the menses], "And the angel of the Lord appeared unto the woman, and said unto her, 'Behold now, thou art barren.' "[108] And even though she was barren and did not bear, and her women neighbors mocked her, saying, "If you want to bear, take a fox skin and burn it with fire until it becomes ashes, and take of them and put it into water, and drink of it three days, each day three times, and you will immediately conceive," even though they [thus] mocked her, the Holy One, blessed be He, harkened to her voice, and at once an angel appeared to her and said, "My daughter, beware, and do not eat anything unclean." And because she observed her impurity, at once she became pregnant.[109]

Many hundred years later, Eliyahu Ba'al Shem gave barren women the same advice the refutation of which by Manoah's wife is praised in the above-mentioned passage. "For pregnancy. Take a fox skin and burn it to dust and ashes, and put its ashes into water and let the woman drink of it three days, and she will become pregnant with the help of God."[110] The same author also recommends putting the gall of a fox into the womb of the barren woman.[111]

Another animal rich in magical powers is the hare, and numerous parts of its body are used in Jewish charms against barrenness. In the "cities of India" the Jews used the skins of hares. "Take the skin of a hare and burn it to dust, and give it to her to drink with wine nine consecutive days every morning, and she will immediately conceive. And the truth is that this is tried and proven."[112] In Egypt to this day, barren Jewish women hang a hare's foot around their necks to ensure conception.[113] Both European and oriental Jewish books of charms advise the use of a hare's womb.

> Pregnancy. Take a hare's womb and dry it thoroughly and pound it well, and let the woman drink the ashes before intercourse in old wine, and the older [the wine] the better. And also her husband should drink of another womb in a similar manner. And take care not to put too much wine on the ashes lest the power of the ashes be annihilated. It is also said that it should be dried precisely in the sun. And this should be done at the beginning of Monday night previous to Tuesday . . . and it can also be done on other nights. It should be done several times. And in another book I found that he should drink of the ashes of the male organs of the hare, and it is best to perform both—this is a great rule in medicines generally.[114]

Both charms, that of the hare's womb and that of the "hare's egg," namely, the male organs of the hare, already were prescribed in the seventeenth century by Eliyahu Ba'al Shem. "Take the egg of a hare and pound it well, and put it into a beverage and give it to the woman to drink on the night of her bath, and she will certainly conceive of a male child."[115] The use of a hare's womb and male parts to bring about pregnancy is not confined to Jewish communities.[116]

Another part of the hare widely used in Jewish communities as a cure for barrenness is the stomach. It has been found that the numerical value (*Gimatria*)[117] of the words *Tazri'a v'yalda* (Conceive seed and bear[118]) equals that of the words *b'qeva arnevet* (in the stomach a hare).[119] Of course, such an equation would only have been sought for and found after the use of a hare's stomach as a cure for barrenness had become customary. In fact, the use of a hare's stomach for this purpose was recommended in the Middle Ages.[120] In the *Sefer Z'khira*, printed in 1729, we read, "For a woman that she may conceive. Take the stomach of a hare and clean it thoroughly, and take care that it touch not the earth, and burn it in a new metal pot which has not yet been used, and burn it to ashes and put the metal [pot] on the burning coals, and then pound it finely and drink it in standing water. And after the bath, before having intercourse, they should both drink of this dust, and thus should they do for three nights before having intercourse, and then she will conceive."[121] It may be interesting to note in passing that in an ancient Anglo-Saxon book of charms there is to be found a very close parallel to this charm. [122]

In other Jewish charms the eating of a hare's stomach, together with other ingredients, is recommended. "Take a hare's stomach and a fish found within another fish and put them into a pan until they dry, and then pound them and give them to her to drink, and she will conceive." [123] Or: "For pregnancy. Take a hare's stomach and let her eat it together with goat's milk or with honey, and she will conceive." [124] Also "the dried stomach of a hare, bear gall, ammonia, and myrrh, powdered and mixed with butter, taken for two days in broth, will help in getting children." [125] The gall and blood of the hare also are efficacious. "Take a hare's gall and mix it with *bonfaisance* oil, and dip into it a piece of cloth and put it into her womb, and she will conceive with the help of God, blessed be He." Or: "A charm for a woman that she conceive. Let her take hare's blood and dry it and grind it to dust, and drink it in a glass of wine, and give also to her husband at the time of the lying, and she will conceive with the help of God." [126] Among other peoples the intestines of a hare are eaten as a cure for barrenness. [127]

The wolf comes next. "If the woman apply a pessary of cotton wool dipped into wolf's blood mixed with vinegar, even though she be sterile she will conceive immediately. Another one: "If she take fish soup and wolf soup and dip into them cotton wool and put it into her womb before having intercourse, even though she be sterile she will conceive immediately." [128] In an earlier source we read: "Take the gall of a pike (hecht) and the gall of a wolf," etc., or, "Take the gall of a wolf with *'atripli*, [129] you will find it with the haberdashers, and let her put it into the womb and she will conceive," or, "Take the womb of a female wolf," etc. [130]

The efficacious parts of the bear are its fat, gall, meat, and milk. "Take bear's fat and let her smear with it her privy parts, and let her husband smear with it his privy parts three nights, and let him have intercourse with her, and she will conceive. [131] Or: "Make a decoction of bear's or wolf's meat as much as a bean. If the animal is male the child will be male, and if it is female the woman will give birth to a daughter." [132] Or: "Let her put bear's gall in wool into her womb." Or: "Take honey which has not been put on fire and bear's milk and porcupine's gall and put it, wrapped in wool, into her womb, and she will conceive." [133] The liver of the porcupine also is efficacious when put into the womb of the barren woman. [134] The wearing of a porcupine's foot around the neck is regarded by the Arab women of Morocco as a charm against barrenness, [135] while the ancient Prussians gave the bride and bridegroom a brew of the sexual organs of a bear and a bull or a he-goat, presumably with a view to ensuring the birth of a male child. [136] In Jewish charms the male parts of a pig are recommended: "A pig's egg [i.e., testicles] dried and pounded and mixed with the intercourse ointment is useful for pregnancy. And if he takes the right egg she will bear a male child and if the left one she will bear a girl.''[137] Or: ''Take the excrement of a pig, dry it, pound it finely, and give it to her to drink, and you should immediately have intercourse with her and she will conceive.''[138] Animal dung and droppings were often recommended by Galen and other ancient writers, and adopted by practitioners down to the time of Quincy's dispensary. They are found in Arabic and Jewish ''dispensaries'' also.[139] In Bosnia and Herzegowina, sterile women drink for a considerable period a soup prepared of an old cock into which are mixed the dried, fried, and pounded testicles of wild boar.[140]

The magical part of the ox, and of cattle in general, is the gall. ''A charm for a woman who has not borne. Take the gall of an ox and make a pessary and dip it into the gall, and put the pessary into her womb for three nights, and on the third night she should lie with her husband, and she should drink no water during that night. And if the gall be that of an ox she will bear a male child, and if that of a cow she will bear a daughter.[141] Or:

> Take the gall of an ox, and it should be precisely one having eggs [male organs] and it should not be castrated [in short, a bull], and make a pessary of a thin cloth and soak it in the gall, and let the pessary swallow the water of the gall thoroughly, and do this for three days before her bath, and let the woman put it into her womb within, and when she has need to urinate let her take it out, and then let her once more dip it into the gall and return it to her womb, and so should she do for three days before the bath and also on the day of the bath, and when she takes the bath she should first remove it and bathe, and after the bath she should dip the pessary once in the gall and return it to her womb until she have intercourse with her husband, and at the time of the intercourse she should remove the pessary and have intercourse with him, and she will conceive with the help of God.[142]

Eliyahu Ba'al Shem advises, ''For a woman that she bear a male child. Take the gall of a cow and wrap it into wool and put it into the mouth[143] of the woman near the time of her menstruation, and assuredly she will bear a male child.''[144] The afterbirth of a cow is recommended as efficacious against barrenness when dried, pounded, and drunk in wine.[145] The galls of an ox and of a pig mixed with honey were advised already by Hippocratean therapy as a cure for barrenness.[146]

In other Jewish charms ox gall is only one of a number of efficacious ingredients. ''Take the horn of a ram and burn it until it becomes ashes, and let her drink it in wine or water mixed with wine. And also take leaves of *finilio*,[147] which is called *yo'ezer* in the language of the Mishna;[148] it may be wet (i.e., fresh) or dry, and pound it, and mix it with the gall of an ox, and put it all on her head at the time of the intercourse, and immediately she will receive the semen and conceive. And this is tried for pregnancy."[149] Or: "Take the hide of a ram and burn it and mix it with the gall of cattle, and let her put it into her womb, and she will conceive."[150] Or: "For a woman that she should conceive. Take a bone which is found in the heart of a deer and hang it round her neck."[151] Or: "In the month of Tammuz[152] when the butcher slaughter a ram, there will be found in its heart a stone. Let the husband of the barren woman take it out so that no man should see it, and let him hang it about her until she conceive, and it will be efficacious."[153] Or: "For pregnancy. Write the name *Horon* on a parchment [made of the skin] of a deer, and wipe it off in clear water, and give it to her to drink."[154]

The magical parts of the sheep are the lungs and liver.

> For a woman who had never had a child. Take the lungs and liver of a sheep and cook it in old, good, and chosen wine, and while it boils the whole should be placed underneath the woman in order that the fumes should enter her body. And when it begins to cool down, let the woman get up and lie down in bed, and let the woman take care lest she should cool down before her husband lie with her, and also after the connection she should take care not to become cold. And all this has to be done in a warm room, well closed that no wind should be able to enter, and it will be efficacious with the help of God.[155]

Other peoples have various other methods of curing barrenness by means of a sheep.[156] The privy parts of a she-goat should be used, according to other Jewish charms. "If you give into the hand of a woman, at the time a man has connection with her, the privy parts of a she-goat, even though she be a woman in her virginity, she will conceive immediately."[157]

Of the elephant the tusk is the efficacious part. "Take the tooth of an elephant which is called *ebolio* [ivory], and grate of it with a knife up to the weight of seven *pshuṭim* [simples], and mix it with one ounce of boiling honey after the foam has been removed from it, and mix it with water and give it to her to drink for three consecutive days, and even though she be sterile she will immediately conceive."[158] Eliyahu Ba'al Shem also advises to put the womb of a mule into the womb of a barren woman.[159] The blood of a bat, too, has fertilizing powers. "Take a bat and slaughter it upon wool and put it over her womb, and after that have intercourse with her, and she will conceive. This too is wondrous."[160] The heart of a mouse gives fertility. "Hang around her the heart of a mouse and she will quickly conceive with the help of God. This is tried and proven."[161] Of the insects, let us mention the spider. "Take a big spider, put it into a small wooden case of equal size, stop the opening with the bark of the same tree or with the shell of a nut, and carry it round the neck."[162]

Jewish popular belief attributes fertilizing powers to the milk of various mammals.

Dog: "Take the milk of a bitch and mix it with what is specified hereafter, and have intercourse with her, and she will conceive immediately." "Take sesame and the blood of a black hen and mix them together, and let her smear with it her privy parts at the time of intercourse, and she will conceive."[163] "Take the milk of a bitch and wash with it her privy parts, and immediately have intercourse with her, and it will be efficacious with the help of God. And this has to be done several times."[164]

Ass: "Take wool and dip it into ass's milk and put it on her navel at the time of intercourse, and she will conceive."[165]

Mare: "For pregnancy. . . . Let the woman drink mare's milk for nine consecutive days without her knowing, and have intercourse with her . . . and she will conceive immediately."[166]

Bear: Of the use of bear's milk we have already heard above.

Cow: "Let the woman wash her womb in milk when having intercourse with her husband, and she will conceive."[167]

Goat: Of the use of goat's milk we have already heard above. Additionally let us mention the following charm. "Take the first milk of a goat before the kid had touched the udder, make a small cheese of it, put it into a new linen cloth, and tie it upon the left arm; it must never be taken off, and the woman will then bear children."[168]

D. Of Human Origin

At the conclusion of the preceding section I spoke of the milk of various animals used as a fertility charm. Folk belief attributes the same potency to mother's milk as well.[169] Eliyahu Ba'al Shem advises, "For a woman, so that she conceive, take mother's milk which is called *mutter milikh* [i.e., German *Muttermilch*], and give her to drink of it a spoonful for three consecutive days on an empty stomach."[170]

Various Jewish books of charms from Europe and the Middle East suggest methods of transferring the power of fertility from a woman who has children to a barren woman by means of the birth stool.

> A woman who has ceased giving birth should sit on the birth stool of a childbearing woman. That is, immediately after the childbearing woman has risen from the birth stool, let her [the other woman] sit in her place on that birth stool. There must, however, be nothing to intervene between her flesh and the birth stool, not even her skirt. And the duration of the sitting should be about half an hour or a little more.[171]

If the same procedure is followed by a woman who has had no children at all, the fertility of the childbearing woman will be transferred to her and she will conceive, but the woman who used the birth stool before her will no longer have children, "and for this reason the women remove the birth stool immediately after the child arrives."[172]

Contact between a fertile woman and another woman can transfer the power of fertility, or some of it, from the first to the second.[173] Among the Sephardi Jews in Safed,

> A woman who gave birth does not enter the house of a bride for forty days [after the birth], because she would harm her and prevent her from conceiving. And if she did enter, the bride should take a piece from the dress of the childbearing woman and soak it in water, and after her immersion [in the ritual bath] she should pour that water on her own body, and this is a charm to make her conceive.[174]

On the other hand, both the bride and the bridegroom, who are in the most blessed period of their lives, convey fertility upon others by their touch. "He who causes a bridegroom and a bride to rejoice will merit that his wife bear male children."[175]

Folk belief attributes fertilizing powers to the umbilical cord.[176] According to a medieval Jewish belief, a barren woman could conceive if she got hold of an umbilical cord, burned it, and then drank the ashes in wine.[177] According to advice followed until a few decades ago by some Sephardi Jews in Palestine, the same charm could give a woman male offspring. "Take a piece from the umbilical cord of the first son and burn it and pound it, and give it to the woman to drink in water or in wine in the night of her immersion, and she will not bear daughters."[178] Or: "When the child comes out of the womb of its mother, let them cut his umbilical cord some four fingers. If they give it to a cock to eat, then all the children the mother will bear after him will be male; and if they give it to a hen, the mother will bear females."[179] Or: "To bear male children. When she gives birth, let her take a little of the umbilical cord and mix it with honey and rose water, and give it to her to drink. And put the rest in a silver case and hang it around her neck, and she will bear males."[180] A German study from the late nineteenth century states that Russian "women, especially Jewesses, are said to suck blood from the child's navel, and in doing so they should swallow three times."[181]

Eating the placenta also is considered a remedy for barrenness.[182] This custom, it seems, was practiced among the Jews of Russia, and Russian immigrants brought it along to America.[183] In another version it is sufficient for the barren woman to sit on the placenta. Barren Sephardi Jewish women in Palestine would sit on the placenta while it was still warm.[184]

Occasionally the placenta of a cow is substituted for a human placenta in Jewish folk custom. In the Middle Ages barren Jewish women ate the dried placenta of a cow, pulverized and mixed into wine.[185] A similar custom was followed until recently by the Sephardi Jews in Palestine. "Let him order the cowherd to stand by when the cow gives birth and take the placenta which is in [*sic*] the calf, and dry it in the sun until it becomes completely dry, and then pound it well until it is like flour, and when the woman gives birth give her a little of that flour that she drink it in wine before the meal, and thenceforth she will bear males."[186]

Among many of the peoples practicing circumcision, the foreskin is considered a potent fertility charm.[187] Among the oriental Jews, barren women would swallow a foreskin in order to become pregnant. This practice also is followed among barren Sephardi women in Safed and Jerusalem. In many cases the *mohel*, the ritual circumciser, would be asked in advance by the husband of a barren woman to put aside the prepuce for her in exchange for a payment.[188] The ingestion of a foreskin is practiced "among the uneducated Jews of Egypt,"[189] and among both Jews and Muslims in Tripoli, Libya.[190] The Jews of Yemen also preserve the prepuce as a remedy for barrenness.[191] Among the Jews of Turkey, a woman who had given birth to one child and then could not conceive again would swallow a prepuce.[192] Several Hebrew books of charms refer to this method of obtaining fertility. "For a barren woman, so that she conceive, let her swallow the foreskin of a circumcised child."[193] Or: "Take the prepuce of a child and dip it in honey, and let her swallow it."[194]

Among the Yemenite Jews also, a variant of the custom is found. They place a metal vessel under the Chair of Elijah, on which the *sandaq* (godfather) sits holding the child in his lap while it is being circumcised, and then they let the bride drink from that vessel.[195] The same custom exists among Sephardi women in Palestine, where both barren women and women who have stopped having children drink the water called "Elijah's water."[196] Among the Jews in Europe other variants are found. In the environs of Warsaw, "childless people . . . are scrupulous to drink from the glass of the circumcision benediction."[197] Elsewhere in Eastern Europe, "a woman who cannot conceive should look at the circumcision knife after the circumcision."[198]

The swallowing of the prepuce is also considered a charm to insure the birth of a male child. "When the prepuce is cut off, the women swallow it as a charm to bear male children."[199]

The question arose whether swallowing the foreskin was permitted by Jewish ritual law, the Halakha.[200] It was debated for several generations, and the gist of the opinions was summed up by the Sephardi chief rabbi of

Tel Aviv, R. Ya'aqov Moshe Toledano, in his book *Yam haGadol.* "I found it necessary to consider the law concerning human flesh, whether it is forbidden by the Tora, and whether it is prohibited because it is a member from a living body and flesh from a living body. And this has a bearing on the custom of women to eat the prepuce of a newborn child as a charm for conception, and the like."[201]

A barren woman also can obtain fertility through direct or indirect contact with a boy or a girl. This belief underlies the custom of seating a small boy-child on the lap of the bride at a certain point in the wedding ceremonies, which is practiced among many Middle Eastern peoples, including the Jews. This assures the bride in advance that she will be fertile, and that she will bear male children.

Folk belief finds powers of fertility also in persons who have a special religious status.[202] Among the Jews of Morocco barren women drink of the water in which the *kohens*, Jews of traditional Aaronic descent, washed their hands on Yom Kippur, the Day of Atonement.[203] In Jerusalem barren women drink of *me kohanim*, "priest water." In Syria, the women who desire pregnancy bring rose water to the synagogue and pour it over the hands of the *kohen* on Yom Kippur, and then, after the end of the fast day, drink the water. Among the Jews of Bukhara, barren women and women who have stopped bearing drink rose water which they poured over the hands of the *kohen* when he pronounced the blessing at the *N'ila* (concluding) prayer on Yom Kippur. Similar customs also are observed by barren Jewish women in Iraq, Persia, and Yemen.[204]

In all the customs described so far, the main purpose is to transfer part of the powers of fertility which dwell in an object or person to the barren woman, and thus to make her fertile. Let us conclude this section with a custom which is based on a belief in the transmigration of souls, in the possibility of transferring a soul which has recently left its body into the womb of the barren woman, and of endowing her with fertility in this manner. If the barren woman performs an act on the basis of this belief, she evidently must establish contact—again directly or indirectly—with the body of the deceased, to which the soul is believed to be still adhering. The means par excellence for effecting such a contact is water.

Both Jewish and Muslim barren women in Tripoli, Libya, drink of the water in which the body of the dead was washed.[205] Among the Jews of Baghdad, it is customary to assure a woman of fertility with the help of the dead as early as at the time of her wedding. The bride enters the chamber in which a dead man is being washed and steps three or four times over the body, in order to make sure she will conceive.[206] Among the Sephardi Jews in Safed, "at the time of the washing of the dead they make satchels filled with *borit* [soap], and wash the body with them. What is left of these satchels, if the deceased was a God-fearing and decent man, is kept, and the [barren] woman washes herself with it at the time of her immersion.''[207]

E. Graves and Snakes

The belief in the fertility-giving powers of saints expresses itself in most cases in a pilgrimage to their tombs by barren women.[208] This custom is found all over the earth, and especially among the peoples of the Middle East[209] and in various Jewish communities. Among the Jews of eastern Europe it is considered ''a charm for pregnancy that the woman carry with her a piece of wood from the roof of the grave of a *tzaddiq* [saint].''[210]

Barren Jewish women in Kurdistan make a pilgrimage to the tomb of R. Shim'on, carrying along a white lamb. Next to the grave there is a well and a stone table. The women wash themselves in the well and then go to the table, on which there are three egg-shaped stones. They lift the stones and let them drop back on the table. If the stones remain upright, the woman knows that she will conceive and bear children; if not, she will remain childless. After the woman gives birth to a child, she brings it to the grave and places it on the ground for a short while.[211] Two separate motifs are combined in this custom. One is the well-known use of water next to the tomb of a saint, and the other an attempt at divining whether the woman's wish would be granted. The degeneration of active magical acts into passive divination procedures is a characteristic feature of decline in the life of folk custom.

A similar phenomenon is known to us from the Yemenite Jews, who practice two customs, one of which is meant to give fertility to the woman in an active manner, and the other of which aims at nothing but divination. A barren woman goes to the tomb of R. Shalom Shabazi, next to which there is a spring, and sings, ''Abba Salim, strengthen my heart and give me my wish!'' Or: ''O, spring, help me and give me a child!''[212] This is an active magico-religious custom. The divination is found in a Yemenite Jewish manuscript from the seventeenth or eighteenth century. ''For pregnancy. Take a glass of water and sprinkle three drops of olive oil into it with the little finger, [and say] with every drop three times, 'Qutiel, Harbiel,' and then let a drop fall, and do this three times. If the drops cling together and rise, [the child] will live, and if they sink and rise not, it will not live.''[213]

According to a European Jewish belief, ''Also this key [to the cemetery] has a virtue for barren women.''[214]

Among many peoples one finds the belief that snakes dwell on graves and that these snakes are but incarnations of the souls of the dead.[215] The idea that the dead body turns into a snake or worm is found in Jewish folk belief as well. A passage in the Babylonian Talmud states, "The spine of a [dead] man, after seven years, becomes a snake."[216] A talmudic legend tells of snakes which guard the graves of saintly men. Rav Kahana died in consequence of the wrath of R. Yoḥanan bar Nappaḥa. Then R. Yoḥanan learned that he had no reason to be angry with Rav Kahana, whereupon he went and stood over the cave in which he was buried and saw that a big snake was coiled around the opening of the cave. R. Yoḥanan said, "Snake, open your mouth [i.e., let your tail go from your mouth, and move away from the opening of the cave], and let the master go in to the disciple." But the snake did not open its mouth. "Let a colleague enter to his colleague!" But it did still not open. "Let the disciple enter to the master!" Whereupon it opened for him. R. Yoḥanan entered, asked for mercy, and raised up Rav Kahana.[217]

A similar legend is reported about the grave of R. Shim'on ben Yoḥai. The entrance of that cave also was guarded by a snake, and when the rabbis brought the body of his son, R. El'azar ben R. Shim'on, to bury him in the same cave, they said to the snake, " 'Open your mouth and let the son enter to his father.' The snake opened for them."[218] The same story is told about the burial of R. Yose, the son of R. El'azar ben R. Shim'on, who also was brought to burial in the same cave.[219] The Palestinian Talmud records that a snake wound itself around the dead body of Bar Kokhba.[220]

Above we have heard about the grave of R. Shalom Shabazi in Yemen, next to which there was a source of water. Ya'aqov Sapir, the nineteenth-century Jewish traveler, describes the Yemenite Jewish belief connected with that grave. "About the grave of R. Salim el-Shibzi: if a person who is not God-fearing goes up there, and does not merit healing, he will find the source dried up, without water; only a snake will be coiled around the entrance."[221]

The Moroccan Jews have a legend which records that when the Jews were ordered by a government decree to transfer the grave of R. Ya'aqov Birdogo to another place, a snake emerged from the grave and showed the people the way, and then stopped on the new spot where the saint wished to rest.[222]

Having thus become acquainted with the connection between the dead and snakes, we shall understand that the dead who endowed barren women with fertility could become transformed in belief and legend into a snake which impregnates them by actual copulation.[223] Another type of legends and folk customs present the snake in its phallic character without any connection with graves or the dead. The comparison of the phallus to the snake, and the concept of the snake as a phallic creature, are widespread in folk imagination everywhere.[224]

Talmudic statements testify to the existence of a belief in the phallic nature of snakes among the Jews in antiquity.

> This woman who sees a snake and does not know whether or not it has designs on her, let her take off her clothes and throw them before the snake. If it coils itself into them, it has designs on her, and if not, it has none. [And if it has designs on her] how can she escape it? Let her have intercourse before the snake [with her husband]. But some say this will make its desire even stronger. Therefore [she should not do that, but] let her take some of her hairs and nail clippings, and cast them at it, and say, "I am menstrually impure." This woman who has been penetrated by a snake (Rashi: "When it desires her, he enters completely in that place" [i.e., the vagina]"), let them spread out her feet and seat her on two barrels, and let him take oil and throw it upon coals, and let him take a basketful of garden cress and aromatic wine, and put it there, and mix it together, and let him take a pair of tongs in his hand, and when the snake smells the fragrance and comes out, let him grasp it and burn it in the fire, for if this is not done, it will return into her.[225]

The snake which injures or attacks women appears as early as in the fourth book of Maccabees (ca. first century C.E.). "And the righteous mother of the seven sons spoke and uttered also these words: 'I was a chaste virgin, and did not go out of my father's house; I guarded the built-up rib.[226] The devil in the desert did not violate me, he who despoils in the field, nor did the Belial snake defile the modesty of my virginity with its seductions. In the period of my flowering I remained tied to my husband.' "[227] In these words there seems to be an allusion to the legend according to which the serpent wanted to marry Eve. "And so we found about the serpent that it planned to slay Adam and marry Eve."[228] According to another Midrash, the serpent, who was none other than Samael (Satan), actually lay with Eve and fathered Cain upon her.[229]

III. Charms against Miscarriage

After a charm for pregnancy had succeeded and a woman conceived, the search began for the means to prevent miscarriage. Folk belief considers the womb a receptacle which can be opened and closed with a key.[230] When the woman receives the semen, her womb must open for her to become pregnant, but thereafter it must remain closed until the day of birth. The Moroccan Jews let a young bachelor tie a belt around the belly of a pregnant woman and lock the belt with a small lock. As long as the lock remained, the womb of the woman would also remain closed and she would not miscarry. When the months of pregnancy were completed, the same youth would unlock the lock, and then the woman would be ready to give birth.[231] The key can, of course, serve to open the womb of a barren woman, that is, enable her to conceive.

> Write these names on seven iron keys, write all these names on each one of them, and then wash those keys in water from seven wells or cisterns, and pour the water over her head after her ablutions. And this is what you should write: "Pishon, Gihon, Hiddeqel, P'rat,[232] Ahnunit, Bantiyya, Lantita, Ahsad, Darya."[233] Thereafter write these names on a glass seven days seven times, and let the writing be blotted out by water, and let her drink the water before the intercourse. And it will help with the aid of God, blessed be He.[234]

The magic rite of locking the womb of a pregnant woman also was practiced in Jerusalem in the nineteenth century. "Pregnant women . . . hang around their necks a locked lock, and throw away the key."[235]

Instead of a lock, the womb of a pregnant woman can be closed, and thus made secure for the fetus, by means of a thread, a kerchief, or so on.

> Immediately at the time of her pregnancy when she feels the child, let her gird herself around her naked body with *qanvos* [canvas] threads, several times. And it is even better if the same is done around the room in which she plans to give birth. And let her not remove the threads from her body. And if there are not enough threads to go around the room, at any rate let her place the threads under the door of the room. And if there are several doors, let her put threads under each of them, and also in the windows, and the hearth, and in every place where there is a hole or an opening in the room. And this is a great mystery.[236]

A similar charm is specified in a Middle Eastern Jewish source.

> For the benefit of a woman that she miscarry not. Take a white thread and a black thread, and let him read over them. "And the Lord said . . . 'This gate shall be shut, it shall not be opened . . . for the Lord the God of Israel hath entered by it, therefore it shall be shut.' "[237] Thus far. And tie it around the belly of the woman until her nine months are up, and then open it. And it will help.[238]

Likewise among the Jews of Jerusalem in the nineteenth century: "The pregnant woman should measure the wall of the Temple (i.e., the Western Wall) with a silk thread, and then should tie it around her hip. Or: take a wrapper of the Tora scroll and tie it around her belly so that she should not lose the blessing of the womb."[239] According to another source, "Pregnant women should measure the Western Wall, or other tombs of saints and holy places, with a silken or woolen thread, and tie the thread around their hips so that they lose not the fruit of their wombs."[240] In other variants, found among the Jews of both Europe and the Middle East, in which parts of living beings, plants, or inanimate objects are tied around the pregnant woman's belly or hung from her neck, the binding represents not only the closing of the womb but also, and sometimes primarily, the fastening of the fetus to the mother's body. A typical example of this is the use of the *t'quma* stone, which I have discussed in some detail elsewhere.[241]

The ruby, whose fertility-giving virtue was presented above, also was believed to be efficacious in preventing miscarriage. "Its virtue is that a woman who wears it will never miscarry."[242] Corals have the same effect.

> A man should teach his wife, when she is pregnant and has reached the ninth month, that she should tie into her shirt a little salt and bread, and three red and beautiful corals which have no holes in them, and when she sees a gentile woman or a Jewish woman who is suspect of eating children or of giving the evil eye to the fetus, she should take a little dust from the earth and say, "Let terror and dread fall upon them," etc. (Exod. 15:16), three times forward and three times backward, and when she says "let them be still as a stone" (ibid.), she should look at the dust, and then, when she says three times forward and backward, as mentioned, let her throw the dust down on the ground.[243]

Among vegetables used as a prevention of miscarriage, the *ethrog* (citron), which forms part of the Sukkot ritual, plays an important role. Pregnant Yemenite Jewish women carry in their dresses the stem (*pitam*) of the *ethrog* as a charm against miscarriage.[244] An eighteenth-century book of charms says, in somewhat confused language, "The Tree of Knowledge was partly grape vine and partly *ethrog*; therefore pregnant women have the custom of removing the stem of the *ethrog* on Hoshana Rabba [the seventh day of the Feast of Sukkot] and of giving money for charity, that it save her from death with her embryo. . . . and let him speak thus: 'Just as a I have a little enjoyment from biting this stem, so did I enjoy the Tree of Knowledge which the Holy One, blessed be He, commanded to Adam and Eve.' "[245]

In oriental Jewish communities, they apply wax as a preventive of miscarriage. "For a woman who miscarries. Take wax and knead it in the milk of a mare, and tie it to the belly of the woman, and she will not miscarry as long as it is on her. And the proof is that if you put it on a hen who is about to lay an egg, it will not be able to as long as it is on it."[246] Honey and yeast have a similar virtue. "For a woman that she should not miscarry. Take honey and besmear with it the entire belly before the fire, and then smear *sauer teig* [i.e., yeast] on a rag and heat it and tie it to her belly."[247]

We have already met the hare as an animal which can cure barrenness. The heart of a hare protects a woman from miscarriage. "If you hang upon her the heart of a hare, dried without salt, she will not miscarry, with the help of God."[248] Or: "Take the heart of a rabbit and put it in leather and let her wear it, and she will not miscarry."[249] The heel of a polecat has the same effect. "For a woman who miscarries. Hang on her the heel of a polecat, and she will never miscarry. And this thing is proven."[250]

Among the reptiles and "creeping things," the snake and the scorpion are efficacious. "A charm that she miscarry not. Let her gird herself with the skin of a snake whose way is to change it every year, and it is often found in houses and courtyards and in the fields. Let her gird it around her naked body all the days of her pregnancy, and she will not miscarry."[251] Or: "Take a live scorpion, and put it into a reed, and seal it with wax, and hang it on her all the time that she is pregnant. And it happened once that they found the scorpion alive after eleven months."[252]

Another folk method of preventing miscarriage is by drinking magic potions. "Let her drink in the days of her pregnancy pounded corals which are called *mirjān*, and she will not miscarry." Or: "Let them slaughter a hen for her name, and let them take out the gizzard, and clean it and burn it in an iron vessel, and the woman should drink its ashes in wine or in a soup, and she will not miscarry, if the fetus is alive. But if it is dead, it will fall out." Or: "A tried and proven charm. Let her drink the ashes of a snake's skin, and she will never miscarry." Or: "Give her the milk of a pregnant she-ass three days every morning on an empty stomach, without her knowledge, and she will no longer miscarry."[253]

The Jews of Morocco give vinegar with oil to drink to a miscarrying woman, early in the morning. Or they take an ounce of honey, an ounce of sugar, seven walnuts, seven almonds, seven dates, and seven raisins, fry them together in oil, and have the woman eat the concoction in the morning on an empty stomach.[254]

The method of another charm is to transfer the danger of, or proclivity to, miscarriage from the woman to an animal. "Let her pass through under the belly of a pregnant mare from one side to the other three times, and what was in the woman will be in the mare, and she will not miscarry." Or: "A charm for a miscarrying woman. Take the intestines of a sheep or goat and wind them around her belly when she is pregnant, and then give it to a pregnant polecat to eat, and the matter shall be turned away with the help of God."[255]

Several magic procedures figure in the advice given by R. Naḥman of Bratzlav to pregnant women. "A charm for a miscarrying woman. Let her carry with her a magnet." (We shall recall that the magnet is also considered a means to enable a barren woman to become pregnant.) Or: "A charm for a miscarrying woman. Let her sell her embryo" (that is, make a fictitious sale of it). Or: "The grinding of a flour and the kneading of the dough for the Passover matzot are a charm for a woman who miscarries." Or: "A woman who loses her children, the remedy for this is that she wash the bride before the huppa." Contact with a bride is familiar to us as a charm for pregnancy. Or: "A woman who miscarries should carry with her dew water." Thus the dew (like rain), which has the virtue of making barren women fertile and resuscitating the dead,[256] also protects the fetus. Finally, two prohibitions. "A woman who miscarries should not wear golden jewels," and "Let her beware on the day of her purification not to let her nail clippings fall on her clothes."[257]

Let us conclude this section with a warning contained in the *Baraita diMassekhet Nidda*, a treatise on ritual purity derived from ancient Palestinian sources and quoted from the thirteenth century on.

> The sages taught and said a pregnant woman should not go frequently to the bath. Why? Because she is in danger . . . and she can either miscarry or have a hemorrhage. . . . If her husband is a learned man, he should not allow his wife, when she is pregnant, to go frequently to the bath. Why? Because the beginning of miscarriage comes from the heat of the bath as she enters it. Why? Because the sinews become sensitive and the source [i.e., the vagina] opens, and she causes death to the child. And the sages also said about the pregnant woman that once she has conceived she should not eat many vegetables. Why? So that it should not damage the heart of the child, which struggles in her womb.[258]

IV. The Prevention of Pregnancy and Birth

The same methods used for achieving conception are resorted to for the opposite purpose, the prevention of pregnancy and birth. In some cases the identity of the methods used for these opposite purposes is clear and logical. If, by means of applying a lock, a kerchief, or a thread, it is possible to close the womb so that the mother should not miscarry, then it stands to reason that the application of the same methods *before* the woman is pregnant can shut her womb and prevent conception. Accordingly, various peoples use a lock for this purpose, which is but one example of the magical binding which, according to widespread folk belief, can deprive both men and women of their copulative powers.[259]

A similar logic underlies those customs in which contact with the earth plays a central role. Just as direct contact with the earth can endow a barren woman with fertility and can assure her of an easy delivery—that is, just as it is possible to transfer by magical means some of the powers of the earth onto the body of the woman—so it is possible to transfer or to return to the earth the woman's fertility, thereby preventing her from conceiving or, if already pregnant, from giving birth.

Various customs expressive of these beliefs were practiced in Jewish communities in the Middle Ages. One of them shows explicitly that the intention was to return something from the woman to the bosom of the earth.[260] The woman stuck the scissors with which the umbilical cord of her child was cut into the soil. As long as the scissors remained in the earth, she could not conceive.[261] Another method was to take the plate from which the woman ate her first meal after the birth and put it under her bed facing downward. If they intended to stop the effect of the charm, they turned the plate upward.[262] In both of these customs the intention was to bury in, or direct into, the earth the woman's fertility, which, according to folk belief, adheres to the utensils she used in connection with, or at the time of, the birth.[263]

Interment figures in the following Jewish charm. In order to prevent a woman from becoming pregnant, they extinguish three burning coals in her menstrual blood, and then they bury the coals. In order to restore her fertility, they dig up the coals and throw them into the fire.[264] In another Jewish charm for the same purpose they bury a pomegranate. If this fruit is buried in the room of a woman in childbed, the birthpangs will be prolonged, or there will be no delivery at all. The remedy against it is to find the buried pomegranate and remove it.[265] The pomegranate is a symbol of fertility; its many seeds stand for children. This meaning of the pomegranate becomes clear from its role in Jewish marriage customs.

The principle of closing the woman's womb by means of magic or symbolically underlies an act of witchcraft described by Rashi, the great Jewish commentator on the Bible and Talmud, who lived in Troyes, France, in the eleventh century.

> Yuḥni, the daughter of Rativi, was a widow, a witch, and when the time came for a woman to give birth, she would close her womb by witchcraft, and after having caused her much suffering, she would say, ''I shall go and ask mercy, perhaps my prayer will be heard.'' Then she would go and cancel her witchery, and the child would emerge. Once she had a day-laborer in her house, and she went to the house of a woman ready to give birth, and the day-laborer heard the noise of the witchery rattling in a vessel as a child rattles in the womb of the mother, and went and opened the lid of the vessel, and the witcheries came out, and the child was born, and then they knew that she was a witch.''[266]

In talmudic times a contraceptive drink, called ''cup of *'aqrin''* (i.e., barrenness) was used. ''A man is not permitted to drink a cup of barrenness to prevent him from begetting, but a woman is allowed to drink a cup of barrenness to prevent her from giving birth.''[267] According to R. Yoḥanan, the ''cup of barrenness'' contained ''one zuz weight of Alexandrian tree resin, one zuz weight of alum, and one zuz weight of garden saffron, pounded and mixed together.''[268] Potions to produce barrenness were known and used by many peoples, and several ancient laws punished those who used them with heavy penalties, not infrequently even with death.[269] Judith, the wife of R. Ḥiyya, took a ''toxin of barrenness'' and is reported to have actually become barren.[270] According to a Midrash, the men of the generation of the Deluge took ''two wives, one for procreation and one for sex. The one who was for procreation sat like a widow all her life, and the one who was for sex drank a cup of barrenness so that she should not conceive, and would sit before her husband like a harlot.''[271]

Another method—which, however, belongs to the world of medicine rather than to that of magic—involved a ball of cotton wool. ''Three women are allowed to use cotton wool at intercourse: the minor, the pregnant woman, and the nursing mother. The minor, so that she should not become pregnant, which may cause her to die; the pregnant woman, because her fetus may become misshapen (*sandal*); and the nursing mother, because she may [if she becomes pregnant again] wean her child prematurely, and it may die.''[272] In antiquity and in the Middle Ages, Jewish women resorted to various forms of witchcraft, of which, however, no details are known. ''A woman made witchery for herself so that she should not bear. All the physicians came to cure her. She said: 'You cannot, because I did it to myself.' ''[273]

Among the Jews of Morocco, a woman who does not want to become pregnant takes a bee, ties it up in a little bundle, and swallows it. She is believed to remain barren for as many years as was the number of bees she swallowed.[274] The same method is used by the Jews of Iraq. ''If the woman eats one bee, she will not become pregnant for one year, and if she eats two, she will not become pregnant for two years.''[275] It seems that the Moroccan form of this charm is the original one: the wrapping up and tying around of the bee or bees stand for the closing of the womb.[276]

Another Moroccan Jewish magical contraceptive is the *'eyn al-harr*, or ''cat's eye.'' This was a white stone with a black spot in the middle, which they set into a ring. As long as a woman wears such a ring she will not become pregnant.[277] This method has a long history among the oriental Jews. According to a fifteenth-century Hebrew source, the *'eyn al-harr* was used for various magic purposes. Abraham haRofe says,

> The stone ''cat's eye,'' which is called in Arabic *'eyn al-harr*—the people of India say that its virtue is that he who wears it will not become impoverished,

and instead of poverty he will reach opulence. . . . And in the cities of the interior of the West [i.e., Morocco] I saw that the women wear it so that they should not become pregnant during all the twenty-four months in which they suckle their first child, lest he come to harm. And also in the Land of Israel, may it be rebuilt and reestablished quickly in our days, some women wear it for this purpose.[278]

Another charm used by Jewish women in Morocco for the same purpose is to grind some gold and drink it mixed with water.[279]

We have heard above that Egyptian Jewish women hang the foot of a hare around their necks in order to become pregnant. The same charm appears in various books of charms for precisely the opposite purpose. "For a woman so that she should not become pregnant, let her hang around her neck the heart or the foot of a hare, or its excrement, or the heart of a mouse. And if she wants never to become pregnant, let her drink the urine of a lamb."[280]

The customs and methods enumerated are based on the belief that it is possible to deprive a woman of her fertility by various means. Here too, as in the customs aiming at giving fertility to a barren woman, one must distinguish between two methods. One intends to remove the powers of fertility from the body of the woman, while the other renders her barren by "tying" or burying something which magically stands for the child, or by closing her womb so that it cannot be impregnated. Folk custom is, of course, far from being systematic, and uses, in addition to these two types of magical procedures, several other means which have no symbolic significance but are effective due to the specific magical powers attributed to them.[281]

V. Charms for Difficult Labor

Among the measures resorted to for facilitating delivery, an important place is held by those which use plants. Plants are living things; they sprout, grow, thrive, and die, and therefore the fruits of plants, or flowers, or beverages made of plants, such as wine, are believed to have the power to endow the woman who ingests them with the powers of fertility and vitality required to bring a difficult labor to a successful conclusion. If the vegetable substance is given to the woman to insert into her vagina, or to use in her bath, the purpose is, in addition to the magical influence, to loosen or dilate her cervix and thus to hasten delivery. When the woman is fumigated with the smoke of plants or of parts of animals which are burned under her body, the purpose seems to be to drive away the demons which are suspected of causing the trouble. Or, just as fumigations can drive away a *dibbuk*, a spirit possessing a person, so, folk logic concludes, can they drive out the child from the body of the mother.

In charms taken from the animal kingdom, the common feature is the intention to transfer to the suffering woman some of the sexual powers which are attributed to certain animals. Since, according to folk belief, great sexual powers are needed for the delivery, one can help the woman who suffers in labor by endowing her with them by means of parts from the bodies of animals, such as a cock, which is the paragon of sexual potency among the birds, and the like. Substances which come out of the body of animals, such as eggs, excrement, and milk, also are considered helpful: if the woman ingests them, or if they are smeared on her body, they will cause the child to come out of her body. The effect of these substances, as well as of other organs taken from the bodies of animals, such as gall, liver, or a horn, is imagined to be entirely mechanical; they cause the ejection of whatever is in the body of the woman, and therefore frequently the magical recipe recommending their use contains the warning that, immediately after delivery, the magical substances must be removed from the woman's body, "lest her entrails come out."

Occasionally the selection of charms expresses the ancient idea that sins cause sterility and prevent delivery. In this case the method recommended is to make a *kappara* (atonement) for the woman.

The idea of the transference of sexual powers underlies those charms in which the substance used is taken from the body of another woman. Mother's milk and the afterbirth are both connected with childbirth, and therefore they have the power, according to folk belief, to help in case of a difficult labor. When the objects used are connected with, or derived from, a man, the idea is to endow the woman with the strength of the male. This is symbolized in the use of the husband's urine, shoe, trousers, belt, or some such item.

It is an ancient belief that the dead can make a woman fertile or pregnant, or can enter her body and be born again from her. These beliefs find expression in several charms whose object is to facilitate delivery by using something taken from the cemetery or used in connection with the dead, such as a shroud.

The earth is a great source of strength and life, and therefore can help a woman who has a difficult delivery. Among the earthly objects are stones, which have male power, according to ancient folk belief. Contact with the earth or a stone, or the eating of some earth or a pulverized stone, will therefore ensure easy delivery. The use of a magnet is based on a different principle: it can attract the child and pull it out of its mother's womb. The ideational association between children and money ("May He multiply our seed and our money like sand,'' says the popular Sabbath song), explains the use of silver coins for facilitating delivery.[282]

Water is an ancient symbol of life ("living water") and is used by many peoples as a charm to ease labor.

An entirely different category of charms are those based on incantations, the invocation of the names of angels, or the use of sacred articles. Some of these charms express belief in the power of the spoken magical word. In most cases people are not satisfied with hanging an amulet inscribed with incantations on the body of the woman; she is made actually to ingest the words. Thus, for instance, the words are written on an amulet and obliterated in water, which then is given to the woman to drink.

Occasionally the imitative magic employed is connected with sacred objects. We have heard that opening a door can, according to folk belief, bring about the opening of the womb of a woman. At times popular custom requires that the door be specifically that of the holy ark in the synagogue.

These remarks have not touched upon all the magical or semimagical methods used to help a woman in difficult labor. But what has been said should suffice to throw some light on the popular thought processes which underlie the use of charms to facilitate delivery. The following pages will show the extraordinary riches of the *materia medica* and the magical methods used in Jewish folk custom at various times and places. The material presented is taken from printed books, manuscripts, and oral information.

As already shown in an earlier section, Jewish folk custom, like the folk customs of other peoples, utilizes *materia medica* taken from the vegetable kingdom, from the animal kingdom, from the bodies of humans, from graves, from the earth, dust, and metals for the purpose of endowing barren women with fertility. The same substances and methods are used to help a woman who has a difficult delivery. While undoubtedly much practical experience has found its way into folk remedies, one must not overestimate the role of empiricism in folk medicine in general and in difficult labor in particular. The very fact that the same *materia* and the same methods are used for both giving fertility to barren women and helping women who have a difficult delivery should indicate that magic rather than practical-physical efficiency is at work in them. Their intent is to mobilize secret magical powers, for which the *materia medica* used are mere receptacles.

Let us begin our survey with charms for difficult labor taken from the vegetable kingdom.[283] In various Jewish communities it is customary to give to the woman an *ethrog* to eat, or the pulverized stem of the ethrog, in order to ease her pains.[284] R. Naḥman of Bratzlav advises, "A woman who loses her children during delivery should put an apple on her head."[285] The Sephardi Jews in Jerusalem give the woman fragrant herbs to smell.[286] In various Ashkenazi communities, it is the custom to give her saffron mixed into wine, brandy, or some other drink.[287] In the oriental Jewish communities of Israel, saffron is famous by its Arabic name, *za'frān*, as a potent charm.[288] Other plants, mixed in wine, also are believed to help the suffering woman. "Take date stones, pound them in a mortar, and give it to her to drink in wine. Take *qoton* [cotton] seed, which is cotton wool, and make it into a dough in wine, and give it to her to drink in water, and she will drop him," i.e., she will quickly be delivered of the child. Or: "Take dry fig leaves and pulverize them, and let her drink them in wine, and she will deliver without pain."[289] Or: "Give her to eat squash in wine, and she will deliver instantly. And if this does not help, take of the squash and mash it and mix it in wine, and give it to her to drink."[290] Or: "Take myrtle *bleter* [leaves], and also *helfn bayn* [German *Elfenbein*, ivory], and pulverize them and give it to her to drink . . . in a warm drink. It is proven."[291] Among the Jews of Dehok in Kurdistan, it is customary to give the woman who suffers in labor a soup made of fig leaves, while in Zakho and 'Amadiyya in Kurdistan, they give her a potion made of *ar'ura* (manna) dissolved in water.[292] Another preventive measure to diminish the birth pangs is taken in advance: "She should not eat radishes while pregnant."[293]

Plants and wine also help the suffering woman when used externally. "A charm for a woman in difficult labor. Let her be washed in wine from the front and from behind."[294] Or: "Hang on her neck some of the leftover *maror* (horseradish, eaten at the Passover seder)."[295] The Jews of Kurdistan use another object connected with the seder night, "a seven-year-old *matzo*." They bake a small *matzo*, the size of a coin, together with the *matzo* eaten at the seder meal. For seven years they put this small *matzo* on the seder plate so that benedictions be said over it. Then they sew it into a small satchel decorated with buttons and rings which have magical significance. In 'Amadiyya the satchel is hung around the neck of the woman as an amulet, while in Zakho she wears it over her heart. In Zakho they also give her water in which the *matzo* was soaked to drink.[296]

In some charms the intention is to influence the functioning of the womb directly. "Take *parisel* [parsley], which in Arabic is called *baqdūnis*, pound it and put it into her womb, and she will deliver instantly. . . . If you put *rota* (*roda*, rue) into her navel, she will deliver instantly, and make sure to take it out of her belly immediately after the delivery lest her entrails come out, God forbid."[297] Similar methods were used among the Jews of Spain in the fourteenth century, when R. Meir Aldabi wrote,

> If the pregnant woman has difficulties in labor, it is useful that she should enter into [i.e., submerge in] water in which *hulb*[298] [Arabic *hulba*, fenugreek] or

manba (Arabic *mumbat*, sprouts), and flax and barley seeds have been cooked, and let her press her hands against her two sides and loins, and let her rub on her hips soft and wet and liquifying oils, such as sesame oil or *zānbari* [Arabic *zān barri*, wild beechnut] oil and the like. And let them make her sneeze with incense, and let her go slowly up and down a slope, and let her drink saffron pulverized and mixed in water or the milk of a bitch, or peanut oil in warm water, or warm water alone, or the juice of leek and its leaven, and dip into it unwashed wool and insert it into her womb.[299]

The following charms were recommended in the seventeenth and eighteenth centuries. ''For a woman who has difficulty in labor. Take *belzen zamen* [*belzen*(?) seeds][300] and tie them in a piece of linen cloth, and tie it to her right thigh, and she will deliver quickly.''[301] Or: ''Put on her belly, that is, on her body and not on the shirt, and also under her right and left armpits, a powder made of *hopfen* [hops], and she will deliver with the help of God, blessed be He.''[302] Or: ''Take yeast which has become strong, and mix it with strong vinegar, and tie it around her hips. And immediately after delivery remove it from her, lest she expel her entrails, God forbid. And then, let her wash and clean her hips of the aforementioned yeast.''[303] Meir Aldabi also recommends that a woman whose fetus has died in her womb should drink ''an infusion of onions.''[304]

In fumigations, substances of both vegetable and animal origin are used. In northeastern Europe and Italy, this method was recommended in the seventeenth century: ''Burn incense under her so that the smoke should enter her body.''[305] Or: ''Wonderful charms for a woman who has difficulty in delivery. Take black pepper and grind it and burn it under her.''[306] Or: ''Let her be fumigated with mustard.''[307] Or: ''Fumigate the woman with *pfersikh shtayn* [stones of peaches] prior to her being seated on the birth stool, and this is a charm to make sure that she will never have birth-pangs.''[308] Or: ''Take a feather of the bird called *vakhtlen* [quail], and black pitch which has never been used for any work, and a spoonful of bran from wheat or barley or rye, and of each the same weight, and put it all on embers and stand it under the woman so that she should receive the smoke into her womb, and she will deliver instantly without pain and without damage, and this is tried and sure, from the wise men of the Ishmaelites [Arabs].''[309] One of the ingredients listed in this complex charm is helpful by itself. ''Fumigate under her with a little *qitrān* [tar], and she will let him drop in any case. Tried and proven.''[310]

Several substances are taken from the animal kingdom and recommended for fumigation. ''Take the nails [i.e., hoofs] of a donkey, and put them on fire in a vessel, and put the vessel under her feet, and fumigate her womb, and she will deliver immediately.'' Or: ''The horn of a goat which is a he-goat [*sic*], its smoke will help a woman who has difficulty in labor, and she will give [i.e., deliver] immediately."[311] Or:

> Take donkey dung and burn it so that its smoke should rise into her nose. Another [method]: Take the eyes of a salted fish which is called *hering*, and also the soul [i.e., the bladder], and fumigate under her. Another [method]: Take of the hoofs of horses that which the blacksmith cuts off with the iron when he puts the iron shoe on the feet of the horse, and fumigate under her until the smoke enters into her body. . . . Another [method]: Take bear dung and fumigate with it, and even if the child is dead. . . . Another [method]: Fumigate with the droppings of pigeons.[312]

Among the Jews of Morocco it is customary to take a plate, put some kohl into it, ignite it, and then put it under the woman who has difficulty in labor.[313] Meir Aldabi advised in the fourteenth century that a woman whose child died in her womb "should be fumigated with donkey dung or with sulphur."[314]

Several of the substances used for fumigation are believed to be effective if taken internally, as well. The following charms were used in the seventeenth century in eastern Europe and Italy.

> Take horse dung and dry it, and mix it in wine or water, and give it to her to drink without her knowledge, and thereby the child will come out even if dead, God forbid. Another one: Take the droppings of mice and dry it well and pulverize it, and let her drink it in wine. Another one: Take the gall of an ox and mix it in water and let her drink it. Another one: Take the milk of a bitch mixed with water or honey, and let her drink it, and the child will come out even if dead, God forbid. And this is proven.[315]

Similar means were used among the Spanish Jews in the fourteenth century. "And if the child died in her entrails, let her drink the milk of a bitch with food, or donkey dung."[316] Or: "Take a frog and burn it to ashes, and take of those ashes the weight of a *qvint*, and put it into a potion to drink, and it will help, with the help of God. Occasionally one must take a male frog and occasionally a female."[317] Or: "Another wonderful charm. Take two eggs which were laid in those days prior to her delivery, and boil them well in water until the water is boiled down to half, and give her to drink that water."[318] Or: "Eggs eaten in the morning prior to eating anything else are very good for the body and facilitate delivery for women."[319]

All kinds of ointments are used externally. "Take the gall of a black hen and smear it on her navel,"[320] or the gall of a black cock, or "black gall" without any further qualification.[321] The Yemenite Jews rub the body of a woman who has difficulty in labor with *semn* (clarified butter).[322]

Tying parts of animals to the woman's body is considered helpful.

"Take cock liver and tie it to the side of the woman, and she will deliver instantly. And remove it immediately lest her entrails come out."[323] In the light of these customs in which hens or cocks figure, one suspects that when, in talmudic times, they tied a hen to the bed of the laboring woman, they did it not to cheer her up, but to facilitate the delivery.[324] Meir Aldabi advised in the fourteenth century, "Let her take between her teeth the antler of a deer or the horn of a goat."[325] This charm reappears with some variation in the seventeenth century in eastern Europe. "Give the right horn of a goat into her hand when she is about to deliver, and she will give birth instantly."[326] They also advised, "Take a snake's skin and put it on her heart."[327]

The Moroccan Jews have an unusual remedy for a woman who has difficulty in childbirth. On rare occasions, so they believe, one can find an object or growth called *wars*[328] in the gall of a cow which had eaten a grass called *qamia*,[329] which can be used for making gold. The *wars* is so valuable that it is worth its weight in gold. When the birthpangs are not sufficiently strong, and for this reason the woman cannot deliver, they dissolve the *wars* in arrack and give it to her to drink. This charm, which is believed to be unfailingly effective, increases the birth pangs and brings the delivery to a successful conclusion.[330] The *wars* is famous among the Sephardi Jews in Jerusalem as well. They called it *arazan* in Ladino, but use it, not for a woman in childbirth, but as a remedy for jaundice. According to them, the *arazan* is a yellow blob of fat found occasionally in the body of a cow (my informant could not say anything more definite about where in the cow's body). They soak it in arrack or in perfumed water and give it to the person suffering from jaundice to drink.[331] The *wars* is similar to the *capra* stone which, according to Italian belief, can be found in the body of a few Indian goats and can be used to cure diseases. The *capra* is mentioned as late as in 1821 in an Italian book of *materia medica*.[332]

The Kurdish Jews make *kappara* for a woman who has a difficult delivery. In 'Amadiyya they slaughter a hen, or, among the rich people, also a lamb, and sprinkle the blood on the place where the delivery is taking place, or on the woman's body. In Zakho they take a cock and a hen—the cock for the expected son and the hen for the mother—and swing them about over the woman's head. Then they slaughter the birds and distribute their meat among the poor.[333]

The charm which recommends that the woman swallow egg white with mother's milk takes us from the animal kingdom to substances derived from the human body. Several books of charms list this combination for a woman in difficult labor.[334] The milk of another woman is useful in itself. "For a woman who has difficulty in labor. If she drinks milk from another nursing woman, she will deliver instantly."[335] Another charm recommends direct bodily contact. "Let another woman put her hand on the belly of the woman in difficult labor and let her say, together with that woman, seven times, 'And he, as a bridegroom, cometh out of his chamber, and rejoiceth as a strong man to run his course' (Ps. 19:6)."[336] The same effect is attributed to the afterbirth. "Take the afterbirth of another woman, burn it to ashes, and give it to her to drink in water. Proven."[337] A substance eliminated from the body of the husband of the laboring woman also has the power to ease her pangs. "Give her to drink some of her husband's urine."[338] Or: "Give her to drink in a shoe of her husband his urine in the amount of one glass."[339] The Jews of Zakho and Senna in Kurdistan pour water into the husband's shoe and the woman in labor drinks it. In Zakho and 'Amadiyya, the woman drinks of the water in which her husband's feet were washed, or the husband hits the woman on her back with his shoe. In Zakho they also tie the husband's shoe on the body of a woman who is afraid that she will miscarry, or who has great difficulties in labor.[340] In the Middle Ages it was customary among both Jews and Christians to give a piece of cloth taken from the husband's vest, trousers, or belt to the woman to wear on her body during pregnancy so that her labor should be easy.[341] Among the Jews of Morocco, the husband shakes his coat-wing over the woman in labor, then strokes her gently with it and says, "I filled you, and let them help you from heaven that it [the child] should come out of you quickly."[342]

A precautionary charm requires that the woman's sons "should not be with her in the house" while she is in labor.[343] The purpose of many customs is to make sure that the woman in childbirth has rest and quiet.[344]

The transition from the human element to earthly substances is indicated by customs in which something taken from a grave or from the cemetery is given to the woman to ease her birthpangs. "Hang on her neck the key of the cemetery," says one instruction which is repeated in numerous sources.[345] The key to the cemetery, which seems to be associated with the idea of "the key of the graves" or "the key of the resurrection of the dead," serves in this case as "the key of childbirth," that is, the key which opens the womb of the woman.[346] Among the Jews of the Caucasus, "if the birthpangs are too violent and too many, they send somebody to the cemetery to bring a handful of earth from the grave of So-and-so. . . . The earth is mixed in water which is given to the suffering woman to drink."[347] The Jews of Poland and Russia pray at graves for women in difficult labor. This is called *q'vorim reissen*, that is, "tearing the graves."[348] In the city of Tunis "there is a coat of the emissary, his honor, the rabbi David Rofe ["physician"] of blessed memory, who died there, and they put this coat on every woman who has difficulty in labor, and then she delivers quickly."[349] Among the Jews of Kurdistan, in Zakho, when a woman suffers in labor they bring a piece of linen large enough to make a shroud for the dead, put it next to her, and say, "Behold, your shroud; this is your shroud; we give it as an atonement to the poor." Then they distribute the linen among the poor.[350]

Dust from under the threshold of the house also has magical curative powers. According to a medieval Jewish custom, if a woman's labor was too difficult they took dust from under the threshold of the room, wrapped it in a piece of cloth, and put it on her womb.[351] Binyamin Ba'al Shem also reports this custom.[352]

The earth plays an interesting role in an incantation rite performed in various Jewish communities.

> Charm for a woman in hard labor. Whisper into her ear this incantation seven times: "Michael, the great [heavenly] prince, heard voices and cries, and asked the Holy One, blessed be He, 'What are the voices and cries I hear?' The Holy One, blessed be He, said to him, 'A gazelle is in labor and cries. Go and tell her [i.e., her child], "Go out, go out, go out, for the earth wants you." And all these thy servants shall come down unto me and prostrate themselves to me, saying, "Get thee out, and all the people that follow thee, and after that I will go out." And he went out (Exod. 11:8). And let him recite this verse *tz'e* [i.e., 91] times, and then let him whisper in her right ear, "It's time, it's time,"[353] and in her left ear, "Go out, go out!" ' " And she will deliver instantly.[354]

To this context belongs, to some extent, the use of a new earthenware vessel on which magic names were written. It was then put on the navel of the woman who had a difficult delivery.[355]

Just as certain stones can give fertility to barren women and can protect pregnant women from miscarriage,[356] so they can help a woman in difficult labor. The ruby in particular has this power; "it is said that it is good for a woman in difficult labor."[357] Isaac Lampronti reports that "the wife of the Hakham Moshe S'faradi was in difficult labor in the year 5445 (1685) in the month of Kislev, and she almost died, and there was in the city of Reggio a blind *hakham*, R. Binyamin Wolf of blessed memory, and he said that they should take a stone called *rubino*, of the size of about two lentils, and grind it and give it to her in red wine to drink, and so they did, and she delivered instantly."[358] The manuscript "Sefer S'gullot v'Hiddot"[359] mentions "red stone," without defining it further, as a charm for hard labor. "Take raven's eggs and cook them in water until hard, and then return them into the raven's nest. Then the raven will bring for them a red stone and put it on the eggs, and they will return to life as they were at first. And wash that stone in water or in wine, and give it to her to drink, and she will deliver instantly."[360] This piece of folklore about the raven who has in his possession a stone which can resuscitate the dead eggs is, of course, based on the talmudic story of R. Y'huda the Indian.[361] Similar powers were attributed to the jasper, which was the stone of Benjamin in the ephod of the high priest. "It will help a woman who has difficulty in delivery."[362] Abraham haRofe, who recommends this, knows also of similar powers possessed by the *galarizide* stone, "which is a stone like ashes . . . and if it is put on the hips it is good for a woman sitting on the birth stool."[363] Another magical stone is the *shaqmaq* (Turkish *çakmak*, steel for striking a flint). "When a woman suffers from cruel birthpangs, put into her palm a *shaqmaq* stone, and let her close her hand tightly around it."[364]

The "S'gullot v'Ḥiddot" recommends another "practical" method to expedite delivery. "For a woman in difficult labor. Take a lodestone which is called *qalamita* (Spanish *calamita*) and put it before the womb, and she will deliver instantly."[365] In fourteenth-century Spain, a variant of this custom was practiced by the Sephardi Jews. "Let her hold between her teeth . . . a lodestone, or the iron or stone from which fire comes out"[366] (that is, a flint stone).

Coins, too, are used in various Jewish communities for the same purpose. The Jews of Egypt "write the name of the woman in labor on a silver coin and put it under her tongue."[367] In other oriental Jewish communities they write on a silver coin the word AMENAM, in which the vowels have the numerical value of 72 (*patah*=6, *segol*=30, *qametz*=16, and *sh'va*=20), and put the coin under the woman's tongue.[368] In Senna, Kurdistan, they put an amulet inscribed by the *hakham* with names of angels on her tongue.[369] In the Warsaw vicinity they place a coin on the navel of a woman in difficult labor, "so that the child should see the penny and hasten to come out to snatch it."[370]

Water, which is believed to be a potent means to fertilize barren women,[371] also figures prominently among the materials employed to facilitate delivery, both in external and internal application. In the Tosefta (second century C.E.) water is mentioned among the other means, either approved or disapproved by the sages, used for this purpose. "He who plugs up the window with a thorn, or ties iron to the bedstead of the woman in labor, or sets a table before her, is guilty of following pagan custom. But to plug up the window with a blanket or with sheaves, or to put a cup of water before her, or to tie a hen next to her to cheer her up—these are not pagan customs."[372] All the methods mentioned in this passage, except the hen, are intended to protect the woman from demons. Plugging up the window with a thorn, blanket, or sheaves prevents the demons from entering the room.[373] Using iron to frighten them off is widespread.[374] Setting a table diverts the demons' attention from the woman to the food; in a like manner, placing a cup of water before the woman serves to protect her, although it also should be remembered that water is a powerful male element which can give her strength. The custom of placing water near a laboring woman is practiced among many peoples.[375] The Jews of Bavaria and Hessen put a barrel or pail of water before the door of the room in which the delivery takes place.[376] Egyptian Jews put a bucket of water under the birth stool or under the bed.[377] Among the Jews of Morocco, the moment the head of the child emerges, somebody pours water on the threshold of the house.[378]

In another type of custom, the woman who has difficult labor is supposed to drink water. Among the Jews of Egypt and in other oriental and Sephardi Jewish communities, drinking water from seven wells is considered to be especially effective.[379] Similarly, in Ashkenazi communities, "For a woman in difficult labor, it is a remedy to give her to drink water from seven wells."[380] The Jews of Afghanistan give her rainwater collected on the seventh day of Passover to drink.[381] And again, in eastern Europe, "For a woman in difficult labor. Take water from the crossroads and give it to her to drink, and it will help with the help of God."[382]

In many places, to increase the power of the water the woman is supposed to drink, they obliterate the words of an incantation, or "names" in it. In the Middle Ages the Jews used to write a magic formula on the four corners of a sheet, then wash the sheet and give the wash water to the woman to drink.[383] Among the Jews of Kurdistan, the *hakham* prepares an amulet with magic words, obliterates them in water, and then the water is given to the woman.[384] The Yemenite Jews write an incantation on the inside of a bowl, fill it with water which obliterates the writing, and then give the water to the woman. In some cases they merely put the bowl on the woman's body.[385] In other oriental Jewish communities they utilize the sanctity inherent in the Tora scroll. "We found in the Kabbala [the advice] to do this to the woman in difficult labor. Take a bowl of water and wash the feet of the staves of the Tora [around which the Tora scroll is wound] in the synagogue, and give her the water to drink."[386] In Senna, Kurdistan, the husband takes the "pomegranates," i.e., the cup-shaped silver decorations which crown the staves of the Tora scroll, to the *hakham*, who fills them with "living water" while reciting psalms, whereupon the husband, without uttering a word, hurries with them to his wife, and she drinks the water while the husband stands behind her.[387]

The Tora scroll figures in numerous remedies for the woman in difficult labor—so much so, in fact, that its use gave rise to many discussions and prohibitions in Sephardi communities. It was, for example, customary to bring a Tora scroll right into the woman's room and to put it there on a table, or into her hands, or even in her lap.[388] This custom aroused the opposition of rabbis and *hakhamim*, who saw in it a desecration of the Tora. But since they recognized that it was impossible to uproot an entrenched custom, they permitted the opening of the holy ark and of a Tora scroll in the synagogue and asking for mercy for the suffering woman.[389] Or, at the utmost, they allowed that the Tora scroll be taken to the door of her house, for "perchance the merit of the Tora will protect her, and not as a charm."[390] However, rabbinical prohibitions often remained without effect when faced with folk custom. In this case, too, the outlawed custom has remained in various oriental Jewish communities. Thus, in Baghdad "they place a Tora scroll in the room of the woman in childbed so as to ease her birthpangs."[391]

In other communities they are content with opening the holy ark. Among the Jews of Alexandria, it is the custom that, when a woman has difficult labor, they go to the synagogue, open the holy ark, recite psalms, and blow the shofar, while others whisper "Get thee out and all the people that follow thee" (Exod. 11:8).[392] In Kurdistan, the *hakham* blows the shofar next to the woman in labor, so that thereby the names of certain angels should penetrate the woman's ears.[393] In Turkey, the Sephardi Jews open the holy ark and read a section from the Tora in the room of the woman in difficult labor.[394] Among the Jews in various places in Russia, e.g., in the environs of Pinsk, this custom has a different form. They tie a string to the door of the holy ark in the synagogue and stretch the string across the streets until it reaches the woman's house, and give its end into her hands. She pulls at the string and thus opens the door. This is considered an unfailing remedy for difficult labor.[395] The opening of the holy ark is, of course, a magical sympathetic act which is supposed to bring about the opening of the woman's womb. In the vicinity of Warsaw, "There is a custom of stretching a string from the holy ark to the woman's bed."[396] Likewise, the Sephardi Jews in Safed

> tie one end of a string to the big toe of the right foot of the woman in labor, and the other end to the Tora scroll in the synagogue, and when she has delivered they immediately cut the string, because she is impure and is forbidden to be tied to the Tora scroll. And this will ease her birthpangs, and she will deliver easily. . . . Another remedy for difficult delivery is to open the doors and windows of the house, and they believe that just as they opened the doors, so God will open the doors of her belly and she will deliver quickly."[397]

Still another method is used around Warsaw.

> Those from whom children are withheld practice scrupulously the opening of the holy ark and the taking out and returning of the Tora scrolls, and they also make sure to be called up to the reading of the Tora on New Year, to the Haftara [the prophetic passage] of Hannah,[398] and for a woman in difficult labor they ask of the man who was called up to the reading of this Haftara on New Year to come to the house of the woman and to recite there that Haftara.

Also: "It is the custom to gird the woman in difficult labor with the wrapper of the Tora scroll."[399]

To the sympathetic-magical acts of opening belongs the custom practiced by the Jews of Poland: the husband undoes the buttons of his trousers.[400]

Another remedy in which the synagogue figures is to give the woman a cup of oil and have her look into it, and then send it to the synagogue to light the lamp. Among the Sephardim in Turkey, and among the European Jews as well, when the labor pains begin they give the woman a cup of oil so that she look into it as into a mirror, and then they send the cup to the synagogue.[401] Among the Jews of Syria, "When the woman sits on the birth stool, it is a charm for easing her birthpangs to bring a vessel with oil, and the woman looks into it and sees her own face in the oil, and then they take this oil and light with it a lamp before the holy ark, for the exaltation of the soul of Rabbi Meir Ba'al haNes ("the miracle worker"), and she will deliver quickly."[402] Among the Sephardim in Safed, "The custom is to give a cup of oil to the woman in labor to look into it, and then they light that oil in the synagogue, and this is a remedy to ease her birthpangs." Or: "A woman in difficult labor pours oil with her own hands from the flask into the cup, and looks into it, and then they light it in the synagogue."[403]

The custom of looking into oil as into a mirror is based on the belief that the image seen in the mirror, oil, or water is the soul, and whatever happens to it will also happen to the person himself.[404] The mirror image of the woman in difficult labor is sent to the synagogue, a holy place, where the demons who obstruct the delivery cannot enter; thereby, it is hoped, the woman will be freed from the influence of the evil spirits. In addition, the lighting of a lamp is symbolic of the beginning of a new life, and by lighting the oil into which the woman has looked, they ensure the emergence of the child from the mother's body and the beginning of its life.

Looking into the oil, which is an active magical act in the customs just listed, has degenerated in some places into the passive act of divination, of finding out what is about to happen without any attempt to influence the outcome. An Italian Hebrew manuscript from the seventeenth to eighteenth centuries reads,

> To know whether the child is dead or alive in the entrails of the woman when she is in very great pain, take a bowl of clear oil, and let her see her face in it. If she sees the face of the child, he is alive, and if not, he is dead. And if he is dead, take a bowl full of honey, and stick her[405] five fingers into it and let her lick each of them separately, and then let her drink a little lukewarm water with honey, and she will deliver instantly.[406]

From another passage in the same manuscript it appears that a person who does not see his image in the bowl is bewitched. "To find out whether a man or a woman is bewitched, take a bowl full of oil, and let the man or the woman look into it. If they are bewitched, they will not see their faces in it, and if they are not, they will see their faces."[407] A bewitched person does not see his mirror image, which is his soul, because the witch has stolen his soul—this is the belief underlying this act of divination. Among various peoples there is the belief that if the reflection of a person is seen in water, a demon or evil spirit will gain control over him by stealing his soul, and, for lack of a soul, the person will have to die.[408] A similar belief may have underlain the talmudic story about a shepherd from the south, who had beautiful eyes and charming locks of hair, and who thought of death the moment he saw his reflection in the water of a well.[409]

VI. Delivery on the Ground

We shall not discuss here delivery out in the open, in the fields, woods, or on the seashore, which are the places where it takes place among numerous primitive peoples,[410] nor delivery upon the earth when it is practiced among peoples who do not use beds and chairs in their daily lives.[411] Among such peoples it is almost inevitable that delivery, too, must take place upon the earth. But if one finds that delivery takes place on the earth among peoples who normally use beds and chairs, one can assume that the custom is the expression of a specific folk belief.[412]

Delivery upon the earth was the practice in the ancient Near East. We have precise knowledge about the posture of the woman in delivery in ancient Egypt, for example, thanks to the paintings in which contemporary artists depicted the birth of gods and kings. These pictures show the woman lying in a bed or sitting on a chair, or, frequently, crouching on the floor[413] or on two bricks placed on the floor.[414] That crouching on the ground was the most usual and most ancient position can be concluded from the fact that in the hieroglyphics the sign for a woman in childbirth shows her in that position.[415] In hieratic Egyptian (from the days of Augustus), the expression "to lay on the earth" is used in the sense of "to give birth."[416] Women gave birth in the same position in ancient Babylonia.[417]

Among the ancient Persians, the birth had to take place upon the earth, for their doctrines demanded that life begin in humility.[418] In ancient Greece also, women gave birth while crouching on the ground. Greek statues show the goddesses of birth in this position.[419] According to Greek belief, the childbearing woman had to be brought in contact with the earth to ensure a successful delivery—that is, that the soul of the child would rise up from the earth.[420] Phaedrus also mentions that the woman in childbirth lay upon the earth.[421]

The Israelite women in Egypt delivered on the *ovnayim*, literally "two stones," but evidently meaning two bricks, which were placed on the ground.[422] Until recently, Persian and Iraqi women delivered in the same manner.[423] Both biblical and later sources attest to the fact that Jewish women gave birth in a crouching position on the ground.[424] According to the nineteenth-century Jewish traveler Yosef Y'huda Chorny, delivery in this position was still practiced in his days among the Jews of the Caucasus. In the town of Derbent, on the shore of the Caspian Sea, "The woman, at the time of parturition, kneels down, and the midwife stands behind her and receives the child."[425] The Jewish women of Afghanistan sit on three stones at the time of childbirth.[426]

Among the Jews of Kurdistan, the woman is delivered in one of several positions. In Senna, the woman steps on two stones, then crouches down on her heels, while three other women support her. In Zakho she kneels on two cushions. In Amadiyya she crouches on her heels, bent forward, and supports herself on a pair of *T*-shaped sticks. They sprinkle earth on the spot where the delivery is to take place so that the child will be born on earth.[427]

To this day many peoples practice the custom of sprinkling some straw on the ground and laying on it the women who are to give birth.[428] Chorny reports from the village of Mamrosh, in the Kyurinsk district of Russia, that the Jewish women give birth on the floor of a special room, on straw.[429] Among the Jews of Bessarabia, it is customary for the woman in childbirth to lie on straw on the floor, especially in the remote villages in which there is no doctor and only midwives assist at the delivery.[430]

Among various other peoples, although delivery takes place on the floor, the woman is laid, not on straw, but upon some other material.[431] The Sephardi Jews in Palestine lay the woman on a straw mat spread on the floor and covered with several blankets.[432] The Jews of Morocco put a mattress on the floor, and the woman lies on it.[433] Again, among other peoples, the woman lies on the naked earth.[434] Among the Persian Jews the woman is laid, immediately upon delivery, on ashes on the floor, and next to her they place the newborn child, leaving both of them there for about half an hour.[435]

VII. Laying the Child upon the Earth

As all folk customs, so the custom of laying the newborn infant upon the earth, which is or was practiced by a very large number of peoples all over the globe, has been given various explanations. According to Gruppe, the intention in this rite is to find out, by listening to the cries of the newborn, whether it is fit to live. Wilutzky writes "By this external sign [i.e., the laying of the child on the ground before the master of the house] the child is brought under the rule of the master of the house." Monseur sees in this custom "a survival of the original custom of delivery upon the earth, which was practiced everywhere." Sartori surmises that one should look for sheer magic as the origin of this custom, one of the many "customs of fertilization." Deubner and Fehrle believe that the purpose is to make the power of the earth penetrate the child, so that it becomes strong. Similarly, E. Goldmann says that the intention is to use the magic forces of the earth in order to provide the child with powers and to protect it from all kinds of dangers. Dieterich sees in the custom a dedication ritual to Mother Earth, who, it is hoped, will protect the child.[436]

Before taking a position in regard to these disparate interpretations, let us summarize briefly the known facts about the custom of laying the newborn on the earth. According to the Roman naturalist Pliny, this was practiced in ancient Rome at the very moment of birth.[437] A special Roman goddess named Levana had the task of lifting the child from the ground.[438] In actual fact, the child's father did so.[439] Among the ancient Greeks the newborn child, or a sick child, was laid in a new furrow in the midst of a wheat field, in order to remove everything evil from it.[440] Similar customs are found among many other peoples to this day.[441] Usually the child is laid on the naked earth,[442] although among some peoples some straw is first placed on the ground.[443]

Since laying the child on the earth has the character of a religio-magical rite, it is understandable that, among those peoples who do not carry it out immediately after birth, care is taken to ensure that the child does not touch earth prior to the time designated for the rite.[444] It seems that the first laying of the child on the earth is something of a test, in which it will be decided whether or not Mother Earth is ready to accept her son and let him live. Occasionally the laying on the earth is accompanied by a ritual washing.[445]

A careful scrutiny of these customs gives the impression that laying the child on the ground most often is intended to endow it with some benefit, but one must not seek a precise definition of it. In some cases it is physical strength, in some wisdom, or diligence, or the like. Moreover, one cannot find a unified or identical concept of the nature of the earth behind these customs. The earth can, of course, endow the newborn child with benefits if she is viewed as man's mother, Mother Earth. But even if it is considered only a storehouse of powers, the physical contact between it and the child can serve the same purpose.

Let us now see what testimonies to the existence of the custom of laying the child on the ground can be found in Jewish sources. As far as ancient times are concerned, we have no direct and explicit witness to the practice of this custom in Israel. But from the accounts speaking of the crouching of the woman on the earth during delivery, one can conclude that the child was laid on the ground,[446] if only because this was the simplest thing to do. If the delivery itself took place on the ground, "under the apple tree," in a garden or field,[447] it is natural that the newborn should be laid on the earth next to its mother.[448]

In the Middle Ages Jews used various charms, some of which show that the child was indeed laid on the earth. When they wanted to protect a child from demons, they took a little of the earth on which the child fell when it was born and tied it around its body for thirty days.[449] One must not assume, of course, that they actually let the child fall on the ground; it is much more likely that the midwife laid it there with all due caution. And since the earth on which the child was laid after its birth protected it from demons, one can assume that the laying of the child on the earth also served to protect it. Binyamin Ba'al Shem, a rabbi who dealt in magic cures, wrote in the seventeenth century in Krotoshin, "So that no evil eye and no witchcraft and no other evil in the world should have power over the newborn child, take dust from that dust on which the child was born and hang it around his neck. He then will be safe from harm and witchcraft."[450] A contemporary and colleague, Eliyahu Ba'al Shem of Chelm, wrote even more explicitly, "To save a child from *benemnis* [i.e., from being exchanged or possessed by demons], when the child is born and is still lying on the ground, take from under it a little dust and tie it in a new piece of linen, and hang it on the neck of the child, and leave it there until after thirty days."[451]

According to another Jewish custom practiced in the eighteenth century, one wishing to safeguard the life of the newborn had to make a ring of silver which the mother collected from nine small girls and put the ring into the child's ear immediately after its birth, even before it was lifted up from the ground.[452] It is difficult to interpret the various features contained in this charm. Let us only mention that silver, as other metals, is used to this day as a protection against demons in oriental Jewish communities. A "Name Shaddai [God]" amulet, made of seven silver rings given by seven pregnant women, appears among the charms used to protect the life of the child.[453] The number nine is known from medieval Jewish charms used to heal the sick.[454] However, what interests us in the present context is that part of the procedure which contains the instruction to put the ring into the child's ear immediately after its birth, *even before it is lifted up from the ground*—that is, the custom of laying the child upon the ground immediately after its birth is taken for granted. On the basis of parallel customs among other peoples, one can assume that here too the purpose was to provide the child with the magical protection of the earth. As we have seen above, among the Persian Jews it is the practice to lay the child on the ground next to its mother and leave it there for about half an hour, which was clearly a religio-magical rite. The Jews of Kurdistan spread some earth on the floor over the spot where the delivery was to take place, so that the child should be born on earth.[455]

The data testifying to the existence of the custom among the Jews in the Middle Ages appear inconclusive in themselves. The two reports quoted do not state explicitly that the newborn child was laid on the ground; they only describe the things to be done after it was lifted up. However, the omission of direct reference to that part of a custom which is taken for granted seems to be a characteristic of reports covering folk tradition. Thus the Roman author Varro, in *Antiquitates Rerum Divinarum*, mentions that the goddess Levana lifts up children from the earth without first describing that they were laid there. On the basis of ancient Roman reports and their modern parallels, Albrecht Dieterich, in his classic *Mutter Erde*, concludes that laying the child on the ground originally was the essential part of the rite, but its importance was subsequently forgotten, while the initially merely complementary act of lifting up assumed the apparently central place in it.[456] In a like manner, in the world of Jewish custom the original importance and significance of the rite of laying was forgotten, and only from reports speaking of the lifting up can we conclude that it did, indeed, exist as a religio-magical act.

VIII. Fruit of the Womb: Fruit of the Earth

Elsewhere I have discussed in some detail the Jewish folk beliefs and customs according to which there is an intrinsic connection and parallelism between man and the earth.[457] Here I want to discuss one additional detail from that circle of ideas and beliefs, namely the view that there is an essential similarity between the newborn child and the fruit of the earth. This view is expressed in the first place in the custom of putting the newborn into a sieve, a winnowing basket, a kneading trough, or a baking pan—that is, into a utensil which is used in processing grain and preparing bread.

The scholar who opened new horizons in our understanding of this equation between the fruit of the womb and the fruit of the earth was Wilhelm Mannhardt, who gave the correct interpretation of these ideas, which go back to the ancient Greek world.[458] The Greeks either put the newborn child into a grain sieve or made its cradle in the shape of the *liknon* (winnow) used to separate grain from chaff. For, like the grain, the child is the fruit of the earth; this is the view expressed symbolically in this act. Shaking or swinging the child in the winnow was believed to rid the child of the powers of evil, but, at the same time, it indicated that the child was considered a being similar or parallel to the grain which jumps out of the chaff at threshing time.[459]

It is not my intention to exhaust the reader by enumerating all the varied details attendant to this custom among many peoples of the world.[460] I shall mention only a few examples I found among the peoples of the Middle East. Among various Bedouin tribes it is customary to receive the child emerging from the mother's body in a sieve.[461] In nineteenth-century Egypt they put the child into a sieve on the seventh day of its life and shook it; they said that this helped the child's stomach.[462] In Upper Egypt, the newborn is laid upon a corn sieve.[463] In Andjra, Morocco, the following rite is carried out on the seventh day of the child's life. They put it in a sieve, on which they first place a bowl of water, henna, and a boiled egg.[464] In Tangier, if the older siblings of a newborn male child died at a tender age, they shake a sieve over his head. They refrain from doing so for a female child, because the rite would cause her never to marry.[465]

To the same circle of ideas belongs the Karelian belief that one must not rock an empty cradle lest "many children come."[466] The conception of the child as grain is recognizable in the earlier northern European cradles which were given the shape of a grain winnow.[467] Popular tradition often attributes a chthonic meaning to the cradle. In many legends the place where the child lies has a connection with the nether world; related to them are the folktales about the golden cradle hidden in the bosom of the earth.[468]

The conjunction between the fruit of the womb and the fruit of the earth also is expressed in customs in which the cradle itself plays no role. In the Balkan lands it is customary to cut the umbilical cord with a knife or a scythe, but not with scissors, lest the next child be a girl.[469] Or, before the child is diapered the first time, for one moment they put on his naked belly a scythe with which straw was cut a short while before. This act will protect the child from bellyaches.[470]

As for the connection between child and grain in the Jewish world, let me add here to the material I gathered elsewhere a few details about placing the child into a sieve, a winnow, or some similar agricultural implement. We have no direct reference to this custom in the Bible, but there is indirect testimony which is confirmed by later Jewish custom. The biblical term *'arisa* means "kneading trough."[471] In the language of the talmudic sages, the same word is used in the sense of a child's cot or cradle, which occasionally could be rocked,[472] or was mounted on wheels,[473] but in most cases was simply a small bed upon which adults also could and did sit.[474]

The transfer of the meaning of *'arisa* from "kneading trough" to "cradle" can be considered an indication that originally the child was put into a kneading trough. If such a custom did exist, one must seek its origin in the view that the fruit of the womb was something similar to the fruit of the earth, upon which are based parallel customs among other peoples.[475]

Later Jewish custom confirms this assumption. In talmudic times, a folk remedy for a child who suffered from shortness of breath was to shake him in a sieve. "Abbaye said: Mother told me, 'This babe who does not breathe, let them swing him in a sieve and he will breathe.' "[476] A medieval German custom which was practiced in Thuringia until modern times constitutes, to some extent, a parallel. If a child was born prematurely and its face was wrinkled, they put it on, or tied it to, the baker's shovel, and in complete silence pushed it three times into the oven from which the loaves of bread had just been removed.[477] The common idea in both customs is that the child's health can be improved by one of the methods which improve or perfect the quality of bread—sifting the flour or introducing the dough into the oven.

Among various Jewish communities such methods of improving the child's condition are used either immediately upon its birth or after it has lived for a number of months or years. Among the Bene Israel of India, the newborn is put into a winnowing pan.[478] The Jews of Kurdistan put the child, for the first three days of its life, in a winnow or a sieve, or the large pan they use in baking bread.[479] Among the Jews of Derbent, in the Caucasus, "the woman, when giving birth, would kneel down and the midwife would stand behind her and receive the child in a wooden bowl."[480] Seeds and winnows appear in the marriage customs of many Jewish communities. Those customs complement the putting of the child in a sieve, a winnow, or a kneading trough. In both, the basis is the equation of the fruit of the womb with the fruit of the earth.

IX. Salting the Child

Because of the widespread use of salt as a seasoning agent and a food preservative, many peoples consider it one of the most important telluric elements.[481] Among the Greeks and Romans, salt was a symbol of permanence, continuity, eternity, and life force.[482] A similar symbolism attached to salt among the ancient Hebrews; hence it had an important role in sacrifices. "And every meat offering of thine shalt thou season with salt; neither shalt thou suffer the salt of the covenant of thy God to be lacking from thy meal offering; with all thine offerings thou shalt offer salt" (Lev. 2:13). Rashi remarks to this verse, "Salt of the covenant—for a covenant has been made with the salt ever since the six days of Creation, when the Lower Waters were promised that they would be offered up on the altar with salt, and at the Water Libation at the Feast of Tabernacles.'' Elsewhere in the Pentateuch, too, the covenant of salt is mentioned. ''All the heave-offerings of the holy things, which the Children of Israel offer unto the Lord, have I given thee, and thy sons and thy daughters with thee, as a due forever; it is an everlasting covenant of salt before the Lord unto thee and to thy seed with thee'' (Num. 18:19). Here Rashi explains, ''A covenant of salt—with the covenant made with the salt which never becomes malodorous.''

According to Ezekiel, the priests used salt in conjunction with the sacrifices (43:25). The same expression, ''covenant of salt,'' occurs in a meaning signifying a bond of eternity in the Book of Chronicles. ''The Lord, the God of Israel, gave the kingdom over Israel to David forever, even to him and to his sons by a covenant of salt'' (2 Chron. 13:5; cf. Ezra 4:14).[483] To this day, religious Jews dip into salt the bread over which they pronounce the benediction, ''Blessed art Thou, O Lord . . . who bringest out bread from the earth,'' before a meal.[484] Salt placed on the table was believed to drive off evil spirits.[485]

Salt has a twofold significance in the Bible in connection with fertility. On the one hand, it symbolizes desolation and barrenness;[486] on the other, it is a means of giving fertility to the earth, animals, and humans. Elisha made the ''miscarrying land'' fertile by casting salt into the bad water, saying, ''Thus saith the Lord: 'I have healed these waters; there shall not be from thence any more death or miscarrying' '' (2 Kings 2:19).[487]

In talmudic times it was customary to put a lump of salt into the womb of an animal which had ceased bearing,[488] and if a mother animal did not want to give suck to its young, they put a lump of salt on her womb. ''Rabban Shim'on ben Gamliel said, 'One takes pity on an animal even on a holiday. What does one do? One puts a lump of salt on her womb, whereupon she will want to suckle her young.' ''[489]

A widespread Jewish custom prescribes that salt, bread, and water be taken into a new house or apartment before one moves into it.[490]

Salt plays an important role as a means to promote human fertility. Many peoples share the belief that salt can augment a woman's fertility and can even open the womb of a barren woman. Salt, therefore, has occupied an important place in marriage ceremonies. For instance, it is put into the clothes of the bride and the groom to make sure that they will be fruitful and multiply, or sprinkled into the bride's shoes, and the like.[491] A medieval Jewish book of folk medicine states that if a woman has a difficult delivery, one should put the eyes of a salted fish under her.[492] In talmudic times, a folk remedy for recurring fever was to weigh a newly minted *zūz*, to go to the *milḥata*, the place where seawater was allowed to evaporate to produce salt, and to weigh a lump of salt against the *zūz*. The salt was then tied under the patient's throat, at the neck of his robe, with a tress of hair.[493] This remedy was given to Abbaye by his foster mother.

On the basis of the great variety of roles salt plays in folk custom, one can assume that salting the newborn child is not a mere hygienic measure, but a rite aimed at establishing contact and connection between the child and the forces of blessing, and especially of fertility, peculiar to salt. The custom of smearing or rubbing powdered salt on the body of the child, or of bathing it in salt water, or of sprinkling salt on it, obtains all over the world.[494]

Salting the newborn is attested among the Hebrews and Jews from biblical times to the present. Ezekiel's remarkable parable of the unwanted and neglected girl-child contains the statement, "In the day thou wast born thy navel was not cut, neither wast thou washed for cleansing, thou wast not salted at all, nor swaddled at all" (Ezek. 16:4). That is, salting the child immediately upon its birth was considered as essential as cutting its umbilical cord, washing, and swaddling it. The custom was retained in talmudic times, moreover, when the rabbis attributed such importance to it that they permitted it even on the Sabbath.[495] Among the Persian Jews, they sprinkle salt on the newborn after it is lifted up from the ground, and then wash it.[496] Among the Jews of Derbent, Caucasus, the midwife receives the child when it emerges, and "then quickly she salts the newborn, whether male or female, and then rinses the salt off its body."[497] Among the Sephardim in Safed, after the newborn is washed in water and rubbed with oil, it is salted.[498]

Hand-in-hand with these customs go the folktales which tell about the birth of man from salt or a salty rock.[499] No such Jewish folktale is known to me, but a biblical aetiological legend tells about the wife of Lot, who was metamorphosed into a pillar of salt (Gen. 19:26). A late Midrash attributes miraculous regenerative powers to that pillar. "And she became a pillar of salt. And she stands there to this day. All day the oxen lick her so that she is reduced to her feet, but by the morning she has grown up again."[500] According to a later, twelfth-century version, "And it came to pass that when she looked behind her she became a pillar of salt. And it is still in that spot to this day. And the oxen which pass by there lick her every day, down to the toes of her feet, and by the morning it grows back."[501] This legend indicates that the pillar of salt was believed to possess the same regenerative powers which were attributed to the red soil of Hebron from which, according to talmudic legend, Adam was formed.[502] This belief, too, can thus be considered as pointing to the fertility-giving powers of salt, which can renew and increase in itself just as it can make man increase and multiply.

X. The Afterbirth and Umbilical Cord

Customs related to the afterbirth occupy a special place in the clusters of customs surrounding childbirth. First of all, in all parts of the world one finds the practice of resorting to various artificial methods to hasten ejection of the afterbirth from the mother's body. These methods are so varied that it would be difficult to summarize them in a general statement. They are presented in considerable detail in the well-known huge compendium on woman in folk custom published by Ploss, Bartels, and Reitzenstein, in which they take up no less than twenty large pages.[503] Here we shall confine ourselves to the Jewish customs which are not mentioned in that work.

According to R. Meir Aldabi, who lived in the fourteenth century and grew up in Spain, "If the child has emerged and the afterbirth remained there, let her be fumigated with the eye of a salted fish or with the nails [sic] of horses, or with the excrement of dogs, or with mustard, or let her drink the milk of a woman who was delivered of a male, if her child is a male, or the milk of a female if she is a female, or let her be fumigated with salted fish."[504] A similar method was used until recently among the Jews of Egypt. "A charm for the woman who delivered. If the afterbirth did not come out, they fumigate her with the excrement of a cat, and then the afterbirth will come out."[505] Eliyahu Ba'al Shem advises, "For a woman who cannot bear the afterbirth. Take three bones which are found in the fish *kerpfn* [carp] in the head, near the ears, and it has three horns, and take three souls [i.e., bladders] from the fish called *herung* [herring], and dry them and pound them to a powder, and give it to her to eat in the juice of a cock called *qabin*(?). Tried and proven."[506] In oriental Jewish communities the following method of fumigation is practiced. "In a manuscript book I found written as follows. 'A woman who delivered and the afterbirth has not yet come out, fumigate her with the excrement of a cat or with the tail of a cat, and it will come out immediately, with the help of God.' "[507] Binyamin Ba'al Shem writes, "Take the afterbirth of another woman, burn it to dust, and give it to her to drink in water. Proven. And likewise also for a woman if the afterbirth remained in her belly. It will help also. Proven."[508]

Many peoples see a kind of twin brother of the newborn in the afterbirth, and preserve it in order to use the powers and special virtues it contains should the need arise.[509] A similar concept underlies the mention of the afterbirth in the deuteronomic curse. "The tender and delicate woman among you . . . her eye shall be evil against the husband of her bosom, and against her son, and against her daughter, and against her afterbirth that cometh out from between her feet, and against her children whom she shall bear" (Deut. 28:56–57). Listing the afterbirth in one breath with husband

and children certainly makes it appear that it was considered something similar to a human being, a twin of a child. How else could the afterbirth be an object of the miserable woman's jealousy? That this is the view underlying the mention of the afterbirth in this context is confirmed by the fact that only Ibn Ezra explains the word *shilya* in the above passage literally, "the place of the child while it dwells in the belly of its mother," while both the Targum and Rashi interpret it as "a small child."

In mishnaic times (first to second centuries C.E.), they used to preserve the afterbirth "so that the child should not get cold," and, specifically, "preserve it in a bowl of oil, or in some clothing, or in a bundle of straw."[510] As with many other customs, here too there was a difference between the way it was carried out by the rich and by the poor. "R. Yose said, 'One even cuts and preserves the afterbirth on a Sabbath, so that the child be warm.' R. Shim'on ben Gamliel said, 'The daughters of kings preserve it in a bowl of oil; the daughters of the rich in cotton sponges; the daughters of the poor in rags.' "[511] This statement shows that the custom was observed among all social classes. And, of course, it could serve its stated purpose of keeping the child warm only if it was believed that a sympathetic magical connection existed between the afterbirth and the child. A similar belief is found among many other peoples.

Most interesting in this context is a statement in the Palestinian Talmud. "This afterbirth, on the Sabbath the rich preserve it in bowls of oil, and the poor in straw and sand. Both bury it in the earth, to give a pledge to the earth."[512] The commentator explains the word "pledge" by adding, "when he will die." This laconic statement expresses a very old and important folk idea: on the very day of his birth, a man must give a pledge to the earth to assure her that he will return to her when he dies. Man is born of earth and to the earth he returns. So that the earth will wait for him patiently, and perhaps also so that she will not demand his return prematurely, the afterbirth is buried as a pledge.[513]

The belief that burying the afterbirth can, so to speak, insure the life of the newborn underlies the custom observed by the Jews of Morocco. If a woman's children habitually die soon after their birth, the next time a child is born to her they bury the afterbirth in a field, in a place not frequented by people, so that the newborn should live and the afterbirth be its atonement.[514] Again the afterbirth substitutes for the child; it is returned to the earth instead of the child. Let us mention here in passing that in mishnaic times it was a popular custom to bury the afterbirth of an animal which miscarried at the crossroads or to hang it on a tree so that it should not miscarry again. This practice was forbidden by the rabbis of the Mishna.[515]

Among the Sephardi Jews in Palestine, the custom is to preserve the afterbirth for two or three days, until the woman in childbed becomes stronger, and then to bury it in the earth.[516] Among the Safed Sephardim, it is the custom "to throw the afterbirth into a latrine, but before doing so they take care lest a cat or a dog eat of it, because that would endanger the child's life and prevent the mother from bearing again."[517] Among Polish and Russian Jews the custom is to bury the afterbirth,[518] while Egyptian Jews preserve the afterbirth in a hidden place.[519]

The same customs are observed among the non-Jewish inhabitants of the Middle East. The Bedouin women of Palestine, after having delivered, go out alone into the desert, dig a pit in the earth, and bury the afterbirth.[520] According to Palestinian Arab belief, the pit is the place of origin of children,[521] and therefore one may assume that the point of the custom is to return to the earth a substitute for the child.

Many peoples use the afterbirth as a medicament or charm, and in a great variety of ways. A few examples will have to suffice. In Obelensk district of Russia, it is believed that the child is born with certain diseases. In order to free him from them, they put the afterbirth on his head and wash him in his mother's urine. In various parts of Italy and Greece, they believe that swellings of glands and similar ailments can be cured by placing an afterbirth on them.[522] Related to this are two folk cures recorded by Abbaye in the name of his foster mother. "Abbaye said: Mother told me, 'This infant which is emaciated, let them bring his mother's afterbirth and stroke his body with it, from its [the afterbirth's] narrow end to its wide end, and if the infant is too fat, from the wide end to the narrow end.' "[523] The eighteenth-century book of folk cures, *Mif'alot Eloqim*, states, "For witchcraft . . . take the afterbirth of a human firstborn, of a male for a male . . . and dry it well and give a little of it, in its mother's milk, to that child to whom the witchery was done."[524]

Various peoples observe the custom of preserving the caul which occasionally covers the child or part of its body when it is born. Such a child is believed to be lucky.[525] In the village of Ma'lula in the Anti-Lebanon, they believe that a child born wrapped in a caul brings luck to his father.[526] In Sidon, the child born in a caul is itself believed to be lucky. Some of the Sidonians dry the caul and the father carries it with him as a good-luck charm.[527] The same belief is attested among the Jews from the Middle Ages on. The *Sefer Ḥasidim* states that he who is born "covered in an armor" (i.e., in a caul) will suffer no harm from demons.[528] Similarly in the nineteenth century, "It seems that our people generally entertained the belief that the child born with a cover [i.e., the caul] over its face, it is a good sign for it that it will be very lucky, and hence the adage about a lucky man, 'He was born in a little shirt,' " and this is also a Russian saying."[529]

Many peoples attribute magical powers to the umbilical cord, or, more precisely, to that part of it which is left attached to the child's body and usually falls off by itself about the fifth day after birth. Very often the cord is wrapped up carefully and preserved, because it is considered a very potent amulet in war, traveling, and other situations. It saves the life of him who carries it, protects him against illness and evil influences, and cures diseases if it is swallowed after it has been pounded to a powder. It secures success in litigation and strengthens understanding. Only a few peoples have an indifferent attitude to the umbilical cord and discard it as unwanted.[530]

As for the connection between the newborn and the umbilical cord, folk custom is based on the principles of sympathetic magic—whatever happens to it also happens to the newborn. If the cord is cast into the sea (as it is done, e.g., in Australia), the child will become a good swimmer or will have good luck in fishing. If it is tied to a tree, the child will become an agile climber and a light mover (thus according to the belief of the people of New Guinea and other islands),[531] or he will become as stong and will live as long as a tree (according to White Russian belief).[532] Some peoples believe that the umbilical cord protects the mother[533] or gives her fertility.[534]

Yemenite Jews bury the afterbirth and the umbilical cord in a deep pit to make sure that they will not fall into the hands of strangers or evil persons. The belief on which this is based is found among many peoples: if somebody has in his hands a part of the body of a person, he has control over him.[535]

The custom of hanging the umbilical cord on the child is widespread.[536] Frequently it is used as a remedy for actual physical diseases. Moroccan Jews put the foreskin and the umbilical cord into the child's pillow. If the child's eyes are diseased, they put the cord into perfumed water and wash his eyes with that water.[537]

The magical power can pass from the umbilical cord itself to the implement with which it was severed; various peoples thus attribute special importance to the implement.[538] The Bene Israel put the knife under the newborn's pillow so that he will be fearless.[539]

The Spanish Jews in the fourteenth and the northeastern European Jews in the seventeenth and eighteenth centuries believed that there was a connection between the umbilical cord and the sex of the next child to be born to the mother. R. Meir Aldabi writes, "Treatment of the newborn. At the beginning, when it comes out of the belly of its mother, let them cut his navel above, at four fingers, and if they give it to a cock to eat, that which will be born after it will be male, and if to a hen, she will bear a female."[540] In the Sephardi community in Safed, it is "customary to dry the foreskin and the umbilical cord, and to put them in a small satchel, and to put that satchel into the pillow on which the newborn is lying, for the women believe that this will make the child quiet, while if they throw it away the child will become unruly."[541] The same custom is observed among the Moroccan Jews.[542]

XI. Protecting Mother and Child

Many are the dangers which threaten mother and child in the period immediately following delivery. Folk belief ascribes these dangers to demons and evil spirits which lie in wait to pounce on them and snatch away their lives. Let us begin our survey of the means of protection used by Jewish folk custom with inanimate substances, and, in the first place, with earth.

The earth, contact with which can give both fertility and strength to the woman who has difficulties in delivery, can also protect the mother and the child from all kinds of dangers. Above we have become acquainted with customs in which the earth serves as a means to cure or to protect the newborn, and elsewhere I have discussed the beliefs according to which contact with the earth can protect man in general from witchcraft and the evil eye.[543] According to medieval Jewish thinking, contact with the earth cured a child suffering from sleeplessness. "Take dust from under the threshold and mix it with mother's milk, and put it on the child's head, and he will sleep in peace."[544] The same charm is resorted to among the Sephardi Jews in the Middle East: "For a crying child. . . . Take dust from the hinges [of the door] of the house in which the child is, and knead it with his mother's milk, and put it on his head in the place where the brain [i.e., the skull] of the child is soft, and he will be cured, with the help of God, blessed be He." Or: "Another one. For a boy who cries too much. Take a little dust from behind seven doors and knead it with his mother's milk, and put it on the middle of his head, and he will lie and not cry."[545]

More complex is the following charm, in which the basic ingredient is dust from beneath the threshold.

> For a woman in childbed so that witchcraft should not harm her. . . . Take dust from the house in which the woman is, from three thresholds of the house, whichever you want, and from four walls of the house a little clay, and a little lime, and pound it thin, and also a little dust from the *bak ofen* [baking oven],[546] and cut from three loaves of bread from the top where they are first well baked, and put it on the fire until it all becomes completely dry, and pound it thin, and the loaves must be baked originally in the name of the woman. And take rye flour and put it in a pan upon the fire so that it be burnt a little, and then take salt, three times a handful, and put it in the pan so that it be burnt a little, and it has to be one after the other. And then mix all this together, and divide it into nine parts, and put each part into a paper. And then ask of a goldsmith that he give you embers, for nothing, as a gift, precisely at dusk, and take one paper with one of the nine parts, and put it on the embers, and fumigate the corner of

the room of the woman in childbed, and at the door and at the oven which is used for cooking and baking. And if the room has several doors, fumigate at every door and also at the windows, and the bed of the woman, and when the paper is consumed, take the second and the third, and fumigate as mentioned. And take the embers which are left over from the fumigation with the pan and put it in a hidden place, and in the second night also fumigate with three candles in the manner mentioned, and in the third night do the same again, and also in the second and third nights take the pans with the remaining coals and hide them, and one must have separate embers for every night, and on the fourth day take the pans with the coals, and go to the water and cast them into it and say nine times *"WIhi no'am"* (Ps. 90), and *"Yoshev b'seter"* (Ps. 91) to their end, and *"Shir lama'alot esa 'eni"* (Ps. 121), and *"Lam' natzeah hashamayim m'saprim k'vod El'"* (Ps. 19) to their end.[547]

As we have seen elsewhere, various peoples attribute healing powers to earth taken from a grave, or which was in some kind of contact with a dead body.[548] Earth taken from the cemetery can also protect the newborn against being "exchanged" by demons.[549] In several places it is believed that earth taken from a grave causes a deep, deathlike sleep.[550] The Sephardi Jews believe, "For sleep. . . . If you want that a man should sleep much, like the dead, and that he should not wake up until you want him to, take dust from a grave of a woman, on a Tuesday, put the dust under his head, and he will not wake up until you remove the dust."[551] The principles of sympathetic magic are clear in this procedure. Contact with earth taken from a grave causes sleep as deep as death.[552]

Various peoples perform a symbolic rite of second birth in order to protect a child's life. If a child is born weak, the rite causes him to be born again, full of strength and vitality. Among the Moroccan Jews, if a child is born whose siblings had died soon after their birth, they take an earthenware barrel or a big earthenware jar called a *tasur*, break off its bottom, and, as soon as the child is born, pass him back and forth through the vessel three times. Such a child, if he is a boy, receives the name Tasur, and if a girl, the name Tasura. The vessel is preserved until the child's wedding, when it is discarded.[553]

Just as in this charm the vessel symbolizes the womb from which the child is reborn, so, in the customs of other peoples, a hole in the ground stands for the womb. Among the Christian villagers of Ma'lula in the Anti-Lebanon, it is the custom that if the children of a couple die at a tender age, they take the smallest child, and, amid much singing, suspend him in a pit in the church of Saint Sergius.[554] Elsewhere in Syria they believe that if a child suffers from an unknown illness, and becomes weaker and weaker, he has been exchanged for a jinn's child. In such a case, his parents take him to the grave of a saint, next to which there is usually a big cistern, and let the

child down into the cistern until he almost touches the water at the bottom.
After a while they pull him up again, and they believe that the jinn has taken
back its own child and returned theirs.[555]

In another connection we have heard of the specific healing power
which folk belief attributes to stones, and especially to precious stones.[556]
We shall therefore not be surprised to learn that various peoples believe that
stones also protect the life of the newborn.[557] Likewise, many peoples hang
a piece of steel or iron around the neck of the newborn, or put it into his
swaddles, as a most reliable apotropaeic measure.[558]

In mishnaic times they used to tie "iron to the leg of the bed of a woman
in childbed."[559] This custom was outlawed by the rabbis, who saw in it an
"Emorite [i.e. pagan] custom," but nevertheless customs similar to it have
survived in various Jewish communities. In the eighteenth century it was
customary among German Jews to put a sword next to the head of a woman
in childbed.[560] The Jews of Afghanistan bring a sword into the room when
the woman is sitting on the birth stool.[561] Among the Sephardi Jews in Syria
and in Palestine, the following charm is used. "A child who cries, his charm
is to write on a knife, near its cutting edge, these names, and put it under his
head at night, and he will no longer cry. And this is what you should write:
'Tarishyorish,' 'Varish,' 'Parish,' three times."[562] Among the Sephardim
in Safed, it is customary "to put a knife and the Book of Psalms under the
pillow on which the infant lies, and thereby the demons will have no power,
and the reason is that the holiness of the book and the virtue of the iron will
cause the demons to flee."[563]

According to another source, "The reason for putting a knife next to the
head of the woman in childbed as a protection is, it seems, that it was first
introduced when they prepared the circumcision knife on the night preceding
the eighth day [on which the rite is performed] if the day of circumcision fell
on a Sabbath [on which day the circumcision must be performed irrespective
of all the Sabbath restrictions, but no carrying of any object is allowed], and
then the matter became confused."[564] Elsewhere the same source states,
"The reason that the circumciser puts the circumcision knife into the pillow
of the newborn on the day preceding the circumcision: because it will serve
as a protection for the child, so that the merit of the circumcision should
protect the child in that night, which is dangerous."[565] Among the Polish
Jews in the Warsaw area, it is customary to put the circumcision knife under
the heads of the mother and of the child on the evening preceding the eighth
day.[566] The Hungarian Jews put an ordinary knife under the pillow of the
woman in childbed.[567]

According to Jewish folk belief, the knife serves as a protection against
demons and evil spirits after birth.[568] Among the Jews of Mattersdorf, one

of the old Seven Communities in western Hungary, the circumciser puts the knife next to the child on the *wachnacht* (watch night, i.e., the night preceding the eighth day). And in order to protect the newborn against the *makhshefe* (witch, that is, Lilith), they also put another knife under the child's pillow, lest he come to harm when no adult is with him.[569] The Bene Israel put the knife with which they cut the umbilical cord under the child's pillow, or at his side, so that he will be afraid of nothing.[570]

Another metal object used as protection against the evil eye is a disk made of silver, copper, or some other metal, with the Hebrew letter *Hē* engraved on it. Such an amulet is hung around the newborn's neck.[571] According to one source, the disk must be made of no other metal but silver, and several names must be engraved on it.

> Children. Let him make a *tabla* [tablet] of silver, of two *dirhams* [drachmas], and it must be purified silver, and let him engrave on one side *Q'ra'Satan* [rend Satan], and on the other side, *Tzmrkd*, and they shall live. And put it on the head of the newborn child. And make also a tablet from purified silver, of eight *dirhams*, and engrave on it the name which is derived from [the first letters of the words in] the biblical verse "There shall be no miscarrying and barren woman" (Exod. 23:26)—*Ltm uba mya*, and also *Lyb'w* [which word contains the first letters of the words in the verse], "There shall be no barren man and barren woman among you" (Deut. 7:14), and put it on the woman before she delivers, and the two aforementioned *tablas* must be immersed in the *miqve* of purity before you apply them.[572]

The Jewish traveler Ya'aqov Sapir reports the following custom from the Jews of Yemen.

> The small children wear around their necks a thick round iron ring which reaches down to the chest. This ring is made of nine kinds of iron, which they collect from nails from nine houses. They make it at a certain time according to the order of the constellations, and with certain incantations. They say that it is good against the evil eye and witchcraft. And this ring is worn by both men and women until the day of their wedding, and after the days of the [wedding] feast they remove them.[573]

Eliyahu Ba'al Shem advises, "To drive away witcheries from the house of the woman in childbed, take a new pot, paying for it whatever the seller asks the first time, and a new comb, also in the same way, and a piece of a new shoe, and new *reyb eyzen* [grater], and embers from the smith, and fumigate in all corners of the room."[574] On the other hand, it is dangerous for a newborn to put iron to his mouth.[575]

In talmudic days various charms were used to protect the life of the newborn. They rubbed his body with an unguent, painted his eyes with kohl, hung knots, a piece of paper, or an amulet around his neck, and so on.[576]

Water, too, can protect mother and child. All over the world it is customary to immerse the newborn in cold water. Because this is often done after the child has been cleansed in some other way, and because the child frequently is immersed in a spring, river, or the sea—that is, in "living" water—one cannot assume that it serves merely the purposes of cleanliness. Rather, it would seem that the intention is to provide the child with some of the powers which the water, like the earth, is believed to have.[577] The ritual character of washing or immersing the newborn is indicated by the Jewish custom as well. Binyamin Ba'al Shem (and similarly Eliyahu Ba'al Shem) writes,

> Take a new earthenware jar, and buy it for whatever the potter wants for it, and take a new lock, and one must be careful not to lock the lock, and when the child is washed the first time, take the water in which he was washed, and put it into that jar, and put the jar under the bed in which the mother lies. And put the lock into the bed open. And if, God forbid, the child falls ill, or something happens [Eliyahu Ba'al Shem writes here, "and if, God forbid, it happens that there is a suspicion of the child's *benemnis* (i.e., that the child is bewitched)], then take the lock and lock it on the child and put it next to him. It is sure, with the help of God, that no evil in the world will befall him.[578]

Among the Bene Israel it is customary that, for several days after the delivery, the midwives take two or three pots of the water in which the child was bathed, swing them around the child, and then pour the water at their own feet.[579] In general, the Bene Israel believe that every person must make three-and-a-half ablutions in his life. The daily ablutions, carried out without any ritual, are considered one half. The ablutions at birth, marriage, and death are considered the three, to which they attribute great importance and which are carried out with festive rituals.[580] Among the Jews of Bavaria and Hessen, the custom is to place a pail or a barrel full of water before the door of the room of the woman in childbed.[581]

Let me quote here two charms recommended by Eliyahu Ba'al Shem, in which water taken internally is the medium for apotropaic powers.

> For a boy or an infant who has sustained a fright from an evil spirit or the evil eye or any other kind of evil happenings or evil afflictions. Buy a new earthenware vessel from the potter and from none other, and the vessel should not be coated, which is called *geglezt* [glazed], and one must give the potter the price he asks the first time, and draw the shape of a *Magen David* [Star of David] on the bowl. . . . And in the middle of the *Magen David* write ten *Sefirot*, and write also the verse "Set Thou a wicked man over him, and let Satan stand at his right hand" (Ps. 109:6), in a reversed order, thus, *Tes Uoht,*

etc., and the verse "There shall no evil befall thee" (Ps. 91:10), also in reverse, thus, *Ereht llahs on live llafeb eeht*, to its end. And give the boy to drink from this vessel until the names [i.e., the words] are blotted out because of the drinking, and it will help with the help of God.

For a woman who has difficulty in delivery, so that one has to suspect that, God forbid, the child has been afflicted by witchcraft which is called *benemen* [bewitching]. Take clear, standing water and put it in a copper cup, and say over the water these verses: "Joseph is a fruitful vine, a fruitful vine by a fountain, its branches run over the wall" (Gen. 49:22) seven times; "Then sang Moses," etc., until "He cast into the sea" (Exod. 15:1–4), also seven times; "Then sang Israel this song: 'Spring up, O well—sing ye unto it—the well which the princes digged, which the nobles of the people delved," etc. (Num. 21:17–18.), seven times. And speak into the right ear of the child, *"Matzpiel patzpatziya* [a mystical angel name], annul all kinds of evil eye, and cause all kinds of bewitching and tying of men and of women, whether Jews or uncircumcised, to separate from this child." Thus speak seven times into his right ear, and seven times into his left ear, and put with your finger which is called *zeret* [little finger], of your right hand a little water from the above-mentioned cup into the mouth of the child, and also sprinkle a little water on his face, and go out, and pour away the water at the crossroads, and return to the house without saying a word, and place the cup under the mother's bed, and let it remain there at least twenty-four hours.[582]

Let us now move on to fire, the third of the four principal elements, and see what role it played as a protection for mother and child. The custom of lighting fire or a candle for the woman in childbed is found among many peoples.[583] According to Jewish legend, there is a connection between fire, which is a sacred symbol of life and fertility,[584] and the child while it is still in its mother's womb.

R. Levi said . . . "It is usual in the world that nobody pays attention to a man who is imprisoned in the jailhouse. If somebody comes and lights a candle for him, the prisoner will be very grateful to him. So the Holy One, blessed be He. The embryo dwells in its mother's womb, and He lights for it a candle there. This is what Job says: 'When His lamp shined above my head' (Job 29:3).[585] As long as the child is in the womb, this candle rests on his head; when he comes out [i.e., is born], an angel taps him on the nose and puts out the candle which is over his head."[586]

The candle also symbolizes the child itself. Rav Huna, it is related in the Talmud, used to pass by the door of R. Abin the carpenter. He saw that R. Abin had the habit of lighting good candles on the eve of the Sabbath, and said, "Two great men will come from here." And there issued from R. Abin Rav Idi ben Abin and Rav Ḥiyya bar Abin. It also is reported of Rav Ḥisda that he used to pass by the door of the parents of Rav Shizvi. He saw that they lighted five candles, and he said, "A great man will issue from here." And Rav Shizvi issued from them. Rav Huna used to quote the proverb, "He who regularly lights the Sabbath candle, his children will become scholars."[587] Similar views were echoed in recent generations. "Through the Hanukkah candles and the Sabbath candles a man will have sons who will become scholars," and "Thanks to paying attention to the candles a man will merit that his wife bear male children."[588]

In talmudic times such importance was attached to the lighting of candles for a woman in childbed that the rabbis permitted it even on the Sabbath, and even for a blind woman if she asked that a birth candle be lit during her delivery.[589] The last-mentioned detail shows that the candle served as a charm for ensuring successful delivery and as a protection for the lives of mother and child. The same purpose was served by lighting a fire for the woman in childbed for thirty days, "even in the period of Tammuz," that is, in midsummer, when it was certainly not needed for warmth.[590]

Jewish custom requires that the newborn be received with a lighted candle when it emerges from the womb. In all parts of the Diaspora the custom is to light a candle or candles next to the woman in childbed.[591] In several Jewish communities it is explicitly acknowledged that this custom is intended to save or protect the lives of mother and child. Thus among the Bene Israel, a dim lamp is left burning in the room of the woman in confinement so that the newborn should not acquire a squint or suffer damage in its sight.[592] Among the Jews of Damascus, "at night one is careful not to leave the woman in childbed in the dark at all, and therefore they light a candle next to her."[593] Among the Sephardim in Safed, "if the woman has difficulties in delivery, they light candles in her room for the exaltation of the souls of Moshe ben Maimon and R. Shim'on ben Yohai, may their merits protect us. Amen."[594]

The symbolic value of the candle and the fire in connection with childbirth is expressed also in the strict prohibition against taking fire in any form out of the confinement room. Although this prohibition applies to all objects found in the room or the house, its application to fire is specifically and emphatically stressed.[595] Among the Polish Jews, "The women do not allow that fire or any burning thing, such as a lighted *papirusa* [cigarette], should be taken out of the confinement room, saying, 'It is forbidden that fire should go out of the confinement room' [in the original Yiddish, *Fun a kinpetarin's shtub tar keyn feyer nisht aroysgehn*]."[596] The Jews of Jerusalem also emphasize that fire, especially, must not be taken from the house of the woman in childbed.[597] Chorny reports from the Jews of Derbent that "it is forbidden to take fire out of that house, and it is also forbidden to borrow any vessel from it."[598] Among the Kurdish Jews, it is forbidden for outsiders to use anything from the house of the woman in childbed in the first week after birth; it also is forbidden to lend a vessel or to take out fire.[599] Among the Jews of Yemen and Aden, it is forbidden to take anything out of the house of the woman in confinement, and this prohibition is especially strict in relation to fire.[600] The same prohibition is observed in Palestine among the Jews of the old Yishuv, the settlers before 1882: "And likewise they will not take on loan anything from the house of the woman in childbed during the first week. Especially fire must not be taken from her house."[601] A Palestinian Arab custom shows most clearly that the candle stands for the newborn. When a child is sick, its parents vow to give the mosque a candle as long as the child's height.[602]

Fumigation, too, provides protection for mother and child. Maimonides decried this custom, in which he saw a remnant of the pagan rite of passing the child through fire for Moloch which was adopted by idolatrous Israelites in biblical times from their pagan neighbors. "And know that traces of this practice have survived even to the present day, because it was widespread in the world. You can see how midwives take a young child wrapped in its swaddling clothes, and after having placed incense of a disagreeable smell on the fire, swing the child in the smoke over that fire. This is certainly a kind of 'passing children through the fire,' and we must not do it."[603] However, as in many other cases, folk custom proved stronger than rabbinical admonition and prohibition, and the fumigation of mother and child has continued to occupy an important place among the apotropaic measures resorted to by many Jewish communities. The Jews of Yemen, e.g., burn incense on the day of birth, on the spot where the delivery took place, on the third day after birth under the body of the mother, and on the fifth day under all the women guests and over seven doors of the house.[604] Among the Jews of Aden, the woman puts incense on the fire, takes the newborn, and swings it over the smoke[605]—thus practicing the precise custom outlawed by Maimonides eight centuries earlier. Such fumigations are practiced among several peoples.[606]

The mirror plays a special role among the birth customs which aim to protect mother and child. According to popular belief among many peoples, Satan or demons lurk in the mirror which hangs near the woman in confinement. In order to prevent these evil beings from harming her, they cover the mirrors during delivery and for as long thereafter as the woman is laid up.[607] According to a belief found in the old Yishuv in Palestine, the woman in childbed must not look into the mirror lest she become cross-eyed, and cross-eyed also will become anybody who looks into a mirror after sunset.[608] The Jews of Morocco follow the reverse: they hang a small mirror at the head of the woman's bed.[609] Interesting is the following charm suggested by Eliyahu Ba'al Shem for a woman who miscarries.

> At times a woman miscarries because of her evil eye, and the charm against it is that she should put some dye in her nostrils,[610] and let her look every day in a mirror, that is *spigel* [mirror], at her nostrils, taking a full glance, and while she looks she should say seven times, "Joseph is a fruitful son, a fruitful vine by a fountain, its branches run over the wall" (Gen. 49:22). And according to the meaning of that which is written, one must look at the left nostril.[611]

Substances taken from the vegetable world figure prominently as protective agents for mother and child. The Bene Israel rub the newborn with turmeric and egg white.[612] The Moroccan Jews use henna for the same purpose: three days after its birth they rub the child's body with oil and sprinkle henna on its limbs.[613] The same custom is followed by the Muslim Moroccans.[614] The Yemenite Jews rub clarified butter on the newborn's body.[615] R. Meir Aldabi advised in the fourteenth century, "Wind strips of pure cotton around the child and put on it a piece dipped into oil, and then anoint its body with oils which contract."[616] The rubbing of the newborn with oil or fat is practiced among many peoples.[617]

A custom reminiscent of the talmudic *parpisa*[618] is practiced in both Sephardi and Ashkenazi communities. The father of the child whose life is endangered is advised "to sow a kind of grain [then let it sprout and grow, and then] cut it, and give it to the poor, and he should not enjoy it."[619] In the Sephardi community of Safed, it is customary to hang over the woman's bed, together with the usual written charms with holy names, verses from the Bible, incantations, and "heads of garlic, and a kind of grass called in the language of the Mishna *pigam* [rue], and in Arabic *ruda*, and one paper [with inscriptions] should be folded and put on the head of the newborn, together with the garlic and the *ruda*."[620] In Jerusalem, among both Sephardim and Ashkenazim, it was customary to hang "twigs of rue over the bed of the woman in confinement, so that the evil eye should not have power, God forbid, over mother and child."[621]

Elsewhere I dealt with the custom observed in various Jewish communities of letting the woman who has difficulties in delivery look into a cup of oil, and then sending it to the synagogue to be used for lighting.[622] R. Naḥman of Bratzlav advised doing this to protect the newborn. "A woman whose children die of the disease called *samke*, that is *zdushin* [Polish "strangulation"], should wash them in oil, and then she should use that oil for a mitzvah [religious commandment].[623]

Eliyahu Ba'al Shem advises fumigation with herbs and spices. "Protection for the woman who is exposed to the danger that her sons are exchanged, which is called *benemnis*. Fumigate the woman in the seventh month with these herbs and spices."[624] Also: "For the taking of children, which is called *benemen*. Take *weyn roytn un wakhholter ber shwartzn kiml* [wine-rue, juniper berry, black caraway] and pound them very fine, and bury them under the hinges of the door, and take a *besin* [broom] and cut it into small pieces before the door, and leave it there eight days, and no witchery will be able to enter there."[625] Or: "For somebody who cannot bring up children. Take *batan wartzil* [(?) root] from the merchants, and *biber gal* [beaver gall],[626] and cook them in three measures of good wine, and it should be cooked thoroughly, and when the child is born wash him with this before any other water touches him, and then put the wash wine in a jar and put the jar under the mother's bed."[627]

The Moroccan Jews use the head of a cock in conjunction with vegetable substances. Immediately after a male child is born, they slaughter a cock and cut off its head. Then they make five little rings of dough, take the head of the cock and a twig of rue, tie all this together, and hang it on the doorpost next to the mezuzah (the small parchment scroll inscribed with Deut. 6:4–9 and 11:13–21, which is fixed in a wooden or metal case to the doorpost of every observant Jewish house), leaving it there until the day of the circumcision. This is considered a "sacrifice" to avert demons and evil spirits.[628]

In the last-mentioned charms, substances derived from vegetables are used with components taken from the animal world. The cock also figures in the following charms. "It is very good to put next to the child, on his right side, the eye of a black cock which was old, and under the child's head the comb of the above-mentioned cock, and also to put next to him the white stones which are found in the cock's gizzard, that is, stones which have the shape of hailstones."[629] Or: "A child who, when born, looks like dead. Take a cock and put it(?) into the anus of the child; then, if it is from God that he should live, the child will live and the cock will die."[630]

Eggs, which are the preeminent symbols of fertility, were used in magical rites whose purpose was to ensure the child's life on the very day of his birth. Among the Jews of Aden, the custom is to break eggs on the spot where the child was born. On the evening of the sixth day after his birth, they take seven eggs, break them against seven doors of the house, and burn incense.[631] The Bene Israel rub egg white on the newborn to prevent skin eruptions.[632] According to the "Sefer S'gullot w'Ḥiddot,"

> For a person possessed, and against demons, and for a woman who loses her children while they are small, God forbid. Take a female lizard [Hebrew

homet], and her sign is that you will find that her body is high and not as slanted as a male, and also you will find in her eggs without a shell, as are found in the hen. And take those eggs and put them in a new copper vessel, and if there is no new one heat it in fire, and put the eggs into it and put it on the fire until the eggs are burned and become ashes, and put those ashes into pure water, and let the woman who loses her children drink of that water soon after her delivery. And also the possessed, and he who has been harmed by demons, should drink of it. And also daub some of the blood [of the lizard] on the four sides of the woman or the possessed man, and also on the middle of the head, and on every place where there is hair, such as the underarms, etc., and put there some of the blood of the lizard, and also take the hand of the lizard and one foot and the head of the lizard, and put them in a piece of material. And when the child is born hang on him all that has been mentioned, and also the possessed and he who has been damaged [by demons] should do all that has been mentioned. And this is proven.[633]

Eliyahu Ba'al Shem recommends the following. "To save the woman in confinement from witcheries, write on a baked egg the name of the holy angel Tarfaniel, and let the woman eat it, and then let her suckle her child."[634] Or: "For witchery, that it should not harm the child from the hour of its birth. Take the egg shells from which the chicks have come out, and take seven pieces of cobwebs, and from nine women pieces of clothing, of nine different colors, and put all this together in a pot over the fire, and fumigate the child and the mother with it."[635] Or: "To save the woman in confinement from witches, take a live spider and put it into virgin wax,[636] and put the wax into a *lo'ez*[637] nut, *un oyf hengin oyf ir* [and hang it on her]."[638]

According to the "Sefer S'gullot w'Ḥiddot," a mouse can have the same beneficial effect.

Another one. Tried and proven. [Transmitted] in the name of our master and rabbi, R. Ḥayyim Vital. Let him take a male mouse which goes under the earth and eats; this mouse is tried and proven that it ruins the crops. Let him take its blood in a piece of cloth, and hang it on her, and when the child is born hang it on him, and as for the mouse itself, dry it and hang it up in the house, and neither a demon nor a harmful spirit, nor an affliction, nor male nor female demons will approach that house in any way.[639]

A custom which was found among East European Jews in the seventeenth and eighteenth centuries, traces of which were found until recently among the Jews of Damascus, had as its purpose the giving of a substitute or atonement for the child whose life was in danger.

A charm for a woman whose children die, God forbid. When she enters the ninth month of her pregnancy, let her go to the place where a bitch has given birth, and let her place her right foot on a little puppy dog and say three times, "Take the dead and give me the live one!" And then let the woman take the little dog on which she stepped, and put it into her lap on her naked body, and let her put its head on her right side and its feet on her left side, and the woman should go with that little dog to the river and remove her belt so that the dog should of itself fall into the river, and she should say again three times, "Take the dead and give me the live one." And this is proven.[640]

The symbolic features of this procedure are completely clear: the woman ties the little dog to her body and then lets him drop; thus the dog is born magically of the woman and condemned to death in place of her own child.

Charms to stop a child from crying too much are "A bone from a dog which it dropped while eating," or "a goat's horn" which is put under the head of the child.[641] Certain biblical verses written on the "parchment [made of the skin] of a deer which was slaughtered in a *kosher*, [ritually pure] manner" and "blotted out in old *kosher* wine and in lukewarm water" can protect a woman whose children die or are being exchanged (*benemen*) if she drinks the wine.[642]

An entirely different concept underlies the custom of the Jews of Afghanistan, who pull the child through the mouth of a wolf's skin.[643] This magic act belongs to the rites of symbolic rebirth, which have been discussed above.

Let us now turn to those charms which require that the mother or the child be brought in contact with human beings possessing special powers. We have already seen that swallowing a foreskin is believed to ensure pregnancy.[644] The same custom is followed by Arab women in Nablus, Palestine, who have lost several children; they swallow it so that the fruit of their wombs will remain alive.[645] East European Jews in the seventeenth and eighteenth centuries had this practice: "So that the newborn child should not become possessed by Lilith, let them put into his mouth the holy covenant [i.e., the foreskin] of a child who was [just] circumcised, and let him [probably his father] take the mezuzah from the house and read the two sections [contained in it] into the right ear of the child, and then return the mezuzah to its place."[646] Among Polish Jews, if a woman lost her children "she would wash the bride before the huppa."[647] Among the Sephardi Jews, "A fine charm for a woman whose children die, God forbid. Take seven rings in charity [i.e., a gift] from seven pregnant women, and let him make of them an [amulet] with the name *Shaddai* [Almighty] on it."[648] Persian, Bukharan and Kurdish Jewish women, as well as women in other oriental Jewish communities, give "Kohen water," that is, the water with which the *kohanim* washed their hands on Yom Kippur, to small children "who cry and are never quiet" and to children who suffer from a bone disease in their feet. These customs were observed both in the old Middle Eastern home countries of these communities and in Palestine after their immigration.[649] Among the Jews of Afghanistan, if a son is born to a couple after their other children have died at a tender age, they celebrate a sham marriage between the newborn child and a woman above sixty, in order thereby to remove the danger which threatens the child's life. In the same way, a sham marriage is arranged for a newborn girl-child with an old man, or else the mother asks for gifts of coins from relatives and friends, makes a small bowl of them, and hangs it around the child's neck.[650]

We have heard above of several customs in which barren women who want to conceive are brought into contact with graves or dead bodies.[651] Contact with the dead also can help, according to folk belief, the newborn whose life is in danger. In Mishnaic times, if a woman felt that the life of her child was endangered, "she pulled [or dragged] him among the dead"— which was forbidden by the rabbis because they saw in it one of "the ways of the Emorites," that is, pagan customs.[652] The Sephardi Jews in Jerusalem sometimes put the cut off and dried hand of a small dead child under the pillow of the newborn whose life they want to protect.[653] The Damascan Jews advise, "When the child is born, sell him to one of the Ḥevra Qadisha [The Holy Society, a charitable organization existing in most Jewish communities] which buries the dead, and let him be the father of the child,"[654] which will thus be saved from death. In the Sephardi community of Safed, they sell the child when it is born "to another man," Jew or Arab, and not specifically to a member of the Ḥevra Qadisha.[655] Similarly, Lithuanian Jews in the seventeenth and eighteenth centuries believed, "He whose children do not survive, God forbid, one person would come and give a *sela'* [coin] to his father and mother as a redemption, and say, 'This is my son and he will live.' It is good to do this."[656]

The Jews of Kurdistan beg for a piece of linen from the women sewing the shrouds of the dead, sew it up into a small satchel, and hang it around the neck of the newborn to protect him.[657] This custom has a most interesting form among the Jews of Damascus. "From the time that the child is born, dress him only in linen. Buy shrouds which are made for the dead and make of them clothes for the child until it grows up to be eight or ten years old, or more."[658] In the Safed Sephardi community also, "the charm of clothing the newborn in linen from the shrouds of the dead" is used.[659] The traditional custom of the East European Jews knows of linen clothes, but without any connection with shrouds. "Clothes of white linen are useful for the living and the dead, for the small and the big, and he who wants to search and discover the virtue of linen clothes which no other garb has—even a newborn whose father is known for having lost his children through Lilith or an evil spirit, this newborn will be safe from all of them."[660] And as for the mothers, "the woman in confinement . . . let her loins be girt with linen."[661]

Clothes paid for with money which the mother got as a gift have the same virtue. In Damascus, "When she is pregnant, even if she is rich, let her go to get charity explicitly, in order to make clothes for the child and to prepare and dress him when he is born, and let her name the child Shahādiyya [Arabic, "witnessing," "testimony"]."[662] In Safed, "Other people give clothes to the newborn as a charity, until it grows up."[663] Traces of this custom are found also in Jerusalem.[664]

Another method to guard the life of the child is not to change his clothes until he grows up. "He whose children die while small, let the mother make him [the next child born] a shirt and let him wear it all the time until he grows up."[665] Among the Jews of Morocco, it is the custom not to wash the swaddling clothes until the child is thirty days old if a woman's other children have died in infancy.[666] The custom of not changing a child's clothes and of letting him walk about at home and in the street with dirty clothes and body also obtains among the Arabs. In Egypt they explain it as a protection against the evil eye, which would strike a clean and nicely dressed child, but will not harm a dirty child wearing rags. For the same reason, the Palestinian Arabs do not wash small children: dirt repels the evil eye.[667] Similar considerations prompt the Egyptians occasionally to let a small boy wear female clothing; the jealous evil eye is not interested in girls.[668]

Folk custom devotes considerable attention to the question of whether it is permitted to dress a male child in female clothes, and vice versa. This exchange of clothing across sex lines is practiced among many peoples. Male children frequently are made to wear girls' clothes in order to protect them from demons.[669] The exchange of clothes often is done at circumcision, marriage, or other significant occasions.[670] Ernest Crawley explains this custom with his "inoculation" theory: the bride and the groom put on each other's clothes, that is, the clothes of the person whom they love and whom they fear, because the other's clothes lessen the "sexual danger"; they try thereby to assimilate themselves to each other, so as to neutralize the danger represented by the other.[671] If this explanation is correct, then doubtless the exchange of clothes at birth serves the same purpose. The "inoculation" of a member of one sex with the powers of the opposite sex must begin immediately after birth. Let us remember that this is not the only example of rites performed at birth with the intention of preparing the newborn for the great hour of marriage. This explanation finds support in the reason Sicilians give for wrapping a newborn girl in a male's shirt, and a newborn boy in a female's shirt. It is done so that the newborn should have luck with the opposite sex.[672]

The custom of putting women's clothes on a child was practiced in the Middle Ages by both Muslims and Jews, and Maimonides strongly condemned it.[673] In modern times, Jewish books of charms and customs reiterate Maimonides's veto.

> Immediately after the delivery one must be careful to wrap a male newborn into the kerchief of a male, and a girl into the kerchief of a female, and this is according to what Rabbi M'naḥem haBavli wrote in the *Ta'ame haMitzvot* [Meanings of the Commandment], and this is his language: "A man shall not put on a woman's garment" (Deut. 22:5), so that he should not come to commit fornication, for the garment will arouse in him thoughts which are worse than a transgression. If he becomes addicted to fornication, he will be punished by a woman's dress—the measure that a man measures will be measured out to him. And I found it written that when the newborn emerges into the air of the world, if the midwife receives a male in the garment of a female, he will be a great fornicator, and if she receives a female child in the garment of a man, she will become a harlot. Therefore [one must receive them] in a new garment, for the garment brings the power of the woman into the man, and the power of the man into the woman." Thus far his language."[674]

It is surprising to what extent these words tally with the explanation Crawley gives for the custom of clothing a person into the garments of the opposite sex. Both R. M'naḥem haBavli and Crawley record the belief that by putting on the garments of the opposite sex something of the powers of that sex are introduced into and absorbed by the individual. But while other peoples conclude that this development is desirable, and hence exchange the sexes' clothes (especially in connection with marriage) in order to inoculate or accustom an individual to the dangerous sexual powers of the opposite sex, the Jewish sages (and possibly the Bible itself?) drew the opposite conclusion: it must not be done lest it lead to fornication. This Jewish prohibition has remained in force until the present time. The Jews of Egypt "make sure to dress the male child in male garments only at the time of his birth, and a female child in female garments. And at times they wrap the child in a new sheet."[675] The Jews of Morocco always take care to wrap the newborn in an entirely new kerchief. Among them, too, the danger of fornication is the basis of this custom.[676] An exception is the custom of the Jews of Transylvania: the first garment they put on a male newborn is his mother's dress, and on a female newborn, a garment of her father.[677]

Sacred objects, which have a role in facilitating delivery, especially the Tora scroll, are also believed to protect the mother and child thereafter. In talmudic days there was a custom, prohibited by the sages, "to put a book or the tefillin [phylacteries] on the child so that he should sleep."[678] And in the *Mahzor Vitri*, the famous eleventh-century prayer book, we read,

> It is the custom that soon after circumcision they gather ten men and take a *ḥumash* [Pentateuch]. And the newborn in the cradle is dressed on the day of circumcision in festive clothes, and they put the book on him and say, "Let this observe what is written in this." And then they say *wayitten l'kha* [a blessing, Gen. 27:28], and all the verses of the blessings, and then he will become wise. And they put in his hand an inkwell and a pen, so that he may become a skilled scribe of the Tora of God.[679]

In the thirteenth century it was the custom among German Jews to put the recently circumcised child on a pillow with a Tora scroll next to his head, and the elders of the community or the rabbis blessed him, saying, "God give thee of the dew of heaven," etc. (Gen. 27:28–36).[680] According to another version, they placed only the Book of Leviticus at his head. " 'This is the book of the generations of Adam' (Gen. 5:1). Herein there is an indication that when they put the boy in the cradle and give him a name they put the book of the Law of the Priests [i.e., Leviticus] next to his head."[681] They still practiced the same custom in the eighteenth century.

> On the thirtieth day after the birth of the child, that is, on the fourth Sabbath, they lay the child in the cradle. Then the child's father takes his great tallit [prayer shawl] and puts it above the child's head, and next to him a silver belt, as well as a page from a rabbinical book or the Talmud, and recites in a loud voice before the children who stand around the cradle the first verse from the fifth book of Moses [Deuteronomy]. Then the children lift up the cradle with the newborn in it, and then they call him by his name, and this is done three times in a row.[682]

This rite is, of course, nothing but the well-known *Holle-Kreisch*.[683]

The custom of placing a copy of the Pentateuch or of Leviticus at the child's head while he is being given a name is practiced in various Ashkenazi Jewish communities.[684] In the Polish and Russian communities, they put the *Sefer Raziel haMal'akh* [Book of the angel Raziel] under the pillow of the woman in childbed to protect her from evil spirits.[685] Various Christian peoples put the Holy Scripture into the child's cradle.[686] The Palestinian Muslim Arabs put the Koran at the head of the newborn who suffers pains, while the Christian Arabs use the Bible for the same purpose.[687]

Both gentiles and Jews isolate the woman in childbed from members of her family, and she remains in this kind of confinement for several weeks after delivery. Among eighteenth-century German Jews, the woman had to remain in her house for six weeks.[688] Among the Jews of Aden, the woman has to remain in isolation for thirty to forty days after delivery, during which time her female neighbors provide food for her. Among the Yemenite Jews, when the young mother goes out of her house for the first time after the period of isolation, she carries the newborn and goes to the mountains with other children and women. When she starts to walk back home, she, and the women with her, throw rue behind their backs, saying, "Do not return, except after three years." Then the whole group returns home, and in the midst of loud trills of joy, the girls pour water on the threshold and the young mother has to enter the house without touching the threshold with her foot.[689]

Among the Bene Israel, the isolation lasts only seven days. On the seventh day, the mother, with the child in her arms, goes in and out of the door several times, while her women friends sprinkle her with water into which turmeric powder is mixed. On the seventh day of the life of a daughter, they put around her handfuls of boiled grain and pieces of coconut, which is a symbol of fertility all over India. On the fortieth day of the life of a male child, or on the eightieth of a female, they hold a plate over the child's head and roll some ten to twenty small balls of boiled rice flour over it. When the balls are about to fall on the ground, the children of the house catch them and eat them right then and there.[690] Among the Jews of Derbent, various prohibitions apply to the newborn's father.

> The father of the child must not wash his body in water, or in the river, or in the bath, or in the sea, for seven weeks after the birth of his child. Likewise he is forbidden to write anything during that time, for they say that this would be a danger for the child. All those seven weeks nobody is allowed to go up to the roof of the house in which the woman is. And it occasionally happens that somebody does not observe this rule, and great quarrels break out, leading to bloodshed.[691]

Furthermore, "the room in which the woman in confinement is, no man or woman is allowed to enter it, except the midwife and the woman's relatives on her mother's side, for seven weeks."[692]

While isolating the mother and child is intended to prevent harm that could be caused by human beings through the evil eye, harm caused by demons and evil spirits is prevented by the magic circle. Elsewhere I had occasion to discuss the magic circle in various religio-magical rites.[693] The basic idea is to protect a person in danger of being harmed by demons, as individuals are especially at the three great stations of the human life cycle—birth, marriage, and death—by drawing a circle around him which the forces of evil are unable to penetrate.

In Ashkenazi communities, the magic circle around the mother and the child is created by nitre, embers, a knife, or a sword. "It is a widespread custom among us Ashkenazim to make a circle around the walls of the room in which the woman in childbirth lies, with *neter* [nitre] or embers, and to write on every wall, 'Adam Eve. Out Lilith.' "[694] Or: "A charm based on a mystery is the custom of the midwives to make a circle around the woman in childbed and around the house with nitre, and this is how those who perform an incantation make a circle around a person."[695] Or: "At the outgoing of the Sabbath, before the Havdala [the ritual separating the Sabbath from the weekdays], the husband should wrap himself in a tallit and stand near the bed of the woman in confinement, and make a circle around her with a new knife which has a black handle, and the child with the cradle should also be there, and the circle he makes should be around the child as well." Then he should pronounce a certain incantation.[696]

It was the custom among eighteenth-century German Jews to place a sword at the head of the woman in childbed. Once every night during the first thirty days after delivery, the woman got up from her bed, took the sword, and made slashing motions with it along the four walls of the room and the floor, in order thus to drive away Lilith.[697] A trace of this custom remained until the twentieth century among the Jews of Hessen-Kassel. They drew a circle around the woman's bed with a knife called a *Krasmesser* (German *Kreismesser*, "circle knife"). In earlier times they used an old cannoneer's sword from Napoleonic days for the same purpose. The rite itself was called *gekrast*, i.e., "circle making."[698] A book of customs which records such a rite does not specify the implement used. "The women at the time of their delivery, when they lie in bed, a circle and partition is made for them so that spirits and Lilin [plural of Lilith] should have no power over them. For the demons are unable to enter from a public place to a private place."[699]

Among the Moroccan Jews in the seventeenth century, it was the custom that, at the beginning of the delivery, the woman's husband or a surrogate drew several circles in her room, as well as on the outer and inner sides of the doors, on the walls, and around her bed. Into each circle he wrote the words, "Adam. Eve. Out Lilith."[700] Until recently it was the custom among Moroccan Jews to take a big knife at every midnight between the delivery and the circumcision, and to make with it motions as if one would cut something alongside the walls of the woman's room, in order to drive away the demons.[701] Finally, the Sephardi Jews in Jerusalem "draw a black line along the walls of the house of the woman in childbed with a piece of coal, as a protection."[702]

XII.[703]

Some general observations can be made on the basis of the foregoing collection of Jewish folk customs and beliefs connected with childbirth.

Regarding the concrete contents of charms, two features are outstanding. One is that many of these charms are found among both Middle Eastern and European, especially east European, Jews. This would lead one to conclude that these charms are part of a common Jewish heritage going back to ancient times when the ancestors of all Diaspora communities lived in Palestine. The other feature is the close similarity between many Jewish charms and those found among the gentiles in whose midst the Jews lived; this is the case especially in those countries in which the Jews had lived for centuries. These close Jewish-gentile correspondences point to mutual influences and to a readiness on the part of the Jews to adopt charms used by the gentiles, and vice versa. We find that Jewish birth customs often prescribe the ingestion of substances of animal origin forbidden by Jewish dietary laws.

For example, a woman is advised to swallow as charms against barrenness, the tongue, gall, and blood of a raven; the skin of a fox; the skin, womb, male organ, stomach, gall, and blood of a hare; the excrement of a pig; grated elephant's tusk; mare's milk. The fact that all of the animals are unclean and ritually forbidden is disregarded. Similarly, no account is taken of the halakhic prohibition of ingesting any part of a human body; charms prescribe the drinking of the ashes of an umbilical cord in wine, the swallowing of a piece of the umbilical cord with honey and rose water, all for the purpose of removing the curse of barrenness. Ashes of a snake's skin and the milk of a she-ass are ingested to prevent miscarriage. Bees wrapped up in a small bundle are swallowed as a contraceptive. The milk of a bitch, donkey dung, and frogs burnt to ashes are ingested as charms for difficult labor. The afterbirth of another woman, burnt to ashes and mixed in water, and the husband's urine are drunk for the same purpose.

The attitude of the rabbis to the ingestion of these ritually unclean and forbidden substances was ambiguous. In general, they took no notice of them and thereby gave them their tacit approval. Occasionally they tried to combat and prohibit them, but some rabbis, among them important scholars, included them in their books of charms and remedies and thus contributed to their popularization.

As for methods resorted to for combating barrenness, preventing conception, facilitating delivery, or protecting mother and child from the Evil Eye and demonic assaults, they are almost exclusively magical in nature. We may add that the same observation can be made of Jewish charms and remedies in general. Although a certain religious feature is present in many cases, e.g., in the form of an incidental reference to "the help of God," the efforts to obtain succor from barrenness, loss of children, or any other trouble, ill, or evil, are based, not on the belief that humble supplication may induce God to help, but on a diametrically opposite assumption—that the performance of certain acts or the use of certain substances will, in itself, bring about the desired effect. The rich variety of procedures prescribed in the books of charms and remedies or reported orally as being followed in various Jewish communities belong to a world of thought and belief full of baleful powers, evil influences, and malevolent spirits, whose power is counterbalanced to some extent by the availability of substances, acts, and words of magic which can be brought to bear upon them. The belief in God and His goodness exists in the magical mind as well, but, characteristically, there is no direct appeal to God or request for divine help in any of the recommended charms. Nor is there anywhere a sense of the essential incompatibility between the belief in the omnipotence and omniscience of God, without whose will nothing is supposed to happen on earth, and the utilization of charms to bring about desired results in a magico-mechanical way.

Notes

"Jewish Birth Customs" consists of several sections, here somewhat revised, and originally published as follows: section I in Hebrew in *Sefer haShana lIhude Amerika* [New York] 10–11 (1949):472–75; section IIA in Hebrew in *Talpioth* [New York] 6 (1953–55):254–57; section IIB in *Folk Lore* [London] 55 (Sept. 1944):115–24; section IIC, ibid. 56 (Dec. 1944–Mar. 1945):208–18; section IID in Hebrew in *Talpioth* 6 (1953–55):244–48; section IIE, ibid., pp. 249–53; section III, ibid., pp. 257–61; section IV, ibid., pp. 262–65; section V in *Sefer haShana lIhude Amerika* 10–11 (1949):475–87; section VI in *Talpioth* 6 (1953–55):265–68; sections VII–X, ibid., pp. 686–705; section XI, ibid., 9 (1965):238–60.

1. On water as a substance fertilizing women, see Raphael Patai, *Adam va'Adama* (Jerusalem, 1942), 1:199ff. On the external use of stones for bestowing fertility on women, ibid., 2:19ff, 103–4, 107. On eating earth for the same purpose, see "Earth Eating," above.

2. The legends of several peoples tell about the births of gods or heroes from stones swallowed by women. The Aztecs attributed the birth of the god Quetzalcoatl to a green stone which his mother, Chimalma, found and swallowed. The Thlinkit Indians on the northwest coast of America had a story about a woman all of whose sons were killed by her brother. She was walking along the shore, crying over the dead, when a big fish took pity on her and told her that she should swallow a stone and drink some seawater. The stone was but the temporary form of the hero Yehl; after his birth from the woman, Yehl took revenge on his uncle (Edwin S. Hartland, *The Legend of Perseus*, 2 vols. [London, 1894–96], 1:112ff., and Hartland, *Primitive Paternity*, 2 vols. [London, 1909–10], 1:11). Similarly in folk custom: in the Banks Islands, women took certain stones to bed with them in order to become pregnant from them (Hartland, *Perseus*, 1:173; *Primitive Paternity*, 1:119). Chinese medical books state that a porridge or juice made of kidney stones can cure barrenness. In various places in France, it was customary until recently for barren women to scrape off a little of the stone statues of certain saints (who in most cases had a priapian or phallic character), and then to drink the powder mixed in water

(Hartland, *Primitive Paternity*, 1:62ff.; Heinrich Ploss, Max and Paul Bartels, and Ferdinand Reitzenstein, *Das Weib* [hereafter Ploss], 11th ed., 3 vols. [Berlin, 1927], 2:323ff.).

3. Abraham haRofe, *Shilte haGibborim* [hereafter title only] (Mantua, 1612), p. 45a; Bahya ben Asher on Exod. 28:17, p. 120. Similarly in *Mid. Talpiyot*, s.v. Efod, p. 61a; *Yalqut Yitzhaq* 90; *Yalqut R'uveni*, T'tzavve 149; *R'fu'a v'Hayyim* (Jerusalem, 1872 [?]) 28a and 35a.

4. R. Ohana, *Mar'e haY'ladim* [hereafter title only], 3d ed. (Jerusalem, 1908), p. 78b, quoting Rabbi Mar Kahana Rabba, *'Anaf Avanim*.

5. *Shilte haGibborim*, p. 45a.

6. Bahya ben Asher on Exod. 28:17, p. 120.

7. *Mar'e haY'ladim*, p. 78b, quoting "a manuscript." The charm against barrenness mentioned in Gen. Rab. 45:2 does not belong here. The correct reading there is not *qame'a* and *himos* (which several scholars identified as haematites, or bloodstone), but *qavu'a* and *mayumas*, as J. Theodor emends in his edition of Gen. Rab. (Berlin, 1912), 1:448, on the basis of the most reliable manuscripts. Mayumas was a licentious pagan feast observed in the port cities of Palestine, Syria, and Italy. *Qavu'a* refers to such a "fixed" feast (see Tos. 'Av. Zar 1:1, ed. Zuckermandel, p. 460), which was celebrated at a certain point in the year (the Mayumas was observed in May). Participation in such an orgiastic feast was considered a fertility charm. However, this is a subject which needs further investigation.

8. A Chinese legend tells how a pearl fell into a maiden's lap and she swallowed it, whereupon she became pregnant. The son born to her later became the emperor Yu. This motif is found also in Koriak legend (Hartland, *Perseus*, 1:112–15; *Primitive Paternity*, 1:11).

9. *Mar'e haY'ladim*, p. 35a, quoting "a manuscript book from Assyria and Babylonia." *Lulu* is the Arabic term for "pearl."

10. In Styria a barren woman scraped off a little of her golden wedding ring and swallowed the dust (Hartland, *Primitive Paternity*, 1:62–63).

11. If the object used is a gun or a rifle, the basis of its fertilizing power is not the metal, but its shape and function, which evoke an association with the penis. In various places in Morocco, barren women tied pieces of cloth torn from their dresses to the barrels of old guns, which were considered holy or even regarded as holy men. In the Moroccan Berber Ait Väryager tribe in the Rif, they placed a gun which was used in a fight against Christians upon the stomach of a barren woman (Edward Westermarch, *Ritual and Belief in Morocco* [London, 1926], 1:73–74).

12. Nahman of Bratzlav, *Sefer haMiddot O Hanhagot Y'sharot* [hereafter *Sefer haMiddot*], s.v. Banim, no. 116, p. 72; cf. *R'fu'a v'Hayyim*, p. 35a.

13. Eliyahu Ba'al Shem, *Toldot Adam* [hereafter title only] (Wilmersdorf, 1808), p. 18a, par. 132.

14. Ibid., p. 136, par. 109. The drawing, of course, is but the widespread magic square whose numbers total thirty-four when added up in any direction. In Arabic numerals:

4	14	15	1
9	7	6	12
5	11	10	8
16	2	3	13

15. Ibid., p. 18b, par. 134.

16. *Sefer haMiddot*, no. 81; ibid., s.v. Herayon, no. 2. Belief in the fertilizing power of iron is expressed in the old Muslim tradition that the female friends of Amina, the mother of

Muhammad, who had ceased having children, suggested that she tie pieces of iron on her arms and neck (Aloys Sprenger, *Mohammad* [Hamburg, 1889], 1:142).

17. *Toldot Adam*, p. 22b, par. 156.

18. *Mar' e haY' ladim*, p. 79a, quoting "a manuscript book from Assyria and Babylon."

19. Gen. 30:14ff.

20. Josephus Flavius, *Antiquities of the Jews* 1:19:8.

21. Much has been written about the mandrake: e.g., Angelo de Gubernatis, *Mythologie des plantes* (Paris, 1878–82), 2:213ff.; Hartland, *Primitive Paternity*, 1:44–47, and *Perseus*, 1:154–55; J. Rendel Harris, *Ascent of Olympus* (Rylands Lectures, 1917), pp. 107ff.; Sir James George Frazer, *Folk-Lore in the Old Testament* (London, 1919), 2:372–97; Warren R. Dawson, in *American Druggist* (August–Dec. 1925); Immanuel Löw, *Die Flora der Juden* (Vienna, 1923–34), 3:363–68; Ploss, 2:333ff.; *HWDA*, 1:312–24; M. M. Banks, in *Folk-Lore* 43 (1932):429–30; C. J. Thompson, *The Mystic Mandrake* (London, 1934); Patai, *Adam va' Adama*, 1:216–20. As to the derivation of the name *dudaim*, see Francis Brown, S. R. Driver, and Charles A. Briggs, *A Hebrew and English Lexicon of the Old Testament* (Boston and New York, 1906), pp. 187, 188.

22. The Sephardi Jews are the descendants of the Jews exiled from Spain and Portugal in the fifteenth century; see Cynthia Crews, in *Folk-Lore* 43 (1932):193ff.

23. Oral communication from Yosef M'yuḥas of Jerusalem. Cf. *Mar' e haY' ladim*, pp. 31a–b; *R'fu' a v' Ḥayyim* (Jerusalem, 1872?), p. 35a.

24. Henry Maundrell, *A Journey from Aleppo to Jerusalem* (Perth, 1800), p. 96, as quoted by Frazer, *Folk-Lore in the Old Testament*, 2:374.

25. Cf. M. Zobel, *Das Jahr des Juden* (Berlin, 1936), p. 116.

26. The letters of the Hebrew alphabet have numerical values and are used as ciphers: *alef* = 1, *bet* = 2, etc. The total numerical value of the letters of the word *'aravah* (willow) equals that of the word *zera'* (seed, progeny). This method of correlating words by means of their numerical equation, called *gimatria* in Hebrew, has occupied an important place in Jewish religious methodology from talmudic times to the latest exegetic authorities. The passage above is quoted from *Ta'ame Minhagim* (Lwow, 1906–7), 2:41b.

27. Ploss, 2:299–300; O. Hovorka and A. Kronfeld, *Vergleichende Volksmedizin* [hereafter Hovorka-Kronfeld], 2 vols. (Stuttgart, 1908–9), 2:514. Thus also according to a sixteenth-century Jewish authority, Tuvya Katz, *Ma'ase Tuvya* (Kraków, 1908), p. 119d.

28. See Raphael Patai, "The 'Control of Rain' in Ancient Palestine," *HUCA* 14 (1939):276–77, where evidence is adduced to show that the Lulav is the Jewish counterpart of the Lebensrute or the Erntestrauss. See also Patai, *Adam va' Adama*, 2:172.

29. *Sefer haMiddot*, s.v. Banim, nos. 59, 137.

30. This book was put at my disposal by Ḥakham Eliyahu Ma'aravi of Damascus.

31. Ruth 4:13.

32. "Sefer S'gullot v'Ḥiddot," manuscript, p. 70b.

33. E.g., in ancient Assyria: F. Delitzsch, *Assyrisches Handwörterbuch* (Leipzig, 1896), p. 670; in ancient Egypt: Adolf Erman, *The Literature of the Ancient Egyptians*, trans. A. M. Blackman (London, 1927), pp. 159ff.; in ancient Rome: Pliny, *Historia Naturalis* 16.95, 25.24; among the Finns: *Kalevala* 50.103–4, 161–62; in France: Paul Sebillot, *Le Folk-lore de France* (Paris, 1904–7), 3:233, 528; in the lands of the Ottoman Empire: Bernhard Stern, *Medizin, Aberglaube, und Geschlechtsleben in der Türkei* (Berlin, 1903), 2:288; in Morocco: Westermarck, *Ritual and Belief*, 1:291, 325, etc. See also Gubernatis, *Mythologie des plantes*, 1:166–67; 2:181–82; Hartland, *Perseus*, 1:76ff., 88–89; and *Primitive Paternity*, 1:56, 32ff.; Hovorka-Kronfeld, 2:513ff.; Sir James George Frazer, *The Golden Bough*, 3d. ed., 12 vols. (London, 1911–20), 2:51, 5:96, 262; Bertel Nyberg, *Kind und Erde* (Helsingfors, 1931), p. 214; *HWDA*, 2:810; Stith Thompson, *Motif-Index of Folk Literature*, 6 vols. (Bloomington, Ind., 1955–58), 5:302.

34. Alpina officinarum Hanse, Rhizoma Galangae; cf. Löw, *Flora*, 3:497.

35. Apparently stands for the biblical *mor ul' vona* = myrrh and frankincense (Cant. 3:6), rendered erroneously *mor l' vana* = white myrrh.

36. *Toldot Adam*, p. 14a, no. 110.
37. Ibid., p. 22b, no. 157.
38. Ibid., p. 17b, no. 127.
39. Ibid., p. 22b, no. 157. Birch juice is drunk for the same purpose by barren women among the Czechs in Bohemia (Hovorka-Kronfeld, 2:515).
40. "Sefer S'gullot v'Hiddot," p. 74b.
41. E.g., the Maori: Frazer, *Golden Bough*, 1:182; cf. ibid., 2:56 (the Hinau tree); the Kara-Kirgiz: Hartland, *Primitive Paternity*, 1:113; and *Perseus*, 1:173; in Morocco: Westermarck, *Ritual and Belief*, 1:77, 202; 2:190–91; among the Hungarians: Hartland, *Primitive Paternity*, 1:40, 73; Hovorka-Kronfeld, 1:269, etc. Cf. also Ploss, 2:331ff.
42. *Mar'e haY'ladim*, p. 81a, quoting "a manuscript."
43. Ibid., p. 35a. A similar Jewish charm is quoted by M. Gaster, "Birth, Jewish," *ERE*, 2:656; see also p. 658.
44. Ammi (*umbelleceae*), cf. Löw, *Flora*, 3:420ff.
45. Y'huda heHasid lived in the eleventh to twelfth centuries.
46. Katz, *Ma'ase Tuvya*, p. 121d.
47. *Toldot Adam*, p. 22b, no. 157.
48. *Urtica urens L.* (stinging nettle) is believed by several peoples to bring about conception (Hovorka-Kronfeld, 1:89; 2:514).
49. *Toldot Adam*, p. 3b, no. 3. As to the *urtica* and *buglosa*, see Löw, *Flora*, 1:293, 296; 3:478–79; 4:170, 173, 481.
50. *Toldot Adam*, p. 7a, no. 59.
51. Ibid., p. 4a, no. 10.
52. Perhaps *inula*; see Löw, *Flora*, 1:421–22.
53. Perhaps *passerina*; see ibid., 2:408.
54. *Toldot Adam*, p. 4a, no. 10.
55. *Secale cornutum*, ergot, *Mutterkorn*; see Löw, *Flora*, 1:40. Among other peoples, it is used as an abortive (Hovorka-Kronfeld, 1:33, 169, 317).
56. Seems to be a misprint for *pigum*, i.e., *ruta graveolens L.*: see Löw, *Flora*, 3:317.
57. *Toldot Adam*, p. 17b, no. 128.
58. "Sefer S'gullot v'Hiddot," pp. 75a–76a.
59. Moshe Reischer, *Sefer Sha'are Y'rushalayim* (Warsaw, 1879), pp. 91–92. This custom also is referred to in the journal *Am Urquell*, vol. 5, p. 225; Stern, *Medizin*, 2:268; Hartland, *Primitive Paternity*, 1:67.
60. "Sefer S'gullot v'Hiddot," p. 67b, quoting a "manuscript book by Rabbi Nathan Omri of blessed memory." Although Celsus counts the *ruta* among the exciting substances, it has acquired among several peoples the reputation of an abortive when taken internally (Hovorka-Kronfeld, 1:171, 356–57).
61. Oral communication from a Moroccan Jewish woman in Jerusalem.
62. *Mar'e haY'ladim*, p. 35a.
63. Ibid., p. 36b, quoting "a manuscript book."
64. Oral communication from a Moroccan Jewish woman in Jerusalem.
65. *Mar'e haY'ladim*, p. 35b. Cumin is used externally by barren women in western Bohemia (Hovorka-Kronfeld, 2:515).
66. *Mar'e haY'ladim*, p. 35a–b, quoting an "Ashkenazi book of medicines and charms."
67. The reference is to the seven days following the cessation of the menstrual flow. After these days of cleansing the woman goes to the ritual bath, and only thereafter is she considered purified and allowed intercourse with her husband.
68. "Sefer S'gullot v'Hiddot," p. 75a. It may be mentioned in passing that in talmudic times garlic was considered efficacious for increasing semen; see B. Yoma 18a.
69. Ploss, 2:312; Hovorka-Kronfeld, 2:419, 514.
70. F. Eckstein, "Brot in Liebeszauber," *ARW* 25 (1927):334–35; Robert Eisler, "Der Fisch als Sexualsymbol," *Imago* 3 (1914):165–96; Angelo de Gubernatis, *Die Tiere in der indogermanischen Mythologie* (Leipzig, 1874), pp. 193–94.

71. Sebillot, *Folk-lore*, 3:353; Hartland, *Perseus*, 1:71ff., and *Primitive Paternity*, 1:7ff.; R. Köhler, *Kleinere Schriften* (Weimar, 1898; Berlin, 1900), 1:179, 387; Thompson, *Motif-Index*, T 511.5.1.

72. Hartland, *Perseus*, 1:155, and *Primitive Paternity*, 1:48ff., 51.

73. Eijub Abela, "Beiträge . . . ," *ZDPV* 7 (1884):115, no. 226.

74. Gen. 48:16.

75. Patai, *Adam va'Adama*, 1:283.

76. *Yalqut R'uveni*, Ps. 72, par. 806.

77. Otto Waser, "Über die äussere Erscheinung der Seele . . . ," *ARW* 16 (1913):358; G. A. van den Bergh van Eysinga, "Altchristliches und Orientalisches," *ZDMG* 60 (1906): 210–12; Wanda V. Bartels, "Die Reihenfolge der Buchstaben im Alphabet," ibid. 69 (1915):55; Max Grunwald, "Zur Vorgeschichte des Sukkothrituals," *Jahrbuch für jüdische Volkskunde* 1 (1923):461.

78. Num. 11:5.

79. B. Yoma 75a.

80. Rashi ad B. Yoma 75a.

81. Rashi ad Job 3:7.

82. B. 'Avoda Zara 29a; see also B. Berakhot 40a and 57b, speaking of the beneficial influence on the health and growth of the body of eating small fish.

83. *Toldot Adam*, p. 35a; Z'kharya ben Ya'aqov Simner, *Sefer Z'khira* [hereafter title only] (Wilmersdorf, 1729), pp. 27b, 54a; Binyamin Binesh Ba'al Shem, *Sefer Amtaḥat Binyamin* [hereafter title only] (Wilmersdorf, 1716), p. 19a; *Mar'e haY'ladim*, p. 15a; cf. also Max Grunwald, "Aus Hausapotheke und Hexenküche," *Jahrbuch für jüdische Volkskunde* 1 (1923):206.

84. *Toldot Adam*, p. 7a, no. 57.

85. Gaster, "Birth, Jewish," p. 656.

86. Oral communication from a Moroccan Jewish woman in Jerusalem. On eating fish for pregnancy, see also Max Grunwald, "Aus Hausapotheke und Hexenkünde," *Mitteilungen zur jüdischen Volkskunde*, no. 1 (1900), p. 56, no. 173.

87. *Toldot Adam*, p. 3b, no. 5.

88. B. Berakhot 57a.

89. Hartland, *Primitive Paternity*, 1:52ff.; cf. *Mélusine*, vol. 7, p. 270.

90. *Toldot Adam*, p. 4a, no. 12; *Mar'e haY'ladim*, pp. 34b, 35b.

91. *Mar'e haY'ladim*, p. 35a, quoting *Sefer R'fu'a v'Ḥayyim*; cf. ibid., p. 75a.

92. *Mar'e haY'ladim*, p. 35a, quoting "manuscript books from Assyria and Babylonia"; cf. "Sefer S'gullot v'Ḥiddot," p. 74b.

93. Hartland, *Perseus*, 1:168.

94. *Mar'e haY'ladim*, p. 34b; *Toldot Adam*, p. 9a, no. 81. The gall of a raven is used by women in Upper Egypt as an aphrodisiac, and, it would seem, as a charm against barrenness (Ploss, 2:311).

95. *Mar'e haY'ladim*, p. 35b.

96. "Sefer S'gullot v'Ḥiddot," p. 75a. Another version of this charm was published by Gaster, "Birth, Jewish," p. 656.

97. Westermarck, *Ritual and Belief*, 2:331–32.

98. *Toldot Adam*, p. 5b, no. 31, in the name of "Aris the physician"; cf. *Mar'e haY'ladim*, p. 34b.

99. *Mar'e haY'ladim*, p. 35a, quoting "a manuscript book."

100. "Sefer S'gullot v'Ḥiddot," p. 75a.

101. Hartland, *Primitive Paternity*, 1:55–56.

102. *Mar'e haY'ladim*, p. 35a.

103. Hartland, *Primitive Paternity*, 1:55–56; 177–78.

104. *Toldot Adam*, p. 17b, no. 129.

105. Y'huda Elzet (J. L. Zlotnick), "MiMinhage Yisrael," *R'shumot* 1 (1918):363.

106. A. Goodrich-Freer, in *Folk-Lore* 15 (1904):186; cf. R. Campbell Thompson, *Semitic Magic* (London, 1908), pp. 102–3.

107. Cf., e.g., Westermarck, *Ritual and Belief*, 1:585; Hartland, *Primitive Paternity*, 1:57, 112; and *Perseus*, 1:114, 157–58; Ploss, 2:315, 334; T. Canaan, *Aberglaube und Volksmedizin im Lande der Bibel* (Hamburg, 1914), 1:116; Hovorka-Kronfeld, 2:516.
108. Judg. 13:3.
109. Hayyim Meir Horowitz, *Tosefta 'Atiqta* (Frankfurt a. M., 1890), pt. 5, p. 19 (Baraita diMassekhet Nidda).
110. *Toldot Adam*, p. 3b, no. 2. Another charm recommends the same use of a fox skin for nine days (Gaster, "Birth, Jewish," p. 656).
111. *Toldot Adam*, p. 3a, no. 1. Nearer to a belief in sympathetic magic is the Transylvanian Saxons' attribution of fertilizing powers to the generative organs of the fox (Hartland, *Perseus*, 1:157).
112. *Mar'e haY'ladim*, p. 35a, quoting "a manuscript book from the cities of India."
113. Oral communication from Ben-Zion Taragan of Alexandria.
114. *Mar'e haY'ladim*, p. 34b.
115. *Toldot Adam*, pp. 2b, no. 6, and 4b, no. 14. Cf. also ibid., p. 11b, no. 96.
116. Hartland, *Perseus*, 1:156; Ploss, 2:313.
117. See n. 26 above.
118. Lev. 12:2.
119. According to Horowitz, *Tosefta 'Atiqta*, pt. 5, p. 19.
120. Cf. Gaster, "Birth, Jewish," p. 656.
121. *Sefer Z'khira*, p. 53b f.; cf. also *Mar'e haY'ladim*, p. 34b.
122. Hartland, *Perseus*, 1:156–57; and *Primitive Paternity*, 1:54–55.
123. "Sefer S'gullot v'Hiddot," p. 75a.
124. Ibid., p. 74a.
125. Gaster, "Birth, Jewish," p. 656.
126. *Mar'e haY'ladim*, p. 35a. Sextus Platonius (330 A.D.) advised the use of hare's blood to facilitate conception (*HWDA*, 2:811).
127. Ploss, 2:311.
128. "Sefer S'gullot v'Hiddot," p. 67a, quoting "a manuscript book of Rav Nathan Omri of blessed memory."
129. Perhaps = *atriplex*; cf. Löw, *Flora*, 4:627, Index, s.v.
130. *Toldot Adam*, p. 3b, no. 5, and p. 3a, no. 1.
131. "Sefer S'gullot v'Hiddot," p. 75a.
132. Gaster, "Birth, Jewish," p. 656.
133. *Toldot Adam*, p. 3, no. 1.
134. Ibid.
135. Ploss, 2:333; not mentioned by Westermarck, *Ritual and Belief*, 2:325–26.
136. Hartland, *Perseus*, 1:156.
137. *Mar'e haY'ladim*, pp. 78a–b.
138. *Toldot Adam*, pp. 35a–b.
139. Gaster, "Birth, Jewish," p. 656.
140. Ploss, 2:313.
141. "Sefer S'gullot v'Hiddot," p. 62a, with the remark, "Copied from an ancient manuscript book."
142. Ibid., p. 74a.
143. Perhaps a euphemism for the privy parts?
144. *Toldot Adam*, p. 4b, no. 13.
145. Gaster, "Birth, Jewish," p. 656.
146. *HWDA*, 2:811. Cow's gall also in Germany (Hovorka-Kronfeld, 2:515).
147. Fennel = *foeniculum capillaceum Gilibert*; cf. Löw, *Flora*, 3:460–61.
148. M. Shabbat 14:3. According to Löw, *Flora*, 1:11, *yo'ezer* = *adiantum capillus Veneris L.*, and thus is not identical with *finilio* = fennel.
149. "Sefer S'gullot v'Hiddot," p. 75a. Horn of a ram pulverized also in Germany (Hovorka-Kronfeld, 2:515).
150. *Mar'e haY'ladim*, p. 35a

151. *Toldot Adam*, pp. 35a–b. Also in other Jewish charms; cf. Gaster, "Birth, Jewish," p. 656. Similarly in ancient Rome and in modern Germany (Hovorka-Kronfeld, 2:515).
152. Approximately corresponding to July-August.
153. *Toldot Adam*, p. 39a.
154. Ibid., p. 4b, no. 15. *Horon* probably stands for *herayon*, pregnancy.
155. *Mar' e haY' ladim*, pp. 34b–35a; cf. *Toldot Adam*, p. 4a, no. 7.
156. Westermarck, *Ritual and Belief*, 2:126; Hovorka-Kronfeld, 2:520; Ploss, 2:311.
157. "Sefer S'gullot v'Hiddot," p. 76a. In Syria barren women were advised to pass under the stomach of an elephant (Abela, "Beiträge," p. 114). Among the Swahili, barren women drink a beverage made of elephant's excrement and various roots (Ploss, 2:312).
158. "Sefer S'gullot v'Hiddot," p. 67b, quoting "a manuscript book of Rav Nathan Omri of blessed memory"; cf. also ibid., p. 74b.
159. *Toldot Adam*, p. 3, no. 1.
160. "Sefer S'gullot v'Hiddot," p. 74b. Bat's blood mixed with ass's milk is drunk by barren women in Danube lands (Ploss, 2:313).
161. *R'fu' a v'Hayyim*, chap. 12, p. 35b.
162. Gaster, "Birth, Jewish," p. 656.
163. "Sefer S'gullot v'Hiddot," p. 74b.
164. *Toldot Adam*, p. 4a, no. 9; *Mar' e haY' ladim*, p. 34b.
165. *Mar' e haY' ladim*, p. 35a.
166. "Sefer S'gullot v'Hiddot," p. 67b, quoting Nathan Omri.
167. *R'fu' a v'Hayyim*, chap. 12, p. 35b.
168. Gaster, "Birth, Jewish," p. 656. For the use of milk by various peoples as a cure for barrenness, see Hartland, *Primitive Paternity*, 1:62, 114; Hovorka-Kronfeld, 2:515, 516, 517.
169. E.g., in Pomerania they used to give a barren woman some milk from a nursing mother as a fertility charm (Hartland, *Primitive Paternity*, 1:70).
170. *Toldot Adam*, p. 35b.
171. Ibid., p. 4a, par. 7; *Mar' e haY' ladim*, p. 15a. According to information supplied by Ben-Zion Taragan of Alexandria, this custom was still practiced in 1942 by Egyptian Jews.
172. *Toldot Adam*, p. 35a. Similarly, in Japan barren women sit in the place where a birth took place shortly before (Hartland, *Primitive Paternity*, 1:113; Ploss, 2:235).
173. Ploss, 2:326ff.
174. Oral communication from Hakham Shim'on Harus of Safed. Among Moroccan tribes there is a belief that women who visit a woman in childbed will absorb some of her *baraka*, "blessed power," and they too will conceive (Westermarck, *Ritual and Belief*, 2:376).
175. *Sefer haMiddot*, s.v. Banim, no. 90.
176. In Olhovitz, Russia, a barren woman was given some water which contained three drops of blood from the child's umbilical cord. Barren women in the Ukraine drank water in which a piece of the umbilical had been soaked. Among the Transylvanian Rumanians a barren woman would eat the dried umbilical and drink some of the blood (Hartland, *Primitive Paternity*, 1:70). Among the natives of Kamchatka, a woman who had given birth and wanted to conceive again soon ate the umbilical of her own child (ibid., 1:71; Hartland, *Perseus*, 1:156; Ploss, 2:312).
177. Gaster, "Birth, Jewish," p. 656.
178. *Mar' e haY' ladim*, p. 18a.
179. Ibid.
180. Ibid., p. 9b, quoting "a manuscript book."
181. Hartland, *Primitive Paternity*, 1:70.
182. In Sicily barren women swallowed a pill made of the dried, powdered placenta (ibid., and Hartland, *Perseus*, 1:162).

183. Hartland, *Primitive Paternity*, 1:70.

184. Oral communication from Mrs. Danon, Tel Aviv. Precisely the same custom was practiced by barren Ruthenian women (Hartland, *Primitive Paternity*, 1:71). Barren Ainu women in Japan sit with uncovered buttocks on the placenta immediately after it was ejected from the womb. Barren Maori women stand with their legs spread over the placenta (Ploss, 2:235). In Bessarabia, the barren women bathed in water containing a placenta (ibid.).

185. Gaster, "Birth, Jewish," p. 656.

186. *Mar'e haY'ladim*, p. 18a. The blood which flows from the mother's body in childbirth also is a charm for pregnancy. In Poland and Hungary, barren women use a flask to collect such blood from a woman giving birth for the first time; they drink the blood mixed with brandy (Hartland, *Primitive Paternity*, 1:70; *Perseus*, 1:162).

187. E.g., among the Masai of East Africa, many women, and especially the barren ones, attend the boys' circumcision ritual, where the boys pelt them with fresh cow dung to make them fertile. Among the neighboring Nandi, the very presence of a barren woman at the circumcision ceremony is considered sufficient to give her fertility (Hartland, *Primitive Paternity*, 1:110; Ploss, 2:328).

188. Oral communication from Ḥakham Shim'on Harus of Safed, Mrs. Danon of Tel Aviv, and Yosef M'yuḥas of Jerusalem.

189. Written communication from Ben-Zion Taragan of Alexandria.

190. Oral communication from Rabbi David Prato, Tel Aviv (later chief rabbi of Rome).

191. Erich Brauer, *Ethnologie der jemenitischen Juden* (Heidelberg, 1934), p. 194.

192. Hartland, *Primitive Paternity*, 1:71.

193. *Mar'e haY'ladim*, p. 78b.

194. Ibid.; cf. also p. 35b.

195. Brauer, *Ethnologie*, p. 194.

196. Efrayim HaR'uveni, "Tzimḥe Bosem baMinhagim haDatiyyim (Fragrant Plants in Religious Customs)," *Tziyyon* [Jerusalem] 4 (1930):102–3.

197. Elzet, "MiMinhage Yisrael," p. 363.

198. Sefer haMiddot, s.v. Herayon and Mohel.

199. *R'fu'a v'Ḥayyim*, chap. 12, p. 35b.

200. Ibid.

201. Ya'aqov Moshe Toledano, *Yam haGadol* (Cairo, 1931), p. 81, par. 53. I am indebted to Ḥakham Shim'on Harus of Safed for having referred me to this source.

202. In India the barren women wash the loincloth of a holy man and then drink the water (Hartland, *Perseus*, 1:161). In Morocco, when a band of the Ḥamādsha, the disciples of Sidi 'Ali ben Ḥamdūsh, perform one of their usual rites and cut their foreheads with axes, the spectators give them lumps of sugar or pieces of bread to dip in their blood or to spit on. The sugar or bread, thus endowed with the holy man's *baraka*, is then eaten by the sick or by barren women. A barren woman also might give her girdle to the head of an 'Esawa band, who fumigates it with benzoin and spits on it. The other members of the company spit on the girdle, and the head of the group gives the woman some milk of which he himself has drunk a little and upon which he and the others have blown (Westermarck, *Ritual and Belief*, 1:203).

203. Oral communication from a Moroccan woman in Jerusalem.

204. HaR'uveni, in *Zion*, p. 102.

205. Oral communication from Rabbi David Prato in Tel Aviv. In Egypt barren Muslim women pass under the stone slab on which the bodies of criminals executed by the sword have been washed, and then wash their own faces in the dirty water. Others step over the body of a man whose head has been cut off (Edward W. Lane, *Manners and Customs of the Modern Egyptians*, Everyman's Library [London, n.d.], pp. 264–65). In Syria a barren woman is advised to stand beneath the body of a man hanged on a tree (Abela, "Beiträge," p. 114). In India barren women "bathe underneath a person who has been hanged" (Theodor Zachariae, "Ein jüdischer Hochzeitsbrauch," *Wiener Zeitschrift für*

die Kunde des Morgenlandes 20 [1906]:296, n. 2). In Morocco a similar act is performed for precisely the opposite purpose: among the Ait Sadden, a woman who wants to become sterile remains at the grave after a man is buried and steps over it three times in the same direction (Westermarck, *Ritual and Belief*, 2:557).

206. Oral communication from Mr. Sasson and Mr. Zekharia of Baghdad.

207. Oral communication from Ḥakham Shim'on Harus of Safed. Barren women in the North American Algonquin tribe crowd around the dying so that the departing soul will enter their bodies and fertilize them (Hartland, *Perseus*, 1:164).

208. Among the South Slavs, barren women make a pilgrimage to the tomb of a woman who died while pregnant, bite off with their teeth a little grass from the grave, call out the dead woman's name, and ask her to endow them with offspring. Then they take earth from the grave and wear it under their girdles (Ploss, 2:328; Frazer, *Golden Bough*, 5:96). Among the Transylvanian gypsies, barren women eat some of the grass which grows on the grave of a woman who died while pregnant (Ploss, 2:328). In North European countries, they put a little earth on the dress of a barren woman when a body is being buried, and then step on the dress, saying, "You too will bring forth a shoot." This process is repeated three times (Nyberg, *Kind und Erde*, p. 259).

209. Ploss, 2:329ff.; *ERE*, 10:242. The saint most famous for his power to give fertility to barren women in the Middle East is Saint George, who has many tombs in various places. In Northern Syria barren women make the pilgrimage to his tomb in Qal'at al-Ḥusayn (S. I. Curtis, *Primitive Semitic Religion Today* [Chicago, 1902], pp. 118ff.). In Morocco, barren women of the Ait Warain tribe go on pilgrimage to the tomb of Sidi 'Esa and immerse themselves in the hot spring next to it. In Andjra, Morocco, they go to the tomb of Mulai 'Abdsslam, and if they bear a son they call him 'Abdsslam. Those from near Ceuta in Morocco go to the tomb of Sidi Nbarak and call the boy by his name. In Fez and other places they tie pieces of their dresses or a few hairs from their heads to the door handle of a holy place in order to be cured of a disease or to become pregnant (Westermarck, *Ritual and Belief*, 1:85, 553–54; 2:404). On Muslim saints as givers of fertility in India, see Frazer, *Golden Bough*, 5:78.

210. *Sefer haMiddot* s.v. Herayon, no. 2, p. 63. Cf. *Ta'ame Minhagim*, 2:42a.

211. Erich Brauer, "Bräuche der Kurdischen Juden," *Almanach des Schocken Verlags 5699* (Berlin, 1938–39), pp. 105–6.

212. Brauer, *Ethnologie*, p. 383; Erich Brauer, "Die Frau bei den südarabischen Juden," *Zeitschrift für Sexualwissenschaft und Sexualpolitic*, 18, no. 3 (1931):171.

213. Samuel Daiches, *Babylonian Oil Magic in the Talmud and in the Later Jewish Literature* (London, 1913), p. 26 (Codex Gaster 128). In West European countries barren women drink water from a well or wash themselves in a spring which flows from the burial place of a Christian saint, from other holy places such as a church, or from a source consecrated to a saint. In India, barren women visit temples which are famous for healing barrenness and there eat some fruit or sweets (Hartland, *Perseus*, 1:159–60; *Primitive Paternity*, 1:34, 64). In northern Palestine, next to the so-called Bath of Solomon, there is a place where hot air rises from the ground, and barren women go there and let the hot air envelop their bodies, believing that the saint buried there thus will make them fertile (Curtiss, *Primitive Semitic Religion Today*, pp. 116–17).

214. *Sefer haMiddot*, s.v. Banim, no. 131. Cf. *Abi'a Ḥiddot* (Livorno, 1879), p. 68b.

215. Thus in ancient Greece the dead were believed to rise from their graves as snakes and eat the food left there for them; see Jane E. Harrison, *Prolegomena to the Study of Greek Religion* (Cambridge, 1909), pp. 326ff.; Sam Wide, "Grabesspende und Toten-schlange," *ARW* 12 (1909):221–23; Erich Kuester, *Die Schlange in der griechischen Kunst und Religion*, Religionsgeschichtliche Versuche und Vorarbeiten 13, no. 2 (Giessen, 1913), pp. 40ff. A typical example of the form these ideas took in the Roman world is Aeneas' uncertainty, when he sees a snake emerge from his father's tomb and taste the food he has offered, whether it is the "genius" of the place or a servant of his father in the world of the dead (Virgil, *Aeneid* 5.84). Among primitive peoples one finds

the same belief in a more tangible form. Among the Zulu: the tribal chieftain becomes a poisonous snake after his death; common men or women become thin brown snakes; an old woman becomes a small black snake. They show great respect for these snakes when visiting the kraal, praise them, and offer them gifts. Among the Bantu tribes: a dead person can become any one of several kinds of animal, but most commonly he becomes a snake. Among the Moki (Hopi) of North America: sorcerers occasionally come out of their graves in the shape of big snakes. Often these snakes can be seen emerging wrapped in the same leaves as those which wrapped the body at burial (Hartland, *Primitive Paternity*, 1:169, 185). All over Africa, as well as elsewhere, the belief is found that the souls of the dead turn into snakes, and for this reason snakes are often taken care of and given gifts of food, especially milk (Frazer, *Golden Bough*, 5:82ff.). On the psychological basis of the equation of the dead and snakes, see Leo Frobenius, *Weltanschauung der Naturvölker* (Berlin, 1898), pp. 55ff.; Carl Meinhof, "Die afrikanischen Religionen," *ARW* 14 (1911):476; Wilhelm Wundt, *Völkerpsychologie* (Stuttgart, 1914–21), 4:145ff.; Kuester, *Die Schlange*, pp. 63ff.

216. B. Bab. Qam. 16a. Cf. Y. Shab. 3b mid. A mouse turns into worms after its death (M. Ḥul. 9:10; B. Ḥul. 127a). Cf. Patai, *Adam va'Adama*, 1:72 and n. 1, ibid.
217. B. Bab. Qam. 117a–b.
218. B. Bab. Metz. 84b.
219. Ibid. 85a.
220. Y. Ta'an 69a top. Cf. the comment of Immanuel Löw in Julius Preuss, *Biblisch-Talmudische Medizin* (Berlin, 1911), p. 124.
221. Ya'aqov Sapir, *Even Sapir* (Lyck, 1866), 1:82a.
222. Ari Ibn-Zaḥav, *B'Sod 'Anlyye haKotel* (Tel Aviv, 1942), pp. 40ff. Similarly, ancient Roman tradition holds that the sacred snake of Aesculapius came of its own accord from Epidaurus to Rome, swam across the Tiber to the island which is in the middle of the river, and chose there a place for its temple (Ludwig Preller, *Römische Mythologie*, 3d ed., 2 vols. (Berlin, 1883), 2:241ff.
223. In ancient Greece barren women made pilgrimages to the temple of Aesculapius (apparently the temple originally was the tomb of the god) and slept upon the sacred ground in the belief that the god would appear in their dreams in the shape of a snake and beget children upon them (Frazer, *Golden Bough*, 5:90; cf. pp. 86ff.; Kuester, *Die Schlange*, pp. 150ff.). On Aesculapius, the god of medicine, whose image was commingled with that of the snake (ibid., pp. 233–37, and sources cited in the notes there). In the mysteries of Sabazios the snake appeared as the incarnation of that god, the giver of fertility. The women carried out a sacred marriage with the god either by letting a live snake slither along their naked bodies under their dresses, or by doing the same with a golden image of a snake, believing that the snake would penetrate their bodies through the vagina (ibid., pp. 148ff.). In West Africa, certain sacred prostitutes were considered to be the wives of the python god. It is generally assumed that there is a close connection between the fertility of the soil and the marriage of these women to the snake god. In British East Africa, weddings are celebrated several times a year between women and the snake god (Frazer, *Golden Bough*, 2:149ff.; 5:66ff.). Similar customs are found in India (ibid., 2:149).
224. Greek legends tell of women who were impregnated by copulating with snakes (Kuester, *Die Schlange*, p. 151, n. 1). Among the Danubian Gypsies, barren women carry out the following rite: in the week of Easter or Pentecost they touch a snake, spit on it twice, sprinkle it with their menstrual blood, and say, "Grow quickly, O snake, so that thereby I should get a child. I am now as thin as you are, and therefore I have no rest. Snake, snake, crawl away from here, and when I become pregnant I shall give you a hat so that the poison of your tongue should increase." These women also wear on their naked bodies as a fertility charm a child's hat in which "snake powder" is wrapped (Hartland, *Perseus*, 1:97, 116; Ploss, 2:334). Among the Awlad Bu'aziz in Morocco, a woman who wants to bear a male child swallows the heart of a snake. Westermarck remarks that the wife of his

own landlord in Morocco had swallowed the hearts of three snakes, one after the other (*Ritual and Belief*, 2:352). In the town of Ḥama in Syria, a barren woman ties a snake's skin around her hips (J. P. van Kasteren, "Aus dem Buche der Weiber," *ZDPV* 18 [1895]:47).

Folk legend complements the picture given by these customs. A Russian folktale tells of the Satan snake who comes every night to the young widow in the form of her dead husband and sleeps with her until morning. In another Russian tale the snake is the husband of a princess. A widespread folktale motif is the one in which the daughter, or the youngest daughter, agrees to marry a snake, which subsequently turns into a handsome youth (Angelo de Gubernatis, *Zoological Mythology*, 2 vols. [London, 1872]). Data about the snake in fertility magic also can be found in Eckstein, "Brot im Liebeszauber," p. 335. At Salli in Morocco, a story is told about a woman whose husband forced her to eat a snake cut into seven pieces, as a result of which seven sons were born to her, each of whom became a holy man (Westermarck, *Ritual and Belief*, 2:353). In many folktales a worm appears as a source of fertility: the woman swallows it in water or in a fruit and becomes pregnant (Hartland, *Perseus*, 1:97, 116; *Primitive Paternity*, 1:9ff.; Thompson, *Motif-Index* T 511.5.2. Many peoples belive that menstruation is caused by the bite of a snake (Ernest Crawley, *The Mystic Rose*, 2 vols. [New York, 1927], 1:231–32; 2:17, 133. For additional data on the phallic nature of the snake among various peoples, see Stern, *Medizin*, 2:140; Kuester, *Die Schlange*, pp. 149–50; Frazer, *Golden Bough*, 5:81–82; *ERE*, 2:406; *HWDA*, 7:1127–28, 1137, 1184.

225. B. Shab. 110a. Cf. Louis Ginzberg, *Legends of the Jews* (Philadelphia, 1947), 5:153; Ludwig Blau, *Altjüdisches Zauberwesen* (Strassbourg, 1898), pp. 76–77.

226. Allusion to womankind, created out of the rib of Adam (Gen. 2:21–22).

227. 4 Macc. 18:7–8.

228. Tos. Sota 4:17, ed. Zuckermandel, p. 301.

229. Pirqe R. Eliezer, chap. 21, and numerous other talmudic and midrashic sources (cf. Robert Graves and Raphael Patai, *Hebrew Myths* [New York, 1964], chap. 14a).

230. Cf. Patai, *Adam va' Adama*, 1:204–5.

231. Oral communication from a Moroccan Jewish woman in Jerusalem.

232. These are the names of the four rivers of Paradise (Gen. 2:10–14).

233. I cannot explain the meaning of these five words.

234. *Mar' e haY' ladim*, p. 79a, quoting "a manuscript book from Assyria and Babylonia."

235. Reischer, *Sefer Sha'are Y'rushalayim*, p. 91; cf. Stern, *Medizin*, 2:289.

236. *Toldot Adam*, p. 6b, no. 44.

237. Ezek. 44:2, with the omission of a few words.

238. *Mar' e haY' ladim*, p. 105b, quoting "a Babylonian manuscript book."

239. Reischer, *Sefer Sha'are Y'rushalayim*, p. 91; cf. Stern, *Medizin*, 2:289; "Sefer S'gullot v'Ḥiddot," p. 71a, quoting "an ancient manuscript book."

240. Luncz, *Y'rushalayim*, 1:27.

241. Cf. Patai, *Adam va' Adama*, 2:28ff.

242. Baḥya ben Asher on Exod. 28:17. Cf. *Sefer Z'khira*, p. 53b; *Amtaḥat Binyamin*, p. 19a; *Mar' e haY' ladim*, p. 16a, quoting "manuscript books from Assyria and Egypt."

243. *Toldot Adam*, p. 15b, no. 118. On coral, see also *Mar' e haY' ladim*, p. 65a; *Abi'a Ḥiddot*, p. 67b; Ploss, 2:505 (diamond as a charm against miscarriage among the ancient Germans).

244. Brauer, *Ethnologie*, p. 181.

245. *Sefer Z'khira*, p. 53b. In Samoa the pregnant women drink a potion made of wild pepper and wild orange leaves (Ploss, 2:505).

246. "S'gullot v'Ḥiddot," p. 67b, quoting "manuscript books from Assyria and Egypt"; *Abi'a Ḥiddot*, p. 67b.

247. *Sefer Z'khira*, p. 53b; *Amtaḥat Binyamin*, p. 19a.

248. *Mar' e haY' ladim*, p. 16a.

249. *Sefer Z'khira*, p. 53b; *Amtaḥat Binyamin*, p. 19a; *Mar' e haY' ladim*, p. 16a, quoting *Sefer b'Derekh Y'shara*.

250. *Mar'e haY'ladim*, p. 78a, quoting *Y'mallet Nafsho*; cf. ibid., p. 16a.
251. *Mar'e haY'ladim*, p. 16a, quoting "a manuscript book by R. Aharon Barazani."
252. Ibid.
253. Ibid., pp. 16bff., and 69a, quoting various sources. Cf. *Abi'a Ḥiddot*, p. 67a. *Amtaḥat Binyamin* recommends the milk of a she-ass (p. 19a). The charm with the eggshell also is found in *Sefer Z'khira*, p. 53a, and a somewhat different version in *Amtaḥat Binyamin*, p. 19a.
254. Oral communication from a Moroccan Jewish woman in Jerusalem.
255. *Mar'e haY'ladim*, p. 16a, quoting "the book of R. Avraham Yaloz."
256. Cf. Patai, *Adam va'Adama*, 1:272–73.
257. *Sefer haMiddot*, s.v. Banim, no. 60; s.v. Mappelet. Cf. *Ta'ame Minhagim*, 2:42a; *Abi'a Ḥiddot*, p. 68b.
258. Ḥayyim Meir Horowitz, *Tosefta 'Atiqta* (Frankfurt a. M., 1890), part 5, p. 28.
259. Cf. Stern, *Medizin*, 2:289; Ploss, 2:302.
260. Cf. the burial of diseases in the earth by burying the nail clippings and the hair of a sick person, practiced, e.g., in Franconia (A. Wuttke, *Der deutsche Volksaberglaube* (Berlin, 1900), p. 331, par. 492ff.
261. Gaster, "Birth, Jewish," p. 656.
262. Ibid., p. 657.
263. In the Orenburg district of Russia, where it is customary to bury the afterbirth in the ground, they believe that if the afterbirth is unearthed and the umbilical cord turned up, the woman will not bear again; if they turn it down, she will conceive again (Ploss, 2:849–50).
264. In a Serbian custom the woman takes several burning embers and extinguishes them in the bath water, saying, "When these embers burn again, then shall I bear a child." If later she wants to become pregnant, she throws the coals into fire (Ploss, 2:301). The Arabs of Palestine dip some cotton wool into the woman's menstrual blood or into the birth blood and bury or burn it to prevent conception (Canaan, *Aberglaube und Volksmedizin*, p. 25). In Galicia the woman collects her menstrual blood in cotton wool, carries it on her body for nine days and nine nights, and then buries it in the earth, saying "I bury you, not for a year, but for ever" (Ploss, 2:302). All the details of this magical procedure, which also are found elsewhere, are clear: the piece of cotton soaked with blood represents the child; the nine days and nine nights stand for the nine months of pregnancy; the burial of the cotton symbolizes the burial of the child and the prevention of pregnancy (Ploss, 2:304).
265. Gaster, "Birth, Jewish," p. 656.
266. Rashi ad B. Sota 22a. The closing of a woman's womb also can be brought about, according to Serbian and Bosnian belief, by closing a door; this therefore can serve as a contraceptive act (Ploss, 2:301). Among various peoples women who do not want to become pregnant throw apples, stones, pegs, seeds, poppies, and embers into a well (ibid., p. 300; B. Kahle, "Noch einmal Kind und Korn," *ARW* 11 [1908]:411; see also B. Kahle, "Aus schwedischem Volkglauben," *Zeitschrift des Vereins für Volkskunde* 10 [1900]: 197). On contraception as a folktale motif, see Thompson, *Motif-Index* T.572.
267. Tos.Yeb. 8:4, ed. Zuckermandel, p. 249.
268. B. Shab. 110a, according to Rashi ibid. Cf. Preuss, *Biblisch-Talmudishe Medizin*, p. 439.
269. *HWDA*, 2:812–13.
270. B. Yeb. 65b.
271. Gen. Rab. 23:3, ed. Theodor-Albeck, p. 222.
272. B. Yeb. 12b. Cf. Tos. Nidda 2:6, p. 642; Preuss, *Biblisch-Talmudische Medizin*, p. 479.
273. *Yalqut Shim'oni* 1, par. 845, quoting *Midrash Esfa*.
274. Oral communication from a Moroccan Jewish woman in Jerusalem.
275. *Mar'e haY'ladim*, p. 29a, quoting "a Babylonian [i.e., Iraqi] manuscript book."
276. Among peoples, e.g., in India, Kamchatka, Egypt, Sudan, British Columbia, South Slavic lands, Hungary (among the Gypsies), barren women swallow bugs, spiders, bees, and so on for precisely the opposite purpose, to conceive (Hartland, *Primitive Paternity*,

1:47ff.) The bee symbolizes human beings in the legends of various peoples (Gubernatis, *Zoological Mythology*).

277. Oral communication from a Moroccan Jewish woman in Jerusalem. Among the Muslim Moroccans the husband wears such a ring, and if he does not want his wife to become pregnant he turns the stone toward the next finger at the time of intercourse (Westermarck, *Ritual and Belief*, 1:459).

278. As reprinted in *Mar'e haY'ladim*, p. 8b, quoting *Shilte haGibborim*, p. 50b.

279. Oral communication from a Moroccan Jewish woman in Jerusalem. In Esthonia the woman swallows mercury to prevent conception (Ploss, 2:302).

280. *Sefer Z'khira*, p. 54a; cf. *R'fu'a v'Hayyim*, chap. 12, p. 36a. In Mecca, a woman who does not want to become pregnant wears a capsule containing hare's excrement between her breasts (Snouck Hurgronje, *Mecca*, as quoted in Ploss, 2:302).

281. The symbolic significance is clearest in those methods in which an actual lock is used for locking the woman's womb. In Bessarabia: the bride who does not want to become pregnant opens a lock, passes once back and forth between the lock and the key, and then locks the lock. As long as the lock remains locked, so will her womb (*HWDA*, 2:813). A woman also can lock her womb to prevent miscarriage.

282. On all these details, see Raphael Patai, *Man and Temple in Ancient Jewish Myth and Ritual* (Edinburgh, 1947), pp. 140ff.; *Adam va'Adama*, 2:19ff.

283. Cf. Wilhelm Mannhardt, *Wald und Feldkulte*, 2d ed. (Berlin, 1877), p. 56; *HWDA*, 3:413.

284. Cf. Johann C. G. Bodenschatz, *Kirchliche Verfassung der heutigen Juden*, 4 vols. (Erlangen and Coburg, 1748–49), 4:57; J. Bergmann, "Sitten und Sagen," *MGWJ* 74 (1930):166; Löw, *Flora*, 3:306, 311.

285. *Sefer haMiddot*, s.v. S'gulla, no. 32; see also *R'fu'a v'Hayyim*, chap. 12, p. 35a, where this custom is mentioned in connection with the Midrash on the Israelite women in Egypt who delivered "under the apple tree." Cf. *Abi'a Hiddot*, p. 68b.

286. Oral communication from Yosef M'yuhas of Jerusalem.

287. *Sefer Z'khira*, p. 27a; *Amtahat Binyamin*, p. 19a; cf. Grunwald. "Aus Hausapotheke und Hexenküche," *Jahrbuch*, p. 211.

288. *Mar'e haY'ladim*, p. 85b.

289. Ibid., p. 70b; *R'fu'a v'Hayyim*, chap. 9, p. 28a.

290. *Toldot Adam*, p. 6b, no. 47.

291. *Amtahat Binyamin*, p. 19a.

292. Cf. Erich Brauer, *Y'hude Kurdistan* (Jerusalem, 1947), p. 131.

293. *Mar'e haY'ladim* p. 70b; *R'fu'a v'Hayyim*, chap. 9, p. 28a. Cf. *Sefer haMiddot*, s.v. Qishuy leda, no. 1; *Abi'a Hiddot*, 68b.

294. See the sources cited in the preceding note; also a written communication from Ben-Zion Taragan of Alexandria.

295. *Mar'e haY'ladim*, p. 70b.

296. Brauer, *Y'hude Kurdistan*, p. 131.

297. *Mar'e haY'ladim*, 70b; cf. *Sefer haMiddot*, s.v. S'gulla, no. 6. Below we shall encounter this warning again; a similar warning was given by Apollonius of Tiana, who advises that one should enter the room of the woman in labor with a live hare hidden in one's clothes, circumambulate the woman once, and in that moment let the hare go free, lest the womb of the woman come out together with the child (Philostratus, *The Life of Apollonius of Tiana* 3.39, Loeb Classical Library, p. 319).

298. Hulba in Arabic is also the name of a tonic prepared of yellowish grains for a woman in childbed (Hans Wehr, *A Dictionary of Modern Written Arabic* [Wiesbaden, 1961], s.v. Hulba. *Note added in 1980*).

299. Meir Aldabi, *Sh'vile Emuna* [hereafter title only], sig. 4, p. 5.

300. According to Ernst Ochs, *Badisches Wörterbuch* (Lahr, Schwarzwald, 1925–40), s.v. Belsenbaum, this tree is the *Traubenkirsche*, or *prunus padus*. (*Note added in 1980*.)

301. *Toldot Adam*, p. 5b, no. 23.

302. Ibid., p. 6b, no. 42.
303. *Amtaḥat Binyamin*, p. 18a. Cf. n. 297 above.
304. *Sh'vile Emuna*, sig. 4, p. 5.
305. *Sefer Z'khira*, p. 27a; likewise in later books of charms and remedies (Grunwald, "Aus Hausapotheke und Hexenküche," *Jahrbuch*, p. 211, no. 189).
306. *Amtaḥat Binyamin*, p. 19a.
307. Ibid.
308. *Toldot Adam*, p. 6a, no. 46.
309. Ibid. p. 12a, no. 98.
310. *Mar'e haY'ladim*, p. 70b; cf. *R'fu'a v'Ḥayyim*, chap. 9, p. 28a; likewise according to a written communication from Ben-Zion Taragan of Alexandria.
311. *Mar'e haY'ladim*, pp. 70b, 78a, quoting *Sh'vile Emuna*; cf. *R'fu'a v'Ḥayyim*, chap. 9, p. 28a.
312. *Amtaḥat Binyamin*, p. 19a.
313. Oral communication by a Moroccan Jewish woman in Jerusalem.
314. *Sh'vile Emuna*, sig. 4, p. 5.
315. *Sefer Z'khira*, p. 27a; cf. *Amtaḥat Binyamin*, p. 19a; *R'fu'a v'Ḥayyim*; Hartland, *Primitive Paternity*, 1:70.
316. *Sh'vile Emuna*, sig. 4, p. 5.
317. *Toldot Adam*, p. 6a, no. 48.
318. *Amtaḥat Binyamin*, p. 18a.
319. Oral communication from Ḥakham Shim'on Harus of Safed; also *Nifla'ot Ma'asekha*, p 36.
320. *Amtaḥat Binyamin*, p. 19a; *R'fu'a v'Ḥayyim*, chap. 9, p. 28a; *Mar'e haY'ladim*, p. 70b.
321. *Toldot Adam*, pp. 6b, no. 45, 38a–b.
322. Brauer, *Ethnologie*, p. 182.
323. "Sefer S'gullot v'Ḥiddot," p. 68b, quoting "a manuscript book by Rav Natan 'Amadi of blessed memory"; see also n. 276 above.
324. Tos. Shab. 6:4, ed. Zuckermandel, p. 117; cf. A. Marmorstein, *Jahrbuch für jüdische Volkskunde* 2(1924–25):365.
325. *Sh'vile Emuna*, Sig. 4, p. 5.
326. *Sefer Z'khira*, p. 27a; *Amtaḥat Binyamin*, p. 19a.
327. *Amtaḥat Binyamin*, p. 19a.
328. *Wars* in Arabic is "saffron," or a plant like the sesame, peculiar to Arabia Felix. (Joseph Catafago, *An Arabic and English Dictionary*, 3d ed. [Beirut, 1975], s.v. wars. *Note added in 1980.*)
329. In Arabic *kāmēh* is "cameo," "precious stone" (Wehr, *Dictionary of Modern Written Arabic*, s.v.). It seems that my informant inadvertently switched the terms, and that originally the story must have been that a *kāmēh* (precious stone) was occasionally found in the intestines of a cow which had eaten *wars* (saffron). *(Note added in 1980.)*
330. Oral communication by a Moroccan Jewish woman in Jerusalem.
331. Oral communication by Yosef Sikron of Jerusalem.
332. Cf. Gubernatis, *Die Tiere*, p. 330.
333. Brauer, *Y'hude Kurdistan*, p. 68.
334. *Sefer Z'khira*, p. 27a; *Amtaḥat Binyamin*, p. 19a; cf. "Sefer S'gullot v'Ḥiddot," pp. 81a, 57b, 87a; *R'fu'a v'Ḥayyim*, chap. 9, p. 28a; Grunwald, "Aus Hausapotheke und Hexenküche," *Jahrbuch*, p. 211, no. 169. According to information supplied by Ben-Zion Taragan, this custom was still practiced in the 1940s in Alexandria. In Morocco, in the Ait Yusi tribe, the midwife warms an egg in the ashes of the hearth and then pours the contents into the mouth of the laboring woman when the child is about to emerge from her body, for this both hastens the delivery and eases the pain (Westermarck, *Ritual and Belief*, 2:371, and additional examples there).
335. *Toldot Adam*, p. 38a; likewise *Amtaḥat Binyamin*, 19a; *Mar'e haY'ladim*, 70b; *R'fu'a v'Ḥayyim*, p. 28a. Similarly among other peoples: *HWDA*, 3:413.

336. *Amtaḥat Binyamin*, p. 19a; *R'fu'a v'Ḥayyim*, p. 28b; *Abi'a Ḥiddot*, p. 68b. The Ait Yusi in Morocco put the kerchief of a woman who is known to have easy deliveries on the head of the woman in labor (Westermarck, *Ritual and Belief*, 2:371).
337. *Amtaḥat Binyamin*, p. 19a.
338. Ibid.
339. *Mar'e haY'ladim*, p. 70b; *R'fu'a v'Ḥayyim*, pp. 28a–b.
340. Erich Brauer, "Birth Customs among the Jews of Kurdistan," *Edoth* 1, no. 2 (1946):69. In Syria and among the South Slavs, the woman in difficult labor is given water in her husband's shoe (Abela, "Beiträge," p. 89; Stern, *Medizin*, 2:299). Among various tribes in Morocco, it is customary for the husband to wash his right foot or his right big toe and to give the wash water to his wife to drink if she has a difficult labor, or the husband steps over his wife several times (Westermarck, *Ritual and Belief*, 2:370). In Syria, if the birth pangs are very strong, they put the husband's shoe under the woman's head without her knowledge (Abela, "Beiträge," pp. 96–97).
341. Moritz Güdemann, *Geschichte des Erziehungswesens und der Cultur der Juden in Frankreich und Deutschland* (Vienna, 1880), p. 214; cf. Jacob Grimm, *Aberglaube*, XL; Wuttke, *Volksaberglaube*, p. 195. More recently they used to put the husband's trousers in front of or on the bed of the woman in difficult labor in order to prevent strong afterpangs (HWDA, 3:415).
342. Oral communication from Yosef Sikron of Jerusalem. A similar custom among the modern Greeks: the husband strikes the woman with his shoe three times on her back and says, "I put on you this burden, and I take it from you now" (Ploss, 3:37).
343. *Sefer haMiddot*, s.v. Qishuy leled, no. 3; cf. *Mar'e haY'ladim*, p. 70b.
344. The belief that the presence of the children and husband of the woman in childbed is harmful to her, and the custom of removing them from the house, are found in the East Indies, in Bosnia, and among the American Indians, Georgians (in the Caucasus), the Armenians, the fellahin of Palestine, and others. See Philip J. Baldensperger, "Birth, Marriage, and Death . . . ," *Palestine Exploration Fund Quarterly Statement* (1894), p. 127; Stern, *Medizin*, 2:293f; Ploss, 2:553–54; Gaster, "Birth, Jewish," pp. 636–37.
345. *Mar'e haY'ladim*, 70a; *R'fu'a v'Ḥayyim*, p. 28a; *Abi'a Ḥiddot*, p. 68b; see also *Sefer haMiddot*, s.v. Banim, no. 23, and s.v. S'gulla.
346. Cf. Patai, *Adam va'Adama*, 1:204–5.
347. Elzet, "MiMinhage Yisrael," p. 366.
348. Ibid.
349. Oral communication from Ḥakham Shim'on Harus of Safed. Similarly, the Arabs of Palestine cover the woman who is in difficult labor with a blanket from a saint's tomb; in Jerusalem they cover her with a blanket from the tomb of Shaykh alḤalili, (Canaan, *Aberglaube und Volksmedizin*, pp. 80, n. 2, 88, n. 3).
350. Brauer, "Birth Customs," p. 69.
351. Gaster, "Birth, Jewish," p. 657.
352. *Amtaḥat Binyamin*, p. 19a.
353. The Hebrew text has *qori, qori*, which seems to be a misspelling of *qeri, qeri*, "it is time."
354. *Mar'e haY'ladim*, p. 70b, quoting *Y'mallet Nafsho*. Cf. Grunwald, "Aus Hausapotheke und Hexenküche," *Mitteilungen*, p. 59; "Sefer S'gullot v'Hiddot," pp. 78a, 87b, quoting "a manuscript book *R'fu'a v'Ḥ ayyim*." Cf. *R'fu'a v'Ḥayyim*, p. 28a; *Abi'a Ḥiddot*, pp. 67a-b. According to Ben-Zion Taragan of Alexandria, this custom is practiced there in a simpler form; cf. *Ta'ame Minhagim*, p. 95b, where a different incantation is mentioned. In Turkey, when the birth pangs were weak they brought earth from a holy place (which could be obtained in the bazaar), filled small bags with it, and tied them to the woman's back. The Muslims used earth which pilgrims had brought from Mecca; the Christians and Jews used earth from Jerusalem (Stern, *Medizin*, 2:297).
355. *Sefer Z'khira*, p. 27a.
356. Patai, *Adam va'Adama*, 2:19–20.

357. *Mar'e haY'ladim*, p. 78b, quoting Rav Mar Kahana, *'Anaf Avanim*. Cf. Baḥya ben Asher on Exod. 28:17, p. 120; *Mid. Talpiyot*, s.v. Ephod, p. 61b; *Yalqut Yitzḥaq* 90; *Yalqut R'uveni*, *T'tzavve* 159; *R'fu'a v'Ḥayyim*, pp. 28a, 35a.
358. Isaac Lampronti, *Paḥad Yitzḥaq*, vol. 5 (Livorno, 5594 [1834]), fol. 206c, s.v. M'qashsha leled.
359. Cf. n. 315 above.
360. "Sefer S'gullot v'Ḥiddot," p. 75b.
361. Patai, *Adam va'Adama*, 2:25.
362. *Shilte haGibborim*; cf. *Mid. Talpiyot*, p. 66a; Patai, *Adam va'Adama*, 2:26.
363. *Shilte haGibborim*, pp. 51a–b; cf. Patai, *Adam v'Adama*, 2:32.
364. *Mar'e haY'ladim*, p. 70b; *R'fu'a v'Ḥayyim*, p. 28a.
365. "Sefer S'gullot v'Ḥiddot," p. 69b.
366. *Sh'vile Emuna*, sig. 4, p. 5.
367. Written communication from Ben-Zion Taragan of Alexandria.
368. *Mar'e haY'ladim*, p. 70a.
369. Brauer, "Birth Customs," p. 69.
370. Elzet, "MiMinhage Yisrael," p. 363.
371. Patai, *Adam va'Adama*, 1:199–200.
372. Tos. Shab. 6:4, ed. Zuckermandel, p. 117.
373. This custom is found among other peoples, e.g., among the Germans, the Greeks, etc., who plug up all the openings in the doors while the woman is in labor (Stern, *Medizin*, 2:294; Wuttke, *Volksaberglaube*, p. 382, par. 581; *HWDA*, s.v. Geburt.
374. On the use of iron as a protection against demons among various peoples, see *ERE*, Index, s.v. Iron.
375. Isidor Scheftelowitz, *Altpalästinensischer Bauernglaube* (Hannover, 1925), p. 71.
376. Ibid., pp. 71–72.
377. Written communication from Ben-Zion Taragan of Alexandria.
378. Oral communication from a Moroccan Jewish woman in Jerusalem.
379. Written communication from Ben-Zion Taragan of Alexandria.
380. *Sefer haMiddot*, s.v. Quishuy leled, no. 2.
381. Erich Brauer, "The Jews of Afghanistan," *Jewish Social Studies* 4 (Apr. 1942):138.
382. *Toldot Adam*, p. 11a, no. 94.
383. Gaster, "Birth, Jewish," p. 657. Women in difficult delivery in Istanbul used to drink the water in which the clothes of a holy man had been washed (Stern, *Medizin*, 2:298).
384. Brauer, *Y'hude Kurdistan*, p. 130.
385. Brauer, *Ethnologie*, p. 183; Brauer, "Die Frau." The use of the *tasa*, a metal bowl inscribed with verses from the Koran, was practiced among the Arabs. The Arabs of Palestine used an earthenware saucer for this purpose, the Ait Waryager in Morocco a bowl, and the Arabs of Egypt a cup or bowl for the cure of all kinds of diseases (Canaan, *Aberglaube*, pp. 80, n. 2, 100, pl. 37; Westermarck, *Ritual and Belief*, 2:372; Edward W. Lane, *Manners and Customs of the Modern Egyptians*, Everyman's Library [London, n.d.] pp. 260ff.).
386. *R'fu'a v'Ḥayyim*, p. 27a–b.
387. Brauer, "Birth Customs," pp. 68–69.
388. Bodenschatz, *Kirchliche Verfassung*, 4:56–57; Paul C. Kirchner, *Jüdisches Zeremoniell* (Nuremburg, 1724), p. 149.
389. *R'fu'a v'Ḥayyim*, pp. 27b–28a; *Abi'a Ḥiddot*, p. 68b, on the basis of various sources; cf. also Elzet, "MiMinhage Yisrael," p. 363.
390. Judah Löb ben Enoch Sundel, *Sh'elot uT'shuvot Ḥinnukh Bet Y'huda* (Frankfurt a.M., 1708), p. 25b, Responsum 71; cf. Yitzḥaq Lampronti, *Paḥad Yitzḥaq*, vol. 4 (Reggio, 1813), fols. 11a and ff., s.v. Yoledet.
391. Y'huda Bergmann, *Ha'Am v'Ruḥo*, p. 112.
392. Exod. 11:8; written communication from Ben-Zion Taragan of Alexandria.
393. Brauer, *Y'hude Kurdistan*, p. 130.

394. Stern, *Medizin*, 2:300.
395. Oral communication from Rabbi Yisrael Dov Kohen of Mount Carmel, Haifa.
396. Elzet, "MiMinhage Yisrael," p. 363.
397. Oral communication from Ḥakham Shim'on Harus of Safed. A parallel to the opening of the Holy Ark can be found in Voigtland and Mecklenburg, Germany, where they believe that one must open all the locks in the house in order to ease the birth pangs (Wuttke, *Volksaberglaube*, p. 378. Similar customs are found in many parts of the world, see *HWDA*, 3:412. An English folktale reports an opposite custom: all the locks must be locked at the time of delivery (Thompson, *Motif-Index* T 582.2). In Turkey, when a woman has difficult labor, her husband asks that the door of the mosque be opened (Stern, *Medizin*, 2:299).
398. 1 Sam. 1:1, where it is related that God hearkened to Hannah's prayer and gave her a son.
399. Elzet, "MiMinhage Yisrael," p. 363.
400. Ibid.
401. Stern, *Medizin*, 2:299. The Turkish Sephardim also bury the kerchief of the woman in labor in the grave of one of her relatives and blow the shofar over her bed, (ibid., pp. 299–300).
402. Oral communication from Rabbi Eliyahu Ma'aravi of Damascus.
403. Oral communication from Ḥakham Shim'on Harus of Safed.
404. Cf. Frazer, *Golden Bough*, 3:92ff.
405. The Hebrew text uses masculine pronouns, but the context shows that it is the woman and not some unnamed man who has to perform the prescribed rite. (*Note added in 1980.*)
406. Cod. Gaster 464, as quoted by Daiches, *Babylonian Oil Magic*, p. 26, One can divine the time of one's death by looking into a cup of oil, (Grunwald, "Aus Hausapotheke und Hexenküche," *Jahrbuch*, p. 205).
407. Cod. Gaster 462, as quoted by Daiches, *Babylonian Oil Magic*, p. 27.
408. Frazer, *Golden Bough*, 2:94; Géza Róheim, *Spiegelzauber* (Leipzig and Vienna, 1919), pp. 123ff.
409. Tos. N'zirut 4:7, ed. Zuckermandel, p. 289; Y. Nazir 51c mid.: Y. Ned. 36d bot.; B. Nazir 4b; B. Ned. 9a; Sifre Naso, chap. 22; Num. Rab., chap. 10, 208b.
410. Cf. Ploss, 2:577–81. In folktales: Thompson, *Motif-Index* T 581. Among the biblical Hebrews: under the apple tree, Song of Sol. 8:5. Among the talmudic Jews: B. Sota 11b, etc. Cf. Patai, *Adam va'Adama*, 1:212ff. On the posture of the woman during delivery, see Ploss, 2:574–99; J. Jarcho, *Postures and Practices during Labor* (New York, 1934).
411. Ploss, 2:750.
412. Cf. *HWDA*, 2:898ff.
413. Ploss, 2:778ff., and esp. figs. 671, 672, 789.
414. Wilhelm Spiegelberg, "Der Ausdruck 'auf die Erde legen' = 'gebären' im Ägyptischen," *ARW* 9 (1906):144–45.
415. Alan Gardiner, *Egyptian Grammar*, 3d ed. (London, 1957), p. 448, B2.
416. Herman Grapow, *Die bildlichen Ausdrücke des Aegyptischen* (Leipzig, 1924), p. 136; Spiegelberg, "Der Ausdruck . . . ," pp. 144–45.
417. Ploss, 2:790–91. Among the native peoples of America also women took this position for delivery; see Ploss, vol. 2, figs. 570, 572, 795, 796, which show women crouching or sitting on the ground. Egyptian women today take the same position (ibid., p. 595, and figs. on pp. 594–96).
418. Cf. *Encyclopaedia Brittanica*, 1911 ed., 18:325.
419. Ernst Samter, *Geburt, Hochzeit, und Tod* (Leipzig and Berlin, 1911), p. 7; Ploss, 2:793.
420. Samter, *Geburt, Hochzeit, und Tod*, pp. 20ff.
421. Phaedrus 1:18. Cf. G. A. Gerhard, "Zur 'Mutter Erde'," *ARW* 17(1914):333ff. In Hungary in the environs of Lake Balaton, women usually deliver while lying in bed; occasionally a woman will crouch down, lean on her hands on the ground, and give birth in this position (Johann Janko, *Ethnographie des . . . Balatongestades* [Vienna, 1906], p. 458).

422. Exod. 1:16; cf. Leopold Löw, *Die Lebensalter in der jüdischen Literatur* (Szegedin, 1875), pp. 74ff.; Albrecht Dieterich, *Mutter Erde* (Leipzig and Berlin), 1925, p. 126; Wilhelm Spiegelberg, *Aegyptologische Randglossen* (Strassburg, 1904), pp. 20–21.

423. Stern, *Medizin*, 2:303.

424. B. Ber. 34b; B. Yeb. 103a; B. Shab. 54b; B. Nid. 31b. Cf. Gaster, "Birth, Jewish," 2:653.

425. Yosef Y'huda Chorny, *Sefer haMassa'ot* (Saint Petersburg, 1884), p. 295; cf. Zvi Kasdai, *Mamlekhet Ararat* (Odessa, 1912), p. 55.

426. Brauer, "Jews of Afghanistan," p. 133.

427. Brauer, *Y'hude Kurdistan*, p. 129.

428. There are scholars who see in this custom a reference to Jesus' birth in a manger; see *HWDA*, 3:413. However, given its presence among many non-Christian peoples, we cannot accept this explanation. In Hungarian villages, women give birth in the middle of a room upon a little pile of straw covered with a sheet (Ploss, 2:584). The same custom has been observed in Finland since ancient days (Kalevala 23.475ff.). In several places in southwest Finland, delivery takes place in the cowshed (Nyberg, *Kind und Erde*, p. 134; cf. p. 255, n. 431). On the cowshed as the place of delivery in folktales, see Thompson, *Motif-Index*, 4:581. In Norway the newborn is called "straw-born" (Nyberg, *Kind und Erde*, p. 133). In Finland, Lettland, Great Russia, Estonia, and among the Votyaks, delivery takes place in the bath hut (Ploss, 2:586–90). According to *A New English Dictionary* (Oxford, 1919), s.v. straw, the expression "in the straw" has been used in England in the sense of giving birth and "out of the straw" in the sense of recovering from childbirth since the seventeenth century. Among the Guri of the Caucasus and the Chinese, it was the custom for delivery to take place on straw in a room which had no wooden floor (Ploss, 2:584–85).

429. Juda Tscherny [hereafter Chorny], "Die kaukasischen Juden," *Globus* 38 (1880):200; cf. Richard Andrée, *Volkskunde der Juden* (Bielefield and Leipzig, 1881), p. 182.

430. Oral communication from a Jew from Bessarabia in Tel Aviv.

431. Various American Indian tribes spread a piece of fur, or grass, or a layer of earth on the floor of the house and cover it with a buffalo skin (Ploss, 2:585). In New Guinea, in the Mawata tribe, the woman lies on a grass bed on the earth (Nyberg, *Kind und Erde*, p. 133). In Hawaii, women give birth in a "delivery hut," lying on the ground on which a piece of cloth is spread (Ploss, 2:593).

432. Oral communication from Mrs. Danon, Tel Aviv, and Yosef M'yuḥas, Jerusalem.

433. Oral communication from a Moroccan Jewish woman in Jerusalem.

434. In India, South Africa, Iceland, etc.; see Dieterich, *Mutter Erde*, pp. 125, 131; Ploss, 2:584; Nyberg, *Kind und Erde*, p. 133.

435. Oral communication from Ḥakham Yishai in Jerusalem.

436. O. Gruppe, *Die Mythologische Literatur aus den Jahren 1898–1905* (Leipzig, 1908), p. 353; Paul Wilutzky, *Vorgeschichte des Rechts*, 3 vols. (Breslau, 1903), 2:111; Nyberg, *Kind und Erde*, p. 158; Eugene Monseur, "La proscription religieuse de l'usage récent," *Revue de l'histoire des religions* 53 (May–June 1903):301–4; Paul Sartori, *Sitte und Brauch*, 2 vols. (Leipzig, 1910, 1914), 1:19, 25, n. 10; Ludwig Deubner, in *ERE*, 2:649, s.v. Birth; Eugen Fehrle, in *HWDA*, 2:898, s.v. Erde; E. Goldmann, "Cartam levare," *Mitteilungen des Instituts für Oesterreichische Geschichtsforschung* 35 (1914):1ff.; Dieterich, *Mutter Erde*, pp. 57, 132, 134.

437. Pliny, *Historia Naturalis* 7.1.

438. Dieterich, *Mutter Erde*, p. 6.

439. The custom of laying the newborn on the earth has been preserved in many places in Italy until modern times (ibid., p. 7).

440. Hesiod, *Opera et die* 463ff.; cf. Dieterich, *Mutter Erde*, p. 98.

441. They have been reported from the ancient Germans, the Scandinavians, the Czechs in Prague, the Slovaks in Hungary, the Swiss, the Italians, the Bosnians and Hercegovinians, the Persians, the Japanese, the Vedda of Ceylon (Sri Lanka), the Toda in India, the

Armenians, the Tupi and Aztecs in South America, the Hottentots, the tribes of the Gold Coast and Lake Victoria in Africa, the Ila-speaking peoples in South Africa, and others. See Berthold Kohlbach, "Der Mythus und Kult der alten Ungarn," *ARW* 2 (1899):355; Dieterich, *Mutter Erde*, pp. 8, 15, 123, 126; Heinrich Ploss and Barbara Klara Renz, *Das Kind* [hereafter Ploss-Renz], 3d ed., 2 vols. (Leipzig, 1911–12), 1:98–99; Samter, *Geburt, Hochzeit, und Tod*, p. 2, n. 4; Hartland, in *ERE*, 2:640; Ludwig Deubner, "Mitteilungen und Hinweise," *ARW* 9 (1906):290; Bernhard Struck, "Niederlegen und Aufheben der Kinder von der Erde," *ARW* 10 (1907):158; Edwin W. Smith and Andrew M. Dale, *The Ila-Speaking Peoples*, 2 vols. (London, 1920), 2:9; Fehrle, in *HWDA*, 2:898–99; Nyberg, *Kind und Erde*, pp. 158ff.

442. E.g., in Bohemia, "so that the child may become strong" (Wuttke, *Volksaberglaube*, p. 381, par. 580).

443. Kalevala 45, 171–72.

444. E.g., in the Baganda tribe near Lake Victoria in Africa, they make sure that the child does not touch the earth in the first few months of its life. When the time comes, they hold a family feast and seat the child on the earth near the door (Struck, "Niederlegen und Aufheben," p. 158). To this context belongs the Javanese belief that the moment in which they lay the child on the earth for the first time is dangerous for it; therefore they put it in a chicken coop, and the mother makes clucking sounds like a hen calling her chicks (James E. Crombie, in *Folk Lore* 6 [1895]:260).

445. In Hungary and in other countries, the Gypsies dig a hole in the ground soon after the birth of a child, pour water into it, and wash the child (Ploss, 2:19). Among the Kwakiutl of British Columbia, the woman delivers while sitting on the lap of another woman over a shallow pit, and the child is allowed to fall into it (Hartland, *Primitive Paternity*, 1:113). A pit or hole in the ground is the usual place where a small infant lies or plays in Asiatic Turkey, Chinese Turkestan, ancient Peru, and Australia, where they even pad the hole with ashes (Nyberg, *Kind und Erde*, pp. 160–61; Fehrle, in *HWDA*, 2:898; Ploss-Renz, 1:289). In Baghdad, where the delivery took place on the floor over a heap of ashes, the child was allowed to fall onto them (Stern, *Medizin*, 2:305). The fellahin of Palestine put red earth into the cradle and lay the child on it (Klein, in *ZDPV*, 4:64). In Bohemia they wrap the child in a sheet and lay it under the table, "so that it may become wise, love to work, and obey its parents" (Wuttke, *Volksaberglaube*, p. 381, par. 581). The custom of laying the newborn under the table also is practiced in Switzerland, Prague, and Hungary (Ploss-Renz, 1:98; Nyberg, *Kind und Erde*, p. 168; Fehrle, in *HWDA*, 2:898).

446. Gaster, "Birth, Jewish," p. 653, assumes that this indeed was the case.

447. Song of Sol. 8:5; cf. B. Sota 11b, etc.

448. Cf. Ezek. 16:5.

449. Gaster, "Birth, Jewish," p. 658.

450. *Amtahat Binyamin*, p. 34a; cf. *Mar'e haY'ladim*, pp. 49a–b.

451. *Toldot Adam*, p. 7a, no. 64.

452. Gaster, "Birth, Jewish," p. 658.

453. See below, sec. X.

454. Cf. Patai, *Adam va'Adama*, 1:241.

455. Brauer, *Y'hude Kurdistan*, p. 129.

456. Dieterich, *Mutter Erde*, p. 6ff.

457. Cf. Patai, *Adam va'Adama*, 1:189ff., 206ff.

458. Cf. Mannhardt, *Wald und Feldkulte*, 3:351, chap. "Kind und Korn."

459. Ibid., 3:370; Dieterich, *Mutter Erde*, pp. 101–2.

460. These are given in Mannhardt, *Wald und Feldkulte*; Dittmar Heubach, *Das Kind in der griechischen Kunst* (Heidelberg, 1903), p. 65; Ploss-Renz, 1:63; Nyberg, *Kind und Erde*, 214ff.

461. Stern, *Medizin*, 2:306.

462. Lane, *Manners and Customs*, 2:243.

463. C. B. Klunzinger, *Upper Egypt* (London, 1878), p. 186.

464. Westermarck, *Ritual and Belief*, 2:390.
465. Ibid., 2:402.
466. Nyberg, *Kind und Erde*, p. 215, according to Finnish sources. In Syria they believe that rocking an empty cradle will give the child a backache.
467. Ibid. The Kwakiutl in British Columbia wrap up a cradle which is no longer needed, together with the bedding which belongs to it, and hide it in a cleft of rock which specifically serves this purpose (Ploss-Renz, 1:293; W. Kobelt, "Die Kwakiūl," *Globus* 57 [1890]:93).
468. Ploss-Renz, 1:293; Nyberg, *Kind und Erde*, pp. 161, 263, n. 547.
469. Stern, *Medizin*, 2:398; Ploss, 2:843, 871.
470. Stern, *Medizin*, 2:335.
471. Thus according to the Targum Onkelos and the Targum Yerushalmi to Num. 15:20–21; Neh. 10:38.
472. Gen. Rab. 53:10, ed. Theodor-Albeck, p. 566; Mid. Tanh. Gen. 53.
473. Tos Kelim Bab. Metz. 8:12, 584.
474. Tos. Mak. 2:4, 6, 439–40. Cf. Eliezer Ben-Yehuda, *Millon*, and the talmudic dictionaries of Levy and Jastrow, s.v. 'arisa. On the double meaning of the word (kneading trough, cradle) see Gaster, "Birth, Jewish," p. 654.
475. Cf. Raphael Patai, " 'Arisah," *JQR* 35 (1944):165–72.
476. B. Shab. 134a. Cf. A. Marmorstein, "Das Sieb im Volksglauben," *ARW* 21 (1922): 235ff. On swinging in folk belief, see also Eugen Fehrle, "Das Sieb im Volksglauben," *ARW* 19 (1916–17):547–51.
477. Wuttke, *Volksaberglaube*, p. 386, par. 588. Here belongs the Hungarian custom according to which a woman who does not want children steps over the kneading trough three times (Heinrich von Wlisloczky, *Aus dem Volksleben der Magyaren* [Munich, 1893], p. 120).
478. Haeem Samuel Kehimkar, *History of the Bene Israel of India* [hereafter *Bene Israel*] (Tel Aviv, 1937), p. 112.
479. Brauer, "Bräuche der Kurdischen Juden," p. 108.
480. Chorny, *Sefer haMassa'ot*, p. 295; cf. Kasdai, *Mamlekhet Ararat*, p. 55.
481. A few among several comprehensive studies of salt in folklore and in cultural history are: Matthias Jacob Schleiden, *Das Salz, seine Geschichte, seine Symbolik, und seine Bedeutung im Menschenleben* (Leipzig, 1875); Victor Hehn, *Das Salz, eine kulturhistorische Studie* (Leipzig, 1919); Ernest Jones, "The Symbolic Significance of Salt in Folklore and Superstition," in *Essays in Applied Psychoanalysis* (London and Vienna, 1923). In the Jewish world: Immanuel Löw, "Das Salz," in *Jewish Studies in Memory of George A. Kohut* (New York, 1935), pp. 429–62.
482. *Iliad* 6.214; Plutarch, *Symposias* 6.10, *Moralia*, vol. 8, Loeb Classical Library (Cambridge, Mass., and London, 1969), p. 513.
483. Let me mention in this connection the statement repeated several times in talmudic sources: "The horn of the altar became damaged, and the service was cancelled that day, until they brought a lump of salt and put it on it so that it should not look damaged" (Tos. Suk. 3:16, 197; cf. Patai, *Adam va'Adama*, 2:168).
484. According to some commentators, this custom is based on the explanation of Rashi to Lev. 2:13 quoted above.
485. *Sefer Z'khira*, p. 18b.
486. Deut. 29:22; Judg. 9:45; Jer. 17:6; Ps. 107:34; Job 39:6.
487. In Ireland and East Prussia, at the time of sowing, the landowner's wife puts salt into the field (Jones, "Symbolic Significance of Salt," p. 123).
488. B. Shab. 128b.
489. Y. Shab. 16c bot. According to Pliny, *Historia Naturalis* 10:85, female mice become pregnant by eating salt. In Belgium they mix salt into the fodder of a pregnant mare or cow so as to make delivery easy. In Normandy they give salt to the cows to increase their milk. In East Friesland and Scotland they put salt in the first milk of a newly calved cow in order

to make her give ample and good-tasting milk. Various peoples put salt into the mouth of a young calf as a protection (Jones, "Symbolic Significance of Salt," p. 121). The Arabs in Morocco hang a lump of salt around the necks of animals as an amulet, and protect threshed grain with salt (Edward Westermarck, *Marriage Ceremonies in Morocco* [London, 1914], pp. 16, 32).

490. This custom is found also among many other peoples; see Jones, "Symbolic Significance of Salt," pp. 119, 129.
491. Ibid., pp. 122, 137.
492. Scheftelowitz, *Altpalästinensischer Bauernglaube*, p. 119, n. 1.
493. B. Shab. 66b, and Rashi ibid.
494. Jones, "Symbolic Significance of Salt," p. 170; Preuss, *Biblisch-talmudische Medizin*, p. 467. Ancient Greek medical advice was that the child should be washed in salt water or that salt should be sprinkled on its body; see Galen, *On the Preservation of Health* 6; Soranus Ephesius, *Gynaecia*, trans. Oswei Temkin (Baltimore, 1956), p. 83; Ploss-Renz, 1:281; cf. Preuss, *Biblisch-talmudische Medizin*, p. 467. On Lesbos the child is washed in water and salt and then a few coins for the midwife are thrown into the vessel used (W. H. D. Rouse, "Folklore Firstfruits from Lesbos," *Folk-Lore* 7 [1896]:145–46. The Samaritans, the Christians in Syria, the Yemenites, and several other Middle Eastern peoples rub salt water on the child's body (William Robertson Smith, *Religion of the Semites*, 3d ed. [London, 1927], p. 594; Sigismund Reich, *Études sur les villages araméens de l'Anti-Liban* [hereafter *Villages araméens*], Documents d'études orientales de l'Institut Francais de Damas, vol. 7, n.d. (ca. 1938), pp. 73–74, and literature on the custom in the Middle East, ibid., p. 74, n. 1; Ploss, 1:260). Among various Moroccan tribes it is customary to put salt under a newborn's head to protect it from jinns and the evil eye (Westermarck, *Ritual and Belief*, 2:379ff.). The Egyptian Arabs put salt next to the child's head for the night, and the next day they sprinkle it about to protect the mother and child from the evil eye (Lane, *Manners and Customs*, p. 510). The Palestinian fellahin rub the newborn's body one or more times with salt or with a mixture of salt, water, and oil, or with salt mixed with red earth (Baldensperger, "Birth, Marriage, and Death," p. 127; F. A. Klein, "Mitteilungen . . . ," *ZDPV*, 4:63). In the village of Jub'adin in the Anti-Lebanon, on the day after its birth they rub the child with salt from head to foot and also put salt on its body for the next three days (Reich, *Villages araméens*, pp. 73–74). The Armenians, Georgians in the Caucasus, Turks and other peoples in Asia Minor sprinkle salt on the newborn and leave him covered with it for twenty-four hours. In Persia they rubbed salt on the newborn after cutting the umbilical cord. Among the Mongols, Kalmucks, and various European peoples (e.g., in Bohemia and Moravia), they wash the newborn with salt water (Ploss, 1:280–81). In Bohemia they explain that the purpose is to strengthen the child. In Oldenburg they put some salt on the tongue of the newborn to protect it from witchcraft (Wuttke, *Volksaberglaube*, pp. 381–82, par. 580). The custom of putting salt on the tongue of the newborn or of immersing him in salt water as a protection against evil influences is found all over Europe. In Holland they put salt into the cradle (Scheftelowitz, *Altpalästinensischer Bauernglaube*, p. 78; Jones, "Symbolic Significance of Salt," p. 121). The ancient Greeks, modern Greeks and Bulgars sprinkle salt on the child right after its birth (Scheftelowitz, *Altpalästinensischer Bauernglaube*, p. 79; Ploss-Renz, 1:280). In the Christian Church the use of salt in connection with baptism was introduced in the fourth century; it has been practiced down to the present (Jones, "Symbolic Significance of Salt," p. 125).

495. B. Shab. 129b.
496. Oral communication from Ḥakham Yishay of Jerusalem.
497. Chorny, *Sefer haMassa'ot*, p. 295; cf. Kasdai, *Mamlekhet Ararat*, p. 55.
498. Oral communication from Ḥakham Shim'on Harus of Safed.
499. Thompson, *Motif-Index* A 1245.4.
500. Pirqe R. Eliezer 25 end.
501. *Sefer haYashar*, Traqlin ed., p. 56.

502. See "Earth Eating," above.

503. Ploss, 2:819–38; see also Smith and Dale, *Ila-Speaking Peoples*, 2:89; Stern, *Medizin*, 2:307.

504. *Sh'vile Emuna*, sig. 5, p. 6.

505. Written communication from Ben-Zion Taragan of Alexandria.

506. *Toldot Adam*, p. 37a.

507. *Mar'e HaY'ladim*, p. 51b.

508. *Amtahat Binyamin*, p. 19a.

509. In many places all over the world they bury the afterbirth, occasionally together with the umbilical cord, under a tree or under the house (Ploss, 2:852ff.; Frazer, *Golden Bough*, 11:160ff.; Smith and Dale, *Ila-Speaking Peoples*, 2:10; Westermarck, *Ritual and Belief*, 2:372–73; Crawley, *Mystic Rose*, 1:151–52; Ploss-Renz, 2:198–99, etc.). In Altmark, Germany, they bury the afterbirth hidden from the rays of the sun and moon, lest the child's face become yellow. In Baden, Württemberg, and Swabian Bavaria, they believe that if the afterbirth is buried under an apple tree, the next child born to the mother will be a girl, and if under a pear tree, it will be a boy (Wuttke, *Volksaberglaube*, p. 378, par. 574). In Macedonia and Bosnia, they bury the afterbirth in the garden or the barn or throw it into a stream, (Stern, *Medizin*, 2:307). Bulgarians bury it under the floor of the room behind the door (Adolf Strauss, *Die Bulgaren* [Leipzig, 1898], p. 283). In some Pacific Islands they wrap the afterbirth in cotton, put it in a pot, and either throw it into the sea or bury it under the house (Ploss, 2:589–90; Frazer, *Golden Bough*, 1:187–88). The Swahili people bury the afterbirth in the very spot where the child was born, so that it will be always attracted to its parents' home. The natives on the Pennefather River in Queensland, Australia, believe that part of the child's soul remains in the afterbirth, and as soon as the afterbirth emerges they bury it in the sand and mark the place with twigs. They believe that Anjea, a supernatural being whose task it is to make babies from mud and insert them into their mothers' wombs, recognizes the spot, takes out the soul, and carries it with him to one of his haunts, where he keeps it until it is wanted for the completion of another child. When Anjea forms the child, he puts into it a part of the soul of its father if it is a male, and if a female, part of the soul of its father's sister. At the proper moment he inserts the child into its mother's womb (Hartland, in *ERE*, 2:639). In one place in Central Celebes they wrap up the afterbirth with spices to keep it from rotting (Frazer, *Golden Bough*, 1:189–90; Scheftelowitz, *Alt-Palästinensischer Bauernglaube*, pp. 23–24). Among European peoples it also is customary to wrap up the afterbirth carefully and to preserve it, e.g., in Styria (Steiermark) and among the Letts, and also to hang it on a tree (Ploss, 2:867ff.). Among various peoples it is customary for a woman to eat the afterbirth as a charm against barrenness and various diseases, e.g., in Germany, Italy, Java, and among Brazilian Indian tribes (ibid., pp. 850, 858). In Mandailing, Indonesia, after they wash the mother and child, they wash the afterbirth and bury it under the house or put it in an earthenware jar, seal it well, and throw it into the river. Thereby they hope to forestall any evil influence the afterbirth could have on the child, which may cause it to have cold feet. (ibid., p. 849). The Gypsies in Transylvania believe that if somebody eats the blood of the afterbirth he will become insensitive to cold, and if somebody complains that he is cold, they tell him, "Eat afterbirth!" (ibid., p. 850). This custom parallels the talmudic custom quoted below.

510. Tos. Shab. 15:3, ed. Zuckermandel, p. 132; cf. Num. Rab. 4:3; B. Nid. 27a.

511. B. Shab. 129b.

512. Y. Shab. 16c bot.

513. Cf. Heinrich Levy, "Beiträge zur Religionsgeschichte und Volkskunde, I. Zu'Mutter Erde'," *ARW*, 29 (1931):187–88. The burial of the afterbirth near the house is considered by the Balinese to be a preparation for death, because they believe that the afterbirth is the brother or sister of the newborn. When someone dies, the soul of his afterbirth comes to show him the way to the heaven of Indra (Ploss, 2:851).

514. Oral communication from a Moroccan Jewish woman in Jerusalem.

515. M. Ḥul. 4:7; cf. B. Ḥul. 77b–78a; Maimonides, *Guide of the Perplexed*, 3.37.
516. Oral communication from Mrs. Danon, Tel Aviv; Rachel Feigenbaum, Jerusalem; and Yosef M'yuḥas, Jerusalem.
517. Written communication from Ḥakham Shim'on Harus of Safed.
518. Oral communication from Rabbi Yisrael Dov Kohen, of Mount Carmel, Haifa.
519. Written communication from Ben-Zion Taragan of Alexandria.
520. Hilma Granqvist, *Marriage Conditions in a Palestinian Village*, 2 vols. (Helsingfors, 1931, 1935), 1:23, n. 2.
521. Patai, *Adam va'Adama*, 2:6.
522. Stern, *Medizin*, 2:307; Ploss, 2:850; *ibid.*, pp. 848ff. for additional examples.
523. B. Shab. 134a.
524. *Mif'alot Eloqim*, p. 212.
525. This belief and custom were found among the ancient Romans and the Germans, Serbs, Danes, Walloons, English, French, Bohemians, Hungarians, Swiss, and others. The English say about a man who is lucky, "He was born in a caul" (Manó Kertész, *Szokásmondások* [Budapest, 1922], p. 105). The Icelanders believe that the guardian spirit of the child, or part of its soul, is in the caul, and therefore it is forbidden to discard it. The caul also brings luck to him who acquires it: in ancient Rome lawyers bought cauls as an amulet for good luck. In Denmark, lawyers tried to obtain cauls as late as the eighteenth century. In England, the caul was an object of commerce as late as in the 1860s, as one can gather from the classified advertisements in contemporary newspapers. The caul was purchased primarily as a charm against shipwreck and for good luck in many fields (Kertész, *Szokásmondások*, p. 105; *ERE*, 2:639; Ploss, 2:861ff.). In East Prussia, Saxony, the Palatinate, and Baden, they believe that a child born in a caul will be very lucky, and they preserve the caul by sewing it into the child's clothes and taking it to baptism with him. Anybody having a caul with him will have good luck in business, in legal matters, and other affairs. If it is buried in the field, the newborn will have good luck, but if it is burned in fire, his luck will be bad, according to Belgian folk belief (Wuttke, *Volksaberglaube*, p. 381, par. 587). On similar beliefs among the Serbs and Greco-Walachians, in Monastir, Bosnia, and Russia, see Stern, *Medizin*, 2:330ff.
526. Reich, 75. *Villages araméens*, p. 75.
527. Abela, "Beiträge," p. 113.
528. *Sefer Ḥasidim*, par. 1463, ed. Wistineczky, p. 354. The text is corrupt and the meaning doubtful. The commentator on the Warsaw, 1818, edition, par. 463, p. 114, opines that the intention is the opposite: he who is born in a caul needs protection from a storm which is but a war of demons. Cf. various sources about the caul in Güdemann, *Geschichte des Erziehungswesens und der Cultur der Juden*, 1:204, n. 6; also Grimm, *Aberglaube*, 4th ed., 2:728.
529. Elzet, "MiMinhage Yisrael," pp. 363–64.
530. Ploss, 2:844.
531. Frazer, *Folk-Lore in the Old Testament*, 3:206–7; *Golden Bough*, 1:182–83; Ploss, 2:845.
532. Ploss, 2:844. Among the Greco-Walachians, in Monastir, the mother preserves the dried umbilical cord and protects it from moisture, lest the child suffer a stomachache. After a few years they show the cord to the child so as to make him lucky (Stern, *Medizin*, 2:308–9). The umbilical cord, like the afterbirth, sometimes is regarded as a brother of the male child or a sister of a female child. Thus, e.g., the Kei islanders, southwest of New Guinea, put the cord in a pot of ashes and place it in the branches of a tree in order to enable it to keep a watchful eye on its sibling (Frazer, *Golden Bough*, 1:186).
533. Among the Ainu of Japan, a mother wore her children's umbilical cords in a small satchel between her breasts; when she died it was buried with her (Ploss, 2:845).
534. In the Ukraine, barren women drink water in which a piece of an umbilical cord has been soaked (Siegfried Seligmann, *Der böse Blick*, 2 vols. [Berlin, 1910], 2:144). In Kamchatka, the woman who has given birth and wants to bear again soon eats the newborn's umbilical cord (Ploss, 2:312, 848).

535. Brauer, *Ethnologie*, p. 183. The same custom is practiced among the Swahili people, but their purpose is to help the child grow. They hang the cord on the child's neck for the first few years of its life, and then they bury it in the same place as the afterbirth (In *ERE*, 2:639). The Maori of New Zealand bury the cord and then plant a tree over it; the growth of the tree indicates whether the child will thrive (Ploss, 2:847). In this tree we recognize, of course, a variant of the *Lebensbaum*, the tree of life; cf. Patai, *Adam va'Adama*, 1:231–32.

536. Cf. Westermarck, *Ritual and Belief*, 2:373; Ploss, 2:845–46.

537. Oral communication from a Moroccan Jewish woman in Jerusalem. The Atyeh also use the umbilical cord for curing eye ailments and other diseases: they hang it up in the kitchen until it dries, and if a child gets sick they soak it and give the water to him to drink. They also wash his afflicted eyes with it or use it for dressing wounds (Ploss, 2:845). Among the Chinese the cord is occasionally kept in a jar; in case of need, they pulverize it and feed it to a sick child (ibid., p. 847). The Annamese also preserve the cord and use it as a remedy for fever in infants (ibid., p. 845). In Baden and Franconia, Germany, they keep the cord, and when the child is six years old, they give it to him to eat in an omelet in order to help his brain develop. In Hessen the cord is sewn into the clothes to make sure it will not get lost. In East Prussia they stick it under the child's blouse when he first goes to school so that he may become a good student (Wuttke, *Volksaberglaube*, p. 380, par. 579, and more examples there). Many peoples believe the cord protects against evil influences (Ploss-Renz, 2:56–61). The South Slavs keep the dried cord, and if a child is bewitched, they grind a piece of it to powder, mix it in water, and give it to him to drink (Seligmann, *Der böse Blick*, 1:292). The Saxons in Transylvania do likewise (Ploss, 2:842). In the Punjab in India, they put a piece of the cord into the mother's and the newborn's clothes as a protection against the evil eye (Seligmann, *Der böse Blick*, 2:144).

538. In the whole Indian archipelago, e.g., they use special knives made of bamboo, although in everyday life they use metal knives. The bamboo knives used for cutting the umbilical cord must not be used for any other purpose (Ploss, 2:842).

539. Kehimkar, *Bene Israel*, p. 112.

540. *Sh'vile Emuna*, sig. 4, p. 6; *Sefer Z'khira*, p. 54a. The Arabs in Syria believe that if they cut the cord too short, the child will not have a pleasant voice (Abela, "Beiträge," p. 114).

541. Oral communication from Ḥakham Shim'on Harus of Safed.

542. Oral communication from a Moroccan Jewish woman in Jerusalem.

543. Cf. Patai, *Adam va'Adama*, 2:113ff.

544. Gaster, "Birth, Jewish," p. 658.

545. *Mar'e haY'ladim*, p. 71a, quoting "a manuscript book"; ibid., p. 71b.

546. In Syria, if a child suffers an earache, they take a little of the yellow clay of which the baking oven is built, put it in water, and smear it over his ears (Abela, "Beiträge," p. 30).

547. *Toldot Adam*, pp. 19a–20b, no. 139. Similar customs are found among other peoples. In Syria, if a man wants to make sure that his daughter will speak well, immediately after her birth he takes dust from under the door of the room in which the delivery took place and smears it on her mouth (Abela, "Beiträge," p. 81). In Voigtland and Silesia, if the child can not sleep, the mother sweeps the room, collects the dust in the middle of the room, and then puts it under the child's head (Wuttke, *Volksaberglaube*, p. 386, par. 587).

548. Patai, *Adam va'Adama*, 2:113–14.

549. In Denmark, they use *Kristenmold* (earth from the cemetery) to protect the child from being exchanged by tying it around the child's neck soon after birth (Nyberg, *Kind und Erde*, pp. 257–58, n. 451).

550. E.g., in Australia, Java, etc. (Frazer, *Golden Bough*, 1:147).

551. *Abi'a Ḥiddot*, p. 83a, quoting "a manuscript book."

552. However, earth taken from other places also can cause deep sleep. In Mettersdorf, after the newborn has slept in the field for the first time, his mother takes home some earth from where the field cradle stood to assure good sleep for the child (Nyberg, *Kind und Erde*, p. 142; Dieterich, *Mutter Erde*, p. 127).

553. Oral communication from a Moroccan Jewish woman in Jerusalem.
554. Reich, *Villages araméens*, p. 71.
555. Stern, *Medizin*, 2:337; Abela, "Beiträge," pp. 84, 106. In India it is the custom that if a child's siblings have died very young, they dig a hole under the framework of the door of the house in which the child was born, and hand the child through it from the outside into the house. The name of the hole is Koni, and if the child is male, they call him Konia, and if a female, Konema (Frazer, *Folk-Lore in the Old Testament*, 3:183). On the widespread rite of passing a sickly newborn across a hole or a cleft in the ground, evidently as an attempt to cause him to be born again, see Nyberg, *Kind und Erde*, pp. 152–53. In Indian folklore one finds an interesting instance of the belief that rebirth, effected with the help of a big earthenware jar, gives new life to a person. In ancient India it was customary to perform a burial rite for a man who was thought to have died in an unknown place. They made a human figure out of 360 leaf stems, and then burned it amid all the rites usually performed at a proper burial. If it happened that the man who was presumed dead reappeared, he continued to be considered dead legally and ritually until a rebirth ceremony was performed. They filled a big earthenware jar, or a barrel, with water and clarified butter, and the man's father recited over it a verse from the Vedas which said that it served as the mother's womb. Then the man got into the vessel, crouched down in it in a fetal position, and remained thus throughout the night without uttering a sound. In the morning they performed all the usual rites of childbirth, and then the adult newborn got out of the vessel through the back (apparently they broke out the bottom). After the performance of the additional rites which normally followed the birth of a child, the man was considered reborn and alive legally. Similar customs were found among the ancient Greeks, and their traces survived until recently among various peoples (Ploss, 2:864–65; cf. Frazer, *Golden Bough*, 1:75).
556. Patai, *Adam va'Adama*, 2:23–24.
557. In modern Greece they used to put a jasper into the child's cradle, in Brandenburg a stone called *Krötenstein*, i.e., "toad-stone," and in Voigtland a *Schreckenstein*, "fright stone." Metals have the same virtue, and especially metal cutting utensils, such as knives, scissors, or needles (Michał Zmigrodsky, *Die Mutter bei den Völkern des arischen Stammes* [Munich, 1886], pp. 115–16; Nyberg, *Kind und Erde*, p. 142). Cf. Georg Graber, "Das Schwert auf dem Brautlager," *ARW* 35 (1938):133–34. Iron is, of course, well known as a protector against demons (Ignaz Goldziher, "Eisen als Schutz gegen Dämonen," *ARW* 10 (1907):41–46; Samter, *Geburt, Hochzeit, und Tod*, pp. 23, 27, 194). In Sweden it is customary to protect the child by putting steel on its cradle (Nyberg, *Kind und Erde*, p. 142).
558. In the Palatinate, Germany, they put iron under the bed of the woman in childbed, "so that the blood of her heart should not spill." In East Prussia they do the same as a protection from witchcraft. In the Upper Palatinate they put a pair of scissors into the cradle as a protection for the child (Wuttke, *Volksaberglaube*, p. 378, para. 575). Almost all over Germany, they stick a knife into the door or the doorpost at the time of delivery (ibid., p. 382, par. 581; cf. Sartori, *Sitte und Brauch*, 1:27). Among other peoples, see *HWDA*, 3:415–16. Among the Arabs, both the Muslims and the Christians, in Palestine, they put a knife or a pair of scissors, stuck into a loaf of bread, next to the child who suffers pain (Canaan, *Aberglaube und Volksmedizin*, p. 80, n. 6).
559. Tos. Shab. 6:4, p. 117.
560. Bodenschatz, *Kirchliche Verfassung*, 4:57.
561. Brauer, "Jews of Afghanistan," p. 133.
562. *Mar'e haY'ladim*, p. 71a, quoting "a manuscript book."
563. Written communication from Ḥakham Shim'on Harus of Safed.
564. *Sefer haMat'amim*, p. 47.
565. Ibid., p. 77.
566. Elzet, "MiMinhage Yisrael," p. 364.
567. Löw, *Lebensalter in der jüdischen Literatur*, p. 77.

568. Elzet, "MiMinhage Yisrael," p. 364.
569. Grunwald, "Zur Vorgeschichte des Sukkothrituals," pp. 455–56.
570. Kehimkar, *Bene Israel*, p. 112. This custom is observed in various tribes in Morocco as a protection against the jinn (Westermarck, *Ritual and Belief*, 2:273, 379–80, 382).
571. *Sefer Z'khira*, p. 29a; *Sefer haMat'amim*, p. 47; cf. *Shulḥan 'Arukh, Yore De'a* 305:15, where another reason is given for hanging a silver disk around the neck of a firstborn who has not yet been redeemed: to remind him, when he grows up, that he must redeem himself.
572. *R'fu'a v'Ḥayyim*, chap. 12, 35a.
573. Ya'aqov Sapir, *Even Sapir*, 1:58b–59a.
574. *Toldot Adam*, p. 19b, no. 137.
575. *Sefer Z'khira*, p. 26b.
576. B. Qid. 73b; cf. M. Shab. 6:9; B. Shab. 66b. (See also *Otzar haG'onim* Shab., the commentators, pars. 126–27. *Note added by Meir Havazelet*).
577. Nyberg, *Kind und Erde*, pp. 95–126, esp. 100, 104. Cf. Ploss-Renz, 1:213, 215–26, 296–306; I. Scheftelowitz, in *ARW* 17 (1914):368–69, 405–6.
578. *Amtaḥat Binyamin*, p. 34a; *Toldot Adam*, p. 6b, no. 3. See also *Mar'e haY'ladim*, p. 57b, quoting "a manuscript book."
579. Kehimkar, *Bene Israel*, p. 113.
580. Ibid., p. 136.
581. Scheftelowitz, in *ARW* 17 (1914):412. Among the Arabs in Egypt it is customary for the midwife to place a jar full of water at the child's head on the seventh day after its birth. (Lane, *Manners and Customs*, p. 511. See also *Otzar haG'onim*, Shab. par. 127. *Note added by Meir Havazelet*.)
582. *Toldot Adam*, pp. 15b, no. 116, 17a, no. 126.
583. *HWDA*, 3:451. Among the Albanians fire has to burn in the house of the woman in childbed for six weeks after delivery (Stern, *Medizin*, 2:315).
584. Cf. 2 Sam. 14:7, 21:17, 22:29; 1 Kings 11:36; Isa. 10:17; Ps. 27:1. Cf. Stanley A. Cook, *The Religion of Ancient Palestine* . . . (London, 1930), pp. 87–88; Mannhardt, *Wald und Feldkulte*, 1:508–9, 2:302–3, 3:135, 190; Frazer, *Golden Bough*, 2:195–96, 230–31. Cf. also Patai, *Adam va'Adama*, 2:218–19.
585. Lev. Rab. 14:2.
586. Seder Y'tzirat haVlad, in Jellinek, *Bet haMidrash*, 1:154. Cf. M. Gaster, *The Chronicles of Jerahmeel* (London, 1899), pp. 19–20, xiii–xiv; M. Güdemann, *Religionsgeschichtliche Studien* (Leipzig, 1876), pp. 7–21.
587. B. Shab. 23b.
588. *Sefer haMiddot*, s.v. Banim, no. 54; cf. no. 91.
589. B. Shab. 128b.
590. Y. Shab. 16c bot. Cf. Lampronti, *Pahad Yitzḥaq*, vol. 4, p. 11a. The magical character of the fire lit for the woman in childbed is shown in the Hottentot custom: the fire is lit at the time of delivery and kept going until the child's navel heals. It is forbidden to cook or take ashes from that fire (Ploss-Renz, 2:194). In ancient Rome they lighted a candle in the room of the woman in confinement to drive away the demons, and the same custom is practiced in modern Greece (Ludwig Deubner, in *ERE*, 2:649).
591. J. D. Eisenstein, ed., *Otzar Yisrael*, 10 vols. (Berlin, Vienna, and London, 1924), 5:108–9, s.v. Yoledet. Cf. Chorny, "Die kaukasischen Juden," p. 200; Andrée, *Volkskunde der Juden*, p. 182; Aaron Fürst, *Sitten und Gebräuche einer Judengasse* (Székesfehérvár, 1908), p. 50 (on Eisenstadt, one of the seven communities in Burgenland).
592. Kehimkar, *Bene Israel*, p. 113.
593. Written communication from R. Eliyahu Ma'aravi of Damascus.
594. Oral communication from Ḥakham Shim'on Harus of Safed. The underlying belief hinted at in these Jewish sources and customs is expressed explicitly in the customs of primitive peoples. In the Amboina and Uliasser islands, "the new-born babe is subject to

the attacks of evil spirits and is put by the fire for his protection'' (Crawley, *Mystic Rose*, 1:74). All over Germany the custom is to have a candle or a lamp burn in the room of the woman in childbed all night and every night until the baptism. In various places three candles are required (Wuttke, *Volksaberglaube*, p. 383, par. 583).

595. Hartland, in *ERE*, 2:638; Stern, *Medizin*, 2:315, 317. In Germany this is observed for nine days or six weeks (Wuttke, *Volksaberglaube*, p. 382, par. 582; *HWDA*, 3:411); in Syria it is observed until the child's navel heals (Abela, "Beiträge," p. 100).

596. Elzet, in *R'shumot*, 1:362.

597. Luncz, *Y'rushalayim*, 1:27; Reischer, *Sefer Sha'are Y'rushalayim* 9 (*Minhage Aretz*).

598. Chorny, *Sefer haMassa'ot*, p. 296; cf. Kasdai, *Mamlekhet Ararat*, pp. 55–56.

599. Brauer, *Y'hude Kurdistan*, p. 133.

600. Brauer, *Ethnologie*, p. 187.

601. Luncz, *Y'rushalayim*, 1:27; cf. Stern, *Medizin*, 2:317–18.

602. Scheftelowitz, *Altpalästinensischer Bauernglaube*, p. 45n; Canaan, *Aberglaube und Volksmedizin*, p. 73.

603. Maimonides, *Guide of the Perplexed* 3, chap. 37, Friedlander trans., p. 178.

604. Brauer, *Ethnologie*, pp. 186–88.

605. Ibid., p. 192.

606. Lane, *Manners and Customs*, 1:316; Stern, *Medizin*, 2:312; Ploss-Renz, 1:283.

607. E.g., in East Prussia, in Brandenburg, among the Slavs, in Gleiwitz, in Hungary, and on the island of Kithnos, Greece (Hartland, in *ERE*, 2:638; Wuttke, *Volksaberglaube*, p. 379, par. 576; Géza Róheim, *Spiegelzauber* (Leipzig, 1919), pp. 112, 174.

608. Stern, *Medizin*, 2:317.

609. Oral communication from a Moroccan Jewish woman in Jerusalem.

610. In Dukkala, Morocco, they put tar into the nostrils of a sick person (Westermarck, *Ritual and Belief*, 1:325).

611. *Toldot Adam*, p. 12b.

612. Kehimkar, *Bene Israel*, pp. 112ff.

613. Oral communication from a Moroccan Jewish woman in Jerusalem.

614. Westermarck, *Ritual and Belief*, 2:383–84.

615. Brauer, *Ethnologie*, p. 184.

616. *Sh'vile Emuna*, p. 6.

617. Ploss-Renz, 1:280. In the Aramaic-speaking villages of the Anti-Lebanon they use myrtle leaves (which also have an important role in their marriage and death customs) to protect the newborn: they grind the leaves, mix them with a little oil, the rind of a pomegranate, and some salt, and put the ointment into a small satchel, and rub the child's body with it (Reich, *Villages araméens*, p. 74).

618. Cf. Patai, *Adam va'Adama*, 1:232. (See also *Otzar haG'onim* Shab. pp. 19–20, 82. *Note added by Meir Havazelet.*)

619. *R'fu'a v'Hayyim*, chap. 12, 35a; and in a somewhat different version in *Sefer haMiddot*, s.v. Banim, no. 64.

620. Oral communication from Hakham Shim'on Harus of Safed. Both garlic and rue also figure among fertility charms.

621. Etta Yellin, *L'Tze'etza'ay*, 2 vols. (Jerusalem, 1938, 1941), 2:51. Among the Arabs of Egypt the birth stool brought by the midwife is decorated with flowers (Lane, *Manners and Customs*, p. 509).

622. See section V above.

623. *Sefer haMiddot*, s.v. Banim, no. 7; in the Traqlin ed., p. 32, no. 114, this charm is given in a corrupt version.

624. *Toldot Adam*, p. 12b, no. 114.

625. Ibid., p. 37a. (*Weyn royten* is the German *Wein-Raute*, a species of rue; *wakholter ber* is the German *Wacholder Beere*, a juniper berry; *kiml* is the German *Kümmel*, caraway; *besin* is the German *Besen*, broom, the shrubs of the genera Cytisus, Genista, and Spartium. I am indebted to Prof. Nathan Susskind for the interpretation of these Yiddish-German terms. *Note added in 1982.*)

626. Cf. Pliny, *Historia Naturalis* 8.30.49.
627. *Toldot Adam*, p. 7b, no. 62.
628. Oral communication from Yosef Sikron of Jerusalem. The slaughtering of a cock or a hen on the occasion of a birth also is practiced among the Muslim Moroccans (Westermarck, *Ritual and Belief*, 2:379–80).
629. *Toldot Adam*, p. 24a, no. 161.
630. *Abi'a Ḥiddot*, p. 46b.
631. Brauer, *Ethnologie*, p. 186.
632. Kehimkar, *Bene Israel*, pp. 112–13.
633. "Sefer S'gullot v'Ḥiddot," p. 55a.
634. *Toldot Adam*, p. 25b, no. 166.
635. Ibid., p. 38a.
636. I.e., wax that has not yet been used; see *Otzar haḤayyim* by R. Y. Tzahalon 6.26, as quoted in Eliezer Ben Y'huda, *Millon*, s.v. B'tula. *Note added by Meir Havazelet.*
637. Possibly *luz*, variously identified as hazelnut, pistachio nut, or almond; see Ben Y'huda, *Millon*, s.v. luz, and Löw, *Flora*, 1:617–18, 620; 3:153–54. *Note added in 1980.*
638. *Toldot Adam*, p. 20a, no. 140.
639. "Sefer S'gullot v'Ḥiddot," p. 55a.
640. *Sefer Z'khira*, p. 27b; *Toldot Adam*, p. 38b; *Amtaḥat Binyamin*, p. 19a; written communication from R. Eliyahu Ma'aravi of Damascus. Cf. the custom of the Muslim Moroccans in connection with a newborn puppy to ensure conception and the birth of a male child (Westermarck, *Ritual and Belief*, 1:585).
641. *Sefer Z'khira*, p. 27b.
642. *Toldot Adam*, pp. 4b, 6a.
643. Brauer, "Jews of Afghanistan," p. 133.
644. See section IID above.
645. Reich, *Villages araméens*, p. 77.
646. *Amtaḥat Binyamin*, p. 34a; *Sefer Z'khira*, pp. 27b, 29b.
647. *Sefer haMiddot*, s.v. Banim, no. 60.
648. *Abi'a Ḥiddot*, p. 46b. Other such amulets are discussed below among metal charms.
649. HaR'uveni, "Tzimḥe Bosem," pp. 102–3.
650. Brauer, "Jews of Afghanistan," pp. 133, 137.
651. See section IE above.
652. Tos. Shab. 6:1, pp. 249–50.
653. Oral communication from Yosef M'yuḥas of Jerusalem. There are many beliefs in Germany in connection with the hand of a dead person, and especially of a dead child. Caressing someone with such a hand can drive away growths, swellings, toothaches, throataches, and other pains. In Oldenberg they first caress a dead person's face with the hand and then caress the afflicted living person with it. The hand or finger of a dead child can make a person invisible, open locked doors, and so on (Wuttke, *Volksaberglaube*, p. 133, pars. 183–84; *HWDA*, 2:229–30).
654. Written communication from R. Eliyahu Ma'aravi of Damascus.
655. Oral communication from Ḥakham Shim'on Harus of Safed.
656. *Sefer Z'khira*, p. 25a.
657. Brauer, "Bräuche," p. 110.
658. Written communication from R. Eliyahu Ma'aravi of Damascus.
659. Oral communication from Ḥakham Shim'on Harus of Safed.
660. *Sefer Z'khira*, p. 53b.
661. *Mif'alot Eloqim*, par. 167.
662. Written communication from R. Eliyahu Ma'aravi of Damascus.
663. Oral communication from Ḥakham Shim'on Harus of Safed.
664. Yellin, *L'Tze'etza'ay*, 1:49.
665. *Sefer haMiddot*, s.v. Banim, no. 134; cf. *R'fu'a v'Ḥayyim*, chap. 12, 35a.
666. Oral communication from Yosef Sikron of Jerusalem.
667. Canaan, *Aberglaube und Volksmedizin*, p. 90.

668. Lane, *Manners and Customs*, p. 58.

669. Examples of such exchanges of clothing at birth are found, e.g., in Germany, India, China, Australia, Guatemala, and among the Basuto (Crawley, *Mystic Rose*, 2:103–4; Frazer, *Folk-Lore in the Old Testament*, 3:184–85, 193).

670. Scheftelowitz, *Altpalästinensischer Bauernglaube*, pp. 54–55; Frazer, *Golden Bough*, 6:253–54; Edward Westermarck, *The History of Human Marriage*, 3 vols. (New York, 1922), 2:519–20.

671. Crawley, *Mystic Rose*, 2:100–101.

672. Wuttke, *Volksaberglaube*, p. 381, par. 580.

673. Maimonides, *Qovetz T' shuvot* 51a; cf. Lane, *Manners and Customs*, p. 53.

674. *M'qore Minhagim* 92; cf. Maimonides, *Guide*, 3:37; *Sefer Z'khira*, p. 27b; *Sefer haMat'amim*, p. 48; *Mar'e haY'ladim*, p. 16b, quoting the Rav ShLaH (*Sh'ne Luḥot haB'rit*).

675. Written communication from Ben-Zion Taragan of Alexandria.

676. Oral communication from a Moroccan Jewish woman in Jerusalem. An exact gentile parallel to this Jewish view is found in Brandenburg, Germany: it is forbidden to wrap a newborn male in a woman's apron or kerchief, lest he become a womanizer. They wrap him in a linen sheet (Wuttke, *Volksaberglaube*, p. 381, par. 580).

677. Oral communication from Aaron Fürst in Jerusalem.

678. Y. Shab. 8b top; Y. 'Er. 26c mid.; cf. *Shulḥan 'Arukh, Yore De'a* 179:9.

679. *Maḥzor Vitry*, ed. Shim'on Horowitz (Nuremberg, 1923), p. 628.

680. Bergmann, "Sitten und Sagen," p. 163.

681. *Sefer Ḥasidim*, ed. Bologna, par. 1040; quoted here from the Warsaw, 1879 ed., p. 224.

682. Bodenschatz, *Kirchliche Verfassung*, 4:65–66; cf. Kirchner, *Jüdisches Zeremoniell*, p. 164.

683. Joseph Perles, "Die Berner Handschrift des kleinen Aruch," in *Jubelschrift zum siebzigsten Geburtstage . . . H. Graetz* (Breslau, 1887), pp. 26–27.

684. Cf. *Sefer Ta'ame Minhagim* 3:85b; *Sefer haMat'amim* 47, quoting *Ma'avar Yabboq*. Cf. Leopold Zunz, *Zur Geschichte und Literatur* (Berlin, 1845), p. 168; Grunwald, "Aus Hausapotheke und Hexenküche," *Mitteilungen*, p. 83; M. L. Bamberger, "Aus meiner Minhagimsammelmappe," *Jahrbuch für jüdische Volkskunde* 1 (1923):329.

685. Gaster, "Birth, Jewish," p. 658.

686. E.g., German folk belief holds that it is forbidden to leave the newborn alone in a room unless a Bible or a prayer book is put under its head or on its bed. Otherwise demons might "exchange" the child (Wuttke, *Volksaberglaube*, pp. 383, par. 583, 379, par. 575).

687. Canaan, *Aberglaube und Volksmedizin*, p. 80, n. 6.

688. Bodenschatz, *Kirchliche Verfassung*, 4:72.

689. Cf. Brauer, *Ethnologie*, pp. 188, 191. This rite is intended to ensure that the woman will have no other child for three years. Among the Albanians the isolation lasts forty days, during which the mother and child must remain in the house. At night they must not even leave the room in which the delivery took place (Stern, *Medizin*, 2:315).

690. Kehimkar, *Bene Israel*, pp. 118, 123. Among the Ila-speakers of Northern Rhodesia the isolation lasts at least six days, after which they perform a rite, centered on the threshold, to remove evil influences (Smith and Dale, *Ila-Speaking Peoples*, 2:11).

691. Chorny, *Sefer haMassa'ot*, p. 296; cf. Kasdai, *Mamlekhet Ararat*, p. 55.

692. Kasdai, *Mamlekhet Ararat*, p. 55.

693. Patai, *Adam va'Adama*, 2:118ff.

694. Perles, "Berner Handschrift," p. 27; cf. M. Gaster, in *MGWJ* 29 (1880):556. (As for the role of Lilith, the arch she-demon, in the Jewish folk imagination, see now Raphael Patai, *The Hebrew Goddess* [New York, 1978], pp. 180–225. *Note added in 1980.*)

695. *Sefer Z'khira*, p. 29a, quoting *Sefer Naftuli*, sec. *WaY'hi*.

696. *Toldot Adam*, p. 24a, no. 162.

697. Bodenschatz, *Kirchliche Verfassung*, 4:57.

698. Julius Dahlberg, ''Volkskunde der Hessen-Kasseler Juden,'' in *Geschichte der jüdischen Gemeinde Kassel* . . . , vol. 1 (Kassel, 1931), p. 157.

699. *Ta'ame Minhagim* 2, 32b, quoting *Sefer haHayyim*, sec. *Sh'mini*.

700. Lancelot Addison, *The Present State of the Jews* (London, 1682), pp. 55–56.

701. Oral communication from a Moroccan Jewish woman in Jerusalem.

702. Luncz, *Y'rushalayim*, 1:27.

703. *Section added in 1982*.

VI.
On the
Peripheries

22. The Jewish Indians of Mexico

In 1939 a series of three articles was published in Yiddish by Meir Berger, a resident of Mexico City, under the title "The 'Red Jews' of Mexico," in the Chicago Yiddish daily *Idisher Kurir* (15, 16, 18 Jan.). The same three articles were published simultaneously in the Philadelphia Yiddish daily *Idishe Velt*. The first two of the three dealt with the beginnings of Jewish settlement in Mexico and with the lawsuits the Inquisition brought against Jews who had escaped from Spain to New Spain—that is, Mexico. The third, which was titled "How do the Grand-children of the Marranos Live in Mexico Today?" in *Idishe Velt* (12 Jan. 1939), described the life of the Indian Jews in present-day Mexico. Berger stated that in 1917, after Mexico adopted its new constitution, the Marranos began to organize, and that "today they number about three thousand in all Mexico."

That there were three thousand descendants of the Marranos, living all over the country and organized into congregations, was repeated in the writings of several authors and travelers who visited Mexico. Marie Syrkin published an article entitled "The Jewish Indians in Mexico" in the *Jewish*

Frontier Anthology 1943–44 (New York, 1945), pp. 509–14, in which she repeated the same number. Egon Erwin Kisch, in his *Entdeckungen in Mexico*, devoted a chapter to the Jewish Indians of Mexico entitled "David's Star in an Indian Village."[1] According to Kisch, there were in the village of Venta Prieta 150 Jews, of whom 37 were adults; all of them belonged to the Tellez or Gonzalez families, who had come two generations earlier from Zamora in the state of Michoacan. In the 10 June 1948 issue of the Tel Aviv daily *Haaretz*, an article titled "Sabbath-Keeping Mexicans," by Benjamin Koralski, stated that "they number a few thousands." During my first visit to Mexico, in the summer of 1948, Rabbi Menahem Coriat, chief rabbi of the Sephardi community in Mexico City, told me that there were two Jewish Indian communities in the city. One was in the Vallejo quarter, headed by *licenciado* (attorney) Ramirez, and the other, twice as big, in the Rio Blanco quarter, headed by Mr. Katz-Hirsh, who was of German-Jewish origin.

All of these reports and statements, and several similar ones,[2] suffer from one basic mistake: they fail to distinguish between two fundamentally dissimilar groups, both of which they consider "Jewish Indians." One of them—as I learned in the course of my fieldwork in Mexico—consists of a very few small and scattered groups of "Jewish Indians," numbering a total of perhaps two hundred or two hundred and fifty, and living in Mexico City, in the village of Venta Prieta, and in a few other places.

The other community, several thousands strong, can in no way be called or considered Jewish Indians. It is a Christian community whose members believe in a special variant of the Christian faith and also observe the biblical Jewish holidays. The name of this community is Iglesia de Dios, that is, the Church of God, and it is but a Mexican version of the Church of God which originated in the United States, where most of its membership is still found. Since we have reason to assume that a considerable part of the Jewish Indians came originally from this Iglesia de Dios and joined the Indian Jewish community, a discussion of its life and doctrines seems in order.

Because most of my fieldwork in Mexico in 1948 was devoted to the Jewish Indians in Venta Prieta, I could not obtain as much information as I would have liked about the origins and history of the Iglesia de Dios in Mexico City. This subject requires a special investigation. But it appears that the church was founded by missionaries from the United States who went to Mexico to proselytize for the American Church of God in the early 1900s. It was not until the second third of the century, however, that the Iglesia de Dios grew to a considerable extent. According to members of the church, whom I interviewed in Mexico City and in Puebla, the Iglesia de

Dios comprised six trends or divisions. Five of them observed Sunday and the Christian holidays, while the sixth, to which my informants belonged, observed the biblical Jewish holidays and the Sabbath, and considered itself the spiritual heir of the ten tribes of Israel. At the same time, they also believed that Jesus was the son of God and the Messiah, and that the day would come when all the Jews would recognize Jesus and therewith become true Jews. For the time being only they, the members of the Iglesia de Dios del Septimo Dia, the Church of God of the Seventh Day, were true Jews.

It was not easy to elicit clear answers from my informants. It required patient probing, and many direct and indirect questions, until the leaders of the church whom I interviewed came forward with unequivocal statements. The church was located at 16 Jose Maria Vigil street in Mexico City, in the Tacubaya quarter. It was a medium-sized room on the second floor of an old house. In front of the chairs, near one wall, there was a reader's desk covered with a white cloth, and on the side which faced the room it was decorated with a Star of David with *Sion* written in the middle. To the right of this pulpit there was a blackboard which, I was told, the teacher of the church used in the lessons he gave to the members. To the left of it stood a piano which was used during the services. The rest of the room was filled with rows of chairs. This was all the furniture, and no external sign indicated anything about the nature or origin of the church's doctrines.

I visited the church on a weekday afternoon, when several members were gathering to receive doctrinal instruction from Roberto Mercado Manzanares, their teacher and leader, to whom I addressed questions about himself, the history of the church, and its doctrines. I am quoting here his answers, as far as possible verbatim, including the contradictions and variations they contained.

About himself Manzanares stated that he was Jewish, and that his parents too were Jews. There were, according to him, many Jews named Manzanares in Uruguay, Guatemala, and Argentina. To my question how his Jewishness and that of the church was expressed, he answered that they considered themselves 90 percent Jews and not more. They were all circumcised; they did not eat pork, they did not work on the Sabbath; they observed the Jewish holidays, New Year, the Day of Atonement, Tabernacles, and so on. They prayed in Spanish and sang only the *Sh'ma' Yisrael* and *HaTiqva* in Hebrew. I asked Manzanares to show me the Hebrew texts of these prayers, but he did not have them. Only when I visited the Iglesia de Dios in Puebla was I able to obtain the texts.

The prayers were printed in two leaflets of four pages each. The first page of both was the same title page;

Iglesia de Dios
Universal Israelita
52 Poniente 1105   Tel. Mexicana 34–18
Puebla, Pue.

The last page of each was blank, and the two inner pages contained the Hebrew texts in Spanish transliteration.

La Sehma

Deuteronomio 6:4–10

Sehma Israel. Adonai Elo
Enum Adonaaaay Ejad
Baruc chen Ke Vu Mayjuto
Leo Laan Vael A Men.

Haticva

Col ol balevav pnimá
Nefesch iehudi homiia,
Ulfatei mizraj cadima
Ain le Sion tzofiia

Od lo avdá ticvatenu
Haticvá mis nostal fain
Li yu tan japsi
Vearseeeenu eree
Zillon Vilurs halain.

Schim u, ajai, beartzot nudi
Et col ajad jozeinu:
qui rac im ajaron haiehudi
Gam ajarit ticvatenu:

  Od lo avdá . . .

La Esperanza

Traduccion

Mientras en el corazón
palpite un alma judía,
y en dirección al oriente
a Sión, la mirada se encamine
nuestra esperanza no se ha perdido
la antigua esperanza
de retornar al pais de nuestros mayores,
a la ciudad donde David moraba.

Escuchad, hermanos mios, en los países
  de mi deambular

La voz de uno de nuestros profetas
"Que sólo con el último judío,
Terminará nuestra esperanza".

Estaremos junto en ese día glorioso
En la tierra de nuestros mayores:
¡¡Viva, viva Palestina!!
nuestros padres dejaron
Lugar que
fin conquistaron.

El Himno que entonó
Moises cuando pasó
el Mar Rojo

Salmo 137: del 1–5

En ke lo e e nu
En ka do ne e nu
En ka mal ke nu
En ke mo shi e nu.

Mi ke lo e nu
Mi ka do ne nu
Mi ke mal kc nu
Mi ke mo shi e nu.

No de le lo e e nu
No de la do ne e nu
No de la mal ke nu
No de la mo shi e nu.

Baruj e lo e nu
Baruj a do ne nu
Baruj ke mal ke nu
Baruj mo shi e nu.

At ta hu he lo he e nu
At ta hu ha do ne e nu
At ta hu mal ke nu
At ta hu mo shi he nu.

Traduccion

No hay como nuestro Dios
No hay como nuestro Senor
No hay como nuestro Rey
No hay como nuestro Salvador.

¿Quién es como nuestro Dios?
¿Quién es como nuestro Senor?
¿Quién es como nuestro Rey?
¿Quién es como nuestro Salvador?

Alabemos a nuestro Dios
Alabemos a nuestro Senor
Alabemos a nuestro Rey
Alabemos a nuestro Salvador.

Bendito sea nuestro Dios
Bendito sea nuestro Senor
Bendito sea nuestro Rey
Bendito sea nuestro Salvador.

Tu eres nuestro Dios
Tu eres nuestro Senor
Tu eres nuestro Rey
Tu eres nuestro Salvador.

The transliteration shows that it was originally prepared by somebody who could read Hebrew and used the Sephardi pronunciation. However, in the course of copying and recopying, more and more errors were made. While the *HaTiqva* and the *En kElohenu* are translated into Spanish, the *Sh'ma' Yisrael* is not. Can it be that this, the most basic prayer of Judaism, was not translated because it proclaims the oneness of God, while the doctrines of the Iglesia de Dios embrace the belief in the Trinity?

Of special interest is the Hebrew text and the Spanish translation of the second stanza of *HaTiqva*. The Hebrew contains, instead of the original words written by Imber, the new version which was substituted in Israel: "Our hope is not yet lost/The hope of two centuries/to be a free nation in our country/The Land of Zion and Jerusalem." This shows that the *HaTiqva* was incorporated into the liturgy of the church not too long ago, or, at least, that there was contact between the leaders of the church and Mexican Zionist circles. The Spanish version, however, which is otherwise literal, contains the translation of the old text of *HaTiqva*: "Our hope is not yet lost/The age-old hope/To return to the land of our fathers/To the city in which David camped."

In the second pamphlet the *En kElohenu* hymn has the title "The Hymn Which Moses Sang When He Passed Through the Red Sea," followed by a source quotation, Psalm 157:1–5 (sic).

About 1930, the Mexico City center of the Iglesia de Dios published (without a date) an eight-page pamphlet, titled *Publicaciones de la Iglesia de Dios—Constitucion Govierno y Doctrina de la Iglesia de Dios*, containing a description of the organization and doctrines of the sect. In several places in it there are allusions or references to Judaism. The paragraph dealing with the constitution of the sect on page 5 states that the Iglesia de Dios has "general offices in Jerusalem, Palestine." Section 8 (pp. 6–7) contains several paragraphs and allusions to the Jewish religion.

Par. 1: The *Biblia*, the Old and the New Testaments, are, and apart from them no other writing is, inspired scripture, and in them is found completely, without error, and clearly, the will of God as directed to man.

Par. 2: Yahweh (Jehova) is God, the creator of the heavens, the earth, the sea, and everything which is in them.

Par. 19: Every year one must celebrate *la Cena del Señor* (the supper of the Lord), at the beginning of the *Pascua* (Passover), on the fourteenth of the month of Nisan, thus following the example given by Jesus.

Par. 21: We must observe the seventh day of the week, from the evening to the evening, as a day of rest sanctified for the Lord.

Par. 34: In the end the people of Israel will be united in Jerusalem.

Several other paragraphs also contain Jewish doctrines in the form in which they are known from the New Testament or from their later Christian reworking. The Christian element is much stronger in these doctrines than the Jewish. Of the holy days mentioned in the Hebrew Bible, these doctrines require only observance of the Sabbath and the Passover night.

It would seem, however, that in the years since the publication of this pamphlet, a certain development in the direction of Judaism has taken place in the Iglesia de Dios. According to the leaders of the sect whom I interviewed in Mexico City and Puebla, they observe all the holy days mentioned in the Hebrew Bible (but not those established later, e.g., Purim and the ninth of Ab), and also keep some of the biblical dietary laws. In Puebla they do not eat pork, the meat of the hare, etc., as specified in the Pentateuch. But they do eat meat and milk together. In Mexico City they do not eat meat with milk, nor even chicken with milk. In Puebla they are not circumcised, but in Mexico City they are, according to the informants interviewed.

On the other hand, their doctrines also contain tenets which are opposed to Jewish monotheism. While I was present in the church in Mexico City, Manzanares addressed a group of students on the meaning of the Star of David. He drew a *Magen David* on the blackboard, wrote *1* to *6* at the six points of the star, and wrote *7* in the middle. "If we philosophize about Creation," he said,

we shall find that the star is the symbol of creation as written in the Bible. Creation took six days, and as against them are the six points of the star. On the seventh day God rested. And when the seventh day of the world eras arrives, all Israel will gather in Jerusalem. To this allude the verses Numbers 24:17, Deuteronomy 18:18, Isaiah 7:14, and Psalms 2:7. All these verses together state that when the Messiah appears, that star will be visible in heaven. The *Historia Universal* of Cesar Cantu, and likewise the history books of Mante, Wells, and others, say that in the year 4004 of the Jewish calendar, and again in 1843, there was a rain of stars.

The star is composed of two triangles—one heavenly triangle and one

earthly triangle. [At this point of his address Manzanares drew two triangles on
the blackboard, one pointing downward, and above it one pointing upward.] In
Genesis 1:26 it is said that God made man in His shape and image. God spoke
in the plural, which shows that He was not alone, but was accompanied by
somebody. In Job 33:4 it is said, "The spirit of God hath made me, and the
breath of the Almighty giveth me life." This verse shows that, in addition to
God, a new person appeared in the Bible, and the name of him is "Jehova."
Also in Job 1:6 "the sons of God" are mentioned. In Job, in the aforementioned verse, it says that the sons of God came to present themselves before
God—that is, here two separate persons are spoken of, God and Jehova. The
meaning of the name Jehova is "messengers." This is the etymology of the
word, which is composed of Hebrew and Aramaic elements. The name Jehova
was known, before the Jews, to the father-in-law of Moses. Jehova and God
are two divine beings. This becomes clear also from what is said in the Bible
about their attributes: among the attributes of Jehova is that he repents, but God
does not repent. Thus it says in Genesis 6:6, "And it repented Jehova that he
had made man." But of God it says in Numbers 23:19, "God is not a man that
He should lie, neither the son of man that He should repent." And also in the
Book of Samuel, in another connection, it is said that Jehova repented that He
had set up Saul to be king (I Sam. 15:35), and that "the Glory of Israel," that
is, God, does not repent (v. 29). Therefore, because of this attribute of Jehova,
in which he resembles man more than God, we shall be justified in locating him
in the heavenly triangle under God, while the other lower corner of this triangle
is the place of Jesus. And, again, the star in its totality, with its six corners,
symbolizes Jehova alone, and the six points of the star stand for the six letters
of the name Jehova.

With these words Manzanares concluded his address, which was one of
a series of talks he gave to veteran members of the church whose intention
was to go out to the provincial towns and villages of Mexico for missionary
work. Manzanares explained to me that the missionary work is very important, because most of the simple people in Mexico still believed that the Jews
were the children of Satan, that they had horns, and that they were salty. The
missionaries go out among the people, talk and preach to them, tell them
about the history of the Jews, and explain that the Jews are at the head of
everything. For is it not that Mary and the saints were Jews, and not
Americans or Spaniards? The missionaries explain to the people that the
Spaniards brought Christianity to Mexico, and also the Inquisition and
idolatry. Once the listeners begin to appreciate these teachings, after a year
"these proselytes become more Jewish than any original Jew." They do not
work on Saturday, observe the Jewish holy days, do not eat pork, and so on.

The Iglesia de Dios is organized centrally, with branches in all the
states of Mexico. The church is headed by an executive of seven (*Los Siete*),
a committee of twelve (*Los Doce*), and a council of seventy (*Los Setenta*),
according to Carlos Garcia, one of the spiritual leaders of the church in the

Tacubaya quarter of Mexico City. However, according to the pamphlet quoted above, the structure of the church is more complex. The pamphlet states that, in addition to these three bodies, there are several more categories and grades in the church. Among them are *Los Ancianos* (the elders), *Los Ayudadores* (the helpers), and *Los Discipulos* (the disciples). One representative from each, the sevens, the twelves, and the seventies, constitute *Los Sobrevedores* (the supervisors), whose task is to visit the places where the missionaries of the church are active and to supervise their work.

I tried to ascertain the principles the church leaders used in selecting the places to which the missionaries are sent. However, I could elicit no clear statement on the subject. All I was told was that the leaders select those localities in which the people will understand the missionaries' message and where they will be given a friendly reception and find understanding. Money is sent to the missionaries from the church headquarters in Mexico City, but not enough to cover all their expenses. In addition, the missionaries must obtain contributions from the local people. In 1945 the Iglesia de Dios had 4,000 members; by 1948, thanks to the success of their missionary work, the membership exceeded 8,000. The church headquarters is at 3731/66 Oriente Street, Colonia Rio Blanco, Mexico City.

My efforts to elicit information on two other questions relating to the position of the church were more successful. I inquired into their doctrines about the divinity of Jesus and into their traditions concerning the origin of the membership.

The first question was received with a certain unwillingness to be forthcoming. The informants knew that I was Jewish, a scholar from Jerusalem, and therefore they tried at first to give a Jewish coloration to their replies. Here is the literal translation of the first answer Manzanares gave to my question: "I believe that Jesus was a great philosopher, a great prophet, like the other prophets of Israel. He was not the Messiah. The Messiah has still to come in the future."

To my question how, if this is their belief concerning Jesus, they can believe in the New Testament, he replied, "In Isaiah, chapter 42, in the beginning of the chapter, it is written that God put His spirit upon His servant, who was Jesus. Also in Isaiah 19:20 it is written that God will send a savior to His people. And apart from this, we believe only in part of the New Testament. We do not believe that Jesus was the son of God and the Messiah."

When I asked that he continue to explain his views, he said, "There are two kinds of Jews: those who believe that the Messiah is yet to come in the future, and those who believe that he has already come. We believe that he has already come. He was Jesus. Other Jews also know that he was the

Messiah. They know this from the Bible, from the words of prophecy, from the calculations of the years, and the like. Also in Zechariah 13:6 there is a proof of this."

Manzanares could not make a definite statement about the origins of the members of the church. But Carlos Garcia came to his aid and answered, "We believe that we are the descendants of the ten tribes of Israel."

I asked, "When did you come to America?"

He answered, "We do not know exactly when we came here. In any event, we came before Cortez, and a proof of it can be found in Isaiah 62:2."

Question: "By what route did your ancestors come from Palestine to America?"

Answer: "We do not know."

Question: "Are all the Indians of America the descendants of the ten tribes of Israel?"

Answer: "Not all the Indians. Only those who are members of the Iglesia de Dios."

Carlos Garcia's brother Alberto, minister of the Iglesia de Dios in Puebla, further clarified this point. According to him, they believe that they are the descendants of the lost ten tribes. "It is," he said, "difficult to say that they are the descendants of the ten tribes by blood [that is, genetically], but they are undoubtedly the descendants of the ten tribes by the spirit." Alberto Garcia also stated that the forefathers of all the present members of the church were Catholics.

In reply to my question, Alberto Garcia summarized the main differences between the Iglesia de Dios and the Ramirez group, that is, the Jewish Indians (see below). "We believe that Jesus was the son of God; they believe that he was one of the Jewish prophets. We pray bareheaded, they with their heads covered. We are not circumcised; they are."

In speaking of the "Ramirez group," Alberto Garcia could not refrain from critical remarks about its leader, Ramirez. "While Ramirez ordered all male members of his group to undergo circumcision, he himself remained uncircumcised. When he finds himself in the company of Christians, he accepts the doctrines of Christianity, but when he is with Jews he denies Jesus." According to Garcia, the members of the Ramirez group claim that they are the descendants of Carvajal, which is not true. (Carvajal was the name of a distinguished New Christian [Marrano] family in sixteenth-century Mexico, several of whose members were burned at the stake by the Inquisition. The two most famous members of the family were Luis de Carvajal y de la Cueva [1539–96?], governor of the New Kingdoms of Leon, who died in jail, and his nephew, Luis de Carvajal el Mozo [1566–96], who was an aide of his uncle and was burned.) Alberto Garcia added the details about the history and doctrines of the Iglesia de Dios repeated in the following three paragraphs.

The Iglesia de Dios was founded in Palestine in A.D. 33. Garcia had in his possession a book of the history of the church which contains all the data about this. In its present form the church was founded in Mexico by men of the Church of God from the United States, about twenty-five years ago (i.e., in 1923). To this day the Mexican church has close connections with the American. All the members of the church in Mexico come from poor families. The Jews of Mexico are rich and proud. Nevertheless, when he sees a Jew, he regards him as a brother, because they themselves believe that they are full Jews. They observe all the holy days mentioned in the Old Testament. The other Jews (i.e., those outside the church), are wrong in their religious belief, but the day will come when all the Jews will accept Jesus. The church in Puebla has one hundred adult members.

They believe that Jesus was the Messiah and the son of God, although in his earthly form he was a Jew. He redeemed the lost ten tribes—this is a specific belief of their own, not shared by the Protestants. Jesus made a new covenant with the House of Israel, according to Jeremiah 31:32. He also fulfilled the priesthood of Melchizedek, and he is the seed promised to Abraham in Genesis 13:15. Jesus died in the middle of the "week" mentioned in Daniel 9:27. He will come a second time, and then all the nations will unite and will be one people. He will also unite all the Jews, and then Palestine will be the queen of all the lands.

The first teacher of the Iglesia de Dios in Mexico was Ezequias Campos. Today, the head of the tribe (i.e., of the church) is Marcus Newman, who is at present in Jerusalem and whose permanent seat is in Salem, Virginia, in the United States.

II.

There can be no doubt that there was a certain connection between the Iglesia de Dios and the founders of the Indian Jewish communities in Mexico. However, for lack of historical documents, and in the absence of any readiness on the part of the Indian Jewish leaders to speak openly about their origin, it is almost impossible to discover any details about that connection.

The heads of the Indian Jewish community in Mexico City, who are more able than their brethren in the village of Venta Prieta to formulate their beliefs and ideas, declare unanimously that all or most of them are the descendants of Spanish Marranos who first arrived in New Spain in the early sixteenth century. These Marranos were among the retinue of Cortez and the other Spanish conquistadores, and quite a few of them achieved high positions and leadership in New Spain. The most important among them was the already mentioned Carvajal family. After the Inquisition became established in New Spain—thus according to the tradition subscribed to by the Jewish Indians in Mexico City—the Marranos were extremely careful about hiding their Jewishness, and about observing outwardly all the laws and rites of Spanish Christianity. Since there were practically no women among the Spanish immigrants in those days, these Marranos married local Indian women, and as a result of these mixed marriages, their offspring came to look more and more like the natives of the country. But, despite all difficulties, the heads of the families remained faithful to the doctrines and traditions of Judaism. When their children reached the age of understanding, the fathers revealed their Jewish origin to them and commanded them not to allow the embers of the old faith to become extinguished. In this manner, in great secrecy and with a gradual narrowing of both forms and content, the Jewish tradition survived in several families from generation to generation.

In the nineteenth and early twentieth centuries, there were a few families in the Indian population of Mexico in which the Jewish tradition still flickered, explained *licenciado* Baltazar Laureano Ramirez, head of the Indian Jewish community of Mexico City. His father, who lived in San Luis Potosi, was one of the faithful, and several more secretly Jewish families could be found in Monterey, Mexico City, and elsewhere. In 1917 Ramirez senior moved to Mexico City and established contact with several Indian Jewish families who lived there, among them the Mendez, Guayevara, and Model families. Especially important was the task of Francisco Rivas, who was professor of Hebrew and Greek at the University of Mexico. According to Ramirez, Rivas, who was known by all as "Papa Rivas," told him about two meetings of the Jewish Indians which took place in Mexico City in 1830 and 1833, and in which the participants resolved to submit to the government an application requesting freedom of thought and religion and equal rights to adherents of all religions. According to Ramirez, these rights were actually granted within a few years in the Mexican constitution, in which the petition of the Jewish Indians had an important part. Ramirez actually took me to the government archives in Mexico City in order to find out whether it was possible to locate that 1883 petition. But it transpired that a few years earlier there was a fire in the archives, in which most of the documents dating from the first half of the nineteenth century were destroyed. Thus we were deprived of the opportunity to check whether there was any historical kernel in the story about the Jewish Indian meetings of 1830 and 1833.

Papa Rivas was the first president of the Jewish Indian community, which was organized in Mexico City before 1920. According to Ramirez, the members of the community learned more about Judaism from Papa Rivas than from their own parents in their childhood and youth, for by the early twentieth century most of the Indian Jews had forgotten almost everything about their Jewish traditions.

It so happens that we have independent evidence about Papa Rivas and his Judaism in the late nineteenth century. Professor Cecil Roth of Oxford, whom I met in New York on 10 March 1949, and with whom I discussed my research among the Jewish Indians of Mexico, called my attention to an article published about forty years earlier in the *Publications of the American Jewish Historical Society* about a Mexican periodical entitled *El Sabado Secreto*. I located the article in volume 23, from 1915, on pages 129–35. Written by Rabbi Martin Zielonka and titled "A Spanish-American Jewish Periodical," it contains an account of a visit Zielonka paid to Mexico City, where he met Professor Francisco Rivas and received from him an almost full series of the periodical, which Rivas had launched in 1889. The title of the periodical was changed several times; once it was *El Sabado Secreto* [The secret sabbath], once *La Luz del Sabado* [The light of the sabbath], and once *El Sabado* [The sabbath]. The masthead on the 9 February 1889 issue reads, "Nuestro periodico solo circulará entre Israelitas," that is, "Our periodical will be circulated only among Israelites." The subsequent issues do not carry this statement. In the opening article, "Nuestro Programa" ("Our Program"), Rivas says, among other things, "We declare Jewish brotherhood, which is a Masonic brotherhood, which is the only universal brotherhood." The editor also explains that the Jews of Mexico are the descendants of Spanish Marranos (this in 1889!). The very fact that in 1889 Francisco Rivas openly declared himself a Jew, and found it possible to publish a paper intended for Jews only, proves that in those days there were Jews in Mexico who considered themselves natives of the country and believed that they were the descendants of Spanish Marranos who had lived in Mexico for centuries and escaped, almost miraculously, the clutches of the Inquisition. It is, therefore, not at all impossible that at least part of the present-day Jewish Indians of Mexico, who likewise consider themselves descendants of Spanish Marranos, are actually of the descent they claim to be. If so, this old Jewish core group was then augmented, from the early twentieth century on, by Indians from the Iglesia de Dios who converted and joined the Jewish Indian group. This, it would seem, is how we must imagine the origin and present composition of the Indian Jewish community in Mexico.

Francisco Rivas himself was a native of Campeche in the Yucatan Peninsula, born in 1850.[3] In the last few years before his death, he used the nom de plume Manuel Puigcerver.[4] Anita Brenner, the well-known American-Mexican-Jewish author, had a discussion with Puigcerver close to the end of his life, and published a brief note about him in the January 1928 issue of the *Menorah Journal* (pp. 100–103), in which she quotes him as telling her,

> I taught Greek in the University for forty years. . . . All Mexico has been taught by a Jew, and they do not know it. . . . My great-great-grandfather was Abrabanel, historian at the court of the King of Spain. He went to Holland when the expulsion came, about which he wrote a beautiful sonnet of farewell, which begins, *Adios, Hispañia, terra bunita, terra de la consolación.* One of his sons, with other families of Jews, came to New Spain. They thought to find a sympathetic refuge, and something of their beloved Spain, which they did until the Inquisition began. After 1570, all of them were Christians—with the outside teeth. My great-grandfather, under the name of Silva, established himself in the territory of Tabasco. . . . the children inherited, with the fortune, the Church's slight doubt of the orthodoxy of the Silvas, and the family was forcibly reduced. Only one escaped, my grandfather, who, under the name of Toledano, and with the friendship of the Archbishop of Campeche, also founded a large and Catholic family, and a large and Jewish fortune.

In the early 1920s a stream of Jewish immigrants began to arrive in Mexico, and most of them settled in the capital. The Catholic press launched a sharp attack on the Jews, and the small group of Indian Jews took council and decided—according to Ramirez—that in the circumstances the best thing to do was "to cooperate with the Christians," to feign acceptance of the religion of the country, and thus to join the ranks of the enemy. However, they did so only in order to spread toleration for the Jews and to work for freedom of thought and religion. This resolution was reached largely under the influence of Papa Rivas, and he was also the author of the decision to convene a meeting of the Indian Jewish leaders and to found a new Christian church, "for the sake of appearances." The meeting took place early in 1925 in Saltillo, in the state of Coahuila, but in the absence of Papa Rivas, who had fallen ill and died in the following year. The participants in the Saltillo meeting were the guests of "brother" Baruj (Barukh) S. Delgado. Delgado, Ramirez, and Mendez were entrusted with the task of organizing the new church, preparing the required declarations, and registering it in a legal form as required by the government.

According to Ramirez, Delgado was a Marrano. However, printed sources make clear that Delgado was a missionary of the Seventh Day Adventist church. The 1920 yearbook of this church, published in Washington, D.C., states that a Mexican brother from Texas has begun missionary work in Saltillo, where he hopes to see the message spread and work established. "This brother, B. S. Delgado, came to us from the Southern

Texas convention'' (p. 203). In the 1921 yearbook, Brother B. Delgado appears among the officers and delegates of the church (p. 146). It is, of course, equally possible that Brother Delgado misled either the Jewish Indians or the Seventh Day Adventists as to his true convictions.

According to Ramirez, he himself coined the name Iglesia de Dios when he registered the new church, following the Saltillo resolution, on 18 February 1925. This registration required a public declaration, which was entered by a notary public as no. 49 in volume 70, page 129, no. 8020 [of an official registry?]. In the course of the next few years, there was a peculiar situation among the Indian Jews. "In the morning I preached about Judaism," Ramirez writes in his letter to me dated 13 February 1949, "and in the evening several others preached about the Gospel." In order to put an end to this situation, the executive of the community resolved, after the anti-Semitic movement subsided, to discontinue the mixed meetings which they held on the Sabbaths with members of other sects. To achieve this, they invited old members to have their sons circumcised, and therefore those whose hearts were not whole with their Judaism of themselves departed from the community. This split took place in 1931–32, and ever since there has been no connection whatsoever between the Jewish Indians and the Iglesia de Dios.

This rather subjective account of the history of the group is undoubtedly influenced by the class aspirations characterizing not only the Jewish Indians of Mexico, but many in the Mexican population in general. While there has been no racial segregation in Mexico—it is generally absent in Latin America, in contrast to the Anglo-Saxon North American countries—Spanish descent has conferred a kind of nobility. To trace one's ancestry to Spain has meant to establish a claim to high status, to a prestigious lineage. It is a frequent phenomenon for an Indian to claim to be a mestizo, and for a mestizo to claim pure Spanish descent. Similarly, for a group like that of the Indian (or mestizo) Jews of Mexico, Spanish descent, even Spanish-Jewish descent, means a step up in the social scale. It is quite probable that this aspiration to higher status was one of the factors, and possibly a most important factor, which motivated some of the Christian Indians to attach themselves to the Indian Jewish community and to deny that they were proselytes.

A similar phenomenon can be observed among the Negro Jews in the United States. The members of these groups are as much African as the Christian blacks of the country. Their adoption of the Jewish religion took place as recently as in the last generation. In physical features there is no difference between them and the other Negros in the United States. Yet these groups declare and insist that they are of Abyssinian descent; they hold allegiance to the Negus, the emperor of Ethiopia, and pray for his well-being and that of his royal house in their synagogue service. The Abyssinians and the Abyssinian Jews, the Falashas, belong primarily to the so-called Caucasoid race, and, apart from the dark skin color, differ considerably in physical features from the Negroid race. But the prestige aspiration works here, too; some Negroes consider it a rise in prestige and status to be taken for descendants of Abyssinians, and their aspiration finds expression in their claim, and perhaps sincere belief, that they are of Abyssinian origin.

While the denial of actual descent and the claim of a different ancestry for social reasons are well-known phenomena, it would be a mistake to consider such motivations the only basis of the emergence of Indian Jewish groups in Mexico. First of all, one must not overlook the possibility that a few remnants of Marrano families of Spanish descent actually survived in Mexico until the nineteenth century, or even into the twentieth. Second, there are other examples of Christian sectarians first approaching the Jewish religious position and then actually converting to Judaism. The Subotniki in Russia and the Sabbath-keepers in Transylvania are examples that readily come to mind. Similarly, one can imagine that some Indian Christian sectarians in Mexico were attracted to Judaism, to a lesser or greater degree. Another, more materialistic consideration may have been the hope that the Jewish immigrants who had recently arrived in Mexico, and some of whom had become quite wealthy, would financially aid their Indian coreligionists. Thus a combination of material, religious, ideological, and spiritual factors may have played a role in the formation of the Indian Jewish groups.

III.

The argument of the Jewish Indians of Mexico that their Marrano ancestors had to marry local Indian women for lack of women in their own ranks is, to some extent, supported by the official censuses of the Mexican government, which show that as late as in the early twentieth century the number of Jewish males exceeded by far that of the Jewish females in the country. Although these censuses do not include the Jewish Indians among the Jews (for even if we accept their leaders' argument concerning the long history of their presence in Mexico, it is clear that Marranos would identify themselves for census purposes as Christians rather than Jews), the male-female ratio among the Jews of the country in the early twentieth century nevertheless presents a parallel to the situation in the sixteenth, when the Marranos first arrived in Mexico. Both in the sixteenth century and in the twentieth, Jews came to Mexico to try their luck in the new country, and in most cases only men came. This situation led to some marriages between Jewish men and Mexican women in the early twentieth century. However, within about twenty years, more and more women immigrated, so that by 1940 the disproportion of the two sexes had almost disappeared. As a result, whatever mixed marriages did take place had no time to result in a visible change in the new generation, and, especially because marriages between Jewish men and Mexican women frequently ended in divorce. In those cases the children usually remained with their mothers, who brought them up in the Mexican Christian tradition. One can assume that in the sixteenth and following centuries the situation was different in that the number of Jewish (or Marrano) women remained small in relation to that of the men, and the offspring of the mixed marriages were brought up in their fathers' houses as Jews, or, more precisely, as Marranos. If so, it is perhaps possible to accept the argument of the Indian Jews about their partly Jewish descent and their claim that mixed marriages resulted in their assimilation, as far as the physical type was concerned, to the Indian or mestizo population of Mexico.

Tables 1 and 2 show the number of Jewish men and women in the Mexican states in 1910 and 1940. They are taken from the official censuses of Mexico. According to table 1, in 1910 there were more than 2.5 times as many Jewish men as women in Mexico. A comparison of the figures in the two tables shows that the number of Jews increased more than fiftyfold in the thirty years from 1910 to 1940, and the number of Jewish women approached that of Jewish men.

Table 1: Jews in Mexico in 1910

State	Males	Females	Total
Aguascalientes	1	—	1
Baja California	1	—	1
Coahuila	10	5	15
Colima	5	2	7
Chihuahua	29	11	40
Distrito Federal (includes Mexico City)	107	42	149
Durango	1	—	1
Hidalgo	1	1	2
Mexico	1	—	1
Michoacán	4	1	5
Nuevo Leon	3	4	7
Puebla	1	—	1
Sonora	17	5	22
Veracruz	2	—	2
Grand Total:	**183**	**71**	**254**

(Source: *Tercer Censo de Poblacion de los Estados Mexicanos*, vol. 2 [1918], p. 30 [Census of 27 Oct. 1910].)

Table 2: Jews in Mexico in 1940

State	Males	Females	Total
Aguascalientes	20	20	40
Baja California T.N.	17	20	37
Baja California T.S.	11	11	22
Campeche	2	3	5
Coahuila	141	128	269
Chiapas	237	226	463
Chihuahua	86	78	164
Distrito Federal (includes Mexico City)	4,886	4,932	9,818
Durango	53	34	87
Guanajuato	33	30	63
Guerrero	75	68	143
Hidalgo	90	97	187
Jalisco	118	117	235
México	181	76	257
Michoacán	57	46	103
Morelos	38	36	74
Nayarit	19	17	36
Nuevo Leon	162	180	342
Oaxaca	19	24	43
Puebla	164	169	333
Queretaro	1	1	2
Quintana Roo	2	—	2
San Luis Potosi	74	78	152
Sinaloa	11	12	23
Sonora	9	10	19
Tabasco	141	144	285
Tamaulipas	97	79	176
Tlaxcala	41	38	79
Veracruz	342	252	594
Yucatan	13	3	16
Zacatecas	49	49	98
Grand Total:	**7,189**	**6,978**	**14,167**

(Source: *Estados Unidos Mexicanos 6° Censo de Poblacion, 1940. Resumen General*. [Secretaria de la Economia Nacional Direccion General de Estadistica, 1943], pp. 14, 52.)

It is clear that in 1910 the Jewish Indians were not registered in the census as Jews. At that time the few Jewish Indian families who can be assumed to have been found in Mexico lived as Marranos and kept their Jewishness carefully hidden. The attitude of Manuel Puigcerver as late as in the 1920s is a case in point. With regard to the 1940 census, however, the matter is not at all clear. By then the Jewish Indians already had organized communities in at least two places, in Mexico City and in the village of Venta Prieta in the state of Hidalgo, so that their Jewishness must have been known to their neighbors. Nevertheless, it seems that the members of their two communities still had themselves registered as Christians in the official census. At least as far as Venta Prieta is concerned, this is indicated by the census figures, according to which there were 187 Jews in the whole state of Hidalgo in 1940. This number could not comprise the Jewish Indians who lived in Venta Prieta, even if we estimate them at only 50, for the number of Jews in the city of Pachuca, the capital of the state, alone amounted to almost 187.

Since there are no official censuses of the Jewish Indians in Mexico, I tried to find some other way to establish their number, at least approximately. The only way to do this was to obtain information from the leaders of the Jewish Indians who maintained close contact with most of the Jewish Indian groups and families in the country. However, before presenting the information I obtained in this manner, I wish to list the family names of those Indian Jews with whom I was able to talk personally.

I myself saw and studied the Jewish Indians in two places only: in Mexico City and in the village of Venta Prieta, located some sixty miles to the north of Mexico City, near Pachuca. In Mexico City I found twelve families of Jewish Indians. I had the opportunity to conduct extended conversations with seven individuals, who belonged to the Ramirez, Carvajal, Espinoza, Salazar, Quiroz, Esquivel, and Garcia families. Each of these families originated outside of Mexico City and had lived in the following places: Ramirez in San Luis Potosi, state of San Luis Potosi; Carvajal in Guanajuato, state of Guanajuato; Espinozo in Tasicuaro, state of Michoacan; Salazar in Saltillo, state of Cuahuila; Quiroz in Aguchitlan, state of Guerrero; Esquivel in Sultepec, state of México; and Garcia in Santa Sicilia Tlalnepantla, state of México. My interlocutor of the Quiroz family admitted that formerly he had been neither Jewish nor Christian, and that his mother had been Catholic. The Salazar declared that his father had been Jewish and his mother Catholic. Both parents of the other five informants had been, according to their testimony, Jewish. The wives of the seven informants also were asserted to be of Jewish descent, except for Quiroz's wife. A daughter of Señora Espinoza had married an Indian who converted to Judaism.

I asked information from the leaders of the Jewish Indian communities of Mexico City and Venta Prieta (between whom there was considerable rivalry) for information concerning the existence of Jewish Indians in other places in Mexico at present. Ramirez, head of the community in Mexico City, gave me the following list: Cocula, state of Guerrero, 25 families (all sugar-cane cultivators); Mexico City, 20 families; Pachuca, state of Hidalgo, 6 families; Calpulalpam, state of Tlaxcala, 6 families (all named Rodriguez); Toluca, state of México, 3 families; Cananea, state of Sonora, 3 families; Monterrey, state of Nuevo Leon, 3 families (named Trevino, Montemaior, and Luna); Saltillo, state of Coahuila, 2 families; San Luis Potosi, state of San Luis Potosi, 2 families; Apipilulco, state of Guerrero, 2 families; Cuautla, state of Morelos, 1 family; Oaxaca, state of Oaxaca, 1 family.

According to Joel Salazar, leader of the Jewish Indians in Venta Prieta, Jewish Indians lived in the following places: Venta Prieta, state of Hidalgo, 10 families (named Perez, Tellez, and Hernandez), comprising 75 to 100 persons; Mexico City, 6 families (Carlos Vargas and Alvarez, 6 persons; Ciro Calderon Quiroz, 10 persons; Joel Salazar, 2 persons; José Martinez, 5 persons; Herlinda Hernandez, widow with two children; Felipe Esquivel, 5 persons); Toluca, state of México, 6 families (Nicolas Villanueva, Antonio Hernandez, Juan Randon, Felicitas Perez, Juan Villanueva, Apollonia Hernandez), ca. 30 persons; Cocula, state of Guerrero, 5 families (David Benitez, Jose Guadarrama, Odon Diaz, Adam Benitez, Candido Sausido), ca. 25–30 persons; Apipilulco, state of Guerrero, 4 families (Benjamin Balna, Macario Hernandez, Abadias Martinez, Tomas Martinez), ca. 20 persons; Cuautla, state of Morelos, 1 family (Daniel Marchan), with 10 children; Oaxaca, state of Oaxaca, 1 family (Juan Pedraza), 6 persons.

Comparison of the two lists reveals that, according to both, Jewish Indian families lived in Mexico City, Toluca, Cocula, Apipilulco, Cuautla, and Oaxaca. As for the number of Jewish families in these places, there is agreement only with regard to the last two, Cuautla and Oaxaca, where, according to both lists, there was one single Indian Jewish family. As for Mexico City, Salazar's list refers to only 6 families, while Ramirez lists 20. On the other hand, the Salazar list doubles the number of families appearing in the Ramirez list in Toluca and Apipilulco. In Cocula, Ramirez has 25 families, Salazar only 5. Ramirez knows of 5 families each in Pachuca, Calpulalpam, Cananea, Monterrey, Saltillo, and San Luis Potosi, which are not mentioned at all in Salazar's list, while the latter knows by name the families in Venta Prieta, not mentioned at all by Ramirez. However, the 6 families living in Pachuca, according to Ramirez, seem to be none other than the families which, in actuality, live in Venta Prieta, which is only three miles from Pachuca, and whom Ramirez did not want to mention because of the quarrel between him and Salazar, whom the Venta Prieta community recognizes as its spiritual head. If so, the Ramirez list contains all the places mentioned by Salazar, and, in addition to them, several others not figuring in the latter's list.

The reason for the gross discrepancy in the number of families and persons especially in three places, in particular—Mexico City, Cocula, and Venta Prieta (or Pachuca in the Ramirez list)—is not hard to find. Mexico City and Cocula are Ramirez communities. In Mexico City he is their actual leader, and in Cocula he visits frequently in order to carry out circumcisions, conduct services, and so on. Venta Prieta, on the other hand, is Salazar's community. Each of these two leaders has a tendency to overstate the numbers of his own community and to understate those of his rival, to the extent of gross exaggerations in both directions. Since Salazar's list contains the names of the families and the numbers of their members it seems to be more reliable, except in the case of Venta Prieta, where Salazar's intent to depict it as a large group made him give an inflated figure. However, what he added in Venta Prieta he deducted from the community in Mexico City, where he passed over in silence families such as those of Carvajal, Espinoza, and even Ramirez himself. The upshot of it all is that one may accept his number, that is, 33 families with 198 to 228 persons, as the probable total of the Jewish Indians in Mexico.

IV.

I traveled from Mexico City to Venta Prieta along the well-paved highway leading to the north, across the maguey country and over the flat, high plateau of the Valle de Mexico, rimmed with a distant crown of bluish mountains. The modern American-made bus, equipped with a constantly blaring radio, traveled with great speed over the narrow highway; in spite of the frequent stops for passengers, sixty miles or more between Mexico City and Pachuca were covered within less than an hour and a half. Some three or four miles before reaching Pachuca, in sight of that town and its mountain ranges, almost in their shadow and hard by the dumpings of scum from their silver mines, was the village of Venta Prieta hugging the right side of the road.

As I walked between the widely scattered houses of the village towards the home of Simon Tellez, my host, the first thing I noticed was that Venta Prieta outwardly differed in no way from the hundreds of Mexican villages founded around the middle of the last century. It had the same square layout with wide but unpaved streets; the same variety of building structure and style, ranging from small low mud huts to brick houses of considerable proportions; the same maguey plants with thick, broad, curved, and thorn-rimmed leaves flanking the houses; the same spacious courtyards and distant fields.

Even a somewhat closer look at the village and its inhabitants revealed nothing unusual. In physical type the people ranged, just as in any other Mexican village, from apparently pure Indian types to mestizos in whom European features were dominant. Their material culture seemed caught in the same process of modernization characteristic of Mexico in general and of the valley in particular, which has found expression in the changing aspects of household furniture, clothing, eating habits, and the like. In the occupational structure of the village, too, nothing atypical could be discovered. There was the usual predominance of agriculture, primarily extensive dry farming with some more intensive work in irrigated fields; the everywhere prevalent domesticated animals—cows, sheep, goats, pigs, horses, donkeys, mules, dogs, chickens, turkeys; the usual complementary industries—the manufacture of pulque, a mild milk-colored beerlike drink which is the fermented sap of the maguey; five or six kilns in which bricks and tiles made of a mixture of mud and cow dung are fired; the familiar signs of rudimentary occupational specialization, either traditional or newfangled, such as the presence of a village baker, a carpenter, a midwife, and four or five shops in which mainly foodstuffs are sold, and drinks—pulque and the fiery tequila.

Typical of the Mexican village was the existence of a school and the consequent decrease of illiteracy, especially in the young generation. Also, in the way the villagers picked the new traits they deemed worth adopting, they had followed the usual Mexican pattern. For, while eschewing some of the things regarded as essential by the civilization from which they borrowed, such as a water-supply unit and an electric lighting system, they had gone to great lengths to install such luxuries as radios (although the electricity had to be generated by wind-wheels) and upholstered furniture.

No outward sign, then, betrayed the presence of a Jewish group in the village—no outward sign, that is, apart from the simple small room adjoining the cowshed and sheep pen of the Tellez families, which served as the synagogue.

During the three months I lived in Venta Prieta, I tried carefully to compare the eight Jewish families with the fifty or so Catholic families in the village, to note the similarities as well as the differences between the two groups. Physically, Jews and Catholics were indistinguishable; both showed the same range of variation from the Indian to the mestizo type. Nor could any difference be discovered between them in language; both groups spoke the same typically Mexican Spanish with its characteristic drawl and slur. Both groups engaged in the same occupation, their basic livelihood being derived from the eight hectares of land allotted to each family by the government a number of years ago. The two groups also seemed identical in behavior and outlook. The religious cleavage often cut across family ties. The only perceptible difference was in the adherence to two different religions. But it was an adherence characterized in both groups by a marked lack of formalized expression or of interest in the respective rituals. There seemed to be a merely sentimental attachment, more accentuated in the Jewish than in the Catholic group.

My purpose in Venta Prieta being to make an anthropological study of the village community, and particularly to investigate the problems of merging and interaction between the Jewish and the Catholic groups, my attention was focused on the present situation and the everyday life of the community. For the purposes of this study, it was of little importance whether the Jewish families in the village were in fact the descendants of early Spanish Jews or of proselytes to Judaism of one or two generations ago. But it was of considerable importance to find out whether they really believed they were descendants of Spanish Marranos, or only made up the story out of an easily understandable desire to gain prestige through relating themselves to the New Christians who had been part of the proud conquistador army of New Spain. I therefore sought out the oldest people in the village and, while asking them to tell me how the village was founded, tried to learn the actual history of its Jewish families.

Sitting in the doorway of her house—one of the few well-built brick houses in Venta Prieta—her white hair framing a bronzed, weather-beaten, and deeply wrinkled face, Señora Trinidad Jiron de Tellez, the oldest member of the Jewish community in the village, told me her story. She was eighty-five. Her grandchildren had told me that some fifty years ago she used to don trousers and go down the shafts of the silver mines in Pachuca to help her husband and sons who were working there to supplement the meager income derived from their fields. Her grandchildren confided that her memory and hearing and sight were somewhat impaired, making her impatient and irritable, but I found Señora Tellez willing enough to talk and firmly decisive in her statements.

"My grandfather," she began after she understood what I wanted of her,

> was Ramon Jiron, and he lived in Morelia in the state of Michoacan. He and his family were Jewish, but all the other inhabitants of the town were Christians. So he had to hide his faith before them, and succeeded in doing this for many years.
>
> One day, however, it became known to his neighbors, and they fell upon his house, dragged him out of it, sewed him into the skin of a newly slaughtered

bull, and threw him into a cauldron of boiling water, where he died a miserable and painful death.

After this happened, my grandmother, Petra Huitron, could not stay any longer in Morelia. So she took her children and went to live in Real del Oro, a mining town in the state of Hidalgo. There her sons worked in the mines. Some years later one of them, also called Ramon Jiron, settled in Pachuca, and he married Guadalupe Salazar. But here too he had troubles on account of his faith, and therefore he decided to settle on the land, away from towns and people, where he and his family could live in peace. Not far from Pachuca there were three *ranchos*, called Cuezco, Pitayas, and Palmar, and the Jiron family rented part of each of them and began working as *arrendatarios* [tenants].

Ramon Jiron the second and his wife had six children, three sons and three daughters, the youngest of whom was I, Trinidad. We lived on a small *ranchito* called La Florida, not far away from here, and there I was married to Manuel Tellez, who came from another Indian Jewish family. Soon after our marriage we moved to the neighborhood of the Smoky Inn, and built the first house here, becoming thus the founders of the village of Venta Prieta. This happened about seventy years ago.

After hearing her story, I looked for its substantiation among other old people in the village. But my endeavors to trace Trinidad's brothers and sisters were only partially successful. Two of her brothers, Placido and Francisco, and one sister, Dorotea, died unmarried or childless, and memory of them had been swallowed up in the stream of days. But the widow of the third brother, Apolonio, as well as his children, grandchildren, and great-grandchildren, still lived in Venta Prieta, as did Trinidad's eldest sister, the ninety-two-year-old Gertrudis. So I first went to see Gertrudis and asked her to tell me the story of her family, without, however, mentioning that I had already spoken to her sister Trinidad. Unfalteringly she told her story, and though more seasoned in years than her sister, she seemed even more firm in her assertions.

My grandfather was Ramon Jiron, and he lived in Zamora in the state of Michoacan. He and his wife, Petra Dias, as well as my own parents, were Catholics. I too am a Catholic. My grandfather was of Spanish descent. His parents wished him to become a priest, but he did not want to and ran away from home. His father pursued him, and as a punishment forced him to dress in a bull's skin. One day, when Ramon was taking a bath, some *arrieros* [workers] passed by, and they gave him a suit of clothes, and he joined them, leaving his parents' house for a second time, and this time for good. This happened after he was already married, and he settled with his wife in Real del Oro.

The rest of her story was largely the same as Trinidad's, with the difference that according to Gertrudis it was she and her husband, Timoteo Volaños, who were the first to settle in Venta Prieta.

The contradictions between the version of the Jewish Trinidad and that of her Catholic sister Gertrudis were as baffling as the likenesses between the two stories were surprising. It seemed to be a well-established family tradition that Ramon Jiron, their grandfather, had been dressed or sewn into a bull's skin, and that this affair had had something to do with his family's departure from the state of Michoacan. The question, however, which the differences in the two versions aroused, namely, whether Ramon Jiron was a Jew or not, could not be answered. There it remained to plague me, though the balance was tipped somewhat in favor of the Catholic version by the statement of Carmen Villalobos, widow of Apolonio Jiron. She and her late husband had been Catholics, she said, as were all their descendants. Of the four sons of Trinidad Tellez still living in Venta Prieta, only two were Jewish, she averred; the other two were Catholics, though not practicing Catholics. Against this evidence, which seemed to point to the truth of the Catholic version of the family tradition, one had to take into consideration the influence of the purely Catholic environment in which the family had lived and was still living, the effect of which would be inevitably to cause considerable disintegration in any Jewish family.

The unanswered question, whether Ramon Jiron was a Jew or a Catholic, had a significance beyond the narrow frame of a single family history. If it could be shown that Ramon Jiron was a Jew, one would have evidence for the existence of at least one Jewish family in the beginning of the last century, at a time when no immigrant European Jews had as yet reached the shores of Mexico. The existence of even a single family at that time, when its Jewishness could not be attributed to later and external Jewish influence and possible conversion, would lend strong support to the otherwise unauthenticated tradition of Jewish remnants, Indian in physical type, evading the claws of the Inquisition and surviving down to the nineteenth century, secretly adhering to their Jewish faith. It would be an indication, even if not conclusive evidence, that at least some of the present-day Indian Jews of Mexico are of mixed Spanish-Jewish and Indian descent. Lacking such evidence, one would have to give at least equal credence to the alternative explanation, which is that the Mexican Indian Jews are a splinter group formed by individuals originally belonging to the Iglesia de Dios.

The religious ideas of the ''Jewish Indians'' of Venta Prieta were so vague in most cases that nowhere could I lay my finger on any definite point indicative of a Christian sectarian past. It is true, as I noted one Saturday morning in the synagogue at the close of the service, that all the worshipers kneeled and bowed low their covered heads while one of the women present said a brief prayer in Spanish. But the Catholic custom of kneeling could equally have penetrated their service from the outside, even though they themselves had been secret Jews for many generations.

On the other hand, the more I probed the more evidence I found of their deep sentimental attachment to Judaism. The most learned in Jewish matters in the community was Guillermo Peña, a man of about forty, with a typical Indian countenance, who worked as a taxi driver in nearby Pachuca. He was constantly overworked and overtired and suffered from lack of sleep. Often, after I had been working in Pachuca—due to lack of electricity in Venta Prieta, I had to take the villagers to Pachuca whenever I wanted to make recordings of their songs—I would seek out Guillermo in the early evening to take me home in his car to Venta Prieta. He was usually asleep behind his wheel. Yet Guillermo found time and energy to decorate the walls of the synagogue with traditional Jewish symbolical pictures and Hebrew inscriptions, to paint religious pictures for private homes, to participate actively in the religious services in the synagogue on Saturdays and holidays, and to teach the young how to read and write in Hebrew.

Again, the fact that some members of the Venta Prieta community did not conceal that they were proselytes converted to Judaism, or half-converted to it, seemed to substantiate the claim of those who asseverated their Jewish descent. The sister of Guillermo Peña, for instance, was the wife of such a proselyte. He was Telesforo Aquiahuatl Sanchez, a true Indian type, the village baker and judge.

The election of a Jew to the office of judge shows that the relationship between the Jews and the Catholics in the village was generally a friendly one. Yet only about twenty years ago, the two groups fought each other with fists and sticks as well as legal arguments. The clash arose over the desire of the Catholics in the village to have the government build a church for them. This the Jewish group opposed, maintaining that the available money should be spent to build a school. The controversy was carried by the contending parties up to the president of Mexico, who finally ruled in favor of the school and sent a detachment of infantry to Venta Prieta to restore law and order. The school was built, and today Jewish and Catholic children study in it side-by-side. The few Catholics who wish to attend mass go to Pachuca or to one of the neighboring villages.

In the Jewish group the lack of religious zeal contrasts remarkably with their ardent wish to be accepted as descendants of the ancient Jews. This wish they expressed unconsciously on many occasions when nothing in the nature of my questioning or of the general conversation called for it. A most interesting demonstration of this was given in connection with the administration of the Rorschach test, with which I planned to supplement the anthropological information concerning the character and inclinations of the villagers gathered by the slow interview technique. Señora Carmen Viqueira de Palerm, of the Clinica de Neuropsiquiatria of the Mexican Seguro Social, kindly offered her help, and on the appointed day she arrived with the ten plates of the test. As it would have been difficult to explain its significance to my villagers, we decided to begin with the adolescent girls in the Tellez families, giving them only preliminary explanation that this was a sort of game in which they were to guess what certain pictures represented. Thus we administered the test to a number of the Tellez and other Jewish families in the village. Next day we visited several non-Jewish families and succeeded in administering the test to them without difficulty. But on the third day, when we again tried to tackle some of the Jews in the village, our troubles began.

We stood in the small narrow courtyard full of goats and sheep before the low mud hut of Herlinda Cruz, a middle-aged woman, one of the few in the village who knew how to read Hebrew, and asked her to undergo the test. We showed her the plates, she took them into her hands, turned them upside down, and then, without any provocation, backed away from us. "No," she said firmly, "I do not want to do it." Then by way of explanation she added, "I am a Jewess. Ruth was the daughter of another people, but she became a Jewess and was accepted, and became the mother of David. I consider myself like Ruth. I am a good Jewess." Her dark eyes were fervent.

Suddenly she turned from us, entered her hut, and immediately emerged again holding in her hand, as final proof of her argument, some four or five Hebrew books: a Bible, several prayer books, and a Hebrew language book. I shall not forget her standing there—in rags, barefoot, amidst her smelly animals, her tall sparse figure towering above the mud hut—holding out proudly, almost triumphantly, her store of Hebrew books.

"Can you read them?" I asked in some confusion.

She nodded; then, choosing one of the books at random, she began to read. Slowly, it is true, stammeringly and with frequent mistakes, but she read the Hebrew text!

The thing did not immediately become clear. But when we met with blunt refusal also on the part of other Jews in the village, accompanied by vigorous assertions of their faithfulness to Judaism, I realized that these people somehow had got the idea that the Rorschach test was a way of finding out whether they were true Jews. So we did the best we could under the circumstances, continuing to make as many tests as possible among the Catholic villagers. I could only hope that perhaps the few tests we had made on the first day would prove sufficient to establish some significant difference between the psychology of the Jews and the Catholics in the village. Señora Viqueira returned to Mexico City with all the protocols of the tests, each written out on a separate sheet of paper.

Some two weeks later I arrived in Mexico City for a short visit, eager to see the analysis of the protocols. Señora Viqueira greeted me with surprising news.

"Imagine," she said, "the protocols of the tests administered to the Jewish subjects are missing!"

An unseen hand had extricated them from her portfolio, and thus another possible clue which might have shed some light on the differential antecedents of the Mexican Indian Jews was lost.

My last visit in Venta Prieta was to the synagogue. A dampness and the sweet fragrance of fresh flowers pervaded the room. It was an early afternoon hour, and the long shafts of the summer sun penetrated the small room through its open door. The flies were whizzing around as if to decide whether to settle upon the unhewn wooden benches or on the colored paper garlands running from the center of the ceiling towards the four walls. I had to bend down in order to avoid the low-hanging paper strips. I sat down and looked up at the ceiling, formed of a whitewashed linen sheet that was torn in many places. Through the rents I could see the rafters of the hollow roof. A simple table, a few chairs, a foot organ, and a cupboard serving as the holy ark with a single Torah scroll in it—the gift of an American rabbi—were the only furnishings of the adobe hut. Ornamental goblets fashioned from bits of gay candy wrappers were pasted to the wall, while two vases filled with field flowers rested on the mud floor before the table. The room was empty of people, and I could undisturbedly contemplate the wallpaintings, the menorah, the Ten Commandments, the Star of David, the lions of Judah, and the almost faultless Hebrew inscriptions around them, the handiwork of Guillermo Peña.

I had attended numerous services in this synagogue and made detailed notes of everything I could hear or observe. In my trunks were hundreds of pages of notes covering many aspects of the life of the Indian Jews in this village, illustrated with photographs, and many hours' lengths of musical recordings. I probably knew more about Venta Prieta than anyone else. Yet on that last visit to the synagogue I found myself pondering a problem. Put aside for a moment the unsolved riddle of the origin of these Indian Jews, I said to myself, and try to utilize all the information you gathered about them to answer one question. These people, who know after all very little about Judaism, who differ in no wise from their neighbors apart from some very vague and indefinite notions about religion, who number only a few dozens within an overwhelming majority of Catholics, what is it that makes them such fervent, eager, and enthusiastic Jews?

Notes

"The Jewish Indians of Mexico" originally was published partly in English in the *Menorah Journal* 38 (Winter 1950):54–67, and partly in Hebrew in *Talpioth* [New York] 5 (1952):828–44. I herewith express my thanks to the Wenner-Gren Foundation for Anthropological Research (formerly the Viking Fund, Inc.) of New York City, and to the Cultural Committee of the Central Organization of the Jews of Mexico for their support in carrying out the fieldwork on which this study is based.

1. Subsequently published in Spanish translation as *Descubrimientos en Mexico* (Mexico City: Nuevo Mundo, 1944). The chapter on the Jewish Indians also was published in the Mexican *Tribuna Israelita*, 5 Jan. 1945, no. 2, pp. 11–14, under the title "Una aldea india baja la estrella de David."
2. Cf., e.g., Victor Alba, "The Redskin Jews of Mexico," *Jewish Chronicle* [London], 7 Jan. 1949; M. M., "Y'hudim Indianim b'Mexico," *Hadoar* [New York], youth supplement, 14 Jan. 1949. In 1944 the American Friends of the Jewish Indians in Mexico published a pamphlet titled *Indian Jews in Mexico* (Thornton, Ark.), which states that there are at least five hundred Jewish Indians in Mexico City, and about the same number in the provincial towns of the republic.
3. Cf. the life history of Francisco Rivas in the *Hebrew Standard* 26, no. 1 (25 Nov. 1892). Unfortunately I was unable to locate a copy.
4. Thus according to a letter by Ramirez dated 13 Feb. 1949.

23. Venta Prieta Revisited

When I informed Simon Téllez, leader of the small, rural "Indian" Jewish community of Venta Prieta, Mexico, that, after an absence of sixteen years, I would like to revisit his family and his village, I did not anticipate the difficulties of obtaining their cooperation—so freely given on my previous visit—in answering my questions and telling me about themselves. I suspected that they might be less cordial towards an inquisitive outsider than they had been in 1948, for I had read several accounts, written by visitors with the intention of presenting sensational discoveries about primitive, half-savage "Jewish Indians," and realized that some of these articles might have reached Venta Prieta. But, not having kept in touch with the community, I was not prepared for the bluntly negative tone of Téllez's reply to my letter, which reached me the day before my scheduled departure for Mexico. "Sr. Patai, with regard to your proposed visit, I don't think that it will be necessary. . . . Sr. Raphael, you did not treat us as brothers in religion, and even less so in race. We were for you nothing more than a subject for one of your informative articles. . . . Please accept my most sincere *Shalom*, with my best wishes, Yours sincerely, Simon Téllez."

These were strong words, especially considering that Spanish is intrinsically a much more courteous language than English, and I knew that they must have expressed even stronger feelings of resentment, silently borne for many years. Should I, then, give up the idea of revisiting Venta Prieta and finding out what had happened to my friends-turned-foes, and what it was they held against me? I was tempted: Mexico had been a study country for me; now it could be what it is for so many Americans, a delightful vacation-land. I considered the possibility for a few minutes, then sat down and wrote a second letter to Simon Téllez, saying that if he and the other villagers did not wish to supply me with additional information, I hoped at least they would not object to my paying my respects in a brief visit, in memory of the friendship we had established in 1948.

At the time of my three-month sojourn as the houseguest of Simon Téllez in the summer of 1948, the Jews of Venta Prieta had been "un-spoiled," in the sense of having had little contact with foreigners, or even with Mexican outsiders, and the reception they accorded me was entirely friendly and gracious. I had been driven to the village which lies to the right of the highway going north from Mexico City, by my friend Eduardo Weinfeld, and taken to the house of Simon Téllez, the largest and best house in the village.

Simon was fifty-one years old at the time, and not only the head of the group of fifty who constituted the Jewish contingent in Venta Prieta, but, as I was soon to find, also the richest and most respected citizen of the village, which then numbered 471 persons. His family consisted of his wife, and two sons, and four daughters. In addition, a fifteen-year-old cousin, Eliza Gonzalez Olvera, also stayed with them, as did four or five non-Jewish workers who slept either in the courtyard or in one of the storerooms.

The luxuriousness of Simon's house, by the village standards, was manifested by its containing, in addition to the bedrooms and a large kitchen, a dining room and a sitting room, the latter furnished with a set of overstuffed easy chairs and sofa, covered in somewhat threadbare red velvet. The house also boasted a bathroom, though without running water. Outside toilet facilities, at the far end of the courtyard, provided a unique feature in the entire village.

The purpose of my visit was briefly explained to Simon. I wanted to spend about three months in Venta Prieta in order to study the life of the village as a whole, and of the Jewish community in particular. I needed a place to sleep and take my meals, and the same accommodations would be required for my interpreter, whom I needed to help me out when my own Spanish proved inadequate. Simon's instantaneous response was cordial. I was to stay in his house, as his guest. His wife, who in any case fed ten to twelve people every day, could easily cook for two more. When, after expressing my gratitude, I indicated that I would, of course, expect to be a paying guest, the suggestion was so disdainfully rejected that I thought it better to postpone the issue until I had time to establish greater familiarity with the Téllez family.

Satisfied with these arrangements in Venta Prieta, I returned to Mexico City to collect my Webster wire recorder and my clothes, and to find out from Dr. Pablo Martinez del Rio whether he had been able to make arrangements with the young anthropologist of Otomi Indian extraction whom he had mentioned as the best suited of his students to serve as my interpreter. To my disappointment, Don Pablo informed me that the young man had been unable to arrange for a leave of absence, but, he said, another of his students was willing to take his place, a young woman named Carmen Sanchez, whose English was even more fluent. He pointed out that a girl interpreter had advantages; she would make it easier for me to approach the women in the village, who might have more time and be more willing to talk than their menfolk.

Carmen turned out to be an attractive girl of twenty-two, with black hair, dark brown eyes, and what is often described as the typical Spanish face. In fact, she had been born in Spain and brought to Mexico by her parents, who had escaped during the Spanish Civil War. A slight Spanish accent readily identified her as a Spaniard, and gave her in the eyes of the Venta Prietans the prestige which in Mexico is associated with everyone and everything of Spanish origin.

We were received warmly everywhere. Everybody seemed to know why we were there, and my interminable questions were patiently answered, while the lips of my informants curved in an ever-present smile reminiscent of the expression so familiar to all students of pre-Columbian art.

The number of my notebooks increased rapidly, and I had to wire to New York for more spools for the recorder (although I could use it only in nearby Pachuca, and not in Venta Prieta itself, which had no electricity). The mosaic of the life of the village with its small group of Jews was slowly pieced together, as was the ''ethnohistory'' of the Jewish families, that special version of their past which they believed, or wanted to believe. In their relaxed, typically Mexican way, they took it for granted that they were Jews, although they knew practically nothing of Jewish religion or history. They had their private myth, which validated their Jewish identity to their own satisfaction. Their religious practices were few and simple: on Friday evenings, Saturday mornings, and Jewish holidays, they assembled in their small, whitewashed adobe synagogue and prayed, mostly in Spanish, but occasionally in halting, faulty Hebrew, reading the prayers aloud for the most part, but occasionally singing them to melodies heard in the synagogues of Mexico City. These were interspersed with Spanish hymns, familiar to me from the Iglesia de Dios (Church of God), a Sabbath-observing Evangelist sect rapidly growing in Mexico at the time. On weekdays, in their daily lives, I could discover no ritual expression of Jewishness, except that they abstained from eating pork and used no milk in cooking meat.

The myth which gave content and color to their lives can be summarized briefly. They were the descendants of the Marranos, those Spanish Jews whom the Inquisition forced to accept Christianity in the fifteenth century, but who secretly continued to adhere to Judaism. (It is a historical fact that among the Spanish conquistadores who seized Mexico were many Marranos, the best known being Louis Carvajal, who was burned at the stake in one of the earliest autos-da-fé staged by the Mexican Inquisition.) The Marranos married local Indian women, and, when their children reached maturity, shared with them the secret of their ancestry. They could do little more, because to observe Judaism, even in greatest secrecy, was a highly dangerous practice under the ever-suspicious eyes of the Inquisition. Within a few generations, the descendants of the Marrano conquerors of New Spain became indistinguishable in appearance from the Mexican Indians, but, though they observed Catholicism like all other Spaniards, they retained the secret knowledge of their Jewish origin and a hope for an open return to the faith of their ancestors.

Their chance came when the Inquisition was finally abolished in Mexico. Many of those who knew of their Marrano descent returned to Judaism, among them one Ramón Jiron, who lived in the town of Morelia in the state of Michoacan. When his Catholic neighbors discovered that Ramón was Jewish, or that he had converted to Judaism, they dragged him from his house, sewed him into a freshly skinned bull's hide, and plunged him into a cauldron of boiling water. His widow left Morelia, settling with her children in Real del Oro, a mining town not far from Pachuca. One of her sons, also named Ramón Jiron, later moved to Pachuca, where he married Guadalupe Salazar, by whom he had six children. Ramón and Guadalupe "had troubles" in Pachuca because of their Jewish religion, and, looking for a new place to live, they rented parts of three nearby ranchos. A young man by the name of Manuel Téllez accompanied the Jirons from Morelia, and, soon after they had become *arrendatarios* (tenant farmers), he married Trinidad, one of the daughters of Ramón and Guadalupe. It was this Trinidad who, in the summer of 1948, when she was eighty-five years old, told me the story of her family. "There, beyond that hill," she said, pointing to the west, "was our first home, the *ranchito* La Florida." Her first children were born there, and some years later they moved to Venta Prieta, which at that time consisted only of four houses, one of them owned by Timoteo Volaños, husband of Trinidad's older sister, Gertrudis.

Gertrudis was still living in Venta Prieta and was ninety-two years old in 1948. She was as definite about her family history as Trinidad, but she knew nothing about her ancestors beyond her grandfather Ramón Jiron the first, and of him, only that he was of Spanish origin. Ramón Jiron had been a good Catholic, she told me, but when his parents wanted him to become a priest, he ran away from home. His father pursued him, caught him, dragged him home, and, as punishment for his disobedience, forced him to wear a bull's skin. One day, when Ramón was taking a bath while alone in the house, some laborers, stopping by, heard his story, took pity on him, gave him a pair of trousers and a shirt, and took him along with them. After wandering about for a time, Ramón settled in Zamorra, Michoacan, where he married Petra Dias. From this point on, the family history as recalled by Gertrudis did not differ essentially from that told by her sister Trinidad.

When I heard these two conflicting stories, each duly confirmed by the respective descendants of the two matriarchs, I had no way of deciding which if either of the two was true. Was Ramón Jiron the elder really a Jew, as his Jewish granddaughter Trinidad maintained, and did some of his children and grandchildren abandon their ancestral faith to accept Catholicism? Or was he a Catholic, as the Catholic Gertrudis attested, and if so, how, when, and why did one branch of his descendants become Jewish? The question was important, because the answer would shed light on the origin of the Venta Prieta Jewish community as a whole, and would illustrate the manner in which Judaism either survived in a hostile Catholic environment for four centuries, or obtained a foothold on an alien, and apparently unfriendly, soil.

My Spanish had improved somewhat by the time of my second visit in the summer of 1964, but I still needed an interpreter to make sure that no misunderstanding crept into my conversation with the Venta Prietans.

As the houses of Venta Prieta loomed up on the right side of the road, I noticed no change at first. The village looked the same; surely the people would be the same too. But this fleeting impression and passing thought both vanished as we made a right turn to cross the little bridge leading over a ditch and hit the still unpaved main street of the village itself. Even before the truck came to a halt in front of Simon Téllez's house, which I had no difficulty in finding, the sound of a blaring jukebox assaulted my ears. I realized that the noise came from the open door of a room to the far right of the house. In 1948, I recalled, that end of the house had been storage space; since then, I found upon entering, it had been converted into a *tienda*, a small shop stocked with a few canned goods, rice, sugar, flour, soap, candles, candy, cigarettes, and the like, and boasting three electrical appliances of our scientific age: a huge ice-cream freezer, the jukebox, and a naked light bulb dangling from a wire in the ceiling.

I did not immediately recognize the young woman behind the counter. "Are you a daughter of Sr. Téllez?" "Yes," she answered, "I am Lilia." The name triggered my memory. Lilia, Simon's youngest daughter, had been eleven in 1948.

She recognized me instantly. (Later I learned that my two letters had been the subject of much discussion, so she had known that I would probably show up within a week or so.) No member of her family was at home, she said, and suggested that she should take me and my interpreter to the house of her cousin, Ruben Olvera Téllez, who was now the *presidente* of their community.

"How old is Ruben?" I asked Lilia.

"Twenty-five." This meant that at the time of my first visit Ruben had been nine years old. That a boy whom I had not even noticed sixteen years earlier should have become the *presidente* of the community brought home to me forcefully that I was facing a different generation, and indeed a different village.

What about the older members of the community? To my inquiry Lilia replied that her grandmother Trinidad had died, as had Trinidad's sister Gertrudis, and several other old people in the village whom I remembered. Although courteous, her reluctance to talk to me about the present life and problems of her people did not diminish, and I felt that I should leave and return later in the afternoon when Ruben would be at home.

I wanted to utilize the remaining hours until five o'clock to check on a theory about the origin of the Téllez family held by a skeptical acquaintance of mine in Mexico City. He believed that the Téllezes had come from a village named Tellez, located close to the highway a few miles south of Venta Prieta, and that all the stories about their Marrano origin and their Michoacan background were pure invention.

At the roadside pointing to Tellez, we turned off the paved highway and traveled three miles over a boulder-strewn path that led to Tellez. After some inquiries we located a young man named Arturo Rodriguez Ortiz, who offered to take us to someone who, he said, knew more about the history of Tellez than anybody. This village historian, Aurelio Meneses Meneses, lived at some distance from the center of Tellez. Meneses, a man in his sixties, answered my questions with the assurance of an expert. No, there was no family named Téllez in the village of Tellez, nor had there ever been such a family there. No person or family from Tellez had ever moved to Venta Prieta. He knew about the Venta Prieta Téllezes; they had not come from Tellez. Then he enumerated all the families that had moved from Tellez to other places, identifying each place by name.

When we returned to Venta Prieta, Ruben was at home and greeted us with reserved dignity. He was a boyish looking young man of slight stature with light brown hair, wearing faintly tinted glasses even indoors. His bearing was marked by an air of authority, and a few days later I had occasion to observe that the children in the synagogue cowered under his admonishing glance, directed from beneath his tinted glasses.

His attitude toward me was at first unfriendly and suspicious. He began by stating peremptorily that they would give me no information whatever, because I had published untrue and derogatory things about the community. I asked him to tell me the basis of this statement, and, after a few more questions, it became apparent that he and other leaders of the community attributed to me certain articles which, in fact, had been written by others. This explained Simon Téllez's letter, and I could imagine how he, his brother Enrique, and his nephew Ruben had discussed the matter and instructed all the members of the community to remain silent if I appeared.

Not having the articles in question at hand, it was difficult for me to convince Ruben that I was not their author. Even after I persuaded him, my cause was still far from won. Following my first visit, Ruben complained, the Jews of Venta Prieta had become a tourist attraction. People came in large numbers, took photographs and moving pictures, talked to them politely, and later wrote about them offensively. Two attitudes especially they resented: that which represented their religion as a hoax maintained for the purpose of obtaining donations from gullible Jewish visitors; and that which viewed them as primitive, uncivilized people. At this point Ruben got up, took a large envelope from a cupboard, and extracted a photograph which he thrust into my hands. "Look at this," he said, "and read the comment on the back."

The picture showed a burro in a stall, nothing else. The caption on the back read, "The Indian Jews of Mexico," and under it appeared the usual stamped caption, "This picture must not be reproduced except by permission from . . ." followed by the name of a commercial photographer. It was obviously one of several photographs taken to show the life of the Jews of Venta Prieta, and the caption merely identified it as belonging to the series called "The Indian Jews of Mexico." But Ruben and the other villagers were deeply offended by it. "We have had more than enough of this," he said, "and decided that we would let nobody take pictures, either of us or our burros, and that we would talk to nobody about ourselves."

From my briefcase I pulled out an offprint of my article published in the Menorah Journal in 1950, and said to Ruben, "If anyone in the village reads

English, ask him to translate this. It's the only thing I have published so far about Venta Prieta. It will show you how I feel about your people. I did not publish anything else precisely because I felt I needed additional information. If, after reading the article, you want to talk to me, write or call me at the Hotel Majestic in Mexico City. If not, just return the offprint, and I will never bother you again.''

A week later, I received a phone call at my hotel from a man who introduced himself as a friend of the Venta Prieta Jews and gave me the telephone number of a Señorita Esther Perez Téllez, who, he said, had a message for me from her relatives in Venta Prieta. When I telephoned, Señorita Perez told me somewhat shyly but in fluent English that Ruben and the others wished me to know that I would be welcome in their synagogue and their homes at any time. She herself, she added, spent every Sunday in Venta Prieta with her family, and would be glad to act as interpreter for me. As it turned out, she proved to be not only a competent interpreter, but my chief source of information during subsequent visits.

Two days later, on a Friday, I took the Pachuca bus and got off at Venta Prieta. I deposited my bag with Ruben's mother and then took a leisurely walk through the broad, half-dusty, half-muddy streets of the village. In the sixteen years since my first visit, the village had become modernized. Electricity had been installed, and from several small grocery stores jukebox music blared, as it did from the Téllez shop. The school had a new, large annex, and next to it a spacious paved courtyard now served as a playground. Many new houses had been built, one of them a two-story building; their brick and concrete construction contrasted sharply with the dark grey adobe of the old crumbling huts. Across the highway to the west, where in 1948 only empty fields had stretched, was a small cluster of new houses. Subsequently I was told that the dumps, which for decades had been removed from the Pachuca silver mines and deposited in fifteen- to twenty-foot heaps to the north of the village, had in recent years been found to contain enough silver to make reworking profitable. Many new workers had therefore settled in the village and built houses for themselves.

In 1948, the synagogue had been the only house of worship; now there was also a Catholic church, a simple, unadorned grey building with a bell on top of its front wall, directly above the entrance. As for the synagogue, the little old adobe structure had disappeared, and had been replaced by a larger building of superior construction, its walls painted turquoise blue, its windows and doors adorned with large iron Stars of David.

Several of the village streets were torn up by deep, narrow ditches, and large concrete pipes attested to work in progress for a sewer system. In 1948, the village had no suitable drinking water. Now water was being piped in.

Along the main street were a number of public taps, under which ran concrete troughs for the cattle. Although this was a great improvement, it had certain disadvantages, too, for around the public faucets the street was muddy and full of dung.

A regular bus service now ran between Pachuca and Venta Prieta every fifteen minutes or so, from early in the morning until eight in the evening; thus Venta Prieta had become practically a suburb of the city. Many more people from the village now regularly worked in Pachuca, and, as I observed the following morning, a few individuals, former Christians who had converted to Judaism, came from Pachuca to attend Sabbath services in the Venta Prieta synagogue.

The negative aspect of this closer contact with the city was that, as usual, the local crafts were being neglected. In 1948, the seven kilns in the village had aroused my interest because, although none of them could have been more than fifty or sixty years old, their shape was surprisingly like smaller temple pyramids of the old Aztec culture, with broad stairways running up their sloping sides. Most of the kilns had been in use in 1948, and I remembered several night-long vigils when teams of young men relayed each other in keeping the fire going for the requisite twenty-four hours. The boys would hurl powdered dung into the kiln with amazing rapidity, while other young men and girls sat around and sang to guitar music, or told stories and teased one another. Firing a kilnload of bricks was thus much more than a purely economic activity; it was something of a minor fiesta, which brought variety, sparkle, and color into the lives of the young villagers. Now, I noticed, the kilns were in disrepair; brickmaking was no longer practiced in the village; Pachuca supplied building materials.

Another thing the village had lost was its bakery. In 1948, there had been one baker in Venta Prieta, Telesforo Aquiahuatl Sanchez, who served also as *juez auxiliar* (auxiliary judge) and was a convert to Judaism. His wife, Concha, who had been instrumental in converting him, was the sister of Guillermo Peña, who had functioned in 1948, as he did in 1964, as a kind of spiritual leader for the congregation. Telesforo's rolls had been crisp and tasty. On my visits to the *panaderia* for the purpose of observing and describing his work routine and sketching his oven, utensils, and house, I always took two or three rolls, after going through a lively argument until he accepted payment. Both Telesforo and his brother-in-law Guillermo had had pure Indian features, and were characterized by that quiet, almost melancholy air which has given rise to the stereotype of *el Indio triste*, the sad Indian. Telesforo still lived in the village, but baked no more; instead, he took the bus each day to his job in Pachuca, and those Venta Prietans who wished to supplement their tortillas with rolls bought them in Pachuca.

The sun was about to set, and I returned to Ruben's house to see whether he had arrived and could take me to the synagogue a little in advance of the Friday evening service. He was there and accompanied me to the next block where the synagogue was located. The reason for erecting a new building, Ruben explained, was that a flood had swept through the village ten years previously and seriously damaged the old adobe structure. The old synagogue had had its entrance directly on the street, but the new one stood back, surrounded by its own grounds, which one entered through a wrought-iron gate. It was then necessary to circle the entire building to reach the entrance at the back. In the old synagogue, the Holy Ark had been placed against the north wall, and I was curious to see whether the leaders of the congregation had become aware of a cardinal rule of synagogue construction which requires that the Ark be placed against the east wall, so that the congregation facing it can direct its prayers towards Jerusalem, the location of the Temple, But no, the Ark stood against the west wall. Many other things, however, both in the equipment of the synagogue and the conducting of the service, attested to an increase in knowledge and orthodoxy.

In the old synagogue— much smaller than the new one, and more primitively furnished—there had been a foot-pedal organ on which Enriqueta, one of the daughters of Simon Téllez, used to accompany the songs and hymns chanted by the congregation. The new building contained no organ; Orthodox Judaism allows no musical instrument in synagogues. I also recalled that in the old synagogue there had been three flower pots flanking the table which stood, covered with a white cloth, between the Ark and the four rows of backless benches. Table, tablecloth in that location, and flowers are all alien to Orthodox synagogues, and they were absent from the new one in Venta Prieta, which, however, boasted nine rows of regular pews, providing a total seating capacity of fifty-four. There was also a seven-branched menorah, a large reading platform, a small lectern, and a stand with a silver bowl in which burned the eternal light—all Orthodox appurtenances which had been absent in the old synagogue.

Another change, although this one had no religious basis, was that while the interior walls of the old synagogue had been decorated by Guillermo Peña with Hebrew inscriptions (a quotation from I Kings 8:57–58) and murals (two rampant lions holding a Star of David between them and supporting on their heads a nine-branched Hanukah candelabrum), all art work was absent from the new synagogue, on whose walls, instead, hung two maps of the state of Israel. In 1948 there was a complete lack of interest in Israel. I had arrived in the village four weeks after the proclamation of Israel's independence and was known by the people to have come from Jerusalem. Moreover, the three months I had spent with them was a time of crucial events, battles, and precarious armistices, a period when the very existence of the newborn state hung in the balance. Yet throughout my stay, nobody ever asked me a single question about Israel. That their attitudes had profoundly changed was evidenced not only by the maps, but also by the fervent desire of several of them to settle in the Jewish state.

With the beginning of the service, more changes became apparent. In the past, the men and boys had worn *sombreros*, the women had covered their heads with scarves or veils, and the girls remained bareheaded. Now, as they entered, the men and boys left their *sombreros* in the last pew and donned small black skullcaps. The tallit, the traditional Jewish prayer shawl with blue stripes and four long fringes had been unknown to them in 1948; now all men and boys wore it. Some of the women now wore small, round, doilylike headcoverings of white lace, as was the custom in the large synagogues of Mexico City. Significantly, too, the men sat on the left of the aisle and the women on the right, which is the Conservative Jewish adaptation of the old Orthodox custom of relegating the women to a separate balcony. The sexes had not been separated in the old Venta Prieta synagogue in 1948.

The service itself, conducted that evening by Guillermo Peña, and on Sabbath morning by him and Xavier Téllez, a son of Simon, resembled those of Reform temples in the United States. They used the prayer book called *Tefila Ritual de Oraciones para todo el Año Rito Sefardi*, edited by Bernardo Schalman and published in Buenos Aires in 1954, which contains the weekday, Sabbath, and holiday prayers in the original Hebrew with a Spanish translation. Most of the prayers were read by Guillermo or Xavier in Spanish; a few were sung by them or by the entire congregation in Hebrew. On Saturday morning, the Torah scroll was taken from the Ark, placed upon the large reading stand, and unrolled, but the weekly section was read by Guillermo, not from the parchment scroll itself in which the Hebrew text is unvocalized, but from a printed Bible, which is much easier to read because it contains the vowel marks. Their knowledge of Hebrew seemed to have improved somewhat since 1948, although many words were still misread, and their pronunciation was a mixture of the Sephardi (Spanish-Jewish) and the Ashkenazi (German-Polish-Jewish) accents. As they entered and took their seats, the girls stretched out their hands to the Ark, then touched their fingers to their lips as if they were not throwing a kiss to it, but drawing one from it. When they read the prayer referring to the "fringes" which serve to remind the Children of Israel of the Lord's commandments (Num. 15:37–41), all of them, men, women and children, performed the same gesture. During the Kiddush, the "Sanctification," all the girls and some of the men held their hands cupped in front of them. And when anybody left the synagogue, he backed out, all the while facing the Ark. The cupping of hands and the backward exit are non-Jewish customs, probably reflecting Christian practices. Another unquestionably Christian custom practiced in 1948 had, however, been abandoned. At that time, towards the end of the service, the congregation knelt while someone spoke a prayer in Spanish— not a traditional prayer from the Bible or the prayer book, but a spontaneous, personal recital of hopes and supplications, addressed to *Jehova nuestro Señor*. In the churches of the Iglesia de Dios, which I visited in 1948 and 1964, I observed the same custom on both occasions.

One thing which had not changed in sixteen years was the uncertainty during the service as to what to do next. Several times Guillermo or Xavier turned to each other, or to Ruben, and a whispered consultation followed, in which evidences of mild disagreement were discernible. Then the reader would continue with the next prayer agreed upon. Apparently the order of the Jewish services in all its fine details had not yet been mastered.

After the Sabbath morning service, I asked Simon and Enrique whether I might take a group picture of the congregation in front of the synagogue. They answered with a polite but definite no; it seemed that their aversion to being photographed was even stronger than their disinclination to being interviewed. But, they said, there would be no objection to my photographing the synagogue itself.

Enrique then invited me to have lunch with him in Pachuca. We were joined by Victor Alarcón Juárez, a man about forty years old and a barber by profession, who had his shop in Pachuca. He had converted to Judaism eight years earlier, he told me during lunch, after having been a member of the Pachuca church of the Adventistas del Septimo Dia (Seventh Day Adventists). It had been his custom for many years now to attend the Sabbath morning prayers in the Venta Prieta synagogue.

Conversation inevitably turned to the Téllez family history, and Enrique recounted a third version of what might be termed the myth of Ramón Jiron and the bull skin. He had heard it, he said, from his mother, Trinidad. There were several discrepancies between Enrique's version and the one I had heard from Trinidad Téllez herself in 1948. According to Enrique, the incident happened to *his* grandfather, Ramón Jiron the second, and not to Ramón the elder, who was Enrique's great-grandfather. This meant that the event occurred much later, when his mother was about ten years old—that is, in 1873. However, the main difference between the two versions was in the accounts of Ramón's death. "Once my grandfather was sewn into the bull's skin," Enrique concluded, "he was left there, and as the skin dried it shrank, gradually compressing his body, until he died in unbearable agony."

Making use of the Pachuca-Venta Prieta bus service, I became a commuter for a few days, staying at a hotel in Pachuca at night and spending my days in Venta Prieta. On the bus on Sunday morning, I ran into José and Esperanza Perez, who had been to town on an errand, and went home with them to meet their daughter Esther.

From Esther, a vital young woman of twenty-eight or twenty-nine, I obtained an insight into the world of the young Jewish generation of Venta Prieta. Ruben, I learned, was elected *presidente* of the community because the younger people felt that it was time for them to move ahead, that it was not sufficient to be Jews in feeling and belief only, but that they must learn as much as possible about Jewish religion, Jewish history, Israel, and other Jewish communities. Although Enrique, the previous *presidente*, had told them many things about their own history, such as that they were descended from Spanish Marranos, they could not believe these stories. "We aren't so much interested in how we *became* Jewish," she said, "but want primarily to live a fully Jewish life."

"We don't know anything about our past," was all they could, or would, say. They were evidently preoccupied with the present and worried about their future. This in itself was something new, contrasting sharply with the carefree attitude of the young adults sixteen years earlier. The atmosphere in the community then had been one of tranquil self-assurance based on the myth of Marrano descent, which had given them, at least in their own eyes, a higher status than that of the other villagers because it imbued them with the prestige of Spanish connections. In 1948, when their Judaism had been little more than the assertion that they were Jews, they wore the legend of their past like a medal of honor. By 1964, the medal had tarnished somewhat; still worn with pride, it imposed duties rather than distinction.

And with the duties had come problems, first and foremost being the one which vexes and perplexes Jews all over the world outside Israel: how to shape the present to insure the future? The most pressing form which this problem took for the young Jews of Venta Prieta was that of finding suitable mates. Mexican folk custom, reinforced by Catholic doctrine, forbids marriage between relatives, even second or third cousins. The Jews of Venta Prieta were as much subject to this prohibition as all the other villagers, and thus the widespread Jewish practice of cousin marriage and other forms of close endogamy, which had enabled small, isolated Jewish communities to maintain themselves in Christian or Muslim lands for many generations, was not possible for them. As a result, most of the boys and girls who had been teenagers in 1948 were still unmarried in 1964, although now they were in their thirties. A few had married Catholics, which involved the usual problems of mixed marrages and their offspring.

"Our most serious problem," said Esther, "is what will become of the children born of the Jewish-Catholic marriages in our village?" Ruben added that in several marriages this had already caused serious trouble, with the Jewish parent insisting that the child go with him (or her) to the synagogue, and the Catholic spouse pulling the child into his own church. "We must try harder to convert the non-Jewish husbands and wives, because if we don't, our group will die out in another twenty or thirty years." To an ear accustomed to the deliberations of Jewish councils, these words of the young Mexican *presidente* had a strangely familiar ring.

Talk of this problem led to a discussion of the wish of several of the group to emigrate to Israel. Awareness of the problem of intermarriage and the acute desire to leave were unquestionably linked. Ruben was vague about the subject of Israel; the immediate predicament in which he and his community were caught up preoccupied him to such an extent that he was unable to visualize settling in a faraway, unknown country. Esther viewed the matter differently. The example of her own young brother who went to an agricultural school in Israel showed her that Israel was a real possibility, and her desire to go there was greatly reinforced by her deep religious conviction. "Living here," she said, "I can't observe the Sabbath rest which is perhaps the most important commandment of my religion. To make a living I have to work, and I can't find a job which wouldn't require me to work on Saturday. I want to go to Israel in order to live a full Jewish life."

But Israel was far and the trip expensive. For several years now, Esther said, she and her family had been working and saving in order to accumulate enough money for the fare. When they have the necessary amount, her father will sell his land, thus obtaining enough money to buy a farm in Israel. "Here, I am miserable; there, I know I'll be happy," she repeatedly assured me.

A few days later, in the plane on my way back to New York, I tried to summarize my impressions of this second visit to Venta Prieta, and it occurred to me that I had gained an insight into a historical process which both spatially and temporally far transcended the narrow limits of that small community: the inevitable sequence of stages which occurs once the seed of Judaism is planted in a group living in a non-Jewish environment.

The first stage is that of naive enchantment with the Jewish religion, based on the eternal myth cycle of Creation, the Fall, the Deluge, the Patriarchs, the Egyptian Slavery, the Exodus, the Sinai Revelation, the Wandering in the Desert, and the Conquest of Canaan. The second stage is that of growing awareness of the duties—ritualistic, behavioral, and moral—imposed upon its members by the Jewish faith. The third stage is one in which the community, or many of its members, feel that Judaism is burdensome, and try to lighten the load by discarding increasingly numerous aspects of it. The fourth stage, that of assimilation, then follows, with individual attempts at adjusting to the gentile environment through intermarriage and secularism. In the fifth stage a reaction sets in against the fourth, with the increasing realization of an imminent danger of "group suicide" and of the urgent necessity of preventing it. The sixth and last stage is reached when efforts are made to avert the danger by imbuing daily life once more with Jewish values, and by embracing Zionism. At the time of my 1948 visit, the Venta Prieta Jews had nearly reached the end of the first stage. In their synagogue services they still sang lustily the Spanish hymns (a heritage of their Iglesia de Dios past) celebrating the Desert Pilgrimage or Heavenly Jerusalem, and were largely unconcerned with the ritualistic framework of Jewish life, although certain signs, such as their willingness to learn Hebrew and to study the Bible, already pointed to the beginnings of the second stage. In 1964, they had just emerged from the fifth stage and had entered into the sixth. They still passively bemoaned the hopelessness of their situation and the danger of their extinction as a separate religious group, but they were already taking practical measures to prevent this, some by trying to intensify their Jewish life, others by going, or planning to go, to Israel.

The acceleration of a historical process and its condensation into approximately two decades was in itself remarkable. Perhaps even more extraordinary was that, within a very few years, the Venta Prietans should have acquired a typically Jewish mentality and outlook, characterized not only by putting a supreme value on group survival, but also by that sense of separateness which so often appears in the derogatory stereotype of the Jew as "clannish."

It was Ruben who gave me a clue to this when I asked him about Victor Alarcón Juárez, the Pachucan barber. "Our community," he said, "consists of our family only, the Téllez and their closest relatives. It is true that Victor, his wife, and children converted about eight years ago, and thus joined our congregation. They had first been Catholics, then Protestants, and now they are Jews. In the beginning, when Victor joined us, he used to come to our synagogue with his entire family of about ten persons. Now, only he, and occasionally one of his sons, still comes to pray with us. We don't accept them, because we can't be sure how they feel, whether they really and fully believe in Judaism."

His words were typical of the Jewish mentality which wards off would-be converts, not because of clannishness, but because it had learned in a long series of historical lessons that converts to Judaism were likely to desert and turn against it. How this historical Jewish posture was acquired by Ruben and the others in the few years of their existence as a community in Venta Prieta was and remains a puzzle to me. But there it was, tangibly, unmistakably governing the attitude of this young man, himself a son of converts, to other, more recent converts, and undoubtedly contributing to the emergence of the stereotype of Jewish clannishness among the Catholics of Venta Prieta.

The main question which had taken me back to the village, concerning the origin of the Jewish community, remained unsolved. I still did not know, nor would anybody probably ever know, whether Ramón Jiron had been Jewish or not, and whether the Jewishness of the Téllez and the other families in Venta Prieta was the result of a return or a conversion. Was it reawakening of the old faith which for many centuries had lain dormant, and, as soon as conditions permitted, reasserted itself? Or was it the result of a gradual moving away from the Catholicism imposed by the conquering Spaniards upon all the natives of Mexico, first to Protestantism, then to the Sabbath-keeping Iglesia de Dios del Septimo Dia, and, finally, once interest in the feasts and laws prescribed in the Old Testament was awakened, to Judaism, whose early history is so powerfully described in the pages of the Bible? The evidence, it seemed to me, pointed in the direction of the latter conclusion. Most important, however, the impression that my Venta Prieta friends were of Christian-sectarian origin was borne in upon me on the eve of my departure from Mexico, when Ruben, Esther, and Esther's brother came to say good-bye to me at my hotel. We spoke of their plans, and Esther complained that they did not receive sufficient help from the Jewish Agency officials or from the Israel Consulate in their endeavor to emigrate to Israel. "They don't consider us Jews," she said, "and, of course, Israel is interested only in the immigration of Jews." I replied that, feeling as Jewish as they did, and observing as much of the Jewish ritual, including circumcision, as they did, it would be only logical for them to undergo an official conversion ceremony before the Mexican rabbinate, in which case they would be accepted as Jews by all concerned. Sixteen years earlier such a suggestion would have been indignantly rejected on the ground that they *were* Jews and the descendants of Jews. No such reaction, however, was forthcoming from Esther and the two boys. As they pondered silently, I added, "You want to reach a goal which is one kilometer away. You have already gone 999 meters, so you might as well go the last meter." The three exchanged glances and then nodded assent. "All right, that's what we'll do," Ruben said, and Esther smiled, whether sadly or gladly I could not tell.

But at that moment it seemed evident that these young people knew that the story of their Jewish ancestry, their Marrano descent, was nothing but a pious fairy tale. And I was struck by the ironic nature of the sacrifice required on the part of these Venta Prietans as the price of their acceptance into the Jewish fold: the expression of their readiness to accept Judaism completely and unconditionally was the strongest indication of their non-Jewish origin, and the tacit admission of this long-denied fact.

Notes

"Venta Prieta Revisited" originally was published in *Midstream*, Mar. 1965, pp. 79–92.

24. The Chuetas
of Majorca

In recent years occasional news items have appeared in the Hebrew and Yiddish press about a group referred to as the "Marranos of Majorca" and their alleged interest in Judaism and Israel. Most recently, one of these reports stated that as a result of a visit by the first Israeli emissary to that Marrano community, several hundred of them expressed their readiness to immigrate to Israel and to return to Judaism. It further stated, that of the 450,000 inhabitants of the island, one half is of Marrano descent, that most of them are poverty-stricken and lack the means to immigrate to Israel, that all of them are sympathetic to Israel, and that some of them belong to Bible study groups. Rarely has a brief journalistic concoction contained so many misconceptions and untruths.

To begin with, there are no "Marranos" in Majorca. The term "Marranos" can legitimately be applied only to crypto-Jews, that is, to Jews who were forced to adopt another religion and who secretly remained loyal to their ancestral faith. Such forced conversions took place in Catholic Spain and Portugal in the Middle Ages. A main purpose of the Inquisition was to track down and punish those among the "new Christians" who secretly continued to adhere or return to Judaism. It was these secret Jews who were contemptuously referred to as "Marranos," i.e., "swine." In the Muslim world, similar forced conversions took place in Persia, mainly in the seventeenth and eighteenth centuries, with the difference, of course, that there they were forced to adopt the Shi'ite variety of Islam, and that following their conversion they were called Jadid al-Islam (New Muslims).

Only a few of the New Christians and New Muslims were able to transmit their secret Jewish heritage to their posterity. By the beginning of the twentieth century, only minute groups of crypto-Jews were found, mainly in Portugal and in the Persian city of Meshhed. All the others succumbed to the pressure of the environment, and the new faith which their fathers were coerced into adopting became, in the course of a few generations, theirs inwardly as well as outwardly. In fact, the typical attitude of these descendants of converts was—and has remained to this day—a greater piety than that of the "old Christians" or "old Muslims," and their typical behavior, a greater meticulousness in all religious observance. At the same time, the typical social situation in which the New Christians and New Muslims found themselves, even after centuries of genuine adherence to the locally dominant faith, was one of isolation. They generally remained a separate group, lived in a separate quarter, married almost exclusively among themselves, and often even frequented their own church. One of these socially isolated groups of Jewish descent is found on the Mediterranean island of Majorca, which has been a Spanish possession for more than seven centuries.

Jews probably first arrived in the Balearic Isles soon after the destruction of Jerusalem by the Romans, when they settled in many parts of the Mediterranean. In Minorca they had a well-established community by the beginning of the fifth century, when they were persecuted at the instigation of Bishop Severus, and some of them converted to Christianity. So far as Majorca is concerned, the sources are silent for another six centuries, but in the twelfth century several synagogues flourished there. When Jaime I took Majorca from the Moors (who had held it since 797) in 1229, he treated the Jews of the island with consideration, granted them liberty, and exempted their synagogues from taxation until 1263.

Although the Inquisition followed the Spanish conquerors to Majorca within a very few years, for about a century and a half the lot of the Jews remained relatively favorable, apart from occasional harrassments, arrests, and fines. In that period the Majorcan Jews grew rich, their commercial enterprises extended all around the Mediterranean, and some of them achieved notable intellectual stature, such as the two cartographers Abraham and Y'huda Cresques, the bibliographer Leo Mosconi, and the rabbi Shim'on ben Tzemah.

At the end of the fourteenth century, the decline of Majorcan Jews began. On 24 August 1391, a mob attacked the Calle (Street), as the Jewish quarter was called, sacked the houses, massacred some three hundred Jews, and forced most of the rest into baptism. Only eight hundred Jews escaped both death and conversion by taking refuge in the royal castle. Following some two decades of respite, a decree issued by Ferdinand of Aragon in 1413 confined the Jews to their quarter and imposed a long list of severe restrictions upon them, including the wearing of a special badge. Another two decades later (1435), a false accusation served as an excuse to imprison and sentence all the Jews to death. Baptism was the only alternative to capital punishment, and within a few days all the Jews of Majorca (over two hundred families) accepted Christianity. A very few managed to make good their escape from the island.

The year 1435 thus marked the end of officially tolerated Judaism on Majorca. Thereafter no Jew was allowed to live on the island, and even foreign Jewish visitors were either limited to a two-week sojourn (in times of "liberal" regimes), or (in stricter days) were seized on their ships before disembarking and questioned in an attempt to extort an admission that they had been baptized—whereupon they were thrown into jail and their property was confiscated. For about two and-a-half centuries the Conversos were actually Marranos, crypto-Jews, who privately and in secret meetings observed Jewish rites and maintained their faith. Although the threatening sword of the Inquisition hung over their heads, this era was a relatively tranquil one for the Marrano Conversos, interrupted only occasionally by outbursts of inquisitorial zeal, as for instance in 1491, when no less than 424 of them were arrested, investigated, fined, and then released. Throughout this period, probably because of insufficient vigilance on the part of the Inquisition, only about a dozen Conversos were burned or otherwise executed for Judaizing, although a large number was tried, "reconciled" (that is, readmitted to church membership after having fully confessed and begged pardon for their heresy), and punished less severely. The double life as outward Christians and secret Jews was not easy, but it was bearable, and the Conversos felt that they and their offspring could continue indefinitely in their successful commercial enterprises and their secretly transmitted and observed Judaism. But this proved to be a false hope.

Toward the end of the seventeenth century, events detrimental to the Conversos followed one after another with increasing frequency. In 1672 it was reported to the Inquisition in Majorca that the "Jews in Majorca were as faithfully Jewish as those living in Leghorn."[1] In 1673, a servant girl described to a priest in great detail the Jewish ceremonies she had seen in the house of a Converso. In 1675, Alonso Lopez, a confessed Marrano, was burned at the stake. In 1677, arrests of Conversos multiplied, and in 1678 no less than 237 were thrown in jail. For more than a year the trials of the Conversos continued, culminating in 1679 in the confiscation of their property, valued at 1.5 million dollars, and in five autos-de-fé, at which a total of 221 Conversos were "reconciled" and sentenced to imprisonment.

About a dozen years later the Holy Office, like a candle that flickers brightly before going out, burst into its last spurt of activity which, in 1691, cost 37 Conversos their lives. Another 49 were tried and convicted, but pardoned. For several decades thereafter trials continued, but the last straggling Conversos caught in the net of the Inquisition were sentenced to noncapital punishment only. From 1722 to 1834, when the Inquisition was finally abolished, no Conversos were tried.

The question as to when the Conversos abandoned their secret adherence to Judaism (or, as the Inquisition saw it, their relapse into heresy), cannot be answered with any accuracy. The process seems to have been gradual; each subsequent generation received a less adequate training in the tenets of Judaism, so that even if they were able to practice, in secrecy, certain religious observances, their ignorance of the Jewish faith increased with each passing generation.

It was due to these circumstances, rather than to the diminished inquisitorial zeal, that following the last autos-de-fé of 1691, only three native Conversos were tried for Judaizing, in 1718, 1720, and 1722 respectively. A belated impartial review of the trials yields convincing evidence of Judaizing in only one of three cases.[2] That the Inquisition, which continued its existence in Majorca for more than a century, remained inactive throughout that period seems evidence enough that no Judaizing tendency could be discovered among the Chuetas, in all probability because there was none. From 1691 on, or, at the latest, from the beginning of the eighteenth century, there were no more Marranos in Marjorca. Their descendants lived on as Chuetas, Christians known to be of Jewish ancestry.

In September 1961, when my collaboration with Robert Graves on a book on Hebrew mythology brought me to Majorca as his guest, I made use of my sojourn there to find out as much as possible about the present-day situation of the Chuetas. With the help of friends (who, to my regret, wish to remain anonymous), I conducted a number of interviews with several natives of the island, both Chuetas and Old Christians (who also stipulated anonymity).

An evaluation of the information thus gathered seems to indicate that no Jewish customs are practiced today by the Chuetas. Nor could any trace of Jewish religious faith be discovered among them. As far as their religion is concerned, they are Catholics, as good as, or even better than, the Old Christians. To call them Marranos is, therefore, completely unjustified.

Yet the Chuetas of Majorca do form a group distinct from the Old Christian majority of the island. Primarily, this separation is due to the fact that in the small insular society the identity of the Chuetas is known to everybody, that the islanders, like the mainland Spaniards, are conservative and subject to inertia, and that they therefore tend to cling to long-established traditions.

And this brings us to the question of stereotypes.

It was a fascinating experience to watch the stereotype of the Chuetas unfold as my informants reported, not what they themselves thought of the Chuetas, but what "most" of the Old Christian Mallorquins believed. The older, uneducated, and superstitious people among the Old Christians, I was told, believed, or used to believe, that on Fridays the tongues of the Chuetas swelled and that they simply would *have* to do something evil on that day—because it was on a Friday that the Jews killed Christ. The Chuetas were also believed to perspire profusely, and, in a general and undefinable way, to behave badly, so much so that to say to an Old Christian, "you behave like a Chueta," was one of the worst insults.

Since the Chuetas were known to be the descendants of Jews, one of whom nineteen centuries ago, was Judas, that name figured prominently in the taunting the Chuetas suffered from the children of the Old Christians. One of the tricks the street urchins used to play on them was to go to the Calle de Plateria (Street of Silversmiths), where the Chuetas lived, light a candle, bend down with it to the ground, and move about in this position as if they were looking for something. When a Chueta would ask what they were looking for, they would yell triumphantly, "For the Testament of Judas!" Or, they would simply march through the Calle singing a doggerel verse,

> Little hammer
> Blue stone,
> Judas-kin,
> Wine-barrel flies!

However, quite apart from such primitive or childish nonsense, my Old Christian informants went on, there are indeed a number of distinct traits which characterize the Chuetas. For one thing, they are most zealous in their observance of the Catholic religion, much more so than most Old Christian Mallorquins. They use a high, whining, nasal intonation in speaking, like priests in the churches. Their overall behavior is subdued, their mannerisms priestly, Jesuitical. They are believed to use expressions and words not used by the Old Christians, although it would be difficult to substantiate this with examples. Also, they accompany their talk with gestures to a much greater extent than the Old Christians.

In their homes, one can perceive an atmosphere of conservatism—for instance, there is no modern furniture. Among the rich Chuetas there is said to be an absence of ostentation—in fact, a tendency to conceal their wealth. They, especially the older ones among them, always wear black suits or dresses.

As to the physical appearance of the Chuetas, my Old Christian informants believed that they can easily be recognized. Their eyes are either darker than those of the true Spaniards, or, according to others, have a melancholy expression which betrays them. They have, it is held, large and prominent noses, and many of them are hook-nosed, to which may be related the nickname *cadafet* applied to Chueta children by their schoolmates. (*Cadafet* is the Mallorquin name for a puffin, a rather rare seabird which has a curious, large, and ugly beak.)

The presence of such a negatively weighted stereotype indicates a definite and persistent dislike for the Chuetas. To obtain information on this subject, about which the Old Christian Mallorquins were rather reticent, I sought out Chueta informants. It was difficult to find any willing to give me information. Several of them froze up as soon as they understood that I wished to speak to them about the Chuetas. They said that they knew absolutely nothing about the Chuetas; or that there were no differences between the Chuetas and the other Mallorquins; or even more simply that they were sorry, but they had no time to talk to me. At last my friends succeeded in locating a Chueta who was willing to talk. He was a professional man, intelligent, well read in Castilian and Catalan, and a deeply religious Catholic, but at the same time exceptionally proud of his Jewish origin. What he had to say about the Chuetas was highly interesting.

As a very young boy, he said, he first became aware of different treatment by his schoolmates. He questioned his parents, and they explained to him that they were "of a different race." Thereafter, he learned about the history of his ancestors. Although his parents had been as good Catholics as any in Palma, he had experienced discrimination, contempt, and hurt. His "racial pride" then developed as a defense mechanism. Hatred of Chuetas, he said, was especially strong among the extremely pious Catholic Mallorquins nicknamed *beatas* (saints). He knew one, he said, who would boast, "I wouldn't give as much as a glass of water to a Chueta!" Under the Republic the situation in this respect had considerably improved, but there was some "anti-Semitism" (anti-Chuetism) in the Falange. At least one high school, the Sagrado Corazon (Sacred Heart), does not accept Chueta children; there are very few priests and nuns from Chueta families; and it is especially difficult for a Chueta to become a Jesuit. The few who succeed are invariably sent away from the island.

The same informant described the Chuetas themselves in terms amounting to a self-stereotype. His description of the physical appearance of the Chuetas—to whom he referred as *Ebreos*, Hebrews—largely coincided with that given by the Old Christians. However, he added one feature: among both the Chuetas and the aristocratic Old Christian Butifaras, there are some redheaded individuals, which he attributed in both cases to long inbreeding. Due to the pressures and the danger in the midst of which the Chuetas had lived for centuries, they had developed, he said, insecure personalities, timidity, and a measure of avarice or frugality. He denied that the Chuetas were in any way different in speech manners, vocabulary, or pronunciation from the Old Christians; but, on the other hand, he claimed that the Chuetas are either extremely talkative or extremely taciturn. Also, they are much more musical than the Old Christians.

Nearly all the Chuetas belong, he said, to the middle class; some are very rich, but he shared the stereotype of the Chuetas held by the Old Christians that even the rich pretend to be poor and would not dream of being ostentatious. They take extremely good care of their possessions, loathe waste, tend to be hoarders, and are conservative by temperament.

Although there are no typical Chueta dishes, they like to eat well and usually spend far more on food than on clothing. In one thing, however, the Chuetas differ from the other Mallorquins: they drink less, and one never sees a drunk Chueta. On the other hand, they are said to be more sensual than the Old Christians, in proof of which their large number of children is cited.

The Chuetas, he thought, dislike working for the government, the army, or the civil service; they all want to be their own bosses, and therefore engage in independent businesses of their own, or in professions.

They are a harder-working lot than the Old Christians, and the more educated ones work hardest. They are better organizers and form a more integrated community, which centers on their church (Santa Eulalia), close to what used to be the ghetto, the Calle (Street) or Juderia (Jewish Quarter), as the section is still called. Nevertheless, the Chuetas are extremely sensitive to the way the Old Christians relate to them: rejection, although frequent in personal contacts, is a painful experience; the rare instances of acceptance are greatly valued. His answer to all the other questions, such as whether the Chuetas had any beliefs, sayings, and customs different from those of the Old Christians, was a categorical no.

Although the origin and history of the Chuetas are known in detail, the meaning of the name "Chueta" has not yet been satisfactorily explained. Some think that it is the diminutive of the name "Jew" in the Majorcan dialect, and means simply "little Jew." Others are of the opinion that, like the French *chouette* (screech owl), it is the name of a bird of ill omen, which may have some likelihood, as another bird nickname, *cadafet*, was also applied to them. On Majorca itself, the current explanation is that it means "pork chop," and that the Conversos were called Chuetas either because they used to sit in front of their shops eating pork chops as proof of their being good Christians, or because they were forced to eat pork chops publicly to prove that they were faithful Catholics. Those who could not bring themselves to do so were promptly burned. Personally I am inclined to dismiss these explanations as apocryphal, and to accept the derivation of the name "Chueta" from a Mallorquin word meaning "pork chops," or, more precisely, the hard, fatty tissue around the loins and kidneys of the pig (suet), which is the least desirable of its edible parts and is more commonly used to make candles or soap. The term "Chueta," therefore, appears to be a refinement of that used in mainland Spain to denote the backsliding Conversos: "swine," or Marranos. The Mallorquins tended to designate social groups by naming them after parts of the pig: "Butifara," the name given to the aristocratic families on the island, means "crackling," the crisp, browned skin of roast pork, or the crisp residue left when hogs' fat is rendered, both of which are regarded as great delicacies. An investigation of Mallorquin designations for ethnic groups or social classes might disclose additional names taken from the pork butchers' terminology.

What actual and objectively verifiable differences do exist today between the Chuetas and the Old Christians? First of all there are occupational specializations. The silversmiths and jewelry shop owners are all Chuetas, most of them still concentrated in the Calle de Plateria of Palma. In Sóller, a small town near the northern shore of the island, most pork butchers, sausagemakers, grocers and drygoods merchants are Chuetas. About half of the musicians in Palma are Chuetas, and piano and violin are Chueta specialties. One very rarely finds a Chueta guitarist; a Chueta trumpeter or drummer, never. Other Chueta specialties are tinsmithing and plumbing. Many are also doctors and dentists.

To an outsider, some family names found in the two extreme classes of Mallorquin society, the Butifaras and the Chuetas, sound deceptively similar, because the Chuetas assumed the names of the noble families which protected them, a custom which dates back to Roman times. But a closer examination discloses slight but important differences between the Butifara and the Chueta versions of the same name: the Butifara Sa Forteza became the Chueta Forteza; Butifara Fúster became Chueta Fustér. An additional difference is that the Chueta names usually have a specific meaning in Spanish or Catalan, while the Old Christian names do not.

A question that inevitably arises as one looks back upon the many centuries of tug-of-war between the Majorcan Inquisition and their favorite victims, the Chuetas, is why the latter did not seek a new environment, in mainland Spain or in some other part of the Mediterranean world, where they could either have joined the local Jewish community or appeared as Catholic Spaniards and been assimilated into the general society within two or three generations? The answer is that when their situation became too dangerous or untenable, they did, in fact, try to leave Majorca. The most outstanding examples of such attempts, both successful and unsuccessful, took place in the 1680s. They were provoked by the sharp increase in the Inquisitorial pressure in the late 1670s. It was in the penitential prisons to which the Conversos were sentenced in 1679, and in which they enjoyed certain comforts and liberties (and were even said to have continued their Judaizing heresies), that they began to formulate plans for their escape from Majorca.

Following their release and finding themselves under constant scrutiny, their resolve to leave the island hardened. The escape began in 1682, with small groups of not more than twenty-five. As more left, the position of those who stayed behind became increasingly dangerous. When news came back of Conversos who, upon their arrival in Nice, Leghorn, or Alexandria, openly returned to Judaism, all the remaining Conversos were suspected of relapse into heresy and a renewed wave of arrests followed.

Early in 1688, their leader, Raphael Valls, succeeded in making arrangements with the captain of an English vessel which lay in the harbor in Palma, and during the night of 7 March, a large group of Conversos boarded the vessel under cover of darkness. A sudden storm prevented the ship from sailing, and before daybreak they had to return to the wharf, only to be immediately arrested by officers of the Inquisition. Next day arrests began of those Conversos who did not participate in the venture, and by 1691 all those of Jewish descent had been seized, many of them tortured, and most had confessed, were "reconciled," and sentenced to penal servitude of varying length; thirty-four were garroted and then burned, and three, among them Raphael Valls, were burned alive.

Another attempt to leave Majorca took place in 1773. By that time the Chuetas no longer lived in fear of loss of life and property. Only the oldest among them remembered the last time a Chueta had been arrested by the Inquisition, half a century earlier. At long last, the descendants of the Conversos had succeeded in convincing their neighbors and the church authorities that they were truly faithful Catholics—which, in fact, must have been the case. But the cessation of arrests and executions did not mean that the Chuetas could live in peace. On the contrary, to the Old Christians the Chuetas were beyond the pale. They rigidly adhered to their statutes of *limpieza* (purity of blood), which made intermarriage with Chuetas the gravest social crime, and even social intercourse with them a practical impossibility. Thus the 400 families still identified as Chuetas in the eighteenth century formed a proscribed and despised class, socially ostracized and excluded from the higher ranks of the Catholic clergy, the female religious orders, the guilds, the army and navy, and public office and service. Strict residential segregation in the ghetto remained the rule.

The Chuetas found this situation increasingly difficult to bear, and in 1773 they took a daring step. They addressed a petition to King Charles III complaining of discrimination, limitations, calumnies, and disabilities. At the same time they seem to have made it known in Majorca that, unless their grievances were satisfied, they would leave the island. The bishop of Majorca, in a supporting letter addressed to the king's council stated that unless something was done to mitigate the injustices they suffered, they might flee to neighboring Minorca, a British possession at the time. In 1781, having received no response, the Chuetas considered wholesale expatriation. However, before their plans could mature, three royal decrees were issued, in 1782, 1785, and 1788, in which the king not only granted all their requests, but made their mistreatment or insult a punishable offense. The emigration plans were then given up, although the royal edicts remained dead letters of the law, and it took several decades before even the most overt and grossest forms of abuse disappeared.

The 1680s and the 1770s were the only two periods when the Chuetas made large-scale, organized attempts or plans to leave Majorca. (On other occasions, as in connection with the 1391 pogroms, only a few individuals or families managed to escape overseas.) But most of the time, throughout the centuries over which the Inquisition cast its menacing shadow, the situation of the Chuetas was sufficiently tolerable to let the advantages of Majorca outweigh its disadvantages. Most were well off economically; they had been natives of the island far longer than those relative newcomers, the Spanish Old Christians; they were members of an "in-group," which, however restricted in its outside contacts, formed a satisfactory social setting; and they were always sustained by the hope that sooner or later the Old Christians would accept them as their equals.

Yet another point must be made in explanation of the Chuetas' clinging to Majorca. It is only we, of the twentieth-century western world, who regard social inequality as a major, intolerable disability. The Chuetas, down to the onset of modern times, and to some extent even to this very day, have always lived in a world where each ethnic or religious group had a social status of its own, a special place within the mosaic of ethnic-religious groups whose totality made up the population picture of any country. In that world, which was most typically represented in and around the Mediterranean, no two ethnic groups had the same status; each had its own privileges as well as disabilities. The status one shared with the group into which one happened to be born was part of one's hereditary endowment in precisely the same way as the color of one's skin, one's height, or mental ability. One had to accept it and bear it through life. If a group as a whole was forced to change its religion, it meant a change of status, but not the abolition of the group as a separate entity. Nor did it mean that thenceforth the individual was liberated from the forces that tied him to his group.

In recent decades, however, a serious threat has arisen to the survival of ethnic groups within the western world. Following the Spanish revolution, the new winds have begun to reach the ranks of relatively static, conservative, and isolated Majorcan society. For the time being, the social distance between the Chuetas and the Old Christians remains a fact. The Chuetas still form a largely endogamous group. But already Chueta–Old Christian intermarriages have begun to occur. Occasional marriages between Chuetas and foreigners (Christians from mainland Spain or from abroad), also contribute to a loosening of the group bonds, as does the spread of liberal views among both Chuetas and educated Old Christians.

The days of the Chuetas of Majorca thus seem numbered. That a few of them may eventually move to Israel and Judaism is a possibility, but not a likelihood. It is almost certain that the rest will merge with the Old Christian majority and disappear as a separate ethnic entity.

Notes

"The Chuetas of Majorca" originally was published in *Midstream*, Spring 1962, pp. 59–68. I wish to express my thanks to the Lucius N. Littauer Foundation and its president, Harry Starr, for a grant which made the preparation of this study possible. In addition to oral information, the major sources used were Baruch Braunstein, *The Chuetas of Majorca* (New York, 1936); Lionel A. Isaacs, *The Jews of Mallorca* (London, 1936); and Antonio Pons, *Los Judios del Reino de Mallorca* (Madrid, 1958).

1. Braunstein, *Chuetas*, p. 59.
2. Ibid., pp. 118–21.

Index

Raphael Patai is an internationally known anthropologist and biblical scholar. He was born in Budapest and studied at the University of Budapest (Dr. Phil., 1933), the University of Breslau, the rabbinical seminaries of Budapest and Breslau, and the Hebrew University, Jerusalem (Ph.D., 1936). He subsequently taught at the Hebrew University and founded and directed the Palestine Institute of Folklore and Ethnology; in 1947 he came to the United States, where he now lives.

Dr. Patai has served as professor of anthropology at Dropsie College and Fairleigh Dickinson University, and as visiting professor at the University of Pennsylvania and at Columbia, Princeton, Ohio State, and New York universities. In addition to several other posts, he has been director of research for the Theodor Herzl Institute and editor of the Herzl Press. Dr. Patai is the author of more than six hundred articles and many books, among them *The Messiah Texts* and *Gates to the Old City*, copublished by Wayne State University Press and Avon Books.

The manuscript was edited by Sherwyn T. Carr and Doreen Broder. The book was designed by Don Ross. The typeface for the text is Times Roman based on a design by Stanley Morison about 1932. The display faces are Times Roman and Letraset's Arnold Bocklin.

The text is printed on 60 lb. Arbor text paper. The book is bound in Holliston Mill's Natural finish cloth over binder's boards.

Manufactured in the United States of America.